EMPLOYMENT LAW: SELECTED FEDERAL AND STATE STATUTES

2012 Edition

LEXISNEXIS LAW SCHOOL PUBLISHING ADVISORY BOARD

EMPLOYMENT LAW: SELECTED FEDERAL AND STATE STATUTES

2012 Edition

Steven L. Willborn
Judge Harry A. Spencer Professor of Law
University of Nebraska-Lincoln

Stewart J. Schwab
Allan R. Tessler Dean & Professor of Law
Cornell Law School

John F. Burton, Jr.
Professor Emeritus, School of Management and Labor Relations
Rutgers, The State University of New Jersey

Gillian L. L. Lester
Associate Dean & Professor of Law
University of California at Berkeley

LexisNexis

ISBN: 978-1-4224-9753-1

NOTE TO USERS
To ensure that you are using the latest materials available in this area, please be sure to periodically check the LexisNexis Law School web site for downloadable updates and supplements at www.lexisnexis.com/lawschool.

Editorial Offices
121 Chanlon Rd, New Providence, NJ 07974 (908) 464-6800
201 Mission St., San Francisco, CA 94105-1831 (415) 908-3200
www.lexisnexis.com

MATTHEW BENDER (2012–Pub.3044)

Table of Contents

PART II.

THE RISE AND FALL OF EMPLOYMENT AT WILL

SARBANES-OXLEY ACT

(Whistleblower and Related Provisions and Regulations)

15 U.S.C. §§ 78j-1(m), 7245; 18 U.S.C. §§ 1513(3), 1514A;
17 C.F.R. § 205.3

§ 301 [15 U.S.C. § 78j-1(m)]. Public company audit committees

(m) Standards relating to audit committees.

(1) Commission rules.

(A) In general. Effective not later than 270 days after the date of enactment of this subsection, the Commission shall, by rule, direct the national securities exchanges and national securities associations to prohibit the listing of any security of an issuer that is not in compliance with the requirements of any portion of paragraphs (2) through (6).

(B) Opportunity to cure defects. The rules of the Commission under subparagraph (A) shall provide for appropriate procedures for an issuer to have an opportunity to cure any defects that would be the basis for a prohibition under subparagraph (A), before the imposition of such prohibition.

(2) Responsibilities relating to registered public accounting firms. The audit committee of each issuer, in its capacity as a committee of the board of directors, shall be directly responsible for the appointment, compensation, and oversight of the work of any registered public accounting firm employed by that issuer (including resolution of disagreements between management and the auditor regarding financial reporting) for the purpose of preparing or issuing an audit report or related work, and each such registered public accounting firm shall report directly to the audit committee.

(3) Independence.

(A) In general. Each member of the audit committee of the issuer shall be a member of the board of directors of the issuer, and shall otherwise be independent.

(B) Criteria. In order to be considered to be independent for purposes of this paragraph, a member of an audit committee of an issuer may not, other than in his or her capacity as a member of the audit committee, the board of directors, or any other board committee—

(i) accept any consulting, advisory, or other compensatory fee from the issuer; or

(ii) be an affiliated person of the issuer or any subsidiary thereof.

(C) Exemption authority. The Commission may exempt from the requirements of subparagraph (B) a particular relationship with respect to audit committee members, as the Commission determines appropriate in light of the circumstances.

(4) Complaints. Each audit committee shall establish procedures for—

(A) the receipt, retention, and treatment of complaints received by the issuer regarding accounting, internal accounting controls, or auditing matters; and

(B) the confidential, anonymous submission by employees of the issuer of concerns regarding questionable accounting or auditing matters.

(5) Authority to engage advisors. Each audit committee shall have the authority to engage independent counsel and other advisers, as it determines necessary to carry out its duties.

(6) Funding. Each issuer shall provide for appropriate funding, as determined by the audit committee, in its capacity as a committee of the board of directors, for payment of compensation—

(A) to the registered public accounting firm employed by the issuer for the purpose of rendering or issuing an audit report; and

(B) to any advisers employed by the audit committee under paragraph (5).

§ 307 [15 U.S.C. § 7245]. Rules of professional responsibility for attorneys

Not later than 180 days after the date of enactment of this Act, the Commission shall issue rules, in the public interest and for the protection of investors, setting forth minimum standards of professional conduct for attorneys appearing and practicing before the Commission in any way in the representation of issuers, including a rule—

(1) requiring an attorney to report evidence of a material violation of securities law or breach of fiduciary duty or similar violation by the company or any agent thereof, to the chief legal counsel or the chief executive officer of the company (or the equivalent thereof); and

(2) if the counsel or officer does not appropriately respond to the evidence (adopting, as necessary, appropriate remedial measures or sanctions with respect to the violation), requiring the attorney to report the evidence to the audit committee of the board of directors of the issuer or to another committee of the board of directors comprised solely of directors not employed directly or indirectly by the issuer, or to the board of directors.

§ 806 [18 U.S.C. § 1514A]. Protection for employees of publicly traded companies who provide evidence of fraud

(a) Whistleblower protection for employees of publicly traded companies. No company with a class of securities registered under section 12 of the Securities Exchange Act of 1934 (15 U.S.C. § 78l), or that is required to file reports under section 15(d) of the Securities Exchange Act of 1934 (15 U.S.C. § 78o(d)), or any officer, employee, contractor, subcontractor, or agent of such company, may discharge, demote, suspend, threaten, harass, or in any other manner discriminate against an employee in the terms and conditions of employment because of any lawful act done by the employee—

(1) to provide information, cause information to be provided, or otherwise assist in an investigation regarding any conduct which the employee reasonably believes constitutes a violation of section 1341, 1343, 1344, or 1348, any rule or regulation of the Securities and Exchange Commission, or any provision of Federal law relating to fraud against shareholders, when the information or assistance is provided to or the investigation is conducted by—

(A) a Federal regulatory or law enforcement agency;

(B) any Member of Congress or any committee of Congress; or

(C) a person with supervisory authority over the employee (or such other person working for the employer who has the authority to investigate, discover, or terminate misconduct); or

(2) to file, cause to be filed, testify, participate in, or otherwise assist in a proceeding filed or about to be filed (with any knowledge of the employer) relating to an alleged violation of section 1341, 1343, 1344, or 1348, any rule or regulation of the Securities and Exchange Commission, or any provision of Federal law relating to fraud against shareholders.

(b) Enforcement Action.

(1) In general. A person who alleges discharge or other discrimination by any person in violation of subsection (a) may seek relief under subsection (c), by—

(A) filing a complaint with the Secretary of Labor; or

(B) if the Secretary has not issued a final decision within 180 days of the filing of the complaint and there is no showing that such delay is due to the bad faith of the claimant, bringing an action at law or equity for de novo review in the appropriate district court of the United States, which shall have jurisdiction over such an action without regard to the amount in controversy.

(2) Procedure.

(A) In general. An action under paragraph (1)(A) shall be governed under the rules and procedures set forth in section 42121(b) of title 49, United States Code.

(B) Exception. Notification made under section 42121(b)(1) of title 49, United States Code, shall be made to the person named in the complaint and to the employer.

(C) Burdens of proof. An action brought under paragraph (1)(B) shall be governed by the legal burdens of proof set forth in section 42121(b) of title 49, United States Code.

(D) Statute of limitations. An action under paragraph (1) shall be commenced not later than 90 days after the date on which the violation occurs.

(c) Remedies.

(1) In general. An employee prevailing in any action under subsection (b)(1) shall be entitled to all relief necessary to make the employee whole.

(2) Compensatory damages. Relief for any action under paragraph (1) shall include—

(A) reinstatement with the same seniority status that the employee would have had, but for the discrimination;

(B) the amount of back pay, with interest; and

(C) compensation for any special damages sustained as a result of the discrimination, including litigation costs, expert witness fees, and reasonable attorney fees.

(d) Rights retained by employee. Nothing in this section shall be deemed to diminish the rights, privileges, or remedies of any employee under any Federal or State law, or under any collective bargaining agreement.

§1107 [18 U.S.C. § 1513(e)]. Retaliation against informants

(e) Whoever knowingly, with the intent to retaliate, takes any action harmful to any person, including interference with the lawful employment or livelihood of any person, for providing to a law enforcement officer any truthful information relating to the commission or possible commission of any Federal offense, shall be fined under this title or imprisoned not more than 10 years, or both.

17 C.F.R. § 205.3. Issuer as Client

(a) Representing an issuer. An attorney appearing and practicing before the Commission in the representation of an issuer owes his or her professional and ethical duties to the issuer as an organization. That the attorney may work with and advise the issuer's officers, directors, or employees in the course of representing the issuer does not make such individuals the attorney's clients.

(b) Duty to report evidence of a material violation.

(1) If an attorney, appearing and practicing before the Commission in the representation of an issuer, becomes aware of evidence of a material violation by the issuer or by any officer, director, employee, or agent of the issuer, the attorney shall report such evidence to the issuer's chief legal officer (or the equivalent thereof) or to both the issuer's chief legal officer and its chief executive officer (or the equivalents thereof) forthwith. By communicating such information to the issuer's officers or directors, an attorney does not reveal client confidences or secrets or privileged or otherwise protected information related to the attorney's representation of an issuer.

(2) The chief legal officer (or the equivalent thereof) shall cause such inquiry into the evidence of a material violation as he or she reasonably believes is appropriate to determine whether the material violation described in the report has occurred, is ongoing, or is about to occur. If the chief legal officer (or the equivalent thereof) determines no material violation has occurred, is ongoing, or is about to occur, he or she shall notify the reporting attorney and advise the reporting attorney of the basis for such determination. Unless the chief legal officer (or the equivalent thereof) reasonably believes that no material violation has occurred, is ongoing, or is about to occur, he or she shall take all reasonable steps to cause the issuer to adopt an appropriate response, and shall advise the reporting attorney thereof. In lieu of causing an inquiry under this paragraph (b), a chief legal officer (or the equivalent thereof) may refer a report of evidence of a material violation to a qualified legal compliance committee under paragraph (c)(2) of this section if the issuer has duly established a qualified legal compliance committee prior to the report of evidence of a material violation.

(3) Unless an attorney who has made a report under paragraph (b)(1) of this section reasonably believes that the chief legal officer or the chief executive officer of the issuer (or the equivalent thereof) has provided an appropriate response within a reasonable time, the attorney shall report the evidence of a material violation to:

(i) The audit committee of the issuer's board of directors;

(ii) Another committee of the issuer's board of directors consisting solely of directors who are not employed, directly or indirectly, by the issuer and are not, in the case of a registered investment company, "interested persons" as defined in section 2(a)(19) of the Investment Company Act of 1940 (15 U.S.C. § 80a-2(a)(19)) (if the issuer's board of directors has no audit committee); or

(iii) The issuer's board of directors (if the issuer's board of directors has no committee consisting solely of directors who are not employed, directly or indirectly, by the issuer and are not, in the case of a registered investment company, "interested persons" as defined in section 2(a)(19) of the Investment Company Act of 1940 (15 U.S.C. § 80a-2(a)(19))).

(4) If an attorney reasonably believes that it would be futile to report evidence of a material violation to the issuer's chief legal officer and chief executive officer (or the equivalents thereof) under paragraph (b)(1) of this section, the attorney may report such evidence as provided under paragraph (b)(3) of this section.

(5) An attorney retained or directed by an issuer to investigate evidence of a material violation reported under paragraph (b)(1), (b)(3), or (b)(4) of this section shall be deemed to be appearing and practicing before the Commission. Directing or retaining an attorney to investigate reported evidence of a material violation does not relieve an officer or director of the issuer to whom such evidence has been reported under paragraph (b)(1), (b)(3), or (b)(4) of this section from a duty to respond to the reporting attorney.

(6) An attorney shall not have any obligation to report evidence of a material violation under this paragraph (b) if:

(i) The attorney was retained or directed by the issuer's chief legal officer (or the equivalent thereof) to investigate such evidence of a material violation and:

(A) The attorney reports the results of such investigation to the chief legal officer (or the equivalent thereof); and

(B) Except where the attorney and the chief legal officer (or the equivalent thereof) each reasonably believes that no material violation has occurred, is ongoing, or is about to occur, the chief legal officer (or the equivalent thereof) reports the results of the investigation to the issuer's board of directors, a committee thereof to whom a report could be made pursuant to paragraph (b)(3) of this section, or a qualified legal compliance committee; or

(ii) The attorney was retained or directed by the chief legal officer (or the equivalent thereof) to assert, consistent with his or her professional obligations, a colorable defense on behalf of the issuer (or the issuer's officer, director, employee, or agent, as the case may be) in any investigation or judicial or administrative proceeding relating to such evidence of a material violation, and the chief legal officer (or the equivalent thereof) provides reasonable and timely reports on the progress and outcome of such proceeding to the issuer's board of directors, a committee thereof to whom a report could be made pursuant to paragraph (b)(3) of this section, or a qualified legal compliance committee.

(7) An attorney shall not have any obligation to report evidence of a material violation under this paragraph (b) if such attorney was retained or directed by a qualified legal compliance committee:

(i) To investigate such evidence of a material violation; or

(ii) To assert, consistent with his or her professional obligations, a colorable defense on behalf of the issuer (or the issuer's officer, director, employee, or agent, as the case may be) in any investigation or judicial or administrative proceeding relating to such evidence of a material violation.

(8) An attorney who receives what he or she reasonably believes is an appropriate and timely response to a report he or she has made pursuant to paragraph (b)(1), (b)(3), or (b)(4) of this section need do nothing more under this section with respect to his or her report.

(9) An attorney who does not reasonably believe that the issuer has made an appropriate response within a reasonable time to the report or reports made pursuant to paragraph (b)(1), (b)(3), or (b)(4) of this section shall explain his or her reasons therefore to the chief legal officer (or the equivalent thereof), the chief executive officer (or the equivalent thereof), and directors to whom the attorney reported the evidence of a material violation pursuant to paragraph (b)(1), (b)(3), or (b)(4) of this section.

(10) An attorney formerly employed or retained by an issuer who has reported evidence of a material violation under this part and reasonably believes that he or she has been discharged for so doing may notify the issuer's board of directors or any committee thereof that he or she believes that he or she has been discharged for reporting evidence of a material violation under this section.

(c) Alternative reporting procedures for attorneys retained or employed by an issuer that has established a qualified legal compliance committee.

(1) If an attorney, appearing and practicing before the Commission in the representation of an issuer, becomes aware of evidence of a material violation by the issuer or by any officer, director, employee, or agent of the issuer, the attorney may, as an alternative to the reporting requirements of paragraph (b) of this section, report such evidence to a qualified legal compliance committee, if the issuer has

previously formed such a committee. An attorney who reports evidence of a material violation to such a qualified legal compliance committee has satisfied his or her obligation to report such evidence and is not required to assess the issuer's response to the reported evidence of a material violation.

(2) A chief legal officer (or the equivalent thereof) may refer a report of evidence of a material violation to a previously established qualified legal compliance committee in lieu of causing an inquiry to be conducted under paragraph (b)(2) of this section. The chief legal officer (or the equivalent thereof) shall inform the reporting attorney that the report has been referred to a qualified legal compliance committee. Thereafter, pursuant to the requirements under § 205.2(k), the qualified legal compliance committee shall be responsible for responding to the evidence of a material violation reported to it under this paragraph (c).

(d) Issuer confidences.

(1) Any report under this section (or the contemporaneous record thereof) or any response thereto (or the contemporaneous record thereof) may be used by an attorney in connection with any investigation, proceeding, or litigation in which the attorney's compliance with this part is in issue.

(2) An attorney appearing and practicing before the Commission in the representation of an issuer may reveal to the Commission, without the issuer's consent, confidential information related to the representation to the extent the attorney reasonably believes necessary:

(i) To prevent the issuer from committing a material violation that is likely to cause substantial injury to the financial interest or property of the issuer or investors;

(ii) To prevent the issuer, in a Commission investigation or administrative proceeding from committing perjury, proscribed in 18 U.S.C. § 1621; suborning perjury, proscribed in 18 U.S.C. § 1622; or committing any act proscribed in 18 U.S.C. § 1001 that is likely to perpetrate a fraud upon the Commission; or(iii) To rectify the consequences of a material violation by the issuer that caused, or may cause, substantial injury to the financial interest or property of the issuer or investors in the furtherance of which the attorney's services were used.

DODD-FRANK WALL STREET REFORM AND CONSUMER PROTECTION ACT

15 USCA § 78u-6

15 USCA § 78u-6 Securities Whistleblower Incentives and Protection

(a) Definitions. In this section the following definitions shall apply:

(1) Covered judicial or administrative action. The term 'covered judicial or administrative action' means any judicial or administrative action brought by the Commission under the securities laws that results in monetary sanctions exceeding $1,000,000.

(2) Fund. The term 'Fund' means the Securities and Exchange Commission Investor Protection Fund.

(3) Original information. The term 'original information' means information that—

(A) is derived from the independent knowledge or analysis of a whistleblower;

(B) is not known to the Commission from any other source, unless the whistleblower is the original source of the information; and

(C) is not exclusively derived from an allegation made in a judicial or administrative hearing, in a governmental report, hearing, audit, or investigation, or from the news media, unless the whistleblower is a source of the information.

(4) Monetary sanctions. The term 'monetary sanctions', when used with respect to any judicial or administrative action, means—

(A) any monies, including penalties, disgorgement, and interest, ordered to be paid; and

(B) any monies deposited into a disgorgement fund or other fund pursuant to section 308(b) of the Sarbanes-Oxley Act of 2002 (15 U.S.C. 7246(b)), as a result of such action or any settlement of such action.

(5) Related action. The term 'related action', when used with respect to any judicial or administrative action brought by the Commission under the securities laws, means any judicial or administrative action brought by an entity described in subclauses (I) through (IV) of subsection (h)(2)(D)(i) that is based upon the original information provided by a whistleblower pursuant to subsection (a) that led to the successful enforcement of the Commission action.

(6) Whistleblower. The term 'whistleblower' means any individual, or 2 or more individuals acting jointly, who provides

information relating to a violation of the securities laws to the Commission, in a manner established, by rule or regulation, by the Commission.

(b) Awards.

(1) In general. In any covered judicial or administrative action, or related action, the Commission, under regulations prescribed by the Commission and subject to subsection (c), shall pay an award or awards to 1 or more whistleblowers who voluntarily provided original information to the Commission that led to the successful enforcement of the covered judicial or administrative action, or related action, in an aggregate amount equal to—

(A) not less than 10 percent, in total, of what has been collected of the monetary sanctions imposed in the action or related actions; and

(B) not more than 30 percent, in total, of what has been collected of the monetary sanctions imposed in the action or related actions.

(2) Payment of awards. Any amount paid under paragraph (1) shall be paid from the Fund.

(c) Determination of Amount of Award; Denial of Award.

(1) Determination of amount of award.

(A) Discretion. The determination of the amount of an award made under subsection (b) shall be in the discretion of the Commission.

(B) Criteria. In determining the amount of an award made under subsection (b), the Commission shall take into account—

(i) the significance of the information provided by the whistleblower to the success of the covered judicial or administrative action;

(ii) the degree of assistance provided by the whistleblower and any legal representative of the whistleblower in a covered judicial or administrative action;

(iii) the programmatic interest of the Commission in deterring violations of the securities laws by making awards to whistleblowers who provide;

(iv) such additional relevant factors as the Commission may establish by rule or regulation.

(2) Denial of award. No award under subsection (b) shall be made—

(A) to any whistleblower who is, or was at the time the whistleblower acquired the original information submitted to the Commission, a member, officer, or employee of—

(i) an appropriate regulatory agency;

(ii) the Department of Justice;

(iii) a self-regulatory organization;

(iv) the Public Company Accounting Oversight Board; or

(v) a law enforcement organization;

(B) to any whistleblower who is convicted of a criminal violation related to the judicial or administrative action for which the whistleblower otherwise could receive an award under this section;

(C) to any whistleblower who gains the information through the performance of an audit of financial statements required under the securities laws and for whom such submission would be contrary to the requirements of section 101A of the Securities Exchange Act of 1934 (15 U.S.C. 78j-1); or

(D) to any whistleblower who fails to submit information to the Commission in such form as the Commission may, by rule, require.

(d) Representation.

(1) Permitted representation. Any whistleblower who makes a claim for an award under subsection (b) may be represented by counsel.

(2) Required representation.

(A) In general. Any whistleblower who anonymously makes a claim for an award under subsection (b) shall be represented by counsel if the whistleblower anonymously submits the information upon which the claim is based.

(B) Disclosure of identity. Prior to the payment of an award, a whistleblower shall disclose the identity of the whistleblower and provide such other information as the Commission may require, directly or through counsel for the whistleblower.

(e) No Contract Necessary. No contract with the Commission is necessary for any whistleblower to receive an award under subsection (b), unless otherwise required by the Commission by rule or regulation.

(f) Appeals. Any determination made under this section, including whether, to whom, or in what amount to make awards, shall be in the discretion of the Commission. Any such determination may beappealed to the appropriate court of appeals of the United States not more than 30 days after the determination is issued by the Commission.The court shall review the determination made by the Commission in accordance with section 706 of title 5, United States Code.

(g) Investor Protection Fund.

(1) Fund established. There is established in the Treasury of the United States a fund to be known as the 'Securities and Exchange Commission Investor Protection Fund'.

(2) Use of fund. The Fund shall be available to the Commission, without further appropriation or fiscal year limitation, for—

(A) paying awards to whistleblowers as provided in subsection (b); and

(B) funding the activities of the Inspector General of the Commission under section 4(i).

(3) Deposits and credits. There shall be deposited into or credited to the Fund an amount equal to—

(A) the amount awarded under subsection (b) from any monetary sanction collected by the Commission in any judicial or administrative action brought by the Commission that is based on information provided by a whistleblower under the securities laws, unless, the balance of the Fund at the time the monetary sanction is collected exceeds $200,000,000;

(B) any monetary sanction added to a disgorgement fund or other fund pursuant to section 308 of the Sarbanes-Oxley Act of 2002 (15 U.S.C. 7246) that is not distributed to the victims for whom the disgorgement fund was established, unless the balance of the disgorgement fund at the time the determination is made not to distribute the monetary sanction to such victims exceeds $100,000,000; and

(C) all income from investments made under paragraph (4).

(4) Investments.

(A) Amounts in fund may be invested. The Commission may request the Secretary of the Treasury to invest the portion of the Fund that is not, in the discretion of the Commission, required to meet the current needs of the Fund.

(B) Eligible investments. Investments shall be made by the Secretary of the Treasury in obligations of the

United States or obligations that are guaranteed as to principal and interest by the United States, with maturities suitable to the needs of the Fund as determined by the Commission on the record.

(C) Interest and proceeds credited. The interest on, and the proceeds from the sale or redemption of, any obligations held in the Fund shall be credited to the Fund.

(5) Reports to congress. Not later than October 30 of each fiscal year beginning after the date of enactment of this subsection, the Commission shall submit to the Committee on Banking, Housing, and Urban Affairs of the Senate, and the Committee on Financial Services of the House of Representatives a report on—

(A) the whistleblower award program, established under this section, including—

(i) a description of the number of awards granted; and

(ii) the types of cases in which awards were granted during the preceding fiscal year;

(B) the balance of the Fund at the beginning of the preceding fiscal year;

(C) the amounts deposited into or credited to the Fund during the preceding fiscal year;

(D) the amount of earnings on investments made under paragraph (4) during the preceding fiscal year;

(E) the amount paid from the Fund during the preceding fiscal year to whistleblowers pursuant to subsection (b);

(F) the balance of the Fund at the end of the preceding fiscal year; and

(G) a complete set of audited financial statements, including—

(i) a balance sheet;

(ii) income statement; and

(iii) cash flow analysis.

(h) Protection of Whistleblowers.

(1) Prohibition against retaliation.

(A) In general. No employer may discharge, demote, suspend, threaten, harass, directly or indirectly, or in any other manner discriminate against, a whistleblower in the terms and conditions of employment because of any lawful act done by the whistleblower—

(i) in providing information to the Commission in accordance with subsection (a); or

(ii) in assisting in any investigation or judicial or administrative action of the Commission based upon or related to such information.

(B) Enforcement.

(i) Cause of action. An individual who alleges discharge or other discrimination in violation of subparagraph (A) may bring an action under this subsection in the appropriate district court of the United States for the relief provided in subparagraph (C).

(ii) Subpoenas. A subpoena requiring the attendance of a witness at a trial or hearing conducted under this section may be served at any place in the United States.

(iii) Statute of limitations.

(I) In general. An action under this subsection may not be brought—

(aa) more than 6 years after the date on which the violation of subparagraph (A) occurred; or

(bb) more than 3 years after the date when facts material to the right of action are known or reasonably should have been known by the employee alleging a violation of subparagraph (A).

(II) Required action within 10 years. Notwithstanding subclause (I), an action under this subsection may not in any circumstance be brought more than 10 years after the date on which the violation occurs.

(C) Relief. Relief for an individual prevailing in an action brought under subparagraph (B) shall include—

(i) reinstatement with the same seniority status that the individual would have had, but for the discrimination;

(ii) 2 times the amount of back pay otherwise owed to the individual, with interest; and

(iii) compensation for litigation costs, expert witness fees, and reasonable attorneys' fees.

(2) Confidentiality.

(A) In general. Unless and until required to be disclosed to a defendant or respondent in connection with a proceeding instituted by the Commission or any entity described in subparagraph (D), all information provided to the Commission by a whistleblower—

(i) in any proceeding in any Federal or State court or administrative agency—

(I) shall be confidential and privileged as an evidentiary matter; and

(II) shall not be subject to civil discovery or other legal process; and

(ii) shall not be subject to disclosure under section 552 of title 5, United States Code (commonly referred to as the Freedom of Information Act) or under any proceeding under that section.

(B) Exempted statute. For purposes of section 552 of title 5, United States Code, this paragraph shall be considered a statute described in subsection (b)(3)(B) of such section 552.

(C) Rule of construction. Nothing in this section is intended to limit, or shall be construed to limit, the ability of the Attorney General to present such evidence to a grand jury or to share such evidence with potential witnesses or defendants in the course of an ongoing criminal investigation.

(D) Availability to government agencies.

(i) In general. Without the loss of its status as confidential and privileged in the hands of the Commission, all information referred to in subparagraph (A) may, in the discretion of the Commission, when determined by the Commission to be necessary to accomplish the purposes of this Act and to protect investors, be made available to—

(I) the Attorney General of the United States;

(II) an appropriate regulatory authority;

(III) a self-regulatory organization;

(IV) a State attorney general in connection with any criminal investigation;

(V) any appropriate State regulatory authority;

(VI) the Public Company Accounting Oversight Board;

(VII) a foreign securities authority; and

(VIII) a foreign law enforcement authority.

(ii) Confidentiality.

(I) In general. Each of the entities described in subclauses (I) through (VI) of clause (i) shall maintain such information as confidential and privileged, in accordance with the requirements established under subparagraph (A).

(II) Foreign authorities. Each of the entities described in subclauses (VII) and (VIII) of clause (i) shall maintain such information in accordance with such assurances of confidentiality as the Commission determines appropriate.

(3) Rights retained. Nothing in this section shall be deemed to diminish the rights, privileges, or remedies of any whistleblower under any Federal or State law, or under any collective bargaining agreement.

(i) Provision of False Information. A whistleblower shall not be entitled to an award under this section if the whistleblower—

(1) knowingly and willfully makes any false, fictitious, or fraudulent statement or representation; or

(2) uses any false writing or document knowing the writing or document contains any false, fictitious, or fraudulent statement or entry.

(j) Rulemaking Authority. The Commission shall have the authority to issue such rules and regulations as may be necessary or appropriate to implement the provisions of this section consistent with the purposes of this section.

MONTANA WRONGFUL DISCHARGE FROM EMPLOYMENT ACT OF 1987

Mont. Code Ann. §§ 39-2-901 to 39-2-914

§39-2-901 [§ 1]. Short title. This part may be cited as the "Wrongful Discharge From Employment Act".

§39-2-902 [§ 2]. Purpose. This part sets forth certain rights and remedies with respect to wrongful discharge. Except as provided in 39-2-912, this part provides the exclusive remedy for a wrongful discharge from employment.

§39-2-903 [§3]. Definitions. In this part, the following definitions apply:

(1) "Constructive discharge" means the voluntary termination of employment by an employee because of a situation created by an act or omission of the employer which an objective, reasonable person would find so intolerable that voluntary termination is the only reasonable alternative. Constructive discharge does not mean voluntary termination because of an employer's refusal to promote the employee or improve wages, responsibilities, or other terms and conditions of employment.

(2) "Discharge" includes a constructive discharge as defined in subsection (1) and any other termination of employment, including resignation, elimination of the job, layoff for lack of work, failure to recall or rehire, and any other cutback in the number of employees for a legitimate business reason.

(3) "Employee" means a person who works for another for hire. The term does not include a person who is an independent contractor.

(4) "Fringe benefits" means the value of any employer-paid vacation leave, sick leave, medical insurance plan, disability insurance plan, life insurance plan, and pension benefit plan in force on the date of the termination.

(5) "Good cause" means reasonable job-related grounds for dismissal based on a failure to satisfactorily perform job duties, disruption of the employer's operation, or other legitimate business reason. The legal use of a

lawful product by an individual off the employer's premises during nonworking hours is not a legitimate business reason, unless the employer acts within the provisions of 39-2-313(3) or (4) [which establish limited exceptions to the statutory ban on discrimination for legal use of products off work].

(6) "Lost wages" means the gross amount of wages that would have been reported to the internal revenue service as gross income on Form W-2 and includes additional compensation deferred at the option of the employee.

(7) "Public policy" means a policy in effect at the time of the discharge concerning the public health, safety, or welfare established by constitutional provision, statute, or administrative rule.

§39-2-904 [§ 4]. Elements of wrongful discharge.

(1) A discharge is wrongful only if:

(a) it was in retaliation for the employee's refusal to violate public policy or for reporting a violation of public policy;

(b) the discharge was not for good cause and the employee had completed the employer's probationary period of employment; or

(c) the employer violated the express provisions of its own written personnel policy.

(2)(a) During a probationary period of employment, the employment may be terminated at the will of either of the employer or the employee on notice to the other for any reason or no reason.

(b) If an employer does not establish a specific probationary period or provide that there is no probationary period prior to or at the time of hire, there is a probationary period of 6 months from the date of hire.

§39-2-905 [§5]. Remedies

(1) If an employer has committed a wrongful discharge, the employee may be awarded lost wages and fringe benefits for a period not to exceed 4 years from the date of discharge, together with interest on the lost wages and fringe benefits. Interim earnings, including amounts the employee could have earned with reasonable diligence, must be deducted from the amount awarded for lost wages. Before interim earnings are deducted from lost wages, there must be deducted from the interim earnings any reasonable amounts expended by the employee in searching for, obtaining, or relocating to new employment.

(2) The employee may recover punitive damages otherwise allowed by law if it is established by clear and convincing evidence that the employer engaged in actual fraud or actual malice in the discharge of the employee in violation of 39-2-904(1).

(3) There is no right under any legal theory to damages for wrongful discharge under this part for pain and suffering, emotional distress,

compensatory damages, punitive damages, or any other form of damages, except as provided for in subsections (1) and (2).

§39-2-911 [§ 6]. Limitation of actions

(1) An action under this part must be filed within 1 year after the date of discharge.

(2) If an employer maintains written internal procedures, other than those specified in 39-2-912, under which an employee may appeal a discharge within the organizational structure of the employer, the employee shall first exhaust those procedures prior to filing an action under this part. The employee's failure to initiate or exhaust available internal procedures is a defense to an action brought under this part. If the employer's internal procedures are not completed within 90 days from the date the employee initiates the internal procedures, the employee may file an action under this part and for purposes of this subsection the employer's internal procedures are considered exhausted. The limitation period in subsection (1) is tolled until the procedures are exhausted. In no case may the provisions of the employer's internal procedures extend the limitation period in subsection (1) more than 120 days.

(3) If the employer maintains written internal procedures under which an employee may appeal a discharge within the organizational structure of the employer, the employer shall within 7 days of the date of the discharge notify the discharged employee of the existence of such procedures and shall supply the discharged employee with a copy of them. If the employer fails to comply with this subsection, the discharged employee need not comply with subsection (2).

§39-2-912 [§ 7]. Exemptions. This part does not apply to a discharge:

(1) that is subject to any other state or federal statute that provides a procedure or remedy for contesting the dispute. Such statutes include those that prohibit discharge for filing complaints, charges, or claims with administrative bodies or that prohibit unlawful discrimination based on race, national origin, sex, age, disability, creed, religion, political belief, color, marital status, and other similar grounds.

(2) of an employee covered by a written collective bargaining agreement or a written contract of employment for a specific term.

§39-2-913 [§ 8]. Preemption of common-law remedies. Except as provided in this part, no claim for discharge may arise from tort or express or implied contract.

§39-2-914 [§ 9]. Arbitration

(1) A party may make a written offer to arbitrate a dispute that otherwise could be adjudicated under this part.

(2) An offer to arbitrate must be in writing and contain the following provisions:

(a) A neutral arbitrator must be selected by mutual agreement or, in the absence of agreement, as provided in 27-5-211.

(b) The arbitration must be governed by the Uniform Arbitration Act, Title 27, chapter 5. If there is a conflict between the Uniform Arbitration Act and this part, this part applies.

(c) The arbitrator is bound by this part.

(3) If a complaint is filed under this part, the offer to arbitrate must be made within 60 days after service of the complaint and must be accepted in writing within 30 days after the date the offer is made.

(4) A discharged employee who makes a valid offer to arbitrate that is accepted by the employer and who prevails in such arbitration is entitled to have the arbitrator's fee and all costs of arbitration paid by the employer.

(5) If a valid offer to arbitrate is made and accepted, arbitration is the exclusive remedy for the wrongful discharge dispute and there is no right to bring or continue a lawsuit under this part. The arbitrator's award is final and binding, subject to review of the arbitrator's decision under the provisions of the Uniform Arbitration Act.

MODEL EMPLOYMENT TERMINATION ACT

National Conference of Commissioners on Uniform State Laws

[Editor's Note: Brackets indicate possible deletions or alternatives for particular state legislatures to consider.]

§ 1. Definitions. In this [Act]:

(1) "Employee" means an individual who works for hire, including an individual employed in a supervisory, managerial, or confidential position, but not an independent contractor.

(2) "Employer" means a person [, excluding this State, a political subdivision, a municipal corporation, or any other governmental subdivision, agency, or instrumentality,] that has employed [five] or more employees for each working day in each of 20 or more calendar weeks in the two-year period next preceding a termination or an employer's filing of a complaint pursuant to Section 5(c), excluding a parent, spouse, child, or other member of the employer's immediate family or of the immediate family of an individual having a controlling interest in the employer.

(3) "Fringe benefit" means vacation leave, sick leave, medical insurance plan, disability insurance plan, life insurance plan, pension benefit plan, or other benefit of economic value, to the extent the leave, plan, or benefit is paid for by the employer.

(4) "Good cause" means (i) a reasonable basis related to an individual employee for termination of the employee's employment in view of relevant factors and circumstances, which may include the employee's duties, responsibilities, conduct on the job or otherwise, job performance, and employment record, or (ii) the exercise of business judgment in good faith by the employer, including setting its economic or institutional goals and

determining methods to achieve those goals, organizing or reorganizing operations, discontinuing, consolidating, or divesting operations or positions or parts of operations or positions, determining the size of its work force and the nature of the positions filled by its work force, and determining and changing standards of performance for positions.

(5) "Good faith" means honesty in fact .

(6) "Pay," as a noun, means hourly wages or periodic salary, including tips, regularly paid and nondiscretionary commissions and bonuses, and regularly paid overtime, but not fringe benefits.

(7) "Person" means an individual, corporation, business trust, estate, trust, partnership, association, joint venture, or any other legal or commercial entity [, excluding government or a governmental subdivision, agency, or instrumentality].

(8) "Termination" means:

(i) a dismissal, including that resulting from the elimination of a position, of an employee by an employer;

(ii) a layoff or suspension of an employee by an employer for more than two consecutive months; or

(iii) a quitting of employment or a retirement by an employee induced by an act or omission of the employer, after notice to the employer of the act or omission without appropriate relief by the employer, so intolerable that under the circumstances a reasonable individual would quit or retire.

§ 2. Scope

(a) This [Act] applies only to a termination that occurs after the effective date of this [Act].

(b) This [Act] does not apply to a termination at the expiration of an express oral or written agreement of employment for a specified duration, which was valid, subsisting, and in effect on the [effective] date of this [Act].

(c) Except as provided in subsection (e), this [Act] displaces and extinguishes all common-law rights and claims of a terminated employee against the employer, its officers, directors, and employees, which are based on the termination or on acts taken or statements made that are reasonably necessary to initiate or effect the termination if the employee's termination requires good cause under Section 3(a), is subject to an agreement for severance pay under Section 4(c), or is permitted by the expiration of an agreement for a specified duration under Section 4(d).

(d) An employee whose termination is not subject to Section 3(a) or 4(d) and who is not a party to an agreement under Section 4 (c) retains all common-law rights and claims.

(e) This [Act] does not displace or extinguish rights or claims of a terminated employee against an employer arising under state or federal statutes or administrative rules or regulations having the force of law [or local ordinances valid under state law], a collective-bargaining agreement between an employer and a labor organization, or an express oral or written agreement relating to employment which does not violate this [Act]. Those rights and claims may not be asserted under this [Act], except as otherwise provided in this [Act]. The existence or adjudication of those rights or claims does not limit the employee's rights or claims under this [Act], except as stated in Section 7(d).

§ 3. Prohibited Terminations

(a) Unless otherwise provided in an agreement for severance pay under Section 4(c) or for a specified duration under Section 4(d), an employer may not terminate the employment of an employee without good cause.

(b) Subsection (a) applies only to an employee who has been employed by the same employer for a total period of one year or more and has worked for the employer for a least 520 hours during the 26 weeks next preceding the termination. A layoff or other break in service is not counted in determining whether an employee's period of employment totals one year, but the employee is considered to be employed during paid vacations and other authorized leaves. If an employee is rehired after a break in service exceeding one year, not counting absences due to labor disputes or authorized leaves, the employee is considered to be newly hired. The 26-week period for purposes of this subsection does not include any week during which the employee was absent because of layoffs of one year or less, paid vacations, authorized leaves, or labor disputes.

§ 4. Agreements between Employer and Employee

(a) A right of an employee under this [Act] may not be waived by agreement except as provided in this section.

(b) By express written agreement, an employer and an employee may provide that the employee's failure to meet specified business-related standards of performance or the employee's commission or omission of specified business-related acts will constitute good cause for termination in proceedings under this [Act]. Those standards or prohibitions are effective only if they have been consistently enforced and they have not been applied to a particular employee in a disparate manner without justification. If the agreement authorizes changes by the employer in the standards or prohibitions, the changes must be clearly communicated to the employee.

(c) By express written agreement, an employer and an employee may mutually waive the requirement of good cause for termination, if the employer agrees that upon the termination of the employee for any reason other than willful misconduct of the employee, the employer will provide severance pay in an amount equal to at least one month's pay for each period of employment totaling one year, up to a maximum total payment equal to 30 months' pay at the employee's rate of pay in effect immediately before the termination. The employer shall make the payment in a lump sum or in a series of monthly installments, none of which may be less than one month's pay plus interest on the principal balance. The lump-sum payment must be made or payment of the monthly installments must begin within 30 days after the employee's termination. An agreement under this subsection constitutes a waiver by the employer and the employee of the right to civil trial, including jury trial, concerning disputes over the nature of the termination and the employee's entitlement to severance pay, and constitutes a stipulation by the parties that those disputes will be subject to the procedures and remedies of this [Act].

(d) The requirement of good cause for termination does not apply to the termination of an employee at the expiration of an express oral or written agreement of employment for a specified duration related to the completion of a specified task, project, undertaking, or assignment. If the employment continues after the expiration of the agreement, Section 3 applies to its termination unless the parties enter into a new express oral or written agreement under this subsection. The period of employment under an agreement described in this subsection counts toward the minimum periods of employment required by Section 3(b).

(e) An employer may provide substantive and procedural rights in addition to those provided by this [Act], either to one or more specific employees by express oral or written agreement, or to employees generally by a written personnel policy or statement, and may provide that those rights are enforceable under the procedures of this [Act].

(f) An employing person and an employee not otherwise subject to this [Act] may become subject to its provisions to the extent provided by express written agreement, in which case the employing person is deemed to be an employer.

(g) An agreement between an employer and an employee subject to this [Act] imposes a duty of good faith in its formation, performance, and enforcement.

(h) By express written agreement, an employer and an employee may settle at any time a claim arising under this [Act].

(i) By express written agreement before or after a dispute or claim arises under this [Act], an employer and an employee may agree to private arbitration or other alternative dispute-resolution procedure for resolving the dispute or claim.

(j) By express written agreement after a dispute or claim arises under this [Act], an employer and an employee may agree to judicial resolution of the dispute or claim.

(k) The substantive provisions of this [Act] apply under an agreement authorized by subsections (i) and (j).

§ 5. Procedure and Limitations

(a) An employee whose employment is terminated may file a complaint and demand for arbitration under this [Act] with the [Commission; Department; Service] not later than 180 days after the effective date of the termination, the date of the breach of an agreement for severance pay under Section 4(c), or the date the employee learns or should have learned of the facts forming the basis of the claim, whichever is latest. The time for filing is suspended while the employee is pursuing the employer's internal remedies and has not been notified in writing by the employer that the internal procedures have been concluded. Resort to an employer's internal procedures is not a condition for filing a complaint under this [Act].

(b) Except when an employee quits, an employer, within 10 business days after a termination, shall mail or deliver to the terminated employee a written statement of the reasons for the termination and a copy of this [Act] or a summary approved by the [Commission; Department; Service].

(c) An employer may file a complaint and demand for arbitration under this [Act] with the [Commission; Department; Service] to determine whether there is good cause for the termination of a named employee. At least 15 business days before filing, the employer shall mail or deliver to the employee a written statement of the employer's intention to file and the factors alleged to constitute good cause for a termination.

(d) The [Commission; Department; Service] shall promptly mail or deliver to the respondent a copy of the complaint and demand for arbitration. Within 21 days after receipt of a complaint, the respondent must file an answer with the [Commission; Department; Service] and mail a copy of the answer to the complainant. The answer of a respondent employer must include a copy of the statement of the reasons for the termination furnished the employee.

[(e) When a complaint is filed, a complainant employee or employer shall pay a filing fee to the [Commission; Department; Service] in [the amount of $______] [an amount not exceeding the maximum filing fee for a civil action in the courts of general jurisdiction of this State]. The [Commission; Department; Service] may waive or defer payment of the filing fee upon a showing of the complainant employee's indigency.]

§ 6. Arbitration; Selection and Powers of Arbitrator; Hearings; Burden of Proof

(a) Except as otherwise provided in this [Act], the [Uniform Arbitration Act] [__________ arbitration act of this State] applies to proceedings under this [Act] as if the parties had agreed to arbitrate under that statute. The [Commission; Department; Service] shall adopt procedural rules to regulate arbitration under this [Act]. The [Administrative Procedure Act and other] statutes of this State applicable to the procedures of state agencies do not apply to arbitration under this [Act].

(b) The [Commission; Department; Service] shall adopt rules specifying the qualifications, method of selection, and appointment of arbitrators. An arbitrator serving under this [Act] exercises the authority of the state.

(c) Subject to rules adopted by the [Commission; Department; Service], all forms of discovery [provided by applicable state statute, rule, or regulation] are available in the discretion of the arbitrator, who shall ensure there is no undue delay, expense, or inconvenience. Upon request, the employer shall provide the complainant or respondent employee a complete copy of the employee's personnel file.

(d) A party may be represented in arbitration by an attorney or other person authorized under the laws of this State to represent an individual in arbitration.

(e) A complainant employee has the burden of proving that a termination was without good cause or that an employer breached an agreement for severance pay under Section 4(c). A complainant employer has the burden of proving that there is good cause for a termination. In all arbitrations, the employer shall present its case first unless the employee alleges that a quitting or retirement was a termination within the meaning of Section 1(8) (iii).

(f) If an employee establishes that a termination was motivated in part by impermissible grounds, the employer, to avoid liability, must establish by a preponderance of the evidence that it would have terminated the employment even in the absence of the impermissible grounds.

§ 7. Awards

(a) Within 30 days after the close of an arbitration hearing or at any later time agreeable to the parties, the arbitrator shall mail or deliver to the parties a written award sustaining or dismissing the complaint, in whole or in part, and specifying appropriate remedies, if any.

(b) An arbitrator may make one or more of the following awards for a termination in violation of this [Act]:

(1) reinstatement to the position of employment the employee held when employment was terminated or, if that is impractical, to a comparable position;

(2) full or partial backpay and reimbursement for lost fringe benefits, with interest, reduced by interim earnings from employment elsewhere, benefits received, and amounts that could have been received with reasonable diligence;

(3) if reinstatement is not awarded, a lump-sum severance payment at the employee's rate of pay in effect before the termination, for a period not exceeding [36 months] after the date of the award, together with the value of fringe benefits lost during that period, reduced by likely earnings and benefits from employment elsewhere, and taking into account such equitable considerations as the employee's length of service with the employer and the reasons for the termination; and

(4) reasonable attorney's fees and costs.

(c) An arbitrator may make either or both of the following awards for a violation of an agreement for severance pay under Section 4(c):

(1) enforcement of the severance pay and other applicable provisions of the agreement, with interest; and

(2) reasonable attorney's fees and costs.

(d) An arbitrator may not make an award except as provided in subsections (b) and (c). The arbitrator may not award damages for pain and suffering, emotional distress, defamation, fraud, or other injury under the common law; punitive damages; compensatory damages; or any other monetary award. In making a monetary award under this section, the arbitrator shall reduce the award by the amount of any monetary award to the employee in another forum for the same conduct of the employer. In making an award, the arbitrator is subject to the rules of issue, fact, and judgment preclusion applicable in courts of record in this State.

(e) If an arbitrator dismisses an employee's complaint and finds it frivolous, unreasonable, or without foundation, the arbitrator may award reasonable attorney's fees and costs to the prevailing employer.

(f) An arbitrator may sustain an employer's complaint and make an award declaring that there is good cause for the termination of a named employee. If the arbitrator dismisses the employer's complaint, the arbitrator may award reasonable attorney's fees and costs to the prevailing employee.

§ 8. Judicial Review and Enforcement

(a) Either party to an arbitration may seek vacation, modification, or enforcement of the arbitrator's award in the [court of general jurisdiction] for the [county] in which the termination occurred or in which the employee resides.

(b) An application for vacation or modification must be filed within [90] days after issuance of the arbitrator's award. An application for enforcement may be filed at any time after the issuance of the arbitrator's award.

(c) The court may vacate or modify an arbitrator's award only if the court finds that:

(1) the award was procured by corruption, fraud, or other improper means;

(2) there was evident partiality by the arbitrator or misconduct prejudicing the rights of a party;

(3) the arbitrator exceeded the powers of an arbitrator;

(4) the arbitrator committed a prejudicial error of law; or

(5) another ground exists for vacating the award under the [Uniform Arbitration Act] [________ arbitration act of this State].

(d) In an application for vacation, modification, or enforcement of the arbitrator's award, the court may award a prevailing employee reasonable attorney's fees and costs. In an application by an employee for vacation of an arbitrator's award, the court may award a prevailing employer reasonable attorney's fees and costs if the court finds the employee's application is frivolous, unreasonable, or without foundation.

§ **9. Posting.** An employer shall post a copy of this [Act] or a summary approved by the [Commission; Department; Service] in a prominent place in the work area. An employer who violates this section is subject to a civil penalty not exceeding [$________]. The [Attorney General] may bring a civil action, on behalf of this State, to impose and collect any civil penalty arising under this section.

§ **10. Retaliation Prohibited and Civil Action Created.** An employer or other employing person may not directly or indirectly take adverse action in retaliation against an individual for filing a complaint, giving testimony, or otherwise lawfully participating in proceedings under this [Act], whether or not the individual is an employee having rights under this [Act]. An employer or other employing person who violates this section is liable to the individual subjected to the adverse action in retaliation for damage caused by the action, punitive damages when appropriate, and reasonable attorney's fees. A separate civil action may be brought to enforce this liability. The employer is also subject to applicable procedures and remedies provided by Sections 5 through 8.

§ **11. Severability Clause.** If any provision of this [Act] or its application to any person or circumstance is held invalid, the invalidity does not affect other provisions or applications of this [Act] which can be given effect without the invalid provision or application, and to this end the provisions of this [Act] are severable. . . .

§ **14. Savings and Transitional Provisions.** This [Act] does not apply to the termination of an employee within six months after the effective date of this [Act] based upon the employee's refusal to enter into an agreement meeting the minimum standards of Section 4(c), which the employer, in the exercise of good faith business judgment, may impose as a condition of continued employment.

LABOR CONTRACT LAW OF THE PEOPLE'S REPUBLIC OF CHINA

Approved by the 28th Conference of the 10th Session of the National People's Congress Standing Committee on June 29, 2007
(unofficial English translation)

Chapter I. General Provisions

Article 1. This Law is formulated for the purposes of improving the labor contractual system, clarifying the rights and obligations of both parties of labor contracts, protecting the legitimate rights and interests of employees, and establishing and developing a harmonious and stable employment relationship.

Article 2. This Law shall apply to the establishment of employment relationship between employees and enterprises, individual economic organizations, private non-enterprise entities, or other organizations (hereafter referred to as employers), and to the formation, fulfillment, change, dissolution, or termination of labor contracts.

The state organs, public institutions, social organizations, and their employees among them there is an employment relationship shall observe this Law in the formation, fulfillment, change, dissolution, or termination of their labor contracts.

Article 3. The principles of lawfulness, fairness, equality, free will, negotiation for agreement and good faith shall be observed in the formation of a labor contract. A labor contract concluded according to the law shall have a binding force. The employer and the employee shall perform the obligations as stipulated in the labor contract.

Article 4. An employer shall establish a sound system of employment rules so as to ensure that its employees enjoy the labor rights and perform the employment obligations.

Where an employer formulates, amends or decides rules or important events concerning the remuneration, working time, break, vacation, work safety and sanitation, insurance and welfare, training of employees, labor discipline, or management of production quota, which are directly related to the interests of the employees, such rules or important events shall be discussed at the meeting of employees' representatives or the general meeting of all employees, and the employer shall also put forward proposals and opinions to the employees and negotiate with the labor union or the employees' representatives on a equal basis to reach agreements on these rules or events.

During the process of execution of a rule or decision about an important event, if the labor union or the employees deems it improper, they may require the employer to amend or improve it through negotiations.

The employer shall make an announcement of the rules and important events which are directly related to the interests of the employees or inform the employees of these rules or events.

Article 5. The labor administrative department of the people's government at the county level or above shall, together with the labor union and the representatives of theenterprise, establish a sound three-party mechanism to coordinate employment relationship and shall jointly seek to solve the major problems related to employment relations.

Article 6. The labor union shall assist and direct the employees when they conclude with the employers and fulfill labor contracts and establish a collective negotiation mechanism with the employers so as to maintain the lawful rights and interests of the employees.

Chapter II. Formation of Labor Contracts

Article 7. An employer establishes an employment relationship with an employee from the date when the employer puts the employee to work. The employer shall prepare a roster of employees for inspection.

Article 8. When an employer hires an employee, it shall faithfully inform him of the work contents, conditions and location, occupational harm, work safety state, remuneration, and other information which the employee requires to be informed. The employer has the right to know the basic information of the employer which is directly related to the labor contract and the employee shall faithfully provide such information.

Article 9. When an employer hires an employee, it shall not detain his identity card or other certificates, nor require him to provide a guaranty or collect money or property from him under any other excuse.

Article 10. A written labor contract shall be concluded in the establishment of an employment relationship.

Where an employment relationship has already been established with an employee but no written labor contract has been entered simultaneously, a written labor contract shall be concluded within one month from the date when the employee begins to work.

Where an employer and an employee conclude a labor contract prior to the employment, the employment relationship is established from the date when the employee begins to work.

Article 11. Where an employer fails to conclude a written labor contract when the employer put his employee to work, if the remuneration stipulated between the employer and the employee is not clear, the remuneration to the new employee shall conform to the provisions of the collective contract. If there is no collective contract or if there is no such stipulation in the collective contract, the principle of equal pay for equal work shall be observed.

Article 12. Labor contracts are classified into fixed-term labor contracts, labor contracts without a fixed term, and the labor contracts that set the completion of specific tasks as the term to end contracts.

Article 13. A fixed-term labor contract refers to a labor contract in which the employer and the employee stipulate the time of termination of the contract. The employer and the employee may conclude a fixed-term labor contract upon negotiation.

Article 14. A labor contract without a fixed term refers to a labor contract in which the employer and the employee stipulate no certain time to end the contract. An employer and an employee may, through negotiations, conclude a labor contract without a fixed term. Under any of the following circumstances, if the employee proposes or agrees to renew or conclude a labor contract, a labor contract without a fixed term shall be concluded unless the employee proposes to conclude a fixed-term labor contract:

1. The employee has already worked for the employer for 10 full years consecutively;

2. When the employer initially adopts the labor contract system or when a state-owned enterprise re-concludes the labor contract due to restructuring, the employee has already worked for this employer for 10 full years consecutively and he attains to the age which is less than 10 years up to the statutory retirement age; or

3. The labor contract is to be renewed after two fixed-term labor contracts have been concluded consecutively, and the employee is not under any of the circumstances as mentioned in Article 39 and Paragraphs (1) and (2) of Article 40 of this Law.

If the employer fails to sign a written labor contract with an employee after the lapse of one full year from the date when the employee begins to work, it shall be deemed that the employer and the employee have concluded a labor contract without a fixed term.

Article 15. A labor contract that sets the completion of a specific task as the term to end the contract refers to the labor contract in which the employer and the employee stipulate that the time period of the contract shall be based on the completion of a specific task.An employer and an employee may, upon negotiation, conclude a labor contract that sets the completion of a specific task to end the contract.

Article 16. A labor contract shall be agreed with by the employer and the employee and shall come into effect after the employer and the employee affix their signatures or seals to the labor contract.The employer and the employee shall each hold one copy of the labor contract.

Article 17. A labor contract shall include the following clauses:

1. The employer's name, domicile, legal representative, or major person-in-charge;

2. The employee's name, domicile, identity card number, or other valid identity certificate number;

3. The time limit for the labor contract;

4. The job descriptions and work locations;

5. The work hours, break time, and vocations;

6. The remunerations;

7. The social security;

8. The employment protection, work conditions, and protection against and prevention of occupational harm; and

9. Other items that shall be included in the labor contract under any laws or regulations.

Apart from the essential clauses as prescribed in the preceding paragraph, the employer and the employee may, in the labor contract, stipulate the probation time period, training, confidentiality, supplementary insurances, welfares and benefits, and other items.

Article 18. If remunerations, work conditions, and other criterions are not expressly stipulated in a labor contract and a dispute is triggered, the employer and the employee may re-negotiate the contract. If no agreement is reached through negotiations, the provisions of the collective contract shall be followed. If there is no collective contract or if there is no such stipulation about the remuneration, the principle of equal pay for equal work shall be observed. If there is no collective contract or if there is no such stipulation about the work conditions and other criterions in the collective contract, the relevant provisions of the state shall be followed.

Article 19. If the term of a labor contract is not less than 3 months but less than 1 year, the probation period shall not exceed one month. If the term of a labor contract is not less than one year but less than 3 years, the probation period shall not exceed 2 months. For a labor contract with a fixed term of 3 years or more or without a fixed term, the probation term shall not exceed 6 months.

An employer can only impose one probation time period on an employee.

For a labor contract that sets the completion of a specific task as the term to end the contract or with a fixed term of less than 3 months, no probation period may be stipulated.

The probation period shall be included in the term of a labor contract. If a labor contract only provides the term of probation, the probation shall be null and void and the term of the probation shall be treated as the term of the labor contract.

Article 20. The wage of an employee during the probation period shall not be lower than the minimum wage for the same position of the same employer or lower than 80% of the wage stipulated in the labor contract, nor may it be lower than the minimum wage of the locality where the employer is located.

Article 21. During the probation period, except when the employee is under any of the circumstances as described in Article 39 and Article 40 (i) and (ii), the employer shall not dissolve the labor contract. If an employer dissolves a labor contract during the probation period, it shall make an explanation.

Article 22. Where an employer pays special training expenses for the special technical training of his employees, the employer may enter an agreement with his employees to specify their service time period.

If an employee violates the stipulation regarding the service time period, he shall pay the employer a penalty for breach of contract. The amount of penalty for breach of contract shall not exceed the training fees provided by the employer. The penalty for breach of a contract in which the employer requires the employee to pay shall not exceed the training expenses attributable to the service time period that is unfulfilled.

The service time period stipulated by the employer and the employee does not affect the promotion of the remuneration of the employee during the probation period under the normal wage adjustment mechanism.

Article 23. An employer may enter an agreement with his employees in the labor contract to require his employees to keep the business secrets and intellectual property of the employer confidential.

For an employee who has the obligation of keeping confidential, the employer and the employee may stipulate non-competition clauses in the labor contract or in the confidentiality agreement and come to an agreement that, when the labor contract is dissolved or terminated, the employee shall be given economic compensations within the non-competition period. If the employee violates the stipulation of non-competition, it shall pay the employer a penalty for breaching the contract.

Article 24. The persons who should be subject to non-competition shall be limited to the senior managers, senior technicians, and the other employees, who have the obligation to keep secrets, of employers. The scope, geographical range and time limit for non-competition shall be stipulated by the employer and the employee. The stipulation on non-competition shall not be contrary to any laws or regulations.

After the dissolution or termination of a labor contract, the non-competition period for any of the persons as mentioned in the preceding paragraph to work in any other employer producing or engaging in products of the same category or engaging in business of the same category as this employer shall not exceed two years.

Article 25. Except for the circumstances as prescribed in Articles 22 and 23 of this Law, the employer shall not stipulate with the employee that the employee shall pay the penalty for breaching contract.

Article 26. The following labor contracts are invalid or are partially invalid if:

1. a party employs the means of deception or coercion or takes advantage of the other party's difficulties to force the other party to conclude a

labor contract or to make an amendment to a labor contract, which is contrary to his will;

2. an employer disclaims its legal liability or denies the employee's rights; or

3. the mandatory provisions of laws or administrative regulations are violated.

If there is any dispute over the invalidating or partially invalidating of a labor contract, the dispute shall be settled by the labor dispute arbitration institution or by the people's court.

Article 27. The invalidity of any part of a labor contract does not affect the validity of the other parts of the contract. The other parts shall still remain valid.

Article 28. If a labor contract has been confirmed to be invalid, the employer shall pay remunerations to his employees who have labored for the employer. The amount of remunerations shall be determined by analogy to the remuneration to the employees taking up the same or similar positions of the employer.

Chapter III. Fulfillment and Change of Labor Contracts

Article 29. An employer and an employee shall, according to the stipulations of the labor contract, fully perform their respective obligations.

Article 30. An employer shall, under the contractual stipulations and the provisions of the state, timely pay its employees the full amount of remunerations.Where an employer defers paying or fails to pay the full amount of remunerations, the employees may apply to the local people's court for an order of payment. The people's court shall issue an order of payment according to the law.

Article 31. An employer shall strictly execute the criterion on production quota, it shall not force any of its employees to work overtime or make any of his employees do so in a disguised form. If an employer arranges overtime work, it shall pay its employee for the overtime work according to the relevant provisions of the state.

Article 32. If an employee refuses to perform dangerous operations ordered by the manager of his employer who violates the safety regulations or forces the employee to risk his life, the employee shall not be deemed to have violated the labor contract.

An employee may criticize, expose to the authorities, or charge against the employer if the work conditions may endanger his life and health.

Article 33. An employer's change of its name, legal representative, key person-in-charge, or investor shall not affect the fulfillment of the labor contracts.

Article 34. In case of merger or split the original labor contracts of the employer still remain valid. Such labor contracts shall be performed by the new employer who succeeds the rights and obligations of the aforesaid employer.

Article 35. An employer and an employee may modify the contents stipulated in the labor contract if they so agree upon negotiations. The modifications to the labor contract shall be made in writing. The employer and the employee shall each hold one copy of the modified labor contract.

Chapter IV. Dissolution and Termination of Labor Contracts

Article 36. An employer and an employee may dissolve the labor contract if they so agree upon negotiations.

Article 37. An employee may dissolve the labor contract if he notifies in writing the employer 30 days in advance. During the probation period, an employee may dissolve the labor contract if he notifies the employer 3 days in advance.

Article 38. Where an employer is under any of the following circumstances, its employees may dissolve the labor contract:

1. It fails to provide labor protection or work conditions as stipulated in the labor contract;
2. It fails to timely pay the full amount of remunerations;
3. It fails to pay social security premiums for the employees;
4. The rules and procedures set up by the employer are contrary to any law or regulation and impair the rights and interests of the employees;
5. The labor contract is invalidated due to the circumstance as mentioned in Article 26 (1) of this Law; or
6. Any other circumstances prescribed by other laws or administrative regulations that authorize employees to dissolve labor contracts.

If an employer forces any employee to work by the means of violence, threat, or illegally restraining personal freedom, or an employer violates the safety regulations to order or forces any employee to perform dangerous operations that endanger the employee's personal life, the employee may immediately dissolve the labor contract without notifying the employer in advance.

Article 39. Where an employee is under any of the following circumstances, his employer may dissolve the labor contract:

1. It is proved that the employee does not meet the recruitment conditions during the probation period;
2. The employee seriously violates the rules and procedures set up by the employer;
3. The employee causes any severe damage to the employer because he seriously neglects his duties or seeks private benefits;
4. The employee simultaneously enters an employment relationship with other employers and thus seriously affects his completion of the tasks of the employer, or the employee refuses to make the ratification after his employer points out the problem;

5. The labor contract is invalidated due to the circumstance as mentioned in Item (1), paragraph 1, Article 26 of this Law; or

6. The employee is under investigation for criminal liabilities according to law.

Article 40. Under any of the following circumstances, the employer may dissolve the labor contract if it notifies the employee in writing 30 days in advance or after it pays the employee an extra month's wages:

1. The employee is sick or is injured for a non-work-related reason and cannot resume his original position after the expiration of the prescribed time period for medical treatment, nor can he assume any other position arranged by the employer;

2. The employee is incompetent to his position or is still so after training or changing his position; or

3. The objective situation, on which the conclusion of the labor contract is based, has changed considerably, the labor contract is unable to be performed and no agreement on changing the contents of the labor contract is reached after negotiations between the employer and the employee.

Article 41. Under any of the following circumstances, if it is necessary to lay off 20 or more employees, or if it is necessary to lay off less than 20 employees but the layoff accounts for 10% of the total number of the employees, the employer shall, 30 days in advance, make an explanation to the labor union or to all its employees. After it has solicited the opinions from the labor union or of the employees, it may lay off the number of employees upon reporting the employee reduction plan to the labor administrative department:

1. It is under revitalization according to the Enterprise Bankruptcy Law;

2. It encounters serious difficulties in production and business operation;

3. The enterprise changes products, makes important technological renovation, or adjusts the methods of its business operation, and it is still necessary to lay off the number of employees after changing the labor contract; or

4. The objective economic situation, on which the labor contract is based, has changed considerably and the employer is unable to perform the labor contract.

The following employees shall be given a priority to be kept when the employer cuts down the number of employees:

1. Those who have concluded a fixed-term labor contract with a long time period;

2. Those who have concluded a labor contract without fixed term; and

3. Those whose family has no other employee and has the aged or minors to support.

If the employer intends to hire new employees within 6 months after it cuts down the number of employees according to the first paragraph of this Article, it shall notify the employees cut down and shall, in the equal conditions, give a priority to the employees cut down.

Article 42. An employer shall not dissolve the labor contract under Articles 40 and 41 of this Law if any of its employees:

1. is engaging in operations exposing him to occupational disease hazards and has not undergone an occupational health check-up before he leaves his position, or is suspected of having an occupational disease and is under diagnosis or medical observation;

2. has been confirmed as having lost or partially lost his capacity to work due to an occupational disease or a work-related injury during his employment with the employer;

3. has contracted an illness or sustained a non-work-related injury and the proscribed time period of medical treatment has not expired;

4. is a female who is in her pregnancy, confinement, or nursing period;

5. has been working for the employer continuously for not less than 15 years and is less than 5 years away from his legal retirement age; or

6. finds himself in other circumstances under which an employer shall not dissolve the labor contract as proscribed in laws or administrative regulations.

Article 43. Where an employer unilaterally dissolves a labor contract, it shall notify the labor union of the reasons in advance. If the employer violates any laws, administrative regulation, or stipulations of the labor contract, the labor union has the power to require the employer to make ratification. The employer shall consider the opinions of the labor union and notify the labor union of the relevant result in writing.

Article 44. A labor contract may be terminated under any of the following circumstances:

1. the term of a labor contract has expired;

2. the employee has begun to enjoy the basic benefits of his pension;

3. the employee is deceased, or is declared dead or missing by the people's court;

4. the employer is declared bankrupt;

5. the employer's business license is revoked or the employer is ordered to close down its business or to dissolve its business entity, or the employer makes a decision to liquidate its business ahead of the schedule; or

6. other circumstances occur as prescribed by other laws or administrative regulations.

Article 45. If a labor contract expires and it is under any of the circumstances as described in Article 42 of this Law, the term of labor contract shall be extended until the disappearance of the relevant circumstance. However, the matters relating to the termination of the labor contract of an employee who has lost or partially lost his capacity to work as prescribed in Article 42 (ii) of this Law shall be handled according to the pertinent provisions on work-related injury insurance.

Article 46. The employer shall, under any of the following circumstances, pay the employee an economic compensation:

1. The employee dissolves the labor contract in pursuance of Article 38 of this Law;

2. The employer proposes to dissolve the labor contract, and it reaches an agreement with the employee on the dissolution through negotiations;

3. The employer dissolves the labor contract according to Article 40 of this Law;

4. The employer dissolves the labor contract according to the first Paragraph of Article 41 of this Law; or

5. The termination of a fixed-term labor contract according to Article 44 (i) of this Law unless the employee refuses to renew the contract even though the conditions offered by the employer are the same as or better than those stipulated in the current contract;

6. The labor contract is terminated according to Article 44(iv) and (v) of this Law; or

7. Other circumstances occur as prescribed by other laws or administrative regulations.

Article 47. An employee shall be given an economic compensation based on the number of years he has worked for the employer and at the rate of one month's wage for each full year he worked. Any period of not less than six months but less than one year shall be counted as one year. The economic compensations payable to an employee for any period of less than six months shall be one-half of his monthly wages.

If the monthly wage of an employee is higher than three times the average monthly wage of employees declared by the people's government at the level of municipality directly under the central government or at the level of a districted city where the employer is located, the rate for the economic compensations to be paid to him shall be three times the average monthly wage of employees and shall be for no more than 12 years of his work.

The term "monthly wage" mentioned in this Article refers to the employee's average monthly wage for the 12 months prior to the dissolution or termination of his labor contract.

Article 48. If an employer dissolves or terminates a labor contract in violation of this Law but the employee demands the continuous fulfillment of the contract, the employer shall do so. If the employee does not demand the continuous fulfillment of the contract or if the continuous fulfillment of the labor contract is impossible, the employer shall pay compensation to the employee according to Article 87 of this Law.

Article 49. The State shall take measures to establish and improve a comprehensive system to ensure that the employees' social security relationship can be transferred from one region to another and can be continued after the transfer.

Article 50. At the time of dissolution or termination of a labor contract, the employer shall issue a document to prove the dissolution or termination of the labor contract and complete, within 15 days, the procedures for the transfer of the employee's personal file and social security relationship.

The employee shall complete the procedures for the handover of his work as agreed upon between both parties. If relevant provisions of this Law require the employer to pay an economic compensation, it shall make a payment upon completion of the procedures for the handover of the employee's work.

The employer shall preserve the labor contracts, which have been dissolved or terminated, for not less than two years for reference purposes.

Chapter V. Special Provisions

Section 3. Part-time Employments

Article 68. "Part-time employment" is a form of labor in which the remuneration is mainly calculated on an hourly basis, the average working hours of a worker per day shall not exceed 4 hours, and the aggregate working hours per week for the same employer shall not exceed 24 hours.

Article 69. Both parties to a part-time employment may reach an oral agreement.

A worker who engages in part-time employment may conclude a labor contract with one or more employers, but a labor contract concluded subsequently may not prejudice the performance of a labor contract previously concluded.

Article 70. No probation period may be stipulated by both parties for a part-time employment.

Article 71. Either of the parties to part-time employment may inform the other party of the termination of labor at any time. Upon the termination of a part-time employment, the employer will pay no economic compensation to the employee.

Article 72. The criterions for the calculation of part-time employment on hourly basis shall not be lower than the minimum hourly wage prescribed by the people's government of the place where the employer is located.

The maximum remuneration settlement and payment cycle for part-time employment shall not exceed 15 days.

. . .

Chapter VII. Legal Liabilities

Article 80. If the rules and procedure of an employer directly related to the employees' interests is contrary to any laws or regulations, the labor administration department shall order the employer to make ratification and give it a warning. If the rules and procedures cause any damage to the employees, the employer shall bear the liability for compensation.

Article 81. If the text of a labor contract provided by an employer does not include the mandatory clauses required by this Law or if an employer fails to deliver a copy of the labor contract to its employee, the labor administration department shall order the employer to make ratification. If any damage is caused to the employee, the employer shall bear the liability for compensation.

Article 82. If an employer fails to conclude a written labor contract with an employee after the lapse of more than one month but less than one year as of the day when it started using him, it shall pay to the worker his monthly wages at double amount.

If an employer fails, in violation of this Law, to conclude with an employee a labor contract without fixed term, it shall pay to the employee his monthly wage at double amount, starting from the date on which a labor contract without fixed term should have been concluded.

Article 83. If an employer stipulates the probation period with an employee to violate this Law, the labor administration department shall order the employer to make ratification. If the illegally stipulated probation has been performed, the employer shall pay compensation to the employee according to the time worked on probation beyond the statutory probation period, at the rate of the employee's monthly wage following the completion of his probation.

Article 84. Where an employer violates this Law by detaining the resident identity cards or other certificates of the employees, the labor administrative department shall order the employer to return the ID and certificates to the employees within a time limit and shall punish the employer according to the relevant laws.

Where an employer violates this Law by collecting money and property from employees in the name of guaranty or in any other excuses, the labor administrative department shall order the employer to return the said property to the employees within a time limit and fine the employer not less than 500 yuan but not more than 2,000 yuan for each person. If any damage is caused to the employees, the employer shall be liable for compensation.

When an employee dissolves or terminates the labor contract in pursuance of law, if the employer retains the archives or other articles of the employees, it shall be punished according to the provisions of the preceding paragraph.

Article 85. Where an employing entity is under any of the following circumstances, the labor administrative department shall order it to pay the remunerations, overtime remunerations or economic compensations within a time limit. If the remuneration is lower than the local minimum wage, the employer shall pay the shortfall. If payment is not made within the time limit, the employer shall be ordered to pay an extra compensation to the employee at a rate of not less than 50 percent and not more than 100 percent of the payable amount:

1. Failing to pay an employee his remunerations in full amount and on time as stipulated in the labor contract or prescribed by the state;

2. Paying an employee the wage below the local minimum wage standard;

3. Arranging overtime work without paying overtime remunerations; or

4. Dissolving or terminating a labor contract without paying the employee the economic compensation under this Law.

Article 86. Where a labor contract is confirmed invalid under Article 26 of this Law and any damage is caused to the other party, the party at fault shall be liable for compensation.

Article 87. If an employer violates this Law by dissolving or terminating the labor contract, it shall pay compensation to the employee at the rate of twice the economic compensations as prescribed in Article 47 of this Law.

Article 88. Where an employer is under any of the following circumstances, it shall be given an administrative punishment. If any crime is constituted, it shall be subject to criminal liabilities. If any damage is caused to the employee, the employer shall be liable for compensation:

1. To force the employee to work by violence, threat or illegal limitation of personal freedom;

2. To illegally command or force any employee to perform dangerous operations endangering the employee's life;

3. To insult, corporally punish, beat, illegally search, or restrain any employee; or

4. To cause damage to the physical or mental health of employees because of poor working conditions or severely polluted environments;

. . .

PART III.

EMPLOYEE PRIVACY

OMNIBUS CRIME CONTROL AND SAFE STREETS ACT

Title III. Wire Interception and Interception of Oral Communications

18 U.S.C. §§ 2510 to 2522

[Editors' note: Inconsistencies in the system of numbering the provisions of the Wiretap Act appear in the statute and are not transcription errors.]

§ 2510. Definitions. As used in this chapter—

(1) "Wire communication" means any aural transfer made in whole or in part through the use of facilities for the transmission of communications by the aid of wire, cable, or other like connection between the point of origin and the point of reception (including the use of such connection in a switching station) furnished or operated by any person engaged in providing or operating such facilities for the transmission of interstate or foreign communications or communications affecting interstate or foreign commerce.

(2) "Oral communication" means any oral communication uttered by a person exhibiting an expectation that such communication is not subject to interception under circumstances justifying such expectation, but such term does not include any electronic communication. . . .

(4) "Intercept" means the aural or other acquisition of the contents of any wire, electronic, or oral communication through the use of any electronic, mechanical, or other device.

(5) "Electronic, mechanical, or other device" means any device or apparatus which can be used to intercept a wire, oral, or electronic communication other than—

(a) Any telephone or telegraph instrument, equipment or facility, or any component thereof,

(i) furnished to the subscriber or user by a provider of wire or electronic communication service in the ordinary course of its business and being used by the subscriber or user in the ordinary course of its business or furnished by such subscriber or user for connection to the facilities of such service and used in the ordinary course of its business; or

(ii) Being used by a provider of wire or electronic communication service in the ordinary course of its business, or by an investigative or law enforcement officer in the ordinary course of his duties. . . .

(8) "Contents", when used with respect to any wire, oral, or electronic communication, includes any information concerning the substance, purport, or meaning of that communication. . . .

(12) "Electronic communication" means any transfer of signs, signals, writing, images, sounds, data, or intelligence of any nature transmitted in whole or in part by a wire, radio, electromagnetic, photo electronic or photo optical system that affects interstate or foreign commerce, but does not include—

(A) any wire or oral communication;

(B) any communication made through a tone-only paging device;

(C) any communication from a tracking device . . . ; or

(D) electronic funds transfer information stored by a financial institution in a communications system used for the electronic storage and transfer of funds.

(13) "User" means any person or entity who—

(A) uses an electronic communication service; and

(B) is duly authorized by the provider of such service to engage in such use.

(14) "Electronic communications system" means any wire, radio, electromagnetic, photo optical or photo electronic facilities for the transmission of wire or electronic communications, and any computer facilities or related electronic equipment for the electronic storage of such communications.

(15) "Electronic communication service" means any service which provides to users thereof the ability to send or receive wire or electronic communications.

(17) "Electronic storage" means—

(A) any temporary, intermediate storage of a wire or electronic communication incidental to the electronic transmission thereof; and

(B) any storage of such communication by an electronic communication service for purposes of backup protection of such communication.

(18) "Aural transfer" means a transfer containing the human voice at any point between and including the point of origin and the point of reception. . . .

§ 2511. Interception and disclosure of wire, oral, or electronic communications prohibited

(1) Except as otherwise specifically provided in this chapter any person who—

(a) Intentionally intercepts, endeavors to intercept, or procures any other person to intercept or endeavor to intercept, any wire, oral, or electronic communication; . . . .

(c) intentionally discloses, or endeavors to disclose, to any other person the contents of any wire, oral, or electronic communication, knowing or having reason to know that the information was obtained through the interception of a wire, oral, or electronic communication in violation of this subsection;

(d) intentionally uses, or endeavors to use, the contents of any wire, oral, or electronic communication, knowing or having reason to know that the information was obtained through the interception of a wire, oral, or electronic communication in violation of this subsection; shall be punished as provided in subsection (4) or shall be subject to suit as provided in subsection (5).

(2)(a)(i) It shall not be unlawful under this chapter for an operator of a switchboard, or an officer, employee, or agent of a provider of wire or electronic communication service, whose facilities are used in the transmission of a wire or electronic communication, to intercept, disclose, or use that communication in the normal course of his employment while engaged in any activity which is a necessary incident to the rendition of his service or to the protection of the rights or property of the provider of that service, except that a provider of wire communication service to the public shall not utilize service observing or random monitoring except for mechanical or service quality control checks;

(d) It shall not be unlawful under this chapter for a person not acting under color of law to intercept a wire, oral, or electronic communication where such person is a party to the communication or where one of the parties to the communication has given prior consent to such interception unless such communication is intercepted for the purpose of committing any criminal or tortuous act in violation of the Constitution or laws of the United States or of any State;

(h) It shall not be unlawful under this chapter—

(ii) for a provider of electronic communication service to record the fact that a wire or electronic communication was initiated or completed in order to protect such provider, another provider furnishing service toward the completion of the wire or electronic communication, or a user of that service, from fraudulent, unlawful or abusive use of such service. . . .

(4)(a) Except as provided in paragraph (b) of this subsection [pertains to satellite communications] or in subsection (5), whoever violates subsection (1) of this section shall be fined under this title or imprisoned not more than five years, or both. . . .

(5)(a)(ii) In an action under this subsection—

(A) if the violation of this chapter is a first offense for the person under paragraph (a) of subsection (4) and such person has not been found liable in a civil action under section 2520 of this title, the Federal Government shall be entitled to appropriate injunctive relief; and

(B) if the violation of this chapter is a second or subsequent offense under paragraph (a) of subsection (4) or such person has been found liable in any prior civil action under section 2520, the person shall be subject to a mandatory $500 civil fine.

(b) The court may use any means within its authority to enforce an injunction issued under paragraph (ii)(A), and shall impose a civil fine of not less than $500 for each violation of such an injunction. . . .

§ 2515. Prohibition of use as evidence of intercepted wire or oral communications

Whenever any wire or oral communication has been intercepted, no part of the contents of such communication and no evidence derived there from may be received in evidence in any trial, hearing, or other proceeding in or before any court, grand jury, department, officer, agency, regulatory body, legislative committee, or other authority of the United States, a State, or a political subdivision thereof if the disclosure of that information would be in violation of this chapter.

§ 2520. Recovery of civil damages authorized

(a) In general. Except as provided in section 2511(2)(a)(ii) [pertains to government foreign intelligence surveillance], any person whose wire, oral, or electronic communication is intercepted, disclosed, or intentionally used in violation of this chapter may in a civil action recover from the person or entity, other than the United States, which engaged in that violation such relief as may be appropriate.

(b) Relief. In an action under this section, appropriate relief includes—

(1) such preliminary and other equitable or declaratory relief as may be appropriate;

(2) damages under subsection (c) and punitive damages in appropriate cases; and

(3) a reasonable attorney's fee and other litigation costs reasonably incurred.

(c) Computation of damages.

(2) In any action under this section, the court may assess as damages whichever is the greater of—

(A) the sum of the actual damages suffered by the plaintiff and any profits made by the violator as a result of the violation; or

(B) statutory damages of whichever is the greater of $100 a day for each day of violation or $10,000.

(d) Defense. A good faith reliance on—

(1) a court warrant or order, a grand jury subpoena, a legislative authorization, or a statutory authorization;

(2) a request of an investigative officer . . . ; or

(3) a good faith determination that section 2511(3) or 2511(2)(i) permitted the conduct complained of;

is a complete defense against any civil or criminal action brought under this chapter or any other law.

(e) Limitation. A civil action under this section may not be commenced later than two years after the date upon which the claimant first has a reasonable opportunity to discover the violation. . . .

§ 2521. Injunction against illegal interception

Whenever it shall appear that any person is engaged or is about to engage in any act which constitutes or will constitute a felony violation of this chapter, the Attorney General may initiate a civil action in a district court of the United States to enjoin such violation. The court shall proceed as soon as practicable to the hearing and determination of such an action, and may, at any time before final determination, enter such a restraining order or prohibition, or take such other action, as is warranted to prevent a continuing and substantial injury to the United States or to any person or class of persons for whose protection the action is brought. A proceeding under this section is governed by the Federal Rules of Civil Procedure, except that, if an indictment has been returned against the respondent, discovery is governed by the Federal Rules of Criminal Procedure.

ELECTRONIC COMMUNICATIONS PRIVACY ACT

18 U.S.C. §§ 2701 to 2711

§ 2701. Unlawful access to stored communications

(a) Offense. Except as provided in subsection (c) of this section whoever—

(1) intentionally accesses without authorization a facility through which an electronic communication service is provided; or

(2) intentionally exceeds an authorization to access that facility;

and thereby obtains, alters, or prevents authorized access to a wire or electronic communication while it is in electronic storage in such system shall be punished as provided in subsection (b) of this section.

(b) Punishment. The punishment for an offense under subsection (a) of this section is—

(1) if the offense is committed for purposes of commercial advantage, malicious destruction or damage, or private commercial gain, or in furtherance of any criminal or tortious act in violation of the Constitution or laws of the United States or any State—

(A) a fine under this title or imprisonment for not more than 5 years, or both, in the case of a first offense under this subparagraph; and

(B) a fine under this title or imprisonment for not more than 10 years, or both, for any subsequent offense under this subparagraph; and

(2) in any other case—

(A) a fine under this title or imprisonment for not more than 1 year or both, in the case of a first offense under this paragraph; and

(B) a fine under this title or imprisonment for not more than 5 years, or both, in the case of an offense under this subparagraph that occurs after a conviction of another offense under this section.

(c) Exceptions. Subsection (a) of this section does not apply with respect to conduct authorized—

(1) by the person or entity providing a wire or electronic communications service; [or]

(2) by a user of that service with respect to a communication of or intended for that user. . . .

§ 2707. Civil action

(a) Cause of action. Except as provided in section 2703(e) [pertains to disclosure required pursuant to court order, warrant, subpoena, etc.], any provider of electronic communication service, subscriber, or other person aggrieved by any violation of this chapter [18 U.S.C. §§ 2701 et seq.] in which the conduct constituting the violation is engaged in with a knowing or intentional state of mind may, in a civil action, recover from the person or entity, other than the United States, which engaged in that violation such relief as may be appropriate.

(b) Relief. In a civil action under this section, appropriate relief includes—

(1) such preliminary and other equitable or declaratory relief as may be appropriate;

(2) damages under subsection (c); and

(3) a reasonable attorney's fee and other litigation costs reasonably incurred.

(c) Damages. The court may assess as damages in a civil action under this section the sum of the actual damages suffered by the plaintiff and any profits made by the violator as a result of the violation, but in no case shall a person entitled to recover receive less than the sum of $1,000. If the violation is willful or intentional, the court may assess punitive damages. In the case of a successful action to enforce liability under this section, the court may assess the costs of the action, together with reasonable attorney fees determined by the court. . . .

(e) Defense. A good faith reliance on—

(1) a court warrant or order, a grand jury subpoena, a legislative authorization, or a statutory authorization . . . ;

(2) a request of an investigative or law enforcement officer . . . ; or

(3) a good faith determination that section 2511(3) permitted the conduct complained of;

is a complete defense to any civil or criminal action brought under this chapter or any other law.

(f) Limitation. A civil action under this section may not be commenced later than two years after the date upon which the claimant first discovered or had a reasonable opportunity to discover the violation. . . .

§ 2708. Exclusivity of remedies

The remedies and sanctions described in this chapter are the only judicial remedies and sanctions for nonconstitutional violations of this chapter. . . .

IOWA PRIVATE SECTOR DRUG-FREE WORKPLACES

Iowa Code § 730.5

§ 730.5:1. Definitions. As used in this section, unless the context otherwise requires:

a. "Alcohol" means ethanol, isopropanol, or methanol.

b. "Confirmed positive test result" means, except for alcohol testing conducted pursuant to subsection 7, paragraph "f", subparagraph (2), the results of a blood, urine, or oral fluid test in which the level of controlled substances or metabolites in the specimen analyzed meets or exceeds nationally accepted standards for determining detectable levels of controlled substances as adopted by the federal substance abuse and mental health services administration. If nationally accepted standards for oral fluid tests have not been adopted by the federal substance abuse and mental health services administration, the standards for determining detectable levels of controlled substances for purposes of determining a confirmed positive test result shall be the same standard that has been established by the federal food and drug administration for the measuring instrument used to perform the oral fluid test.

c. "Drug" means a substance considered a controlled substance and included in schedule I, II, III, IV, or V under the federal Controlled Substances Act, 21 U.S.C. § 801 et seq. . . .

g. "Medical review officer" means a licensed physician, osteopathic physician, chiropractor, nurse practitioner, or physician assistant authorized to practice in any state of the United States, who is responsible for receiving laboratory results generated by an employer's drug or alcohol testing program, and who has knowledge of substance abuse disorders and has appropriate medical training to interpret and evaluate an individual's confirmed positive test result together with the individual's medical history and any other relevant biomedical information.

h. "Prospective employee" means a person who has made application, whether written or oral, to an employer to become an employee.

i. "Reasonable suspicion drug or alcohol testing" means drug or alcohol testing based upon evidence that an employee is using or has used alcohol or other drugs in violation of the employer's written policy drawn from specific objective and articulable facts and reasonable inferences drawn from those facts in light of experience. For purposes of this paragraph, facts and inferences may be based upon, but not limited to, any of the following:

(1) Observable phenomena while at work such as direct observation of alcohol or drug use or abuse or of the physical symptoms or manifestations of being impaired due to alcohol or other drug use.

(2) Abnormal conduct or erratic behavior while at work or a significant deterioration in work performance.

(3) A report of alcohol or other drug use provided by a reliable and credible source.

(4) Evidence that an individual has tampered with any drug or alcohol test during the individual's employment with the current employer.

(5) Evidence that an employee has caused an accident while at work which resulted in an injury to a person for which injury, if suffered by an employee, a record or report could be required under chapter 88, or resulted in damage to property, including to equipment, in an amount reasonably estimated at the time of the accident to exceed one thousand dollars.

(6) Evidence that an employee has manufactured, sold, distributed, solicited, possessed, used, or transferred drugs while working or while on the employer's premises or while operating the employer's vehicle, machinery, or equipment.

j. "Safety-sensitive position" means a job wherein an accident could cause loss of human life, serious bodily injury, or significant property or environmental damage, including a job with duties that include immediate supervision of a person in a job that meets the requirement of this paragraph.

k. "Sample" means such sample from the human body capable of revealing the presence of alcohol or other drugs, or their metabolites, which shall include only urine, saliva, breath, and blood. However, "sample" does not mean blood except as authorized pursuant to subsection 7, paragraph "l".

l. "Unannounced drug or alcohol testing" means testing for the purposes of detecting drugs or alcohol which is conducted on a periodic basis, without advance notice of the test to employees, other than employees whose duties include responsibility for administration of the employer's drug or alcohol testing program, subject to testing prior to the day of testing, and without individualized suspicion. The selection of employees to be tested from the pool of employees subject to testing shall be done based on a neutral and objective selection process by an entity independent from the employer and shall be made by a computer-based random number generator that is matched with employees' social security numbers, payroll identification numbers, or other comparable identifying numbers in which each member of the employee population subject to testing has an equal chance of selection for initial testing, regardless of whether the employee has been selected or tested previously. The random selection process shall be conducted through a computer program that records each selection attempt by date, time, and employee number.

§ 730.5:2. Applicability. This section does not apply to drug or alcohol tests conducted on employees required to be tested pursuant to federal statutes, federal regulations, or orders issued pursuant to federal law. In addition, an employer, through its written policy, may exclude from the pools of employees subject to unannounced drug or alcohol testing pursuant to subsection 8, paragraph "a", employee populations required to be tested as described in this subsection.

§ 730.5:3. Testing optional. This section does not require or create a legal duty on an employer to conduct drug or alcohol testing and the requirements of this section shall not be construed to encourage, discourage, restrict, limit, prohibit, or require such testing. In addition, an employer may implement and require drug or alcohol testing at some but not all of the work sites of the employer and the requirements of this section shall only apply to the employer and employees who are at the work sites where drug or alcohol testing pursuant to this section has been implemented. A cause of action shall not arise in favor of any person against an employer or agent of an employer based on the failure of the employer to establish a program or policy on substance abuse prevention or to implement any component of testing as permitted by this section.

§ 730.5:4. Testing as condition of employment—requirements. To the extent provided in subsection 8, an employer may test employees and prospective employees for the presence of drugs or alcohol as a condition of continued employment or hiring. An employer shall adhere to the requirements of this section concerning the conduct of such testing and the use and disposition of the results of such testing.

§ 730.5:5. Collection of samples. In conducting drug or alcohol testing, an employer may require the collection of samples from its employees and prospective employees, and may require presentation of reliable individual identification from the person being tested to the person collecting the samples. Collection of a sample shall be in conformance with the requirements of this section. The employer may designate the type of sample to be used for this testing.

. . . .

§ 730.5:7. Testing procedures. All sample collection and testing for drugs or alcohol under this section shall be performed in accordance with the following conditions:

a. The collection of samples shall be performed under sanitary conditions and with regard for the privacy of the individual from whom the specimen is being obtained and in a manner reasonably calculated to preclude contamination or substitution of the specimen. If the sample collected is urine, procedures shall be established to provide for individual privacy in the collection of the sample unless there is a reasonable suspicion that a particular individual subject to testing may alter or substitute the urine specimen to be provided, or has previously altered or substituted a urine specimen provided pursuant to a drug or alcohol test. For purposes of this paragraph, "individual privacy" means a location at the collection site where urination can occur in private, which has been secured by visual inspection to ensure that other persons are not present, which provides that undetected access to the location is not possible during urination, and which provides for the ability to effectively restrict access to the location during the time the specimen is provided. If an individual is providing a urine sample and collection of the urine sample is directly monitored or observed by another individual, the individual who is directly monitoring or observing the collection shall be of the same gender as the individual from whom the urine sample is being collected.

b. Collection of a urine sample for testing of current employees shall be performed so that the specimen is split into two components at the time of collection in the presence of the individual from whom the sample or specimen is collected. The second portion of the specimen or sample shall be of sufficient quantity to permit a second, independent confirmatory test as provided in paragraph "i". The sample shall be split such that the primary sample contains at least thirty milliliters and the secondary sample contains at least fifteen milliliters. Both portions of the sample shall be forwarded to the laboratory conducting the initial confirmatory testing. In addition to any requirements for storage of the initial sample that may be imposed upon the laboratory as a condition for certification or approval, the laboratory shall store the second portion of any sample until receipt of a confirmed negative test result or for a period of at least forty-five calendar days following the completion of the initial confirmatory testing, if the first portion yielded a confirmed positive test result.

c. Sample collections shall be documented, and the procedure for documentation shall include the following:

(1) Samples, except for samples collected for alcohol testing conducted pursuant to paragraph "f", subparagraph (2), shall be labeled so as to reasonably preclude the possibility of misidentification

of the person tested in relation to the test result provided, and samples shall be handled and tracked in a manner such that control and accountability are maintained from initial collection to each stage in handling, testing, and storage, through final disposition.

(2) An employee or prospective employee shall be provided an opportunity to provide any information which may be considered relevant to the test, including identification of prescription or nonprescription drugs currently or recently used, or other relevant medical information. To assist an employee or prospective employee in providing the information described in this subparagraph, the employer shall provide an employee or prospective employee with a list of the drugs to be tested.

d. Sample collection, storage, and transportation to the place of testing shall be performed so as to reasonably preclude the possibility of sample contamination, adulteration, or misidentification.

e. All confirmatory drug testing shall be conducted at a laboratory certified by the United States department of health and human services' substance abuse and mental health services administration or approved under rules adopted by the Iowa department of public health.

f. Drug or alcohol testing shall include confirmation of any initial positive test results. An employer may take adverse employment action, including refusal to hire a prospective employee, based on a confirmed positive test result for drugs or alcohol.

(1) For drug or alcohol testing, except for alcohol testing conducted pursuant to subparagraph (2), confirmation shall be by use of a different chemical process than was used in the initial screen for drugs or alcohol. The confirmatory drug or alcohol test shall be a chromatographic technique such as gas chromatography/mass spectrometry, or another comparably reliable analytical method.

(2) Notwithstanding any provision of this section to the contrary, alcohol testing, including initial and confirmatory testing, may be conducted pursuant to requirements established by the employer's written policy. The written policy shall include requirements governing evidential breath testing devices, alcohol screening devices, and the qualifications for personnel administering initial and confirmatory testing, which shall be consistent with regulations adopted as of January 1, 1999, by the United States department of transportation governing alcohol testing required to be conducted pursuant to the federal Omnibus Transportation Employee Testing Act of 1991.

(3) Notwithstanding any provision of this section to the contrary, collection of an oral fluid sample for testing shall be performed in the presence of the individual from whom the sample or specimen is collected. The specimen or sample shall be of sufficient quantity to permit a second, independent, confirmatory test as provided in paragraph "i". In addition to any requirement for storage of the initial sample that may be imposed upon the laboratory as a condition for

certification or approval, the laboratory shall store the unused portion of any sample until receipt of a confirmed negative test result or for a period of at least forty-five calendar days following the completion of the initial confirmatory testing, if the portion yielded a confirmed positive test result.

g. A medical review officer shall, prior to the results being reported to an employer, review and interpret any confirmed positive test results, including both quantitative and qualitative test results, to ensure that the chain of custody is complete and sufficient on its face and that any information provided by the individual pursuant to paragraph "c", subparagraph (2), is considered. However, this paragraph shall not apply to alcohol testing conducted pursuant to paragraph "f", subparagraph (2).

h. In conducting drug or alcohol testing pursuant to this section, the laboratory, the medical review officer, and the employer shall ensure, to the extent feasible, that the testing only measure, and the records concerning the testing only show or make use of information regarding, alcohol or drugs in the body.

i. (1) If a confirmed positive test result for drugs or alcohol for a current employee is reported to the employer by the medical review officer, the employer shall notify the employee in writing by certified mail, return receipt requested, of the results of the test, the employee's right to request and obtain a confirmatory test of the second sample collected pursuant to paragraph "b" at an approved laboratory of the employee's choice, and the fee payable by the employee to the employer for reimbursement of expenses concerning the test. The fee charged an employee shall be an amount that represents the costs associated with conducting the second confirmatory test, which shall be consistent with the employer's cost for conducting the initial confirmatory test on an employee's sample. If the employee, in person or by certified mail, return receipt requested, requests a second confirmatory test, identifies an approved laboratory to conduct the test, and pays the employer the fee for the test within seven days from the date the employer mails by certified mail, return receipt requested, the written notice to the employee of the employee's right to request a test, a second confirmatory test shall be conducted at the laboratory chosen by the employee. The results of the second confirmatory test shall be reported to the medical review officer who reviewed the initial confirmatory test results and the medical review officer shall review the results and issue a report to the employer on whether the results of the second confirmatory test confirmed the initial confirmatory test as to the presence of a specific drug or alcohol. If the results of the second test do not confirm the results of the initial confirmatory test, the employer shall reimburse the employee for the fee paid by the employee for the second test and the initial confirmatory test shall not be considered a confirmed positive test result for drugs or alcohol for purposes of taking disciplinary action pursuant to subsection 10.

(2) If a confirmed positive test result for drugs or alcohol for a prospective employee is reported to the employer by the medical review officer, the employer shall notify the prospective employee in writing of the results of the test, of the name and address of the medical review officer who made the report, and of the prospective employee's right to request records under subsection 13. . . .

§ 730.5:8. Drug or alcohol testing. Employers may conduct drug or alcohol testing as provided in this subsection:

a. Employers may conduct unannounced drug or alcohol testing of employees who are selected from any of the following pools of employees:

(1) The entire employee population at a particular work site of the employer except for employees not subject to testing pursuant to a collective bargaining agreement, or employees who are not scheduled to be at work at the time the testing is conducted because of the status of the employees or who have been excused from work pursuant to the employer's work policy prior to the time the testing is announced to employees.

(2) The entire full-time active employee population at a particular work site except for employees not subject to testing pursuant to a collective bargaining agreement, or employees who are not scheduled to be at work at the time the testing is to be conducted because of the status of the employee or who have been excused from work pursuant to the employer's working policy.

(3) All employees at a particular work site who are in a pool of employees in a safety-sensitive position and who are scheduled to be at work at the time testing is conducted, other than employees not subject to testing pursuant to a collective bargaining agreement, or employees who are not scheduled to be at work at the time the testing is to be conducted or who have been excused from work pursuant to the employer's work policy prior to the time the testing is announced to employees.

b. Employers may conduct drug or alcohol testing of employees during, and after completion of, drug or alcohol rehabilitation.

c. Employers may conduct reasonable suspicion drug or alcohol testing.

d. Employers may conduct drug or alcohol testing of prospective employees.

e. Employers may conduct drug or alcohol testing as required by federal law or regulation or by law enforcement.

f. Employers may conduct drug or alcohol testing in investigating accidents in the workplace in which the accident resulted in an injury to a person for which injury, if suffered by an employee, a record or report could be required under chapter 88, or resulted in damage to property, including to equipment, in an amount reasonably estimated at the time of the accident to exceed one thousand dollars.

§ 730.5:9. Written policy and other testing requirements.

a.(1) Drug or alcohol testing or retesting by an employer shall be carried out within the terms of a written policy which has been provided to every employee subject to testing, and is available for review by employees and prospective employees. If an employee or prospective employee is a minor, the employer shall provide a copy of the written policy to a parent of the employee or prospective employee and shall obtain a receipt or acknowledgment from the parent that a copy of the policy has been received. Providing a copy of the written policy to a parent of a minor by certified mail, return receipt requested, shall satisfy the requirements of this subparagraph. . . .

b. The employer's written policy shall provide uniform requirements for what disciplinary or rehabilitative actions an employer shall take against an employee or prospective employee upon receipt of a confirmed positive test result for drugs or alcohol or upon the refusal of the employee or prospective employee to provide a testing sample. The policy shall provide that any action taken against an employee or prospective employee shall be based only on the results of the drug or alcohol test. The written policy shall also provide that if rehabilitation is required pursuant to paragraph "g", the employer shall not take adverse employment action against the employee so long as the employee complies with the requirements of rehabilitation and successfully completes rehabilitation. . . .

§ 730.5:10. Disciplinary procedures.

a. Upon receipt of a confirmed positive test result for drugs or alcohol which indicates a violation of the employer's written policy, or upon the refusal of an employee or prospective employee to provide a testing sample, an employer may use that test result or test refusal as a valid basis for disciplinary or rehabilitative actions pursuant to the requirements of the employer's written policy and the requirements of this section, which may include, among other actions, the following:

(1) A requirement that the employee enroll in an employer -provided or approved rehabilitation, treatment, or counseling program, which may include additional drug or alcohol testing, participation in and successful completion of which may be a condition of continued employment, and the costs of which may or may not be covered by the employer's health plan or policies.

(2) Suspension of the employee, with or without pay, for a designated period of time.

(3) Termination of employment.

(4) Refusal to hire a prospective employee.

(5) Other adverse employment action in conformance with the employer's written policy and procedures, including any relevant collective bargaining agreement provisions.

b. Following a drug or alcohol test, but prior to receipt of the final results of the drug or alcohol test, an employer may suspend a current employee, with or without pay, pending the outcome of the test. An employee who has been suspended shall be reinstated by the employer, with back pay, and interest on such amount at eighteen percent per annum compounded annually, if applicable, if the result of the test is not a confirmed positive test result for drugs or alcohol which indicates a violation of the employer's written policy.

§ 730.5:11. Employer immunity. A cause of action shall not arise against an employer who has established a policy and initiated a testing program in accordance with the testing and policy safeguards provided for under this section, for any of the following:

a. Testing or taking action based on the results of a positive drug or alcohol test result, indicating the presence of drugs or alcohol, in good faith, or on the refusal of an employee or prospective employee to submit to a drug or alcohol test.

b. Failure to test for drugs or alcohol, or failure to test for a specific drug or controlled substance.

c. Failure to test for, or if tested for, failure to detect, any specific drug or other controlled substance.

d. Termination or suspension of any substance abuse prevention or testing program or policy.

e. Any action taken related to a false negative drug or alcohol test result.

§ 730.5:12. Employer liability—false positive test results.

a. Except as otherwise provided in paragraph "b", a cause of action shall not arise against an employer who has established a program of drug or alcohol testing in accordance with this section, unless all of the following conditions exist:

(1) The employer's action was based on a false positive test result.

(2) The employer knew or clearly should have known that the test result was in error and ignored the correct test result because of reckless, malicious, or negligent disregard for the truth, or the willful intent to deceive or to be deceived.

b. A cause of action for defamation, libel, slander, or damage to reputation shall not arise against an employer establishing a program of drug or alcohol testing in accordance with this section unless all of the following apply:

(1) The employer discloses the test results to a person other than the employer, an authorized employee, agent, or representative of the employer, the tested employee or the tested applicant for employment, an authorized substance abuse treatment program or employee assistance program, or an authorized agent or representative of the tested employee or applicant.

(2) The test results disclosed incorrectly indicate the presence of alcohol or drugs.

(3) The employer negligently discloses the results.

c. In any cause of action based upon a false positive test result, all of the following conditions apply:

(1) The results of a drug or alcohol test conducted in compliance with this section are presumed to be valid.

(2) An employer shall not be liable for monetary damages if the employer's reliance on the false positive test result was reasonable and in good faith.

§ 730.5:13. Confidentiality of results—exception.

a. All communications received by an employer relevant to employee or prospective employee drug or alcohol test results, or otherwise received through the employer's drug or alcohol testing program, are confidential communications and shall not be used or received in evidence, obtained in discovery, or disclosed in any public or private proceeding, except as otherwise provided or authorized by this section.

b. An employee, or a prospective employee, who is the subject of a drug or alcohol test conducted under this section pursuant to an employer's written policy and for whom a confirmed positive test result is reported shall, upon written request, have access to any records relating to the employee's drug or alcohol test, including records of the laboratory where the testing was conducted and any records relating to the results of any relevant certification or review by a medical review officer. However, a prospective employee shall be entitled to records under this paragraph only if the prospective employee requests the records within fifteen calendar days from the date the employer provided the prospective employee written notice of the results of a drug or alcohol test as provided in subsection 7, paragraph "i", subparagraph (2).

c. Except as provided by this section and as necessary to conduct drug or alcohol testing under this section and to file a report pursuant to subsection 16, a laboratory and a medical review officer conducting drug or alcohol testing under this section shall not use or disclose to any person any personally identifiable information regarding such testing, including the names of individuals tested, even if unaccompanied by the results of the test.

d. An employer may use and disclose information concerning the results of a drug or alcohol test conducted pursuant to this section under any of the following circumstances:

(1) In an arbitration proceeding pursuant to a collective bargaining agreement, or an administrative agency proceeding or judicial proceeding under workers' compensation laws or unemployment compensation laws or under common or statutory laws where action taken by the employer based on the test is relevant or is challenged.

(2) To any federal agency or other unit of the federal government as required under federal law, regulation or order, or in accordance with compliance requirements of a federal government contract.

(3) To any agency of this state authorized to license individuals if the employee tested is licensed by that agency and the rules of that agency require such disclosure.

(4) To a union representing the employee if such disclosure would be required by federal labor laws.

(5) To a substance abuse evaluation or treatment facility or professional for the purpose of evaluation or treatment of the employee. However, positive test results from an employer drug or alcohol testing program shall not be used as evidence in any criminal action against the employee or prospective employee tested.

§ 730.5:14. Civil penalties—jurisdiction.

a. Any laboratory or medical review officer which discloses information in violation of the provisions of subsection 7, paragraph "h" or "k", or any employer who, through the selection process described in subsection 1, paragraph "l", improperly targets or exempts employees subject to unannounced drug or alcohol testing, shall be subject to a civil penalty of one thousand dollars for each violation. The attorney general or the attorney general's designee may maintain a civil action to enforce this subsection. Any civil penalty recovered shall be deposited in the general fund of the state.

b. A laboratory or medical review officer involved in the conducting of a drug or alcohol test pursuant to this section shall be deemed to have the necessary contact with this state for the purpose of subjecting the laboratory or medical review officer to the jurisdiction of the courts of this state.

§ 730.5:15. Civil remedies. This section may be enforced through a civil action.

a. A person who violates this section or who aids in the violation of this section, is liable to an aggrieved employee or prospective employee for affirmative relief including reinstatement or hiring, with or without back pay, or any other equitable relief as the court deems appropriate including attorney fees and court costs.

b. When a person commits, is committing, or proposes to commit, an act in violation of this section, an injunction may be granted through an action in district court to prohibit the person from continuing such acts. The action for injunctive relief may be brought by an aggrieved employee or prospective employee, the county attorney, or the attorney general. In an action brought under this subsection alleging that an employer has required or requested a drug or alcohol test in violation of this section, the employer has the burden of proving that the requirements of this section were met. . . .

UTAH DRUG AND ALCOHOL TESTING STATUTE

Utah Code Ann. §§ 34-38-1 to 34-38-15

§ 34-38-1. Legislative findings—Purpose and intent of chapter

(1) The Legislature finds that a healthy and productive work force, safe working conditions free from the effects of drugs and alcohol, and maintenance of the quality of products produced and services rendered in this state, are important to employers, employees, and the general public. The Legislature further finds that the abuse of drugs and alcohol creates a variety of workplace problems, including increased injuries on the job, increased absenteeism, increased financial burden on health and benefit programs, increased workplace theft, decreased employee morale, decreased productivity, and a decline in the quality of products and services.

(2) The Legislature does not intend to prohibit an employee from seeking damages or job reinstatement if action is taken by the employer on the basis of an inaccurate test result.

§ 34-38-2. Definitions

For purposes of this chapter:

(1) "Alcohol" means ethyl alcohol or ethanol.

(2) "Drugs" means a substance recognized as a drug in the United States Pharmacopoeia, the National Formulary, the Homeopathic Pharmacopoeia, or other drug compendia, or supplement to any of those compendia.

(3)(a) "Employer" means a person, including a public utility or transit district, that has one or more workers or operators employed in the same business, or in or about the same establishment, under any contract of hire, express or implied, oral or written. "Employer" does not include the federal or state government, or other local political subdivisions.

(4) "Employee" means an individual in the service of an employer, for compensation.

(5) "Failed test" means a confirmed drug or alcohol test that indicates that the sample tested is:

(a) positive;

(b) adulterated; or

(c) substituted.

(6) "Inaccurate test result" means a test result that is treated as a positive test result, when the sample should not have resulted in a positive test result.

(7) "Licensed physician" means an individual who is licensed:

(a) as a doctor of medicine under Title 58, Chapter 67, Utah Medical Practice Act, or similar law of another state; or

(b) as an osteopathic physician or surgeon under Title 58, Chapter 68, Utah Osteopic Medical Practice Act, or similar law of another state.

(8) "Prospective employee" means an individual who applies to an employer, either in writing or orally, to become the employer's employee.

(9) "Sample" means urine, blood, breath, saliva, or hair.

§ 34-38-3. Testing for drugs or alcohol

(1) If an employer tests an employee or prospective employee for the presence of drugs or alcohol as a condition of hiring or continued employment, the employer is protected from liability as provided in this chapter if the employer complies with this chapter. However, employers and management in general shall submit to the testing themselves on a periodic basis. . . .

§ 34-38-4. Samples—Identification and collection

In order to test reliably for the presence of drugs or alcohol, an employer may require samples from his employees and prospective employees, and may require presentation of reliable identification to the person collecting the samples. Collection of the sample shall be in conformance with the requirements of Section 34-38-6. The employer may designate the type of sample to be used for testing.

§ 34-38-5. Time of testing—Cost of testing and transportation

(1) Any drug or alcohol testing by an employer shall occur during or immediately after the regular work period of current employees and shall be deemed work time for purposes of compensation and benefits for current employees.

(2) An employer shall pay all costs of testing for drugs or alcohol required by the employer, including the cost of transportation if the testing of a current employee is conducted at a place other than the workplace.

§ 34-38-6. Requirements for collection and testing

(1) The collection and testing of a sample for drugs and alcohol under this chapter shall be performed in accordance with this chapter.

(2) The collection of a sample shall be performed under reasonable and sanitary conditions.

(3) A sample shall be collected and tested:

(a) with due regard to the privacy of the individual being tested; and

(b) in a manner reasonably calculated to prevent substitutions or interference with the collection or testing of a reliable sample.

(4) The sample collection shall be documented. The documentation procedures required by this Subsection (4) include:

(a) labeling of a sample so as reasonably to preclude the probability of erroneous identification of test results; and

(b) an opportunity for the employee or prospective employee to provide notification of any information that the employee or prospective employee considers relevant to the test, including:

(i) identification of currently or recently used prescription or nonprescription drugs; or

(ii) other relevant medical information.

(5) Sample collection, storage, and transportation to the place of testing shall be performed so as reasonably to preclude the probability of sample contamination or adulteration.

(6)(a) Testing of a sample shall conform to scientifically accepted analytical methods and procedures.

(b) Before a test of a sample may be considered a failed test and used as a basis for an action by an employer under Section 34–38–8, testing of the sample shall include a confirmation test:

(i) by gas chromatography, gas chromatography-mass spectroscopy, or other comparably reliable analytical method; and

(ii) if the sample used for a test is a urine sample, by a laboratory that is certified by the United States Department of Health and Human Services under the National Laboratory Certification Program.

§ 34-38-7. Employer's written testing policy—Purposes and requirements for collection and testing—Employer's use of test results

(1) Testing or retesting for the presence of drugs or alcohol by an employer shall be carried out within the terms of a written policy which has been distributed to employees and is available for review by prospective employees.

(2) Within the terms of his written policy, an employer may require the collection and testing of samples for the following purposes:

(a) investigation of possible individual employee impairment;

(b) investigation of accidents in the workplace or incidents of workplace theft;

(c) maintenance of safety for employees or the general public; or

(d) maintenance of productivity, quality of products or services, or security of property or information.

(3) The collection and testing of samples shall be conducted in accordance with Sections 34-38-4, 34-38-5, and 34-38-6, and need not be limited to circumstances where there are indications of individual, job-related impairment of an employee or prospective employee.

(4) The employer's use and disposition of all drug or alcohol test results are subject to the limitations of Sections 34-38-8 and 34-38-13.

§ 34-38-8. Employer's disciplinary or rehabilitative actions

(1) An employer may take an action described in Subsection (2) if:

(a) the employer receives a test result that:

(i) indicates a failed test;

(ii) is confirmed as required by Subsection 34–38–6(6); and

(iii) indicates a violation of the employer's written policy; or

(b) an employee or prospective employee refuses to provide a sample.

(2) An employer may use a test result or a refusal described in Subsection (1) as the basis for disciplinary or rehabilitative actions, which may include the following:

(a) a requirement that the employee enroll in an employer-approved rehabilitation, treatment, or counseling program, which may include additional drug or alcohol testing, as a condition of continued employment;

(b) suspension of the employee with or without pay for a period of time;

(c) termination of employment;

(d) refusal to hire a prospective employee; or

(e) other disciplinary measures in conformance with the employer's usual procedures, including a collective bargaining agreement.

§ 34-38-9. No cause of action for failure to test or detect or for termination of testing program

No cause of action arises in favor of any person against an employer who has established a policy and initiated a testing program in accordance with this chapter, for any of the following:

(1) failure to test for drugs or alcohol, or failure to test for a specific drug or other substance;

(2) failure to test for, or if tested for, failure to detect, any specific drug or other substance, disease, infectious agent, virus, or other physical abnormality, problem, or defect of any kind; or

(3) termination or suspension of any drug or alcohol testing program or policy.

§ 34-38-10. No cause of action arises against employer unless false test result—Presumption and limitation of damages in claim against employer

(1) A cause of action may not arise in favor of a person against an employer who establishes a program of drug or alcohol testing in accordance with this chapter, and who takes an action under Section 34-38-8, unless the employer takes the action on the basis of an inaccurate test result.

(2) If a person bringing a claim, including a claim under Section 34-38-11, alleges that an employer's action is based on an inaccurate test result:

(a) there is a rebuttable presumption that the test result is valid if the employer complies with Section 34-38-6; and

(b) the employer is not liable for monetary damages if the employer's reliance on an inaccurate test result is reasonable and in good faith.

(3)(a) There is a rebuttable presumption that the employer complies with Section 34-38-6 if as part of the employer's drug and alcohol testing program a licensed physician who is trained in the interpretation of drug and alcohol test results:

(i) provides medical assessment of a result that indicates a failed test;

(ii) requests re-analysis of a test result if necessary; and

(iii) makes a determination whether or not alcohol or other drug use has occurred.

(b) A court may find that an employer complies with Section 34-38-6 notwithstanding that the employer's drug and alcohol testing program does not include an action described in Subsection (3)(a).

§ 34-38-11. Bases for cause of action for defamation, libel, slander, or damage to reputation

No cause of action for defamation of character, libel, slander, or damage to reputation arises in favor of any person against an employer who has established a program of drug or alcohol testing in accordance with this chapter, unless:

(1) the results of that test were disclosed to any person other than the employer, an authorized employee or agent of the employer, the tested employee, or the tested prospective employee;

(2) the information disclosed is based on an inaccurate test result;

(3) an inaccurate test result is disclosed with malice; and

(4) all elements of an action for defamation of character, libel, slander, or damage to reputation as established by statute or common law, are satisfied.

§ 34-38-12. No cause of action for failure of employer to establish testing program

No cause of action arises in favor of any person based upon the failure of an employer to establish a program or policy of drug or alcohol testing.

§ 34-38-13. Confidentiality of test-related information

(1) For purposes of this section, "test-related information" means the following received by the employer through the employer's drug or alcohol testing program:

(a) information;

(b) interviews;

(c) reports;

(d) statements;

(e) memoranda; or

(f) test results.

(2) Except as provided in Subsections (3) and (6), test-related information is a confidential communication and may not be:

(a) used or received in evidence;

(b) obtained in discovery; or

(c) disclosed in any public or private proceeding.

(3) Test-related information:

(a) shall be disclosed to the Division of Occupational and Professional Licensing.

(b) may only be used in a proceeding related to:

(i) an action taken by the Division of Occupational and Professional Licensing under Section 58-1-401 [pertains to denial of occupational or professional licenses] when the Division of Occupational and Professional Licensing is taking action in whole or in part on the basis of test-related information disclosed under Subsection (3)(a);

(ii) an action taken by an employer under Section 34-38-8; or

(iii) an action under Section 34-38-11.

(4) Test-related information shall be the property of the employer.

(5) An employer is entitled to use a drug or alcohol test result as a basis for action under Section 34-38-8.

(6) An employer may not be examined as a witness with regard to test-related information, except:.

(a) in a proceeding related to an action taken by the employer under Section 34-38-8;

(b) in an action under Section 34-38-11; or

(c) in an action described in Subsection (3)(b)(i).

§ 34-38-14. Employee not "disabled"

An employee or prospective employee whose drug or alcohol test result is confirmed as positive in accordance with this chapter may not, because of those results alone, be defined as a person with a "disability" for purposes of Title 34A, Chapter 5, Utah Antidiscrimination Act.

§ 34-38-15. No physician-patient relationship created

A physician-patient relationship is not created between an employee or prospective employee, and the employer or any person performing the test, solely by the establishment of a drug or alcohol testing program in the workplace.

VERMONT DRUG AND ALCOHOL TESTING STATUTE

Vt. Stat. Ann. tit. 21 §§ 511 to 520

§ 511. Definitions

As used in this subchapter:

(1) "Applicant for employment" means an individual seeking or being sought for employment with an employer.

(2) "Designated laboratory" means a laboratory designated by the department of health under section 518 of this title.

(3) "Drug" means a drug listed or classified by the U.S. Drug Enforcement Administration as a Schedule I drug, or its metabolites, and alcohol. It shall also mean other drugs or their metabolites which are likely to cause impairment of the individual on the job, which are: amitriptyline, amphetamines, barbiturates, benzodiazepines, cannabinoids, cocaine, doxepin, glutethimide, hydromorphone, imipramine, meperidine, methadone, methaqualone, opiates, oxycodone, pentazocine, phenytoin, phencyclidine, phenothiazines, and propoxyphene. In addition, the commissioner of health may, pursuant to chapter 25 of Title 3, add drugs to this list not recognized as being commonly abused and likely to cause impairment of the employee on the job at the time of the passage of this act.

(4) "Drug test" means the procedure of taking and analyzing body fluids or materials from the body for the purpose of detecting the presence of a regulated drug as defined in chapter 84 of Title 18 or a drug as defined in subdivision (4) of this section.

(5) "Employee" means any person who may be permitted, required or directed by any employer, in consideration of direct or indirect gain or profit, to perform services.

(6) "Employer" means any individual, organization, or governmental body including partnership, association, trustee, estate, corporation, joint stock company, insurance company or legal representative, whether domestic or foreign, or the receiver, trustee in bankruptcy, trustee or successor thereof, and any common carrier by mail, motor, water, air or express company doing business in or operating within this state, which has one or more

individuals performing services for it within this state, or which has offered or may offer employment to one or more individuals.

(7) "Employment agency" means a person who undertakes, with or without compensation, to procure, refer, recruit or place for an employer or person, the opportunity to work for an employer.

(8) "Collector" means an individual certified by a United States Health and Human Services approved collector certification program for each type of specimen to be collected. A "collector" shall be recertified every three years and may not be an employee of the employer for the purposes of performing a drug test based on probable cause.

§ 512. Drug testing of applicants; prohibitions; exceptions

(a) General prohibition. Except as provided in subsection (b) of this section, an employer or an employment agency shall not, as a condition of employment, do any of the following:

(1) Request or require that an applicant for employment take or submit to a drug test.

(2) Administer or attempt to administer a drug test to an applicant for employment.

(3) Request or require that an applicant for employment consent, directly or indirectly, to a practice prohibited under this subchapter.

(b) Exception. An employer may require an applicant for employment to submit to a drug test only if all of the following conditions are met:

(1) Conditional offer of employment. The applicant has been given an offer of employment conditioned on the applicant receiving a negative test result.

(2) Notice. The applicant received written notice of the drug testing procedure and a list of the drugs to be tested. The notice shall also state that therapeutic levels of medically-prescribed drugs tested will not be reported. The notice required under this subdivision may not be waived by the applicant.

(3) Administration. The drug test is administered in accordance with section 514 of this title.

§ 513. Drug testing of employees; prohibitions; exceptions

(a) General prohibition. Except as provided in subsection (c) of this section, an employer shall not, as a condition of employment, promotion or change of status of employment, or as an expressed or implied condition of a benefit or privilege of employment, do any of the following:

(1) Request or require that an employee take or submit to a drug test.

(2) Administer or attempt to administer a drug test to an employee.

(3) Request or require that an employee consent, directly or indirectly, to a practice prohibited under this subchapter.

(b) Random or company-wide tests. An employer shall not request, require or conduct random or company-wide drug tests except when such testing is required by federal law or regulation.

(c) Exception. Notwithstanding the prohibition in subsection (a) of this section, an employer may require an individual employee to submit to a drug test if all the following conditions are met:

(1) Probable cause. The employer or an agent of the employer has probable cause to believe the employee is using or is under the influence of a drug on the job.

(2) Employee assistance program. The employer has available for the employee tested a bona fide rehabilitation program for alcohol or drug abuse and such program is provided by the employer or is available to the extent provided by a policy of health insurance or under contract by a nonprofit hospital service corporation.

(3) Employee may not be terminated. The employee may not be terminated if the test result is positive and the employee agrees to participate in and then successfully completes the employee assistance program; however, the employee may be suspended only for the period of time necessary to complete the program, but in no event longer than three months. The employee may be terminated if, after completion of an employee assistance program, the employer subsequently administers a drug test in compliance with subdivisions (1) and (4) of this subsection and the test result is positive.

(4) Administration of test. The drug test is administered in accordance with section 514 of this title.

§ 514. Administration of tests

An employer may request an applicant for employment or an employee to submit to a drug test pursuant to this subchapter, provided the drug testing is performed in compliance with all the following requirements:

(1) Drugs to be tested. The test shall be administered only to detect the presence of alcohol or drugs, as defined in subdivision 511(3) of this title, at nontherapeutic levels.

(2) Written policy. The employer shall provide all persons tested with a written policy that identifies the circumstances under which persons may be required to submit to drug tests, the particular test procedures, the drugs that will be screened, a statement that over-the-counter medications and other substances may result in a positive test and the consequences of a positive test result. The employer's policy shall incorporate all provisions of this section.

(3) Blood samples. An employer may not request or require that a blood sample be drawn for the purpose of administering a drug test.

(4) Designated laboratory. The employer shall use only a laboratory designated by the department of health.

(5) Chain of custody. The collector shall establish a chain of custody procedure for both sample collection and testing that will assure the anonymity of the individual being tested and verify the identity of each sample and test result.

(6) Urinalysis procedure. If a urinalysis procedure is used to screen for drugs, the employer shall:

(A) require the laboratory performing the test to confirm any sample that tests positive by testing the sample by gas chromatography with mass spectrometry or an equivalent scientifically accepted method that provides quantitative data about the detected drug or drug metabolites; and

(B) provide the person tested with an opportunity, at his or her request and expense, to have a blood sample drawn at the time the urine sample is provided, and preserved in such a way that it can be tested later for the presence of drugs.

(7) Laboratory reports. A laboratory may report that a urine sample is positive only if both the initial test and confirmation test are positive for the particular drug. Test results shall only be provided by written report in accordance with subdivision (9) of this section.

(8) Negative test results. The detection of a drug at a therapeutic level as defined by the commissioner of health shall be reported as a negative test result. The laboratory's report shall not contain any information indicating the presence of a drug at a therapeutic level as defined by the commissioner.

(9) Information to be supplied. The laboratory shall provide the medical review officer with a written report of the drug test result. The medical review officer shall review the report, and discuss the results and options available with the individual tested. The written report shall include all of the following information:

(A) The unique identifier code of the person tested.

(B) The type of test conducted for both initial screening and confirmation.

(C) The results of each test.

(D) The detection level, meaning the cut-off or measure used to distinguish positive and negative samples, on both the initial screening and confirmation procedures.

(E) The name and address of the laboratory.

(F) Any other information provided by the laboratory concerning that person's test.

(10) Preservation of samples. The collector shall ensure that a portion of any positive sample is preserved in a condition that will permit accurate retesting for a period of not less than 90 days after the person tested receives the result.

(11) Medical review officer. The employer shall contract with or employ a certified medical review officer who shall be a licensed physician with knowledge of the medical use of prescription drugs and the pharmacology and toxicology of illicit drugs. The medical review officer shall review and evaluate all drug test results, assure compliance with this section and sections 515 and 516 of this title, report the results of all tests to the individual tested, and report only confirmed drug test results to the employer.

(12) Collector. The employer shall designate a collector to collect specimens from job applicants and employees. The collector may be an employee for the purposes of collecting specimens from job applicants. The collector may not be an employee for the purposes of collecting specimens from employees for drug testing based on probable cause.

§ 515. Positive test results; opportunity to retest

(a) A medical review officer shall contact personally an employee or applicant who has a positive test result and explain the results and why the results may not be accurate.

(b) The medical review officer shall provide any applicant or employee who has a positive test result with an opportunity to retest a portion of the sample at an independent laboratory at the expense of the person tested and shall consider the results of the retest.

§ 516. Confidentiality

(a) Any health care information about an individual to be tested shall be taken only by a medical review officer and shall be confidential and shall not be released to anyone except the individual tested, and may not be obtained by court order or process, except as provided in this subchapter.

(b) Employers, medical review officers, laboratories and their agents, who receive or have access to information about drug test results, shall keep all information confidential. Release of such information under any other circumstance shall be solely pursuant to a written consent form signed voluntarily by the person tested, except where such release is compelled by a court of competent jurisdiction in connection with an action brought under this subchapter. A medical review officer shall not reveal the identity of an individual being tested to any person, including the laboratory.

(c) If information about drug test results is released contrary to the provisions of this subchapter, it shall be inadmissible as evidence in any judicial or quasi-judicial proceeding, except in a court of competent jurisdiction in connection with an action brought under this subchapter.

§ 517. Employer's authority

This subchapter shall not restrict an employer's authority to prohibit the non-prescribed use of drugs or alcohol during work hours, or restrict an employer's authority to discipline, suspend or dismiss an employee for being under the influence of drugs or alcohol during work hours, except as that authority is restricted under subsection 513(c)(3) of this title in reference to participation in an employee assistance program or suspension. . . .

§ 519. Enforcement

(a) **Private right of action.** An applicant or employee aggrieved by a violation of this subchapter may bring a civil action for injunctive relief, damages, court costs and attorney's fees.

(b) **Burden of proof.** In a private right of action alleging that an employer has violated this subchapter, the employer has the burden of proving that the requirements of sections 513, 514 and 516 of this title have been satisfied. In any civil action alleging that a laboratory has violated the reporting or confidentiality sections of this subchapter, the laboratory shall have the burden of proving that the requirements of sections 514 and 516 of this title have been satisfied.

(c) **State action to obtain civil penalty.** A person who violates any provision of this subchapter shall be subject to a civil penalty of not less than $500.00 nor more than $2,000.00.

(d) **State action to obtain criminal penalty.** A person who knowingly violates any provision of this subchapter shall be fined not less than $500.00 nor more than $1,000.00 or shall be imprisoned not more than six months, or both. . . .

EMPLOYEE POLYGRAPH PROTECTION ACT

29 U.S.C. §§ 2001–2009

§ 2001 [§ 2]. Definitions. As used in this chapter: . . .

(2) Employer. The term "employer" includes any person acting directly or indirectly in the interest of an employer in relation to an employee or prospective employee.

(3) Lie detector. The term "lie detector" includes a polygraph, deceptograph, voice stress analyzer, psychological stress evaluator, or any other similar device (whether mechanical or electrical) that is used, or the results of which are used, for the purpose of rendering a diagnostic opinion regarding the honesty or dishonesty of an individual.

(4) Polygraph. The term "polygraph" means an instrument that—

(A) records continuously, visually, permanently, and simultaneously changes in cardiovascular, respiratory, and electrodermal patterns as minimum instrumentation standards; and

(B) is used, or the results of which are used, for the purpose of rendering a diagnostic opinion regarding the honesty or dishonesty of an individual.

§ 2002 [§ 3]. Prohibitions on lie detector use. Except as provided in sections 2006 and 2007 of this title, it shall be unlawful for any employer engaged in or affecting commerce or in the production of goods for commerce—

(1) directly or indirectly, to require, request, suggest, or cause any employee or prospective employee to take or submit to any lie detector test;

(2) to use, accept, refer to, or inquire concerning the results of any lie detector test of any employee or prospective employee;

(3) to discharge, discipline, discriminate against in any manner, or deny employment or promotion to, or threaten to take any such action against—

(A) any employee or prospective employee who refuses, declines, or fails to take or submit to any lie detector test; . . .

(B) any employee or prospective employee on the basis of the results of any lie detector test; . . .

(4) to discharge, discipline, discriminate against in any manner, or deny employment or promotion to, or threaten to take any such action against, any employee or prospective employee because—

(A) such employee or prospective employee has filed any complaint or instituted or caused to be instituted any proceeding under or related to this chapter;

(B) such employee or prospective employee has testified or is about to testify in any such proceeding; or

(C) of the exercise by such employee or prospective employee, on behalf of such employee or another person, of any right afforded by this chapter.

§ 2005 [§ 6]. Enforcement provisions

(a) Civil penalties

(1) In general. Subject to paragraph (2), any employer who violates any provision of this chapter may be assessed a civil penalty of not more than $10,000.

(2) Determination of amount. In determining the amount of any penalty under paragraph (1), the Secretary shall take into account the previous record of the person in terms of compliance with this chapter and the gravity of the violation.

(b) Injunctive actions by the Secretary. The Secretary may bring an action under this section to restrain violations of this chapter. The Solicitor of Labor may appear for and represent the Secretary in any litigation brought under this chapter. In any action brought under this section, the district courts of the United States shall have jurisdiction, for cause shown, to issue temporary or permanent restraining orders and injunctions to require compliance with this chapter, including such legal or equitable relief incident thereto as may be appropriate, including, but not limited to, employment, reinstatement, promotion, and the payment of lost wages and benefits.

(c) Private civil actions

(1) Liability. An employer who violates this chapter shall be liable to the employee or prospective employee affected by such violation. Such employer shall be liable for such legal or equitable relief as may be appropriate, including, but not limited to, employment, reinstatement, promotion, and the payment of lost wages and benefits.

(2) Court. An action to recover the liability prescribed in paragraph (1) may be maintained against the employer in any Federal or State court of competent jurisdiction by an employee or prospective employee for or on behalf of such employee, prospective employee, and other employees or prospective employees similarly situated. No such action may be commenced more than 3 years after the date of the alleged violation.

(3) Costs. The court, in its discretion, may allow the prevailing party (other than the United States) reasonable costs, including attorney's fees.

(d) Waiver of rights prohibited. The rights and procedures provided by this chapter may not be waived by contract or otherwise, unless such waiver is part of a written settlement agreed to and signed by the parties to the pending action or complaint under this chapter.

§ 2006 [§ 7]. Exemptions

(a) No application to Governmental employers. This chapter shall not apply with respect to the United States Government, any State or local government, or any political subdivision of a State or local government.

(b) National defense and security exemption

(1) National defense. Nothing in this chapter shall be construed to prohibit the administration, by the Federal Government, in the performance of any counterintelligence function, of any lie detector test to—

(A) any expert or consultant under contract to the Department of Defense or any employee of any contractor of such Department; or

(B) any expert or consultant under contract with the Department of Energy in connection with the atomic energy defense activities of such Department or any employee of any contractor of such Department in connection with such activities.

(2) Security. Nothing in this chapter shall be construed to prohibit the administration, by the Federal Government, in the performance of any intelligence or counterintelligence function, of any lie detector test to—

(A)(i) any individual employed by, assigned to, or detailed to, the National Security Agency, the Defense Intelligence Agency, National Geospatial-Intelligence Agency, or the Central Intelligence Agency,

(ii) any expert or consultant under contract to any such agency;

(iii) any employee of a contractor to any such agency;

(iv) any individual applying for a position in any such agency; or

(v) any individual assigned to a space where sensitive cryptologic information is produced, processed, or stored for any such agency; or

(B) any expert, or consultant (or employee of such expert or consultant) under contract with any Federal Government department, agency, or program whose duties involve access to information that has been classified at the level of top secret or designated as being within a special access program under section 4.2(a) of Executive Order 12356 (or a successor Executive order).

(c) FBI contractors exemption. Nothing in this chapter shall be construed to prohibit the administration, by the Federal Government, in the performance of any counterintelligence function, of any lie detector test to an employee of a contractor of the Federal Bureau of Investigation of the Department of Justice who is engaged in the performance of any work under the contract with such Bureau.

(d) Limited exemption for ongoing investigations. Subject to sections 2007 and 2009 of this title, this chapter shall not prohibit an employer from requesting an employee to submit to a polygraph test if—

(1) the test is administered in connection with an ongoing investigation involving economic loss or injury to the employer's business, such as theft, embezzlement, misappropriation, or an act of unlawful industrial espionage or sabotage;

(2) the employee had access to the property that is the subject of the investigation;

(3) the employer has a reasonable suspicion that the employee was involved in the incident or activity under investigation; and

(4) the employer executes a statement, provided to the examinee before the test, that—

(A) sets forth with particularity the specific incident or activity being investigated and the basis for testing particular employees;

(B) is signed by a person (other than a polygraph examiner) authorized to legally bind the employer;

(C) is retained by the employer for at least 3 years; and

(D) contains at a minimum—

(i) an identification of the specific economic loss or injury to the business of the employer;

(ii) a statement indicating that the employee had access to the property that is the subject of the investigation; and

(iii) a statement describing the basis of the employer's reasonable suspicion that the employee was involved in the incident or activity under investigation.

(e) Exemption for security services

(1) In general. Subject to paragraph (2) and sections 2007 and 2009 of this title, this chapter shall not prohibit the use of polygraph tests on prospective employees by any private employer whose primary business purpose consists of providing armored car personnel, personnel engaged in the design, installation, and maintenance of security alarm systems, or other uniformed or plainclothes security personnel and whose function includes protection of—

(A) facilities, materials, or operations having a significant impact on the health or safety of any State or political subdivision thereof, or the national security of the United States, as determined under rules and regulations issued by the Secretary within 90 days after June 27, 1988, including—

(i) facilities engaged in the production, transmission, or distribution of electric or nuclear power;

(ii) public water supply facilities;

(iii) shipments or storage of radioactive or other toxic waste materials; and

(iv) public transportation; or

(B) currency, negotiable securities, precious commodities or instruments, or proprietary information.

(2) Access. The exemption provided under this subsection shall not apply if the test is administered to a prospective employee who would not be employed to protect facilities, materials, operations, or assets referred to in paragraph (1).

(f) Exemption for drug security, drug theft, or drug diversion investigations

(1) In general. Subject to paragraph (2) and sections 2007 and 2009 of this title, this chapter shall not prohibit the use of a polygraph test by any employer authorized to manufacture, distribute, or dispense a controlled substance listed in schedule I, II, III, or IV of section 812 of Title 21.

(2) Access. The exemption provided under this subsection shall apply—

(A) if the test is administered to a prospective employee who would have direct access to the manufacture, storage, distribution, or sale of any such controlled substance; or

(B) in the case of a test administered to a current employee, if—

(i) the test is administered in connection with an ongoing investigation of criminal or other misconduct involving, or potentially involving, loss or injury to the manufacture, distribution, or dispensing of any such controlled substance by such employer; and

(ii) the employee had access to the person or property that is the subject of the investigation.

§ 2007 [§ 8]. Restrictions on use of exemptions

(a) Test as basis for adverse employment action

(1) Under ongoing investigations exemption. Except as provided in paragraph (2), the exemption under subsection (d) of section 2006 of this title shall not apply if an employee is discharged, disciplined, denied employment or promotion, or otherwise discriminated against in any manner on the basis of the analysis of a polygraph test chart or the refusal to take a polygraph test, without additional supporting evidence. The evidence required by such subsection may serve as additional supporting evidence.

(2) Under other exemptions. In the case of an exemption described in subsection (e) or (f) of such section, the exemption shall not apply if the results of an analysis of a polygraph test chart are used, or the refusal to take a polygraph test is used, as the sole basis upon which an adverse employment action described in paragraph (1) is taken against an employee or prospective employee.

(b) Rights of examinee. The exemptions provided under subsections (d), (e), and (f) of section 2006 of this title shall not apply unless the requirements described in the following paragraphs are met:

(1) All phases. Throughout all phases of the test—

(A) the examinee shall be permitted to terminate the test at any time;

(B) the examinee is not asked questions in a manner designed to degrade, or needlessly intrude on, such examinee;

(C) the examinee is not asked any question concerning—

(i) religious beliefs or affiliations;

(ii) beliefs or opinions regarding racial matters;

(iii) political beliefs or affiliations;

(iv) any matter relating to sexual behavior; and

(v) beliefs, affiliations, opinions, or lawful activities regarding unions or labor organizations; and

(D) the examiner does not conduct the test if there is sufficient written evidence by a physician that the examinee is suffering from a medical or psychological condition or undergoing treatment that might cause abnormal responses during the actual testing phase.

(2) Pretest phase. During the pretest phase, the prospective examinee—

(A) is provided with reasonable written notice of the date, time, and location of the test, and of such examinee's right to obtain and consult with legal counsel or an employee representative before each phase of the test;

(B) is informed in writing of the nature and characteristics of the tests and of the instruments involved;

(C) is informed, in writing—

(i) whether the testing area contains a two-way mirror, a camera, or any other device through which the test can be observed;

(ii) whether any other device, including any device for recording or monitoring the test, will be used; or

(iii) that the employer or the examinee may (with mutual knowledge) make a recording of the test;

(D) is read and signs a written notice informing such examinee—

(i) that the examinee cannot be required to take the test as a condition of employment;

(ii) that any statement made during the test may constitute additional supporting evidence for the purposes of an adverse employment action described in subsection (a) of this section;

(iii) of the limitations imposed under this section;

(iv) of the legal rights and remedies available to the examinee if the polygraph test is not conducted in accordance with this chapter; and

(v) of the legal rights and remedies of the employer under this chapter (including the rights of the employer under section 2008(c)(2) of this title); and

(E) is provided an opportunity to review all questions to be asked during the test and is informed of the right to terminate the test at any time.

(3) Actual testing phase. During the actual testing phase, the examiner does not ask such examinee any question relevant during the test that was not presented in writing for review to such examinee before the test.

(4) **Post-test phase.** Before any adverse employment action, the employer shall—

(A) further interview the examinee on the basis of the results of the test; and

(B) provide the examinee with—

(i) a written copy of any opinion or conclusion rendered as a result of the test; and

(ii) a copy of the questions asked during the test along with the corresponding charted responses.

(5) **Maximum number and minimum duration of tests.** The examiner shall not conduct and complete more than five polygraph tests on a calendar day on which the test is given, and shall not conduct any such test for less than a 90-minute duration.

(c) **Qualifications and requirements of examiners.** The exemptions provided under subsections (d), (e), and (f) of section 2006 of this title shall not apply unless the individual who conducts the polygraph test satisfies the requirements under the following paragraphs:

(1) **Qualifications.** The examiner—

(A) has a valid and current license granted by licensing and regulatory authorities in the State in which the test is to be conducted, if so required by the State; and

(B) maintains a minimum of a $50,000 bond or an equivalent amount of professional liability coverage.

(2) **Requirements.** The examiner—

(A) renders any opinion or conclusion regarding the test—

(i) in writing and solely on the basis of an analysis of polygraph test charts;

(ii) that does not contain information other than admissions, information, case facts, and interpretation of the charts relevant to the purpose and stated objectives of the test; and

(iii) that does not include any recommendation concerning the employment of the examinee; and

(B) maintains all opinions, reports, charts, written questions, lists, and other records relating to the test for a minimum period of 3 years after administration of the test.

§ 2008 [§ 9]. Disclosure of information

(a) **In general.** A person, other than the examinee, may not disclose information obtained during a polygraph test, except as provided in this section.

(b) Permitted disclosures. A polygraph examiner may disclose information acquired from a polygraph test only to—

(1) the examinee or any other person specifically designated in writing by the examinee;

(2) the employer that requested the test; or

(3) any court, governmental agency, arbitrator, or mediator, in accordance with due process of law, pursuant to an order from a court of competent jurisdiction.

(c) Disclosure by employer. An employer (other than an employer described in subsection (a), (b), or (c) of section 2006 of this title) for whom a polygraph test is conducted may disclose information from the test only to—

(1) a person in accordance with subsection (b) of this section; of

(2) a governmental agency, but only insofar as the disclosed information is an admission of criminal conduct.

§ 2009 [§ 10]. Effect on other laws and agreements. Except as provided in subsections (a), (b), and (c) of section 2006 of this title, this chapter shall not preempt any provision of any State or local law or of any negotiated collective bargaining agreement that prohibits lie detector tests or is more restrictive with respect to lie detector tests than any provision of this chapter.

PART V.

PROHIBITIONS ON STATUS DISCRIMINATION

TITLE VII OF THE CIVIL RIGHTS ACT OF 1964

42 U.S.C. §§ 2000e to 2000e–17

§ 701 [§ 2000e]. Definitions. For the purposes of this title—

(a) The term "person" includes one or more individuals, governments, governmental agencies, political subdivisions, labor unions, partnerships, associations, corporations, legal representatives, mutual companies, joint-stock companies, trusts, unincorporated organizations, trustees, trustees in cases under Title 11, or receivers.

(b) The term "employer" means a person engaged in an industry affecting commerce who has fifteen or more employees for each working day in each of twenty or more calendar weeks in the current or preceding calendar year, and any agent of such a person, but such term does not include (1) the United States, a corporation wholly owned by the Government of the United States, an Indian tribe, or any department or agency of the District of Columbia subject by statute to procedures of the competitive service (as defined in section 2102 of Title 5), or (2) a bona fide private membership club (other than a labor organization) which is exempt from taxation under section 501(c) of Title 26. . . .

(c) The term "employment agency" means any person regularly undertaking with or without compensation to procure employees for an employer or to procure for employees opportunities to work for an employer and includes an agent of such a person.

(d) The term "labor organization" means a labor organization engaged in an industry affecting commerce, and any agent of such an organization, and includes any organization of any kind, any agency, or employee representation committee, group, association, or plan so engaged in which employees participate and which exists for the purpose, in whole or in part, of dealing with employers concerning grievances, labor disputes, wages, rates of pay, hours, or other terms or conditions of employment, and any conference, general committee, joint or system board, or joint council so engaged which is subordinate to a national or international labor organization.

(e) A labor organization shall be deemed to be engaged in an industry affecting commerce if (1) it maintains or operates a hiring hall . . . which procures employees for an employer . . . or (2) the number of its members [is] fifteen or more . . ., and such labor organization—

> (1) is the certified representative of employees under the provisions of the National Labor Relations Act, as amended, or the Railway Labor Act, as amended; [or]
>
> (2) although not certified, is a national or international labor organization or a local labor organization recognized or acting as the representative of employees of an employer or employers engaged in an industry affecting commerce. . . .

(f) The term "employee" means an individual employed by an employer, except that the term "employee" shall not include any person elected to public office in any State or political subdivision of any State by the qualified voters thereof, or any person chosen by such officer to be on such officer's personal staff, or an appointee on the policy making level or an immediate adviser with respect to the exercise of the constitutional or legal powers of the office. The exemption set forth in the preceding sentence shall not include employees subject to the civil service laws of a State government, governmental agency or political subdivision. With respect to employment in a foreign country, such term includes an individual who is a citizen of the United States.

(g) The term "commerce" means trade, traffic, commerce, transportation, transmission, or communication among the several States; or between a State and any place outside thereof; or within the District of Columbia, or a possession of the United States; or between points in the same State but through a point outside thereof.

(h) The term "industry affecting commerce" means any activity, business, or industry in commerce or in which a labor dispute would hinder or obstruct commerce or the free flow of commerce and includes any activity or industry "affecting commerce" within the meaning of the Labor-Management Reporting and Disclosure Act of 1959, and further includes any governmental industry, business, or activity.

(i) The term "State" includes a State of the United States, the District of Columbia, Puerto Rico, the Virgin Islands, American Samoa, Guam, Wake Island, the Canal Zone, and Outer Continental Shelf lands defined in the Outer Continental Shelf Lands Act.

(j) The term "religion" includes all aspects of religious observance and practice, as well as belief, unless an employer demonstrates that he is unable to reasonably accommodate to an employee's or prospective employee's religious observance or practice without undue hardship on the conduct of the employer's business.

(k) The terms "because of sex" or "on the basis of sex" include, but are not limited to, because of or on the basis of pregnancy, childbirth, or related medical conditions; and women affected by pregnancy, childbirth, or related medical conditions shall be treated the same for all employment-related purposes, including receipt of benefits under fringe benefit programs, as other persons not so affected but similar in their ability or inability to work, and nothing in section 703(h) shall be interpreted to permit otherwise. This subsection shall not require an employer to pay for health insurance benefits for abortion, except where the life of the mother would be endangered if the fetus were carried to term, or except where medical complications have arisen from an abortion: Provided, That nothing herein shall preclude an employer from providing abortion benefits or otherwise affect bargaining agreements in regard to abortion.

(l) The term "complaining party" means the Commission, the Attorney General, or a person who may bring an action or proceeding under this title.

(m) The term "demonstrates" means meets the burdens of production and persuasion.

(n) The term "respondent" means an employer, employment agency, labor organization, joint labor-management committee controlling apprenticeship or other training or retraining program, including an on-the-job training program, or Federal entity subject to section 717.

§ 702 [§ 2000e-1]. Applicability to foreign and religious employment

(a) This title shall not apply to an employer with respect to the employment of aliens outside any State, or to a religious corporation, association, educational institution, or society with respect to the employment of individuals of a particular religion to perform work connected with the carrying on by such corporation, association, educational institution, or society of its activities.

(b) It shall not be unlawful under section 703 or 704 for an employer (or a corporation controlled by an employer), labor organization, employment agency, or joint labor-management committee controlling apprenticeship or other training or retraining (including on-the-job training programs) to take any action otherwise prohibited by such section, with respect to an employee in a workplace in a foreign country if compliance with such section would cause such employer (or such corporation), such organization, such agency, or such committee to violate the law of the foreign country in which such workplace is located.

(c)(1) If an employer controls a corporation whose place of incorporation is a foreign country, any practice prohibited by section 703 or 704 engaged in by such corporation shall be presumed to be engaged in by such employer.

(2) Sections 703 and 704 shall not apply with respect to the foreign operations of an employer that is a foreign person not controlled by an American employer.

(3) For purposes of this subsection, the determination of whether an employer controls a corporation shall be based on—

(A) the interrelation of operations;

(B) the common management;

(C) the centralized control of labor relations; and

(D) the common ownership or financial control, of the employer and the corporation.

§ 703 [§ 2000e-2]. Unlawful employment practices

(a) It shall be an unlawful employment practice for an employer—

(1) to fail or refuse to hire or to discharge any individual, or otherwise to discriminate against any individual with respect to his compensation, terms, conditions, or privileges of employment, because of such individual's race, color, religion, sex, or national origin; or

(2) to limit, segregate, or classify his employees or applicants for employment in any way which would deprive or tend to deprive any individual of employment opportunities or otherwise adversely affect his status as an employee, because of such individual's race, color, religion, sex, or national origin.

(b) It shall be an unlawful employment practice for an employment agency to fail or refuse to refer for employment, or otherwise to discriminate against, any individual because of his race, color, religion, sex, or national origin, or to classify or refer for employment any individual on the basis of his race, color, religion, sex, or national origin.

(c) It shall be an unlawful employment practice for a labor organization—

(1) to exclude or to expel from its membership, or otherwise to discriminate against, any individual because of his race, color, religion, sex, or national origin;

(2) to limit, segregate, or classify its membership or applicants for membership, or to classify or fail or refuse to refer for employment any individual, in any way which would deprive or tend to deprive any individual of employment opportunities, or would limit such employment opportunities or otherwise adversely affect his status as an employee or as an applicant for employment, because of such individual's race, color, religion, sex, or national origin; or

(3) to cause or attempt to cause an employer to discriminate against an individual in violation of this section.

(d) It shall be an unlawful employment practice for any employer, labor organization, or joint labor-management committee controlling apprenticeship or other training or retraining, including on-the-job training programs to discriminate against any individual because of his race, color, religion, sex, or national origin in admission to, or employment in, any program established to provide apprenticeship or other training.

(e) Notwithstanding any other provision of this title, (1) it shall not be an unlawful employment practice for an employer to hire and employ employees, for an employment agency to classify, or refer for employment any individual, for a labor organization to classify its membership or to classify or refer for employment any individual, or for an employer, labor organization, or joint labor-management committee controlling apprenticeship or other training or retraining programs to admit or employ any individual in any such program, on the basis of his religion, sex, or national origin in those certain instances where religion, sex, or national origin is a bona fide occupational qualification reasonably necessary to the normal operation of that particular business or enterprise, and (2) it shall not be an unlawful employment practice for a school, college, university, or other educational institution or institution of learning to hire and employ employees of a particular religion if such school, college, university, or other educational institution or institution of learning is, in whole or in substantial part, owned, supported, controlled, or managed by a particular religion or by a particular religious corporation, association, or society, or if the curriculum of such school, college, university, or other educational institution or institution of learning is directed toward the propagation of a particular religion. . . .

(h) Notwithstanding any other provision of this title, it shall not be an unlawful employment practice for an employer to apply different standards of compensation, or different terms, conditions, or privileges of employment pursuant to a bona fide seniority or merit system, or a system which measures earnings by quantity or quality of production or to employees who work in different locations, provided that such differences are not the result of an intention to discriminate because of race, color, religion, sex, or national origin, nor shall it be an unlawful employment practice for an employer to give and to act upon the results of any professionally developed ability test provided that such test, its administration or action upon the results is not designed, intended or used to discriminate because of race, color, religion, sex or national origin. It shall not be an unlawful employment practice under this title for any employer to differentiate upon the basis of sex in determining the amount of the wages or compensation paid or to be paid to employees of such employer if such differentiation is authorized by the provisions of section 206(d) of [the Fair Labor Standards Act].

(i) Nothing contained in this title shall apply to any business or enterprise on or near an Indian reservation with respect to any publicly announced employment practice of such business or enterprise under which a preferential treatment is given to any individual because he is an Indian living on or near a reservation.

(j) Nothing contained in this title shall be interpreted to require any employer, employment agency, labor organization, or joint labor-management committee subject to this title to grant preferential treatment to any individual or to any group because of the race, color, religion, sex, or national origin of such individual or group on account of an imbalance which may exist with respect to the total number or percentage of persons of any race, color, religion, sex, or national origin employed by any employer, referred or classified for employment by any employment agency or labor organization, admitted to membership or classified by any labor organization, or admitted to, or employed in, any apprenticeship or other training program, in comparison with the total number or percentage of persons of such race, color, religion, sex, or national origin in any community, State, section, or other area, or in the available work force in any community, State, section, or other area.

(k)(1)(A) An unlawful employment practice based on disparate impact is established under this title only if—

(i) a complaining party demonstrates that a respondent uses a particular employment practice that causes a disparate impact on the basis of race, color, religion, sex, or national origin and the respondent fails to demonstrate that the challenged practice is job related for the position in question and consistent with business necessity; or

(ii) the complaining party makes the demonstration described in subparagraph (C) with respect to an alternative employment practice and the respondent refuses to adopt such alternative employment practice.

(B)(i) With respect to demonstrating that a particular employment practice causes a disparate impact as described in subparagraph (A)(i), the complaining party shall demonstrate that each particular challenged employment practice causes a disparate impact, except that if the complaining party can demonstrate to the court that the elements of a respondent's decision making process are not capable of separation for analysis, the decision making process may be analyzed as one employment practice.

(ii) If the respondent demonstrates that a specific employment practice does not cause the disparate impact, the respondent shall not be required to demonstrate that such practice is required by business necessity.

(C) The demonstration referred to by subparagraph (A)(ii) shall be in accordance with the law as it existed on June 4, 1989, with respect to the concept of "alternative employment practice".

(2) A demonstration that an employment practice is required by business necessity may not be used as a defense against a claim of intentional discrimination under this title.

(3) Notwithstanding any other provision of this title, a rule barring the employment of an individual who currently and knowingly uses or possesses a controlled substance, as defined in schedules I and II of section 102(6) of the Controlled Substances Act, other than the use or possession of a drug taken under the supervision of a licensed health care professional, or any other use or possession authorized by the Controlled Substances Act or any other provision of Federal law, shall be considered an unlawful employment practice under this title only if such rule is adopted or applied with an intent to discriminate because of race, color, religion, sex, or national origin.

(l) It shall be an unlawful employment practice for a respondent, in connection with the selection or referral of applicants or candidates for employment or promotion, to adjust the scores of, use different cutoff scores for, or otherwise alter the results of, employment related tests on the basis of race, color, religion, sex, or national origin.

(m) Except as otherwise provided in this title, an unlawful employment practice is established when the complaining party demonstrates that race, color, religion, sex, or national origin was a motivating factor for any employment practice, even though other factors also motivated the practice.

(n)(1)(A) Notwithstanding any other provision of law, and except as provided in paragraph (2), an employment practice that implements and is within the scope of a litigated or consent judgment or order that resolves a claim of employment discrimination under the Constitution or Federal civil rights laws may not be challenged under the circumstances described in subparagraph (B).

(B) A practice described in subparagraph (A) may not be challenged in a claim under the Constitution or Federal civil rights laws—

(i) by a person who, prior to the entry of the judgment or order described in subparagraph (A), had—

(I) actual notice of the proposed judgment or order sufficient to apprise such person that such judgment or order might adversely affect the interests and legal rights of such person and that an opportunity was available to present objections to such judgment or order by a future date certain; and

(II) a reasonable opportunity to present objections to such judgment or order; or

(ii) by a person whose interests were adequately represented by another person who had previously challenged the judgment or order on the same legal grounds and with a similar factual situation, unless there has been an intervening change in law or fact.

(2) Nothing in this subsection shall be construed to—

(A) alter the standards for intervention under rule 24 of the Federal Rules of Civil Procedure or apply to the rights of parties who have successfully intervened pursuant to such rule in the proceeding in which the parties intervened;

(B) apply to the rights of parties to the action in which a litigated or consent judgment or order was entered, or of members of a class represented or sought to be represented in such action, or of members of a group on whose behalf relief was sought in such action by the Federal Government;

(C) prevent challenges to a litigated or consent judgment or order on the ground that such judgment or order was obtained through collusion or fraud, or is transparently invalid or was entered by a court lacking subject matter jurisdiction; or

(D) authorize or permit the denial to any person of the due process of law required by the Constitution.

(3) Any action not precluded under this subsection that challenges an employment consent judgment or order described in paragraph (1) shall be brought in the court, and if possible before the judge, that entered such judgment or order. Nothing in this subsection shall preclude a transfer of such action pursuant to section 1404 of title 28.

§ 704 [§ 2000e-3]. Other unlawful employment practices

(a) It shall be an unlawful employment practice for an employer to discriminate against any of his employees or applicants for employment, for an employment agency, or joint labor-management committee controlling apprenticeship or other training or retraining, including on-the-job training programs, to discriminate against any individual, or for a labor organization to discriminate against any member thereof or applicant for membership, because he has opposed any practice made an unlawful employment practice by this title, or because he has made a charge, testified assisted, or participated in any manner in an investigation, proceeding, or hearing under this title.

(b) It shall be an unlawful employment practice for an employer, labor organization, employment agency, or joint labor-management committee controlling apprenticeship or other training or retraining, including on-the- job training programs, to print or publish or cause to be printed or published any notice or advertisement relating to employment by such an employer or membership in or any classification or referral for employment by such a labor organization, or relating to any classification or referral for employment by such an employment agency, or relating to admission to, or employment in, any program established to provide apprenticeship or other training by such a joint labor-management committee, indicating any preference, limitation, specification, or discrimination, based on race, color, religion, sex, or national origin, except that such a notice or advertisement may indicate a preference, limitation, specification, or discrimination based on religion, sex, or national origin when religion, sex, or national origin is a bona fide occupational qualification for employment.

§ 705 [§ 2000e-4]. Equal Employment Opportunity Commission

(a) There is hereby created a Commission to be known as the Equal Employment Opportunity Commission, which shall be composed of five members, not more than three of whom shall be members of the same political party. Members of the Commission shall be appointed by the President by and with the advice and consent of the Senate for a term of five years. . . . The President shall designate one member to serve as Chairman of the Commission, and one member to serve as Vice Chairman. . . .

(b)(1) There shall be a General Counsel of the Commission appointed by the President, by and with the advice and consent of the Senate, for a term of four years. The General Counsel shall have responsibility for the conduct of litigation as provided in sections [706 and 707]. The General Counsel shall have such other duties as the Commission may prescribe or as may be provided by law and shall concur with the Chairman of the Commission on the appointment and supervision of regional attorneys. . . .

(g) The Commission shall have power—

(1) to cooperate with and, with their consent, utilize regional, State, local, and other agencies, both public and private, and individuals;

(2) to pay to witnesses whose depositions are taken or who are summoned before the Commission or any of its agents the same witness and mileage fees as are paid to witnesses in the courts of the United States;

(3) to furnish to persons subject to this title such technical assistance as they may request to further their compliance with this title or an order issued thereunder;

(4) upon the request of (i) any employer, whose employees or some of them, or (ii) any labor organization, whose members or some of them, refuse or threaten to refuse to cooperate in effectuating the provisions of this title, to assist in such effectuation by conciliation or such other remedial action as is provided by this title;

(5) to make such technical studies as are appropriate to effectuate the purposes and policies of this title and to make the results of such studies available to the public;

(6) to intervene in a civil action brought under section [§ 706] by an aggrieved party against a respondent other than a government, governmental agency or political subdivision. . . .

§ 706 [§ 2000e-5]. Enforcement provisions

(a) The Commission is empowered, as hereinafter provided, to prevent any person from engaging in any unlawful employment practice as set forth in section 703 or 704.

(b) Whenever a charge is filed by or on behalf of a person claiming to be aggrieved, or by a member of the Commission, alleging that an employer, employment agency, labor organization, or joint labor-management committee controlling apprenticeship or other training or retraining, including on-the-job training programs, has engaged in an unlawful employment practice, the Commission shall serve a notice of the charge (including the date, place and circumstances of the alleged unlawful employment practice) on such employer, employment agency, labor organization, or joint labor-management committee (hereinafter referred to as the "respondent") within ten days, and shall make an investigation thereof. Charges shall be in writing under oath or affirmation and shall contain such information and be in such form as the Commission requires. Charges shall not be made public by the Commission. If the Commission determines after such investigation that there is not reasonable cause to believe that the charge is true, it shall dismiss the charge and promptly notify the person claiming to be aggrieved and the respondent of its action. In determining whether reasonable cause exists, the Commission shall accord substantial weight to final findings and orders made by State or local authorities in proceedings commenced under State or local law pursuant to the requirements of subsections (c) and (d) of this section. If the Commission determines after such investigation that there is reasonable cause to believe that the charge is true, the Commission shall endeavor to eliminate any such alleged unlawful employment practice by informal methods of conference, conciliation, and persuasion. Nothing said or done during and as a part of such informal endeavors may be made public by the Commission, its officers or employees, or used as evidence in a subsequent proceeding without the written consent of the persons concerned. Any person who makes public information in violation of this subsection shall be fined not more than $1,000 or imprisoned for not more than one year, or both. The Commission shall make its determination on reasonable cause as promptly as possible and, so far as practicable, not later than one hundred and twenty days from the filing of the charge or, where applicable under subsection (c) or (d) of this section, from the date upon which the Commission is authorized to take action with respect to the charge.

(c) In the case of an alleged unlawful employment practice occurring in a State, or political subdivision of a State, which has a State or local law prohibiting the unlawful employment practice alleged and establishing or authorizing a State or local authority to grant or seek relief from such practice or to institute criminal proceedings with respect thereto upon receiving notice thereof, no charge may be filed under subsection (b) of this section by the person aggrieved before the expiration of sixty days after proceedings have been commenced under the State or local law, unless such proceedings have been earlier terminated, provided that such sixty-day period shall be extended to one hundred and twenty days during the first year after the effective date of such State or local law. If any requirement for the commencement of such proceedings is imposed by a State or local authority other than a requirement of the filing of a written and signed statement of the facts upon which the proceeding is based, the proceeding shall be deemed to have been commenced for the purposes of this subsection at the time such statement is sent by registered mail to the appropriate State or local authority.

(d) In the case of any charge filed by a member of the Commission alleging an unlawful employment practice occurring in a State or political subdivision of a State which has a State or local law prohibiting the practice alleged and establishing or authorizing a State or local authority to grant or seek relief from such practice or to institute criminal proceedings with respect thereto upon receiving notice thereof, the Commission shall, before taking any action with respect to such charge, notify the appropriate State or local officials and, upon request, afford them a reasonable time, but not less than sixty days (provided that such sixty-day period shall be extended to one hundred and twenty days during the first year after the effective day of such State or local law), unless a shorter period is requested, to act under such State or local law to remedy the practice alleged.

(e)(1) A charge under this section shall be filed within one hundred and eighty days after the alleged unlawful employment practice occurred and notice of the charge (including the date, place and circumstances of the alleged unlawful employment practice) shall be served upon the person against whom such charge is made within ten days thereafter, except that in a case of an unlawful employment practice with respect to which the person aggrieved has initially instituted proceedings with a State or local agency with authority to grant or seek relief from such practice or to institute criminal proceedings with respect thereto upon receiving notice thereof, such charge shall be filed by or on behalf of the person aggrieved within three hundred days after the alleged unlawful employment practice occurred, or within thirty days after receiving notice that the State or local agency has terminated the proceedings under the State or local law, whichever is earlier, and a copy of such charge shall be filed by the Commission with the State or local agency.

(2) For purposes of this section, an unlawful employment practice occurs, with respect to a seniority system that has been adopted for an intentionally discriminatory purpose in violation of this title (whether or not that discriminatory purpose is apparent on the face of the seniority provision), when the seniority system is adopted, when an individual becomes subject to the seniority system, or when a person

aggrieved is injured by the application of the seniority system or provision of the system.

(f)(1) If within thirty days after a charge is filed with the Commission or within thirty days after expiration of any period of reference under subsection (c) or (d) of this section, the Commission has been unable to secure from the respondent a conciliation agreement acceptable to the Commission, the Commission may bring a civil action against any respondent not a government, governmental agency, or political subdivision named in the charge. In the case of a respondent which is a government, governmental agency, or political subdivision, if the Commission has been unable to secure from the respondent a conciliation agreement acceptable to the Commission, the Commission shall take no further action and shall refer the case to the Attorney General who may bring a civil action against such respondent in the appropriate United States district court. The person or persons aggrieved shall have the right to intervene in a civil action brought by the Commission or the Attorney General in a case involving a government, governmental agency, or political subdivision. If a charge filed with the Commission pursuant to subsection (b) of this section is dismissed by the Commission, or if within one hundred and eighty days from the filing of such charge or the expiration of any period of reference under subsection (c) or (d) of this section, whichever is later, the Commission has not filed a civil action under this section or the Attorney General has not filed a civil action in a case involving a government, governmental agency, or political subdivision, or the Commission has not entered into a conciliation agreement to which the person aggrieved is a party, the Commission, or the Attorney General in a case involving a government, governmental agency, or political subdivision, shall so notify the person aggrieved and within ninety days after the giving of such notice a civil action may be brought against the respondent named in the charge (A) by the person claiming to be aggrieved or (B) if such charge was filed by a member of the Commission, by any person whom the charge alleges was aggrieved by the alleged unlawful employment practice. Upon application by the complainant and in such circumstances as the court may deem just, the court may appoint an attorney for such complainant and may authorize the commencement of the action without the payment of fees, costs, or security. Upon timely application, the court may, in its discretion, permit the Commission, or the Attorney General in a case involving a government, governmental agency, or political subdivision, to intervene in such civil action upon certification that the case is of general public importance. Upon request, the court may, in its discretion, stay further proceedings for not more than sixty days pending the termination of State or local proceedings described in subsection (c) or (d) of this section or further efforts of the Commission to obtain voluntary compliance.

(2) Whenever a charge is filed with the Commission and the Commission concludes on the basis of a preliminary investigation that prompt judicial action is necessary to carry out the purposes of this Act, the Commission, or the Attorney General in a case involving a government, governmental agency, or political subdivision, may bring an action for appropriate temporary or preliminary relief pending final disposition of such charge. Any temporary restraining order or other order granting preliminary or temporary relief shall be issued in accordance with rule 65 of the Federal Rules of Civil Procedure. It shall be the duty of a court having jurisdiction over proceedings under this section to assign cases for hearing at the earliest practicable date and to cause such cases to be in every way expedited.

(3) Each United States district court and each United States court of a place subject to the jurisdiction of the United States shall have jurisdiction of actions brought under this title. Such an action may be brought in any judicial district in the State in which the unlawful employment practice is alleged to have been committed, in the judicial district in which the employment records relevant to such practice are maintained and administered, or in the judicial district in which the aggrieved person would have worked but for the alleged unlawful employment practice, but if the respondent is not found within any such district, such an action may be brought within the judicial district in which the respondent has his principal office. For purposes of sections 1404 and 1406 of Title 28, the judicial district in which the respondent has his principal office shall in all cases be considered a district in which the action might have been brought.

(4) It shall be the duty of the chief judge of the district (or in his absence, the acting chief judge) in which the case is pending immediately to designate a judge in such district to hear and determine the case. In the event that no judge in the district is available to hear and determine the case, the chief judge of the district, or the acting chief judge, as the case may be, shall certify this fact to the chief judge of the circuit (or in his absence, the acting chief judge) who shall then designate a district or circuit judge of the circuit to hear and determine the case.

(5) It shall be the duty of the judge designated pursuant to this subsection to assign the case for hearing at the earliest practicable date and to cause the case to be in every way expedited. If such judge has not scheduled the case for trial within one hundred and twenty days after issue has been joined, that judge may appoint a master pursuant to rule 53 of the Federal Rules of Civil Procedure.

(g)(1) If the court finds that the respondent has intentionally engaged in or is intentionally engaging in an unlawful employment practice charged in the complaint, the court may enjoin the respondent from engaging in such unlawful employment practice, and order such affirmative action as may be appropriate, which may include, but is not limited to, reinstatement or hiring of employees, with or without back pay (payable by the employer, employment agency, or labor organization, as the case may be, responsible for the unlawful employment practice), or any other equitable relief as the court deems appropriate. Back pay liability shall not accrue from a date more than two years prior to the filing of a charge with the Commission. Interim earnings or amounts earnable with reasonable diligence by the person or persons discriminated against shall operate to reduce the back pay otherwise allowable.

(2)(A) No order of the court shall require the admission or reinstatement of an individual as a member of a union, or the hiring, reinstatement, or promotion of an individual as an employee, or the payment to him of any back pay, if such individual was refused admission, suspended, or expelled, or was refused employment or advancement or was suspended or discharged for any reason other than discrimination on account of race, color, religion, sex, or national origin or in violation of section 704(a).

(B) On a claim in which an individual proves a violation under section 703(m) and a respondent demonstrates that the respondent would have taken the same action in the absence of the impermissible motivating factor, the court—

(i) may grant declaratory relief, injunctive relief (except as provided in clause (ii)), and attorney's fees and costs demonstrated to be directly attributable only to the pursuit of a claim under section 703(m); and

(ii) shall not award damages or issue an order requiring any admission, reinstatement, hiring, promotion, or payment, described in subparagraph (A).

(h) The provisions of chapter 6 of Title 29 [the Norris-LaGuardia Act] shall not apply with respect to civil actions brought under this section.

(i) In any case in which an employer, employment agency, or labor organization fails to comply with an order of a court issued in a civil action brought under this section, the Commission may commence proceedings to compel compliance with such order.

(j) Any civil action brought under this section and any proceedings brought under subsection (i) of this section shall be subject to appeal as provided in sections 1291 and 1292, Title 28.

(k) In any action or proceeding under this title the court, in its discretion, may allow the prevailing party, other than the Commission or the United States, a reasonable attorney's fee (including expert fees) as part of the costs, and the Commission and the United States shall be liable for costs the same as a private person.

§ 707 [§ 2000e-6]. Civil actions by Attorney General

(a) Whenever the Attorney General has reasonable cause to believe that any person or group of persons is engaged in a pattern or practice of resistance to the full enjoyment of any of the rights secured by this title, and that the pattern or practice is of such a nature and is intended to deny the full exercise of the rights herein described, the Attorney General may bring a civil action in the appropriate district court of the United States by filing with it a complaint (1) signed by him (or in his absence the Acting Attorney General), (2) setting forth facts pertaining to such pattern or practice, and (3) requesting such relief, including an application for a permanent or temporary injunction, restraining order or other order against the person or persons responsible for such pattern or practice, as he deems necessary to insure the full enjoyment of the rights herein described.

(b) The district courts of the United States shall have and shall exercise jurisdiction of proceedings instituted pursuant to this section. . . .

(c) Effective two years after March 24, 1972, the functions of the Attorney General under this section shall be transferred to the Commission, together with such personnel, property, records, and unexpended balances of appropriations, allocations, and other funds employed, used, held, available, or to be made available in connection with such functions unless the President submits, and neither House of Congress vetoes, a reorganization plan pursuant to chapter 9 of Title 5, inconsistent with the provisions of this subsection. . . .

(e) Subsequent to March 24, 1972, the Commission shall have authority to investigate and act on a charge of a pattern or practice of discrimination, whether filed by or on behalf of a person claiming to be aggrieved or by a member of the Commission. All such actions shall be conducted in accordance with the procedures set forth in section 706.

§ 708 [§ 2000e-7]. Effect on State laws. Nothing in this title shall be deemed to exempt or relieve any person from any liability, duty, penalty, or punishment provided by any present or future law of any State or political subdivision of a State, other than any such law which purports to require or permit the doing of any act which would be an unlawful employment practice under this title.

§ 709 [§ 2000e-8]. Investigations

(a) In connection with any investigation of a charge filed under section [706], the Commission or its designated representative shall at all reasonable times have access to, for the purposes of examination, and the right to copy any evidence of any person being investigated or proceeded against that relates to unlawful employment practices covered by this title and is relevant to the charge under investigation.

(b) The Commission may cooperate with State and local agencies charged with the administration of State fair employment practices laws and, with the consent of such agencies, may, for the purpose of carrying out its functions and duties under this title and within the limitation of funds appropriated specifically for such purpose, engage in and contribute to the cost of research and other projects of mutual interest undertaken by such agencies, and utilize the services of such agencies and their employees, and, notwithstanding any other provision of law, pay by advance or reimbursement such agencies and their employees for services rendered to assist the Commission in carrying out this title. In furtherance of such cooperative efforts, the Commission may enter into written agreements with such State or local agencies and such agreements may include provisions under which the Commission shall refrain from processing a charge in any cases or class of cases specified in such agreements or under which the Commission shall relieve any person or class of persons in such State or locality from requirements imposed under this section. The Commission shall rescind any such agreement whenever it determines that the agreement no longer serves the interest of effective enforcement of this title.

(c) Every employer, employment agency, and labor organization subject to this title shall (1) make and keep such records relevant to the determinations of whether unlawful employment practices have been or are being committed, (2) preserve such records for such periods, and (3) make such reports therefrom as the Commission shall prescribe by regulation or order, after public hearing, as reasonable, necessary, or appropriate for the enforcement of this title or the regulations or orders thereunder. . . .

(e) It shall be unlawful for any officer or employee of the Commission to make public in any manner whatever any information obtained by the Commission pursuant to its authority under this section prior to the institution of any proceeding under this title involving such information. Any officer or employee of the Commission who shall make public in any manner whatever any information in violation of this subsection shall be guilty of a misdemeanor and upon conviction thereof, shall be fined not more than $1,000, or imprisoned not more than one year.

§ 710 [§ 2000e-9]. Conduct of hearings and investigations pursuant to section [11 of the National Labor Relations Act]. For the purpose of all hearings and investigations conducted by the Commission or its duly authorized agents or agencies, section [11 of the National Labor Relations Act] shall apply.

§ 711 [§ 2000e-10]. Posting of notices; penalties

(a) Every employer, employment agency, and labor organization, as the case may be, shall post and keep posted in conspicuous places upon its premises where notices to employees, applicants for employment, and members are customarily posted a notice to be prepared or approved by the Commission setting forth excerpts from or, summaries of, the pertinent provisions of this title and information pertinent to the filing of a complaint.

(b) A willful violation of this section shall be punishable by a fine of not more than $100 for each separate offense.

§ 712 [§ 2000e-11]. Veterans' special rights or preference. Nothing contained in this title shall be construed to repeal or modify any Federal, State, territorial, or local law creating special rights or preference for veterans.

§ 713 [§ 2000e-12]. Regulations; conformity of regulations with administrative procedure provisions; reliance on interpretations and instructions of Commission

(a) The Commission shall have authority from time to time to issue, amend, or rescind suitable procedural regulations to carry out the provisions of this title. Regulations issued under this section shall be in conformity with the standards and limitations of subchapter II of chapter 5 of Title 5.

(b) In any action or proceeding based on any alleged unlawful employment practice, no person shall be subject to any liability or punishment for or on account of (1) the commission by such person of an unlawful employment practice if he pleads and proves that the act or omission complained of was in good faith, in conformity with, and in reliance on any written interpretation or opinion of the Commission, or (2) the failure of such person to publish and file any information required by any provision of this title if he pleads and proves that he failed to publish and file such information in good faith, in conformity with the instructions of the Commission issued under this title regarding the filing of such information. Such a defense, if established, shall be a bar to the action or proceeding, notwithstanding that (A) after such act or omission, such interpretation or opinion is modified or rescinded or is determined by judicial authority to be invalid or of no legal effect, or (B) after publishing or filing the description and annual reports, such publication or filing is determined by judicial authority not to be in conformity with the requirements of this title. . . .

§ 717 [§ 2000e-16]. Employment by Federal Government

(a) All personnel actions affecting employees or applicants for employment (except with regard to aliens employed outside the limits of the United States) in military departments as defined in section 102 of Title 5, in executive agencies as defined in section 105 of Title 5 (including employees and applicants for employment who are paid from nonappropriated funds), in the United States Postal Service and the Postal Rate Commission, in those units of the Government of the District of Columbia having positions in the competitive service, and in those units of the judicial branch of the Federal Government having positions in the competitive service, in the Smithsonian Institution, and in the Government Printing Office, the Government Accountability Office, and the Library of Congress shall be made free from any discrimination based on race, color, religion, sex, or national origin.

(b) Except as otherwise provided in this subsection, the Equal Employment Opportunity Commission shall have authority to enforce the provisions of subsection (a) of this section through appropriate remedies, including reinstatement or hiring of employees with or without back pay, as will effectuate the policies of this section, and shall issue such rules, regulations, orders and instructions as it deems necessary and appropriate to carry out its responsibilities under this section. The Equal Employment Opportunity Commission shall—

(1) be responsible for the annual review and approval of a national and regional equal employment opportunity plan which each department and agency and each appropriate unit referred to in subsection (a) of this section shall submit in order to maintain an affirmative program of equal employment opportunity for all such employees and applicants for employment;

(2) be responsible for the review and evaluation of the operation of all agency equal employment opportunity programs, periodically obtaining and publishing (on at least a semiannual basis) progress reports from each such department, agency, or unit; and

(3) consult with and solicit the recommendations of interested individuals, groups, and organizations relating to equal employment opportunity.

The head of each such department, agency, or unit shall comply with such rules, regulations, orders, and instructions which shall include a provision that an employee or applicant for employment shall be notified of any final action taken on any complaint of discrimination filed by him thereunder. The plan submitted by each department, agency, and unit shall include, but not be limited to—

(1) provision for the establishment of training and education programs designed to provide a maximum opportunity for employees to advance so as to perform at their highest potential; and

(2) a description of the qualifications in terms of training and experience relating to equal employment opportunity for the principal and operating officials of each such department, agency, or unit responsible for carrying out the equal employment opportunity program and of the allocation of personnel and resources proposed by such department, agency, or unit to carry out its equal employment opportunity program.

With respect to employment in the Library of Congress, authorities granted in this subsection to the Equal Employment Opportunity Commission shall be exercised by the Librarian of Congress.

(c) Within 90 days of receipt of notice of final action taken by a department, agency, or unit referred to in subsection (a) of this section, or by the Equal Employment Opportunity Commission upon an appeal from a decision or order of such department, agency, or unit on a complaint of discrimination based on race, color, religion, sex or national origin, brought pursuant to subsection (a) of this section, Executive Order 11478 or any succeeding Executive orders, or after one hundred and eighty days from the filing of the initial charge with the department, agency, or unit or with the Equal Employment Opportunity Commission on appeal from a decision or order of such department, agency, or unit until such time as final action may be taken by a department, agency, or unit, an employee or applicant for employment, if aggrieved by the final disposition of his complaint, or by the failure to take final action on his complaint, may file a civil action as provided in section [706] in which civil action the head of the department, agency, or unit, as appropriate, shall be the defendant.

(d) The provisions of section [706](f) through (k), as applicable, shall govern civil actions brought hereunder, and the same interest to compensate for delay in payment shall be available as in cases involving nonpublic parties.

(e) Nothing contained in this Act shall relieve any Government agency or official of its or his primary responsibility to assure nondiscrimination in employment as required by the Constitution and statutes or of its or his responsibilities under Executive Order 11478 relating to equal employment opportunity in the Federal Government. . . .

NINETEENTH CENTURY CIVIL RIGHTS ACTS

42 U.S.C. §§ 1981, 1981a, 1983, 1988

§ 1981. Equal rights under the law

(a) All persons within the jurisdiction of the United States shall have the same right in every State and Territory to make and enforce contracts, to sue, be parties, give evidence, and to the full and equal benefit of all laws and proceedings for the security of persons and property as is enjoyed by white citizens, and shall be subject to like punishment, pains, penalties, taxes, licenses, and exactions of every kind, and to no other.

(b) For purposes of this section, the term "make and enforce contracts" includes the making, performance, modification, and termination of contracts, and the enjoyment of all benefits, privileges, terms, and conditions of the contractual relationship.

(c) The rights protected by this section are protected against impairment by nongovernmental discrimination and impairment under color of State law.

§ 1981a. Damages in cases of intentional discrimination in employment

(a)(1) In an action brought by a complaining party under section 706 or 717 of the Civil Rights Act of 1964 against a respondent who engaged in unlawful intentional discrimination (not an employment practice that is unlawful because of its disparate impact) prohibited under section 703, 704, or 717 of the Act, and provided that the complaining party cannot recover under [42 U.S.C. § 1981], the complaining party may recover compensatory and punitive damages as allowed in subsection (b), in addition to any relief authorized by section 706(g) of the Civil Rights Act of 1964, from the respondent.

(2) In an action brought by a complaining party under the powers, remedies, and procedures set forth in section 706 or 717 of the Civil Rights Act of 1964 (as provided in section 107(a) of the Americans with Disabilities Act of 1990 and section 505(a)(1) of the Rehabilitation Act of 1973, respectively) against a respondent who engaged in unlawful intentional discrimination (not an employment practice that is unlawful because of its disparate impact) under section 501 of the Rehabilitation Act of 1973 and the regulations implementing section 501, or who violated the requirements of section 501 of the Act or the regulations implementing section 501 concerning the provision of a reasonable accommodation,

or section 102 of the Americans with Disabilities Act of 1990, or committed a violation of section 102(b)(5) of the Act, against an individual, the complaining party may recover compensatory and punitive damages as allowed in subsection (b), in addition to any relief authorized by section 706(g) of the Civil Rights Act of 1964, from the respondent.

(3) In cases where a discriminatory practice involves the provision of a reasonable accommodation pursuant to section 102(b)(5) of the Americans with Disabilities Act of 1990 or regulations implementing section 501 of the Rehabilitation Act of 1973, damages may not be awarded under this section where the covered entity demonstrates good faith efforts, in consultation with the person with the disability who has informed the covered entity that accommodation is needed, to identify and make a reasonable accommodation that would provide such individual with an equally effective opportunity and would not cause an undue hardship on the operation of the business.

(b)(1) A complaining party may recover punitive damages under this section against a respondent (other than a government, government agency or political subdivision) if the complaining party demonstrates that the respondent engaged in a discriminatory practice or discriminatory practices with malice or with reckless indifference to the federally protected rights of an aggrieved individual.

(2) Compensatory damages awarded under this section shall not include backpay, interest on backpay, or any other type of relief authorized under section 706(g) of the Civil Rights Act of 1964.

(3) The sum of the amount of compensatory damages awarded under this section for future pecuniary losses, emotional pain, suffering, inconvenience, mental anguish, loss of enjoyment of life, and other nonpecuniary losses, and the amount of punitive damages awarded under this section, shall not exceed, for each complaining party—

(A) in the case of a respondent who has more than 14 and fewer than 101 employees in each of 20 or more calendar weeks in the current or preceding calendar year, $50,000;

(B) in the case of a respondent who has more than 100 and fewer than 201 employees in each of 20 or more calendar weeks in the current or preceding calendar year, $100,000; and

(C) in the case of a respondent who has more than 200 and fewer than 501 employees in each of 20 or more calendar weeks in the current or preceding calendar year, $200,000; and

(D) in the case of a respondent who has more than 500 employees in each of 20 or more calendar weeks in the current or preceding calendar year, $300,000.

(4) Nothing in this section shall be construed to limit the scope of, or the relief available under [42 U.S.C. § 1981].

(c) If a complaining party seeks compensatory or punitive damages under this section—

(1) any party may demand a trial by jury; and

(2) the court shall not inform the jury of the limitations described in subsection (b)(3) of this section.

(d) As used in this section:

(1) The term "complaining party" means—

(A) in the case of a person seeking to bring an action under subsection (a)(1) of this section, the Equal Employment Opportunity Commission, the Attorney General, or a person who may bring an action or proceeding under title VII of the Civil Rights Act of 1964; or

(B) in the case of a person seeking to bring an action under subsection (a)(2) of this section, the Equal Employment Opportunity Commission, the Attorney General, a person who may bring an action or proceeding under section 505(a)(1) of the Rehabilitation Act of 1973 or a person who may bring an action or proceeding under title I of the Americans with Disabilities Act of 1990.

(2) The term "discriminatory practice" means the discrimination described in paragraph (1), or the discrimination or the violation described in paragraph (2), of subsection (a) of this section.

§ 1983. Civil action for deprivation of rights. Every person who, under color of any statute, ordinance, regulation, custom, or usage, of any State or Territory or the District of Columbia, subjects, or causes to be subjected, any citizen of the United States or other person within the jurisdiction thereof to the deprivation of any rights, privileges, or immunities secured by the Constitution and laws, shall be liable to the party injured in an action at law, suit in equity, or other proper proceeding for redress, except that in any action brought against a judicial officer for an act or omission taken in such judicial officer's judicial capacity, injunctive relief shall not be granted unless a declaratory decree was violated or declaratory relief was unavailable. For the purposes of this section, any Act of Congress applicable exclusively to the District of Columbia shall be considered to be a statute of the District of Columbia.

§ 1988. Proceedings in vindication of civil rights; attorney's fees. . .

(b) In any action or proceeding to enforce a provision of sections [1981, 1981a, or 1983] of this title, . . . the court, in its discretion, may allow the prevailing party, other than the United States, a reasonable attorney's fee as part of the costs, except that in any action brought against a judicial officer for an act or omission taken in such officer's judicial capacity such officer shall not be held liable for any costs, including attorney's fees, unless such action was clearly in excess of such officer's jurisdiction.

(c) In awarding an attorney's fee under subsection (b) in any action or proceeding to enforce a provision of section 1981 or 1981a of this title the court, in its discretion, may include expert fees as part of the attorney's fee.

REHABILITATION ACT OF 1973

29 U.S.C. §§ 705, 791, 793 794a

§ 8 [§ 705]. Definitions. For the purposes of this Act: . . .

(20)(B) Subject to subparagraphs (C), (D), (E), and (F), the term "individual with a disability" means, for purposes of . . . [this Act], any person who has a disability as defined in [Section 3 of the Americans with Disabilities Act].

(C)(i) For purposes of title V of this Act, the term "individual with a disability" does not include an individual who is currently engaging in the illegal use of drugs, when a covered entity acts on the basis of such use.

(ii) Nothing in clause (i) shall be construed to exclude as an individual with disabilities an individual who—

(I) has successfully completed a supervised drug rehabilitation program and is no longer engaging in the illegal use of drugs, or has otherwise been rehabilitated successfully and is no longer engaging in such use;

(II) is participating in a supervised rehabilitation program and is no longer engaging in such use; or

(III) is erroneously regarded as engaging in such use, but is not engaging in such use;

except that it shall not be a violation of this Act for a covered entity to adopt or administer reasonable policies or procedures, including but not limited to drug testing, designed to ensure that an individual described in subclause (I) or (II) is no longer engaging in the illegal use of drugs. . . .

(v) For purposes of sections 793 and 794 of this title as such sections relate to employment, the term "individual with a disability" does not include any individual who is an alcoholic whose current use of alcohol prevents such individual from performing the duties of the job in question or whose employment, by reason of such current alcohol abuse, would constitute a direct threat to property or the safety of others.

(D) For the purpose of sections 793 and 794 of this title, as such sections relate to employment, such term does not include an individual who has a currently contagious disease or infection and who, by reason of such disease or infection, would constitute a direct threat to the health or safety of other individuals or who, by reason of the currently contagious disease or infection, is unable to perform the duties of the job.

(E) For the purposes of sections 791, 793, and 794 of this title—

(i) for purposes of the application of subparagraph (B) to such sections, the term "impairment" does not include homosexuality or bisexuality; and

(ii) therefore the term "individual with a disability" does not include an individual on the basis of homosexuality or bisexuality.

(F) For the purposes of sections 791, 793, and 794 of this title, the term "individual with a disability" does not include an individual on the basis of—

(i) transvestism, transsexualism, pedophilia, exhibitionism, voyeurism, gender identity disorders not resulting from physical impairments, or other sexual behavior disorders;

(ii) compulsive gambling, kleptomania, or pyromania; or

(iii) psychoactive substance abuse disorders resulting from current illegal use of drugs. . . .

§ 501 [§ 791]. Employment of individuals with disabilities. . .

(b) Each department, agency, and instrumentality (including the United States Postal Service and the Postal Rate Commission) in the executive branch shall, within one hundred and eighty days after September 26, 1973, submit to the Commission and to the Committee an affirmative action program plan for the hiring, placement, and advancement of individuals with disabilities in such department, agency, or instrumentality. Such plan shall include a description of the extent to which and methods whereby the special needs of employees with disabilities are being met. Such plan shall be updated annually, and shall be reviewed annually and approved by the Commission if the Commission determines, after consultation with the Committee, that such plan provides sufficient assurances, procedures and commitments to provide adequate hiring, placement, and advancement opportunities for individuals with disabilities. . . .

§ 503 [§ 793]. Employment under federal contracts

(a) Any contract in excess of $10,000 entered into by any Federal department or agency for the procurement of personal property and nonpersonal services (including construction) for the United States shall contain a provision requiring that the party contracting with the United States shall take affirmative action to employ and advance in employment qualified individuals with disabilities. The provisions of this section shall apply to any subcontract in excess of $10,000 entered into by a prime contractor in carrying out any contract for the procurement of personal property and nonpersonal services (including construction) for the United States. . . .

(b) If any individual with a disability believes any contractor has failed or refused to comply with the provisions of a contract with the United States, relating to employment of individuals with disabilities, such individual may file a complaint with the Department of Labor. The Department shall promptly investigate such complaint and shall take such action thereon as the facts and circumstances warrant, consistent with the terms of such contract and the laws and regulations applicable thereto. . . .

(d) The standards used to determine whether this section has been violated in a complaint alleging nonaffirmative action employment discrimination under this section shall be the standards applied under title I of the Americans with Disabilities Act and the provisions of sections 501 through 504, and 510, of the Americans with Disabilities Act, as such sections relate to employment.

§ 504 [§ 794]. Nondiscrimination under federal grants and programs

(a) No otherwise qualified individual with a disability in the United States, as defined in section 705(20) of this title, shall, solely by reason of her or his disability, be excluded from the participation in, be denied the benefits of, or be subjected to discrimination under any program or activity receiving Federal financial assistance or under any program or activity conducted by any Executive agency or by the United States Postal Service. . . .

(b) For the purposes of this section, the term "program or activity" means all of the operations of—

(1)(A) a department, agency, special purpose district, or other instrumentality of a State or of a local government; or

(B) the entity of such State or local government that distributes such assistance and each such department or agency (and each other State or local government entity) to which the assistance is extended, in the case of assistance to a State or local government;

(2)(A) a college, university, or other postsecondary institution, or a public system of higher education; or

(B) a local educational agency (as defined in section 7801 of Title 20), system of vocational education, or other school system;

(3)(A) an entire corporation, partnership, or other private organization, or an entire sole proprietorship—

(i) if assistance is extended to such corporation, partnership, private organization, or sole proprietorship as a whole; or

(ii) which is principally engaged in the business of providing education, health care, housing, social service, or parks and recreation; or

(B) the entire plant or other comparable, geographically separate facility to which Federal financial assistance is extended, in the case of any other corporation, partnership, private organization, or sole proprietorship; or

(4) any other entity which is established by two or more of the entities described in paragraph (1), (2), or (3);

any part of which is extended Federal financial assistance.

(c) Small providers are not required by subsection (a) of this section to make significant structural alterations to their existing facilities for the purpose of assuring program accessibility, if alternative means of providing the services are available. The terms used in this subsection shall be construed with reference to the regulations existing on March 22, 1988.

(d) The standards used to determine whether this section has been violated in a complaint alleging employment discrimination under this section shall be the standards applied under title I of the Americans with Disabilities Act of 1990 and the provisions of sections 501 through 504, and 510, of the Americans with Disabilities Act of 1990, as such sections relate to employment.

§ 505 [§ 794a]. Remedies and attorney's fees

(a)(1) The remedies, procedures, and rights set forth in section 717 of the Civil Rights Act of 1964, including the application of sections 706(f) through 706(k), shall be available with respect to any complaint under section 791 of this title, to any employee or applicant for employment aggrieved by the final disposition of such complaint, or by the failure to take final action on such complaint. In fashioning an equitable or affirmative action remedy under such section, a court may take into account the reasonableness of the cost of any necessary work place accommodation, and the availability of alternatives therefor or other appropriate relief in order to achieve an equitable and appropriate remedy.

(2) The remedies, procedures, and rights set forth in Title VI of the Civil Rights Act of 1964 shall be available to any person aggrieved by any act or failure to act by any recipient of Federal assistance or Federal provider of such assistance under section 794 of this title.

(b) In any action or proceeding to enforce or charge a violation of a provision of this title, the court, in its discretion, may allow the prevailing party, other than the United States, a reasonable attorney's fee as part of the costs.

AMERICANS WITH DISABILITIES ACT

(Introductory, Employment and Miscellaneous Sections)
42 U.S.C. §§ 12101–12213

§ 2 [§ 12101]. Findings and purposes

(a) The Congress finds that—

(1) physical or mental disabilities in no way diminish a person's right to fully participate in all aspects of society, yet many people with physical or mental disabilities have been precluded from doing so because of discrimination; others who have a record of a disability or are regarded as having a disability also have been subject to discrimination;

(2) historically, society has tended to isolate and segregate individuals with disabilities, and, despite some improvements, such forms of discrimination against individuals with disabilities continue to be a serious and pervasive social problem;

(3) discrimination against individuals with disabilities persists in such critical areas as employment, housing, public accommodations, education, transportation, communication, recreation, institutionalization, health services, voting, and access to public services;

(4) unlike individuals who have experienced discrimination on the basis of race, color, sex, national origin, religion, or age, individuals who have experienced discrimination on the basis of disability have often had no legal recourse to redress such discrimination;

(5) individuals with disabilities continually encounter various forms of discrimination, including outright intentional exclusion, the discriminatory effects of architectural, transportation, and communication barriers, overprotective rules and policies, failure to make modifications to existing facilities and practices, exclusionary qualification standards and criteria, segregation, and relegation to lesser services, programs, activities, benefits, jobs, or other opportunities;

(6) census data, national polls, and other studies have documented that people with disabilities, as a group, occupy an inferior status in our society, and are severely disadvantaged socially, vocationally, economically, and educationally;

(7) the Nation's proper goals regarding individuals with disabilities are to assure equality of opportunity, full participation, independent living, and economic self-sufficiency for such individuals; and

(8) the continuing existence of unfair and unnecessary discrimination and prejudice denies people with disabilities the opportunity to compete on an equal basis and to pursue those opportunities for which our free society is justifiably famous, and costs the United States billions of dollars in unnecessary expenses resulting from dependency and nonproductivity.

(b) It is the purpose of this Act—

(1) to provide a clear and comprehensive national mandate for the elimination of discrimination against individuals with disabilities;

(2) to provide clear, strong, consistent, enforceable standards addressing discrimination against individuals with disabilities;

(3) to ensure that the Federal Government plays a central role in enforcing the standards established in this Act on behalf of individuals with disabilities; and

(4) to invoke the sweep of congressional authority, including the power to enforce the fourteenth amendment and to regulate commerce, in order to address the major areas of discrimination faced day-to-day by people with disabilities.

§ 3 [§ 12102]. Definition of disability. As used in this Act:

(1) The term "disability" means, with respect to an individual—

(A) a physical or mental impairment that substantially limits one or more major life activities of such individual;

(B) a record of such an impairment; or

(C) being regarded as having such an impairment (as described in paragraph (3)).

(2)(A) For purposes of paragraph (1), major life activities include, but are not limited to, caring for oneself, performing manual tasks, seeing, hearing, eating, sleeping, walking, standing, lifting, bending, speaking, breathing, learning, reading, concentrating, thinking, communicating, and working.

(B) For purposes of paragraph (1), a major life activity also includes the operation of a major bodily function, including but not limited to, functions of the immune system, normal cell growth, digestive, bowel, bladder, neurological, brain, respiratory, circulatory, endocrine, and reproductive functions.

(3) For purposes of paragraph (1)(C):

(A) An individual meets the requirement of "being regarded as having such an impairment" if the individual establishes that he or she has been subjected to an action prohibited under this Act because of an actual or perceived physical or mental impairment whether or not the impairment limits or is perceived to limit a major life activity.

(B) Paragraph (1)(C) shall not apply to impairments that are transitory and minor. A transitory impairment is an impairment with an actual or expected duration of 6 months or less.

(4) The definition of "disability" in paragraph (1) shall be construed in accordance with the following:

(A) The definition of disability in this Act shall be construed in favor of broad coverage of individuals under this Act, to the maximum extent permitted by the terms of this Act.

(B) The term "substantially limits" shall be interpreted consistently with the findings and purposes of the ADA Amendments Act of 2008.

(C) An impairment that substantially limits one major life activity need not limit other major life activities in order to be considered a disability.

(D) An impairment that is episodic or in remission is a disability if it would substantially limit a major life activity when active.

(E)(i) The determination of whether an impairment substantially limits a major life activity shall be made without regard to the ameliorative effects of mitigating measures such as—

(I) medication, medical supplies, equipment, or appliances, low-vision devices (which do not include ordinary eyeglasses or contact lenses), prosthetics including limbs and devices, hearing aids and cochlear implants or other implantable hearing devices, mobility devices, or oxygen therapy equipment and supplies;

(II) use of assistive technology;

(III) reasonable accommodations or auxiliary aids or services; or

(IV) learned behavioral or adaptive neurological modifications.

(ii) The ameliorative effects of the mitigating measure of ordinary eyeglasses or contact lenses shall be considered in determining whether an impairment substantially limits a major life activity.

(iii) As used in this subparagraph—

(I) the term "ordinary eyeglasses or contact lenses" means lenses that are intended to fully correct visual acuity or eliminate refractive error; and

(II) the term "low-vision devices" means devices that magnify, enhance, or otherwise augment a visual image.

§ 4 [§ 12103]. Additional definitions. As used in this Act:

(1) The term "auxiliary aids and services" includes—

(A) qualified interpreters or other effective methods of making aurally delivered materials available to individuals with hearing impairments;

(B) qualified readers, taped texts, or other efective methods of making visually delivered materials available to individuals with visual impairments;

(C) acquisition or modification of equipment or devices; and

(D) other similar services and actions.

(2) The term "State" means each of the several States, the District of Columbia, the Commonwealth of Puerto Rico, Guam, American Samoa, the Virgin Islands of the United States, the Trust Territory of the Pacific Islands, and the Commonwealth of the Northern Mariana Islands.

TITLE I–EMPLOYMENT

§ 101 [§ 12111]. Definitions. As used in this title:

(1) The term "Commission" means the Equal Employment Opportunity Commission established by section [705 of Title VII].

(2) The term "covered entity" means an employer, employment agency, labor organization, or joint labor-management committee.

(3) The term "direct threat" means a significant risk to the health or safety of others that cannot be eliminated by reasonable accommodation.

(4) The term "employee" means an individual employed by an employer. With respect to employment in a foreign country, such term includes an individual who is a citizen of the United States.

(5)(A) The term "employer" means a person engaged in an industry affecting commerce who has 15 or more employees for each working day in each of 20 or more calendar weeks in the current or preceding calendar year, and any agent of such person. . . .

(B) The term "employer" does not include—

(i) the United States, a corporation wholly owned by the government of the United States, or an Indian tribe; or

(ii) a bona fide private membership club (other than a labor organization) that is exempt from taxation under section 501(c) of Title 26.

(6)(A) The term "illegal use of drugs" means the use of drugs, the possession or distribution of which is unlawful under the Controlled Substances Act [21 U.S.C. § 801 et seq.]. Such term does not include the use of a drug taken under supervision by a licensed health care professional, or other uses authorized by the Controlled Substances Act or other provisions of Federal law.

(B) The term "drug" means a controlled substance, as defined in schedules I through V of section 202 of the Controlled Substances Act [21 U.S.C. § 812].

(7) The terms "person", "labor organization", "employment agency", "commerce", and "industry affecting commerce", shall have the same meaning given such terms in section [701 of Title VII].

(8) The term "qualified individual" means an individual who, with or without reasonable accommodation, can perform the essential functions of the employment position that such individual holds or desires. For the purposes of this title, consideration shall be given to the employer's judgment as to what functions of a job are essential, and if an employer has prepared a written description before advertising or interviewing applicants for the job, this description shall be considered evidence of the essential functions of the job.

(9) The term "reasonable accommodation" may include—

(A) making existing facilities used by employees readily accessible to and usable by individuals with disabilities; and

(B) job restructuring, part-time or modified work schedules, reassignment to a vacant position, acquisition or modification of equipment or devices, appropriate adjustment or modifications of examinations, training materials or policies, the provision of qualified readers or interpreters, and other similar accommodations for individuals with disabilities.

(10)(A) The term "undue hardship" means an action requiring significant difficulty or expense, when considered in light of the factors set forth in subparagraph (B).

(B) In determining whether an accommodation would impose an undue hardship on a covered entity, factors to be considered include—

(i) the nature and cost of the accommodation needed under this title;

(ii) the overall financial resources of the facility or facilities involved in the provision of the reasonable accommodation; the number of persons employed at such facility; the effect on expenses and resources, or the impact otherwise of such accommodation upon the operation of the facility;

(iii) the overall financial resources of the covered entity; the overall size of the business of a covered entity with respect to the number of its employees; the number, type, and location of its facilities; and

(iv) the type of operation or operations of the covered entity, including the composition, structure, and functions of the workforce of such entity; the geographic separateness, administrative, or fiscal relationship of the facility or facilities in question to the covered entity.

§ 102 [§ 12112]. Discrimination

(a) No covered entity shall discriminate against a qualified individual on the basis of disability in regard to job application procedures, the hiring, advancement, or discharge of employees, employee compensation, job training, and other terms, conditions, and privileges of employment.

(b) As used in subsection (a) of this section, the term "discriminate" includes—

(1) limiting, segregating, or classifying a job applicant or employee in a way that adversely affects the opportunities or status of such applicant or employee because of the disability of such applicant or employee;

(2) participating in a contractual or other arrangement or relationship that has the effect of subjecting a covered entity's qualified applicant or employee with a disability to the discrimination prohibited by this title (such relationship includes a relationship with an employment or referral agency, labor union, an organization providing fringe benefits to an employee of the covered entity, or an organization providing training and apprenticeship programs);

(3) utilizing standards, criteria, or methods of administration—

(A) that have the effect of discrimination on the basis of disability; or

(B) that perpetuate the discrimination of others who are subject to common administrative control;

(4) excluding or otherwise denying equal jobs or benefits to a qualified individual because of the known disability of an individual with whom the qualified individual is known to have a relationship or association;

(5)(A) not making reasonable accommodations to the known physical or mental limitations of an otherwise qualified individual with a disability who is an applicant or employee, unless such covered entity can demonstrate that the accommodation would impose an undue hardship on the operation of the business of such covered entity; or

(B) denying employment opportunities to a job applicant or employee who is an otherwise qualified individual with a disability, if such denial is based on the need of such covered entity to make reasonable accommodation to the physical or mental impairments of the employee or applicant;

(6) using qualification standards, employment tests or other selection criteria that screen out or tend to screen out an individual with a disability or a class of individuals with disabilities unless the standard, test or other selection criteria, as used by the covered entity, is shown to be job-related for the position in question and is consistent with business necessity; and

(7) failing to select and administer tests concerning employment in the most effective manner to ensure that, when such test is administered to a job applicant or employee who has a disability that impairs sensory, manual, or speaking skills, such test results accurately reflect the skills, aptitude, or whatever other factor of such applicant or employee that such test purports to measure, rather than reflecting the impaired sensory, manual, or speaking skills of such employee or applicant (except where such skills are the factors that the test purports to measure).

(c)(1) It shall not be unlawful under this section for a covered entity to take any action that constitutes discrimination under this section with respect to an employee in a workplace in a foreign country if compliance with this section would cause such covered entity to violate the law of the foreign country in which such workplace is located.

(2)(A) If an employer controls a corporation whose place of incorporation is a foreign country, any practice that constitutes discrimination under this section and is engaged in by such corporation shall be presumed to be engaged in by such employer.

(B) This section shall not apply with respect to the foreign operations of an employer that is a foreign person not controlled by an American employer.

(C) For purposes of this paragraph, the determination of whether an employer controls a corporation shall be based on—

(i) the interrelation of operations;

(ii) the common management;

(iii) the centralized control of labor relations; and

(iv) the common ownership or financial control, of the employer and the corporation.

(d)(1) The prohibition against discrimination as referred to in subsection (a) of this section shall include medical examinations and inquiries.

(2)(A) Except as provided in paragraph (3), a covered entity shall not conduct a medical examination or make inquiries of a job applicant as to whether such applicant is an individual with a disability or as to the nature or severity of such disability.

(B) A covered entity may make preemployment inquiries into the ability of an applicant to perform job-related functions.

(3) A covered entity may require a medical examination after an offer of employment has been made to a job applicant and prior to the commencement of the employment duties of such applicant, and may condition an offer of employment on the results of such examination, if—

(A) all entering employees are subjected to such an examination regardless of disability;

(B) information obtained regarding the medical condition or history of the applicant is collected and maintained on separate forms and in separate medical files and is treated as a confidential medical record, except that—

(i) supervisors and managers may be informed regarding necessary restrictions on the work or duties of the employee and necessary accommodations;

(ii) first aid and safety personnel may be informed, when appropriate, if the disability might require emergency treatment; and

(iii) government officials investigating compliance with this Act shall be provided relevant information on request; and

(C) the results of such examination are used only in accordance with this title.

(4)(A) A covered entity shall not require a medical examination and shall not make inquiries of an employee as to whether such employee is an individual with a disability or as to the nature or severity of the disability, unless such examination or inquiry is shown to be job-related and consistent with business necessity.

(B) A covered entity may conduct voluntary medical examinations, including voluntary medical histories, which are part of an employee health program available to employees at that work site. A covered entity may make inquiries into the ability of an employee to perform job-related functions.

(C) Information obtained under subparagraph (B) regarding the medical condition or history of any employee are subject to the requirements of subparagraphs (B) and (C) of paragraph (3).

§ 103 [§ 12113]. Defenses

(a) It may be a defense to a charge of discrimination under this Act that an alleged application of qualification standards, tests, or selection criteria that screen out or tend to screen out or otherwise deny a job or benefit to an individual with a disability has been shown to be job-related and consistent with business necessity, and such performance cannot be accomplished by reasonable accommodation, as required under this title.

(b) The term "qualification standards" may include a requirement that an individual shall not pose a direct threat to the health or safety of other individuals in the workplace.

(c) Notwithstanding section 12102(4)(E)(ii) of this title, a covered entity shall not use qualification standards, employment tests, or other selection criteria based on an individual's uncorrected vision unless the standard, test, or other selection criteria, as used by the covered entity, is shown to be job-related for the position in question and consistent with business necessity.

(d)(1) This title shall not prohibit a religious corporation, association, educational institution, or society from giving preference in employment to individuals of a particular religion to perform work connected with the carrying on by such corporation, association, educational institution, or society of its activities.

(2) Under this title, a religious organization may require that all applicants and employees conform to the religious tenets of such organization.

(e)(1) The Secretary of Health and Human Services, not later than 6 months after July 26, 1990, shall—

(A) review all infectious and communicable diseases which may be transmitted through handling the food supply;

(B) publish a list of infectious and communicable diseases which are transmitted through handling the food supply;

(C) publish the methods by which such diseases are transmitted; and

(D) widely disseminate such information regarding the list of diseases and their modes of transmissability to the general public.

Such list shall be updated annually.

(2) In any case in which an individual has an infectious or communicable disease that is transmitted to others through the handling of food, that is included on the list developed by the Secretary of Health and Human Services under paragraph (1), and which cannot be eliminated by reasonable accommodation, a covered entity may refuse to assign or continue to assign such individual to a job involving food handling.

(3) Nothing in this Act shall be construed to preempt, modify, or amend any State, county, or local law, ordinance, or regulation applicable to food handling which is designed to protect the public health from individuals who pose a significant risk to the health or safety of others, which cannot be eliminated by reasonable accommodation, pursuant to the list of infectious or communicable diseases and the modes of transmissability published by the Secretary of Health and Human Services.

§ 104 [§ 12114]. Illegal use of drugs and alcohol

(a) For purposes of this title, the term "qualified individual with a disability" shall not include any employee or applicant who is currently engaging in the illegal use of drugs, when the covered entity acts on the basis of such use.

(b) Nothing in subsection (a) of this section shall be construed to exclude as a qualified individual with a disability an individual who—

(1) has successfully completed a supervised drug rehabilitation program and is no longer engaging in the illegal use of drugs, or has otherwise been rehabilitated successfully and is no longer engaging in such use;

(2) is participating in a supervised rehabilitation program and is no longer engaging in such use; or

(3) is erroneously regarded as engaging in such use, but is not engaging in such use;

except that it shall not be a violation of this Act for a covered entity to adopt or administer reasonable policies or procedures, including but not limited to drug testing, designed to ensure that an individual described in paragraph (1) or (2) is no longer engaging in the illegal use of drugs.

(c) A covered entity—

(1) may prohibit the illegal use of drugs and the use of alcohol at the workplace by all employees;

(2) may require that employees shall not be under the influence of alcohol or be engaging in the illegal use of drugs at the workplace;

(3) may require that employees behave in conformance with the requirements established under the Drug-Free Workplace Act of 1988 [41 U.S.C. § 701 et seq.];

(4) may hold an employee who engages in the illegal use of drugs or who is an alcoholic to the same qualification standards for employment or job performance and behavior that such entity holds other employees, even if any unsatisfactory performance or behavior is related to the drug use or alcoholism of such employee; and

(5) may, with respect to Federal regulations regarding alcohol and the illegal use of drugs, require that—

(A) employees comply with the standards established in such regulations of the Department of Defense, if the employees of the covered entity are employed in an industry subject to such regulations, including complying with regulations (if any) that apply to employment in sensitive positions in such an industry, in the case of employees of the covered entity who are employed in such positions (as defined in the regulations of the Department of Defense);

(B) employees comply with the standards established in such regulations of the Nuclear Regulatory Commission, if the employees of the covered entity are employed in an industry subject to such regulations, including complying with regulations (if any) that apply to employment in sensitive positions in such an industry, in the case of employees of the covered entity who are employed in such positions (as defined in the regulations of the Nuclear Regulatory Commission); and

(C) employees comply with the standards established in such regulations of the Department of Transportation, if the employees of the covered entity are employed in a transportation industry subject to such regulations, including complying with such regulations (if any) that apply to employment in sensitive positions in such an industry, in the case of employees of the covered entity who are employed in such positions (as defined in the regulations of the Department of Transportation).

(d)(1) For purposes of this title, a test to determine the illegal use of drugs shall not be considered a medical examination.

(2) Nothing in this title shall be construed to encourage, prohibit, or authorize the conducting of drug testing for the illegal use of drugs by job applicants or employees or making employment decisions based on such test results.

(e) Nothing in this title shall be construed to encourage, prohibit, restrict, or authorize the otherwise lawful exercise by entities subject to the jurisdiction of the Department of Transportation of authority to—

(1) test employees of such entities in, and applicants for, positions involving safety-sensitive duties for the illegal use of drugs and for on-duty impairment by alcohol; and

(2) remove such persons who test positive for illegal use of drugs and on-duty impairment by alcohol pursuant to paragraph (1) from safety-sensitive duties in implementing subsection (c) of this section.

§ 105 [§ 12115]. Posting notices. Every employer, employment agency, labor organization, or joint labor-management committee covered under this title shall post notices in an accessible format to applicants, employees, and members describing the applicable provisions of this Act, in the manner prescribed by section [§ 711 of Title VII].

§ 106 [§ 12116]. Regulations. Not later than 1 year after July 26, 1990, the Commission shall issue regulations in an accessible format to carry out this title in accordance with subchapter II of chapter 5 of Title 5.

§ 107 [§ 12117]. Enforcement

(a) The powers, remedies, and procedures set forth in sections [705, 706, 707, 709, and 710 of Title VII] shall be the powers, remedies, and procedures this title provides to the Commission, to the Attorney General, or to any person alleging discrimination on the basis of disability in violation of any provision of this Act, or regulations promulgated under section [106], concerning employment.

(b) The agencies with enforcement authority for actions which allege employment discrimination under this title and under the Rehabilitation Act of 1973 [29 U.S.C. § 701 et seq.] shall develop procedures to ensure that administrative complaints filed under this title and under the Rehabilitation Act of 1973 are dealt with in a manner that avoids duplication of effort and prevents imposition of inconsistent or conflicting standards for the same requirements under this title and the Rehabilitation Act of 1973. The Commission, the Attorney General, and the Office of Federal Contract Compliance Programs shall establish such coordinating mechanisms (similar to provisions contained in the joint regulations promulgated by the Commission and the Attorney

General at part 42 of title 28 and part 1691 of title 29, Code of Federal Regulations, and the Memorandum of Understanding between the Commission and the Office of Federal Contract Compliance Programs dated January 16, 1981 (46 Fed. Reg. 7435, January 23, 1981)) in regulations implementing this title and Rehabilitation Act of 1973 not later than 18 months after July 26, 1990.

TITLE V - MISCELLANEOUS PROVISIONS

§ 501 [§ 12201]. Construction

(a) Except as otherwise provided in this Act, nothing in this Act shall be construed to apply a lesser standard than the standards applied under title V of the Rehabilitation Act of 1973 [29 U.S.C. § 790 et seq.] or the regulations issued by Federal agencies pursuant to such title.

(b) Nothing in this Act shall be construed to invalidate or limit the remedies, rights, and procedures of any Federal law or law of any State or political subdivision of any State or jurisdiction that provides greater or equal protection for the rights of individuals with disabilities than are afforded by this Act. Nothing in this Act shall be construed to preclude the prohibition of, or the imposition of restrictions on, smoking in places of employment covered by title I of this Act, in transportation covered by title II or III of this Act, or in places of public accommodation covered by title III of this Act.

(c) [The employment sections] of this Act shall not be construed to prohibit or restrict—

(1) an insurer, hospital or medical service company, health maintenance organization, or any agent, or entity that administers benefit plans, or similar organizations from underwriting risks, classifying risks, or administering such risks that are based on or not inconsistent with State law; or

(2) a person or organization covered by this Act from establishing, sponsoring, observing or administering the terms of a bona fide benefit plan that are based on underwriting risks, classifying risks, or administering such risks that are based on or not inconsistent with State law; or

(3) a person or organization covered by this Act from establishing, sponsoring, observing or administering the terms of a bona fide benefit plan that is not subject to State laws that regulate insurance.

Paragraphs (1), (2), and (3) shall not be used as a subterfuge to evade the purposes of [the employment sections of this Act].

(d) Nothing in this Act shall be construed to require an individual with a disability to accept an accommodation, aid, service, opportunity, or benefit which such individual chooses not to accept.

(e) Nothing in this Act alters the standards for determining eligibility for benefits under State Worker's compensation laws or under State and Federal disability benefit programs.. . .

(g) Nothing in this chapter shall provide the basis for a claim by an individual without a disability that the individual was subject to discrimination because of the individual's lack of disability.

(h) [A covered entity as defined in § 12111] need not provide a reasonable accommodation or a reasonable modification to policies, practices, or procedures to an individual who meets the definition of disability in section 12102(1) of this Act solely under subparagraph (C) of such section.

§ 502 [§ 12202]. State immunity. A State shall not be immune under the eleventh amendment to the Constitution of the United States from an action in Federal or State court of competent jurisdiction for a violation of this Act. In any action against a State for a violation of the requirements of this Act, remedies (including remedies both at law and in equity) are available for such a violation to the same extent as such remedies are available for such a violation in an action against any public or private entity other than a State.

§ 503 [§ 12203]. Prohibition against retaliation and coercion

(a) No person shall discriminate against any individual because such individual has opposed any act or practice made unlawful by this Act or because such individual made a charge, testified, assisted, or participated in any manner in an investigation, proceeding, or hearing under this Act.

(b) It shall be unlawful to coerce, intimidate, threaten, or interfere with any individual in the exercise or enjoyment of, or on account of his or her having exercised or enjoyed, or on account of his or her having aided or encouraged any other individual in the exercise or enjoyment of, any right granted or protected by this Act.

(c) The remedies and procedures available under section [107] shall be available to aggrieved persons for violations of subsections (a) and (b) of this section. . . .

§ 505 [§ 12205]. Attorney's fees. In any action or administrative proceeding commenced pursuant to this Act, the court or agency, in its discretion, may allow the prevailing party, other than the United States, a reasonable attorney's fee, including litigation expenses, and costs, and the United States shall be liable for the foregoing the same as a private individual.

§ 505a [§ 12205a]. Rule of construction regarding regulatory authority. The authority to issue regulations granted to the Equal Employment Opportunity Commission, the Attorney General, and the Secretary of Transportation under this Act includes the authority to issue regulations implementing the definitions of disability in section 12102 of this Act (including rules of construction) and the definitions in section 12103 of this title, consistent with the ADA Amendments Act of 2008. . . .

§ 508 [§ 12208]. Transvestites. For the purposes of this Act, the term "disabled" or "disability" shall not apply to an individual solely because that individual is a transvestite. . . .

§ 510 [§ 12210]. Illegal use of drugs

(a) For purposes of this Act, the term "individual with a disability" does not include an individual who is currently engaging in the illegal use of drugs, when the covered entity acts on the basis of such use.

(b) Nothing in subsection (a) of this section shall be construed to exclude as an individual with a disability an individual who—

(1) has successfully completed a supervised drug rehabilitation program and is no longer engaging in the illegal use of drugs, or has otherwise been rehabilitated successfully and is no longer engaging in such use;

(2) is participating in a supervised rehabilitation program and is no longer engaging in such use; or

(3) is erroneously regarded as engaging in such use, but is not engaging in such use;

except that it shall not be a violation of this Act for a covered entity to adopt or administer reasonable policies or procedures, including but not limited to drug testing, designed to ensure that an individual described in paragraph (1) or (2) is no longer engaging in the illegal use of drugs; however, nothing in this section shall be construed to encourage, prohibit, restrict, or authorize the conducting of testing for the illegal use of drugs.

(c) Notwithstanding subsection (a) of this section and section [511(b)(3)], an individual shall not be denied health services, or services provided in connection with drug rehabilitation, on the basis of the current illegal use of drugs if the individual is otherwise entitled to such services.

(d)(1) The term "illegal use of drugs" means the use of drugs, the possession or distribution of which is unlawful under the Controlled Substances Act [21 U.S.C. § 801 et seq.]. Such term does not include the use of a drug taken under supervision by a licensed health care professional, or other uses authorized by the Controlled Substances Act or other provisions of Federal law.

(2) The term "drug" means a controlled substance, as defined in schedules I through V of section 202 of the Controlled Substances Act [21 U.S.C. § 812].

§ 511 [§ 12211]. Definitions

(a) For purposes of the definition of "disability" in section [3(2)] of this [Act], homosexuality and bisexuality are not impairments and as such are not disabilities under this Act.

(b) Under this Act, the term "disability" shall not include—

(1) transvestism, transsexualism, pedophilia, exhibitionism, voyeurism, gender identity disorders not resulting from physical impairments, or other sexual behavior disorders;

(2) compulsive gambling, kleptomania, or pyromania; or

(3) psychoactive substance use disorders resulting from current illegal use of drugs.

§ 513 [§ 12212]. Alternative means of dispute resolution. Where appropriate and to the extent authorized by law, the use of alternative means of dispute resolution, including settlement negotiations, conciliation, facilitation, mediation, factfinding, minitrials, and arbitration, is encouraged to resolve disputes arising under this Act.

AGE DISCRIMINATION IN EMPLOYMENT ACT

29 U.S.C. §§ 621–634

§ 2 [§ 621]. Congressional statement of findings and purpose

(a) The Congress hereby finds and declares that—

(1) in the face of rising productivity and affluence, older workers find themselves disadvantaged in their efforts to retain employment, and especially to regain employment when displaced from jobs;

(2) the setting of arbitrary age limits regardless of potential for job performance has become a common practice, and certain otherwise desirable practices may work to the disadvantage of older persons;

(3) the incidence of unemployment, especially long-term unemployment with resultant deterioration of skill, morale, and employer acceptability is, relative to the younger ages, high among older workers; their numbers are great and growing; and their employment problems grave;

(4) the existence in industries affecting commerce, of arbitrary discrimination in employment because of age, burdens commerce and the free flow of goods in commerce.

(b) It is therefore the purpose of this Act to promote employment of older persons based on their ability rather than age; to prohibit arbitrary age discrimination in employment; to help employers and workers find ways of meeting problems arising from the impact of age on employment. . . .

§ 4 [§ 623]. Prohibition of age discrimination

(a) It shall be unlawful for an employer—

(1) to fail or refuse to hire or to discharge any individual or otherwise discriminate against any individual with respect to his

compensation, terms, conditions, or privileges of employment, because of such individual's age;

(2) to limit, segregate, or classify his employees in any way which would deprive or tend to deprive any individual of employment opportunities or otherwise adversely affect his status as an employee, because of such individual's age; or

(3) to reduce the wage rate of any employee in order to comply with this Act.

(b) It shall be unlawful for an employment agency to fail or refuse to refer for employment, or otherwise to discriminate against, any individual because of such individual's age, or to classify or refer for employment any individual on the basis of such individual's age.

(c) It shall be unlawful for a labor organization—

(1) to exclude or to expel from its membership, or otherwise to discriminate against, any individual because of his age;

(2) to limit, segregate, or classify its membership, or to classify or fail or refuse to refer for employment any individual, in any way which would deprive or tend to deprive any individual of employment opportunities, or would limit such employment opportunities or otherwise adversely affect his status as an employee or as an applicant for employment, because of such individual's age;

(3) to cause or attempt to cause an employer to discriminate against an individual in violation of this section.

(d) It shall be unlawful for an employer to discriminate against any of his employees or applicants for employment, for an employment agency to discriminate against any individual, or for a labor organization to discriminate against any member thereof or applicant for membership, because such individual, member or applicant for membership has opposed any practice made unlawful by this section, or because such individual, member or applicant for membership has made a charge, testified, assisted, or participated in any manner in an investigation, proceeding, or litigation under this Act.

(e) It shall be unlawful for an employer, labor organization, or employment agency to print or publish, or cause to be printed or published, any notice or advertisement relating to employment by such an employer or membership in or any classification or referral for employment by such a labor organization, or relating to any classification or referral for employment by such an employment agency, indicating any preference, limitation, specification, or discrimination, based on age.

(f) It shall not be unlawful for an employer, employment agency, or labor organization—

(1) to take any action otherwise prohibited under subsections (a), (b), (c), or (e) of this section where age is a bona fide occupational qualification reasonably necessary to the normal operation of the particular business, or where the differentiation is based on reasonable

factors other than age, or where such practices involve an employee in a workplace in a foreign country, and compliance with such subsections would cause such employer, or a corporation controlled by such employer, to violate the laws of the country in which such workplace is located;

(2) to take any action otherwise prohibited under subsection (a), (b), (c), or (e) of this section—

(A) to observe the terms of a bona fide seniority system that is not intended to evade the purposes of this Act, except that no such seniority system shall require or permit the involuntary retirement of any individual specified by section 12(a) because of the age of such individual; or

(B) to observe the terms of a bona fide employee benefit plan—

(i) where, for each benefit or benefit package, the actual amount of payment made or cost incurred on behalf of an older worker is no less than that made or incurred on behalf of a younger worker, as permissible under section 1625.10, title 29, Code of Federal Regulations (as in effect on June 22, 1989); or

(ii) that is a voluntary early retirement incentive plan consistent with the relevant purpose or purposes of this Act.

Notwithstanding clause (i) or (ii) of subparagraph (B), no such employee benefit plan or voluntary early retirement incentive plan shall excuse the failure to hire any individual, and no such employee benefit plan shall require or permit the involuntary retirement of any individual specified by section 12(a) because of the age of such individual. An employer, employment agency, or labor organization acting under subparagraph (A), or under clause (i) or (ii) of subparagraph (B), shall have the burden of proving that such actions are lawful in any civil enforcement proceeding brought under this Act; or

(3) to discharge or otherwise discipline an individual for good cause.

(g) [Repealed.]

(h)(1) If an employer controls a corporation whose place of incorporation is in a foreign country, any practice by such corporation prohibited under this section shall be presumed to be such practice by such employer.

(2) The prohibitions of this section shall not apply where the employer is a foreign person not controlled by an American employer.

(3) For the purpose of this subsection the determination of whether an employer controls a corporation shall be based upon the—

(A) interrelation of operations,

(B) common management,

(C) centralized control of labor relations, and

(D) common ownership or financial control, of the employer and the corporation.

(i)(1) Except as otherwise provided in this subsection, it shall be unlawful for an employer, an employment agency, a labor organization, or any combination thereof to establish or maintain an employee pension benefit plan which requires or permits—

(A) in the case of a defined benefit plan, the cessation of an employee's benefit accrual, or the reduction of the rate of an employee's benefit accrual, because of age, or

(B) in the case of a defined contribution plan, the cessation of allocations to an employee's account, or the reduction of the rate at which amounts are allocated to an employee's account, because of age.

(2) Nothing in this section shall be construed to prohibit an employer, employment agency, or labor organization from observing any provision of an employee pension benefit plan to the extent that such provision imposes (without regard to age) a limitation on the amount of benefits that the plan provides or a limitation on the number of years of service or years of participation which are taken into account for purposes of determining benefit accrual under the plan.

(3) In the case of any employee who, as of the end of any plan year under a defined benefit plan, has attained normal retirement age under such plan—

(A) if distribution of benefits under such plan with respect to such employee has commenced as of the end of such plan year, then any requirement of this subsection for continued accrual of benefits under such plan with respect to such employee during such plan year shall be treated as satisfied to the extent of the actuarial equivalent of in-service distribution of benefits, and

(B) if distribution of benefits under such plan with respect to such employee has not commenced as of the end of such year in accordance with section 1056(a)(3) of [ERISA] and section 401(a)(14)(C) of [the Internal Revenue Code] and the payment of benefits under such plan with respect to such employee is not suspended during such plan year pursuant to section 1053(a)(3)(B) of [ERISA] or section 411(a)(3)(B) of [the Internal Revenue Code], then any requirement of this subsection for continued accrual of benefits under such plan with respect to such employee during such plan year shall be treated as satisfied to the extent of any adjustment in the benefit payable under the plan during such plan year attributable to the delay in the distribution of benefits after the attainment of normal retirement age.

The provisions of this paragraph shall apply in accordance with regulations of the Secretary of the Treasury. Such regulations shall provide for the application of the preceding provisions of this paragraph to all employee pension benefit plans subject to this subsection and may provide for the application of such provisions, in the case of any such employee, with respect to any period of time within a plan year.

(4) Compliance with the requirements of this subsection with respect to an employee pension benefit plan shall constitute compliance with the requirements of this section relating to benefit accrual under such plan.

(5) Paragraph (1) shall not apply with respect to any employee who is a highly compensated employee (within the meaning of section 414(q) of [the Internal Revenue Code]) to the extent provided in regulations prescribed by the Secretary of the Treasury. . . .

(6) A plan shall not be treated as failing to meet the requirements of paragraph (1) solely because the subsidized portion of any early retirement benefit is disregarded in determining benefit accruals or it is a plan permitted by subsection (m) of this section.. . .

(8) A plan shall not be treated as failing to meet the requirements of this section solely because such plan provides a normal retirement age described in section 1002(24)(B) of [ERISA] and section 411(a)(8)(B) of [the Internal Revenue Code].

(9) For purposes of this subsection—

(A) The terms "employee pension benefit plan", "defined benefit plan", "defined contribution plan", and "normal retirement age" have the meanings provided such terms in section 1002 of [ERISA].

(B) The term "compensation" has the meaning provided by section 414(s) of [the Internal Revenue Code].

(j) It shall not be unlawful for an employer which is a State, a political subdivision of a State, an agency or instrumentality of a State or a political subdivision of a State, or an interstate agency to fail or refuse to hire or to discharge any individual because of such individual's age if such action is taken—

(1) with respect to the employment of an individual as a firefighter or as a law enforcement officer, the employer has complied with section 3(d)(2) of the Age Discrimination in Employment Amendments of 1996 if the individual was discharged after the date described in such section, and the individual has attained—

(A) the age of hiring or retirement, respectively, in effect under applicable State or local law on March 3, 1983; or

(B)(i) if the individual was not hired, the age of hiring in effect on the date of such failure or refusal to hire under applicable State or local law enacted after September 30, 1996; or

(ii) if applicable State or local law was enacted after September 30, 1996, and the individual was discharged, the higher of—

(I) the age of retirement in effect on the date of such discharge under such law; and

(II) age 55; and

(2) pursuant to a bona fide hiring or retirement plan that is not a subterfuge to evade the purposes of this chapter.

(k) A seniority system or employee benefit plan shall comply with this Act regardless of the date of adoption of such system or plan.

(l) Notwithstanding clause (i) or (ii) of subsection (f)(2)(B) of this section—

(1)(A) It shall not be a violation of subsection (a), (b), (c), or (e) of this section solely because—

(i) an employee pension benefit plan (as defined in section 1002(2) of [ERISA]) provides for the attainment of a minimum age as a condition of eligibility for normal or early retirement benefits; or

(ii) a defined benefit plan (as defined in section 1002(35) of [ERISA]) provides for—

(I) payments that constitute the subsidized portion of an early retirement benefit; or

(II) social security supplements for plan participants that commence before the age and terminate at the age (specified by the plan) when participants are eligible to receive reduced or unreduced old-age insurance benefits under title II of the Social Security Act [42 U.S.C. §§ 401 et seq.], and that do not exceed such old-age insurance benefits. . . .

(2)(A) It shall not be a violation of subsection (a), (b), (c), or (e) of this section solely because following a contingent event unrelated to age—

(i) the value of any retiree health benefits received by an individual eligible for an immediate pension;

(ii) the value of any additional pension benefits that are made available solely as a result of the contingent event unrelated to age and following which the individual is eligible for not less than an immediate and unreduced pension; or

(iii) the values described in both clauses (i) and (ii); are deducted from severance pay made available as a result of the contingent event unrelated to age.

(B) For an individual who receives immediate pension benefits that are actuarially reduced under subparagraph (A)(i), the amount of the deduction available pursuant to subparagraph (A)(i) shall be reduced by the same percentage as the reduction in the pension benefits.

(C) For purposes of this paragraph, severance pay shall include that portion of supplemental unemployment compensation benefits (as described in section 501(c)(17) of [the Internal Revenue Code]) that—

(i) constitutes additional benefits of up to 52 weeks;

(ii) has the primary purpose and effect of continuing benefits until an individual becomes eligible for an immediate and unreduced pension; and

(iii) is discontinued once the individual becomes eligible for an immediate and unreduced pension.

(D) For purposes of this paragraph and solely in order to make the deduction authorized under this paragraph the term "retiree health benefits" means benefits provided pursuant to a group health plan covering retirees, for which (determined as of the contingent event unrelated to age)—

(i) the package of benefits provided by the employer for the retirees who are below age 65 is at least comparable to benefits provided under title XVIII of the Social Security Act [42 U.S.C. §§ 1395 et seq.];

(ii) the package of benefits provided by the employer for the retirees who are age 65 and above is at least comparable to that offered under a plan that provides a benefit package with one-fourth the value of benefits provided under title XVIII of such Act; or

(iii) the package of benefits provided by the employer is as described in clauses (i) and (ii).

(E)(i) If the obligation of the employer to provide retiree health benefits is of limited duration, the value for each individual shall be calculated at a rate of $3,000 per year for benefit years before age 65, and $750 per year for benefit years beginning at age 65 and above.

(ii) If the obligation of the employer to provide retiree health benefits is of unlimited duration, the value for each individual shall be calculated at a rate of $48,000 for individuals below age 65, and $24,000 for individuals age 65 and above.

(iii) The values described in clauses (i) and (ii) shall be calculated based on the age of the individual as of the date of the contingent event unrelated to age. The values are effective on October 16, 1990, and shall be adjusted on an annual basis, with respect to a contingent event that occurs subsequent to the first year after October 16, 1990, based on the medical component of the Consumer Price Index for all-urban consumers published by the Department of Labor.

(iv) If an individual is required to pay a premium for retiree health benefits, the value calculated pursuant to this subparagraph shall be reduced by whatever percentage of the overall premium the individual is required to pay.

(F) If an employer that has implemented a deduction pursuant to subparagraph (A) fails to fulfill the obligation described in subparagraph (E), any aggrieved individual may bring an action for specific performance of the obligation described in subparagraph (E). The relief shall be in addition to any other remedies provided under Federal or State law.

(3) It shall not be a violation of subsection (a), (b), (c), or (e) of this section solely because an employer provides a bona fide employee benefit plan or plans under which long-term disability benefits received by an individual are reduced by any pension benefits (other than those attributable to employee contributions)—

(A) paid to the individual that the individual voluntarily elects to receive; or

(B) for which an individual who has attained the later of age 62 or normal retirement age is eligible.

(m) Notwithstanding subsection (f)(2)(b), it shall not be a violation of subsection (a), (b), (c), or (e) solely because a plan of an institution of higher education (as defined in section 1001 of Title 20) offers employees who are serving under a contract of unlimited tenure (or similar arrangement providing for unlimited tenure) supplemental benefits upon voluntary retirement that are reduced or eliminated on the basis of age, if—

(1) such institution does not implement with respect to such employees any age-based reduction or cessation of benefits that are not such supplemental benefits, except as permitted by other provisions of this chapter;

(2) such supplemental benefits are in addition to any retirement or severance benefits which have been offered generally to employees serving under a contract of unlimited tenure (or similar arrangement providing for unlimited tenure), independent of any early retirement or exit-incentive plan, within the preceding 365 days; and

(3) any employee who attains the minimum age and satisfies all non-age-based conditions for receiving a benefit under the plan has an opportunity lasting not less than 180 days to elect to retire and to receive the maximum benefit that could then be elected by a younger but otherwise similarly situated employee, and the plan does not require retirement to occur sooner than 180 days after such election. . . .

§ 6 [§ 625]. Administration. The Secretary shall have the power—

(a) to make delegations, to appoint such agents and employees, and to pay for technical assistance on a fee for service basis, as he deems necessary to assist him in the performance of his functions under this Act;

(b) to cooperate with regional, State, local, and other agencies, and to cooperate with and furnish technical assistance to employers, labor organizations, and employment agencies to aid in effectuating the purposes of this Act.

§ 7 [§ 626]. Recordkeeping, investigation, and enforcement

(a) The Equal Employment Opportunity Commission shall have the power to make investigations and require the keeping of records necessary or appropriate for the administration of this Act in accordance with the powers and procedures provided in sections 209 and 211 of [the Fair Labor Standards Act].

(b) The provisions of this Act shall be enforced in accordance with the powers, remedies, and procedures provided in sections 211(b), 216 (except for subsection (a) thereof), and 217 of [the Fair Labor Standards Act], and subsection (c) of this section. Any act prohibited under section 4 of this title shall be deemed to be a prohibited act under section 215 of [the Fair Labor Standards Act]. Amounts owing to a person as a result of a violation of this Act shall be deemed to be unpaid minimum wages or unpaid overtime compensation for purposes of sections 216 and 217 of [the Fair Labor Standards Act]: Provided, That liquidated damages shall be payable only in cases of willful violations of this Act. In any action brought to enforce this Act the court shall have jurisdiction to grant such legal or equitable relief as may be appropriate to effectuate the purposes of this Act, including without limitation judgments compelling employment, reinstatement or promotion, or enforcing the liability for amounts deemed to be unpaid minimum wages or unpaid overtime compensation under this section. Before instituting any action under this section, the Equal Employment Opportunity Commission shall attempt to eliminate the discriminatory practice or practices alleged, and to effect voluntary compliance with the requirements of this Act through informal methods of conciliation, conference, and persuasion.

(c)(1) Any person aggrieved may bring a civil action in any court of competent jurisdiction for such legal or equitable relief as will effectuate the purposes of this Act: Provided, That the right of any person to bring such action shall terminate upon the commencement of an action by the Equal Employment Opportunity Commission to enforce the right of such employee under this Act.

(2) In an action brought under paragraph (1), a person shall be entitled to a trial by jury of any issue of fact in any such action for recovery of amounts owing as a result of a violation of this Act, regardless of whether equitable relief is sought by any party in such action.

(d) No civil action may be commenced by an individual under this section until 60 days after a charge alleging unlawful discrimination has been filed with the Equal Employment Opportunity Commission. Such a charge shall be filed—

(A) within 180 days after the alleged unlawful practice occurred; or

(B) in a case to which section 14(b) applies, within 300 days after the alleged unlawful practice occurred, or within 30 days after receipt by the individual of notice of termination of proceedings under State law, whichever is earlier.

Upon receiving such a charge, the Commission shall promptly notify all persons named in such charge as prospective defendants in the action and shall promptly seek to eliminate any alleged unlawful practice by informal methods of conciliation, conference, and persuasion.

(e) Section 259 of [the Portal-to-Portal Act] shall apply to actions under this Act. If a charge filed with the Commission under this Act is dismissed or the proceedings of the Commission are otherwise terminated by the Commission, the Commission shall notify the person aggrieved. A civil action may be brought under this section by a person defined in Section 11(a) against the respondent named in the charge within 90 days after the date of the receipt of such notice.

(f)(1) An individual may not waive any right or claim under this Act unless the waiver is knowing and voluntary. Except as provided in paragraph (2), a waiver may not be considered knowing and voluntary unless at a minimum—

(A) the waiver is part of an agreement between the individual and the employer that is written in a manner calculated to be understood by such individual, or by the average individual eligible to participate;

(B) the waiver specifically refers to rights or claims arising under this Act;

(C) the individual does not waive rights or claims that may arise after the date the waiver is executed;

(D) the individual waives rights or claims only in exchange for consideration in addition to anything of value to which the individual already is entitled;

(E) the individual is advised in writing to consult with an attorney prior to executing the agreement;

(F)(i) the individual is given a period of at least 21 days within which to consider the agreement; or

(ii) if a waiver is requested in connection with an exit incentive or other employment termination program offered to a group or class of employees, the individual is given a period of at least 45 days within which to consider the agreement;

(G) the agreement provides that for a period of at least 7 days following the execution of such agreement, the individual may revoke the agreement, and the agreement shall not become effective or enforceable until the revocation period has expired;

(H) if a waiver is requested in connection with an exit incentive or other employment termination program offered to a group or class of employees, the employer (at the commencement of the period specified in subparagraph (F)) informs the individual in writing in a manner calculated to be understood by the average individual eligible to participate, as to—

(i) any class, unit, or group of individuals covered by such program, any eligibility factors for such program, and any time limits applicable to such program; and

(ii) the job titles and ages of all individuals eligible or selected for the program, and the ages of all individuals in the same job classification or organizational unit who are not eligible or selected for the program.

(2) A waiver in settlement of a charge filed with the Equal Employment Opportunity Commission, or an action filed in court by the individual or the individual's representative, alleging age discrimination of a kind prohibited under section 4 or 15 may not be considered knowing and voluntary unless at a minimum—

(A) subparagraphs (A) through (E) of paragraph (1) have been met; and

(B) the individual is given a reasonable period of time within which to consider the settlement agreement.

(3) In any dispute that may arise over whether any of the requirements, conditions, and circumstances set forth in subparagraph

(A), (B), (C), (D), (E), (F), (G), or (H) of paragraph (1), or subparagraph (A) or (B) of paragraph (2), have been met, the party asserting the validity of a waiver shall have the burden of proving in a court of competent jurisdiction that a waiver was knowing and voluntary pursuant to paragraph (1) or (2).

(4) No waiver agreement may affect the Commission's rights and responsibilities to enforce this Act. No waiver may be used to justify interfering with the protected right of an employee to file a charge or participate in an investigation or proceeding conducted by the Commission.

§ 8 [§ 627]. Notices to be posted. Every employer, employment agency, and labor organization shall post and keep posted in conspicuous places upon its premises a notice to be prepared or approved by the Equal Employment Opportunity Commission setting forth information as the Commission deems appropriate to effectuate the purposes of this Act.

§ 9 [§628]. Rules and regulations; exemptions. In accordance with the provisions of subchapter II of chapter 5 of Title 5, the Equal Employment Opportunity Commission may issue such rules and regulations as it may consider necessary or appropriate for carrying out this Act, and may establish such reasonable exemptions to and from any or all provisions of this Act as it may find necessary and proper in the public interest.

§ 10 [§629]. Criminal penalties. Whoever shall forcibly resist, oppose, impede, intimidate or interfere with a duly authorized representative of the Equal Employment Opportunity Commission while it is engaged in the performance of duties under this Act shall be punished by a fine of not more than $500 or by imprisonment for not more than one year, or by both: Provided, however, That no person shall be imprisoned under this section except when there has been a prior conviction hereunder.

§ 11 [§ 630]. Definitions. For the purposes of this Act—

(a) The term "person" means one or more individuals, partnerships, associations, labor organizations, corporations, business trusts, legal representatives, or any organized groups of persons.

(b) The term "employer" means a person engaged in an industry affecting commerce who has twenty or more employees for each working day in each of twenty or more calendar weeks in the current or preceding calendar year. . . . The term also means (1) any agent of such a person, and (2) a State or political subdivision of a State and any agency or instrumentality of a State or a political subdivision of a State, and any interstate agency, but such term does not include the United States, or a corporation wholly owned by the Government of the United States.

(c) The term "employment agency" means any person regularly undertaking with or without compensation to procure employees for an employer and includes an agent of such a person; but shall not include an agency of the United States.

(d) The term "labor organization" means a labor organization engaged in an industry affecting commerce, and any agent of such an organization, and includes any organization of any kind, any agency, or employee representation committee, group, association, or plan so engaged in which employees participate and which exists for the purpose, in whole or in part, of dealing with employers concerning grievances, labor disputes, wages, rates of pay, hours, or other terms or conditions of employment, and any conference, general committee, joint or system board, or joint council so engaged which is subordinate to a national or international labor organization. . . .

(f) The term "employee" means an individual employed by any employer except that the term "employee" shall not include any person elected to public office in any State or political subdivision of any State by the qualified voters thereof, or any person chosen by such officer to be on such officer's personal staff, or an appointee on the policymaking level or an immediate adviser with respect to the exercise of the constitutional or legal powers of the office. The exemption set forth in the preceding sentence shall not include employees subject to the civil service laws of a State government, governmental agency, or political subdivision. The term "employee" includes any individual who is a citizen of the United States employed by an employer in a workplace in a foreign country.

(g) The term "commerce" means trade, traffic, commerce, transportation, transmission, or communication among the several States; or between a State and any place outside thereof; or within the District of Columbia, or a possession of the United States; or between points in the same State but through a point outside thereof.

(h) The term "industry affecting commerce" means any activity, business, or industry in commerce or in which a labor dispute would hinder or obstruct commerce or the free flow of commerce and includes any activity or industry "affecting commerce" within the meaning of the Labor-Management Reporting and Disclosure Act of 1959 [29 U.S.C. § 401 et seq.].

(i) The term "State" includes a State of the United States, the District of Columbia, Puerto Rico, the Virgin Islands, American Samoa, Guam, Wake Island, the Canal Zone, and Outer Continental Shelf lands defined in the Outer Continental Shelf Lands Act [43 U.S.C. § 1331 et seq.].

(j) The term "firefighter" means an employee, the duties of whose position are primarily to perform work directly connected with the control and extinguishment of fires or the maintenance and use of firefighting apparatus and equipment, including an employee engaged in this activity who is transferred to a supervisory or administrative position.

(k) The term "law enforcement officer" means an employee, the duties of whose position are primarily the investigation, apprehension, or detention of individuals suspected or convicted of offenses against the criminal laws of a State, including an employee engaged in this activity who is transferred to a supervisory or administrative position. For the purpose of this subsection, "detention" includes the duties of employees assigned to guard individuals incarcerated in any penal institution.

(l) The term "compensation, terms, conditions, or privileges of employment" encompasses all employee benefits, including such benefits provided pursuant to a bona fide employee benefit plan.

§ 12 [§631]. Age limits

(a) The prohibitions in this Act shall be limited to individuals who are at least 40 years of age.

(b) In the case of any personnel action affecting employees or applicants for employment which is subject to the provisions of section 15, the prohibitions established in section 15 shall be limited to individuals who are at least 40 years of age.

(c)(1) Nothing in this Act shall be construed to prohibit compulsory retirement of any employee who has attained 65 years of age and who, for the 2-year period immediately before retirement, is employed in a bona fide executive or a high policymaking position, if such employee is entitled to an immediate nonforfeitable annual retirement benefit from a pension, profit-sharing, savings, or deferred compensation plan, or any combination of such plans, of the employer of such employee, which equals, in the aggregate, at least $44,000.

(2) In applying the retirement benefit test of paragraph (1) of this subsection, if any such retirement benefit is in a form other than a straight life annuity (with no ancillary benefits), or if employees contribute to any such plan or make rollover contributions, such benefit shall be adjusted in accordance with regulations prescribed by the Equal Employment Opportunity Commission, after consultation with the Secretary of the Treasury, so that the benefit is the equivalent of a straight life annuity (with no ancillary benefits) under a plan to which employees do not contribute and under which no rollover contributions are made. . . .

§ 14 [§ 633]. Federal-State relationship

(a) Nothing in this Act shall affect the jurisdiction of any agency of any State performing like functions with regard to discriminatory employment practices on account of age except that upon commencement of action under this Act such action shall supersede any State action.

(b) In the case of an alleged unlawful practice occurring in a State which has a law prohibiting discrimination in employment because of age and establishing or authorizing a State authority to grant or seek relief from such discriminatory practice, no suit may be brought under section 7 before the expiration of sixty days after proceedings have been commenced under the State law, unless such proceedings have been earlier terminated: Provided,

That such sixty-day period shall be extended to one hundred and twenty days during the first year after the effective date of such State law. If any requirement for the commencement of such proceedings is imposed by a State authority other than a requirement of the filing of a written and signed statement of the facts upon which the proceeding is based, the proceeding shall be deemed to have been commenced for the purposes of this subsection at the time such statement is sent by registered mail to the appropriate State authority.

§ 15 [§ 633a]. Nondiscrimination on account of age in Federal Government employment

(a) All personnel actions affecting employees or applicants for employment who are at least 40 years of age (except personnel actions with regard to aliens employed outside the limits of the United States) in military departments as defined in section 102 of Title 5, in executive agencies as defined in section 105 of Title 5 (including employees and applicants for employment who are paid from nonappropriated funds), in the United States Postal Service and the Postal RCommission, in those units in the government of the District of Columbia having positions in the competitive service, and in those units of the judicial branch of the Federal Government having positions in the competitive service, in the Smithsonian Institution, and in the Government Printing Office, the Government Accountability Office, and the Library of Congress shall be made free from any discrimination based on age.

(b) Except as otherwise provided in this subsection, the Equal Employment Opportunity Commission is authorized to enforce the provisions of subsection (a) of this section through appropriate remedies, including reinstatement or hiring of employees with or without backpay, as will effectuate the policies of this section. The Equal Employment Opportunity Commission shall issue such rules, regulations, orders, and instructions as it deems necessary and appropriate to carry out its responsibilities under this section. The Equal Employment Opportunity Commission shall—

(1) be responsible for the review and evaluation of the operation of all agency programs designed to carry out the policy of this section, periodically obtaining and publishing (on at least a semiannual basis) progress reports from each department, agency, or unit referred to in subsection (a) of this section;

(2) consult with and solicit the recommendations of interested individuals, groups, and organizations relating to nondiscrimination in employment on account of age; and

(3) provide for the acceptance and processing of complaints of discrimination in Federal employment on account of age.

The head of each such department, agency, or unit shall comply with such rules, regulations, orders, and instructions of the Equal Employment Opportunity Commission which shall include a provision that an employee or applicant for employment shall be notified of any final action taken on any complaint of discrimination filed by him thereunder. Reasonable exemptions to the provisions of this section may be established by the Commission but only when the Commission has established a maximum age requirement on the basis of a determination that age is a bona fide occupational qualification necessary to the performance of the duties of the position. With respect to employment in the Library of Congress, authorities granted in this subsection to the Equal Employment Opportunity Commission shall be exercised by the Librarian of Congress.

(c) Any person aggrieved may bring a civil action in any Federal district court of competent jurisdiction for such legal or equitable relief as will effectuate the purposes of this Act.

(d) When the individual has not filed a complaint concerning age discrimination with the Commission, no civil action may be commenced by any individual under this section until the individual has given the Commission not less than thirty days' notice of an intent to file such action. Such notice shall be filed within one hundred and eighty days after the alleged unlawful practice occurred. Upon receiving a notice of intent to sue, the Commission shall promptly notify all persons named therein as prospective defendants in the action and take any appropriate action to assure the elimination of any unlawful practice.

(e) Nothing contained in this section shall relieve any Government agency or official of the responsibility to assure nondiscrimination on account of age in employment as required under any provision of Federal law.

(f) Any personnel action of any department, agency, or other entity referred to in subsection (a) of this section shall not be subject to, or affected by, any provision of this Act, other than the provisions of section and the provisions of this section. . . .

GENETIC INFORMATION NONDISCRIMINATION ACT

42 U.S.C. §§ 2000ff - 2000ff-10

§ 2. [§ 2000ff note]. Findings

Congress makes the following findings:

(1) Deciphering the sequence of the human genome and other advances in genetics open major new opportunities for medical progress. New knowledge about the genetic basis of illness will allow for earlier detection of illnesses, often before symptoms have begun. Genetic testing can allow individuals to take steps to reduce the likelihood that they will contract a particular disorder. New knowledge about genetics may allow for the development of better therapies that are more effective against disease or have fewer side effects than current treatments. These advances give rise to the potential misuse of genetic information to discriminate in health insurance and employment.

(2) The early science of genetics became the basis of State laws that provided for the sterilization of persons having presumed genetic "defects" such as mental retardation, mental disease, epilepsy, blindness, and hearing loss, among other conditions. The first sterilization law was enacted in the State of Indiana in 1907. By 1981, a majority of States adopted sterilization laws to "correct" apparent genetic traits or tendencies. Many of these State laws have since been repealed, and many have been modified to include essential constitution requirements of due process and equal protection. However, the current explosion in the science of genetics, and the history of sterilization laws by the States based on early genetic science, compels Congressional action in this area.

(3) Although genes are facially neutral markers, many genetic conditions and disorders are associated with particular racial and ethnic groups and gender. Because some genetic traits are most prevalent in particular groups, members of a particular group may be stigmatized or discriminated against as a result of that genetic information. This form of discrimination was evident in the 1970s, which saw the advent of programs to screen and identify carriers of sickle cell anemia, a disease which afflicts African-Americans. Once again, State legislatures began to enact discriminatory laws in the area, and in the early 1970s began mandating genetic screening of all African-Americans for sickle cell anemia, leading to discrimination and unnecessary fear. To alleviate some of this stigma, Congress in 1972 passed the National Sickle Cell Anemia Control Act, which withholds Federal funding from States unless sickle cell testing is voluntary.

(4) Congress has been informed of examples of genetic discrimination in the workplace. These include the use of pre-employment genetic screening at Lawrence Berkeley Laboratory, which led to a court decision in favor of employees in that case *Norman-Bloodsaw v. Lawrence Berkeley Laboratory* (135 F.3d 1260, 1269 (9th Cir. 1998)). Congress clearly has a compelling public interest in relieving the fear of discrimination and in prohibiting its actual practice in employment and health insurance.

(5) Federal law addressing genetic discrimination in health insurance and employment is incomplete in both the scope and depth of its protections. Moreover, while many States have enacted some type of genetic non-discrimination law, these laws vary widely with respect to their approach, application, and level of protection. Congress has collected substantial evidence that the American public and the medical community find the existing patchwork of State and Federal laws to be confusing and inadequate to protect them from discrimination. Therefore Federal legislation establishing a national and uniform basic standard is necessary to fully protect the public from discrimination and allay their concerns about the potential for discrimination, thereby allowing individuals to take advantage of genetic testing, technologies, research, and new therapies.

TITLE II - PROHIBITING EMPLOYMENT DISCRIMINATION ON THE BASIS OF GENETIC INFORMATION

§ 201. [§ 2000ff]. Definitions

In this title:

(1) The term "Commission" means the Equal Employment Opportunity Commission as created by section 705 of the Civil Rights Act of 1964 (42 U.S.C. § 2000 e-4).

(2)(A) The term "employee" means—

(i) an employee (including an applicant), as defined in section 701(f) of the Civil Rights Act of 1964 (42 U.S.C. § 2000e(f));

(ii) a State employee (including an applicant) described in section 304(a) of the Government Employee Rights Act of 1991 (42 U.S.C. § 2000e-16c(a));

(iii) a covered employee (including an applicant), as defined in section 101 of the Congressional Accountability Act of 1995 (2 U.S.C. § 1301);

(iv) a covered employee (including an applicant), as defined in section 411(c) of title 3, United States Code; or

(v) an employee or applicant to which section 717(a) of the Civil Rights Act of 1964 (42 U.S.C. § 2000e-16(a)) applies.

(B) The term "employer" means—

(i) an employer (as defined in section 701(b) of the Civil Rights Act of 1964 (42 U.S.C. § 2000e(b)));

(ii) an entity employing a State employee described in section 304(a) of the Government Employee Rights Act of 1991;

(iii) an employing office, as defined in section 411(c) of title 3, United States Code;

(iv) an employing office, as defined in section 101 of title 3, United States Code; or

(v) an entity to which section 717(a) of the Civil Rights Act of 1964 applies.

(C) The terms "employment agency" and "labor organization" have the meanings given the terms in section 701 of the Civil Rights Act of 1964 (42 U.S.C. § 2000e).

(D) The term "member", with respect to a labor organization, includes an applicant for membership in a labor organization.

(3) The term "family member" means, with respect to an individual—

(A) a dependent (as such term is used for purposes of section 701(f)(2) of the Employment Retirement Income Security Act of 1974) of such individual, and

(B) any other individual who is a first-degree, second-degree, third-degree or fourth-degree relative of such individual or of an individual described in subparagraph (A).

(4)(A) The term "genetic information" means, with respect to any individual, information about—

(i) such individual's genetic tests,

(ii) the genetic tests of family members of such individual, and

(iii) the manifestation of a disease or disorder in family members of such individual.

(B) Such term includes, with respect to any individual, any request for, or receipt of, genetic services, or participation in clinical research which includes genetic services, by such individual or any family member of such individual.

(C) The term "genetic information" shall not include information about the sex or age of any individual.

(5) The term "genetic monitoring" means the periodic examination of employees to evaluate acquired modifications to their genetic material, such as chromosomal damage or evidence of increased occurrence of mutations, that may have developed in the course of employment due to exposure to toxic substances in the workplace, in order to identify, evaluate, and respond to the effects of or control adverse environmental exposures in the workplace.

(6) The term "genetic services" means—

(A) a genetic test;

(B) genetic counseling (including obtaining, interpreting, or assessing genetic information); or

(C) genetic education.

(7)(A) The term "genetic test" means an analysis of human DNA, RNA, chromosomes, proteins, or metabolites, that detects genotypes, mutations, or chromosomal changes.

(B) The term "genetic test" does not mean an analysis of proteins or metabolites that does not detect genotypes, mutations, or chromosomal changes.

§ 202. [§ 2000ff-1]. Employer Practices

(a) It shall be an unlawful employment practice for an employer—

(1) to fail or refuse to hire, or to discharge, any employee, or otherwise to discriminate against any employee with respect to the compensation, terms, conditions, or privileges of employment of the employee, because of genetic information with respect to the employee; or

(2) to limit, segregate, or classify the employees of the employer in any way that would deprive or tend to deprive any employee of employment opportunities or otherwise adversely affect the status of the employee as an employee, because of genetic information with respect to the employee.

(b) It shall be an unlawful employment practice for an employer to request, require, or purchase genetic information with respect to an employee or a family member of the employee except—

(1) where an employer inadvertently requests or requires family medical history of the employee or family member of the employee;

(2) where—

(A) health or genetic services are offered by the employer, including such services offered as part of a wellness program;

(B) the employee provides prior, knowing, voluntary, and written authorization;

(C) only the employee (or family member if the family member is receiving genetic services) and the licensed health care professional or board certified genetic counselor involved in providing such services receive individually identifiable information concerning the results of such services; and

(D) any individually identifiable genetic information provided under subparagraph (C) in connection with the services provided under subparagraph (A) is only available for purposes of such services and shall not be disclosed to the employer except in aggregate terms that do not disclose the identity of specific employees;

(3) where an employer requests or requires family medical history from the employee to comply with the certification provisions of section 103 of the Family and Medical Leave Act of 1993 (29 U.S.C. § 2613) or such requirements under State family and medical leave laws;

(4) where an employer purchases documents that are commercially and publicly available (including newspaper, magazines, periodicals, and books, but not including medical databases or court records) that include family medical history;

(5) where the information involved is to be used for genetic monitoring of the biological effects of toxic substances in the workplace, but only if—

(A) the employer provides written notice of the genetic monitoring to the employee;

(B)(i) the employee provides prior, knowing, voluntary, and written authorization; or

(ii) the genetic monitoring is required by Federal or State law;

(C) the employee is informed of individual monitoring results;

(D) the monitoring is in compliance with—

(i) any Federal genetic monitoring regulations, including any such regulations that may be promulgated by the Secretary of Labor pursuant to the Occupational Safety and Health Act of 1970 (29 U.S.C.

§ 651 *et seq.*), the Federal Mine Safety and Health Act of 1977 (30 U.S.C § 801 *et seq.*), or the Atomic Energy Act of 1954 (42 U.S.C. § 2011 *et seq.*); or

(ii) State genetic monitoring regulations, in the case of a State that is implementing genetic monitoring regulations under the authority of the Occupational Safety and Health Act of 1970 (29 U.S.C. § 651 *et seq.*); and

(E) the employer, excluding any licensed health care professional or board certified genetic counselor that is involved in the genetic monitoring program, receives the results of the monitoring in aggregate terms that do not disclose the identity of specific employees; or

(6) where the employer conducts DNA analysis for law enforcement purposes as a forensic laboratory or for purposes of human genetic information of such employer's employees, but only to the extent that such genetic information is used for analysis of DNA identification markers for quality control to detect sample contamination.

(c) In the case of information to which any of the paragraphs (1) through (6) of subsection (b) applies, such information may not be used in violation of paragraph (1) or (2) of subsection (a) or treated or disclosed in a manner that violates section 206.

§ 203. [§ 2000ff-2]. Employment Agency Practices

(a) It shall be an unlawful employment practice for an employment agency—

(1) to fail or refuse to refer for employment, or otherwise to discriminate with respect to the individual;

(2) to limit, segregate, or classify individuals or fail or refuse to refer for employment any individual in any way that would deprive or tend to deprive any individual of employment opportunities, or otherwise adversely affect the status of the individual as an employee, because of genetic information with respect to the individual; or

(3) to cause or attempt to cause an employer to discriminate against an individual in violation of this title.

(b) It shall be an unlawful employment practice for an employment agency to request, require, or purchase genetic information with respect to an individual or a family member of the individual except—

(1) where an employment agency inadvertently requests or requires family medical history of the individual or family member of the individual;

(2) where—

(A) health or genetic services are offered by the employment agency, including such services offered as part of a wellness program;

(B) the individual provides prior, knowing, voluntary and written authorization;

(C) only the individual (or family member if the family member is receiving genetic services) and the licensed health care professional or board certified genetic counselor involved in providing such receive individually identifiable information concerning the results of such services; and

(D) any individually identifiable genetic information provided under subparagraph (C) in connection with the services provided under subparagraph (A) is only available for purposes of such services and shall not be disclosed to the employment agency except in aggregate terms that do not disclose the identity of specific individuals;

(3) where an employment agency requests or requires family medical history from the individual to comply with the certification provisions of section 103 of the Family and Medical Leave Act of 1993 (29 U.S.C. § 2613) or such requirements under State family and medical leave laws;

(4) where an employment agency purchases documents that are commercially and publicly available (including newspapers, magazines, periodical, and books, but not including medical databases or court records) that include family medical history; or

(5) where the information involved is to be used for genetic monitoring of the biological effects of toxic substances in the workplace, but only if—

(A) the employment agency provides written notice of the genetic monitoring to the individual;

(B)(i) the individual provides prior, knowing, voluntary, and written authorization; or

(ii) the genetic monitoring is required by Federal or State law;

(C) the individual is informed of individual monitoring results;

(D) the monitoring is in compliance with—

(i) any Federal genetic monitoring regulations, including any such regulations that may be promulgated by the Secretary of Labor pursuant to the Occupational Safety and Health Act of 1970 (29 U.S.C. § 651 *et seq.*), the Federal Mine Safety and Health Act of 1977 (30 U.S.C. § 801 *et seq.*), or the Atomic Energy Act of 1954 (42 U.S.C. § 2011 *et seq.*); or

(ii) State genetic monitoring regulations, in the case of a State that is implementing genetic monitoring regulations under the authority of the Occupational Safety and Health Act of 1970 (29 U.S.C. § 651 *et seq.*); and

(E) the employment agency, excluding any licensed health care professional or board certified genetic counselor that is involved in the genetic monitoring program, receives the results of the monitoring only in aggregate terms that do not disclose the identity of specific individuals.

(c) In the case of information to which any of paragraphs (1) through (5) of subsection (b) applies, such information may not be used in violation of paragraph (1), (2), or (3) of subsection (a) or treated or disclosed in a manner that violates section 206.

§ 204. [§ 2000ff-3]. Labor Organization Practices

(a) It shall be an unlawful employment practice for a labor organization—

(1) to exclude or to expel from the membership of the organization, or otherwise to discriminate against, any member because of genetic information with respect to the member;

(2) to limit, segregate, or classify the members of the organization, or fail or refuse to refer for employment any member, in any way that would deprive or tend to deprive any member of employment opportunities, or otherwise adversely affect the status of the member as an employee, because of genetic information with respect to the number; or

(3) to cause or attempt to cause an employer to discriminate against a member in violation of this title.

(b) It shall be an unlawful employment practice for a labor organization to request, require, or purchase genetic information with respect to a member or a family member of the member except—

(1) where a labor organization inadvertently requests or requires family medical history of the member or family member of the member;

(2) where—

(A) health or genetic services are offered by the labor organization, including such services offered as part of a wellness program;

(B) the member provides prior, knowing, voluntary, and written authorization;

(C) only the member (or family member if the family member is receiving genetic services) and the licensed health care professional or board certified genetic counselor involved in providing such services receive individually identifiable information concerning the results of such services; and

(D) any individually identifiable genetic information provided under subparagraph (C) in connection with the services provided under subparagraph (A) is only available for purposes of such services and shall not be disclosed to the labor organization except in aggregate terms that do not disclose the identity of specific members;

(3) where a labor organization requests or requires family medical history from the members to comply with the certification provisions of section 103 of the Family and Medical Leave Act of 1993 (29 U.S.C. § 2613) or such requirements under State family and medical leave laws;

(4) where a labor organization purchases documents that are commercially and publicly available (including newspapers, magazines, periodicals, and books, but not including medical databases or court records) that include family medical history; or

(5) where the information involved is to be used for genetic monitoring of the biological effects of toxic substances in the workplace, but only if—

(A) the labor organization provides written notice of the genetic monitoring to the member;

(B)(i) the member provides prior, knowing, voluntary, and written authorization; or

(ii) the genetic monitoring is required by Federal or State law;

(C) the member is informed of individual monitoring results;

(D) the monitoring is in compliance with—

(i) any Federal genetic monitoring regulations, including any such regulations that may be promulgated by the Secretary of Labor pursuant to the Occupation Safety and Health Act of 1970 (29 U.S.C. § 651 *et seq.*), the Federal Mine Safety and Health Act of 1977 (30 U.S.C. § 801 *et seq.*), or the Atomic Energy Act of 1954 (42 U.S.C. § 2011 *et seq.*); or

(ii) State genetic monitoring regulations, in the case of a State that is implementing genetic monitoring regulations under the authority of the Occupation Safety and Health Act of 1970 (29 U.S.C. § 651 *et seq.*); and

(E) the labor organization, excluding any licensed health care professional or board certified genetic counselor that is involved in the genetic monitoring program, receives the results of the monitoring only in aggregate terms that do not disclose the identity of specific members.

(c) In the case of information to which any of paragraphs (1) through (5) of subsection (b) applies, such information may not be used in violation of paragraph (1), (2), or (3) of subsection (a) or treated or disclosed in a manner that violates section 206.

§ 205. [§ 2000ff-4]. Training Programs

(a) It shall be an unlawful employment practice for any employer, labor organization, or joint labor-management committee controlling apprenticeship or other training or retraining, including on-the-job training programs—

(1) to discriminate against any individual because of genetic information with respect to the individual in admission to, or employment in, any program established to provide apprenticeship or other training or retraining;

(2) to limit, segregate, or classify the applicants for or participants in such apprenticeship or other training or retraining, or fail or refuse to refer for employment any individual, in any way that would deprive or tend to deprive any individual of employment opportunities, or otherwise adversely affect the status of the individual as an employee, because of genetic information with respect to the individual; or

(3) to cause or attempt to cause an employer to discriminate against an applicant for or a participant in such apprenticeship or other training or retraining in violation of this title.

(b) It shall be an unlawful employment practice for an employer, labor organization, or joint labor-management committee described in subsection (a) to request, require, or purchase genetic information with respect to an individual or a family member of the individual except—

(1) where the employer, labor organization, or joint labor-management committee inadvertently requests or requires family medical history of the individual or family member of the individual;

(2) where—

(A) health or genetic services are offered by the employer, labor organization, or joint labor-management committee, including such services offered as part of a wellness program;

(B) the individual provides prior, knowing, voluntary, and written authorization;

(C) only the individual (or family member if the family member is receiving genetic services) and the licensed health care professional or board certified genetic counselor involved in providing such services receive individually identifiable concerning the results of such services; and

(D) any individually identifiable information provided under subparagraph (C) in connection with the services provided under subparagraph (A) is only available for purposes of such services and shall not be disclosed to the employer, labor organization, or joint labor-management committee except in aggregate terms that do not disclose the identity of specific individuals;

(3) where the employer, labor organization, or joint-management committee requests or requires family medical history from the individual to comply with the certification provisions of section 103 of the Family and Medical Leave Act of 1993 (29 U.S.C. § 2613) or such requirements under State family and medical leave laws;

(4) where the employer, labor organization, or joint-management committee purchases documents that are commercially and publicly available (including newspaper, magazines, periodicals, and books, but not including medical databases or court records) that include family medical history;

(5) where the information involved is to be used for genetic monitoring of the biological effects of toxic substances in the workplace, but only if—

(A) the employer, labor organization, or joint labor-management committee provides written notice of the genetic monitoring to the individual;

(B)(i) the individual provides prior, knowing, voluntary, and written authorization; or

(ii) the genetic monitoring is required by Federal or State law;

(C) the individual is informed of individual monitoring results;

(D) the monitoring is in compliance with—

(i) any Federal genetic monitoring regulations, including any such regulations that may be promulgated by the Secretary of Labor pursuant to the Occupational Safety and Health Act of 1970 (29 U.S.C. § 651 *et seq.*), the Federal Mine Safety and Health Act of 1977 (30 U.S.C. § 801 *et seq.*), or the Atomic Energy Act of 1954 (42 U.S.C. § 2011 *et seq.*); or

(ii) State genetic monitoring regulations, in the case of a State that is implementing genetic monitoring regulations under the authority of the

Occupational Safety and Health Act of 1970 (29 U.S.C. § 651 *et seq.*); and

(E) the employer, labor organization, or joint labor-management committee, excluding any licensed health care professional or board certified genetic counselor that is involved in the genetic monitoring program, receives the results of the monitoring only in aggregate terms that do not disclose the identity of specific individuals; or

(6) where the employer conducts DNA analysis for law enforcement purposes as a forensic laboratory or for purposes of human remains identification, and requests or requires genetic information of such employer's apprentices or trainees, but only to the extent that such genetic information is used for analysis of DNA identification markers for quality control to detect sample contamination.

(c) In the case of information to which any of paragraphs (1) through (6) of subsection (b) applies, such information may not be used in violation of paragraph (1), (2), or (3) of subsection (a) or treated or disclosed in a manner that violates section 206.

§ 206. [§ 2000ff-5]. Confidentiality of Genetic Information

(a) If an employer, employment agency, labor organization, or joint labor-management committee possesses genetic information about an employee or member, such information shall be maintained on separate forms and in separate medical files and be treated as a confidential medical record of the employee or member. An employer, employment agency, labor organization, or joint labor-management committee shall be considered to be in compliance with the maintenance of information subject to this subsection with respect to genetic information subject to this subsection that is maintained and treated as a confidential medical record under section 102(d)(3)(B) of the Americans with Disabilities Act (42 U.S.C. § 12112(d)(3)(B)).

(b) An employer, employment agency, labor organization, or joint-management committee shall not disclose genetic information concerning an employee or member except—

(1) to the employee or member of a labor organization (or family member if the family member is receiving the genetic services) at the written request of the employee or member of such organization;

(2) to an occupational or other health researcher if the research is conducted in compliance with the regulations and protections provided for under part 46 of title 45, Code of Federal Regulations;

(3) in response to an order of a court, except that—

(A) the employer, employment agency, labor organization, or joint labor-management committee may disclose only the genetic information expressly authorized by such order; and

(B) if the court order was secured without the knowledge of the employee or member to whom the information refers, the employer, employment agency, labor organization, or joint labor-management committee shall inform the employee or member of the court order and any genetic information that was disclosed pursuant to such order;

(4) to government officials who are investigating compliance with this title if the information is relevant to the investigation;

(5) to the extent that such disclosure is made in connection with the employee's compliance with the certification provisions of section 103 of the Family and Medical Leave Act of 1993 (29 U.S.C. § 2613) or such requirements under State family and medical leave laws; or

(6) to a Federal, State, or local public health agency only with regard to information that is described in section 201(4)(A)(iii) and that concerns a contagious disease that presents an imminent hazard of death or life-threatening illness, and that the employee whose family member or family members is or are the subject of a disclosure under this paragraph is notified of such disclosure.

(c) With respect to the regulations promulgated by the Secretary of Health and Human Services under part C of title XI of the Social Security Act (42 U.S.C. § 1320d *et seq.*) and section 264 of the Health Insurance Portability and Accountability Act of 1996 (42 U.S.C. § 1320d-2 note), this title does not prohibit a covered entity under such regulations from any use or disclosure of health information that is authorized for the covered entity under such regulations. The previous sentence does not affect the authority of such Secretary to modify such regulations.

§ 207. [§ 2000ff-6]. Remedies and Enforcement

(a)(1) The powers, procedures, and remedies provided in sections 705, 706, 707, 709, 710, and 711 of the Civil Rights Act of 1964 (42 U.S.C. § 2000e-4 et seq.) to the Commission, the Attorney General, or any person, respectively, alleging an unlawful employment practice in violation of this title against an employee described in section 201(2)(A)(I), except as provided in paragraphs (2) and (3).

(2) The powers, remedies and procedures provided in subsections (b) and (c) of section 722 of the Revised Statutes of the United States (42 U.S.C. § 1988) shall be powers, remedies and procedures this title provides to the Commission, the Attorney General, or any person, alleging such a practice.

(3) The powers, remedies and procedures provided in section 1977A of the Revised Statutes of the United States (42 U.S.C. § 1981a), including the limitations contained in subsection (b)(3) of such

section 1977A, shall be powers, remedies, and procedures this title provides to the Commission, the Attorney General, or any person, alleging such a practice (not an employment practice specifically excluded from coverage under section 1977A(a)(1) of the Revised Statutes of the United States).

(b)(1) The powers, remedies, and procedures provided in sections 302 and 304 of the Government Employee Rights Act of 1991 (42 U.S.C. § 2000e-16b, 2000e-16c) to the Commission, or any person, alleging a violation of section 302(a)(1) of that Act (42 U.S.C. § 2000e-16b(a)(1)) shall be the powers, remedies, and procedures this title provides to the Commission, or any person, respectively, alleging an unlawful employment practice in violation of this title against an employee described in section 201(2)(A)(ii), except as provided in paragraphs (2) and (3).

(2) The powers, remedies and procedures provided in subsections (b) and (c) of section 722 of the Revised Statutes of United States (42 U.S.C. § 1988), shall be the powers, remedies and procedures this title provides to the Commission, or any person, alleging such a practice.

(3) The powers, remedies and procedures provided in section 1977A of the Revised Statutes of the United States (42 U.S.C. § 1981a), including the limitations contained in subsection (b)(3) of such section 1977A, shall be powers, remedies and procedures this title provides to the Commission, or any person, alleging such practice (not an employment practice specifically excluded from coverage under section 1977A(a)(1) of the Revised Statutes of the United States).

(c)(1) The powers, remedies and procedures provided in the Congressional Accountability Act of 1995 (2 U.S.C. § 1301 *et seq.*) to the Board (as defined in section 101 of that Act (2 U.S.C. § 1301)), or any person, alleging a violation of section 201(a)(1) of that Act (42 U.S.C. § 1331(a)(1)) shall be the powers, remedies, and procedures this title provides to that Board, or any person, alleging an unlawful employment practice in violation of this title against an employee described in section 201(2)(A)(iii), except as provided in paragraphs (2) and (3).

(2) The powers, remedies and procedures provided in subsections (b) and (c) of section 722 of the Revised Statutes of the United States (42 U.S.C. § 1988), shall be powers, remedies, and procedures this title provides to that Board, or any person, alleging such a practice.

(3) The powers, remedies and procedures provided in section 1977A of the Revised Statutes of the United States (42 U.S.C. § 1981a), including the limitations contained in subsection (b)(3) of such section 1977A, shall be powers, remedies and procedures this title provides to that Board, or any person, alleging such a practice (not an

employment practice specifically excluded from coverage under section 1977A(a)(1) of the Revised Statutes of the United States).

(4) With respect to a claim alleging a practice described in paragraph (1), title III of the Congressional Accountability Act of 1995 (2 U.S.C. § 1381 *et seq.*) shall apply in the same manner as such title applies with respect to a claim alleging a violation of section 201(a)(1) of such Act (2 U.S.C. § 1311(a)(1)).

(d)(1) The powers, remedies and procedures provided in chapter 5 of title 3, United States Code, to the President, the Commission, the Merit Systems Protection Board, or any person, alleging a violation of section 411(a)(1) of that title, shall be the powers, remedies and procedures this title provides to the President, the Commission, such Board, or any person, respectively, alleging an unlawful employment practice in violation of this title against an employee described in section 201(2)(A)(iv), except as provided in paragraphs (2) and (3).

(2) The powers, remedies and procedures provided in subsections (b) and (c) of section 722 of the Revised Statutes of the United States (42 U.S.C. § 1988), shall be powers, remedies and procedures this title provides to the President, the Commission, such Board, or any person, alleging such a practice.

(3) The powers, remedies and procedures provided in section 1977A of the Revised Statutes of the United States (42 U.S.C. § 1981a), including the limitations contained in subsection (b)(3) of such section 1977A, shall be powers, remedies and procedures this title provides to the President, the Commission, such Board, or any person, alleging such a practice (not an employment practice specifically excluded from coverage under section 1977A(a)(1) of the Revised Statutes of the United States).

(e)(1) The powers, remedies and procedures provided in section 717 of the Civil Rights Act of 1964 (42 U.S.C. § 2000e-16) to the Commission, the Attorney General, the Librarian of Congress, or any person, alleging a violation of that section shall be the powers, remedies and procedures this title provides to the Commission, the Attorney General, the Librarian of Congress, or any person, respectively, alleging an unlawful employment practice in violation of this title against an employee or applicant described in section 201(2)(A)(v), except as provided in paragraphs (2) and (3).

(2) The powers, remedies and procedures provided in subsections (b) and (c) of section 722 of the Revised Statutes of the United States (42 U.S.C. § 1988), shall be powers, remedies and procedures this title provides to the Commission, the Attorney General, the Librarian of Congress, or any person, alleging such a practice.

(3) The powers, remedies and procedures provided in section 1977A of the Revised Statutes of the United States (42 U.S.C. § 1981a), including the limitations contained in subsection (b)(3) of such

section 1977A, shall be powers, remedies and procedures this title provides to the Commission, the Attorney General, the Librarian of Congress, or any person, alleging such a practice (not an employment practice specifically excluded from coverage under section 1977A(a)(1) of the Revised Statutes of the United States).

(f) No person shall discriminate against any individual because such individual has opposed any act or practice made unlawful by this title or because such individual made a charge, testified, assisted, or participated in any manner in an investigation, proceeding or hearing under this title. The remedies and procedures otherwise provided for under this section shall be available to aggrieved individuals with respect to violations of this subsection.

(g) In this section, the term "Commission" means the Equal Employment Opportunity Commission.

§ 208. [§ 2000ff-7]. Disparate Impact

(a) Notwithstanding any other provision of this Act, "disparate impact", as that term is used in section 703(k) of the Civil Rights Act of 1964 (42 U.S.C. § 2000e-2(k)), on the basis of genetic information does not establish a cause of action under this Act.

(b) On the date that is 6 years after the date of enactment of this Act [May 21, 2008], there shall be established a commission, to be known as the Genetic Nondiscrimination Study Commission (referred to in this section as the "Commission") to review the developing science of genetics and to make recommendations to Congress regarding whether to provide a disparate impact cause of action under this Act.

[Provisions omitted regarding establishment of Commission.]

§ 209. [§ 2000ff-8]. Construction

(a) Nothing in this title shall be construed to—

(1) limit the rights or protections of an individual under any other Federal or State statute that provides equal or greater protection to an individual than the rights or protections provided for under this title, including the protections of an individual under the Americans with Disabilities Act of 1990 (42 U.S.C. § 12101 *et seq.*) (including coverage afforded to individuals under section 102 of such Act (42 U.S.C. § 12112)), or under the Rehabilitation Act of 1973 (29 U.S.C. § 701 *et seq.*);

(2)(A) limit the rights or protections of an individual to bring an action under this title against an employer, employment agency, labor organization, or joint labor-management committee for a violation of this title; or

(B) provide for enforcement of, or penalties for violation of, any requirement or prohibition applicable to any employer, employment agency, labor organization, or joint labor-management committee subject to enforcement for a violation under—

(i) the amendments made by title I of this Act;

(ii)(I) subsection (a) of section 701 of the Employee Retirement Income Security Act of 1974 as such section applies with respect to genetic information pursuant to subsection (b)(1)(B) of such section;

(II) section 702(a)(1)(F) of such Act; or

(III) section 702(B)(1) of such Act as such section applies with respect to genetic information as a health status-related factor;

(iii)(I) subsection (a) of section 2701 of the Public Health Service Act as such section applies with respect to genetic information pursuant to subsection (b)(1)(B) of such section;

(II) section 2702(a)(1)(F) of such Act; or

(III) section 2702(b)(1) of such Act as such section applies with respect to genetic information as a health status-related factor; or

(iv)(I) subsection (a) of section 9801 of the Internal Revenue Code of 1986 as such section applies with respect to genetic information pursuant to subsection (b)(1)B) of such section;

(II) section 9802(a)(1)(F) of such Act; or

(III) section 9802(b)(1) of such Act as such section applies with respect to genetic information as a health status-related factor;

(3) apply to the Armed Forces Repository of Specimen Samples for the Identification of Remains;

(4) limit or expand the protections, rights, or obligations of employees or employers under applicable workers' compensation laws;

(5) limit the authority of a Federal department or agency to conduct or sponsor occupational or other health research that is conducted in compliance with the regulations contained in part 46 of title 45, Code of Federal Regulations (or any corresponding or similar regulation or rule);

(6) limit the statutory or regulatory authority of the Occupational Safety and Health Administration or the Mine Safety and

Health Administration to promulgate or enforce workplace safety and health laws and regulations; or

(7) require any specific benefit for an employee or member or a family member of an employee or member under any group health plan or health insurance issuer offering group health insurance coverage in connection with a group health plan.

(b) Any reference in this title to genetic information concerning an individual or family member of an individual shall—

(1) with respect to such an individual or family member of an individual who is a pregnant woman, include genetic information of any fetus carried by such pregnant woman; and

(2) with respect to an individual or family member utilizing an assisted reproductive technology, include genetic information of any embryo legally held by the individual or family member.

(c) With respect to a group health plan, or a health insurance issuer offering group health insurance coverage in connection with a group health plan, this title does not prohibit any activity of such plan or issuer that is authorized for the plan or issuer under any provision of law referred to in clauses (i) through (iv) of subsection (a)(2)(B).

§ 210. [§ 2000ff-9]. Medical Information That is Not Genetic Information

An employer, employment agency, labor organization, or joint labor-management committee shall not be considered to be in violation of this title based on the use, acquisition, or disclosure of medical information that is not genetic information about a manifested disease, disorder, or pathological condition of an employee or member, including a manifested disease, disorder, or pathological condition that has or may have a genetic basis.

§ 211. [§ 2000ff-10]. Regulations

Not later than 1 year after the date of enactment of this title [May 21, 2008], the Commission shall issue final regulations to carry out this title. . . .

PART VI.

REGULATION OF COMPENSATION

FAIR LABOR STANDARDS ACT

29 U.S.C. §§ 201–219

§ 201. Short title. This chapter may be cited as the "Fair Labor Standards Act of 1938".

§ 202. Congressional finding and declaration of policy

(a) The Congress finds that the existence, in industries engaged in commerce or in the production of goods for commerce, of labor conditions detrimental to the maintenance of the minimum standard of living necessary for health, efficiency, and general well-being of workers (1) causes commerce and the channels and instrumentalities of commerce to be used to spread and perpetuate such labor conditions among the workers of the several States; (2) burdens commerce and the free flow of goods in commerce; (3) constitutes an unfair method of competition in commerce; (4) leads to labor disputes burdening and obstructing commerce and the free flow of goods in commerce; and (5) interferes with the orderly and fair marketing of goods in commerce. That Congress further finds that the employment of persons in domestic service in households affects commerce.

(b) It is declared to be the policy of this chapter, through the exercise by Congress of its power to regulate commerce among the several States and with foreign nations, to correct and as rapidly as practicable to eliminate the conditions above referred to in such industries without substantially curtailing employment or earning power.

§ 203. Definitions. As used in this chapter—

(a) "Person" means an individual, partnership, association, corporation, business trust, legal representative, or any organized group of persons.

(b) "Commerce" means trade, commerce, transportation, transmission, or communication among the several States or between any State and any place outside thereof.

(c) "State" means any State of the United States or the District of Columbia or any Territory or possession of the United States.

(d) "Employer" includes any person acting directly or indirectly in the interest of an employer in relation to an employee and includes a public agency, but does not include any labor organization (other than when acting as an employer) or anyone acting in the capacity of officer or agent of such labor organization.

(e)(1) Except as provided in paragraphs (2), (3), and (4) the term "employee" means any individual employed by an employer.

(2) In the case of an individual employed by a public agency, such term means—

(A) any individual employed by the Government of the United States—

(i) as a civilian in the military departments (as defined in section 102 of Title 5),

(ii) in any executive agency (as defined in section 105 of such title),

(iii) in any unit of the judicial branch of the Government which has positions in the competitive service,

(iv) in a nonappropriated fund instrumentality under the jurisdiction of the Armed Forces,

(v) in the Library of Congress, or

(vi) the Government Printing Office;

(B) any individual employed by the United States Postal Service or the Postal Rate Commission; and

(C) any individual employed by a State, political subdivision of a State, or an interstate governmental agency, other than such an individual—

(i) who is not subject to the civil service laws of the State, political subdivision, or agency which employs him; and

(ii) who—

(I) holds a public elective office of that State, political subdivision, or agency,

(II) is selected by the holder of such an office to be a member of his personal staff,

(III) is appointed by such an officeholder to serve on a policymaking level,

(IV) is an immediate adviser to such an officeholder with respect to the constitutional or legal powers of his office, or

(V) is an employee in the legislative branch or legislative body of that State, political subdivision, or agency and is not employed by the legislative library of such State, political subdivision, or agency.

(3) For purposes of subsection (u) of this section, such term does not include any individual employed by an employer engaged in agriculture if such individual is the parent, spouse, child, or other member of the employer's immediate family.

(4)(A) The term "employee" does not include any individual who volunnteers to perform services for a public agency which is a State, a political subdivision of a State, or an interstate governmental agency, if—

(i) the individual receives no compensation or is paid expenses, reasonable benefits, or a nominal fee to perform the services for which the individual volunteered; and

(ii) such services are not the same type of services which the individual is employed to perform for such public agency.

(B) An employee of a public agency which is a State, political subdivision of a State, or an interstate governmental agency may volunteer to perform services for any other State, political subdivision, or interstate governmental agency, including a State, political subdivision or agency with which the employing State, political subdivision, or agency has a mutual aid agreement.

(f) "Agriculture" includes farming in all its branches and among other things includes the cultivation and tillage of the soil, dairying, the production, cultivation, growing, and harvesting of any agricultural or horticultural commodities (including commodities defined as agricultural commodities in section 1141j(g) of Title 12), the raising of livestock, bees, fur-bearing animals, or poultry, and any practices (including any forestry or lumbering operations) performed by a farmer or on a farm as an incident to or in conjunction with such farming operations, including preparation for market, delivery to storage or to market or to carriers for transportation to market.

(g) "Employ" includes to suffer or permit to work.

(h) "Industry" means a trade, business, industry, or other activity, or branch or group thereof, in which individuals are gainfully employed.

(i) "Goods" means goods (including ships and marine equipment), wares, products, commodities, merchandise, or articles or subjects of commerce of any character, or any part or ingredient thereof, but does not include goods after their delivery into the actual physical possession of the ultimate consumer thereof other than a producer, manufacturer, or processor thereof.

(j) "Produced" means produced, manufactured, mined, handled, or in any other manner worked on in any State; and for the purposes of this chapter an employee shall be deemed to have been engaged in the production of goods if such employee was employed in producing, manufacturing, mining, handling, transporting, or in any other manner working on such goods, or in any closely related process or occupation directly essential to the production thereof, in any State.

(k) "Sale" or "sell" includes any sale, exchange, contract to sell, consignment for sale, shipment for sale, or other disposition.

(l) "Oppressive child labor" means a condition of employment under which

> (1) any employee under the age of sixteen years is employed by an employer (other than a parent or a person standing in place of a parent employing his own child or a child in his custody under the age of sixteen years in an occupation other than manufacturing or mining or an occupation found by the Secretary of Labor to be particularly hazardous for the employment of children between the ages of sixteen and eighteen years or detrimental to their health or well-being) in any occupation, or
>
> (2) any employee between the ages of sixteen and eighteen years is employed by an employer in any occupation which the Secretary of Labor shall find and by order declare to be particularly hazardous for the employment of children between such ages or detrimental to their health or well-being; but oppressive child labor shall not be deemed to exist by virtue of the employment in any occupation of any person with respect to whom the employer shall have on file an unexpired certificate issued and held pursuant to regulations of the Secretary of Labor certifying that such person is above the oppressive child-labor age. The Secretary of Labor shall provide by regulation or by order that the employment of employees between the ages of fourteen and sixteen years in occupations other than manufacturing and mining shall not be deemed to constitute oppressive child labor if and to the extent that the Secretary of Labor determines that such employment is confined to periods which will not interfere with their schooling and to conditions which will not interfere with their health and well-being.

(m) "Wage" paid to any employee includes the reasonable cost, as determined by the Administrator [Secretary], to the employer of furnishing such employee with board, lodging, or other facilities, if such board, lodging, or other facilities are customarily furnished by such employer to his employees: Provided, That the cost of board, lodging, or other facilities shall not be included as a part of the wage paid to any employee to the extent it is excluded there from under the terms of a bona fide collective-bargaining agreement applicable to the particular employee: Provided further, That the Secretary is authorized to determine the fair value of such board, lodging, or other facilities for defined classes of employees and in defined areas, based on average cost to the employer or to groups of employers similarly situated, or average value to groups of employees, or other appropriate measures of fair value. Such evaluations, where applicable and pertinent, shall be used in lieu of actual measure of cost in determining the wage paid to any employee. In determining the wage an employer is required to pay a tipped employee, the amount paid such employee by the employee's employer shall be an amount equal to—

(1) the cash wage paid such employee which for purposes of such determination shall be not less than the cash wage required to be paid such an employee on the date of enactment of this paragraph; and

(2) an additional amount on account of the tips received by such employee which amount is equal to the difference between the wage specified in paragraph (1) and the wage in effect under section 206(a)(1) of this title.

The additional amount on account of tips may not exceed the value of the tips actually received by an employee. The preceding 2 sentences shall not apply with respect to any tipped employee unless such employee has been informed by the employer of the provisions of this subsection, and all tips received by such employee have been retained by the employee, except that this subsection shall not be construed to prohibit the pooling of tips among employees who customarily and regularly receive tips. . . .

(o) Hours Worked. In determining for the purposes of sections 206 and 207 of this title the hours for which an employee is employed, there shall be excluded any time spent in changing clothes or washing at the beginning or end of each workday which was excluded from measured working time during the week involved by the express terms of or by custom or practice under a bona fide collective-bargaining agreement applicable to the particular employee. . . .

(q) "Secretary" means the Secretary of Labor.

(r)(1) "Enterprise" means the related activities performed (either through unified operation or common control) by any person or persons for a common business purpose, and includes all such activities whether performed in one or more establishments or by one or more corporate or other organizational units including departments of an establishment operated through leasing arrangements, but shall not include the related activities performed for such enterprise by an independent contractor. Within the meaning of this subsection, a retail or service establishment which is under independent ownership shall not be deemed to be so operated or controlled as to be other than a separate and distinct enterprise by reason of any arrangement, which includes, but is not necessarily limited to, an agreement (A) that it will sell, or sell only, certain goods specified by a particular manufacturer, distributor, or advertiser, or (B) that it will join with other such establishments in the same industry for the purpose of collective purchasing, or (C) that it will have the exclusive right to sell the goods or use the brand name of a manufacturer, distributor, or advertiser within a specified area, or by reason of the fact that it occupies premises leased to it by a person who also leases premises to other retail or service establishments.

(2) For purposes of paragraph (1), the activities performed by any person or persons

(A) in connection with the operation of a hospital, an institution primarily engaged in the care of the sick, the aged, the mentally ill or defective who reside on the premises of such institution, a school for mentally or physically handicapped or gifted children, a preschool, elementary or secondary school, or an institution of higher education (regardless of whether or not such hospital, institution, or school is operated for profit or not for profit), or

(B) in connection with the operation of a street, suburban or interurban electric railway, or local trolley or motorbus carrier, if the rates and services of such railway or carrier are subject to regulation by a State or local agency (regardless of whether or not such railway or carrier is public or private or operated for profit or not for profit), or

(C) in connection with the activities of a public agency,

shall be deemed to be activities performed for a business purpose.

(s)(1) "Enterprise engaged in commerce or in the production of goods for commerce" means an enterprise that—

(A)(i) has employees engaged in commerce or in the production of goods for commerce, or that has employees handling, selling, or otherwise working on goods or materials that have been moved in or produced for commerce by any person; and

(ii) is an enterprise whose annual gross volume of sales made or business done is not less than $500,000 (exclusive of excise taxes at the retail level that are separately stated);

(B) is engaged in the operation of a hospital, an institution primarily engaged in the care of the sick, the aged, or the mentally ill or defective who reside on the premises of such institution, a school for mentally or physically handicapped or gifted children, a preschool, elementary or secondary school, or an institution of higher education (regardless of whether or not such hospital, institution, or school is public or private or operated for profit or not for profit); or

(C) is an activity of a public agency.

(2) Any establishment that has as its only regular employees the owner thereof or the parent, spouse, child or other member of the immediate family of such owner shall not be considered to be an enterprise engaged in commerce or in the production of goods for commerce or a part of such an enterprise. The sales of such an establishment shall not be included for the purpose of determining the annual gross volume of sales of any enterprise for the purpose of this subsection.

(t) "Tipped employee" means any employee engaged in an occupation in which he customarily and regularly receives more than $30 a month in tips. . . .

§ 204. Administration

(a) Creation of Wage and Hour Division in Department of Labor; Administrator. There is created in the Department of Labor a Wage and Hour Division which shall be under the direction of an Administrator, to be known as the Administrator of the Wage and Hour Division (in this chapter referred to as the "Administrator"). The Administrator shall be appointed by the President, by and with the advice and consent of the Senate.

§ 206. Minimum wage

(a) Employees engaged in commerce; . . . agricultural employees. Every employer shall pay to each of his employees who in any workweek is engaged in commerce or in the production of goods for commerce, or is employed in an enterprise engaged in commerce or in the production of goods for commerce, wages at the following rates:

(1) except as otherwise provided in this section, not less than—

(C) $7.25 an hour. . . .

(d) Prohibition of Sex Discrimination

(1) No employer having employees subject to any provisions of this section shall discriminate, within any establishment in which such employees are employed, between employees on the basis of sex by paying wages to employees in such establishment at a rate less than the rate at which he pays wages to employees of the opposite sex in such establishment for equal work on jobs the performance of which requires equal skill, effort, and responsibility, and which are performed under similar working conditions, except where such payment is made

pursuant to (i) a seniority system; (ii) a merit system; (iii) a system which measures earnings by quantity or quality of production; or (iv) a differential based on any other factor other than sex: *Provided,* That an employer who is paying a wage rate differential in violation of this subsection shall not, in order to comply with the provisions of this subsection, reduce the wage rate of any employee.

(2) No labor organization, or its agents, representing employees of an employer having employees subject to any provisions of this section shall cause or attempt to cause such an employer to discriminate against an employee in violation of paragraph (1) of this subsection.

(3) For purposes of administration and enforcement, any amounts owing to any employee which have been withheld in violation of this subsection shall be deemed to be unpaid minimum wages or unpaid overtime compensation under this chapter

(f) Employees in domestic service. Any employee—

(1) who in any workweek is employed in domestic service in a household shall be paid wages at a rate not less than the wage rate in effect under subsection (a)(1) of this section unless such employee's compensation for such service would not because of section 209(a)(6) of the Social Security Act [42 U.S.C. § 409(a)(6)] constitute wages for the purposes of title II of such Act [42 U.S.C. §§ 401 et seq.], or

(2) who in any workweek—

(A) is employed in domestic service in one or more households, and

(B) is so employed for more than 8 hours in the aggregate, shall be paid wages for such employment in such workweek at a rate not less than the wage rate in effect under subsection (a)(1) of this section.

(g) Newly hired employees who are less than 20 years old.

(1) In lieu of the rate prescribed by subsection (a)(1) of this section, any employer may pay any employee of such employer, during the first 90 consecutive calendar days after such employee is initially employed by such employer, a wage which is not less than $4.25 an hour.

(2) No employer may take any action to displace employees (including partial displacements such as reduction in hours, wages, or employment benefits) for purposes of hiring individuals at the wage authorized in paragraph (1).

(3) Any employer who violates this subsection shall be considered to have violated section 215(a)(3) of this title.

(4) This subsection shall only apply to an employee who has not attained the age of 20 years.

§ 207. Maximum hours

(a) Employees engaged in interstate commerce; additional applicability to employees pursuant to subsequent amendatory provisions

(1) Except as otherwise provided in this section, no employer shall employ any of his employees who in any workweek is engaged in commerce or in the production of goods for commerce, or is employed in an enterprise engaged in commerce or in the production of goods for commerce, for a workweek longer than forty hours unless such employee receives compensation for his employment in excess of the hours above specified at a rate not less than one and one-half times the regular rate at which he is employed. . .

(b) Employment pursuant to collective bargaining agreement; employment by independently owned and controlled local enterprise engaged in distribution of petroleum products. No employer shall be deemed to have violated subsection (a) of this section by employing any employee for a workweek in excess of that specified in such subsection without paying the compensation for overtime employment prescribed therein if such employee is so employed.

(1) in pursuance of an agreement, made as a result of collective bargaining by representatives of employees certified as bona fide by the National Labor Relations Board, which provides that no employee shall be employed more than one thousand and forty hours during any period of twenty-six consecutive weeks; or

(2) in pursuance of an agreement, made as a result of collective bargaining by representatives of employees certified as bona fide by the National Labor Relations Board, which provides that during a specified period of fifty-two consecutive weeks the employee shall be employed not more than two thousand two hundred and forty hours and shall be guaranteed not less than one thousand eight hundred and forty hours (or not less than forty-six weeks at the normal number of hours worked per week, but not less than thirty hours per week) and not more than two thousand and eighty hours of employment for which he shall receive compensation for all hours guaranteed or worked at rates not less than those applicable under the agreement to the work performed and for all hours in excess of the guaranty which are also in excess of the maximum workweek applicable to such employee under subsection (a) of this section or two thousand and eighty in such period at rates not less than one and one-half times the regular rate at which he is employed; or

(3) by an independently owned and controlled local enterprise (including an enterprise with more than one bulk storage establishment) engaged in the wholesale or bulk distribution of petroleum products if—

(A) the annual gross volume of sales of such enterprise is less than $1,000,000 exclusive of excise taxes,

(B) more than 75 per centum of such enterprise's annual dollar volume of sales is made within the State in which such enterprise is located, and

(C) not more than 25 per centum of the annual dollar volume of sales of such enterprise is to customers who are engaged in the bulk distribution of such products for resale,and such employee receives compensation for employment in excess of forty hours in any workweek at a rate not less than one and one-half times the minimum wage rate applicable to him under section 206 of this title, and if such employee receives compensation for employment in excess of twelve hours in any workday, or for employment in excess of fifty-six hours in any workweek, as the case may be, at a rate not less than one and one-half times the regular rate at which he is employed.

[(c) & (d) Repealed.]

(e) Definition of "regular rate" of employment. As used in this section the "regular rate" at which an employee is employed shall be deemed to include all remuneration for employment paid to, or on behalf of, the employee, but shall not be deemed to include—

(1) sums paid as gifts; payments in the nature of gifts made at Christmas time or on other special occasions, as a reward for service, the amounts of which are not measured by or dependent on hours worked, production, or efficiency;

(2) payments made for occasional periods when no work is performed due to vacation, holiday, illness, failure of the employer to provide sufficient work, or other similar cause; reasonable payments for traveling expenses, or other expenses, incurred by an employee in the furtherance of his employer's interests and properly reimbursable by the employer; and other similar payments to an employee which are not made as compensation for his hours of employment;

(3) sums paid in recognition of services performed during a given period if either, (a) both the fact that payment is to be made and the amount of the payment are determined at the sole discretion of the employer at or near the end of the period and not pursuant to any prior contract, agreement, or promise causing the employee to expect such payments regularly; or (b) the payments are made pursuant to a bona fide profit-sharing plan or trust or bona fide thrift or savings plan, meeting the requirements of the Administrator set forth in appropriate regulations which he shall issue, having due regard among other relevant factors, to the extent to which the amounts paid to the employee are determined without regard to hours of work, production, or efficiency; or (c) the payments are talent fees (as such talent fees are defined and

delimited by regulations of the Administrator) paid to performers, including announcers, on radio and television programs;

(4) contributions irrevocably made by an employer to a trustee or third person pursuant to a bona fide plan for providing old-age, retirement, life, accident, or health insurance or similar benefits for employees;

(5) extra compensation provided by a premium rate paid for certain hours worked by the employee in any day or workweek because such hours are hours worked in excess of eight in a day or in excess of the maximum workweek applicable to such employee under subsection (a) of this section or in excess of the employee's normal working hours or regular working hours, as the case may be;

(6) extra compensation provided by a premium rate paid for work by the employee on Saturdays, Sundays, holidays, or regular days of rest, or on the sixth or seventh day of the workweek, where such premium rate is not less than one and one-half times the rate established in good faith for like work performed in non overtime hours on other days;

(7) extra compensation provided by a premium rate paid to the employee, in pursuance of an applicable employment contract or collective-bargaining agreement, for work outside of the hours established in good faith by the contract or agreement as the basic, normal, or regular workday (not exceeding eight hours) or workweek (not exceeding the maximum workweek applicable to such employee under subsection (a) of this section), where such premium rate is not less than one and one-half times the rate established in good faith by the contract or agreement for like work performed during such workday or workweek; or

(8) any value or income derived from employer-provided grants or rights provided pursuant to a stock option, stock appreciation right, or bona fide employee stock purchase program which is not otherwise excludable under any of paragraphs (1) through (7) if—

(A) grants are made pursuant to a program, the terms and conditions of which are communicated to participating employees either at the beginning of the employee's participation in the program or at the time of the grant;

(B) in the case of stock options and stock appreciation rights, the grant or right cannot be exercisable for a period of at least 6 months after the time of grant (except that grants or rights may become exercisable because of an employee's death, disability, retirement, or a change in corporate ownership, or other circumstances permitted by regulation), and the exercise price is at least 85 percent of the fair market value of the stock at the time of grant;

(C) exercise of any grant or right is voluntary; and

(D) any determinations regarding the award of, and the amount of, employer-provided grants or rights that are based on performance are—

(i) made based upon meeting previously established performance criteria (which may include hours of work, efficiency, or productivity) of any business unit consisting of at least 10 employees or of a facility, except that, any determinations may be based on length of service or minimum schedule of hours or days of work; or

(ii) made based upon the past performance (which may include any criteria) of one or more employees in a given period so long as the determination is in the sole discretion of the employer and not pursuant to any prior contract.

(f) Employment necessitating irregular hours of work. No employer shall be deemed to have violated subsection (a) of this section by employing any employee for a workweek in excess of the maximum workweek applicable to such employee under subsection (a) of this section if such employee is employed pursuant to a bona fide individual contract, or pursuant to an agreement made as a result of collective bargaining by representatives of employees, if the duties of such employee necessitate irregular hours of work, and the contract or agreement (1) specifies a regular rate of pay of not less than the minimum hourly rate provided in subsection (a) or (b) of section 206 of this title (whichever may be applicable) and compensation at not less than one and one-half times such rate for all hours worked in excess of such maximum workweek, and (2) provides a weekly guaranty of pay for not more than sixty hours based on the rates so specified.

(g) Employment at piece rates. No employer shall be deemed to have violated subsection (a) of this section by employing any employee for a workweek in excess of the maximum workweek applicable to such employee under such subsection if, pursuant to an agreement or understanding arrived at between the employer and the employee before performance of the work, the amount paid to the employee for the number of hours worked by him in such workweek in excess of the maximum workweek applicable to such employee under such subsection—

(1) in the case of an employee employed at piece rates, is computed at piece rates not less than one and one-half times the bona fide piece rates applicable to the same work when performed during no overtime hours; or

(2) in the case of an employee performing two or more kinds of work for which different hourly or piece rates have been established, is computed at rates not less than one and one-half times

such bona fide rates applicable to the same work when performed during no overtime hours; or

(3) is computed at a rate not less than one and one-half times the rate established by such agreement or understanding as the basic rate to be used in computing overtime compensation there under: Provided, That the rate so established shall be authorized by regulation by the Administrator as being substantially equivalent to the average hourly earnings of the employee, exclusive of overtime premiums, in the particular work over a representative period of time; and if

(i) the employee's average hourly earnings for the workweek exclusive of payments described in paragraphs (1) through (7) of subsection (e) of this section are not less than the minimum hourly rate required by applicable law, and

(ii) extra overtime compensation is properly computed and paid on other forms of additional pay required to be included in computing the regular rate.

(h) Extra compensation creditable toward overtime compensation.

(1) Except as provided in paragraph (2), sums excluded from the regular rate pursuant to subsection (e) shall not be creditable toward wages required under section 6 or overtime compensation required under this section.

(2) Extra compensation paid as described in paragraphs (5), (6), and (7) of subsection (e) shall be creditable toward overtime compensation payable pursuant to this section.

(i) Employment by retail or service establishment. No employer shall be deemed to have violated subsection (a) of this section by employing any employee of a retail or service establishment for a workweek in excess of the applicable workweek specified therein, if (1) the regular rate of pay of such employee is in excess of one and one-half times the minimum hourly rate applicable to him under section 206 of this title, and (2) more than half his compensation for a representative period (not less than one month) represents commissions on goods or services. In determining the proportion of compensation representing commissions, all earnings resulting from the application of a bona fide commission rate shall be deemed commissions on goods or services without regard to whether the computed commissions exceed the draw or guarantee.

(j) Employment in hospital or establishment engaged in care of sick, aged or mentally ill. No employer engaged in the operation of a hospital or an establishment which is an institution primarily engaged in the care of the sick, the aged, or the mentally ill or defective who reside on the premises shall be deemed to have violated subsection (a) of this section if, pursuant to an agreement or understanding arrived at between the employer and the employee before performance of the work, a work period of fourteen consecutive days is accepted in lieu of the workweek of seven consecutive days for purposes of overtime computation and if, for his employment in excess of eight hours and any workday and in excess of eighty hours in such fourteen-day period, the employee receives compensation at a rate not less than one and one-half times the regular rate at which he is employed.

(k) Employment by public agency engaged in fire protection or law enforcement activities. No public agency shall be deemed to have violated subsection (a) of this section with respect to the employment of any employee in fire protection activities or any employee in law enforcement activities (including security personnel in correctional institutions) if—

(1) in a work period of 28 consecutive days the employee receives for tours of duty which in the aggregate exceed the lesser of (A) 216 hours, or (B) the average number of hours (as determined by the Secretary pursuant to section 6(c)(3) of the Fair Labor Standards Amendments of 1974) in tours of duty of employees engaged in such activities in work periods of 28 consecutive days in calendar year 1975; or

(2) in the case of such an employee to whom a work period of at least 7 but less than 28 days applies, in his work period the employee receives for tours of duty which in the aggregate exceed a number of hours which bears the same ratio to the number of consecutive days in his work period as 216 hours (or if lower, the number of hours referred to in clause (B) of paragraph (1)) bears to 28 days, compensation at a rate not less than one and one-half times the regular rate at which he is employed.

(l) Employment in domestic service in one or more households. No employer shall employ any employee in domestic service in one or more households for a workweek longer than forty hours unless such employee receives compensation for such employment in accordance with subsection (a) of this section.

(m) Employment in tobacco industry. For a period or periods of not more than fourteen workweeks in the aggregate in any calendar year, any employer may employ any employee for a workweek in excess of that specified in subsection (a) of this section without paying the compensation for overtime employment prescribed in such subsection, if such employee—

(1) is employed by such employer—

(A) to provide services (including stripping and grading) necessary and incidental to the sale at auction of green leaf tobacco of type 11, 12, 13, 14, 21, 22, 23, 24, 31, 35, 36, or 37 (as such types are defined by the Secretary of Agriculture), or in auction sale, buying, handling, stemming, redrying, packing, and storing of such tobacco,

(B) in auction sale, buying, handling, sorting, grading, packing, or storing green leaf tobacco of type 32 (as such type is defined by the Secretary of Agriculture), or

(C) in auction sale, buying, handling, stripping, sorting, grading, sizing, packing, or stemming prior to packing, of perishable cigar leaf tobacco of type 41, 42, 43, 44, 45, 46, 51, 52, 53, 54, 55, 61, or 62 (as such types are defined by the Secretary of Agriculture); and

(2) receives for—

(A) such employment by such employer which is in excess of ten hours in any workday, and

(B) such employment by such employer which is in excess of forty-eight hours in any workweek, compensation at a rate not less than one and one-half times the regular rate at which he is employed.

An employer who receives an exemption under this subsection shall not be eligible for any other exemption under this section.

(n) Employment by street, suburban or interurban electric railway, or local trolley or motorbus carrier. In the case of an employee of an employer engaged in the business of operating a street, suburban or interurban electric railway, or local trolley or motorbus carrier (regardless of whether or not such railway or carrier is public or private or operated for profit or not for profit), in determining the hours of employment of such an employee to which the rate prescribed by subsection (a) of this section applies there shall be excluded the hours such employee was employed in charter activities by such employer if (1) the employee's employment in such activities was pursuant to an agreement or understanding with his employer arrived at before engaging in such employment, and (2) if employment in such activities is not part of such employee's regular employment.

(o) Compensatory time

(1) Employees of a public agency which is a State, a political subdivision of a State, or an interstate governmental agency may receive, in accordance with this subsection and in lieu of overtime compensation, compensatory time off at a rate not less than one and one-half hours for each hour of employment for which overtime compensation is required by this section.

(2) A public agency may provide compensatory time under paragraph (1) only—

(A) pursuant to—

(i) applicable provisions of a collective bargaining agreement, memorandum of understanding, or any other agreement between the public agency and representatives of such employees; or

(ii) in the case of employees not covered by subclause (i), an agreement or understanding arrived at between the employer and employee before the performance of the work; and

(B) if the employee has not accrued compensatory time in excess of the limit applicable to the employee prescribed by paragraph (3).

In the case of employees described in clause (A)(ii) hired prior to April 15, 1986, the regular practice in effect on April 15, 1986, with respect to compensatory time off for such employees in lieu of the receipt of overtime compensation, shall constitute an agreement or understanding under such clause (A)(ii). Except as provided in the previous sentence, the provision of compensatory time off to such employees for hours worked after April 14, 1986, shall be in accordance with this subsection.

(3)(A) If the work of an employee for which compensatory time may be provided included work in a public safety activity, an emergency response activity, or a seasonal activity, the employee engaged in such work may accrue not more than 480 hours of compensatory time for hours worked after April 15, 1986. If such work was any other work, the employee engaged in such work may accrue not more than 240 hours of compensatory time for hours worked after April 15, 1986. Any such employee who, after April 15, 1986, has accrued 480 or 240 hours, as the case may be, of compensatory time off shall, for additional overtime hours of work, be paid overtime compensation.

(B) If compensation is paid to an employee for accrued compensatory time off, such compensation shall be paid at the regular rate earned by the employee at the time the employee receives such payment.

(4) An employee who has accrued compensatory time off authorized to be provided under paragraph (1) shall, upon termination of employment, be paid for the unused compensatory time at a rate of compensation not less than—

(A) the average regular rate received by such employee during the last 3 years of the employee's employment, or

(B) the final regular rate received by such employee, whichever is higher.

(5) An employee of a public agency which is a State, political subdivision of a State, or an interstate governmental agency—

(A) who has accrued compensatory time off authorized to be provided under paragraph (1), and

(B) who has requested the use of such compensatory time, shall be permitted by the employee's employer to use such time within a reasonable period after making the request if the use of the compensatory time does not unduly disrupt the operations of the public agency.

(6) The hours an employee of a public agency performs court reporting transcript preparation duties shall not be considered as hours worked for purposes of subsection (a) of this section if—

(A) such employee is paid at a per-page rate which is not less than—

(i) the maximum rate established by State law or local ordinance for the jurisdiction of such public agency,

(ii) the maximum rate otherwise established by a judicial or administrative officer and in effect on July 1, 1995, or

(iii) the rate freely negotiated between the employee and the party requesting the transcript, other than the judge who presided over the proceedings being transcribed, and

(B) the hours spent performing such duties are outside of the hours such employee performs other work (including hours for which the agency requires the employee's attendance) pursuant to the employment relationship with such public agency.

For purposes of this section, the amount paid such employee in accordance with subparagraph (A) for the performance of court reporting transcript preparation duties, shall not be considered in the calculation of the regular rate at which such employee is employed.

(7) For purposes of this subsection—

(A) the term "overtime compensation" means the compensation required by subsection (a), and

(B) the terms "compensatory time" and "compensatory time off" mean hours during which an employee is not working, which are not counted as hours worked during the applicable workweek or other work period for purposes of overtime compensation, and for which the employee is compensated at the employee's regular rate.

(p) Special detail work for fire protection and law enforcement employees; occasional or sporadic employment; substitution

(1) If an individual who is employed by a State, political subdivision of a State, or an interstate governmental agency in fire protection or law enforcement activities (including activities of security personnel in correctional institutions) and who, solely at such individual's option, agrees to be employed on a special detail by a separate or independent employer in fire protection, law enforcement, or related activities, the hours such individual was employed by such separate and independent employer shall be excluded by the public agency employing such individual in the calculation of the hours for which the

employee is entitled to overtime compensation under this section if the public agency—

(A) requires that its employees engaged in fire protection, law enforcement, or security activities be hired by a separate and independent employer to perform the special detail,

(B) facilitates the employment of such employees by a separate and independent employer, or

(C) otherwise affects the condition of employment of such employees by a separate and independent employer.

(2) If an employee of a public agency which is a State, political subdivision of a State, or an interstate governmental agency undertakes, on an occasional or sporadic basis and solely at the employee's option, part-time employment for the public agency which is in a different capacity from any capacity in which the employee is regularly employed with the public agency, the hours such employee was employed in performing the different employment shall be excluded by the public agency in the calculation of the hours for which the employee is entitled to overtime compensation under this section.

(3) If an individual who is employed in any capacity by a public agency which is a State, political subdivision of a State, or an interstate governmental agency, agrees, with the approval of the public agency and solely at the option of such individual, to substitute during scheduled work hours for another individual who is employed by such agency in the same capacity, the hours such employee worked as a substitute shall be excluded by the public agency in the calculation of the hours for which the employee is entitled to overtime compensation under this section.

(q) Maximum hour exemption for employees receiving remedial education. Any employer may employ any employee for a period or periods of not more than 10 hours in the aggregate in any workweek in excess of the maximum workweek specified in subsection (a) of this section without paying the compensation for overtime employment prescribed in such subsection, if during such period or periods the employee is receiving remedial education that is—

(1) provided to employees who lack a high school diploma or educational attainment at the eighth grade level;

(2) designed to provide reading and other basic skills at an eighth grade level or below; and

(3) does not include job specific training. . . .

(r)(1) An employer shall provide—

A. a reasonable break time for an employee to express breast milk for her nursing child for 1 year after the child's birth each time such employee has need to express the milk; and

B. a place, other than a bathroom, that is shielded from view and free from intrusion from coworkers and the public, which may be used by an employee to express breast milk.

(2) An employer shall not be required to compensate an employee receiving reasonable break time under paragraph (1) for any work time spent for such purpose.

(3) An employer that employs less than 50 employees shall not be subject to the requirements of this subsection, if such requirements would impose an undue hardship by causing the employer significant difficulty or expense when considered in relation to the size, financial resources, nature, or structure of the employer's business.

(4) Nothing in this subsection shall preempt a State law that provides greater protections to employees than the protections provided for under this subsection.

§ 211. Investigations, inspections, records, and homework regulations

(a) The Administrator or his designated representatives may investigate and gather data regarding the wages, hours, and other conditions and practices of employment in any industry subject to this chapter, and may enter and inspect such places and such records (and make such transcriptions thereof), question such employees, and investigate such facts, conditions, practices, or matters as he may deem necessary or appropriate to determine whether any person has violated any provision of this chapter, or which may aid in the enforcement of the provisions of this chapter. Except as provided in section 212 of this title and in subsection (b) of this section, the Administrator shall utilize the bureaus and divisions of the Department of Labor for all the investigations and inspections necessary under this section. Except as provided in section 212 of this title, the Secretary of Labor shall bring all actions under section 217 of this title to restrain violations of this chapter.

(b) With the consent and cooperation of State agencies charged with the administration of State labor laws, the Administrator and the Secretary of Labor may, for the purpose of carrying out their respective functions and duties under this chapter, utilize the services of State and local agencies and their employees and, notwithstanding any other provision of law, may reimburse such State and local agencies and their employees for services rendered for such purposes.

(c) Every employer subject to any provision of this chapter or of any order issued under this chapter shall make, keep, and preserve such records of the persons employed by him and of the wages, hours, and other conditions and practices of employment maintained by him, and shall preserve such records for such periods of time, and shall make such reports there from to the

Administrator as he shall prescribe by regulation or order as necessary or appropriate for the enforcement of the provisions of this chapter or the regulations or orders there under. The employer of an employee who performs substitute work described in section 207(p)(3) of this title may not be required under this subsection to keep a record of the hours of the substitute work.

(d) The Administrator is authorized to make such regulations and orders regulating, restricting, or prohibiting industrial homework as are necessary or appropriate to prevent the circumvention or evasion of and to safeguard the minimum wage rate prescribed in this chapter, and all existing regulations or orders of the Administrator relating to industrial homework are continued in full force and effect.

§ 212. Child labor provisions

(a) No producer, manufacturer, or dealer shall ship or deliver for shipment in commerce any goods produced in an establishment situated in the United States in or about which within thirty days prior to the removal of such goods there from any oppressive child labor has been employed: Provided, That any such shipment or delivery for shipment of such goods by a purchaser who acquired them in good faith in reliance on written assurance from the producer, manufacturer, or dealer that the goods were produced in compliance with the requirements of this section, and who acquired such goods for value without notice of any such violation, shall not be deemed prohibited by this subsection: And provided further, That a prosecution and conviction of a defendant for the shipment or delivery for shipment of any goods under the conditions herein prohibited shall be a bar to any further prosecution against the same defendant for shipments or deliveries for shipment of any such goods before the beginning of said prosecution.

(b) The Secretary of Labor or any of his authorized representatives, shall make all investigations and inspections under section 211(a) of this title with respect to the employment of minors, and, subject to the direction and control of the Attorney General, shall bring all actions under section 217 of this title to enjoin any act or practice which is unlawful by reason of the existence of oppressive child labor, and shall administer all other provisions of this chapter relating to oppressive child labor.

(c) No employer shall employ any oppressive child labor in commerce or in the production of goods for commerce or in any enterprise engaged in commerce or in the production of goods for commerce.

(d) In order to carry out the objectives of this section, the Secretary may by regulation require employers to obtain from any employee proof of age.

§ 213. Exemptions

(a) Minimum wage and maximum hour requirements. The provisions of section 206 (except subsection (d) in the case of paragraph (1) of this subsection) and section 207 of this title shall not apply with respect to—

(1) any employee employed in a bona fide executive, administrative, or professional capacity (including any employee employed in the capacity of academic administrative personnel or teacher in elementary or secondary schools), or in the capacity of outside salesman (as such terms are defined and delimited from time to time by regulations of the Secretary, subject to the provisions of subchapter II of chapter 5 of Title 5, except that an employee of a retail or service establishment shall not be excluded from the definition of employee employed in a bona fide executive or administrative capacity because of the number of hours in his workweek which he devotes to activities not directly or closely related to the performance of executive or administrative activities, if less than 40 per centum of his hours worked in the workweek are devoted to such activities); or

[(2) Repealed.]

(3) any employee employed by an establishment which is an amusement or recreational establishment, organized camp, or religious or nonprofit educational conference center, if (A) it does not operate for more than seven months in any calendar year, or (B) during the preceding calendar year, its average receipts for any six months of such year were not more than 33 1/3 per centum of its average receipts for the other six months of such year, except that the exemption from sections 206 and 207 of this title provided by this paragraph does not apply with respect to any employee of a private entity engaged in providing services or facilities (other than, in the case of the exemption from section 206 of this title, a private entity engaged in providing services and facilities directly related to skiing) in a national park or a national forest, or on land in the National Wildlife Refuge System, under a contract with the Secretary of the Interior or the Secretary of Agriculture; or

[(4) Repealed.]

(5) any employee employed in the catching, taking, propagating, harvesting, cultivating, or farming of any kind of fish, shellfish, crustacean, sponges, seaweeds, or other aquatic forms of animal and vegetable life, or in the first processing, canning or packing such marine products at sea as an incident to, or in conjunction with, such fishing operations, including the going to and returning from work and loading and unloading when performed by any such employee; or

(6) any employee employed in agriculture (A) if such employee is employed by an employer who did not, during any calendar quarter during the preceding calendar year, use more than five hundred man-days of agricultural labor, (B) if such employee is the parent, spouse, child, or other member of his employer's immediate family, (C) if such employee (i) is employed as a hand harvest laborer and is paid on a piece rate basis in an operation which has been, and is customarily and generally recognized as having been, paid on a piece rate basis in

the region of employment, (ii) commutes daily from his permanent residence to the farm on which he is so employed, and (iii) has been employed in agriculture less than thirteen weeks during the preceding calendar year, (D) if such employee (other than an employee described in clause (C) of this subsection) (i) is sixteen years of age or under and is employed as a hand harvest laborer, is paid on a piece rate basis in an operation which has been, and is customarily and generally recognized as having been, paid on a piece rate basis in the region of employment, (ii) is employed on the same farm as his parent or person standing in the place of his parent, and (iii) is paid at the same piece rate as employees over age sixteen are paid on the same farm, or (E) if such employee is principally engaged in the range production of livestock; or

(7) any employee to the extent that such employee is exempted by regulations, order, or certificate of the Secretary issued under section 214 of this title; or

(8) any employee employed in connection with the publication of any weekly, semiweekly, or daily newspaper with a circulation of less than four thousand the major part of which circulation is within the county where published or counties contiguous thereto; or

[(9) Repealed.]

(10) any switchboard operator employed by an independently owned public telephone company which has not more than seven hundred and fifty stations; or

[(11) Repealed.]

(12) any employee employed as a seaman on a vessel other than an American vessel; or

[(13) Repealed.]

(14) any agricultural employee employed in the growing and harvesting of shade-grown tobacco who is engaged in the processing (including, but not limited to, drying, curing, fermenting, bulking, rebulking, sorting, grading, aging, and baling) of such tobacco, prior to the stemming process, for use as cigar wrapper tobacco; or

(15) any employee employed on a casual basis in domestic service employment to provide babysitting services or any employee employed in domestic service employment to provide companionship services for individuals who (because of age or infirmity) are unable to care for themselves (as such terms are defined and delimited by regulations of the Secretary); or

(16) A criminal investigator who is paid availability pay under section 5545a of Title 5; or

(17) any employee who is a computer systems analyst, computer programmer, software engineer, or other similarly skilled worker, whose primary duty is—

(A) the application of systems analysis techniques and procedures, including consulting with users, to determine hardware, software, or system functional specifications;

(B) the design, development, documentation, analysis, creation, testing, or modification of computer systems or programs, including prototypes, based on and related to user or system design specifications;

(C) the design, documentation, testing, creation, or modification of computer programs related to machine operating systems; or

(D) a combination of duties described in subparagraphs (A), (B), and (C) the performance of which requires the same level skills, and who, in the case of an employee who is compensated on an hourly basis, is compensated at a rate of not less than $27.63 an hour.

(b) Maximum hour requirements. The provisions of section 207 of this title shall not apply with respect to—

(1) any employee with respect to whom the Secretary of Transportation has power to establish qualifications and maximum hours of service pursuant to the provisions of section 31502 of Title 49; or

(2) any employee of an employer engaged in the operation of a rail carrier subject to part A of subtitle IV of Title 49; or

(3) any employee of a carrier by air subject to the provisions title II of the Railway Labor Act [45 U.S.C. §§ 181 et seq.]; or

[(4) Repealed.]

(5) any individual employed as an outside buyer of poultry, eggs, cream, or milk, in their raw or natural state; or

(6) any employee employed as a seaman; or

[(7) & (8) Repealed.]

(9) any employee employed as an announcer, news editor, or chief engineer by a radio or television station the major studio of which is located

(A) in a city or town of one hundred thousand population or less, according to the latest available decennial census figures as compiled by the Bureau of the Census, except where such city or town is part of a standard metropolitan statistical area, as defined and designated by the Office of Management and Budget, which has a total population in excess of one hundred thousand, or

(B) in a city or town of twenty-five thousand population or less, which is part of such an area but is at least 40 airline miles from the principal city in such area; or

(10)(A) any salesman, partsman, or mechanic primarily engaged in selling or servicing automobiles, trucks, or farm implements, if he is employed by a nonmanufacturing establishment primarily engaged in the business of selling such vehicles or implements to ultimate purchasers; or

(B) any salesman primarily engaged in selling trailers, boats, or aircraft, if he is employed by a nonmanufacturing establishment primarily engaged in the business of selling trailers, boats, or aircraft to ultimate purchasers; or

(11) any employee employed as a driver or driver's helper making local deliveries, who is compensated for such employment on the basis of trip rates, or other delivery payment plan, if the Secretary shall find that such plan has the general purpose and effect of reducing hours worked by such employees to, or below, the maximum workweek applicable to them under section 207(a) of this title; or

(12) any employee employed in agriculture or in connection with the operation or maintenance of ditches, canals, reservoirs, or waterways, not owned or operated for profit, or operated on a sharecrop basis, and which are used exclusively for supply and storing of water for agricultural purposes; or

(13) any employee with respect to his employment in agriculture by a farmer, notwithstanding other employment of such employee in connection with livestock auction operations in which such farmer is engaged as an adjunct to the raising of livestock, either on his own account or in conjunction with other farmers, if such employee (A) is primarily employed during his workweek in agriculture by such farmer, and (B) is paid for his employment in connection with such livestock auction operations at a wage rate not less than that prescribed by section 206(a)(1) of this title; or

(14) any employee employed within the area of production (as defined by the Secretary) by an establishment commonly recognized as a country elevator, including such an establishment which sells products and services used in the operation of a farm, if no more than five employees are employed in the establishment in such operations; or

(15) any employee engaged in the processing of maple sap into sugar (other than refined sugar) or syrup; or

(16) any employee engaged (A) in the transportation and preparation for transportation of fruits or vegetables, whether or not performed by the farmer, from the farm to a place of first processing or first marketing within the same State, or (B) in transportation, whether or not performed by the farmer, between the farm and any point within the same State of persons employed or to be employed in the harvesting of fruits or vegetables; or

(17) any driver employed by an employer engaged in the business of operating taxicabs; or

[(18) & (19) Repealed.]

(20) any employee of a public agency who in any workweek is employed in fire protection activities or any employee of a public agency who in any workweek is employed in law enforcement activities (including security personnel in correctional institutions), if the public agency employs during the workweek less than 5 employees in fire protection or law enforcement activities, as the case may be; or

(21) any employee who is employed in domestic service in a household and who resides in such household; or

[(22) & (23) Repealed.]

(24) any employee who is employed with his spouse by a nonprofit educational institution to serve as the parents of children—

(A) who are orphans or one of whose natural parents is deceased, or

(B) who are enrolled in such institution and reside in residential facilities of the institution, while such children are in residence at such institution, if such employee and his spouse reside in such facilities, receive, without cost, board and lodging from such institution, and are together compensated, on a cash basis, at an annual rate of not less than $10,000; or

[(25) & (26) Repealed.]

(27) any employee employed by an establishment which is a motion picture theater; or

(28) any employee employed in planting or tending trees, cruising, surveying, or felling timber, or in preparing or transporting logs or other forestry products to the mill, processing plant, railroad, or other transportation terminal, if the number of employees employed by his employer in such forestry or lumbering operations does not exceed eight; or

(29) any employee of an amusement or recreational establishment located in a national park or national forest or on land in the National Wildlife Refuge System if such employee (A) is an employee of a private entity engaged in providing services or facilities in a national park or national forest, or on land in the National Wildlife Refuge System, under a contract with the Secretary of the Interior or the Secretary of Agriculture, and (B) receives compensation for employment in excess of fifty-six hours in any workweek at a rate not less than one and one-half times the regular rate at which he is employed; or

(30) A criminal investigator who is paid availability pay under section 5545a of Title 5.

(c) Child labor requirements

(1) Except as provided in paragraph (2) or (4), the provisions of section 212 of this title relating to child labor shall not apply to

any employee employed in agriculture outside of school hours for the school district where such employee is living while he is so employed, if such employee—

(A) is less than twelve years of age and (i) is employed by his parent, or by a person standing in the place of his parent, on a farm owned or operated by such parent or person, or (ii) is employed, with the consent of his parent or person standing in the place of his parent, on a farm, none of the employees of which are (because of subsection (a)(6)(A) of this section) required to be paid at the wage rate prescribed by section 206(a)(5) of this title,

(B) is twelve years or thirteen years of age and (i) such employment is with the consent of his parent or person standing in the place of his parent, or (ii) his parent or such person is employed on the same farm as such employee, or

(C) is fourteen years of age or older.

(2) The provisions of section 212 of this title relating to child labor shall apply to an employee below the age of sixteen employed in agriculture in an occupation that the Secretary of Labor finds and declares to be particularly hazardous for the employment of children below the age of sixteen, except where such employee is employed by his parent or by a person standing in the place of his parent on a farm owned or operated by such parent or person.

(3) The provisions of section 212 of this title relating to child labor shall not apply to any child employed as an actor or performer in motion pictures or theatrical productions, or in radio or television productions.

(4)(A) An employer or group of employers may apply to the Secretary for a waiver of the application of section 212 of this title to the employment for not more than eight weeks in any calendar year of individuals who are less than twelve years of age, but not less than ten years of age, as hand harvest laborers in an agricultural operation which has been, and is customarily and generally recognized as being, paid on a piece rate basis in the region in which such individuals would be employed. The Secretary may not grant such a waiver unless he finds, based on objective data submitted by the applicant, that—

(i) the crop to be harvested is one with a particularly short harvesting season and the application of section 212 of this title would cause severe economic disruption in the industry of the employer or group of employers applying for the waiver;

(ii) the employment of the individuals to whom the waiver would apply would not be deleterious to their health or well-being;

(iii) the level and type of pesticides and other chemicals used would not have an adverse effect on the health or well-being of the individuals to whom the waiver would apply;

(iv) individuals age twelve and above are not available for such employment; and

(v) the industry of such employer or group of employers has traditionally and substantially employed individuals under twelve years of age without displacing substantial job opportunities for individuals over sixteen years of age.

(B) Any waiver granted by the Secretary under subparagraph (A) shall require that—

(i) the individuals employed under such waiver be employed outside of school hours for the school district where they are living while so employed;

(ii) such individuals while so employed commute daily from their permanent residence to the farm on which they are so employed; and

(iii) such individuals be employed under such waiver (I) for not more than eight weeks between June 1 and October 15 of any calendar year, and (II) in accordance with such other terms and conditions as the Secretary shall prescribe for such individuals' protection.

(5)(A) In the administration and enforcement of the child labor provisions of this chapter, employees who are 16 and 17 years of age shall be permitted to load materials into, but not operate or unload materials from, scrap paper balers and paper box compactors—

(i) that are safe for 16- and 17-year-old employees loading the scrap paper balers or paper box compactors; and

(ii) that cannot be operated while being loaded.

(B) For purposes of subparagraph (A), scrap paper balers and paper box compactors shall be considered safe for 16- or 17-year-old employees to load only if—

(i)(I) the scrap paper balers and paper box compactors meet the American National Standards Institute's Standard ANSI Z245.5-1990 for scrap paper balers and Standard ANSI Z245.2-1992 for paper box compactors; or

(II) the scrap paper balers and paper box compactors meet an applicable standard that is adopted by the American National Standards Institute after August 6, 1996, and that is certified by the Secretary to be at least as protective of the safety of minors as the standard described in subclause (I);

(ii) the scrap paper balers and paper box compactors include an on-off switch incorporating a key-lock or other system and the control of the system is maintained in the custody of employees who are 18 years of age or older;

(iii) the on-off switch of the scrap paper balers and paper box compactors is maintained in an off position when the scrap paper balers and paper box compactors are not in operation; and

(iv) the employer of 16- and 17-year-old employees provides notice, and posts a notice, on the scrap paper balers and paper box compactors stating that—

(I) the scrap paper balers and paper box compactors meet the applicable standard described in clause (i);

(II) 16- and 17-year-old employees may only load the scrap paper balers and paper box compactors; and

(III) any employee under the age of 18 may not operate or unload the scrap paper balers and paper box compactors.

The Secretary shall publish in the Federal Register a standard that is adopted by the American National Standards Institute for scrap paper balers or paper box compactors and certified by the Secretary to be protective of the safety of minors under clause (i)(II).

(C)(i) Employers shall prepare and submit to the Secretary reports—

(I) on any injury to an employee under the age of 18 that requires medical treatment (other than first aid) resulting from the employee's contact with a scrap paper baler or paper box compactor during the loading, operation, or unloading of the baler or compactor; and

(II) on any fatality of an employee under the age of 18 resulting from the employee's contact with a scrap paper baler or paper box compactor during the loading, operation, or unloading of the baler or compactor.

(ii) The reports described in clause (i) shall be used by the Secretary to determine whether or not the implementation of subparagraph (A) has had any effect on the safety of children.

(iii) The reports described in clause (i) shall provide—

(I) the name, telephone number, and address of the employer and the address of the place of employment where the incident occurred;

(II) the name, telephone number, and address of the employee who suffered an injury or death as a result of the incident;

(III) the date of the incident;

(IV) a description of the injury and a narrative describing how the incident occurred; and

(V) the name of the manufacturer and the model number of the scrap paper baler or paper box compactor involved in the incident.

(iv) The reports described in clause (i) shall be submitted to the Secretary promptly, but not later than 10 days after the date on which an incident relating to an injury or death occurred.

(v) The Secretary may not rely solely on the reports described in clause (i) as the basis for making a determination that any of the employers described in clause (i) has violated a provision of section 212 of this title relating to oppressive child labor or a regulation or order issued pursuant to section 212 of this title. The Secretary shall, prior to making such a determination, conduct an investigation and inspection in accordance with section 212(b) of this title.

(vi) The reporting requirements of this subparagraph shall expire 2 years after August, 6 1996.

(6) In the administration and enforcement of the child labor provisions of this act, employees who are under 17 years of age may not drive automobiles or trucks on public roadways. Employees who are 17 years of age may drive automobiles or trucks on public roadways only if—

(A) such driving is restricted to daylight hours;

(B) the employee holds a State license valid for the type of driving involved in the job performed and has no records of any moving violation at the time of hire;

(C) the employee has successfully completed a State approved driver education course;

(D) the automobile or truck is equipped with a seat belt for the driver and any passengers and the employee's employer has instructed the employee that the seat belts must be used when driving the automobile or truck;

(E) the automobile or truck does not exceed 6,000 pounds of gross vehicle weight;

(F) such driving does not involve—

(i) the towing of vehicles;

(ii) route deliveries or route sales;

(iii) the transportation for hire of property, goods, or passengers;

(iv) urgent, time-sensitive deliveries;

(v) more than two trips away from the primary place of employment in any single day for the purpose of delivering goods of the employee's employer to a customer (other than urgent, time-sensitive deliveries);

(vi) more than two trips away from the primary place of employment in any single day for the purpose of transporting passengers (other than employees of the employer);

(vii) transporting more than three passengers (including employees of the employer); or

(viii) driving beyond a 30 mile radius from the employee's place of employment; and

(G) such driving is only occasional and incidental to the employee's employment.

For purposes of subparagraph (G), the term "occasional and incidental" is no more than one-third of an employee's worktime in any workday and no more than 20 percent of an employee's worktime in any workweek.

(7)(A)(i) Subject to subparagraph (B), in the administration and enforcement of the child labor provisions of this Act, it shall not be considered oppressive child labor for a new entrant into the workforce to be employed inside or outside places of business where machinery is used to process wood products.

(ii) In this paragraph, the term "new entrant into the workforce" means an individual who—

(I) is under the age of 18 and at least the age of 14, and

(II) by statute or judicial order is exempt from compulsory school attendance beyond the eighth grade.

(B) The employment of a new entrant into the workforce under subparagraph (A) shall be permitted—

(i) if the entrant is supervised by an adult relative of the entrant or is supervised by an adult member of the same religious sect or division as the entrant;

(ii) if the entrant does not operate or assist in the operation of power-driven woodworking machines;

(iii) if the entrant is protected from wood particles or other flying debris within the workplace by a barrier appropriate to the potential hazard of such wood particles or flying debris or by maintaining a sufficient distance from machinery in operation; and

(iv) if the entrant is required to use personal protective equipment to prevent exposure to excessive levels of noise and saw dust.

(d) **Delivery of newspapers and wreath making**. The provisions of sections 206, 207, and 212 of this title shall not apply with respect to any employee engaged in the delivery of newspapers to the consumer or to any home worker engaged in the making of wreaths composed principally of natural holly, pine, cedar, or other evergreens (including the harvesting of the evergreens or other forest products used in making such wreaths).

(e) **Maximum hours requirements and minimum wage employees.** The provisions of section 207 of this title shall not apply with respect to employees for whom the Secretary of Labor is authorized to establish minimum wage rates as provided in section 206(a)(3) of this title, except with respect to employees for whom such rates are in effect; and with respect to such employees the Secretary may make rules and regulations providing reasonable limitations and allowing reasonable variations, tolerances, and exemptions to and from any or all of the provisions of section 207 of this title if he shall find, after a public hearing on the matter, and taking into account the factor set forth in section 206(a)(3) of this title, that economic conditions warrant such action.

(f) **Employment in foreign countries and certain United States territories**. The provisions of sections 206, 207, 211 and 212 of this title shall not apply with respect to any employee whose services during the workweek are performed in a workplace within a foreign country or within territory under the jurisdiction of the United States other than the following: a State of the United States; the District of Columbia; Puerto Rico; the Virgin Islands; outer Continental Shelf lands defined in the Outer Continental Shelf Lands Act [ch. 345, 67 Stat. 462] [43 U.S.C. §§ 1331 et seq.]; American Samoa; Guam; Wake Island; Eniwetok Atoll; Kwajalein Atoll; and Johnston Island.

(g) Certain employment in retail or service establishments, agriculture. The exemption from section 206 of this title provided by paragraph (6) of subsection (a) of this section shall not apply with respect to any employee employed by an establishment (1) which controls, is controlled by, or is under common control with, another establishment the activities of which are not related for a common business purpose to, but materially support the activities of the establishment employing such employee; and (2) whose annual gross volume of sales made or business done, when combined with the annual gross volume of sales made or business done by each establishment which controls, is controlled by, or is under common control with, the establishment employing such employee, exceeds $10,000,000 (exclusive of excise taxes at the retail level which are separately stated).

(h) Maximum hour requirement: fourteen workweek limitation. The provisions of section 207 of this title shall not apply for a period or periods of not more than fourteen workweeks in the aggregate in any calendar year to any employee who—

(1) is employed by such employer—

(A) exclusively to provide services necessary and incidental to the ginning of cotton in an establishment primarily engaged in the ginning of cotton;

(B) exclusively to provide services necessary and incidental to the receiving, handling, and storing of raw cotton and the compressing of raw cotton when performed at a cotton warehouse or compress-warehouse facility, other than one operated in conjunction with a cotton mill, primarily engaged in storing and compressing;

(C) exclusively to provide services necessary and incidental to the receiving, handling, storing, and processing of cottonseed in an establishment primarily engaged in the receiving, handling, storing, and processing of cottonseed; or

(D) exclusively to provide services necessary and incidental to the processing of sugar cane or sugar beets in an establishment primarily engaged in the processing of sugar cane or sugar beets; and

(2) receives for—

(A) such employment by such employer which is in excess of ten hours in any workday, and

(B) such employment by such employer which is in excess of forty-eight hours in any workweek, compensation at a rate not less than one and one-half times the regular rate at which he is employed.

Any employer who receives an exemption under this subsection shall not be eligible for any other exemption under this section or section 207 of this title.

(i) Cotton ginning. The provisions of section 207 of this title shall not apply for a period or periods of not more than fourteen workweeks in the aggregate in any period of fifty-two consecutive weeks to any employee who—

(1) is engaged in the ginning of cotton for market in any place of employment located in a county where cotton is grown in commercial quantities; and

(2) receives for any such employment during such work weeks—

(A) in excess of ten hours in any workday, and

(B) in excess of forty-eight hours in any workweek, compensation at a rate not less than one and one-half times the regular rate at which he is employed. No week included in any fifty-two week period for purposes of the preceding sentence may be included for such purposes in any other fifty-two week period.

(j) Process of sugar beets, sugar beet molasses, or sugar cane. The provisions of section 207 of this title shall not apply for a period or periods of not more than fourteen workweeks in the aggregate in any period of fifty-two consecutive weeks to any employee who—

(1) is engaged in the processing of sugar beets, sugar beet molasses, or sugar cane into sugar (other than refined sugar) or syrup; and

(2) receives for any such employment during such work weeks—

(A) in excess of ten hours in any workday, and

(B) in excess of forty-eight hours in any workweek, compensation at a rate not less than one and one-half times the regular rate at which he is employed. No week included in any fifty-two week period for purposes of the preceding sentence may be included for such purposes in any other fifty-two week period.

§ 214. Employment under special certificates

(a) Learners, apprentices, messengers. The Secretary, to the extent necessary in order to prevent curtailment of opportunities for employment, shall by regulations or by orders provide for the employment of learners, of apprentices, and of messengers employed primarily in delivering letters and messages, under special certificates issued pursuant to regulations of the Secretary, at such wages lower than the minimum wage applicable under section 206 of this title and subject to such limitations as to time, number, proportion, and length of service as the Secretary shall prescribe.

(b) Students

(1)(A) The Secretary, to the extent necessary in order to prevent curtailment of opportunities for employment, shall by special certificate issued under a regulation or order provide, in accordance with subparagraph (B), for the employment, at a wage rate not less than 85 per centum of the otherwise applicable wage rate in effect under section 206 of this title or not less than $1.60 an hour, whichever is the higher, of full-time students (regardless of age but in compliance with applicable child labor laws) in retail or service establishments.

(B) Except as provided in paragraph (4)(B), during any month in which full-time students are to be employed in any retail or service establishment under certificates issued under this subsection the proportion of student hours of employment to the total hours of employment of all employees in such establishment may not exceed—

(i) in the case of a retail or service establishment whose employees (other than employees engaged in commerce or in the production of goods for commerce) were covered by this chapter before the effective date of the Fair Labor Standards Amendments of 1974—

(I) the proportion of student hours of employment to the total hours of employment of all employees in such establishment for the corresponding month of the immediately preceding twelve-month period,

(II) the maximum proportion for any corresponding month of student hours of employment to the total hours of employment of all employees in such establishment applicable to the issuance of certificates under this section at any time before the effective date of the Fair Labor Standards Amendments of 1974 for the employment of students by such employer, or

(III) a proportion equal to one-tenth of the total hours of employment of all employees in such establishment, whichever is greater;

(ii) in the case of retail or service establishment whose employees (other than employees engaged in commerce or in the production of goods for commerce) are covered for the first time on or after the effective date of the Fair Labor Standards Amendments of 1974—

(I) the proportion of hours of employment of students in such establishment to the total hours of employment of all employees in such establishment for the corresponding month of the twelve-month period immediately prior to the effective date of such Amendments,

(II) the proportion of student hours of employment to the total hours of employment of all employees in such establishment for the corresponding month of the immediately preceding twelve-month period, or

(III) a proportion equal to one-tenth of the total hours of employment of all employees in such establishment, whichever is greater; or

(iii) in the case of a retail or service establishment for which records of student hours worked are not available, the proportion of student hours of employment to the total hours of employment of all employees based on the practice during the immediately preceding twelve-month period in (I) similar establishments of the same employer in the same general metropolitan area in which such establishment is located, (II) similar establishments of the same or nearby communities if such establishment is not in a metropolitan area, or (III) other establishments of the same general character operating in the community or the nearest comparable community.

For purpose of clauses (i), (ii), and (iii) of this subparagraph, the term "student hours of employment" means hours during which students are employed in a retail or service establishment under certificates issued under this subsection.

(2) The Secretary, to the extent necessary in order to prevent curtailment of opportunities for employment, shall by special certificate issued under a regulation or order provide for the employment, at a wage rate not less than 85 per centum of the wage rate in effect under section 206(a)(5) of this title or not less than $1.30 an hour, whichever is the higher, of full-time students (regardless of age but in compliance with applicable child labor laws) in any occupation in agriculture.

(3) The Secretary, to the extent necessary in order to prevent curtailment of opportunities for employment, shall by special certificate issued under a regulation or order provide for the employment by an institution of higher education, at a wage rate not less than 85

per centum of the otherwise applicable wage rate in effect under section 206 of this title or not less than $1.60 an hour, whichever is the higher, of full-time students (regardless of age but in compliance with applicable child labor laws) who are enrolled in such institution. The Secretary shall by regulation prescribe standards and requirements to insure that this paragraph will not create a substantial probability of reducing the full-time employment opportunities of persons other than those to whom the minimum wage rate authorized by this paragraph is applicable.

(4)(A) A special certificate issued under paragraph (1), (2), or (3) shall provide that the student or students for whom it is issued shall, except during vacation periods, be employed on a part-time basis and not in excess of twenty hours in any workweek.

(B) If the issuance of a special certificate under paragraph (1) or (2) for an employer will cause the number of students employed by such employer under special certificates issued under this subsection to exceed six, the Secretary may not issue such a special certificate for the employment of a student by such employer unless the Secretary finds employment of such student will not create a substantial probability of reducing the full-time employment opportunities of persons other than those employed under special certificates issued under this subsection. If the issuance of a special certificate under paragraph (1) or (2) for an employer will not cause the number of students employed by such employer under special certificates issued under this subsection to exceed six—

(i) the Secretary may issue a special certificate under paragraph (1) or (2) for the employment of a student by such employer if such employer certifies to the Secretary that the employment of such student will not reduce the full- time employment opportunities of persons other than those employed under special certificates issued under this subsection, and

(ii) in the case of an employer which is a retail or service establishment, subparagraph (B) of paragraph (1) shall not apply with respect to the issuance of special certificates for such employer under such paragraph.

The requirement of this subparagraph shall not apply in the case of the issuance of special certificates under paragraph (3) for the employment of full-time students by institutions of higher education; except that if the Secretary determines that an institution of higher education is employing students under certificates issued under paragraph (3) but in violation of the requirements of that paragraph or of regulations issued thereunder, the requirements of this subparagraph shall apply with respect to the issuance of special certificates under paragraph (3) for the employment of students by such institution.

(C) No special certificate may be issued under this subsection unless the employer for whom the certificate is to be issued provides evidence satisfactory to the Secretary of the student status of the employees to be employed under such special certificate.

(D) To minimize paperwork for, and to encourage, small businesses to employ students under special certificates issued under paragraphs (1) and (2), the Secretary shall, by regulation or order, prescribe a simplified application form to be used by employers in applying for such a certificate for the employment of not more than six full-time students. Such an application shall require only—

(i) a listing of the name, address, and business of the applicant employer,

(ii) a listing of the date the applicant began business, and

(iii) the certification that the employment of such full-time students will not reduce the full-time employment opportunities of persons other than persons employed under special certificates.

(c) Handicapped workers.

(1) The Secretary, to the extent necessary to prevent curtailment of opportunities for employment, shall by regulation or order provide for the employment, under special certificates, of individuals (including individuals employed in agriculture) whose earning or productive capacity is impaired by age, physical or mental deficiency, or injury, at wages which are—

(A) lower than the minimum wage applicable under section 206 of this title,

(B) commensurate with those paid to no handicapped workers, employed in the vicinity in which the individuals under the certificates are employed, for essentially the same type, quality, and quantity of work, and

(C) related to the individual's productivity.

(2) The Secretary shall not issue a certificate under paragraph (1) unless the employer provides written assurances to the Secretary that—

(A) in the case of individuals paid on an hourly rate basis, wages paid in accordance with paragraph (1) will be reviewed by the employer at periodic intervals at least once every six months, and

(B) wages paid in accordance with paragraph (1) will be adjusted by the employer at periodic intervals, at least once each year, to reflect changes in the prevailing wage paid to experienced no handicapped individuals employed in the locality for essentially the same type of work.

(3) Notwithstanding paragraph (1), no employer shall be permitted to reduce the hourly wage rate prescribed by certificate under this subsection in effect on June 1, 1986, of any handicapped individual for a period of two years from such date without prior authorization of the Secretary.

(4) Nothing in this subsection shall be construed to prohibit an employer from maintaining or establishing work activities centers to provide therapeutic activities for handicapped clients.

(5)(A) Notwithstanding any other provision of this subsection, any employee receiving a special minimum wage at a rate specified pursuant to this subsection or the parent or guardian of such an employee may petition the Secretary to obtain a review of such special minimum wage rate. An employee or the employee's parent or guardian may file such a petition for and in behalf of the employee or in behalf of the employee and other employees similarly situated. No employee may be a party to any such action unless the employee or the employee's parent or guardian gives consent in writing to become such a party and such consent is filed with the Secretary.

(B) Upon receipt of a petition filed in accordance with subparagraph (A), the Secretary within ten days shall assign the petition to an administrative law judge appointed pursuant to section 3105 of Title 5. The administrative law judge shall conduct a hearing on the record in accordance with section 554 of Title 5 with respect to such petition within thirty days after assignment.

(C) In any such proceeding, the employer shall have the burden of demonstrating that the special minimum wage rate is justified as necessary in order to prevent curtailment of opportunities for employment.

(D) In determining whether any special minimum wage rate is justified pursuant to subparagraph (C), the administrative law judge shall consider—

(i) the productivity of the employee or employees identified in the petition and the conditions under which such productivity was measured; and

(ii) the productivity of other employees performing work of essentially the same type and quality for other employers in the same vicinity.

(E) The administrative law judge shall issue a decision within thirty days after the hearing provided for in subparagraph (B). Such action shall be deemed to be a final agency action unless within thirty days the Secretary grants a request to review the decision of the administrative law judge. Either the petitioner or the employer may request review by the Secretary within fifteen days of the date of issuance of the decision by the administrative law judge.

(F) The Secretary, within thirty days after receiving a request for review, shall review the record and either adopt the decision of the administrative law judge or issue exceptions. The decision of the administrative law judge, together with any exceptions, shall be deemed to be a final agency action.

(G) A final agency action shall be subject to judicial review pursuant to chapter 7 of Title 5. An action seeking such review shall be brought within thirty days of a final agency action described in subparagraph (F).

(d) Employment by schools. The Secretary may by regulation or order provide that sections 206 and 207 of this title shall not apply with respect to the employment by any elementary or secondary school of its students if such employment constitutes, as determined under regulations prescribed by the Secretary, an integral part of the regular education program provided by such school and such employment is in accordance with applicable child labor laws.

§ 215. Prohibited acts; prima facie evidence

(a) After the expiration of one hundred and twenty days from June 25, 1938, it shall be unlawful for any person—

(1) to transport, offer for transportation, ship, deliver, or sell in commerce, or to ship, deliver, or sell with knowledge that shipment or delivery or sale thereof in commerce is intended, any goods in the production of which any employee was employed in violation of section 206 or section 207 of this title, or in violation of any regulation or order of the Administrator issued under section 214 of this title; except that no provision of this chapter shall impose any liability upon any common carrier for the transportation in commerce in the regular course of its business of any goods not produced by such common carrier, and no provision of this chapter shall excuse any common carrier from its obligation to accept any goods for transportation; and except that any such transportation, offer, shipment, delivery, or sale of such goods by a purchaser who acquired them in good faith in reliance on written assurance from the producer that the goods were produced in compliance with the requirements of this chapter, and who acquired such goods for value without notice of any such violation, shall not be deemed unlawful;

(2) to violate any of the provisions of section 206 or section 207 of this title, or any of the provisions of any regulation or order of the Administrator issued under section 214 of this title;

(3) to discharge or in any other manner discriminate against any employee because such employee has filed any complaint or instituted or caused to be instituted any proceeding under or related to this chapter, or has testified or is about to testify in any such proceeding, or has served or is about to serve on an industry committee;

(4) to violate any of the provisions of section 212 of this title;

(5) to violate any of the provisions of section 211(c) of this title, or any regulation or order made or continued in effect under the provisions of section 211(d) of this title, or to make any statement, report, or record filed or kept pursuant to the provisions of such section or of any regulation or order thereunder, knowing such statement, report, or record to be false in a material respect.

(b) For the purposes of subsection (a)(1) of this section proof that any employee was employed in any place of employment where goods shipped or sold in commerce were produced, within ninety days prior to the removal of the goods from such place of employment, shall be prima facie evidence that such employee was engaged in the production of such goods.

§ 216. Penalties.

(a) Any person who willfully violates any of the provisions of section 215 of this title shall upon conviction thereof be subject to a fine of not more than $10,000, or to imprisonment for not more than six months, or both. No person shall be imprisoned under this subsection except for an offense committed after the conviction of such person for a prior offense under this subsection.

(b) Any employer who violates the provisions of section 206 or section 207 of this title shall be liable to the employee or employees affected in the amount of their unpaid minimum wages, or their unpaid overtime compensation, as the case may be, and in an additional equal amount as liquidated damages. Any employer who violates the provisions of section 215(a)(3) of this title shall be liable for such legal or equitable relief as may be appropriate to effectuate the purposes of section 215(a)(3) of this title, including without limitation employment, reinstatement, promotion, and the payment of wages lost and an additional equal amount as liquidated damages. An action to recover the liability prescribed in either of the preceding sentences may be maintained against any employer (including a public agency) in any Federal or State court of competent jurisdiction by any one or more employees for and in behalf of himself or themselves and other employees similarly situated. No employee shall be a party plaintiff to any such action unless he gives his consent in writing to become such a party and such consent is filed in the court in which such action is brought. The court in such action shall, in addition to any judgment awarded to the plaintiff or plaintiffs, allow a reasonable attorney's fee to be paid by the defendant, and costs of the action. The right provided by this subsection to bring an action by or on behalf of any employee, and the right of any employee to become a party plaintiff to any such action, shall terminate upon the filing of a complaint by the Secretary of Labor in an action under section 217 of this title in which (1) restraint is sought of any further delay in the payment of unpaid minimum wages, or the amount of unpaid overtime compensation, as the case may be, owing to such employee under section 206 or section 207 of this title by an employer liable therefor under the provisions of this subsection or (2) legal or equitable relief is sought as a result of alleged violations of section 215(a)(3) of this title.

(c) The Secretary is authorized to supervise the payment of the unpaid minimum wages or the unpaid overtime compensation owing to any employee or employees under section 206 or section 207 of this title, and the agreement of any employee to accept such payment shall upon payment in full constitute a waiver by such employee of any right he may have under subsection (b) of this section to such unpaid minimum wages or unpaid overtime compensation and an additional equal amount as liquidated damages. The Secretary may bring an action in any court of competent jurisdiction to recover the amount of unpaid minimum wages or overtime compensation and an equal amount as liquidated damages. The right provided by subsection (b) of this section to bring an action by or on behalf of any employee to recover the liability specified in the first sentence of such subsection and of any employee to become a party plaintiff to any such action shall terminate upon the filing of a complaint by the Secretary in an action under this subsection in which a recovery is sought of unpaid minimum wages or unpaid overtime compensation under sections 206 and 207 of this title or liquidated or other damages provided by this subsection owing to such employee by an employer liable under the provisions of subsection (b) of this section, unless such action is dismissed without prejudice on motion of the Secretary. Any sums thus recovered by the Secretary of Labor on behalf of an employee pursuant to this subsection shall be held in a special deposit account and shall be paid, on order of the Secretary of Labor, directly to the employee or employees affected. Any such sums not paid to an employee because of inability to do so within a period of three years shall be covered into the Treasury of the United States as miscellaneous receipts. In determining when an action is commenced by the Secretary of Labor under this subsection for the purposes of the statutes of limitations provided in section 255(a) of this title, it shall be considered to be commenced in the case of any individual claimant on the date when the complaint is filed if he is specifically named as a party plaintiff in the complaint, or if his name did not so appear, on the subsequent date on which his name is added as a party plaintiff in such action. . . .

(e)(1)(A) Any person who violates the provisions of sections 212 or 213(c) of this title, relating to child labor, or any regulation issued pursuant to such sections, shall be subject to a civil penalty not to exceed—

(i) $11,000 for each employee who was the subject of such a violation; or

(ii) $50,000 with regard to each such violation that causes the death or serious injury of any employee under the age of 18 years, which penalty may be doubled where the violation is a repeated or willful violation.

(B) For purposes of subparagraph (A), the term "serious injury" means—

(i) permanent loss or substantial impairment of one of the senses (sight, hearing, taste, smell, tactile sensation);

(ii) permanent loss or substantial impairment of the function of a bodily member, organ, or mental faculty, including the loss of all or part of an arm, leg, foot, hand or other body part; or

(iii) permanent paralysis or substantial impairment that causes loss of movement or mobility of an arm, leg, foot, hand or other body part.

(2) Any person who repeatedly or willfully violates section 206 or 207, relating to wages, shall be subject to a civil penalty not to exceed $1,100 for each such violation.

(3) In determining the amount of any penalty under this subsection, the appropriateness of such penalty to the size of the business of the person charged and the gravity of the violation shall be considered. The amount of any penalty under this subsection, when finally determined, may be—

(A) deducted from any sums owing by the United States to the person charged;

(B) recovered in a civil action brought by the Secretary in any court of competent jurisdiction, in which litigation the Secretary shall be represented by the Solicitor of Labor; or

(C) ordered by the court, in an action brought for a violation of section 215(a)(4) of this title or a repeated or willful violation of section 215(a)(2) of this title, to be paid to the Secretary.

(4) Any administrative determination by the Secretary of the amount of any penalty under this subsection shall be final, unless within 15 days after receipt of notice thereof by certified mail the person charged with the violation takes exception to the determination that the violations for which the penalty is imposed occurred, in which event final determination of the penalty shall be made in an administrative

proceeding after opportunity for hearing in accordance with section 554 of Title 5, and regulations to be promulgated by the Secretary.

(5) Except for civil penalties collected for violations of section 212 of this title, sums collected as penalties pursuant to this section shall be applied toward reimbursement of the costs of determining the violations and assessing and collecting such penalties, in accordance with the provision of section 9a of this title. Civil penalties collected for violations of section 212 of this title shall be deposited in the general fund of the Treasury.

§ 217. Injunction proceedings. The district courts, together with the United States District Court for the District of the Canal Zone, the District Court of the Virgin Islands, and the District Court of Guam shall have jurisdiction, for cause shown, to restrain violations of section 215 of this title, including in the case of violations of section 215(a)(2) of this title the restraint of any withholding of payment of minimum wages or overtime compensation found by the court to be due to employees under this chapter (except sums which employees are barred from recovering, at the time of the commencement of the action to restrain the violations, by virtue of the provisions of section 255 of this title).

§ 218. Relation to other laws.

(a) No provision of this chapter or of any order thereunder shall excuse noncompliance with any Federal or State law or municipal ordinance establishing a minimum wage higher than the minimum wage established under this chapter or a maximum workweek lower than the maximum workweek established under this chapter, and no provision of this chapter relating to the employment of child labor shall justify noncompliance with any Federal or State law or municipal ordinance establishing a higher standard than the standard established under this chapter. No provision of this chapter shall justify any employer in reducing a wage paid by him which is in excess of the applicable minimum wage under this chapter, or justify any employer in increasing hours of employment maintained by him which are shorter than the maximum hours applicable under this chapter.

§ 219. Separability of provisions. If any provision of this chapter or the application of such provision to any person or circumstance is held invalid, the remainder of this chapter and the application of such provision to other persons or circumstances shall not be affected thereby.

PORTAL-TO-PORTAL ACT

29 U.S.C. §§ 251-262

§ 255. Statute of limitations. Any action . . . for unpaid minimum wages, unpaid overtime compensation, or liquidated damages, under the Fair Labor Standards Act of 1938, as amended [29 U.S.C. §§ 201 et seq.] . . . —

(a). . . may be commenced within two years after the cause of action accrued, and every such action shall be forever barred unless commenced within two years after the cause of action accrued, except that a cause of action arising out of a willful violation may be commenced within three years after the cause of action accrued. . . .

§ 256. Determination of commencement of future actions. In determining when an action is commenced for the purposes of section 255 of this title, an action . . . shall be considered to be commenced on the date when the complaint is filed; except that in the case of a collective or class action instituted under the Fair Labor Standards Act of 1938, as amended, or the Bacon-Davis Act, it shall be considered to be commenced in the case of any individual claimant—

(a) on the date when the complaint is filed, if he is specifically named as a party plaintiff in the complaint and his written consent to become a party plaintiff is filed on such date in the court in which the action is brought; or

(b) if such written consent was not so filed or if his name did not so appear – on the subsequent date on which such written consent is filed in the court in which the action was commenced.

§ 259. Reliance in future on administrative rulings

(a) [N]o employer shall be subject to any liability or punishment for or on account of the failure of the employer to pay minimum wages or overtime compensation under the Fair Labor Standards Act of 1938, as amended . . . if he pleads and proves that the act or omission complained of was in good faith in conformity with and in reliance on any written administrative regulation, order, ruling, approval, or interpretation of the agency of the United States [authorized to administer the statute] or any administrative practice or enforcement policy of such agency with respect to the class of employers to which he belonged. Such a defense, if established, shall be a bar to the action or proceeding, notwithstanding that after such act or omission, such administrative regulation, order, ruling, approval, interpretation practice, or enforcement policy is modified or rescinded or is determined by judicial authority to be invalid or of no legal effect. . . .

§ **260. Liquidated damages.** In any action . . . to recover unpaid minimum wages, unpaid overtime compensation, or liquidated damages, under the Fair Labor Standards Act of 1938, as amended [29 U.S.C. §§ 201 et seq.], if the employer shows to the satisfaction of the court that the act or omission giving rise to such action was in good faith and that he had reasonable grounds for believing that his act or omission was not a violation of the Fair Labor Standards Act of 1938, as amended, the court may, in its sound discretion, award no liquidated damages or award any amount thereof not to exceed the amount specified in section 216 of this title.

WAGE PAYMENT LAWS — SELECTED EXCERPTS

A. FORM OF PAYMENT

MICHIGAN WAGES AND FRINGE BENEFITS ACT

Mich. Comp. Laws Ann. § 408.476

§ 408.476. Payment of wages in United States currency, negotiable check or draft; deposit of employee's wages in savings institution

(1) An employer or agent of an employer may pay wages to an employee by any of the following methods that protect the earnings of the employee from garnishment as required by 15 USC 1673, to the same extent they would be exempt while held by the employer:

(a) Payment in United States currency.

(b) Payment by a negotiable check or draft payable on presentation at a financial institution or other established place of business without discount in United States currency.

(c) Direct deposit or electronic transfer to the employee's account at a financial institution.

(d) Issuing a payroll debit card that complies with subsection (6).

(2) Except as provided in section 283a of the management and budget act, 1984 PA 431, MCL 18.1283a, or in subsection (4), an employer or agent of an employer shall not deposit an employee's wages in a bank, credit union, or savings and loan association without the full, free, and written consent of the employee, obtained without intimidation, coercion, or fear of discharge or reprisal for refusal to permit the deposit.

(3) Except as provided in subsection (4), an employer or agent of an employer shall not issue a payroll debit card to an employee under subsection (1)(d) without the full, free, and written consent of the employee, obtained without intimidation, coercion, or fear of discharge or reprisal for refusal to accept the payroll debit card. However, an employer paying wages by payroll debit card to 1 or more of its employees as of January 1, 2005 may pay wages to any of its employees by payroll debit card without obtaining the consent described in this act.

(4) An employer or agent of an employer may require employees to receive wages only through direct deposit or a payroll debit card that complies with subsection (6) if the employer has provided the employee with all of the following:

(a) A written form that allows the employee the option to receive wages either by direct deposit to the employee's account at a financial institution or through a payroll debit card.

(b) A statement indicating that, except for an employee currently paid by direct deposit or any employee of an employer paying wages by payroll debit card to 1 or more of its employees on January 1, 2005, failure to return the form within 30 days with the account information necessary to implement direct deposit will be presumed to indicate consent to receiving wages through a payroll debit card. If an employee is currently paid by direct deposit, the method of payment shall not be changed to payroll debit card without written consent of the employee.

(c) Written disclosure of all of the following concerning the payroll debit card:

(i) The terms and conditions for use, including an itemized list of any and all fees.

(ii) The methods for accessing wages without charge.

(iii) A statement that, if the payroll debit card is used outside of the specified network of automatic teller machines, both the payroll card issuer and the operator of the automatic teller machine may impose charges.

(iv) The methods to obtain free balance inquiries.

(v) The employee's right to elect to change the method of receiving wages at any time, as provided in subsection (5).

(vi) That the payroll debit card does not provide access to a savings or checking account.

(5) An employee may request a change in the method of receiving wages established under subsection (4) at any time. The employer shall take no longer than 1 pay period to implement the change after the employer receives the request and any information necessary to implement the request. An employer shall allow an employee to select payment by direct deposit or electronic transfer under subsection (4) freely, without intimidation, coercion, or fear of discharge or reprisal for the choice.

(6) An employer shall not pay wages by issuing a payroll debit card unless the payroll debit card has all of the following characteristics:

(a) Entitles the employee to make at least 1 withdrawal or transfer without charge each pay period, but not more frequently than once per week, for any amount the employee elects up to the balance accessible through the card.

(b) Allows no changes in fees or terms of service unless the employee has received a written notice at least 21 days in advance of the date that the changes take effect identifying the changes.

(c) Provides a method for the employee to make an unlimited number of balance inquiries without charge, either electronically or by telephone.

(d) Is not linked to any form of credit, including a loan against future pay or a cash advance on future pay.

(7) An employer shall not require an employee to pay any fees or costs incurred by the employer in connection with paying wages or establishing a process for paying wages by a method described in subsection (1)(c) or (d).

(8) As used in this section:

(a) "Federally insured financial institution" means a state or nationally chartered bank or a state or federally chartered savings and loan association, savings bank, or credit union whose deposits are insured by an agency of the United States government and which maintains a principal office or branch office located in this state under the laws of this state or the United States.

(b) "Payroll debit card" means a stored-value card issued by a federally insured financial institution that provides an employee with immediate access for withdrawal or transfer of his or her wages through a network of automatic teller machines. The term includes a card commonly known as a payroll debit card, payroll card, and paycard.

B. PAY PERIODS

MASSACHUSETTS WAGE PAYMENT LAW

Mass. Gen. Laws Ann. ch.149, § 148

§ 148. Payment of wages; commissions; exemption by contract; persons deemed employers; provision for cashing check or draft; violation of statute. Every person having employees in his service shall pay weekly or bi-weekly each such employee the wages earned by him to within six days of the termination of the pay period during which the wages were earned if employed for five or six days in a calendar week, or to within seven days of the termination of the pay period during which the wages were earned if such employee is employed seven days in a calendar week, or in the case of an employee who has worked for a period of less than five days, hereinafter called a casual employee, shall, within seven days after the termination of such period, pay the wages earned by such casual employee during such period, but any employee leaving his employment shall be paid in full on the following regular pay day, and, in the absence of a regular pay day, on the following Saturday; and any employee discharged from such employment shall be paid in full on the day of his discharge, or in Boston as soon as the laws requiring pay rolls, bills and accounts to be certified shall have been complied with; and the commonwealth, its departments, officers, boards and commissions shall so pay every mechanic, workman and laborer employed by it or them, and every person employed in any other capacity by it or them in any penal or charitable institution, and every county and city shall so pay every employee engaged in its business the wages or salary earned by him, unless such mechanic, workman, laborer or employee requests in writing to be paid in a different manner; and every town shall so pay each employee engaged in its business if so required by him; but an employee absent from his regular place of labor at a time fixed for payment shall be paid thereafter on demand; provided, however, that the department of public utilities, after hearing, may authorize a railroad corporation or a parlor or sleeping car corporation to pay the wages of any of its employees less frequently than weekly, if such employees prefer less frequent payments, and if their interests and the interests of the public will not suffer thereby; and provided, further, that employees engaged in a bona fide executive, administrative or professional capacity as determined by the attorney general and employees whose salaries are regularly paid on a weekly basis or at a weekly rate for a work week of substantially the same number of hours from week to week may be paid bi-weekly or semi-monthly unless such employee elects at his own option to be paid monthly; and provided, further, that employees engaged in agricultural work may be paid their wages monthly; in either case, however, failure by a railroad corporation or a parlor or sleeping car corporation to pay its employees their wages as authorized by the said department, or by an employer of employees engaged in agricultural work to pay monthly the wages of his or her employees, shall be deemed a violation of this section; and provided, further, that an employer may make payment of wages prior to the time that they are required to be paid under the provisions of this section, and such wages together with any wages already earned and due under this section, if any, may be paid weekly, bi-weekly, or semi-monthly to a salaried employee, but in no event shall wages remain unpaid by an employer for more than six days from the termination of the pay period in which such wages were earned by the employee. For the purposes of this section the words salaried employee shall mean any employee whose remuneration is on a weekly, bi-weekly, semi-monthly, monthly or annual basis, even though deductions or increases may be made in a particular pay period. The word "wages" shall include any holiday or vacation payments due an employee under an oral or written agreement. An employer, when paying an employee his wage, shall furnish to such employee a suitable pay slip, check stub or envelope showing the name of the employer, the name of the employee, the day, month, year, number of hours worked, and hourly rate, and the amounts of deductions or increases made for the pay period.

Compensation paid to public and non-public school teachers shall be deemed to be fully earned at the end of the school year, and proportionately earned during the school year; provided, however, that payment of such compensation may be deferred to the extent that equal payments may be established for a 12 month period including amounts payable in July and August subsequent to the end of the school year.

Every railroad corporation shall furnish each employee with a statement accompanying each payment of wages listing current accrued total earnings and taxes and shall also furnish said employee with each such payment a listing of his daily wages and the method used to compute such wages.

This section shall apply, so far as apt, to the payment of commissions when the amount of such commissions, less allowable or authorized deductions, has been definitely determined and has become due and payable to such employee, and commissions so determined and due such employees shall be subject to the provisions of section one hundred and fifty.

This section shall not apply to an employee of a hospital which is supported in part by contributions from the commonwealth or from any city or town, nor to an employee of an incorporated hospital which provides treatment to patients free of charge, or which is conducted as a public charity, unless such employee requests such hospital to pay him weekly. This section shall not apply to an employee of a co-operative association if he is a shareholder therein, unless he requests such association to pay him weekly, nor to casual employees as hereinbefore defined employed by the commonwealth or by any county, city or town.

No person shall by a special contract with an employee or by any other means exempt himself from this section or from section one hundred and fifty. The president and treasurer of a corporation and any officers or agents having the management of such corporation shall be deemed to be the employers of the employees of the corporation within the meaning of this section. Every public officer whose duty it is to pay money, approve, audit or verify pay rolls, or perform any other official act relative to payment of any public employees, shall be deemed to be an employer of such employees, and shall be responsible under this section for any failure to perform his official duty relative to the payment of their wages or salaries, unless he is prevented from performing the same through no fault on his part.

Any employer paying wages to an employee by check or draft shall provide for such employee such facilities for the cashing of such check or draft at a bank or elsewhere, without charge by deduction from the face amount thereof or otherwise, as shall be deemed by the attorney general to be reasonable. The state treasurer may in his discretion in writing exempt himself and any other public officer from the provisions of this paragraph.

An employer paying his employees on a weekly basis on July first, nineteen hundred and ninety-two shall, prior to paying said employees on a bi-weekly basis, provide each employee with written notice of such change at least ninety days in advance of the first such bi-weekly paycheck.

Whoever violates this section shall be punished or shall be subject to a civil citation or order as provided in section 27C [providing for civil penalties of up to $25,000 per violation and criminal penalties of up to $50,000 and two years imprisonment.].

IOWA WAGE PAYMENT COLLECTION LAW

Iowa Code Ann. § 91A.3

§ 91A.3. Mode of payment–bond of farm labor contractor

1. An employer shall pay all wages due its employees, less any lawful deductions specified in section 91A.5, at least in monthly, semimonthly, or biweekly installments on regular paydays which are at consistent intervals from each other and which are designated in advance by the employer. However,

if any of these wages due its employees are determined on a commission basis, the employer may, upon agreement with the employee, pay only a credit against such wages. If such credit is paid, the employer shall, at regular intervals, pay any difference between a credit paid against wages determined on a commission basis and such wages actually earned on a commission basis. These regular intervals shall not be separated by more than twelve months. A regular payday shall not be more than twelve days, excluding Sundays and legal holidays, after the end of the period in which the wages were earned. An employer and employee may, upon written agreement which shall be maintained as a record, vary the provisions of this subsection.

2. The wages paid under subsection 1 shall be paid in United States currency or by written instrument issued by the employer and negotiable on demand at full face value for such currency, unless the employee has agreed in writing to receive a part of or all wages in kind or in other form.

3. a. The wages paid under subsection 1 shall be paid at the employee's normal place of employment during normal employment hours or at a place and hour mutually agreed upon by the employer and employee, or the employee may elect to have the wages sent for direct deposit, on or by the regular payday of the employee, into a financial institution designated by the employee. Upon written request by the employee, wages due may be sent to the employee by mail. The employer shall maintain a copy of the request for as long as it is effective and for at least two years thereafter. An employee hired on or after July 1, 2005, may be required, as a condition of employment, to participate in direct deposit of the employee's wages in a financial institution of the employee's choice unless any of the following conditions exist:

(1) The costs to the employee of establishing and maintaining an account for purposes of the direct deposit would effectively reduce the employee's wages to a level below the minimum wage provided under section 91D.1.

(2) The employee would incur fees charged to the employee's account as a result of the direct deposit.

(3) The provisions of a collective bargaining agreement mutually agreed upon by the employer and the employee organization prohibit the employer from requiring an employee to sign up for direct deposit as a condition of hire.

b. If the employer fails to pay an employee's wages on or by the regular payday in accordance with this subsection, the employer is liable for the amount of any overdraft charge if the overdraft is created on the employee's account because of the employer's failure to pay the wages on or by the regular payday. The overdraft charges may be the basis for a claim under section 91A.10 and for damages under section 91A.8.

4. The wages paid under subsection 1 may be delivered to a designee of the employee who is so designated in writing or may be sent to the employee by any reasonable means requested by the employee in writing. A designee under this subsection shall not also be an assignee or buyer of wages under section 539.4 nor a garnisher of the employee under chapter 642, unless the designee complies with the provisions of section 539.4 and chapter 642.

5. If an employee is absent from the normal place of employment on the regular payday, the employer shall, upon demand of the employee made within the first seven days following the regular payday, pay the wages, less any lawful deductions specified in section 91A.5, which were due on that regular payday. However, if demand is not made within this seven-day period, the employer shall, upon demand of the employee, pay the wages which were due on a regular payday within the first seven days following the day on which demand is made.

6. Expenses by the employee which are authorized by the employer and incurred by the employee shall either be reimbursed in advance of expenditure or be reimbursed not later than thirty days after the employee's submission of an expense claim. If the employer refuses to pay all or part of each claim, the employer shall submit to the employee a written justification of such refusal within the same time period in which expense claims are paid under this subsection. . . .

C. WAGE PAYMENTS AFTER SEPARATION FROM EMPLOYMENT

UTAH PAYMENT OF WAGES LAW
Utah Code Ann. § 34-28-5

§ 34-28-5. Separation from payroll – Resignation – Cessation because of industrial dispute

(1)(a) Whenever an employer separates an employee from the employer's payroll the unpaid wages of the employee become due immediately, and the employer shall pay the wages to the employee within 24 hours of the time of separation at the specified place of payment.

(b)(i) In the case of failure to pay wages due an employee within 24 hours of written demand, the wages of the employee shall continue from the date of demand until paid, but in no event to exceed 60 days, at the same rate which the employee received at the time of separation.

(ii) The employee may recover the penalty thus accruing to the employee in a civil action. This action must be commenced within 60 days from the date of separation.

(iii) An employee who has not made a written demand for payment is not entitled to any penalty under Subsection (1)(b).

(2) If an employee does not have a written contract for a definite period and resigns the employee's employment, the wages earned and unpaid together with any deposit hold by the employer and properly belonging to the resigned employee for the performance of the employee's employment duties become due and payable on the next regular payday.

(3) If work ceases as the result of an industrial dispute, the wages earned and unpaid at the time of this cessation become due and payable at the next regular payday, as provided in Section 34-28-3, including, without abatement or reduction, all amounts due all persons whose work has been suspended as a result of the industrial dispute, together with any deposit or other guaranty held by the employer for the faithful performance of the duties of the employment.

(4) This section does not apply to the earnings of a sales agent employed on a commission basis who has custody of accounts, money, or goods of the sales agent's principal if the net amount due the agent is determined only after an audit or verification of sales, accounts, funds, or stocks.

NEVADA PAYMENT AND COLLECTION OF WAGES AND OTHER BENEFITS LAW

Nev. Rev. Stat. §§ 608.020 to 608.040

§ 608.020. Discharge of employee: Immediate payment. Whenever an employer discharges an employee, the wages and compensation earned and unpaid at the time of such discharge shall become due and payable immediately.

§ 608.030. Payment of employee who resigns or quits his employment. Whenever an employee resigns or quits his employment, the wages and compensation earned and unpaid at the time of his resignation or quitting must be paid no later than:

1. The day on which he would have regularly been paid the wages or compensation; or

2. Seven days after he resigns or quits, whichever is earlier.

§ 608.040. Penalty for failure to pay discharged or quitting employee

1. If an employer fails to pay:

(a) Within 3 days after the wages or compensation of a discharged employee becomes due; or

(b) On the day the wages or compensation is due to an employee who resigns or quits, the wages or compensation of the employee continues at the same rate from the day he resigned, quit or was discharged until paid or for 30 days, whichever is less.

2. Any employee who secretes or absents himself to avoid payment of his wages or compensation, or refuses to accept them when fully tendered to

him, is not entitled to receive the payment thereof for the time he secretes or absents himself to avoid payment.

COLORADO WAGE PAYMENT LAW

Colo. Rev. Stat. § 8-4-109

§ 8-4-109. Termination of employment — payments required — civil penalties payments to surviving spouse or heir

(1)(a) When an interruption in the employer-employee relationship by volition of the employer occurs, the wages or compensation for labor or service earned, vested, determinable, and unpaid at the time of such discharge is due and payable immediately. If at such time the employer's accounting unit, responsible for the drawing of payroll checks, is not regularly scheduled to be operational, then the wages due the separated employee shall be made available to the employee no later than six hours after the start of such employer's accounting unit's next regular workday; except that, if the accounting unit is located off the work site, the employer shall deliver the check for wages due the separated employee no later than twenty-four hours after the start of such employer's accounting unit's next regular workday to one of the following locations selected by the employer:

(I) The work site;

(II) The employer's local office; or

(III) The employee's last-known mailing address.

(b) When an employee quits or resigns such employee's employment, the wages or compensation shall become due and payable upon the next regular payday. When a separation of employment occurs, the employer shall make the separated employee's check for wages due available at one of the following locations selected by the employer:

(I) The work site;

(II) The employer's local office; or

(III) The employee's last-known mailing address.

(2) Nothing in subsection (1) of this section shall limit the right of an employer to set off any deductions pursuant to section 8-4-105 owing by the employee to the employer or require the payment at the time employment is severed of compensation not yet fully earned under the compensation agreement between the employee and employer, whether written or oral

(3)(a) If an employer refuses to pay wages or compensation in accordance with subsection (1) of this section, the employee or his or her designated agent shall make a written demand for the payment within sixty days after the date of separation and shall state in the demand where such payment can be received.

(a.5) If the employer disputes the amount of wages or compensation claimed by an employee under this article and if, within fourteen days after the employee's demand, the employer makes a legal tender of the amount that the employer in good faith believes is due, the employer shall not be liable for any penalty unless, in a legal action, the employee recovers a greater sum than the amount so tendered.

(b) If an employee's earned, vested, and determinable wages or compensation are not mailed to the place of receipt specified in a demand for payment and postmarked within fourteen days after the receipt of such demand, the employer shall be liable to the employee for the wages or compensation, and a penalty of the sum of the following amounts of wages or compensation due or, if greater, the employee's average daily earnings for each day, not to exceed ten days, until such payment or other settlement satisfactory to the employee is made:

(I) One hundred twenty-five percent of that amount of such wages or compensation up to and including seven thousand five hundred dollars; and

(II) Fifty percent of that amount of such wages or compensation that exceed seven thousand five hundred dollars.

(c) If the employee can show that the employer's failure to pay is willful, the penalty required under paragraph (b) of this subsection (3) shall increase by fifty percent. Evidence that a judgment has, within the previous five years, ben entered against the employer for failure to pay wages or compensation shall be admissible as evidence of willful conduct.

(d) The daily earnings penalty shall not begin to accrue until the employer receives the written demand set forth in paragraph (a) of this subsection (3). The employee or his or her designated agent may commence a civil action to recover the penalty set forth in this subsection (3). Any employee or his or her designated agent who has not made a written demand for the payment within sixty days after the date of separation or who has otherwise not been available to receive payment shall not be entitled to any such penalty under this subsection (3). A payment under this subsection (3) shall be made in the form of a check draft or voucher in the name of the employee.

(4) If, at the time of the death of any employee, an employer is indebted to the employee for wages or compensation, and no personal representative of the employee's estate has been appointed, such employer shall pay the amount earned, vested, and determinable to the deceased employee's surviving spouse. If there is no surviving spouse, the employer shall pay the amount due to the deceased employee's next legal heir upon the request of such heir. If a personal representative for the employee has been appointed and is known to the employer prior to payment of the amount due to the spouse or other legal

heir, the employer shall pay the amount due to such personal representative upon the request of such representative. The employer shall require proof of a claimant's relationship to the deceased employee by affidavit and require such claimant to acknowledge the receipt of any payment in writing. Any payments made by the employer pursuant to the provisions of this section shall operate as a full and complete discharge of the employer's indebtedness to the extent of the payment, and no employer shall thereafter be liable to the deceased employee's estate or to the deceased employee's personal representative. Any amounts received by a surviving spouse or legal heir shall be considered in diminution of the allowance to the spouse or legal heir pursuant to the "Colorado Probate Code", articles 10 to 17 of title 15, C.R.S. Nothing in this section shall create a substantive right that does not exist in any agreement between the employer and the employee.

D. DEDUCTIONS FROM WAGES

OREGON WAGE PAYMENT LAW

Or. Rev. Stat. §§ 652.610, 652.615

§ 652.610. Itemized statement of amounts and purposes of deductions required

(1) All persons, firms, partnerships, associations, cooperative associations, corporations, municipal corporations, the state and its political subdivisions, except the federal government and its agencies, employing, in this state, during any calendar month one or more persons, and withholding for any purpose any sum of money from the wages, salary or commission earned by an employee, shall provide the employee on regular paydays with a statement sufficiently itemized to show the amount and purpose of the deductions made during the respective period of service that the payment covers.

(2) The itemized statement shall be furnished to the employee at the time payment of wages, salary or commission is made, and may be attached to or be a part of the check, draft, voucher or other instrument by which payment is made, or may be delivered separately from the instrument.

(3) An employer may not withhold, deduct or divert any portion of an employee's wages unless:

(a) The employer is required to do so by law;

(b) The deductions are authorized in writing by the employee, are for the employee's benefit and are recorded in the employer's books;

(c) The employee has voluntarily signed an authorization for a deduction for any other item, provided that the ultimate recipient of the money withheld is not the employer and that the deduction is recorded in the employer's books;

(d) The deduction is authorized by a collective bargaining agreement to which the employer is a party;

(e) The deduction is authorized under ORS 18.736; or

(f) The deduction is made from the payment of wages upon termination of employment and is authorized pursuant to a written agreement between the employee and employer for the repayment of a loan made to the employee by the employer, if all of the following conditions are met:

(A) The employee has voluntarily signed the agreement;

(B) The loan was paid to the employee in cash or other medium permitted by ORS 652.110;

(C) The loan was made solely for the employee's benefit and was not used, either directly or indirectly, for any purpose required by the employer or connected with the employee's employment with the employer;

(D) The amount of the deduction at termination of employment does not exceed the amount permitted to be garnished under ORS 18.385; and

(E) The deduction is recorded in the employer's books.

(4) When an employer deducts an amount from an employee's wages as required or authorized by law or agreement, the employer shall pay the amount deducted to the appropriate recipient as required by the law or agreement. The employer shall pay the amount deducted within the time required by the law or the agreement or, if the time for payment is not specified by the law or agreement, within seven days after the date the wages from which the deductions are made are due. Failure to pay the amount as required constitutes an unlawful deduction.

(5) This section does not:

(a) Prohibit the withholding of amounts authorized in writing by the employee to be contributed by the employee to charitable organizations, including contributions made pursuant to ORS 243.666 and 663.110;

(b) Prohibit deductions by check-off dues to labor organizations or service fees when the deductions are not otherwise prohibited by law; or

(c) Diminish or enlarge the right of any person to assert and enforce a lawful setoff or counterclaim or to attach, take, reach or apply an employee's compensation on due legal process.

§ 652.615. Remedy for violation of ORS 652.610. There is hereby created a private cause of action for a violation of ORS 652.610(3) for actual damages or $200, whichever is greater. In any such action the court may award to the prevailing party, in addition to costs and disbursements, reasonable attorney fees.

NEW JERSEY WAGE PAYMENT LAW

N.J. Stat. Ann. § 34:11-4.4

§ 34:11-4.4. Withholding or diverting wages

No employer may withhold or divert any portion of an employee's wages unless:

a. The employer is required or empowered to do so by New Jersey or United States law; or

b. The amounts withheld or diverted are for:

(1) Contributions authorized either in writing by employees, or under a collective bargaining agreement, to employee welfare, insurance, hospitalization, medical or surgical or both, pension, retirement, and profit-sharing plans, and to plans establishing individual retirement annuities on a group or individual basis, as defined by section 408(b) of the Federal Internal Revenue Code of 1986 (26 U.S.C. § 408(b)) or individual retirement accounts at any State or federally chartered bank, savings bank, or savings and loan association, as defined by section 408(a) of the Federal Internal Revenue Code of 1986 (26 U.S.C. § 408(a)), for the employee, his spouse or both.

(2) Contributions authorized either in writing by employees, or under a collective bargaining agreement, for payment into company-operated thrift plans; or security option or security purchase plans to buy securities of the employing corporation, an affiliated corporation, or other corporations at market price or less, provided such securities are listed on a stock exchange or are marketable over the counter.

(3) Payments authorized by employees for payment into employee personal savings accounts, such as payments to a credit union, savings fund society, savings and loan or building and loan association; and payments to banks for Christmas, vacation, or other savings funds; provided all such deductions are approved by the employer.

(4) Payments for company products purchased in accordance with a periodic payment schedule contained in the original purchase agreement; payments for employer loans to employees, in accordance with a periodic payment schedule contained in the original loan agreement; payments for safety equipment; payments for the purchase of United States Government bonds; payments to correct payroll errors; and payments of costs and related fees for the replacement of employee identification, which is used to allow employees access to sterile or secured areas of airports, in accordance with a fee schedule described in any airline media plan approved by the federal Transportation Security Administration; provided all such deductions are approved by the employer.

(5) Contributions authorized by employees for organized and generally recognized charities; provided the deductions for such contributions are approved by the employer.

(6) Payments authorized by employees or their collective bargaining agents for the rental of work clothing or uniforms or for the laundering or dry cleaning of work clothing or uniforms; provided the deductions for such payments are approved by the employer.

(7) Labor organization dues and initiation fees, and such other labor organization charges permitted by law.

(8) Contributions authorized in writing by employees, pursuant to a collective bargaining agreement, to a political committee, continuing political committee, or both, as defined in section 3 of P.L. 1973, c. 83 (C. 19:44A-3), established by the employees' labor union for the purpose of making contributions to aid or promote the nomination, election or defeat of any candidate for a public office of the State or of a county, municipality or school district or the passage or defeat of any public question, subject to the conditions specified in section 2 of P.L. 1991, c. 190 (C. 34:11-4.4a).

(9) Contributions authorized in writing by employees to any political committee or continuing political committee, other than a committee provided for in paragraph (8) of this subsection, for the purpose of making contributions to aid or promote the nomination, election or defeat of any candidate for a public office of the State or of a county, municipality or school district or the passage or defeat of any public question, subject to the conditions specified in section 2 of P.L. 1991, c. 190 (C. 34:11-4.4a); in making a payroll deduction pursuant to this paragraph the administrative expenses incurred by the employer shall be borne by such committee, at the option of the employer.

(10) Payments authorized by employees for employer-sponsored programs for the purchase of insurance or annuities on a group or individual basis, if otherwise permitted by law.

(11) Such other contributions, deductions and payments as the Commissioner of Labor may authorize by regulation as proper and in conformity with the intent and purpose of this act, if such deductions are approved by the employer.

E. ASSIGNMENTS OF WAGES

MARYLAND ASSIGNMENT OF WAGES LAW

Md. Com. Law Code Ann. §§ 15-302 to 15-305

§ 15-302. Requisites of assignment

(a) **In general**. An assignment of wages is not valid unless:

(1) The assignment is:

(i) In writing;

(ii) Signed and acknowledged by the assignor before a notary public in and for the county where he resides; and

(iii) Entered the same day on the docket of the court by the clerk; and

(2) Within three days from the execution and acknowledgment of the assignment, a copy of the assignment with the certificate of acknowledgment is served on the assignor's employer in the same manner as the Maryland Rules provide for service of a summons.

(b) Assignment by a married assignor. An assignment of wages by a married person is not valid unless also executed and acknowledged by the assignor's spouse in the manner required by subsection (a) of this section.

(c) Certain assignments void. An assignment of wages to be earned in whole or in part more than six months after the making of the assignment is void.

§ 15-303. Proof of service on employer

(a) Admission in writing. Proof of the service made in accordance with § 15-302(a)(2) of this subtitle shall be by written admission of the assignor's employer on the original assignment.

(b) Filing. Within two days from the date of service, the original assignment with the employer's written admission shall be filed with the clerk of the court.

§ 15-304. Affidavit as to interest on loan. The assignor's acknowledgment of assignment shall include his affidavit stating that he has not paid and will not pay directly or indirectly on any sum borrowed, an effective rate of simple interest, as defined in § 12-101 of this article, of more than 6 percent per annum.

§ 15-305. Injunction

(a) When injunction permitted. If an assignee files or threatens to file an action to enforce any assignment of wages which does not comply with any provision of this subtitle, on petition of the assignor or his employer, a court of equity may enjoin the threatened or attempted enforcement of the assignment.

(b) Remedies at law and in equity may coexist. The fact that a petitioner has a complete and adequate remedy at law does not constitute a defense to the maintenance of an action in equity to enjoin the threatened or attempted enforcement of the assignment.

DISTRICT OF COLUMBIA WAGE ASSIGNMENT LAW

D.C. Code Ann. § 28-2305

§ 28-2305. Contract to assign future salary or wages

(a) A contract attempting or purporting to transfer or assign salary or wages to be earned by the debtor, if made in the District of Columbia, is invalid and contrary to public policy and unenforceable, and if made outside the District of Columbia, is unenforceable in any court within the District of Columbia.

(b) Whoever, in the District of Columbia demands or receives from a debtor an assignment of salary or wages to be thereafter earned by the debtor, or notifies an employer that he holds an assignment of such salary or wages, upon conviction shall be fined not more than $200 or imprisoned not more than sixty days. Prosecutions under this subsection shall be upon information filed in the Criminal Division of the Superior Court of the District of Columbia by the Attorney General of the District of Columbia or one of his assistants.

CALIFORNIA ASSIGNMENT OF WAGES STATUTE

Cal. Labor Code § 300

§ 300. Validity and exceptions

(a) As used in this section, the phrase "assignment of wages" includes the sale or assignment of, or giving of an order for, wages or salary but does not include an order or assignment made pursuant to Chapter 8 (commencing with Section 5200) of Part 5 of Division 9 of the Family Code or Section 3088 of the Probate Code.

(b) No assignment of wages, earned or to be earned, is valid unless all of the following conditions are satisfied:

(1) The assignment is contained in a separate written instrument, signed by the person by whom the wages or salary have been earned or are to be earned, and identifying specifically the transaction to which the assignment relates.

(2) Where the assignment is made by a married person, the written consent of the spouse of the person making the assignment is attached to the assignment. No such consent is required of any married person (A) after entry of a judgment decreeing a legal separation from such person's spouse or (B) if the married person and the spouse of the married person are living separate and apart after entry of an interlocutory judgment of dissolution of their marriage, if a written statement by the person making the assignment, setting forth such facts, is attached to or included in the assignment.

(3) Where the assignment is made by a minor, the written consent of a parent or guardian of the minor is attached to the assignment.

(4) Where the assignment is made by a person who is unmarried or who is an adult or who is both unmarried and an adult, a written statement by the person making the assignment, setting forth such facts, is attached to or included in the assignment.

(5) No other assignment exists in connection with the same transaction or series of transactions and a written statement by

the person making the assignment to that effect is attached to or included in the assignment.

(6) A copy of the assignment and of the written statement provided for in paragraphs (2), (4), and (5), authenticated by a notary public, is filed with the employer, accompanied by an itemized statement of the amount then due to the assignee.

(7) At the time the assignment is filed with the employer, no other assignment of wages of the employee is subject to payment and no earnings withholding order against the employee's wages or salary is in force.

(c) Under any assignment of wages, a sum not to exceed 50 per centum of the assignor's wages or salary shall be withheld by, and be collectible from, the assignor's employer at the time of each payment of such wages or salary.

(d) The employer is entitled to rely upon the statements of fact in the written statement provided for in paragraphs (2), (4), and (5) of subdivision (b), without the necessity of inquiring into the truth thereof, and the employer shall incur no liability whatsoever by reason of any payments made by the employer to an assignee under any assignment in reliance upon the facts so stated.

(e) An assignment of wages to be earned is revocable at any time by the maker thereof. Any power of attorney to assign or collect wages or salary is revocable at any time by the maker thereof. No revocation of such an assignment or power of attorney is effective as to the employer until the employer receives written notice of revocation from the maker.

(f) No assignment of wages, earned or to be earned, is valid under any circumstances if the wages or salary earned or to be earned are paid under a plan for payment at a central place or places established under the provisions of Section 204a.

(g) This section does not apply to deductions which the employer may be requested by the employee to make for the payment of life, retirement, disability or unemployment insurance premiums, for the payment of taxes owing from the employee, for contribution to funds, plans or systems providing for death, retirement, disability, unemployment, or other benefits, for the payment for goods or services furnished by the employer to the employee or the employee's family at the request of the employee, or for charitable, educational, patriotic or similar purposes.

(h) No assignment of wages is valid unless at the time of the making thereof, such wages or salary have been earned, except for necessities of life and then only to the person or persons furnishing such necessities of life directly and then only for the amount needed to furnish such necessities.

F. GARNISHMENT

NEBRASKA GARNISHMENT LAW

Neb. Rev. Stat. § 25-1558

§ 25-1558. Wages; subject to garnishment; amount; exceptions

(1) Except as provided in subsection (2) of this section, the maximum part of the aggregate disposable earnings of an individual for any work week which is subject to garnishment shall not exceed the lesser of the following amounts:

(a) Twenty-five percent of his or her disposable earnings for that week;

(b) The amount by which his or her disposable earnings for that week exceed thirty times the federal minimum hourly wage prescribed by section 206(a)(1) of Title 29 of the United States Code in effect at the time earnings are payable; or

(c) Fifteen percent of his or her disposable earnings for that week, if the individual is a head of a family.

(2) The restrictions of subsection (1) of this section shall not apply in the case of:

(a) Any order of any court for the support of any persons;

(b) Any order of any court of bankruptcy under Chapter XIII of the Bankruptcy Act; or

(c) Any debt due for any state or federal tax.

(3) No court shall make, execute, or enforce any order or process in violation of this section. The exemptions allowed in this section shall be granted to any person so entitled without any further proceedings.

(4) For the purposes of this section:

(a) Earnings shall mean compensation paid or payable by an employer to an employee for personal services, whether denominated as wages, salary, commission, bonus, or otherwise, and includes periodic payments pursuant to a pension or retirement program;

(b) Disposable earnings shall mean that part of the earnings of any individual remaining after the deduction from those earnings of any amounts required by law to be withheld;

(c) Garnishment shall mean any legal or equitable procedure through which the earnings of any individual are required to be withheld for payment of any debt; and

(d) Head of a family shall mean an individual who actually supports and maintains one or more individuals who are closely connected with him or her by blood relationship, relationship by marriage, by adoption, or by guardianship, and whose right to exercise family control and provide for the dependent individuals is based upon some moral or legal obligation.

(5) Every assignment, sale, transfer, pledge, or mortgage of the wages or salary of an individual which is exempted by this section, to the extent of the exemption provided by this section, shall be void and unenforceable by any process of law.

(6) No employer shall discharge any employee by reason of the fact that his or her earnings have been subjected to garnishment for any one indebtedness.

(7) In the case of earnings for any pay period other than a week, the Commissioner of Labor shall by regulation prescribe a multiple of the federal minimum hourly wage equivalent in effect to that set forth in this section.

FEDERAL UNEMPLOYMENT TAX ACT

26 U.S.C. § 3301-3311

§ 3301. Rate of tax. There is hereby imposed on every employer (as defined in section 3306(a)) for each calendar year an excise tax, with respect to having individuals in his employ, equal to—

(1) 6.2 percent in the case of calendar years 1988 through 2010 and the first 6 months of calendar year 2011; or

(2) 6.0 percent in the case of the remainder of calendar year 2011 and each calendar year thereafter;

of the total wages (as defined in section 3306(b)) paid by him during the calendar year (or portion of the calendar year) with respect to employment (as defined in section 3306(c)).

§ 3302. Credits against tax

(a) Contributions to state unemployment funds

(1) The taxpayer may, to the extent provided in this subsection and subsection (c), credit against the tax imposed by section 3301 the amount of contributions paid by him into an unemployment fund maintained during the taxable year under the unemployment compensation law of a State which is certified as provided in section 3304 for the 12-month period ending on October 31 of such year. . . .

(b) Additional credit. In addition to the credit allowed under subsection (a), a taxpayer may credit against the tax imposed by section 3301 for any taxable year an amount, with respect to the unemployment compensation law of each State certified as provided in section 3303 for the 12-month period ending on October 31 of such year, or with respect to any provisions thereof so certified, equal to the amount, if any, by which the contributions required to be paid by him with respect to the taxable year were less than the contributions such taxpayer would have been required to pay if throughout the taxable year he had been subject under such State law to the highest rate applied thereunder in such 12-month period to any person having individuals in his employ, or to a rate of 5.4%, whichever rate is lower.

(c) Limit on total credits

(1) The total credits allowed to a taxpayer under this section shall not exceed 90 percent of the tax against which such credits are allowable. . . .

§ 3304. Approval of State laws

(a) Requirements. The Secretary of Labor shall approve any State law submitted to him, within 30 days of such submission, which he finds provides that—

(1) all compensation is to be paid through public employment offices or such other agencies as the Secretary of Labor may approve; . . .

(3) all money received in the unemployment fund shall (except for refunds of sums erroneously paid into such fund and except for refunds paid in accordance with the provisions of section 3305(b)) immediately upon such receipt be paid over to the Secretary of the Treasury to the credit of the Unemployment Trust Fund established by section 904 of the Social Security Act (42 U.S.C. 1104); . . .

(5) compensation shall not be denied in such State to any otherwise eligible individual for refusing to accept new work under any of the following conditions:

(A) if the position offered is vacant due directly to a strike, lockout, or other labor dispute;

(B) if the wages, hours, or other conditions of the work offered are substantially less favorable to the individual than those prevailing for similar work in the locality;

(C) if as a condition of being employed the individual would be required to join a company union or to resign from or refrain from joining any bona fide labor organization;

(6)(A) compensation is payable on the basis of service to which section 3309(a)(1) applies, in the same amount, on the same terms, and subject to the same conditions as compensation payable on the basis of other service subject to such law; except that —

(i) with respect to services in an instructional, research, or principal administrative capacity for an educational institution to which section 3309(a)(1) applies, compensation shall not be payable based on such services for any week commencing during the period between two successive academic years or terms (or, when an agreement provides instead for a similar period between two regular but not successive terms, during such period) to any individual if such individual performs such services in the first of such academic years (or terms) and if there is a contract or reasonable assurance that such individual will perform services in any such capacity for any educational institution in the second of such academic years or terms, . . .

(9)(A) compensation shall not be denied or reduced to any individual solely because he files a claim in another State (or a contiguous country with which the United States has an agreement with respect to unemployment compensation) or because he resides in another State (or such a contiguous country) at the time he files a claim for unemployment compensation;

(B) the State shall participate in any arrangements for the payment of compensation on the basis of combining an individual's wages and employment covered under the State law with his wages and employment covered under the unemployment compensation law of other States which are approved by the Secretary of Labor in consultation with the State unemployment compensation agencies as reasonably calculated to assure the prompt and full payment of compensation in such situations. Any such arrangement shall include provisions for (i) applying the base period of a single State law to a claim involving the combining of an individual's wages and employment covered under two or more State laws, and (ii) avoiding duplicate use of wages and employment by reason of such combining;

(10) compensation shall not be denied to any individual by reason of cancellation of wage credits or total reduction or his benefit rights for any cause other than discharge for misconduct connected with his work, fraud in connection with a claim for compensation, or receipt of disqualifying income;

(11) extended compensation shall be payable as provided by the Federal-State Extended Unemployment Compensation Act of 1970.

(12) no person shall be denied compensation under such State law solely on the basis of pregnancy or termination of pregnancy;

(13) compensation shall not be payable to any individual on the basis of any services, substantially all of which consist of participating in sports or athletic events or training or preparing to so participate, for any week which commences during the period between two successive sport seasons (or similar periods) if such individual performed such services in the first of such seasons (or similar periods) and there is a reasonable assurance that such individual will perform such services in the later of such seasons (or similar periods);

(14)(A) compensation shall not be payable on the basis of services performed by an alien unless such alien is an individual who was lawfully admitted for permanent residence at the time such services were performed, was lawfully present for purposes of performing such services, or was permanently residing in the United States under color of law at the time such services were performed (including an alien who was lawfully present in the United States as a result of the application of the provisions of section 212(d)(5) of the Immigration and Nationality Act). . . ;

(15)(A) subject to subparagraph (B), the amount of compensation payable to an individual for any week which begins after March 31, 1980, and which begins in a period with respect to which such individual is receiving a governmental or other pension, retirement or retired pay, annuity, or any other similar periodic payment which is based on the previous work of such individual shall be reduced (but not below zero) by an amount equal to the amount of such pension, retirement or retired pay, annuity, or other payment, which is reasonably attributable to such week except that—

(i) the requirements of this paragraph shall apply to any pension, retirement or retired pay, annuity, or similar periodic payment only if—

(I) such pension, retirement or retired pay, annuity, or similar payment is under a plan maintained (or contributed to) by a base period employer or chargeable employer (as determined under applicable law), and

(II) in the case of such a payment not made under the Social Security Act or the Railroad Retirement Act of 1974 (or the corresponding provisions of prior law), services performed for such employer by the individual after the beginning of the base period (or remuneration for such services) affect eligibility for, or increase the amount of, such pension, retirement or retired pay, annuity, or similar payment, and

(ii) the State law may provide for limitations on the amount of any such a reduction to take into account contributions made by the individual for the pension, retirement or retired pay, annuity, or other similar periodic payment. . . .

§ 3306. Definitions

(a) Employer. For purposes of this chapter—

(1) In general. The term "employer" means, with respect to any calendar year, any person who—

(A) during any calendar quarter in the calendar year or the preceding calendar year paid wages of $1,500 or more, or

(B) on each of some 20 days during the calendar year or during the preceding calendar year, each day being in a different calendar week, employed at least one individual in employment for some portion of the day.

For purposes of this paragraph, there shall not be taken into account any wages paid to, or employment of, an employee performing domestic services referred to in paragraph (3).

(2) Agricultural labor. In the case of agricultural labor, the term "employer" means, with respect to any calendar year, any person who—

(A) during any calendar quarter in the calendar year or the preceding calendar year paid wages of $20,000 or more for agricultural labor, or

(B) on each of some 20 days during the calendar year or during the preceding calendar year, each day being in a different calendar week, employed at least 10 individuals in employment in agricultural labor for some portion of the day.

(3) Domestic service. In the case of domestic service in a private home, local college club, or local chapter of a college fraternity or sorority, the term "employer" means, with respect to any calendar year, any person who during any calendar quarter in the calendar year or the preceding calendar year paid wages in cash of $1,000 or more for such service.

(4) Special rule. A person treated as an employer under paragraph (3) shall not be treated as an employer with respect to wages paid for any service other than domestic service referred to in paragraph (3) unless such person is treated as an employer under paragraph (1) or (2) with respect to such other service. . . .

§ 3310. Judicial review

(a) In general. Whenever under section 3303(b) or section 3304(c) the Secretary of Labor makes a finding pursuant to which he is required to withhold a certification with respect to a State under such section, such State may, within 60 days after the Governor of the State has been notified of such action, file with the United States court of appeals for the circuit in which such State is located or with the United States Court of Appeals for the District of Columbia, a petition for review of such action. A copy of the petition shall be forthwith transmitted by the clerk of the court to the Secretary of Labor. The Secretary of Labor thereupon shall file in the court the record of the proceedings on which he based his action as provided in section 2112 of title 28 of the United States Code.

. . .

NORTH CAROLINA EMPLOYMENT SECURITY LAW

N.C. Gen. Stat. §§ 96-1 through 96-29

§ 96-9. Contributions

(b) Rate of Contributions

(1) **Beginning Rate**. The standard beginning rate of contributions for an employer is a percentage of wages paid by the employer during a calendar year for employment occurring during that year. The rate is [2.25% for employment occurring after 1986, 1.8% for employment occurring after 1993, and 1.2% for employment occurring after 1995].

(2) **Experience Rating**

a. **Waiting Period for Rate Reduction**. No employer's contribution rate shall be reduced below the standard rate for any calendar year until its account has been chargeable with benefits for at least 12 calendar months ending July 31 immediately preceding the computation date. . . .

b. **Credit Ratio**. The Commission shall, for each year, compute a credit reserve ratio for each employer whose account has a credit balance. An employer's credit reserve ratio shall be the quotient obtained by dividing the credit balance of the employer's account as of July 31 of each year by the total taxable payroll of the employer for the 36 calendar-month period ending June 30 preceding the computation date. Credit balance as used in this section means the total of all contributions paid and credited for all past periods in accordance with the provisions of G.S. § 96-9 (c)(1) together with all other lawful credits to the account of the employer less the total benefits charged to the account of the employer for all past periods.

c. **Debit Ratio**. The Commission shall for each year compute a debit ratio for each employer whose account shows that the total of all its contributions paid and credited for all past periods in accordance with G.S. 96-9 (c)(1) together with all other lawful credits is less than the total benefits charged to its account for all past periods. An employer's debit ratio shall be the quotient obtained by dividing the debit balance of the employer's account as of July 31 of each year by the total taxable payroll of the employer for the 36 calendar-month period ending June 30 preceding the computation date. The amount arrived at by subtracting the total amount of all contributions paid and credited for all past periods in accordance with the provisions of G.S. 96-9 (c)(1) together with all other lawful credits of the employer from the total amount of all benefits charged to the account of the employer for such periods is the employer's debit balance. . . .

(3)d. Rate schedule A, B, C, D, E, F, G, H, or I appearing on the line opposite the fund ratio in the following Fund Ratio Schedules table shall be applicable in determining and assigning each eligible employer's contribution rate for the calendar year immediately following the computation date. The fund ratio is the total amount available for benefits in the Unemployment Insurance Fund on the computation date divided by the total amount of the taxable payroll of all subject employers for the 12-month period ending June 30 preceding the computation date.

FUND RATIO SCHEDULES

When the Fund Ratio Is:

As Much As	*But Less Than*	*Applicable Schedule*
—	2.0%	A
2.0%	3.0%	B
3.0%	4.0%	C
4.0%	5.0%	D
5.0%	6.0%	E
6.0%	7.0%	F
7.0%	8.0%	G
8.0%	9.0%	H
9.0% and in excess thereof		I

. . .

d3. The standard contribution rate set by subdivision (b)(1) of this section applies to an employer unless the employer's account has a credit balance. Beginning January 1, 1999, the contribution rate of an employer whose account has a credit balance is determined in accordance with the rate set in the following Experience Rating Formula table for the applicable rate schedule. The contribution rate of an employer whose contribution rate is determined by this Experience Rating Formula table shall be reduced by (50%) for any year in which the balance in the Unemployment Insurance Fund equals or exceeds $800,000,000 on the computation date and the fund ratio determined on that date is less than 5% and shall be reduced 60% for any year in which the balance in the Unemployment Insurance Fund equals or exceeds $800,000,000 on the computation date, and the fund ratio determined on that date is 5% or more.

EXPERIENCE RATING FORMULA

When The Credit Ratio Is:

As Much As	*But Less Than*	*Rate Schedules (%)*								
		A	B	C	D	E	F	G	H	I
—	0.2%	2.16	2.16	2.16	2.16	2.00	1.84	1.68	1.52	1.36
0.2%	0.4%	2.16	2.16	2.16	2.00	1.84	1.68	1.52	1.36	1.20
0.4%	0.6%	2.16	2.16	2.00	1.84	1.68	1.52	1.36	1.20	1.04
0.6%	0.8%	2.16	2.00	1.84	1.68	1.52	1.36	1.20	1.04	0.88
0.8%	1.0%	2.00	1.84	1.68	1.52	1.36	1.20	1.04	0.88	0.72
1.0%	1.2%	1.84	1.68	1.52	1.36	1.20	1.04	0.88	0.72	0.64
1.2%	1.4%	1.68	1.52	1.36	1.20	1.04	0.88	0.72	0.64	0.56
1.4%	1.6%	1.52	1.36	1.20	1.04	0.88	0.72	0.64	0.56	0.48
1.6%	1.8%	1.36	1.20	1.04	0.88	0.72	0.64	0.56	0.48	0.40
1.8%	2.0%	1.20	1.04	0.88	0.72	0.64	0.56	0.48	0.40	0.32
2.0%	2.2%	1.04	0.88	0.72	0.64	0.56	0.48	0.40	0.32	0.24
2.2%	2.4%	0.88	0.72	0.64	0.56	0.48	0.40	0.32	0.24	0.16
2.4%	2.6%	0.72	0.64	0.56	0.48	0.40	0.32	0.24	0.16	0.12
2.6%	2.8%	0.64	0.56	0.48	0.40	0.32	0.24	0.16	0.12	0.08
2.8%	3.0%	0.56	0.48	0.40	0.32	0.24	0.16	0.12	0.08	0.07
3.0%	3.2%	0.48	0.40	0.32	0.24	0.16	0.12	0.08	0.07	0.06
3.2%	3.4%	0.40	0.32	0.24	0.16	0.12	0.08	0.07	0.06	0.06
3.4%	3.6%	0.32	0.24	0.16	0.12	0.08	0.07	0.06	0.06	0.05
3.6%	3.8%	0.24	0.15	0.12	0.08	0.07	0.06	0.06	0.05	0.04
3.8%	4.0%	0.16	0.12	0.08	0.07	0.06	0.06	0.05	0.04	0.03
4.0% and over		0.00	0.00	0.00	0.00	0.00	0.00	0.00	0.00	0.00

e. For any calendar year that the training and reemployment contribution in G.S. 96-6.1 applies, each employer whose account as of any computation date occurring after August 1, 1964, shows a debit balance shall be assigned the rate of contributions appearing on the line opposite his debit ratio as set forth in the following Rate Schedule for Overdrawn Accounts:

RATE SCHEDULE FOR OVERDRAWN ACCOUNTS BEGINNING WITH THE CALENDAR YEAR 1978

When The Debit Ratio Is:

As Much As	*But Less Than*	*Assigned Rate*
0.0%	0.3%	2.3%
0.3	0.6	2.5
0.6	0.9	2.6
0.9	1.2	2.8
1.2	1.5	3.0
1.5	1.8	3.1
1.8	2.1	3.3
2.1	2.4	3.4
2.4	2.7	3.6
2.7	3.0	3.8
3.0	3.3	3.9
3.3	3.6	4.1
3.6	3.9	4.2
3.9	4.2	4.4
4.2	4.5	4.6
4.5	4.8	4.8
4.8	5.1	5.0
5.1	5.4	5.2
5.4 and over		5.4

. . .

(c)(2) Charging of benefit payments.

a. Benefits paid shall be allocated to the account of each base period employer in the proportion that the base period wages paid to an eligible individual in any calendar quarter by each such employer bears to the total wages paid by all base period employers during the base period, except as hereinafter provided in paragraphs b, c, and d of this subdivision, G.S. 96-9(d)(2)c, and 96-12.01G. The amount so allocated shall be multiplied by one hundred twenty percent (120%) and charged to that employer's account. Benefits paid shall be charged to employers' accounts upon the basis of benefits paid to claimants whose benefit years have expired.

b. Any benefits paid to any claimant under a claim filed for a period occurring after the date of such separations as are set forth in this paragraph and based on wages paid prior to the date of (i) the leaving of work by the claimant without good cause attributable to the employer; (ii) the discharge of claimant for misconduct in connection with his work; (iii) the discharge of the claimant for substantial fault as that term may be defined in G.S. 96-14; (iv) the discharge of the claimant solely for a bona fide inability to do the work for which he was hired but only where the claimant's period of employment was 100 days or less; (v) separations made disqualifying under G.S. 96-14(2b) and (6a); or (vi) separation due to leaving for disability or health condition; or (vii) separation of claimant solely as the result of an undue family hardship shall not be charged to the account of an employer by whom the claimant was employed at the time of such separation; provided, however, said employer promptly furnishes the Commission with such notices regarding any separation of the individual from work as are or may be required by the regulations of the Commission.

No benefit charges shall be made to the account of any employer who has furnished work to an individual who, because of the loss of employment with one or more other employers, becomes eligible for partial benefits while still being furnished work by such employer on substantially the same basis and substantially the same amount as had been made available to such individual during his base period whether the employments were simultaneous or successive; provided, that such employer makes a written request for non-charging of benefits in accordance with Commission regulations and procedures.

No benefit charges shall be made to the account of any employer for the benefit years ending on or before June 30, 1992, where benefits were paid as a result of a discharge due directly to the reemployment of a veteran mandated by the Veteran's Reemployment Rights Law, 38 USCA §2021, et seq.

No benefit charges shall be made to the account of any employer where benefits are paid as a result of a decision by an Adjudicator, Appeals Referee or the Commission if such decision to pay benefits is ultimately reversed; nor shall any such benefits paid be deemed to constitute an overpayment under G.S. 96-18(g)(2), the provisions thereof notwithstanding. Provided, an overpayment of benefits paid shall be established in order to provide for the waiting period required by G.S. 96-13(c).

c. Any benefits paid to any claimant who is attending a vocational school or training program as provided in G.S. 96-13(a)(3) shall not be charged to the account of the base period employer(s).

d. Any benefits paid to any claimant under the following conditions shall not be charged to the account of the base period employer(s):

1. The benefits are paid for unemployment due directly to a major natural disaster, and

2. The President has declared the disaster pursuant to the Disaster Relief Act of 1970, 42 USCA 4401, et seq., and

3. The benefits are paid to claimants who would have been eligible for disaster unemployment assistance under this Act, if

they had not received unemployment insurance benefits with respect to that unemployment.

. . .

§ 96-12. Benefits

(b)(1)b. An individual who is totally unemployed shall be paid the individual's weekly benefit amount. The weekly benefit amount for an individual is the amount of the high-quarter wages paid to the individual in the individual's base period, divided by 26 and, if the quotient is not a whole dollar, rounded to the next lower whole dollar. If this amount is less than fifteen dollars ($15.00), the individual is not eligible for benefits.

(2) Each August 1, the Commission shall calculate the maximum weekly benefit amount available to an individual. The maximum weekly benefit amount is sixty-six and two-thirds percent (66 2/3%) of the average weekly insured wage rounded, if the amount is not a whole dollar, to the next lower whole dollar. The maximum weekly benefit amount set on August 1 of a year applies to an individual whose benefit year begins on or after that date and before August 1 of the following year. . . .

(c) Partial Weekly Benefit. An individual who is partially unemployed or part-totally employed shall be paid a portion of the individual's weekly benefit amount. The portion payable is the difference between the individual's weekly benefit amount and any part of the wages or remuneration that is payable to the individual for a week for which benefits are claimed and that exceeds ten percent (10%) of the individual's average weekly wage in the highest quarter of the individual's base period rounded, if the amount is not a whole dollar, to the next lower whole dollar. . . .

(d) Duration of Benefits. The total benefits paid to an individual shall not be less than the minimum total benefit and shall not exceed the lesser of the maximum total benefit or the individual's total benefit amount. The total benefit amount for an individual is determined by dividing the individual's base-period wages by the individual's high-quarter wages, multiplying that quotient by eight and two thirds, rounding the result to the nearest whole number, and then multiplying the resulting amount by the individual's weekly benefit amount. The minimum total benefit for an individual is 13 times the individual's weekly benefit amount. The maximum total benefit for an individual is 26 times the individual's weekly benefit amount, unless the benefits are extended further in accordance with G.S. 96-12.01. . . .

(g) Income Tax Withholding. When an individual files a new claim for unemployment compensation, the individual shall be advised in writing at the time of filing that:

(1) Unemployment compensation is subject to federal and State individual income tax.

(2) Requirements exist pertaining to estimated tax payments.

(3) The individual may elect to have federal individual income tax deducted and withheld from the individual's payment of unemployment compensation in an amount specified in section 3402 of the Internal Revenue Code. . . .

(4) The individual may elect to have State individual income tax deducted and withheld from the individual's payment of unemployment compensation in an amount determined by the individual.

(5) The individual may change a previously elected withholding status. . . .

§ 96-13. Benefit eligibility conditions

(a) An unemployed individual shall be eligible to receive benefits with respect to any week only if the Commission finds that—

(1) The individual has registered for work at and thereafter has continued to report at an employment office as directed by the commission in accordance with such regulations as the Commission may prescribe;

(2) The Individual has made a claim for benefits in accordance with the provisions of G.S. 96-15(a);

(3) The individual is able to work, and is available for work: Provided that, unless temporarily excused by Commission regulations, no individual shall be deemed available for work unless he establishes to the satisfaction of the Commission that he is actively seeking work: Provided further, that an individual customarily employed in seasonal employment shall, during the period of nonseasonal operations, show to the satisfaction of the Commission that such individual is actively seeking employment which such individual is qualified to perform by past experience or training during such nonseasonal period: Provided further, however, that no individual shall be considered available for work for any week not to exceed two in any calendar year in which the Commission finds that his unemployment is due to a vacation. In administering this proviso, benefits shall be paid or denied on a payroll-week basis as established by the employing unit. A week of unemployment due to a vacation as provided herein means any payroll week within which the equivalent of three customary full-time working days consist of a vacation period. For the purpose of this subdivision, any unemployment which is caused by a vacation period and which occurs in the calendar year following that within which the vacation period begins shall be deemed to have occurred in the calendar year within which such vacation period begins. For purposes of this subdivision, no individual shall be deemed available for work during any week that the individual tests positive for a controlled substance if (i) the test

is a controlled substance examination administered under Article 20 of Chapter 95 of the General Statutes, (ii) the test is required as a condition of hire for a job, and (iii) the job would be suitable work for the claimant. The employer shall report to the Commission, in accordance with regulations adopted by the Commission, each claimant that tests positive for a controlled substance under this subdivision. An unemployed individual shall not be disqualified for eligibility for unemployment compensation solely on the basis that the individual is in school.

(4) No individual shall be deemed able to work under this subsection during any week for which that person is receiving or is applying for benefits under any other State or federal law based on his temporary total or permanent total disability. Provided that if compensation is denied to any individual for any week under the foregoing sentence and such individual is later determined not to be totally disabled, such individual shall be entitled to a retroactive payment of the compensation for each week for which the individual filed a timely claim for compensation and for which the compensation was denied solely by reason of the foregoing sentence.

(5) The individual has participated in reemployment services, if the Division referred the individual to these services after determining, through use of a worker profiling system, that the individual would likely exhaust regular benefits and would need reemployment services to make a successful transition to new employment, unless the individual establishes justifiable cause for failing to participate in the services.

(6) Notwithstanding any other provisions of this Chapter, an unemployed individual shall not be ineligible for unemployment compensation benefits under any provision of the Employment Security Law relating to availability for work, active search for work, or refusal to accept work solely because the individual is seeking only part-time work as defined in G.S. 96-8(29), provided that a majority of weeks of work in the individual's base period include part-time work.

(b)(1) The payment of benefits to any individual based on services for nonprofit organizations, hospitals, or State hospitals and State institutions of higher education, other institutions of higher education, or secondary schools and subdivisions of secondary schools subject to this Chapter shall be in the same manner and under the same conditions of the laws of this Chapter as applied to individuals whose benefit rights are based on other services subject to this Chapter. Except that with respect to services in the educational institutions listed above:

a. In an instructional, research, or principal administrative capacity, compensation shall not be payable based on such services for any week commencing during the period between two successive academic years or terms, or, when an agreement provides instead for a similar period between two regular but not successive terms, during that period, to any individual if he performs such services in the first of the academic years or terms and if there is a contract or reasonable assurance that the individual will perform services in any such capacity for any educational institution in the second of the academic years or terms; and,

b. In any other capacity for an educational institution:

1. Compensation shall be denied on the basis of such services for any week which commences during a period between two successive academic years or terms if the individual performs such services in the first of the academic years or terms and there is a reasonable assurance that the individual will perform such services in the second of the academic years or terms, except that

2. If compensation is denied to any individual for any week under subclause 1 and the individual was not offered an opportunity to perform such services for the educational institution for the second of the academic years or terms, the individual shall be entitled to a retroactive payment of the compensation for each week for which the individual filed a timely claim for compensation and for which compensation was denied solely by reason of subclause 1; and,

c. With respect to any services described in clause a or b, compensation payable on the basis of such services shall be denied to any individual for any week which commences during an established and customary vacation period or holiday recess, and there is a reasonable assurance that such individual will perform such services in the period immediately following the vacation period or holiday recess; and,

d. With respect to any services described in clause a or b, compensation on the basis of services in any such capacity shall be denied as specified in clauses a, b, and c. to any individual who performed such services in an educational institution while in the employ of an educational service agency, and for this purpose the term "educational service agency" means a governmental agency or governmental entity which is established and operated exclusively for the purpose of providing such services to one or more educational institutions; and,

e. With respect to any services to which G.S. 96-13(b)(1) applies, if such services are provided to or on behalf of an educational institution, compensation shall be denied under the same circumstances as described in clauses a through d.

(c) Beginning February 16, 1977, an unemployed individual shall be eligible to receive benefits with respect to any week only if the Commission finds that he has been totally, partially, or part-totally unemployed for a waiting period of one week with respect to each benefit year. No week shall be counted as a week of unemployment for waiting-period credit under this provision unless the claimant except for the provisions of this subdivision was otherwise eligible for benefits. As to claims filed on or after September 5, 1999, the waiting period for a benefit year shall not be required of any claimant if all of the following conditions are met:

(1) The benefits are to be paid for unemployment due directly to a major natural disaster.

(2) The President of the United States has declared the disaster pursuant to the Disaster Relief Act of 1970, 42 U.S.C.A. 4401, et seq.

(3) The benefits are to be paid to claimants who would have been eligible for disaster unemployment assistance if they had not been eligible to receive unemployment insurance benefits with respect to that unemployment.

(4) The claimant files for a waiver of the waiting period week within 30 days after the date of notification or mailing of the notice of the right to have the waiting period week waived. The Employment Security Commission, for good cause shown, may at any time in its discretion, with or without motion or notice, order the period enlarged if the request for an enlargement of time is made before the expiration of the period originally prescribed or as extended by a previous order. After expiration of the specified period, the Employment Security Commission may permit the act to be done where the failure to act was a result of excusable neglect.

The benefits paid as a result of the waiver of the waiting period week shall not be charged to the account or accounts of the base period employer or employers in accordance with G.S. 96-9(c)(2)d. The Employment Security Commission shall implement regulations prescribing the procedure for the waiver of the waiting period week in accordance with G.S. 96-4(b).

(c1) As to claims filed on or after January 29, 2003, the waiting period for a benefit year shall not be required of a claimant if all of the following conditions are met:

(1) The benefits are to be paid for unemployment due directly to a major industrial disaster that destroys substantially all of the physical facilities of a manufacturing plant.

(2) The Governor has acknowledged the disaster through the creation of such task forces as are needed to coordinate State assistance to the manufacturer and its employees.

(3) The Governor has issued an Executive Order directing and authorizing the Employment Security Commission to waive the waiting week for employees of the manufacturer.

(4) The Employment Security Commission shall implement regulations prescribing the procedure for the waiver of the waiting period week in accordance with G.S. 96-4(b). . . .

§ 96-14. Disqualification for benefits. An individual shall be disqualified for benefits:

(1) For the duration of his unemployment beginning with the first day of the first week after the disqualifying act occurs with respect to which week an individual files a claim for benefits if it is determined by the Commission that such individual is, at the time such claim is filed, unemployed because he left work without good cause attributable to the employer.

Where an individual is discharged or leaves work due solely to a disability incurred or other health condition, whether or not related to the work, he shall not be disqualified for benefits if the individual shows:

a. That, at the time of leaving, an adequate disability or health condition of the employee, of a minor child who is in the legally recognized custody of the individual, of an aged or disabled parent of the individual, or of a disabled member of the individual's immediate family, either medically diagnosed or otherwise shown by competent evidence, existed to justify the leaving; and

b. That, at a reasonable time prior to leaving, the individual gave the employer notice of the disability or health condition.

Where an employee is notified by the employer that such employee will be separated from employment on some future date and the employee leaves work prior to this date because of the impending separation, the employee shall be deemed to have left work voluntarily and the leaving shall be without good cause attributable to the employer. However, if the employee shows to the satisfaction of the Commission that it was impracticable or unduly burdensome for the employee to work until the announced separation date, the permanent disqualification imposed for leaving work without good cause attributable to the employer may be reduced to the greater of four weeks or the period running from the beginning of the week during which the claim for benefits was made until the end of the week of the announced separation date.

An employer's placing an individual on a bona fide disciplinary suspension of 10 or fewer consecutive calendar days shall not constitute good cause for leaving work.

(1a) Where an individual leaves work, the burden of showing good cause attributable to the employer rests on said individual, and the burden shall not be shifted to the employer.

(1b) Where an individual leaves work due solely to a unilateral and permanent reduction in work hours of more than twenty percent (20%) of the customary scheduled full-time work hours in the establishment, plant, or industry in which he was employed, said leaving shall constitute good cause attributable to the employer for leaving work. Provided however that if said reduction is temporary or was occasioned by malfeasance, misfeasance or nonfeasance on the part of the individual, such reduction in work hours shall not constitute good cause attributable to the employer for leaving work.

(1c) Where an individual leaves work due solely to a unilateral and permanent reduction in his rate of pay of more than fifteen percent (15%), said leaving shall constitute good cause attributable to the employer for leaving work. Provided however that if said reduction is temporary or was occasioned by malfeasance, misfeasance or nonfeasance on the part of the individual, such reduction in pay shall not constitute good cause attributable to the employer for leaving work.

(1d) For the purposes of this Chapter, any claimant leaving work to accompany the claimant's spouse to a new place of residence where that spouse has secured work in a location that is too far removed for the claimant reasonably to continue his or her work shall constitute good cause for leaving work. Notwithstanding the other provisions of this subdivision, any claimant leaving work to accompany the claimant's spouse to a new place of residence because the spouse has been reassigned from one military assignment to another shall be deemed good cause for leaving work. Benefits paid on the basis of this subdivision shall not be charged to the account of the employer.

(1e) For the duration of an individual's unemployment, beginning with the first day of the first week after the disqualifying act occurs with respect to which week an individual files a claim for benefits, if it is determined by the Commission that such individual is, at the time such claim is filed, unemployed because the individual, without good cause attributable to the employer and after receiving notice from the employer, refused to return to work for a former employer when recalled within four weeks from a layoff, or when recalled in any week in which the work search requirements under G.S. 96-13 have been waived. As used in this subsection, the term "layoff" means a temporary separation from work due to no work available for the individual at the time of separation from work and the individual is retained on the employer's payroll and is a continuing employee subject to recall by the employer.

(1f) For the purposes of this Chapter, any claimant's leaving work, or discharge, if the claimant has been adjudged an aggrieved party as set forth by Chapter 50B of the General Statutes or there is evidence of domestic violence, sexual offense, or stalking, or the claimant has been granted program participant status pursuant to G.S. 15C-4 as the result of domestic violence committed upon the claimant or upon a minor child with or in the custody of the claimant by a person who has or has had a familial relationship with the claimant or minor child, shall constitute good cause for leaving work. Benefits paid on the basis of this section shall be noncharged. Evidence of domestic violence, sexual offense, or stalking may include: (i) law enforcement, court, or federal agency records or files; (ii) documentation from a domestic violence or sexual assault program if the claimant is alleged to be a victim of domestic violence or sexual assault; or (iii) documentation from a religious, medical, or other professional from whom the claimant has sought assistance in dealing with the alleged domestic violence, sexual abuse, or stalking. This provision is only applicable to the claimant and claimant's spouse, parents, and children under 18 years of age, whether the relationship is a biological, step-, half-, or in-law relationship.

(1g) For purposes of this Chapter, separation or discharge solely due to an inability to accept work during a particular shift as a result of an undue family hardship shall constitute good cause for leaving work. Benefits paid on the basis of this section shall not be charged to the account of the employer.

(2) For the duration of the individual's unemployment beginning with the first day of the first week after the disqualifying act occurs with respect to which week an individual files a claim for benefits if it is determined by the Commission that such individual is, at the time such claim is filed, unemployed because he or she was discharged for misconduct connected with the work. Misconduct connected with the work is defined as conduct evincing such willful or wanton disregard of an employer's interest as is found in deliberate violations or disregard of standards of behavior which the employer has the right to expect of an employee, or in carelessness or negligence of such degree or recurrence as to manifest equal culpability, wrongful intent or evil design, or to show an intentional and substantial disregard of the employer's interests or of the employee's duties and obligations to the employer.

"Discharge for misconduct with the work" as used in this section is defined to include but not be limited to separation initiated by an employer for reporting to work significantly impaired by alcohol or illegal drugs; consuming alcohol or illegal drugs on employer's premises; conviction by a court of competent jurisdiction for manufacturing, selling, or distribution of a controlled substance punishable under G.S. 90-95(a)(1) or G.S. 90-95(a)(2) while in the employ of said employer. This phrase does not include discharge or employer-initiated separation of a severely disabled veteran, as defined in G.S. 96–8, for acts or omissions of the veteran that the Commission determines are attributed to a disability incurred or aggravated in the line of duty during active military service, or to the veteran's absence from work to obtain care and treatment of a disability incurred or aggravated in the line of duty during active military service.

(2a) For a period of not less than four nor more than 13 weeks beginning with the first day of the first week during which or after the disqualifying act occurs with respect to which week an individual files a claim for benefits if it is determined by the Commission that such individual is, at the time the claim is filed, unemployed because he was discharged for substantial fault on his part connected with his work not rising to the level of misconduct. Substantial fault is defined to include those acts or omissions of employees over which they exercised reasonable control and which violate reasonable requirements of the job but shall not include (1) minor infractions of rules unless such infractions are repeated after a warning was received by the employee, (2) inadvertent mistakes made by the employee, nor (3) failures to perform work because of insufficient skill, ability, or equipment. Upon a finding of discharge under this subsection, the individual shall be disqualified for a period of nine weeks unless, based on findings by the Commission of aggravating or mitigating circumstances, the period of disqualification is lengthened or shortened within the limits set out above. The length of the disqualification so set by the Commission shall not be disturbed by a reviewing court except upon a finding of plain error. . . .

(3) For the duration of his unemployment beginning with the first day of the first week in which the disqualifying act occurs if it is determined by the Commission that such individual has failed without good cause (i) to apply for available suitable work when so directed by the employment office of the Commission; or (ii) to accept suitable work when offered him; or (iii) to return to his customary self-employment (if any) when so directed by the Commission. Provided further, an otherwise eligible individual who is attending a vocational school or training program which has been approved by the Commission for such individual shall not be denied benefits because he refuses to apply for or accept suitable work during such period of training.

In determining whether or not any work is suitable for an individual, the Commission shall consider the degree of risk involved to his health, safety, and morals, his physical fitness and prior training, his experience and prior earnings, his length of unemployment and prospects for securing local work in his customary occupation, and the distance of the available work from his residence.

Notwithstanding any other provisions of this Chapter, no work shall be deemed suitable and benefits shall not be denied under this Chapter to any otherwise eligible individual for refusing to accept new work under any of the following conditions:

a. If the position offered is vacant due directly to a strike, lockout, or other labor dispute;

b. If the remuneration, hours, or other conditions of the work offered are substantially less favorable to the individual than those prevailing for similar work in the locality;

c. If as a condition of being employed the individual would be required to join a company union or to resign from or refrain from joining any bona fide labor organization;

d. If the position offered is full-time work and the individual meets the part-time worker requirements of G.S. 96–13(a)(6).

(4) For the duration of his unemployment beginning with the first day of the first week after the disqualifying act occurs with respect to which week an individual files a claim for benefits if it is determined by the Commission that:

a. Such individual has failed without good cause to attend a vocational school or training program when so directed by the Commission;

b. Such individual has discontinued his training course without good cause; or

c. If the individual is separated from his training course or vocational school due to misconduct.

(5) For any week with respect to which the Commission finds that his total or partial unemployment is caused by a labor dispute in active progress on or after July 1, 1961, at the factory, establishment, or other premises at which he is or was last employed or caused after such date by a labor dispute at another place within this State which is owned or operated by the same employing unit which owns or operates the factory, establishment, or other premises at which he is or was last employed and which supplies materials or services necessary to the continued and usual operation of the premises at which he is or was last employed. Provided, that an individual disqualified under the provisions of this subdivision shall continue to be disqualified thereunder after the labor dispute has ceased to be in active progress for such period of time as is reasonably necessary and required to physically resume operations in the method of operating in use at the plant, factory, or establishment of the employing unit.

(6) If the Commission finds he is customarily self-employed and can reasonably return to self-employment.

(6a) For the duration of his unemployment beginning with the first day of the first week during which or after the disqualifying act occurs with respect to which week an individual files a claim for benefits if it is determined by the Commission that the individual is, at the time the claim is filed, unemployed because the individual's ownership share of the employing entity was voluntarily sold and, at the time of the sale:

a. The employing entity was a corporation and the individual held five percent (5%) or more of the outstanding shares of the voting stock of the corporation;

b. The employing entity was a partnership, limited or general, and the individual was a limited or general partner; or

c. The employing entity was a proprietorship, and the individual was a proprietor.

. . .

(9) . . . The amount of benefits payable to an individual for any week which begins after July 1, 1981, and which begins in a period with respect to which such individual is receiving a governmental or other pension, retirement or retired pay, annuity, or other similar periodic payment which is based on the previous work of such individual shall be reduced (but not below zero) by the amounts of any such pension, retirement or retired pay, annuity, or other payment contributed to in part or in total by the individual's base period employers; provided, however, that the amount of all payments received by an individual under the Railroad Retirement Act shall be deducted from the individual's benefit amount. Provided further, that all such reduced weekly benefit

amounts shall be rounded to the nearest lower full dollar amount (if not a full dollar amount).

(10) Any employee disqualified for the duration of his unemployment due to the provisions of (1), (2), (2B), (3), (4), or (6A) above may have that permanent disqualification removed if he meets the following three conditions:

a. Returns to work for at least five weeks and is paid cumulative wages of at least 10 times his weekly benefit amount;

b. Subsequently becomes unemployed through no fault of his own; and

c. Meets the availability requirements of the law.

Any time certain disqualification imposed by the provisions of subsections (1), (1D), and (2A) shall be removed by serving the disqualification imposed as provided by this subsection.

Provided for good cause shown the Commission in its discretion may as to any permanent disqualification provided in this Chapter reduce the disqualification period to a time certain but not less than five weeks. The maximum amount of benefits due any individual whose permanent disqualification is changed to a time certain shall be reduced by an amount determined by multiplying the number of weeks of disqualification by the weekly benefit amount.

Provided further, any permanent disqualification pursuant to the provisions of (1), (2), (3), (4), or (6A) shall terminate two years after the effective date of the beginning of said disqualification.

. . .

(12) Notwithstanding any other provision of this Chapter, no otherwise eligible individual shall be denied benefits for any weeks if it is determined by the Commission that such individual is, at the time such claim is filed, unemployed because he left work solely as a result of a lack of work caused by the bankruptcy of his employer.

WORKER ADJUSTMENT AND RETRAINING NOTIFICATION ACT

29 U.S.C. §§ 2101-2109

§ 2101. Definitions; exclusions from definition of loss of employment

(a) Definitions. As used in this chapter—

(1) the term "employer" means any business enterprise that employs—

(A) 100 or more employees, excluding part-time employees; or

(B) 100 or more employees who in the aggregate work at least 4,000 hours per week (exclusive of hours of overtime);

(2) the term "plant closing" means the permanent or temporary shutdown of a single site of employment, or one or more facilities or operating units within a single site of employment, if the shutdown results in an employment loss at the single site of employment during any 30-day period for 50 or more employees excluding any part-time employees;

(3) the term "mass layoff" means a reduction in force which—

(A) is not the result of a plant closing; and

(B) results in an employment loss at the single site of employment during any 30-day period for—

(i)(I) at least 33 percent of the employees (excluding any part-time employees); and

(II) at least 50 employees (excluding any part-time employees); or

(ii) at least 500 employees (excluding any part-time employees);

(4) the term "representative" means an exclusive representative of employees within the meaning of section 159(a) or 158(f) of this title or section 152 of Title 45;

(5) the term "affected employees" means employees who may reasonably be expected to experience an employment loss as a consequence of a proposed plant closing or mass layoff by their employer;

(6) subject to subsection (b) of this section, the term "employment loss" means (A) an employment termination, other than a discharge for cause, voluntary departure, or retirement, (B) a layoff exceeding 6 months, or (C) a reduction in hours of work of more than 50 percent during each month of any 6-month period;

(7) the term "unit of local government" means any general purpose political subdivision of a State which has the power to levy taxes and spend funds, as well as general corporate and police powers; and

(8) the term "part-time employee" means an employee who is employed for an average of fewer than 20 hours per week or who has been employed for fewer than 6 of the 12 months preceding the date on which notice is required.

(b) Exclusions from definition of employment loss

(1) In the case of a sale of part or all of an employer's business, the seller shall be responsible for providing notice for any plant closing or mass layoff in accordance with section 2102 of this title, up to and including the effective date of the sale. After the effective date of the sale of part or all of an employer's business, the purchaser shall be responsible for providing notice for any plant closing or mass layoff in accordance with section 2102 of this title. Notwithstanding any other provision of this chapter, any person who is an employee of the seller (other than a part-time employee) as of the effective date of the sale shall be considered an employee of the purchaser immediately after the effective date of the sale.

(2) Notwithstanding subsection (a)(6) of this section, an employee may not be considered to have experienced an employment loss if the closing or layoff is the result of the relocation or consolidation of part or all of the employer's business and, prior to the closing or layoff—

(A) the employer offers to transfer the employee to a different site of employment within a reasonable commuting distance with no more than a 6-month break in employment; or

(B) the employer offers to transfer the employee to any other site of employment regardless of distance with no more than a 6-month break in employment, and the employee accepts within 30 days of the offer or of the closing or layoff, whichever is later.

§ 2102. Notice required before plant closings and mass layoffs

(a) Notice to employees, state dislocated worker units, and local governments. An employer shall not order a plant closing or mass layoff until the end of a 60-day period after the employer serves written notice of such an order—

(1) to each representative of the affected employees as of the time of the notice or, if there is no such representative at that time, to each affected employee; and

(2) to the State or entity designated by the State to carry out rapid response activities under section 134(a)(2)(A) of the Workforce Investment Act of 1998 [20 U.S.C. § 2864(a)(2)(A)], and the chief elected official of the unit of local government within which such closing or layoff is to occur.

If there is more than one such unit, the unit of local government which the employer shall notify is the unit of local government to which the employer pays the highest taxes for the year preceding the year for which the determination is made.

(b) Reduction of notification period

(1) An employer may order the shutdown of a single site of employment before the conclusion of the 60-day period if as of the time that notice would have been required the employer was actively seeking capital or business which, if obtained, would have enabled the employer to avoid or postpone the shutdown and the employer reasonably and in good faith believed that giving the notice required would have precluded the employer from obtaining the needed capital or business.

(2)(A) An employer may order a plant closing or mass layoff before the conclusion of the 60-day period if the closing or mass layoff is caused by business circumstances that were not reasonably foreseeable as of the time that notice would have been required.

(B) No notice under this chapter shall be required if the plant closing or mass layoff is due to any form of natural disaster, such as a flood, earthquake, or the drought currently ravaging the farmlands of the United States.

(3) An employer relying on this subsection shall give as much notice as is practicable and at that time shall give a brief statement of the basis for reducing the notification period.

(c) Extension of layoff period. A layoff of more than 6 months which, at its outset, was announced to be a layoff of 6 months or less, shall be treated as an employment loss under this chapter unless—

(1) the extension beyond 6 months is caused by business circumstances (including unforeseeable changes in price or cost) not reasonably foreseeable at the time of the initial layoff; and

(2) notice is given at the time it becomes reasonably foreseeable that the extension beyond 6 months will be required.

(d) Determinations with respect to employment loss. For purposes of this section, in determining whether a plant closing or mass layoff has occurred or will occur, employment losses for 2 or more groups at a single site of employment, each of which is less than the minimum number of employees specified in section 2101(a)(2) or (3) of this title but which in the aggregate exceed that minimum number, and which occur within any 90-day period shall be considered to be a plant closing or mass layoff unless the employer demonstrates that the employment losses are the result of separate and distinct actions and causes and are not an attempt by the employer to evade the requirements of this chapter.

§ 2103. Exemptions. This chapter shall not apply to a plant closing or mass layoff if—

(1) the closing is of a temporary facility or the closing or layoff is the result of the completion of a particular project or undertaking, and the affected employees were hired with the understanding that their employment was limited to the duration of the facility or the project or undertaking; or

(2) the closing or layoff constitutes a strike or constitutes a lockout not intended to evade the requirements of this chapter. Nothing in this chapter shall require an employer to serve written notice pursuant to section 2102(a) of this title when permanently replacing a person who is deemed to be an economic striker under the National Labor Relations Act [29 U.S.C.A. § 151 et seq.]: Provided, That nothing in this chapter shall be deemed to validate or invalidate any judicial or administrative ruling relating to the hiring of permanent replacements for economic strikers under the National Labor Relations Act.

§ 2104. Administration and enforcement of requirements

(a) Civil actions against employers

(1) Any employer who orders a plant closing or mass layoff in violation of section 2102 of this title shall be liable to each aggrieved employee who suffers an employment loss as a result of such closing or layoff for—

(A) back pay for each day of violation at a rate of compensation not less than the higher of—

(i) the average regular rate received by such employee during the last 3 years of the employee's employment; or

(ii) the final regular rate received by such employee; and

(B) benefits under an employee benefit plan described in section 1002(3) of this title, including the cost of medical expenses incurred during the employment loss which would have been covered under an employee benefit plan if the employment loss had not occurred.

Such liability shall be calculated for the period of the violation, up to a maximum of 60 days, but in no event for more than one-half the number of days the employee was employed by the employer.

(2) The amount for which an employer is liable under paragraph (1) shall be reduced by—

(A) any wages paid by the employer to the employee for the period of the violation;

(B) any voluntary and unconditional payment by the employer to the employee that is not required by any legal obligation; and

(C) any payment by the employer to a third party or trustee (such as premiums for health benefits or payments to a defined contribution pension plan) on behalf of and attributable to the employee for the period of the violation.

In addition, any liability incurred under paragraph (1) with respect to a defined benefit pension plan may be reduced by crediting the employee with service for all purposes under such a plan for the period of the violation.

(3) Any employer who violates the provisions of section 2102 of this title with respect to a unit of local government shall be subject to a civil penalty of not more than $500 for each day of such violation, except that such penalty shall not apply if the employer pays to each aggrieved employee the amount for which the employer is liable to that employee within 3 weeks from the date the employer orders the shutdown or layoff.

(4) If an employer which has violated this chapter proves to the satisfaction of the court that the act or omission that violated this chapter was in good faith and that the employer had reasonable grounds for believing that the act or omission was not a violation of this chapter the court may, in its discretion, reduce the amount of the liability or penalty provided for in this section.

(5) A person seeking to enforce such liability, including a representative of employees or a unit of local government aggrieved under paragraph (1) or (3), may sue either for such person or for other persons similarly situated, or both, in any district court of the United States for any district in which the violation is alleged to have occurred, or in which the employer transacts business.

(6) In any such suit, the court, in its discretion, may allow the prevailing party a reasonable attorney's fee as part of the costs.

(7) For purposes of this subsection, the term, "aggrieved employee" means an employee who has worked for the employer ordering the plant closing or mass layoff and who, as a result of the failure by the employer to comply with section 2102 of this title did not receive timely notice either directly or through his or her representative as required by section 2102 of this title.

(b) Exclusivity of remedies. The remedies provided for in this section shall be the exclusive remedies for any violation of this chapter. Under this chapter, a Federal court shall not have authority to enjoin a plant closing or mass layoff.

§ 2105. Procedures in addition to other rights of employees. The rights and remedies provided to employees by this chapter are in addition to, and not in lieu of, any other contractual or statutory rights and remedies of the employees, and are not intended to alter or affect such rights and remedies, except that the period of notification required by this chapter shall run concurrently with any period of notification required by contract or by any other statute.

§ 2106. Procedures encouraged where not required. It is the sense of Congress that an employer who is not required to comply with the notice requirements of section 2102 of this title should, to the extent possible, provide notice to its employees about a proposal to close a plant or permanently reduce its workforce.

§ 2107. Authority to prescribe regulations

(a) The Secretary of Labor shall prescribe such regulations as may be necessary to carry out this chapter. Such regulations shall, at a minimum, include interpretative regulations describing the methods by which employers may provide for appropriate service of notice as required by this chapter.

(b) The mailing of notice to an employee's last known address or inclusion of notice in the employee's paycheck will be considered acceptable methods for fulfillment of the employer's obligation to give notice to each affected employee under this chapter.

§ 2108. Effect on other laws. The giving of notice pursuant to this chapter, if done in good faith compliance with this chapter, shall not constitute a violation of the National Labor Relations Act [29 U.S.C.A. § 151 et seq.] or the Railway Labor Act [45 U.S.C.A. § 151 et seq.].

§ 2109. Report on employment and international competitiveness. Two years after Aug. 4, 1988, the Comptroller General shall submit to the Committee on Small Business of both the House and Senate, the Committee on Labor and Human Resources, and the Committee on Education and Labor a report containing a detailed and objective analysis of the effect of this chapter on employers (especially small- and medium-sized businesses), the economy (international competitiveness), and employees (in terms of levels and conditions of employment). The Comptroller General shall assess both costs and benefits, including the effect on productivity, competitiveness, unemployment rates and compensation, and worker retraining and readjustment.

PART VII.

EMPLOYEE BENEFITS

FAMILY AND MEDICAL LEAVE ACT

29 U.S.C. §§ 2601 et. seq.

§ 2 [§ 2601]. Findings and purposes

(a) Congress finds that—

(1) the number of single-parent households and two-parent households in which the single parent or both parents work is increasing significantly;

(2) it is important for the development of children and the family unit that fathers and mothers be able to participate in early childrearing and the care of family members who have serious health conditions;

(3) the lack of employment policies to accommodate working parents can force individuals to choose between job security and parenting;

(4) there is inadequate job security for employees who have serious health conditions that prevent them from working for temporary periods;

(5) due to the nature of the roles of men and women in our society, the primary responsibility for family caretaking often falls on women, and such responsibility affects the working lives of women more than it affects the working lives of men; and

(6) employment standards that apply to one gender only have serious potential for encouraging employers to discriminate against employees and applicants for employment who are of that gender.

(b) It is the purpose of this Act—

(1) to balance the demands of the workplace with the needs of families, to promote the stability and economic security of families, and to promote national interests in preserving family integrity;

(2) to entitle employees to take reasonable leave for medical reasons, for the birth or adoption of a child, and for the care of a child, spouse, or parent who has a serious health condition;

(3) to accomplish the purposes described in paragraphs (1) and (2) in a manner that accommodates the legitimate interests of employers;

(4) to accomplish the purposes described in paragraphs (1) and (2) in a manner that, consistent with the Equal Protection Clause of the Fourteenth Amendment, minimizes the potential for employment discrimination on the basis of sex by ensuring generally that leave is available for eligible medical reasons (including maternity-related disability) and for compelling family reasons, on a gender-neutral basis; and

(5) to promote the goal of equal employment opportunity for women and men, pursuant to such clause.

§ 101 [§ 2611] Definitions. As used in this subchapter:

(1) The terms "commerce" and "industry or activity affecting commerce" mean any activity, business, or industry in commerce or in which a labor dispute would hinder or obstruct commerce or the free flow of commerce, and include "commerce" and any "industry affecting commerce", as defined in paragraphs (1) and (3) of Section 501 of the Labor Management Relations Act, 1947 [29 U.S.C. § 142].

(2)(A) The term "eligible employee" means an employee who has been employed—

(i) for at least 12 months by the employer with respect to whom leave is requested under section 102; and

(ii) for at least 1,250 hours of service with such employer during the previous 12-month period.

(B) The term "eligible employee" does not include—

(i) any Federal officer or employee covered under subchapter V of chapter 63 of Title 5; or

(ii) any employee of an employer who is employed at a worksite at which such employer employs less than 50 employees if the total number of employees employed by that employer within 75 miles of that worksite is less than 50.

(C) For purposes of determining whether an employee meets the hours of service requirement specified in subparagraph (A)(ii), the legal standards established under section 7 of the Fair Labor Standards Act of 1938 [29 U.S.C. § 207] shall apply.

(D) [Special rules for airline flight crews omitted].

(3) The terms "employ", "employee", and "State" have the same meanings given such terms in subsections (c), (e), and (g) of section 3 of the Fair Labor Standards Act of 1938 [29 U.S.C. § 203].

(4)(A) The term "employer"—

(i) means any person engaged in commerce or in any industry or activity affecting commerce who employs 50 or more employees for each working day during each of 20 or more calendar workweeks in the current or preceding calendar year;

(ii) includes—

(I) any person who acts, directly or indirectly, in the interest of an employer to any of the employees of such employer; and

(II) any successor in interest of an employer;

(iii) includes any "public agency", as defined in section 3(x) of the Fair Labor Standards Act of 1938 [29 U.S.C. § 203(x)]; and

(iv) includes the General Accountability Office and the Library of Congress.

(B) For purposes of subparagraph (A)(iii), a public agency shall be considered to be a person engaged in commerce or in an industry or activity affecting commerce.

(5) The term "employment benefits" means all benefits provided or made available to employees by an employer, including group life insurance, health insurance, disability insurance, sick leave, annual leave, educational benefits, and pensions, regardless of whether such benefits are provided by a practice or written policy of an employer or through an "employee benefit plan", as defined in section 3(3) of the Employee Retirement Income Security Act of 1974 [29 U.S.C. § 1002(3)].

(6) The term "health care provider" means—

(A) a doctor of medicine or osteopathy who is authorized to practice medicine or surgery (as appropriate) by the State in which the doctor practices; or

(B) any other person determined by the Secretary to be capable of providing health care services.

(7) The term "parent" means the biological parent of an employee or an individual who stood in loco parentis to an employee when the employee was a son or daughter.

(8) The term "person" has the same meaning given such term in section 3(a) of the Fair Labor Standards Act of 1938 [29 U.S.C. § 203(a)].

(9) The term "reduced leave schedule" means a leave schedule that reduces the usual number of hours per workweek, or hours per workday, of an employee.

(10) The term "Secretary" means the Secretary of Labor.

(11) The term "serious health condition" means an illness, injury, impairment, or physical or mental condition that involves—

(A) inpatient care in a hospital, hospice, or residential medical care facility; or

(B) continuing treatment by a health care provider.

(12) The term "son or daughter" means a biological, adopted, or foster child, a stepchild, a legal ward, or a child of a person standing in loco parentis, who is—

(A) under 18 years of age; or

(B) 18 years of age or older and incapable of self-care because of a mental or physical disability.

(13) The term "spouse" means a husband or wife, as the case may be.

(14) The term "covered active duty" means—

(A) in the case of a member of a regular component of the Armed Forces, duty during the deployment of the member with the Armed Forces to a foreign country; and

(B) in the case of a member of a reserve component of the Armed Forces, duty during the deployment of the member with the Armed Forces to a foreign country under a call o order to active duty under a provision of law referred to in section 101(a)(13)(B) of title 10.

(15) The term "covered servicemember" means—

(A) a member of the Armed Forces (including a member of the National Guard or Reserves) who is undergoing medical treatment, recuperation, or therapy, is otherwise in outpatient status, or is otherwise on the temporary disability retired list, for a serious injury or illness; or

(B) a veteran who is undergoing medical treatment, recuperation, or therapy, for a serious injury or illness and who was a member of the Armed Forces (including a member of the National Guard or Reserves) at any time during the period of 5 years preceding the date on which the veteran undergoes that medical treatment, recuperation, or therapy.

(16) The term "outpatient status," with respect to a covered servicemember, means the status of a member of the Armed Forces assigned to—

(A) a military medical treatment facility as an outpatient; or

(B) a unit established for the purpose of providing command and control of members of the Armed Forces receiving medical care as outpatients.

(17) The term "next of kin," used with respect to an individual, means the nearest blood relative of that individual.

(18) The term "serious injury or illness"—

(A) in the case of a member of the Armed Forces (including a member of the National Guard or Reserves), means an injury or illness that was incurred by the member in line of duty on active duty in the Armed Forces (or existed before the beginning of the member's active duty and was aggravated by service in line of duty on active duty in the Armed Forces) and that may render the member medically unfit to perform the duties of the member's office, grade, rank, or rating; and

(B) in the case of a veteran who was a member of the Armed Forces (including a member of t he National Guard or Reserves) at any time during a period described in paragraph 15(B), means a qualifying (as defined by the Secretary of Labor) injury or illness that was incurred by the member in line of duty on active duty in the Armed Forces (or existed before the beginning of the member's active duty and was aggravated by service in line of duty on active duty in the Armed Forces) and that manifested itself before or after the member became a veteran.

(19) The term "veteran" has the meaning given the term in section 101 of title 38.

§ 102 [§ 2612]. Leave requirement

(a)(1) Subject to section 103, an eligible employee shall be entitled to a total of 12 workweeks of leave during any 12-month period for one or more of the following:

(A) Because of the birth of a son or daughter of the employee and in order to care for such son or daughter.

(B) Because of the placement of a son or daughter with the employee for adoption or foster care.

(C) In order to care for the spouse, or a son, daughter, or parent, of the employee, if such spouse, son, daughter, or parent has a serious health condition.

(D) Because of a serious health condition that makes the employee unable to perform the functions of the position of such employee.

(E) Because of any qualifiying emergency (as the Secretary shall, by regulation, determine) arising out of the fact that the spouse, or a son, daughter, or parent of the employee is on covered active duty (or has been notified of an impending call or order to covered active duty) in the Armed Forces.

(2) The entitlement to leave under subparagraphs (A) and (B) of paragraph (1) for a birth or placement of a son or daughter shall expire at the end of the 12-month period beginning on the date of such birth or placement.

(3) Subject to section 103, an eligible employee who is the spouse, son, daughter, parent, or next of kin of a covered servicemember shall be entitled to a total of 26 workweeks of leave during a 12-month period to care for the servicemember. The leave described in this paragraph shall only be available during a single 12-month period.

(4) During the single 12-month period described in paragraph (3), an eligible employee shall be entitled to a combined total of 26 workweeks of leave under paragraphs (1) and (3). Nothing in this paragraph shall be construed to limit the availability of leave under paragraph (1) during any other 12-month period. . . .

(b)(1) Leave under subparagraph (A) or (B) of subsection (a)(1) shall not be taken by an employee intermittently or on a reduced leave schedule unless the employee and the employer of the employee agree otherwise. Subject to paragraph (2), subsection (e)(2) of this section, and subsection (b)(5) or (f) (as appropriate) of section 103, leave under subparagraph (C) or (D) of subsection (a)(1) or under subsection (a)(3) of this section may be taken intermittently or on a reduced leave schedule when medically necessary. The taking of leave intermittently or on a reduced leave schedule pursuant to this paragraph shall not result in a reduction in the total amount of leave to which the employee is entitled under subsection (a) of this section beyond the amount of leave actually taken.

(2) If an employee requests intermittent leave, or leave on a reduced leave schedule, under subparagraph (C) or (D) of subsection (a)(1) of this section or under subsection (a)(3) of this section, that is foreseeable based on planned medical treatment, the employer may require such employee to transfer temporarily to an available alternative position offered by the employer for which the employee is qualified and that—

(A) has equivalent pay and benefits; and

(B) better accommodates recurring periods of leave than the regular employment position of the employee.

(c) Except as provided in subsection (d) of this section, leave granted under subsection (a) may consist of unpaid leave. Where an employee is otherwise exempt under regulations issued by the Secretary pursuant to section 13(a)(1) of the Fair Labor Standards Act of 1938 [29 U.S.C. § 213(a)(1)], the compliance of an employer with this subchapter by providing unpaid leave shall not affect the exempt status of the employee under such section.

(d)(1) If an employer provides paid leave for fewer than 12 workweeks (or 26 workweeks in the case of leave provided under subsection (a)(3) of this section), the additional weeks of leave necessary to attain the 12 workweeks (or 26 workweeks, as appropriate) of leave required under this subchapter may be provided without compensation.

(2)(A) An eligible employee may elect, or an employer may require the employee, to substitute any of the accrued paid vacation leave, personal leave, or family leave of the employee for leave provided under subparagraph (A), (B), (C), or (E) of subsection (a)(1) of this section for any part of the 12-week period of such leave under such subsection.

(B) An eligible employee may elect, or an employer may require the employee, to substitute any of the accrued paid vacation leave, personal leave, or medical or sick leave of the employee for leave provided under subparagraph (C) or (D) of subsection (a)(1) for any part of the 12-week period of such leave under such subsection, except that nothing in this subchapter shall require an employer to provide paid sick leave or paid medical leave in any situation in which such employer would not normally provide any such paid leave. An eligible employee may elect, or an employer may require the employee, to substitute any of the accrued paid vacation leave, personal leave, family leave, or medical or sick leave of the employee for leave provided under subsection (a)(3) of this section for any part of the 26-week period of such leave under such subsection, except that nothing in this subchapter requires an employer to provide paid sick leave or paid medical leave in any situation in which the employer would not normally provide any such paid leave.

(e)(1) In any case in which the necessity for leave under subparagraph (A) or (B) of subsection (a)(1) of this section is foreseeable based on an expected birth or placement, the employee shall provide the employer with not less than 30 days' notice, before the date the leave is to begin, of the employee's intention to take leave under such subparagraph, except that if the date of the birth or placement requires leave to begin in less than 30 days, the employee shall provide such notice as is practicable.

(2) In any case in which the necessity for leave under subparagraph (C) or (D) of subsection (a)(1) of this section is foreseeable based on planned medical treatment, the employee—

(A) shall make a reasonable effort to schedule the treatment so as not to disrupt unduly the operations of the employer, subject to the approval of the health care provider of the employee or the health care provider of the son, daughter, spouse, parent, or covered servicemember of the employee, as appropriate; and

(B) shall provide the employer with not less than 30 days' notice, before the date the leave is to begin, of the employee's intention to take leave under such subparagraph, except that if the date of the treatment requires leave to begin in less than 30 days, the employee shall provide such notice as is practicable.

(3) In any case in which the necessity for leave under subsection (a)(1)(E) of this section is foreseeable, whether because the

spouse, or a son, daughter, or parent, of the employee is on covered active duty, or because of notification of an impending call or order to covered active duty, the employee shall provide such notice to the employer as is reasonable and practicable.

(f)(1) In any case in which a husband and wife entitled to leave under subsection (a) of this section are employed by the same employer, the aggregate number of workweeks of leave to which both may be entitled may be limited to 12 workweeks during any 12-month period, if such leave is taken—

(A) under subparagraph (A) or (B) of subsection (a)(1) of this section; or

(B) to care for a sick parent under subparagraph (C) of such subsection.

(2)(A) The aggregate number of workweeks of leave to which both that husband and wife may be entitled under subsection (a) of this section may be limited to 26 workweeks during the single 12-month period described in subsection (a)(3) of this section if the leave is—

(i) leave under subsection (a)(3) of this section; or

(ii) a combination of leave under subsection (a)(3) of this section and leave described in paragraph (1).

(B) If the leave taken by the husband and wife includes leave described in paragraph (1), the limitation in paragraph (1) shall apply to the leave described in paragraph (1).

§ 103 [§ 2613]. Certification

(a) An employer may require that a request for leave under subparagraph (C) or (D) of paragraph (1) or paragraph (3) of section 102(a) be supported by a certification issued by the health care provider of the eligible employee or of the son, daughter, spouse, or parent of the employee, or of the next of kin of an individual in the case of leave taken under such paragraph (3), as appropriate. The employee shall provide, in a timely manner, a copy of such certification to the employer.

(b) Certification provided under subsection (a) shall be sufficient if it states—

(1) the date on which the serious health condition commenced;

(2) the probable duration of the condition;

(3) the appropriate medical facts within the knowledge of the health care provider regarding the condition;

(4)(A) for purposes of leave under section 102(a)(1)(C), a statement that the eligible employee is needed to care for the son, daughter, spouse, or parent and an estimate of the amount of time that such employee is needed to care for the son, daughter, spouse, or parent; and

(B) for purposes of leave under section 102(a)(1)(D), a statement that the employee is unable to perform the functions of the position of the employee;

(5) in the case of certification for intermittent leave, or leave on a reduced leave schedule, for planned medical treatment, the dates on which such treatment is expected to be given and the duration of such treatment;

(6) in the case of certification for intermittent leave, or leave on a reduced leave schedule, under section 102(a)(1)(D), a statement of the medical necessity for the intermittent leave or leave on a reduced leave schedule, and the expected duration of the intermittent leave or reduced leave schedule; and

(7) in the case of certification for intermittent leave, or leave on a reduced leave schedule, under section 102(a)(1)(C), a statement that the employee's intermittent leave or leave on a reduced leave schedule is necessary for the care of the son, daughter, parent, or spouse who has a serious health condition, or will assist in their recovery, and the expected duration and schedule of the intermittent leave or reduced leave schedule.

(c)(1) In any case in which the employer has reason to doubt the validity of the certification provided under subsection (a) for leave under subparagraph (C) or (D) of section 102(a)(1), the employer may require, at the expense of the employer, that the eligible employee obtain the opinion of a second health care provider designated or approved by the employer concerning any information certified under subsection (b) for such leave.

(2) A health care provider designated or approved under paragraph (1) shall not be employed on a regular basis by the employer.

(d)(1) In any case in which the second opinion described in subsection (c) differs from the opinion in the original certification provided under subsection (a) of this section, the employer may require, at the expense of the employer, that the employee obtain the opinion of a third health care provider designated or approved jointly by the employer and the employee concerning the information certified under subsection (b) of this section.

(2) The opinion of the third health care provider concerning the information certified under subsection (b) shall be considered to be final and shall be binding on the employer and the employee.

(e) The employer may require that the eligible employee obtain subsequent recertifications on a reasonable basis.

(f) An employer may require that a request for leave under section 102(a)(1)(E) be supported by a certification issued at such time and in such manner as the Secretary may by regulation prescribe. If the Secretary issues a regulation requiring such certification, the employee shall provide, in a timely manner, a copy of such certification to the employer.

§ 104 [§ 2614]. Employment and benefits protection

(a)(1) Except as provided in subsection (b), any eligible employee who takes leave under section 102 for the intended purpose of the leave shall be entitled, on return from such leave—

(A) to be restored by the employer to the position of employment held by the employee when the leave commenced; or

(B) to be restored to an equivalent position with equivalent employment benefits, pay, and other terms and conditions of employment.

(2) The taking of leave under section 102 shall not result in the loss of any employment benefit accrued prior to the date on which the leave commenced.

(3) Nothing in this section shall be construed to entitle any restored employee to—

(A) the accrual of any seniority or employment benefits during any period of leave; or

(B) any right, benefit, or position of employment other than any right, benefit, or position to which the employee would have been entitled had the employee not taken the leave.

(4) As a condition of restoration under paragraph (1) for an employee who has taken leave under section 102(a)(1)(D), the employer may have a uniformly applied practice or policy that requires each such employee to receive certification from the health care provider of the employee that the employee is able to resume work, except that nothing in this paragraph shall supersede a valid State or local law or a collective bargaining agreement that governs the return to work of such employees.

(5) Nothing in this subsection shall be construed to prohibit an employer from requiring an employee on leave under section 102 to report periodically to the employer on the status and intention of the employee to return to work.

(b)(1) An employer may deny restoration under subsection (a) of this section to any eligible employee described in paragraph (2) if—

(A) such denial is necessary to prevent substantial and grievous economic injury to the operations of the employer;

(B) the employer notifies the employee of the intent of the employer to deny restoration on such basis at the time the employer determines that such injury would occur; and

(C) in any case in which the leave has commenced, the employee elects not to return to employment after receiving such notice.

(2) An eligible employee described in paragraph (1) is a salaried eligible employee who is among the highest paid 10 percent of the employees employed by the employer within 75 miles of the facility at which the employee is employed.

(c)(1) Except as provided in paragraph (2), during any period that an eligible employee takes leave under section 102, the employer shall maintain coverage under any "group health plan" (as defined in section 5000(b)(1) of the Internal Revenue Code of 1986 [26 U.S.C. § 5000(b)(1)]) for the duration of such leave at the level and under the conditions coverage would have been provided if the employee had continued in employment continuously for the duration of such leave.

(2) The employer may recover the premium that the employer paid for maintaining coverage for the employee under such group health plan during any period of unpaid leave under section 102 if—

(A) the employee fails to return from leave under section 102 after the period of leave to which the employee is entitled has expired; and

(B) the employee fails to return to work for a reason other than—

(i) the continuation, recurrence, or onset of a serious health condition that entitles the employee to leave under subparagraph (C) or (D) of section 102(a)(1); or

(ii) other circumstances beyond the control of the employee.

(3)(A) An employer may require that a claim that an employee is unable to return to work because of the continuation, recurrence, or onset of the serious health condition described in paragraph (2)(B)(i) be supported by—

(i) a certification issued by the health care provider of the son, daughter, spouse, or parent of the employee, as appropriate, in the case of an employee unable to return to work because of a condition specified in section 102(a)(1)(C);

(ii) a certification issued by the health care provider of the eligible employee, in the case of an employee unable to return to work because of a condition specified in section 102(a)(1)(D); or

(iii) a certification issued by the health care provider of the servicemember being cared for by the employee, in the case of an employee unable to return to work because of a condition specified in section 102(a)(3).

(B) The employee shall provide, in a timely manner, a copy of such certification to the employer.

(C)(i) The certification described in subparagraph (A)(ii) shall be sufficient if the certification states that a serious health condition prevented the employee from being able to perform the functions of the position of the employee on the date that the leave of the employee expired.

(ii) The certification described in subparagraph (A)(i) shall be sufficient if the certification states that the employee is needed to care for the son, daughter, spouse, or parent who has a serious health condition on the date that the leave of the employee expired.

§ 105 [§ 2615]. Prohibited acts

(a)(1) It shall be unlawful for any employer to interfere with, restrain, or deny the exercise of or the attempt to exercise, any right provided under this subchapter.

(2) It shall be unlawful for any employer to discharge or in any other manner discriminate against any individual for opposing any practice made unlawful by this subchapter.

(b) It shall be unlawful for any person to discharge or in any other manner discriminate against any individual because such individual—

(1) has filed any charge, or has instituted or caused to be instituted any proceeding, under or related to this subchapter;

(2) has given, or is about to give, any information in connection with any inquiry or proceeding relating to any right provided under this subchapter; or

(3) has testified, or is about to testify, in any inquiry or proceeding relating to any right provided under this subchapter.

§ 106 [§ 2616]. Investigative authority

(a) To ensure compliance with the provisions of this subchapter, or any regulation or order issued under this subchapter, the Secretary shall have, subject to subsection (c) of this section, the investigative authority provided under section 11(a) of the Fair Labor Standards Act of 1938 [29 U.S.C. § 211(a)].

(b) Any employer shall make, keep, and preserve records pertaining to compliance with this title in accordance with section 11(c) of the Fair Labor Standards Act of 1938 [29 U.S.C. § 211(c)] and in accordance with regulations issued by the Secretary.

(c) The Secretary shall not under the authority of this section require any employer or any plan, fund, or program to submit to the Secretary any books or records more than once during any 12-month period, unless the Secretary has reasonable cause to believe there may exist a violation of this subchapter or any regulation or order issued pursuant to this subchapter, or is investigating a charge pursuant to section 107(b).

(d) For the purposes of any investigation provided for in this section, the Secretary shall have the subpoena authority provided for under section 9 of the Fair Labor Standards Act of 1938 [29 U.S.C. § 209].

§ 107 [§ 2617]. Enforcement

(a)(1) Any employer who violates section 105 shall be liable to any eligible employee affected—

(A) for damages equal to—

(i) the amount of—

(I) any wages, salary, employment benefits, or other compensation denied or lost to such employee by reason of the violation; or

(II) in a case in which wages, salary, employment benefits, or other compensation have not been denied or lost to the employee, any actual monetary losses sustained by the employee as a direct result of the violation, such as the cost of providing care, up to a sum equal to 12 weeks of wages or salary for the employee;

(ii) the interest on the amount described in clause (i) calculated at the prevailing rate; and

(iii) an additional amount as liquidated damages equal to the sum of the amount described in clause (i) and the interest described in clause (ii), except that if an employer who has violated section 105 proves to the satisfaction of the court that the act or omission which violated section 105 was in good faith and that the employer had reasonable grounds for believing that the act or omission was not a violation of section 105, such court may, in the discretion of the court, reduce the amount of the liability to the amount and interest determined under clauses (i) and (ii), respectively; and

(B) for such equitable relief as may be appropriate, including employment, reinstatement, and promotion.

(2) An action to recover the damages or equitable relief prescribed in paragraph (1) may be maintained against any employer (including a public agency) in any Federal or State court of competent jurisdiction by any one or more employees for and in behalf of—

(A) the employees; or

(B) the employees and other employees similarly situated.

(3) The court in such an action shall, in addition to any judgment awarded to the plaintiff, allow a reasonable attorney's fee, reasonable expert witness fees, and other costs of the action to be paid by the defendant.

(4) The right provided by paragraph (2) to bring an action by or on behalf of any employee shall terminate—

(A) on the filing of a complaint by the Secretary in an action under subsection (d) in which restraint is sought of any further delay in the payment of the amount described in paragraph (1)(A) to such employee by an employer responsible under paragraph (1) for the payment; or

(B) on the filing of a complaint by the Secretary in an action under subsection (b) in which a recovery is sought of the damages described in paragraph (1)(A) owing to an eligible employee by an employer liable under paragraph (1), unless the action described in subparagraph (A) or (B) is dismissed without prejudice on motion of the Secretary.

(b)(1) The Secretary shall receive, investigate, and attempt to resolve complaints of violations of section 105 in the same manner that the Secretary receives, investigates, and attempts to resolve complaints of violations of sections 6 and 7 of the Fair Labor Standards Act of 1938 [29 U.S.C. §§ 206-07].

(2) The Secretary may bring an action in any court of competent jurisdiction to recover the damages described in subsection (a)(1)(A).

(3) Any sums recovered by the Secretary pursuant to paragraph (2) shall be held in a special deposit account and shall be paid, on order of the Secretary, directly to each employee affected. Any such sums not paid to an employee because of inability to do so within a period of 3 years shall be deposited into the Treasury of the United States as miscellaneous receipts.

(c)(1) Except as provided in paragraph (2), an action may be brought under this section not later than 2 years after the date of the last event constituting the alleged violation for which the action is brought.

(2) In the case of such action brought for a willful violation of section 105, such action may be brought within 3 years of the date of the last event constituting the alleged violation for which such action is brought.

(3) In determining when an action is commenced by the Secretary under this section for the purposes of this subsection, it shall be considered to be commenced on the date when the complaint is filed.

(d) The district courts of the United States shall have jurisdiction, for cause shown, in an action brought by the Secretary—

(1) to restrain violations of section 105, including the restraint of any withholding of payment of wages, salary, employment benefits, or other compensation, plus interest, found by the court to be due to eligible employees; or

(2) to award such other equitable relief as may be appropriate, including employment, reinstatement, and promotion.

(e) The Solicitor of Labor may appear for and represent the Secretary on any litigation brought under this section. . . .

§ 109 [§ 2619]. Notice

(a) Each employer shall post and keep posted, in conspicuous places on the premises of the employer where notices to employees and applicants for employment are customarily posted, a notice, to be prepared or approved by the Secretary, setting forth excerpts from, or summaries of, the pertinent provisions of this subchapter and information pertaining to the filing of a charge.

(b) Any employer that willfully violates this section may be assessed a civil money penalty not to exceed $100 for each separate offense. . . .

§ 401 [§ 2651]. Effect on other laws

(a) Nothing in this Act or any amendment made by this Act shall be construed to modify or affect any Federal or State law prohibiting discrimination on the basis of race, religion, color, national origin, sex, age, or disability.

(b) Nothing in this Act or any amendment made by this Act shall be construed to supersede any provision of any State or local law that provides greater family or medical leave rights than the rights established under this Act or any amendment made by this Act.

§ 402 [§ 2652]. Effect on existing employment benefits

(a) Nothing in this Act or any amendment made by this Act shall be construed to diminish the obligation of an employer to comply with any collective bargaining agreement or any employment benefit program or plan that provides greater family or medical leave rights to employees than the rights established under this Act or any amendment made by this Act.

(b) The rights established for employees under this Act or any amendment made by this Act shall not be diminished by any collective bargaining agreement or any employment benefit program or plan.

§ 403 [§ 2653]. Encouragement of more generous leave policies. Nothing in this Act or any amendment made by this Act shall be construed to discourage employers from adopting or retaining leave policies more generous than any policies that comply with the requirements under this Act or any amendment made by this Act.

UNIFORMED SERVICES EMPLOYMENT AND REEMPLOYMENT RIGHTS ACT

38 U.S.C. §§ 4301 to 4334

§ 4301. Purposes; sense of Congress.

(a) The purposes of this chapter are—

(1) to encourage noncareer service in the uniformed services by eliminating or minimizing the disadvantages to civilian careers and employment which can result from such service;

(2) to minimize the disruption to the lives of persons performing service in the uniformed services as well as to their employers, their fellow employees, and their communities, by providing for the prompt reemployment of such persons upon their completion of such service; and

(3) to prohibit discrimination against persons because of their service in the uniformed services.

(b) It is the sense of Congress that the Federal Government should be a model employer in carrying out the provisions of this chapter.

§ 4302. Relation to other law and plans or agreements.

(a) Nothing in this chapter shall supersede, nullify or diminish any Federal or State law (including any local law or ordinance), contract, agreement, policy, plan, practice, or other matter that establishes a right or benefit that is more beneficial to, or is in addition to, a right or benefit provided for such person in this chapter.

(b) This chapter supersedes any State law (including any local law or ordinance), contract, agreement, policy, plan, practice, or other matter that reduces, limits, or eliminates in any manner any right or benefit provided by this chapter, including the establishment of additional prerequisites to the exercise of any such right or the receipt of any such benefit.

§ 4303. Definitions. For the purposes of this chapter—

(1) The term "Attorney General" means the Attorney General of the United States or any person designated by the Attorney General to carry out a responsibility of the Attorney General under this chapter.

(2) The term "benefit", "benefit of employment", or "rights and benefits" means any advantage, profit, privilege, gain, status, account, or interest (other than wages or salary for work performed) that accrues by reason of an employment contract or agreement or an employer policy, plan, or practice and includes rights and benefits under a pension plan, a health plan, an employee stock ownership plan, insurance coverage and awards, bonuses, severance pay, supplemental unemployment benefits, vacations, and the opportunity to select work hours or location of employment.

(3) The term "employee" means any person employed by an employer. Such term includes any person who is a citizen, national, or permanent resident alien of the United States employed in a workplace in a foreign country by an employer that is an entity incorporated or otherwise organized in the United States or that is controlled by an entity organized in the United States, within the meaning of section 4319(c) of this title.

(4)(A) Except as provided in subparagraphs (B) and (C), the term "employer" means any person, institution, organization, or other entity that pays salary or wages for work performed or that has control over employment opportunities, including—

(i) a person, institution, organization, or other entity to whom the employer has delegated the performance of employment-related responsibilities;

(ii) the Federal Government;

(iii) a State;

(iv) any successor in interest to a person, institution, organization, or other entity referred to in this subparagraph; and

(v) a person, institution, organization, or other entity that has denied initial employment in violation of section 4311.

(B) In the case of a National Guard technician employed under section 709 of title 32, the term "employer" means the adjutant general of the State in which the technician is employed.

(C) Except as an actual employer of employees, an employee pension benefit plan described in section 3(2) of the Employee Retirement Income Security Act of 1974 (29 U.S.C. § 1002(2)) shall be deemed to be an employer only with respect to the obligation to provide benefits described in section 4318.

(D)(i) Whether the term "successor in interest" applies with respect to an entity described in subparagraph (A) for purposes of clause (iv) of such subparagraph shall be determined on a case-by-case basis using a multi-factor test that considers the following factors:

(I) Substantial continuity of business operations.

(II) Use of the same or similar facilities.

(III) Continuity of work force.

(IV) Similarity of jobs and working conditions.

(V) Similarity of supervisory personnel.

(VI) Similarity of machinery, equipment, and production methods.

(VII) Similarity of products of services.

(ii) The entity's lack of notice or awareness of a potential or pending claim under this chapter at the time of a merger, acquisition, or other form of succession shall not be considered when applying the multi-factor test under clause (i).

(5) The term "Federal executive agency" includes the United States Postal Service, the Postal Rate Commission, any nonappropriated fund instrumentality of the United States, any Executive agency (as that term is defined in section 105 of title 5) other than an agency referred to in section 2302(a)(2)(C)(ii) of title 5, and any military department (as that term is defined in section 102 of title 5) with respect to the civilian employees of that department.

(6) The term "Federal Government" includes any Federal executive agency, the legislative branch of the United States, and the judicial branch of the United States.

(7) The term "health plan" means an insurance policy or contract, medical or hospital service agreement, membership or subscription contract, or other arrangement under which health services for individuals are provided or the expenses of such services are paid.

(8) The term "notice" means (with respect to subchapter II [38 U.S.C. §§ 4311 *et seq.*]) any written or verbal notification of an obligation or intention to perform service in the uniformed services provided to an employer by the employee who will perform such service or by the uniformed service in which such service is to be performed.

(9) The term "qualified", with respect to an employment position, means having the ability to perform the essential tasks of the position.

(10) The term "reasonable efforts", in the case of actions required of an employer under this chapter, means actions, including training provided by an employer, that do not place an undue hardship on the employer.

(11) Notwithstanding section 101 [38 U.S.C. § 101], the term "Secretary" means the Secretary of Labor or any person designated by such Secretary to carry out an activity under this chapter.

(12) The term "seniority" means longevity in employment together with any benefits of employment which accrue with, or are determined by, longevity in employment.

(13) The term "service in the uniformed services" means the performance of duty on a voluntary or involuntary basis in a uniformed service under competent authority and includes active duty, active duty for training, initial active duty for training, inactive duty training, full-time National Guard duty, a period for which a person is absent from a position of employment for the purpose of an examination to determine the fitness of the person to perform any such duty, and a period for which a person is absent from employment for the purpose of performing funeral honors duty as authorized by section 12503 of title 10 or section 115 of title 32.

(14) The term "State" means each of the several States of the United States, the District of Columbia, the Commonwealth of Puerto Rico, Guam, the Virgin Islands, and other territories of the United States (including the agencies and political subdivisions thereof).

(15) The term "undue hardship", in the case of actions taken by an employer, means actions requiring significant difficulty or expense, when considered in light of—

(A) the nature and cost of the action needed under this chapter;

(B) the overall financial resources of the facility or facilities involved in the provision of the action; the number of persons employed at such facility; the effect on expenses and resources, or the impact otherwise of such action upon the operation of the facility;

(C) the overall financial resources of the employer; the overall size of the business of an employer with respect to the number of its employees; the number, type, and location of its facilities; and

(D) the type of operation or operations of the employer, including the composition, structure, and functions of the work force of such employer; the geographic separateness, administrative, or fiscal relationship of the facility or facilities in question to the employer.

(16) The term "uniformed services" means the Armed Forces, the Army National Guard and the Air National Guard when engaged in active duty for training, inactive duty training, or full-time National Guard duty, the commissioned corps of the Public Health Service, and any other category of persons designated by the President in time of war or national emergency.

§ 4304. Character of service. A person's entitlement to the benefits of this chapter by reason of the service of such person in one of the uniformed services terminates upon the occurrence of any of the following events:

(1) A separation of such person from such uniformed service with a dishonorable or bad conduct discharge.

(2) A separation of such person from such uniformed service under other than honorable conditions, as characterized pursuant to regulations prescribed by the Secretary concerned.

(3) A dismissal of such person permitted under section 1161(a) of title 10.

(4) A dropping of such person from the rolls pursuant to section 1161(b) of title 10.

§ 4311. Discrimination against persons who serve in the uniformed services and acts of reprisal prohibited.

(a) A person who is a member of, applies to be a member of, performs, has performed, applies to perform, or has an obligation to perform service in a uniformed service shall not be denied initial employment, reemployment, retention in employment, promotion, or any benefit of employment by an employer on the basis of that membership, application for membership, performance of service, application for service, or obligation.

(b) An employer may not discriminate in employment against or take any adverse employment action against any person because such person (1) has taken an action to enforce a protection afforded any person under this chapter, (2) has testified or otherwise made a statement in or in connection with any proceeding under this chapter, (3) has assisted or otherwise participated in an investigation under this chapter, or (4) has exercised a right provided for in this chapter. The prohibition in this subsection shall apply with respect to a person regardless of whether that person has performed service in the uniformed services.

(c) An employer shall be considered to have engaged in actions prohibited—

(1) under subsection (a), if the person's membership, application for membership, service, application for service, or obligation for service in the uniformed services is a motivating factor in the employer's action, unless the employer can prove that the action would have been taken in the absence of such membership, application for membership, service, application for service, or obligation for service; or

(2) under subsection (b), if the person's (A) action to enforce a protection afforded any person under this chapter, (B) testimony or making of a statement in or in connection with any proceeding under this chapter, (C) assistance or other participation in an investigation under this chapter, or (D) exercise of a right provided for in this chapter, is a motivating factor in the employer's action, unless the employer can prove that the action would have been taken in the absence of such person's enforcement action, testimony, statement, assistance, participation, or exercise of a right.

(d) The prohibitions in subsections (a) and (b) shall apply to any position of employment, including a position that is described in section 4312(d)(1)(C) of this title.

§ 4312. Reemployment rights of persons who serve in the uniformed services.

(a) Subject to subsections (b), (c), and (d) and to section 4304, any person whose absence from a position of employment is necessitated by reason of service in the uniformed services shall be entitled to the reemployment rights and benefits and other employment benefits of this chapter if—

(1) the person (or an appropriate officer of the uniformed service in which such service is performed) has given advance written or verbal notice of such service to such person's employer;

(2) the cumulative length of the absence and of all previous absences from a position of employment with that employer by reason of service in the uniformed services does not exceed five years; and

(3) except as provided in subsection (f), the person reports to, or submits an application for reemployment to, such employer in accordance with the provisions of subsection (e).

(b) No notice is required under subsection (a)(1) if the giving of such notice is precluded by military necessity or, under all of the relevant circumstances, the giving of such notice is otherwise impossible or unreasonable. A determination of military necessity for the purposes of this subsection shall be made pursuant to regulations prescribed by the Secretary of Defense and shall not be subject to judicial review.

(c) Subsection (a) shall apply to a person who is absent from a position of employment by reason of service in the uniformed services if such person's cumulative period of service in the uniformed services, with respect to the employer relationship for which a person seeks reemployment, does not exceed five years, except that any such period of service shall not include any service—

(1) that is required, beyond five years, to complete an initial period of obligated service;

(2) during which such person was unable to obtain orders releasing such person from a period of service in the uniformed services

before the expiration of such five-year period and such inability was through no fault of such person;

(3) performed as required pursuant to section 10147 of title 10, under section 502(a) or 503 of title 32, or to fulfill additional training requirements determined and certified in writing by the Secretary concerned, to be necessary for professional development, or for completion of skill training or retraining; or

(4) performed by a member of a uniformed service who is—

(A) ordered to or retained on active duty under section 688, 12301(a), 12301(g), 12302, 12304, or 12305 of title 10 or under section 331, 332, 359, 360, 367, or 712 of title 14;

(B) ordered to or retained on active duty (other than for training) under any provision of law because of a war or national emergency declared by the President or the Congress, as determined by the Secretary concerned;

(C) ordered to active duty (other than for training) in support, as determined by the Secretary concerned, of an operational mission for which personnel have been ordered to active duty under section 12304 of title 10;

(D) ordered to active duty in support, as determined by the Secretary concerned, of a critical mission or requirement of the uniformed services; or

(E) called into Federal service as a member of the National Guard under chapter 15 of title 10 [10 U.S.C. §§ 331 *et seq.*] or under section 12406 of title 10.

(d)(1) An employer is not required to reemploy a person under this chapter if—

(A) the employer's circumstances have so changed as to make such reemployment impossible or unreasonable;

(B) in the case of a person entitled to reemployment under subsection (a)(3), (a)(4), or (b)(2)(B) of section 4313, such employment would impose an undue hardship on the employer; or

(C) the employment from which the person leaves to serve in the uniformed services is for a brief, nonrecurrent period and there is no reasonable expectation that such employment will continue indefinitely or for a significant period.

(2) In any proceeding involving an issue of whether—

(A) any reemployment referred to in paragraph (1) is impossible or unreasonable because of a change in an employer's circumstances,

(B) any accommodation, training, or effort referred to in subsection (a)(3), (a)(4), or (b)(2)(B) of section 4313 would impose an undue hardship on the employer, or

(C) the employment referred to in paragraph (1)(C) is for a brief, nonrecurrent period and there is no reasonable expectation that such employment will continue indefinitely or for a significant period, the employer shall have the burden of proving the impossibility or unreasonableness, undue hardship, or the brief or nonrecurrent nature of the employment without a reasonable expectation of continuing indefinitely or for a significant period.

(e)(1) Subject to paragraph (2), a person referred to in subsection (a) shall, upon the completion of a period of service in the uniformed services, notify the employer referred to in such subsection of the person's intent to return to a position of employment with such employer as follows:

(A) In the case of a person whose period of service in the uniformed services was less than 31 days, by reporting to the employer—

(i) not later than the beginning of the first full regularly scheduled work period on the first full calendar day following the completion of the period of service and the expiration of eight hours after a period allowing for the safe transportation of the person from the place of that service to the person's residence; or

(ii) as soon as possible after the expiration of the eight-hour period referred to in clause (i), if reporting within the period referred to in such clause is impossible or unreasonable through no fault of the person.

(B) In the case of a person who is absent from a position of employment for a period of any length for the purposes of an examination to determine the person's fitness to perform service in the uniformed services, by reporting in the manner and time referred to in subparagraph (A).

(C) In the case of a person whose period of service in the uniformed services was for more than 30 days but less than 181 days, by submitting an application for reemployment with the employer not later than 14 days after the completion of the period of service or if submitting such application within such period is impossible or unreasonable through no fault of the person, the next first full calendar day when submission of such application becomes possible.

(D) In the case of a person whose period of service in the uniformed services was for more than 180 days, by submitting an application for reemployment with the employer not later than 90 days after the completion of the period of service.

(2)(A) A person who is hospitalized for, or convalescing from, an illness or injury incurred in, or aggravated during, the performance of service in the uniformed services shall, at the end of the period that is necessary for the person to recover from such illness or injury, report to the person's employer (in the case of a person described in subparagraph (A) or (B) of paragraph (1)) or submit an application for reemployment with such employer (in the case of a person described in subparagraph (C) or (D) of such paragraph). Except as provided in subparagraph (B), such period of recovery may not exceed two years.

(B) Such two-year period shall be extended by the minimum time required to accommodate the circumstances beyond such person's control which make reporting within the period specified in subparagraph (A) impossible or unreasonable.

(3) A person who fails to report or apply for employment or reemployment within the appropriate period specified in this subsection shall not automatically forfeit such person's entitlement to the rights and benefits referred to in subsection (a) but shall be subject to the conduct rules, established policy, and general practices of the employer pertaining to explanations and discipline with respect to absence from scheduled work.

(f)(1) A person who submits an application for reemployment in accordance with subparagraph (C) or (D) of subsection (e)(1) or subsection (e)(2) shall provide to the person's employer (upon the request of such employer) documentation to establish that—

(A) the person's application is timely;

(B) the person has not exceeded the service limitations set forth in subsection (a)(2) (except as permitted under subsection (c)); and

(C) the person's entitlement to the benefits under this chapter has not been terminated pursuant to section 4304.

(2) Documentation of any matter referred to in paragraph (1) that satisfies regulations prescribed by the Secretary shall satisfy the documentation requirements in such paragraph.

(3)(A) Except as provided in subparagraph (B), the failure of a person to provide documentation that satisfies regulations prescribed pursuant to paragraph (2) shall not be a basis for denying reemployment in accordance with the provisions of this chapter if the failure occurs because such documentation does not exist or is not readily available at the time of the request of the employer. If, after such reemployment, documentation becomes available that establishes that such person does not meet one or more of the requirements referred to in subparagraphs (A), (B), and (C) of paragraph (1), the employer of such person may terminate the employment of the person and the provision of any rights or benefits afforded the person under this chapter.

(B) An employer who reemploys a person absent from a position of employment for more than 90 days may require that the person provide the employer with the documentation referred to in subparagraph (A) before beginning to treat the person as not having incurred a break in service for pension purposes under section 4318(a)(2)(A).

(4) An employer may not delay or attempt to defeat a reemployment obligation by demanding documentation that does not then exist or is not then readily available.

(g) The right of a person to reemployment under this section shall not entitle such person to retention, preference, or displacement rights over any person with a superior claim under the provisions of title 5, United States Code, relating to veterans and other preference eligibles.

(h) In any determination of a person's entitlement to protection under this chapter, the timing, frequency, and duration of the person's training or service, or the nature of such training or service (including voluntary service) in the uniformed services, shall not be a basis for denying protection of this chapter if the service does not exceed the limitations set forth in subsection (c) and the notice requirements established in subsection (a)(1) and the notification requirements established in subsection (e) are met.

§ 4313. Reemployment positions.

(a) Subject to subsection (b) (in the case of any employee) and sections 4314 and 4315 (in the case of an employee of the Federal Government), a person entitled to reemployment under section 4312, upon completion of a period of service in the uniformed services, shall be promptly reemployed in a position of employment in accordance with the following order of priority:

(1) Except as provided in paragraphs (3) and (4), in the case of a person whose period of service in the uniformed services was for less than 91 days—

(A) in the position of employment in which the person would have been employed if the continuous employment of such person with the employer had not been interrupted by such service, the duties of which the person is qualified to perform; or

(B) in the position of employment in which the person was employed on the date of the commencement of the service in the uniformed services, only if the person is not qualified to perform the duties of the position referred to in subparagraph (A) after reasonable efforts by the employer to qualify the person.

(2) Except as provided in paragraphs (3) and (4), in the case of a person whose period of service in the uniformed services was for more than 90 days—

(A) in the position of employment in which the person would have been employed if the continuous employment of such person with the employer had not been interrupted by such service, or a position of like seniority, status and pay, the duties of which the person is qualified to perform; or

(B) in the position of employment in which the person was employed on the date of the commencement of the service in the uniformed services, or a position of like seniority, status and pay, the duties of which the person is qualified to perform, only if the person is not qualified to perform the duties of a position referred to in subparagraph (A) after reasonable efforts by the employer to qualify the person.

(3) In the case of a person who has a disability incurred in, or aggravated during, such service, and who (after reasonable efforts by the employer to accommodate the disability) is not qualified due to such disability to be employed in the position of employment in which the person would have been employed if the continuous employment of such person with the employer had not been interrupted by such service—

(A) in any other position which is equivalent in seniority, status, and pay, the duties of which the person is qualified to perform or would become qualified to perform with reasonable efforts by the employer; or

(B) if not employed under subparagraph (A), in a position which is the nearest approximation to a position referred to in subparagraph (A) in terms of seniority, status, and pay consistent with circumstances of such person's case.

(4) In the case of a person who (A) is not qualified to be employed in (i) the position of employment in which the person would have been employed if the continuous employment of such person with the employer had not been interrupted by such service, or (ii) in the position of employment in which such person was employed on the date of the commencement of the service in the uniformed services for any reason (other than disability incurred in, or aggravated during, service in the uniformed services), and (B) cannot become qualified with reasonable efforts by the employer, in any other position which is the nearest approximation to a position referred to first in clause (A)(i) and then

in clause (A)(ii) which such person is qualified to perform, with full seniority.

(b)(1) If two or more persons are entitled to reemployment under section 4312 in the same position of employment and more than one of them has reported for such reemployment, the person who left the position first shall have the prior right to reemployment in that position.

(2) Any person entitled to reemployment under section 4312 who is not reemployed in a position of employment by reason of paragraph (1) shall be entitled to be reemployed as follows:

(A) Except as provided in subparagraph (B), in any other position of employment referred to in subsection (a)(1) or (a)(2), as the case may be (in the order of priority set out in the applicable subsection), that provides a similar status and pay to a position of employment referred to in paragraph (1) of this subsection, consistent with the circumstances of such person's case, with full seniority.

(B) In the case of a person who has a disability incurred in, or aggravated during, a period of service in the uniformed services that requires reasonable efforts by the employer for the person to be able to perform the duties of the position of employment, in any other position referred to in subsection (a)(3) (in the order of priority set out in that subsection) that provides a similar status and pay to a position referred to in paragraph (1) of this subsection, consistent with circumstances of such person's case, with full seniority.

§ 4314. Reemployment by the Federal Government.

(a) Except as provided in subsections (b), (c), and (d), if a person is entitled to reemployment by the Federal Government under section 4312, such person shall be reemployed in a position of employment as described in section 4313.

(b)(1) If the Director of the Office of Personnel Management makes a determination described in paragraph (2) with respect to a person who was employed by a Federal executive agency at the time the person entered the service from which the person seeks reemployment under this section, the Director shall—

(A) identify a position of like seniority, status, and pay at another Federal executive agency that satisfies the requirements of section 4313 and for which the person is qualified; and

(B) ensure that the person is offered such position.

(2) The Director shall carry out the duties referred to in subparagraphs (A) and (B) of paragraph (1) if the Director determines that—

(A) the Federal executive agency that employed the person referred to in such paragraph no longer exists and the functions of such agency have not been transferred to another Federal executive agency; or

(B) it is impossible or unreasonable for the agency to reemploy the person.

(c) If the employer of a person described in subsection (a) was, at the time such person entered the service from which such person seeks reemployment under this section, a part of the judicial branch or the legislative branch of the Federal Government, and such employer determines that it is impossible or unreasonable for such employer to reemploy such person, such person shall, upon application to the Director of the Office of Personnel Management, be ensured an offer of employment in an alternative position in a Federal executive agency on the basis described in subsection (b).

(d) If the adjutant general of a State determines that it is impossible or unreasonable to reemploy a person who was a National Guard technician employed under section 709 of title 32, such person shall, upon application to the Director of the Office of Personnel Management, be ensured an offer of employment in an alternative position in a Federal executive agency on the basis described in subsection (b).

§ 4315. Reemployment by certain Federal agencies.

(a) The head of each agency referred to in section 2302(a)(2)(C)(ii) of title 5 shall prescribe procedures for ensuring that the rights under this chapter apply to the employees of such agency.

(b) In prescribing procedures under subsection (a), the head of an agency referred to in that subsection shall ensure, to the maximum extent practicable, that the procedures of the agency for reemploying persons who serve in the uniformed services provide for the reemployment of such persons in the agency in a manner similar to the manner of reemployment described in section 4313.

(c)(1) The procedures prescribed under subsection (a) shall designate an official at the agency who shall determine whether or not the reemployment of a person referred to in subsection (b) by the agency is impossible or unreasonable.

(2) Upon making a determination that the reemployment by the agency of a person referred to in subsection (b) is impossible or unreasonable, the official referred to in paragraph (1) shall notify the person and the Director of the Office of Personnel Management of such determination.

(3) A determination pursuant to this subsection shall not be subject to judicial review.

(4) The head of each agency referred to in subsection (a) shall submit to the Select Committee on Intelligence and the Committee on Veterans' Affairs of the Senate and the Permanent Select Committee on Intelligence and the Committee on Veterans' Affairs of the House of Representatives on an annual basis a report on the number of persons whose reemployment with the agency was determined under this subsection to be impossible or unreasonable during the year preceding the report, including the reason for each such determination.

(d)(1) Except as provided in this section, nothing in this section, section 4313, or section 4325 shall be construed to exempt any agency referred to in subsection (a) from compliance with any other substantive provision of this chapter.

(2) This section may not be construed—

(A) as prohibiting an employee of an agency referred to in subsection (a) from seeking information from the Secretary regarding assistance in seeking reemployment from the agency under this chapter, alternative employment in the Federal Government under this chapter, or information relating to the rights and obligations of employee and Federal agencies under this chapter; or

(B) as prohibiting such an agency from voluntarily cooperating with or seeking assistance in or of clarification from the Secretary or the Director of the Office of Personnel Management of any matter arising under this chapter.

(e) The Director of the Office of Personnel Management shall ensure the offer of employment to a person in a position in a Federal executive agency on the basis described in subsection (b) if—

(1) the person was an employee of an agency referred to in section 2302(a)(2)(C)(ii) of title 5 at the time the person entered the service from which the person seeks reemployment under this section;

(2) the appropriate officer of the agency determines under subsection (c) that reemployment of the person by the agency is impossible or unreasonable; and

(3) the person submits an application to the Director for an offer of employment under this subsection.

§ 4316. Rights, benefits, and obligations of persons absent from employment for service in a uniformed service.

(a) A person who is reemployed under this chapter is entitled to the seniority and other rights and benefits determined by seniority that the person had on the date of the commencement of service in the uniformed services plus the additional seniority and rights and benefits that such person would have attained if the person had remained continuously employed.

(b)(1) Subject to paragraphs (2) through (6), a person who is absent from a position of employment by reason of service in the uniformed services shall be—

(A) deemed to be on furlough or leave of absence while performing such service; and

(B) entitled to such other rights and benefits not determined by seniority as are generally provided by the employer of the person to employees having similar seniority, status, and pay who are on furlough or leave of absence under a contract, agreement, policy, practice, or plan in effect at the commencement of such service or established while such person performs such service.

(2)(A) Subject to subparagraph (B), a person who—

(i) is absent from a position of employment by reason of service in the uniformed services, and

(ii) knowingly provides written notice of intent not to return to a position of employment after service in the uniformed service, is not entitled to rights and benefits under paragraph (1)(B).

(B) For the purposes of subparagraph (A), the employer shall have the burden of proving that a person knowingly provided clear written notice of intent not to return to a position of employment after service in the uniformed service and, in doing so, was aware of the specific rights and benefits to be lost under subparagraph (A).

(3) A person deemed to be on furlough or leave of absence under this subsection while serving in the uniformed services shall not be entitled under this subsection to any benefits to which the person would not otherwise be entitled if the person had remained continuously employed.

(4) Such person may be required to pay the employee cost, if any, of any funded benefit continued pursuant to paragraph (1) to the extent other employees on furlough or leave of absence are so required.

(5) The entitlement of a person to coverage under a health plan is provided for under section 4317.

(6) The entitlement of a person to a right or benefit under an employee pension benefit plan is provided for under section 4318.

(c) A person who is reemployed by an employer under this chapter shall not be discharged from such employment, except for cause—

(1) within one year after the date of such reemployment, if the person's period of service before the reemployment was more than 180 days; or

(2) within 180 days after the date of such reemployment, if the person's period of service before the reemployment was more than 30 days but less than 181 days.

(d) Any person whose employment with an employer is interrupted by a period of service in the uniformed services shall be permitted, upon request of that person, to use during such period of service any vacation, annual, or similar leave with pay accrued by the person before the commencement of such service. No employer may require any such person to use vacation, annual, or similar leave during such period of service.

(e)(1) An employer shall grant an employee who is a member of a reserve component an authorized leave of absence from a position of employment to allow that employee to perform funeral honors duty as authorized by section 12503 of title 10 or section 115 of title 32.

(2) For purposes of section 4312(e)(1) of this title, an employee who takes an authorized leave of absence under paragraph (1) is deemed to have notified the employer of the employee's intent to return to such position of employment.

§ 4317. Health plans.

(a)(1) In any case in which a person (or the person's dependents) has coverage under a health plan in connection with the person's position of employment, including a group health plan (as defined in section 607(1) of the Employee Retirement Income Security Act of 1974 [29 U.S.C. § 1167(1)]), and such person is absent from such position of employment by reason of service in the uniformed services, or such person becomes eligible for medical and dental care under chapter 55 of title 10 by reason of subsection (d) of section 1074 of that title, the plan shall provide that the person may elect to continue such coverage as provided in this subsection. The maximum period of coverage of a person and the person's dependents under such an election shall be the lesser of—

(A) the 24-month period beginning on the date on which the person's absence begins; or

(B) the day after the date on which the person fails to apply for or return to a position of employment, as determined under section 4312(e).

(2) A person who elects to continue health-plan coverage under this paragraph may be required to pay not more than 102 percent of the full premium under the plan (determined in the same manner as the applicable premium under section 4980B(f)(4) of the Internal Revenue Code of 1986 [26 U.S.C. § 4980B(f)(4)]) associated with such coverage for the employer's other employees, except that in the case of a person who performs service in the uniformed services for

less than 31 days, such person may not be required to pay more than the employee share, if any, for such coverage.

(3) In the case of a health plan that is a multiemployer plan, as defined in section 3(37) of the Employee Retirement Income Security Act of 1974 [29 U.S.C. § 1002(37)], any liability under the plan for employer contributions and benefits arising under this paragraph shall be allocated—

(A) by the plan in such manner as the plan sponsor shall provide; or

(B) if the sponsor does not provide—

(i) to the last employer employing the person before the period served by the person in the uniformed services, or

(ii) if such last employer is no longer functional, to the plan.

(b)(1) Except as provided in paragraph (2), in the case of a person whose coverage under a health plan was terminated by reason of service in the uniformed services, or by reason of the person's having become eligible for medical and dental care under chapter 55 of title 10 [10 U.S.C. §§ 1071 *et seq.*] by reason of subsection (d) of section 1074 of that title [10 U.S.C. § 1074], an exclusion or waiting period may not be imposed in connection with the reinstatement of such coverage upon reemployment under this chapter if an exclusion or waiting period would not have been imposed under a health plan had coverage of such person by such plan not been terminated as a result of such service or eligibility. This paragraph applies to the person who is reemployed and to any individual who is covered by such plan by reason of the reinstatement of the coverage of such person.

(2) Paragraph (1) shall not apply to the coverage of any illness or injury determined by the Secretary of Veterans Affairs to have been incurred in, or aggravated during, performance of service in the uniformed services.

(3) In the case of a person whose coverage under a health plan is terminated by reason of the person having become eligible for medical and dental care under chapter 55 of title 10 by reason of subsection (d) of section 1074 of that title but who subsequently does not commence a period of active duty under the order to active duty that established such eligibility because the order is canceled before such active duty commences, the provisions of paragraph (1) relating to any exclusion or waiting period in connection with the reinstatement of coverage under a health plan shall apply to such person's continued employment, upon the termination of such eligibility for medical and dental care under chapter 55 of title 10 [10 U.S.C. §§ 1071 *et seq.*] that is incident to the cancellation of such order, in the same manner as if

the person had become reemployed upon such termination of eligibility.

§ 4318. Employee pension benefit plans.

(a)(1)(A) Except as provided in subparagraph (B), in the case of a right provided pursuant to an employee pension benefit plan (including those described in sections 3(2) and 3(33) of the Employee Retirement Income Security Act of 1974 [29 U.S.C. § 1002(2), (33)]) or a right provided under any Federal or State law governing pension benefits for governmental employees, the right to pension benefits of a person reemployed under this chapter shall be determined under this section.

(B) In the case of benefits under the Thrift Savings Plan, the rights of a person reemployed under this chapter shall be those rights provided in section 8432b of title 5. The first sentence of this subparagraph shall not be construed to affect any other right or benefit under this chapter.

(2)(A) A person reemployed under this chapter shall be treated as not having incurred a break in service with the employer or employers maintaining the plan by reason of such person's period or periods of service in the uniformed services.

(B) Each period served by a person in the uniformed services shall, upon reemployment under this chapter, be deemed to constitute service with the employer or employers maintaining the plan for the purpose of determining the nonforfeitability of the person's accrued benefits and for the purpose of determining the accrual of benefits under the plan.

(b)(1) An employer reemploying a person under this chapter shall, with respect to a period of service described in subsection (a)(2)(B), be liable to an employee pension benefit plan for funding any obligation of the plan to provide the benefits described in subsection (a)(2) and shall allocate the amount of any employer contribution for the person in the same manner and to the same extent the allocation occurs for other employees during the period of service. For purposes of determining the amount of such liability and any obligation of the plan, earnings and forfeitures shall not be included. For purposes of determining the amount of such liability and for purposes of section 515 of the Employee Retirement Income Security Act of 1974 [29 U.S.C. § 1145] or any similar Federal or State law governing pension benefits for governmental employees, service in the uniformed services that is deemed under subsection (a) to be service with the employer shall be deemed to be service with the employer under the terms of the plan or any applicable collective bargaining agreement. In the case of a multiemployer plan, as defined in section 3(37) of the Employee Retirement Income Security Act of 1974 [29 U.S.C. § 1002(37)], any liability of the plan described in this paragraph shall be allocated—

(A) by the plan in such manner as the sponsor maintaining the plan shall provide; or

(B) if the sponsor does not provide—

(i) to the last employer employing the person before the period served by the person in the uniformed services, or

(ii) if such last employer is no longer functional, to the plan.

(2) A person reemployed under this chapter shall be entitled to accrued benefits pursuant to subsection (a) that are contingent on the making of, or derived from, employee contributions or elective deferrals (as defined in section 402(g)(3) of the Internal Revenue Code of 1986 [26 U.S.C. § 402(g)(3)]) only to the extent the person makes payment to the plan with respect to such contributions or deferrals. No such payment may exceed the amount the person would have been permitted or required to contribute had the person remained continuously employed by the employer throughout the period of service described in subsection (a)(2)(B). Any payment to the plan described in this paragraph shall be made during the period beginning with the date of reemployment and whose duration is three times the period of the person's service in the uniformed services, such payment period not to exceed five years.

(3) For purposes of computing an employer's liability under paragraph (1) or the employee's contributions under paragraph (2), the employee's compensation during the period of service described in subsection (a)(2)(B) shall be computed—

(A) at the rate the employee would have received but for the period of service described in subsection (a)(2)(B), or

(B) in the case that the determination of such rate is not reasonably certain, on the basis of the employee's average rate of compensation during the 12-month period immediately preceding such period (or, if shorter, the period of employment immediately preceding such period).

(c) Any employer who reemploys a person under this chapter and who is an employer contributing to a multiemployer plan, as defined in section 3(37) of the Employee Retirement Income Security Act of 1974 [29 U.S.C. § 1002(37)], under which benefits are or may be payable to such person by reason of the obligations set forth in this chapter, shall, within 30 days after the date of such reemployment, provide information, in writing, of such reemployment to the administrator of such plan. . . .

§ 4322. Enforcement of employment or reemployment rights.

(a) A person who claims that—

(1) such person is entitled under this chapter to employment or reemployment rights or benefits with respect to employment by an employer; and

(2)(A) such employer has failed or refused, or is about to fail or refuse, to comply with the provisions of this chapter; or

(B) in the case that the employer is a Federal executive agency, such employer or the Office of Personnel Management has failed or refused, or is about to fail or refuse, to comply with the provisions of this chapter, may file a complaint with the Secretary in accordance with subsection (b), and the Secretary shall investigate such complaint.

(b) Such complaint shall be in writing, be in such form as the Secretary may prescribe, include the name and address of the employer against whom the complaint is filed, and contain a summary of the allegations that form the basis for the complaint.

(c)(1) Not later than five days after the Secretary received a complaint submitted by a person under subsection (a), the Secretary shall notify such person in writing of his or her rights with respect to such complaint under this section and section 4323 or 4324, as the case may be.

(2) The Secretary shall, upon request, provide technical assistance to a potential claimant with respect to a complaint under this subsection, and when appropriate, to such claimant's employer.

(d) The Secretary shall investigate each complaint submitted pursuant to subsection (a). If the Secretary determines as a result of the investigation that the action alleged in such complaint occurred, the Secretary shall attempt to resolve the complaint by making reasonable efforts to ensure that the person or entity named in the complaint complies with the provisions of this chapter.

(e) If the efforts of the Secretary with respect to any complaint filed under subsection (a) do not resolve the complaint, the Secretary shall notify the person who submitted the complaint of—

(1) the results of the Secretary's investigation; and

(2) the complainant's entitlement to proceed under the enforcement of rights provisions provided under section 4323 (in the case of a person submitting a complaint against a State or private employer) or section 4324 (in the case of a person submitting a complaint against a Federal executive agency or the Office of Personnel Management).

(f) Any action required by subsections (d) and (e) with respect to a complaint submitted by a person to the Secretary under subsection (a) shall be completed by the Secretary not later than 90 days after receipt of such complaint.

(g) This subchapter does not apply to any action relating to benefits to be provided under the Thrift Savings Plan under title 5.

§ 4323. Enforcement of rights with respect to a State or private employer.

(a)(1) A person who receives from the Secretary a notification pursuant to section 4322(e) of this title of an unsuccessful effort to resolve a complaint relating to a State (as an employer) or a private employer may request that the Secretary refer the complaint to the Attorney General. Not later than 60 days after the Secretary receives such a request with respect to a complaint, the Secretary shall refer the complaint to the Attorney General. If the Attorney General is reasonably satisfied that the person on whose behalf the complaint is referred is entitled to the rights or benefits sought, the Attorney General may appear on behalf of, and act as attorney for, the person on whose behalf the complaint is submitted and commence an action for relief under this chapter for such person. In the case of such an action against a State (as an employer), the action shall be brought in the name of the United States as the plaintiff in the action.

(2) Not later than 60 days after the date the Attorney General receives a referral under paragraph (1), the Attorney General shall—

(A) make a decision whether to appear on behalf of, and act as attorney for, the person on whose behalf the complaint is submitted; and

(B) notify such person in writing of such decision.

(3) A person may commence an action for relief with respect to a complaint against a State (as an employer) or a private employer if the person—

(A) has chosen not to apply to the Secretary for assistance under section 4322(a) of this title;

(B) has chosen not to request that the Secretary refer the complaint to the Attorney General under paragraph (1); or

(C) has been refused representation by the Attorney General with respect to the complaint under such paragraph.

(b)(1) In the case of an action against a State (as an employer) or a private employer commenced by the United States, the district courts of the United States shall have jurisdiction over the action.

(2) In the case of an action against a State (as an employer) by a person, the action may be brought in a State court of competent jurisdiction in accordance with the laws of the State.

(3) In the case of an action against a private employer by a person, the district courts of the United States shall have jurisdiction of the action.

(c)(1) In the case of an action by the United States against a State (as an employer), the action may proceed in the United States district court for any district in which the State exercises any authority or carries out any function.

(2) In the case of an action against a private employer, the action may proceed in the United States district court for any district in which the private employer of the person maintains a place of business.

(d)(1) In any action under this section, the court may award relief as follows:

(A) The court may require the employer to comply with the provisions of this chapter.

(B) The court may require the employer to compensate the person for any loss of wages or benefits suffered by reason of such employer's failure to comply with the provisions of this chapter.

(C) The court may require the employer to pay the person an amount equal to the amount referred to in subparagraph (B) as liquidated damages, if the court determines that the employer's failure to comply with the provisions of this chapter was willful.

(2)(A) Any compensation awarded under subparagraph (B) or (C) of paragraph (1) shall be in addition to, and shall not diminish, any of the other rights and benefits provided for under this chapter.

(B) In the case of an action commenced in the name of the United States for which the relief includes compensation awarded under subparagraph (B) or (C) of paragraph (1), such compensation shall be held in a special deposit account and shall be paid, on order of the Attorney General, directly to the person. If the compensation is not paid to the person because of inability to do so within a period of 3 years, the compensation shall be covered into the Treasury of the United States as miscellaneous receipts.

(3) A State shall be subject to the same remedies, including prejudgment interest, as may be imposed upon any private employer under this section.

(e) The court shall use, in any case in which the court determines it is appropriate, its full equity powers, including temporary or permanent injunctions, temporary restraining orders, and contempt orders, to vindicate fully the rights or benefits of persons under this chapter.

(f) An action under this chapter may be initiated only by a person claiming rights or benefits under this chapter under subsection (a) or by the United States under subsection (a)(1).

(g) In any action under this chapter, only an employer or a potential employer, as the case may be, shall be a necessary party respondent.

(h)(1) No fees or court costs may be charged or taxed against any person claiming rights under this chapter.

(2) In any action or proceeding to enforce a provision of this chapter by a person under subsection (a)(2) who obtained private counsel for such action or proceeding, the court may award any such person who prevails in such action or proceeding reasonable attorney fees, expert witness fees, and other litigation expenses.

(i) In this section, the term "private employer" includes a political subdivision of a State. . . .

§ 4334. Notice of rights and duties.

(a) Each employer shall provide to persons entitled to rights and benefits under this chapter a notice of the rights, benefits, and obligations of such persons and such employers under this chapter. The requirement for the provision of notice under this section may be met by the posting of the notice where employers customarily place notices for employees.

(b) The Secretary shall provide to employers the text of the notice to be provided under this section.

EMPLOYEE RETIREMENT INCOME SECURITY ACT

(Including COBRA, HIPAA, the Newborns' and Mothers' Health Protection Act, and the Mental Health Parity Act)
29 U.S.C. §§ 1001-1461

Title I – Protection of Employee Benefit Rights

Subtitle A – General Provisions

Part 5 – Administration and Enforcement

Part 6 – Continuation Coverage and Additional Standards for Group Health Plans [COBRA]

Part 7 – Group Health Plan Requirements

Subpart A – Requirements Relating to Portability, Access, and Renewability [HIPAA]

Subpart B – Other Requirements

Subpart C – General Provisions

Title IV – Plan Termination Insurance

Subtitle A – Pension Benefit Guaranty Corporation

Title I – Protection of Employee Benefit Rights

Subtitle A – General Provisions

§ 2 [§ 1001]. Congressional findings and declaration of policy

(a) Benefit plans as affecting interstate commerce and the Federal taxing power. The Congress finds that the growth in size, scope, and numbers of employee benefit plans in recent years has been rapid and substantial; that the operational scope and economic impact of such plans is increasingly interstate; that the continued well-being and security of millions of employees and their dependents are directly affected by these plans; that they are affected with a national public interest; that they have become an important factor affecting the stability of employment and the successful development of industrial relations; that they have become an important factor in commerce because of the interstate character of their activities, and of the activities of their participants, and the employers, employee organizations, and other entities by which they are established or maintained; that a large volume of the activities of such plans is carried on by means of the mails and instrumentalities of interstate commerce; that owing to the lack of employee information and adequate safeguards concerning their operation, it is desirable in the interests of employees and their beneficiaries, and to provide for the general welfare and the free flow of commerce, that disclosure be made and safeguards be provided with respect to the establishment, operation, and administration of such plans; that they substantially affect the revenues of the United States because they are afforded preferential Federal tax treatment; that despite the enormous growth in such plans many employees with long years of employment are losing anticipated retirement benefits owing to the lack of vesting provisions in such plans; that owing to the inadequacy of current minimum standards, the soundness and stability of plans with respect to adequate funds to pay promised benefits may be endangered; that owing to the termination of plans before requisite funds have been accumulated, employees and their beneficiaries have been deprived of anticipated benefits;

and that it is therefore desirable in the interests of employees and their beneficiaries, for the protection of the revenue of the United States, and to provide for the free flow of commerce, that minimum standards be provided assuring the equitable character of such plans and their financial soundness.

(b) Protection of interstate commerce and beneficiaries by requiring disclosure and reporting, setting standards of conduct, etc., for fiduciaries. It is hereby declared to be the policy of this Act to protect interstate commerce and the interests of participants in employee benefit plans and their beneficiaries, by requiring the disclosure and reporting to participants and beneficiaries of financial and other information with respect thereto, by establishing standards of conduct, responsibility, and obligation for fiduciaries of employee benefit plans, and by providing for appropriate remedies, sanctions, and ready access to the Federal courts.

(c) Protection of interstate commerce, the Federal taxing power, and beneficiaries by vesting of accrued benefits, setting minimum standards of funding, requiring termination insurance. It is hereby further declared to be the policy of this Act to protect interstate commerce, the Federal taxing power, and the interests of participants in private pension plans and their beneficiaries by improving the equitable character and the soundness of such plans by requiring them to vest the accrued benefits of employees with significant periods of service, to meet minimum standards of funding, and by requiring plan termination insurance. . . .

§ 3 [§ 1002]. Definitions. For purposes of this title:

(1) The terms "employee welfare benefit plan" and "welfare plan" mean any plan, fund, or program which was heretofore or is hereafter established or maintained by an employer or by an employee organization, or by both, to the extent that such plan, fund, or program was established or is maintained for the purpose of providing for its participants or their beneficiaries, through the purchase of insurance or otherwise, (A) medical, surgical, or hospital care or benefits, or benefits in the event of sickness, accident, disability, death or unemployment, or vacation benefits, apprenticeship or other training programs, or day care centers, scholarship funds, or prepaid legal services, or (B) any benefit described in section 302(c) of [the Labor Management Relations Act] (other than pensions on retirement or death, and insurance to provide such pensions).

(2)(A) Except as provided in subparagraph (B), the terms "employee pension benefit plan" and "pension plan" mean any plan, fund, or program which was heretofore or is hereafter established or maintained by an employer or by an employee organization, or by both, to the extent that by its express terms or as a result of surrounding circumstances such plan, fund, or program—

(i) provides retirement income to employees, or

(ii) results in a deferral of income by employees for periods extending to the termination of covered employment or beyond, regardless of the method of calculating the contributions made to the plan, the method of calculating the benefits under the plan or the method of distributing benefits from the plan. A distribution from a plan, fund, or program shall not be treated as made in a form other than retirement income or as a distribution prior to termination of covered employment solely because such distribution is made to an employee who has attained age 62 and who is not separated from employment at the time of such distribution.

(B) The Secretary may by regulation prescribe rules consistent with the standards and purposes of this Act providing one or more exempt categories under which—

(i) severance pay arrangements, and

(ii) supplemental retirement income payments, under which the pension benefits of retirees or their beneficiaries are supplemented to take into account some portion or all of the increases in the cost of living (as determined by the Secretary of Labor) since retirement, shall, for purposes of this title, be treated as welfare plans rather than pension plans. In the case of any arrangement or payment a principal effect of which is the evasion of the standards or purposes of this Act applicable to pension plans, such arrangement or payment shall be treated as a pension plan. An applicable voluntary early retirement incentive plan . . . and an applicable employment retention plan . . . shall for purposes of this Act, be treated as a welfare plan (and not a pension plan) with respect to such payments and supplements.

(3) The term "employee benefit plan" or "plan" means an employee welfare benefit plan or an employee pension benefit plan or a plan which is both an employee welfare benefit plan and an employee pension benefit plan.

(4) The term "employee organization" means any labor union or any organization of any kind, or any agency or employee representation committee, association, group, or plan, in which employees participate and which exists for the purpose, in whole or in part, of dealing with employers concerning an employee benefit plan, or other matters incidental to employment relationships; or any employees' beneficiary association organized for the purpose in whole or in part, of establishing such a plan.

(5) The term "employer" means any person acting directly as an employer, or indirectly in the interest of an employer, in relation to an employee benefit plan; and includes a group or association of employers acting for an employer in such capacity.

(6) The term "employee" means any individual employed by an employer.

(7) The term "participant" means any employee or former employee of an employer, or any member or former member of an employee organization, who is or may become eligible to receive a benefit of any type from an employee benefit plan which covers employees of such employer or members of such organization, or whose beneficiaries may be eligible to receive any such benefit.

(8) The term "beneficiary" means a person designated by a participant, or by the terms of an employee benefit plan, who is or may become entitled to a benefit thereunder.

(9) The term "person" means an individual, partnership, joint venture, corporation, mutual company, joint-stock company, trust, estate, unincorporated organization, association, or employee organization.

(10) The term "State" includes any State of the United States, the District of Columbia, Puerto Rico, the Virgin Islands, American Samoa, Guam, Wake Island, and the Canal Zone. The term "United States" when used in the geographic sense means the States and the Outer Continental Shelf lands defined in the Outer Continental Shelf Lands Act [43 U.S.C. §§ 1331-1343].

(11) The term "commerce" means trade, traffic, commerce, transportation, or communication between any State and any place outside thereof.

(12) The term "industry or activity affecting commerce" means any activity, business, or industry in commerce or in which a labor dispute would hinder or obstruct commerce or the free flow of commerce, and includes any activity or industry "affecting commerce" within the meaning of the Labor Management Relations Act, 1947 [29 U.S.C. §§ 141 et seq.] or the Railway Labor Act [45 U.S.C. §§ 151 et seq.]

(13) The term "Secretary" means the Secretary of Labor.

(14) The term "party in interest" means, as to an employee benefit plan—

(A) any fiduciary (including, but not limited to, any administrator, officer, trustee, or custodian), counsel, or employee of such employee benefit plan;

(B) a person providing services to such plan;

(C) an employer any of whose employees are covered by such plan;

(D) an employee organization any of whose members are covered by such plan;

(E) an owner, direct or indirect, of 50 percent or more of—

(i) the combined voting power of all classes of stock entitled to vote or the total value of shares of all classes of stock of a corporation.

(ii) the capital interest or the profits interest of a partnership, or

(iii) the beneficial interest of a trust or unincorporated enterprise, which is an employer or an employee organization described in subparagraph (C) or (D);

(F) a relative (as defined in paragraph (15)) of any individual described in subparagraph (A), (B), (C), or (E);

(G) a corporation, partnership, or trust or estate of which (or in which) 50 percent or more of—

(i) the combined voting power of all classes of stock entitled to vote or the total value of shares of all classes of stock of such corporation,

(ii) the capital interest or profits interest of such partnership, or

(iii) the beneficial interest of such trust or estate, is owned directly or indirectly, or held by persons described in subparagraph (A), (B), (C), (D), or (E);

(H) an employee, officer, director (or an individual having powers or responsibilities similar to those of officers or directors), or a 10 percent or more shareholder directly or indirectly, of a person described in subparagraph (B), (C), (D), (E), or (G), or of the employee benefit plan; or

(I) a 10 percent or more (directly or indirectly in capital or profits) partner or joint venturer of a person described in subparagraph (B), (C), (D), (E), or (G). . . .

(15) The term "relative" means a spouse, ancestor, lineal descendant, or spouse of a lineal descendant.

(16)(A) The term "administrator" means—

(i) the person specifically so designated by the terms of the instrument under which the plan is operated;

(ii) if an administrator is not so designated, the plan sponsor; or

(iii) in the case of a plan for which an administrator is not designated and a plan sponsor cannot be identified, such other person as the Secretary may by regulation prescribe.

(B) The term "plan sponsor" means (i) the employer in the case of an employee benefit plan established or maintained by a single employer, (ii) the employee organization in the case of a plan established or maintained by an employee organization, or (iii) in the case of a plan established or maintained by two or more employers or jointly by one or more employers and one or more employee organizations, the association, committee, joint board of trustees, or other similar group of representatives of the parties who establish or maintain the plan. . . .

(19) The term "nonforfeitable" when used with respect to a pension benefit or right means a claim obtained by a participant or his beneficiary to that part of an immediate or deferred benefit under a pension plan which arises from the participant's service, which is unconditional, and which is legally enforceable against the plan. For purposes of this paragraph, a right to an accrued benefit derived from employer contributions shall not be treated as forfeitable merely because the plan contains a provision described in section 203(a)(3). . . .

(21)(A) Except as otherwise provided in subparagraph (B), a person is a fiduciary with respect to a plan to the extent (i) he exercises any discretionary authority or discretionary control respecting management of such plan or exercises any authority or control respecting management or disposition of its assets, (ii) he renders investment advice for a fee or other compensation, direct or indirect, with respect to any moneys or other property of such plan, or has any authority or responsibility to do so, or (iii) he has any discretionary authority or discretionary responsibility in the administration of such plan. Such term includes any person designated under section 405(c)(1)(B). . . .

(22) The term "normal retirement benefit" means the greater of the early retirement benefit under the plan, or the benefit under the plan commencing at normal retirement age. The normal retirement benefit shall be determined without regard to—

(A) medical benefits, and

(B) disability benefits not in excess of the qualified disability benefit.

For purposes of this paragraph, a qualified disability benefit is a disability benefit provided by a plan which does not exceed the benefit which would be provided for the participant if he separated from the service at normal retirement age. For purposes of this paragraph, the early retirement benefit under a plan shall be determined without regard to any benefit under the plan which the Secretary of the Treasury finds to be a benefit described in section 204(b)(1)(G).

(23) The term "accrued benefit" means—

(A) in the case of a defined benefit plan, the individual's accrued benefit determined under the plan and, except as provided in section 204(c)(3), expressed in the form of an annual benefit commencing at normal retirement age, or

(B) in the case of a plan which is an individual account plan, the balance of the individual's account.

The accrued benefit of an employee shall not be less than the amount determined under section 204(c)(2)(B) with respect to the employee's accumulated contribution.

(24) The term "normal retirement age" means the earlier of—

(A) the time a plan participant attains normal retirement age under the plan, or

(B) the later of—

(i) the time a plan participant attains age 65, or

(ii) the 5th anniversary of the time a plan participant commenced participation in the plan.

(25) The term "vested liabilities" means the present value of the immediate or deferred benefits available at normal retirement age for participants and their beneficiaries which are nonforfeitable.

(26) The term "current value" means fair market value where available and otherwise the fair value as determined in good faith by a trustee or a named fiduciary (as defined in section 402(a)(2)) pursuant to the terms of the plan and in accordance with regulations of the Secretary, assuming an orderly liquidation at the time of such determination.

(27) The term "present value", with respect to a liability, means the value adjusted to reflect anticipated events. . . .

(28) The term "normal service cost" or "normal cost" means the annual cost of future pension benefits and administrative expenses assigned, under an actuarial cost method, to years subsequent to a particular valuation date of a pension plan. . . .

(29) The term "accrued liability" means the excess of the present value, as of a particular valuation date of a pension plan, of the projected future benefit costs and administrative expenses for all plan participants and beneficiaries over the present value of future contributions for the normal cost of all applicable plan participants and beneficiaries. . . .

(30) The term "unfunded accrued liability" means the excess of the accrued liability, under an actuarial cost method which so provides, over the present value of the assets of a pension plan. . . .

(32) The term "governmental plan" means a plan established or maintained for its employees by the Government of the United States, by the government of any State or political subdivision thereof, or by any agency or instrumentality of any of the foregoing. . . .

(33)(A) The term "church plan" means a plan established and maintained . . . by a church or by a convention or association of churches which is exempt from tax under section 501 of [the Internal Revenue Code]. . . .

(34) The term "individual account plan" or "defined contribution plan" means a pension plan which provides for an individual account for each participant and for benefits based solely upon the amount contributed to the participant's account, and any income, expenses, gains and losses, and any forfeitures of accounts of other participants which may be allocated to such participant's account.

(35) The term "defined benefit plan" means a pension plan other than an individual account plan; except that a pension plan which is not an individual account plan and which provides a benefit derived from employer contributions which is based partly on the balance of the separate account of a participant—

(A) for the purposes of section 202 shall be treated as an individual account plan, and

(B) for the purposes of paragraph (23) of this section and section 204 shall be treated as an individual account plan to the extent the benefits are based upon the separate account of a participant and as a defined benefit plan with respect to the remaining portion of benefits under the plan.

(36) The term "excess benefit plan" means a plan maintained by an employer solely for the purpose of providing benefits for certain employees in excess of the limitations on contributions and benefits imposed by section 415 of [the Internal Revenue Code] on plans to which that section applies, without regard to whether the plan is funded. . . .

(37)(A) The term "multiemployer plan" means a plan—

(i) to which more than one employer is required to contribute,

(ii) which is maintained pursuant to one or more collective bargaining agreements between one or more employee organizations and more than one employer, and

(iii) which satisfies such other requirements as the Secretary may prescribe by regulation. . . .

(38) The term "investment manager" means any fiduciary (other than a trustee or named fiduciary, as defined in section 402(a)(2))—

(A) who has the power to manage, acquire, or dispose of any asset of a plan;

(B) who is (i) registered as an investment adviser under the Investment Advisers Act of 1940 [15 U.S.C. §§ 80b-1 et seq.] or under the laws of any State; (ii) [is registered as an investment advisor under State law; (iii) is a bank, as defined in that Act; or (iv) is an insurance company qualified to perform services described in subparagraph (A) under the laws of more than one State; and

(C) has acknowledged in writing that he is a fiduciary with respect to the plan.

(39) The terms "plan year" and "fiscal year of the plan" mean, with respect to a plan, the calendar, policy, or fiscal year on which the records of the plan are kept.

(40)(A) The term "multiple employer welfare arrangement" means an employee welfare benefit plan, or any other arrangement (other than an employee welfare benefit plan), which is established or maintained for the purpose of offering or providing any benefit described in paragraph (1) to the employees of two or more employers (including one or more self-employed individuals), or to their beneficiaries . . .

(41) The term "single-employer plan" means a plan which is not a multiemployer plan.

§ 4 [§ 1003]. Coverage

(a) Except as provided in subsection (b) or (c) of this section and in sections 201, 301, and 401, this title shall apply to any employee benefit plan if it is established or maintained—

(1) by any employer engaged in commerce or in any industry or activity affecting commerce; or

(2) by any employee organization or organizations representing employees engaged in commerce or in any industry or activity affecting commerce; or

(3) by both.

(b) The provisions of this title shall not apply to any employee benefit plan if—

(1) such plan is a governmental plan (as defined in section 3(32));

(2) such plan is a church plan (as defined in section 3(33)) with respect to which no election has been made under section 410(d) of [the Internal Revenue Code];

(3) such plan is maintained solely for the purpose of complying with applicable workmen's compensation laws or unemployment compensation or disability insurance laws;

(4) such plan is maintained outside of the United States primarily for the benefit of persons substantially all of whom are nonresident aliens; or

(5) such plan is an excess benefit plan (as defined in section 3(36)) and is unfunded.

The provisions of part 7 of subtitle B [§§ 701 et seq.] shall not apply to a health insurance issuer (as defined in section 733(b)(2)) solely by reason of health insurance coverage (as defined in section 733(b)(1)) provided by such issuer in connection with a group health plan (as defined in section 733(a)(1)) if the provisions of this title do not apply to such group health plan.

(c) If a pension plan allows an employee to elect to make voluntary employee contributions to accounts and annuities as provided in section 408(q) [of the Internal Revenue Code], such accounts and annuities (and contributions thereto) shall not be treated as part of such plan (or as a separate pension plan) for purposes of any provision of this Act other than section 403(c), 404, or 405 (relating to exclusive benefit, and fiduciary and co-fiduciary responsibilities) and part 5 of this subchapter (relating to administration and enforcement. Such provisions shall apply to such accounts and annuities in a manner similar to their application to a simplified employee pension plan under section 408(k) of [the Internal Revenue Code].

Subtitle B – Regulatory Provisions

Part 1 – Reporting and Disclosure

§ 101 [§ 1021]. Duty of disclosure and reporting

(a) Summary plan description and information to be furnished to participants and beneficiaries. The administrator of each employee benefit plan shall cause to be furnished in accordance with section

104(b) to each participant covered under the plan and to each beneficiary who is receiving benefits under the plan—

(1) a summary plan description described in section 102(a)(1); and

(2) the information described in subsection (f) and sections 104(b)(3) and 105(a) and (c).

(b) Reports to be filed with Secretary of Labor. The administrator shall, in accordance with section 104(a), file with the Secretary—

(1) the annual report containing the information required by section 103; and

(2) terminal and supplementary reports as required by subsection (c) of this section.

(c) Terminal and supplementary reports

(1) Each administrator of an employee pension benefit plan which is winding up its affairs (without regard to the number of participants remaining in the plan) shall, in accordance with regulations prescribed by the Secretary, file such terminal reports as the Secretary may consider necessary. A copy of such report shall also be filed with the Pension Benefit Guaranty Corporation.

(2) The Secretary may require terminal reports to be filed with regard to any employee welfare benefit plan which is winding up its affairs in accordance with regulations promulgated by the Secretary.

(3) The Secretary may require that a plan described in paragraph (1) or (2) file a supplementary or terminal report with the annual report in the year such plan is terminated and that a copy of such supplementary or terminal report in the case of a plan described in paragraph (1) be also filed with the Pension Benefit Guaranty Corporation. . . .

(h) Simple retirement accounts

(1) Except as provided in this subsection, no report shall be required under this section by an employer maintaining a qualified salary reduction arrangement under section 408(p) of [the Internal Revenue Code].

(2) The trustee of any simple retirement account established pursuant to a qualified salary reduction arrangement under section 408(p) of [the Internal Revenue Code] shall provide to the employer maintaining the arrangement each year a description containing the following information:

(A) The name and address of the employer and the trustee.

(B) The requirements for eligibility for participation.

(C) The benefits provided with respect to the arrangement.

(D) The time and method of making elections with respect to the arrangement.

(E) The procedures for, and effects of, withdrawals (including rollovers) from the arrangement.

(3) The employer shall notify each employee immediately before the period for which an election described in section 408(p)(5)(C) of [the Internal Revenue Code] may be made of the employee's opportunity to make such election. Such notice shall include a copy of the description described in paragraph (2).

(i) Notice of blackout periods to participant or beneficiary under individual account plan.

(1) In advance of the commencement of any blackout period with respect to an individual account plan, the plan administrator shall notify the plan participants and beneficiaries who are affected by such action in accordance with this subsection.

(2)(A) The notices described in paragraph (1) shall be written in a manner calculated to be understood by the average plan participant and shall include—

(i) the reasons for the blackout period,

(ii) an identification of the investments and other rights affected,

(iii) the expected beginning date and length of the blackout period,

(iv) in the case of investments affected, a statement that the participant or beneficiary should evaluate the appropriateness of their current investment decisions in light of their inability to direct or diversify assets credited to their accounts during the blackout period, and

(v) such other matters as the Secretary may require by regulation.

(B) Except as otherwise provided in this subsection, notices described in paragraph (1) shall be furnished to all participants and beneficiaries under the plan to whom the blackout period applies at least 30 days in advance of the blackout period.

(C) In any case in which—

(i) a deferral of the blackout period would violate the requirements of subparagraph (A) or (B) of section 404(a)(1), and a fiduciary of the plan reasonably so determines in writing, or

(ii) the inability to provide the 30-day advance notice is due to events that were unforeseeable or circumstances beyond the reasonable control of the plan administrator, and a fiduciary of the plan reasonably so determines in writing, subparagraph (B) shall not apply, and the notice shall be furnished to all participants and beneficiaries under the plan to whom the blackout period applies as soon as reasonably possible under the circumstances unless such a notice in advance of the termination of the blackout period is impracticable.

(D) The notice required to be provided under this subsection shall be in writing, except that such notice may be in electronic or other form to the extent that such form is reasonably accessible to the recipient. . . .

(4) If, following the furnishing of the notice pursuant to this subsection, there is a change in the beginning date or length of the blackout period (specified in such notice pursuant to paragraph (2)(A)(iii)), the administrator shall provide affected participants and beneficiaries notice of the change as soon as reasonably practicable. In relation to the extended blackout period, such notice shall meet the requirements of paragraph (2)(D) and shall specify any material change in the matters referred to in clauses (i) through (v) of paragraph (2)(A). . . .

(6) The Secretary shall issue guidance and model notices which meet the requirements of this subsection.

(7) For purposes of this subsection—

(A) The term "blackout period" means, in connection with an individual account plan, any period for which any ability of participants or beneficiaries under the plan, which is otherwise available under the terms of such plan, to direct or diversify assets credited to their accounts, to obtain loans from the plan, or to obtain distributions from the plan is temporarily suspended, limited, or restricted, if such suspension, limitation, or restriction is for any period of more than 3 consecutive business days. . . .

(m) Notice of right to divest. Not later than 30 days before the first date on which an applicable individual of an applicable individual account plan is eligible to exercise the right under section 204(j) to direct the proceeds from the divestment of employer securities with respect to any type of contributions, the administrator shall provide to such individual a notice—

(1) setting forth such right under such section, and

(2) describing the importance of diversifying the investment of retirement account assets.

The notice required by this subsection shall be written in a manner calculated to be understood by the average plan participant and may be delivered in written, electronic, or other appropriate form to the extent that such form is reasonably accessible to the recipient.

§ 102 [§ 1022]. Summary plan description

(a) A summary plan description of any employee benefit plan shall be furnished to participants and beneficiaries as provided in section 104(b). The summary plan description shall include the information described in subsection (b) of this section, shall be written in a manner calculated to be understood by the average plan participant, and shall be sufficiently accurate and comprehensive to reasonably apprise such participants and beneficiaries of their rights and obligations under the plan. A summary of any material modification in the terms of the plan and any change in the information required under subsection (b) of this section shall be written in a manner calculated to be understood by the average plan participant and shall be furnished in accordance with section 104(b)(1).

(b) The summary plan description shall contain the following information: The name and type of administration of the plan; in the case of a group health plan (as defined in section 733(a)(1)), whether a health insurance issuer (as defined in section 733(b)(2)) is responsible for the financing or administration (including payment of claims) of the plan and (if so) the name and address of such issuer; the name and address of the person designated as agent for the service of legal process, if such person is not the administrator; the name and address of the administrator; names, titles, and addresses of any trustee or trustees (if they are persons different from the administrator); a description of the relevant provisions of any applicable collective bargaining agreement; the plan's requirements respecting eligibility for participation and benefits; a description of the provisions providing for nonforfeitable pension benefits; circumstances which may result in disqualification, ineligibility, or denial or loss of benefits; the source of financing of the plan and the identity of any organization through which benefits are provided; the date of the end of the plan year and whether the records of the plan are kept on a calendar, policy, or fiscal year basis; the procedures to be followed in presenting claims for benefits under the plan including the office at the Department of Labor through which participants and beneficiaries may seek assistance or information regarding their rights under this Act and the Health Insurance Portability and Accountability Act of 1996 with respect to health benefits that are offered through a group health plan (as defined in section 733(a)(1)), the remedies available under the plan for the redress of claims which are denied in whole or in part (including procedures required under section 503), and if the employer so elects for purposes of complying with section 701(f)(3)(B)(i), the model notice applicable to the State in which the participants and beneficiaries reside.

§ 103 [§ 1023]. Annual Reports

[This section requires employee benefit plans to publish annual reports and specifies the information that must be included in them. In general terms, the reports must include a financial statement, an opinion by a qualified public accountant on the financial statement, an actuarial statement, and an opinion by an enrolled actuary on the actuarial statement.]

§ 104 [§ 1024]. Filing and Furnishing of Information

[This section requires annual reports, plan descriptions and summary plan descriptions to be filed with the Secretary. It also requires that participants and beneficiaries receiving benefits be furnished with summary plan descriptions and summaries of the annual report, and that other relevant information (annual reports, plan description, collective bargaining agreements, etc.) be made available to them.]

§ 105 [§ 1025]. Reporting of Participant's Benefit Rights

(a) Requirements to provide pension benefit statements.

(1)(A) The administrator of an individual account plan (other than a one-participant retirement plan described in section 101(i)(8)(B)) shall furnish a pension benefit statement—

(i) at least once each calendar quarter to a participant or beneficiary who has the right to direct the investment of assets in his or her account under the plan,

(ii) at least once each calendar year to a participant or beneficiary who has his or her own account under the plan but does not have the right to direct the investment of assets in that account, and

(iii) upon written request to a plan beneficiary not described in clause (i) or (ii).

(B) The administrator of a defined benefit plan (other than a one-participant retirement plan described in section 101(i)(8)(B)) shall furnish a pension benefit statement—

(i) at least once every 3 years to each participant with a nonforfeitable accrued benefit and who is employed by the employer maintaining the plan at the time the statement is furnished, and

(ii) to a participant or beneficiary of the plan upon written request.

Information furnished upon clause (i) to a participant may be based on reasonable estimates determined under regulations prescribed by the Secretary, in consultation with the Pension Benefit Guaranty Corporation.

(2)(A) A pension benefit statement under paragraph (1)—

(i) shall indicate, on the basis of the latest available information—

(I) the total benefits accrued, and

(II) the nonforfeitable benefits, if any, which have accrued, or the earliest date on which benefits will become nonforfeitable,

(ii) shall include an explanation of any permitted disparity under section 401(l) [of the Internal Revenue Code] or any floor-offset arrangement that may be applied in determining any accrued benefits described in clause (i),

(iii) shall be written in a manner calculated to be understood by the average plan participant, and

(iv) may be delivered in written, electronic, or other appropriate form to the extent such form is reasonably accessible to the participant or beneficiary.

(B) In the case of an individual account plan, any pension benefit statement under clause (i) or (ii) of paragraph (1)(A) shall include—

(i) the value of each investment to which assets in the individual account have been allocated, determined as of the most recent valuation date under the plan, including the value of any assets held in the form of employer securities, without regard to whether such securities were contributed by the plan sponsor or acquired at the direction of the plan or of the participant or beneficiary, and

(ii) in the case of a pension benefit statement under paragraph (1)(A)(i)—

(I) an explanation of any limitations or restrictions on any right of the participant or beneficiary under the plan to direct an investment,

(II) an explanation, written in a manner calculated to be understood by the average plan participant, of the importance, for the long-term retirement security of participants and beneficiaries of a well-balanced and diversified investment portfolio, including a statement of the risk that holding more than 20 percent of a portfolio in the security of one entity (such as employer securities) may not be adequately diversified, and

(III) a notice directing the participant or beneficiary to the Internet website of the Department of Labor for sources of information on individual investing and diversification. . . .

(b) Limitation on number of statements. In no case shall a participant or beneficiary be entitled under this section to receive more than 1 statement described in subparagraph (A)(iii) or (B)(ii) of subsection (a)(1) of this section, whichever is applicable, in any 12 month period. . . .

Part 2 – Participation and Vesting

§ 201 [§ 1051]. Coverage. This part shall apply to any employee benefit plan described in section 4(a) (and not exempted under section 4(b)) other than—

(1) an employee welfare benefit plan;

(2) a plan which is unfunded and is maintained by an employer primarily for the purpose of providing deferred compensation for a select group of management or highly compensated employees;

(3)(A) a plan established and maintained by a society, order, or association described in section 501(c)(8) or (9) of [the Internal Revenue Code], if no part of the contributions to or under such plan are made by employers of participants in such plan, or

(B) a trust described in section 501(c)(18) of [the Internal Revenue Code];

(4) a plan is established and maintained by a labor organization described in section 501(c)(5) of [the Internal Revenue Code] and which does not at any time after September 2, 1974, provide for employer contributions;

(5) any agreement providing payments to a retired partner or a deceased partner's successor in interest, as described in section 736 of [the Internal Revenue Code];

(6) an individual retirement account or annuity described in section 408 of [the Internal Revenue Code], or a retirement bond described in section 409 of [the Internal Revenue Code] (as effective for obligations issued before January 1, 1984);

(7) an excess benefit plan; or

(8) any plan, fund or program under which an employer, all of whose stock is directly or indirectly owned by employees, former employees or their beneficiaries, proposes through an unfunded arrangement to compensate retired employees for benefits which were forfeited by such employees under a pension plan maintained by a former employer prior to the date such pension plan became subject to this Act.

§ 202 [§ 1052]. Minimum participation standards

(a)(1)(A) No pension plan may require, as a condition of participation in the plan, that an employee complete a period of service with the employer or employers maintaining the plan extending beyond the later of the following dates—

(i) the date on which the employee attains the age of 21; or

(ii) the date on which he completes 1 year of service.

(B)(i) In the case of any plan which provides that after not more than 2 years of service each participant has a right to 100 percent of his accrued benefit under the plan which is nonforfeitable at the time such benefit accrues, clause (ii) of subparagraph (A) shall be applied by substituting "2 years of service" for "1 year of service".

(ii) In the case of any plan maintained exclusively for employees of an educational organization (as defined in section 170(b)(1)(A)(ii) of [the Internal Revenue Code]) by an employer which is exempt from tax under section 501(a) of [the Internal Revenue Code], which provides that each participant having at least 1 year of service has a right to 100 percent of his accrued benefit under the plan which is nonforfeitable at the time such benefit accrues, clause (i) of subparagraph (A) shall be applied by substituting "26" for "21". This clause shall not apply to any plan to which clause (i) applies.

(2) No pension plan may exclude from participation (on the basis of age) employees who have attained a specified age.

[The remainder of this section deals with issues that arise in applying the participation standards. The section defines "year of service" and "hour of service" (which is used in the definition of "year of service"). The section also provides guidance on how to deal with breaks in service, including breaks caused by the birth or adoption of a child.]

§ 203 [§ 1053]. Minimum vesting standards

(a) Nonforfeitability requirements. Each pension plan shall provide that an employee's right to his normal retirement benefit is nonforfeitable upon the attainment of normal retirement age and in addition shall satisfy the requirements of paragraphs (1) and (2) of this subsection.

(1) A plan satisfies the requirements of this paragraph if an employee's rights in his accrued benefit derived from his own contributions are nonforfeitable.

(2)(A)(i) In the case of a defined benefit plan, a plan satisfies the requirements of this paragraph if it satisfies the requirements of clause (ii) or (iii).

(ii) A plan satisfies the requirements of this clause if an employee who has completed at least 5 years of service has a nonforfeitable right to 100 percent of the employee's accrued benefit derived from employer contributions.

(iii) A plan satisfies the requirements of this clause if an employee has a nonforfeitable right to a percentage of the employee's accrued benefit derived from employer contributions determined under the following table:

Years of service:	The nonforfeitable percentage is:
3	20
4	40
5	60
6	80
7 or more	100.

(B)(i) In the case of an individual account plan, a plan satisfies the requirements of this paragraph if it satisfies the requirements of clause (ii) or (iii).

(ii) A plan satisfies the requirements of this clause if an employee who has completed at least 3 years of service has a nonforfeitable right to 100 percent of the employee's accrued benefit derived from employer contributions.

(iii) A plan satisfies the requirements of this clause if an employee has a nonforfeitable right to a percentage of the employee's accrued benefit derived from employer contributions determined under the following table:

Years of service:	The nonforfeitable percentage is:
2	20
3	40
4	60
5	80
6 or more	100.

(3)(A) A right to an accrued benefit derived from employer contributions shall not be treated as forfeitable solely because the plan provides that it is not payable if the participant dies (except in the case of a survivor annuity which is payable as provided in section 205).

(B) A right to an accrued benefit derived from employer contributions shall not be treated as forfeitable solely because the plan provides that the payment of benefits is suspended for such period as the employee is employed, subsequent to the commencement of payment of such benefits—

(i) in the case of a plan other than a multiemployer plan, by an employer who maintains the plan under which such benefits were being paid; and

(ii) in the case of a multiemployer plan, in the same industry, in the same trade or craft, and the same geographic area covered by the plan, as when such benefits commenced.

The Secretary shall prescribe such regulations as may be necessary to carry out the purposes of this subparagraph, including regulations with respect to the meaning of the term "employed". . . .

(b) Computation of period of service

(1) In computing the period of service under the plan for purposes of determining the nonforfeitable percentage under subsection (a)(2) of this section, all of an employee's years of service with the employer or employers maintaining the plan shall be taken into account, except that the following may be disregarded:

(A) years of service before age 18;

(B) years of service during a period for which the employee declined to contribute to a plan requiring employee contributions;

(C) years of service with an employer during any period for which the employer did not maintain the plan or a predecessor plan, defined by the Secretary of the Treasury;

(D) service not required to be taken into account under paragraph (3);

(E) years of service before January 1, 1971, unless the employee has had at least 3 years of service after December 31, 1970;

(F) years of service before this part first applies to the plan if such service would have been disregarded under the rules of the plan with regard to breaks in service, as in effect on the applicable date; and

(G) in the case of a multiemployer plan, years of service—

(i) with an employer after—

(I) a complete withdrawal of such employer from the plan (within the meaning of section 4203), or

(II) to the extent permitted by regulations prescribed by the Secretary of the Treasury, a partial withdrawal described in section 4205(b)(2)(A)(i) in connection with the decertification of the collective bargaining representative; and

(ii) with any employer under the plan after the termination date of the plan under section 4048.

(2)(A) For purposes of this section, except as provided in subparagraph (C), the term "year of service" means a calendar year, plan year, or other 12-consecutive month period designated by the plan (and not prohibited under regulations prescribed by the Secretary) during which the participant has completed 1,000 hours of service.

(B) For purposes of this section, the term "hour of service" has the meaning provided by section 202(a)(3)(C).

(C) In the case of any seasonal industry where the customary period of employment is less than 1,000 hours during a calendar year, the term "year of service" shall be such period as determined under regulations of the Secretary.

(D) For purposes of this section, in the case of any maritime industry, 125 days of service shall be treated as 1,000 hours of service. The Secretary may prescribe regulations to carry out the purposes of this subparagraph.

(3)(A) For purposes of this paragraph, the term "1-year break in service" means a calendar year, plan year, or other 12-consecutive-month period designated by the plan (and not prohibited under regulations prescribed by the Secretary) during which the participant has not completed more than 500 hours of service.

(B) For purposes of paragraph (1), in the case of any employee who has any 1-year break in service, years of service before such break shall not be required to be taken into account until he has completed a year of service after his return.

(C) For purposes of paragraph (1), in the case of any participant in an individual account plan or an insured defined benefit plan which satisfies the requirements of subsection 204(b)(1)(F) who has 5 consecutive 1-year breaks in service, years of service after such 5-year period shall not be required to be taken into account for purposes of determining the nonforfeitable percentage of his accrued benefit derived from employer contributions which accrued before such 5-year period.

(D)(i) For purposes of paragraph (1), in the case of a nonvested participant, years of service with the employer or employers maintaining the plan before any period of consecutive 1-year breaks in service shall not be required to be taken into account if the number of consecutive 1-year breaks in service within such period equals or exceeds the greater of—

(I) 5, or

(II) the aggregate number of years of service before such period.

(ii) If any years of service are not required to be taken into account by reason of a period of breaks in service to which clause (i) applies, such years of service shall not be taken into account in applying clause (i) to a subsequent period of breaks in service.

(iii) For purposes of clause (i), the term "nonvested participant" means a participant who does not have any nonforfeitable right under the plan to an accrued benefit derived from employer contributions.

(E)(i) In the case of each individual who is absent from work for any period—

(I) by reason of the pregnancy of the individual,

(II) by reason of the birth of a child of the individual,

(III) by reason of the placement of a child with the individual in connection with the adoption of such child by such individual, or

(IV) for purposes of caring for such child for a period beginning immediately following such birth or placement, the plan shall treat as hours of service, solely for purposes of determining under this paragraph whether a 1-year break in service has occurred, the hours described in clause (ii).

(ii) The hours described in this clause are—

(I) the hours of service which otherwise would normally have been credited to such individual but for such absence, or

(II) in any case in which the plan is unable to determine the hours described in subclause (I), 8 hours of service per day of absence, except that the total number of hours treated as hours of service under this clause by reason of such pregnancy or placement shall not exceed 501 hours.

(iii) The hours described in clause (ii) shall be treated as hours of service as provided in this subparagraph—

(I) only in the year in which the absence from work begins, if a participant would be prevented from incurring a 1-year break in service in such year solely because the period of absence is treated as hours of service as provided in clause (i); or

(II) in any other case, in the immediately following year.

(iv) For purposes of this subparagraph, the term "year" means the period used in computations pursuant to paragraph (2).

(v) A plan may provide that no credit will be given pursuant to this subparagraph unless the individual furnishes to the plan administrator such timely information as the plan may reasonably require to establish—

(I) that the absence from work is for reasons referred to in clause (i), and

(II) the number of days for which there was such an absence. . . .

(c) Plan amendments altering vesting schedule

(1)(A) A plan amendment changing any vesting schedule under the plan shall be treated as not satisfying the requirements of subsection (a)(2) of this section if the nonforfeitable percentage of the accrued benefit derived from employer contributions (determined as of the later of the date such amendment is adopted, or the date such amendment becomes effective) of any employee who is a participant in the plan is less than such nonforfeitable percentage computed under the plan without regard to such amendment.

(B) A plan amendment changing any vesting schedule under the plan shall be treated as not satisfying the requirements of subsection (a)(2) of this section unless each participant having not less than 3 years of service is permitted to elect, within a reasonable period after adoption of such amendment, to have his nonforfeitable percentage computed under the plan without regard to such amendment.

(2) Subsection (a) of this section shall not apply to benefits which may not be provided for designated employees in the event of early termination of the plan under provisions of the plan adopted pursuant to regulations prescribed by the Secretary of the Treasury to

preclude the discrimination prohibited by section 401(a)(4) of [the Internal Revenue Code].

(d) Nonforfeitable benefits after lesser period and in greater amounts than required. A pension plan may allow for nonforfeitable benefits after a lesser period and in greater amounts than are required by this part.

(e) Consent for distribution; present value; covered distributions

(1) If the present value of any nonforfeitable benefit with respect to a participant in a plan exceeds $5,000, the plan shall provide that such benefit may not be immediately distributed without the consent of the participant. . .

(f) Special rules for plans computing acccrued benefits by reference to hypothetical account balance or equivalent amounts.

(1) An applicable defined benefit plan shall not be treated as failing to meet—

(A) subject to paragraph (2), the requirements of subsection (a)(2) of this section, or

(B) the requirements of section 204(c) or 205(g), or the requirements of subsection (e), with respect to accrued benefits derived from employer contributions,

solely because the present value of the accrued benefit (or any portion thereof) of any participant is, under the terms of the plan, equal to the amount expressed as the balance in the hypothetical account described in paragraph (3) or as an accumulated percentage of the participant's final average compensation.

(2) In the case of an applicable defined benefit plan, such plan shall be treated as meeting the requirements of subsection (a)(2) of this section only if an employee who has completed at least 3 years of service has a nonforfeitable right to 100 percent of the employee's accrued benefit derived from employer contributions.

(3) For purposes of this subsection—

(A) The term "applicable defined benefit plan" means a defined benefit plan under which the accrued benefit (or any portion thereof) is calculated as the balance of a hypothetical account maintained for the participant or as an accumulated percentage of the participant's final average compensation. . . .

§ 204 [§ 1054]. Benefit accrual requirements

(a) Satisfaction of requirements by pension plans. Each pension plan shall satisfy the requirements of subsection (b)(3) of this section, and—

(1) in the case of a defined benefit plan, shall satisfy the requirements of subsection (b)(1) of this section; and

(2) in the case of a defined contribution plan, shall satisfy the requirements of subsection (b)(2) of this section.

(b) Enumeration of plan requirements

(1)(A) A defined benefit plan satisfies the requirements of this paragraph if the accrued benefit to which each participant is entitled upon his separation from the service is not less than—

(i) 3 percent of the normal retirement benefit to which he would be entitled at the normal retirement age if he commenced participation at the earliest possible entry age under the plan and served continuously until the earlier of age 65 or the normal retirement age specified under the plan, multiplied by

(ii) the number of years (not in excess of 33 1/3) of his participation in the plan. . . .

(B) A defined benefit plan satisfies the requirements of this paragraph of a particular plan year if under the plan the accrued benefit payable at the normal retirement age is equal to the normal retirement benefit and the annual rate at which any individual who is or could be a participant can accrue the retirement benefits payable at normal retirement age under the plan for any later plan year is not more than 133 1/3 percent of the annual rate at which he can accrue benefits for any plan year beginning on or after such particular plan year and before such later plan year. . . .

(C) A defined benefit plan satisfies the requirements of this paragraph if the accrued benefit to which any participant is entitled upon his separation from the service is not less than a fraction of the annual benefit commencing at normal retirement age to which he would be entitled under the plan as in effect on the date of his separation if he continued to earn annually until normal retirement age the same rate of compensation upon which his normal retirement benefit would be computed under the plan, determined as if he had attained normal retirement age on the date any such determination is made (but taking into account no more than the 10 years of service immediately preceding his separation from service). Such fraction shall be a fraction, not exceeding 1, the numerator of which is the total number of his years of participation in the plan (as of the date of his separation from the service) and the denominator of which is the total number of years he would have participated in the plan if he separated from the service at the normal retirement age. . . .

(2)(A) A defined contribution plan satisfies the requirements of this paragraph if, under the plan, allocations to the employee's account are not ceased, and the rate at which amounts are allocated to the employee's account is not reduced, because of the attainment of any age. . . .

(3) A plan satisfies the requirements of this paragraph if—

(A) in the case of a defined benefit plan, the plan requires separate accounting for the portion of each employee's accrued benefit derived from any voluntary employee contributions permitted under the plan; and

(B) in the case of any plan which is not a defined benefit plan, the plan requires separate accounting for each employee's accrued benefit. . . .

(g) Decrease of accrued benefits through amendment of plan

(1) The accrued benefit of a participant under a plan may not be decreased by an amendment of the plan, other than an amendment described in section 302(c)(8) or 4281. . . .

(j) Diversification requirements for certain individual accounts plans.

(1) An applicable individual account plan shall meet the diversification requirements of paragraphs (2), (3), and (4).

(2) In the case of the portion of an applicable individual's account attributable to employee contributions and elective deferrals which is invested in employer securities, a plan meets the requirements of this paragraph if the applicable individual may elect to direct the plan to divest any such securities and to reinvest an equivalent amount in other investment options meeting the requirements of paragraph (4).

(3) In the case of the portion of the account attributable to employer contributions other than elective deferrals which is invested in employer securities, a plan meets the requirements of this paragraph if each applicable individual who—

(A) is a participant who has completed at least 3 years of service, or

(B) is a beneficiary of a participant described in subparagraph (A) or of a deceased participant, may elect to direct the plan to divest any such securities and to reinvest an equivalent amount in other investment options meeting the requirements of paragraph (4).

(4)(A) The requirements of this paragraph are met if the plan offers not less than 3 investment options, other than employer securities, to which an applicable individual may direct the proceeds from the divestment of employer securities pursuant to this subsection, each of which is diversified and has materially different risk and return characteristics.

(B)(i) A plan shall not be treated as failing to meet the requirements of this paragraph merely because the plan limits the time for divestment and reinvestment to periodic, reasonable opportunities occurring no less frequently than quarterly.

(ii) Except as provided in regulations, a plan shall not meet the requirements of this paragraph if the plan imposes restrictions or conditions with respect to the investment of employer securities which are not imposed on the investment of other assets of the plan. This subparagraph shall not apply to any restrictions or conditions imposed by reason of the application of securities laws. . . .

§ 205 [§ 1055]. Requirement of joint and survivor annuity and preretirement survivor annuity

(a) Required contents for applicable plans. Each pension plan to which this section applies shall provide that—

(1) in the case of a vested participant who does not die before the annuity starting date, the accrued benefit payable to such participant shall be provided in the form of a qualified joint and survivor annuity, and

(2) in the case of a vested participant who dies before the annuity starting date and who has a surviving spouse, a qualified preretirement survivor annuity shall be provided to the surviving spouse of such participant.

(b) Applicable plans

(1) This section shall apply to—

(A) any defined benefit plan,

(B) any individual account plan which is subject to the funding standards of section 302, and

(C) any participant under any other individual account plan unless—

(i) such plan provides that the participant's nonforfeitable accrued benefit . . . is payable in full, on the death of the participant, to the participant's surviving spouse (or, if there is no surviving spouse or the surviving spouse consents in the manner required under subsection (c)(2), to a designated beneficiary),

(ii) such participant does not elect the payment of benefits in the form of a life annuity, and

(iii) with respect to such participant, such plan is not a direct or indirect transferee . . . of a plan which is described in subparagraph (A) or (B) or to which this clause applied with respect to the participant.

(c) Plans meeting requirements of section

(1) A plan meets the requirements of this section only if—

(A) under the plan, each participant—

(i) may elect at any time during the applicable election period to waive the qualified joint and survivor annuity form of benefit or the qualified preretirement survivor annuity form of benefit (or both),

(ii) if the participant elects a waiver under clause (i), may elect the qualified survivor annuity at any time during the applicable election period, and (ii) may revoke any such election at any time during the applicable election period, and

(B) the plan meets the requirements of paragraphs (2), (3), and (4).

(2) Each plan shall provide that an election under paragraph (1)(A)(i) shall not take effect unless—

(A)(i) the spouse of the participant consents in writing to such election,

(ii) such election designates a beneficiary (or a form of benefits) which may not be changed without spousal consent (or the consent of the spouse expressly permits designations by the participant without any requirement of further consent by the spouse), and (iii) the spouse's consent acknowledges the effect of such election and is witnessed by a plan representative or a notary public, or

(B) it is established to the satisfaction of a plan representative that the consent required under subparagraph (A) may not be obtained because there is no spouse, because the spouse cannot be located, or because of such other circumstances as the Secretary of the Treasury may by regulations prescribe.

Any consent by a spouse (or establishment that the consent of a spouse may not be obtained) under the preceding sentence shall be effective only with respect to such spouse.

(3)(A) Each plan shall provide to each participant, within a reasonable period of time before the annuity starting date (and consistent with such regulations as the Secretary of the Treasury may prescribe) a written explanation of—

(i) the terms and conditions of the qualified joint and survivor annuity,

(ii) the participant's right to make, and the effect of, an election under paragraph (1) to waive the joint and survivor annuity form of benefit,

(iii) the rights of the participant's spouse under paragraph (2), and

(iv) the right to make, and the effect of, a revocation of an election under paragraph (1).

(B)(i) Each plan shall provide to each participant, within the applicable period with respect to such participant (and consistent with such regulations as the Secretary may prescribe), a written explanation with respect to the qualified preretirement survivor annuity comparable to that required under subparagraph (A). . . .

(4) Each plan shall provide that, if this section applies to a participant when part or all of the participant's accrued benefit is to be used as security for a loan, no portion of the participant's accrued benefit may be used as security for such loan unless—

(A) the spouse of the participant (if any) consents in writing to such use during the 90-day period ending on the date on which the loan is to be so secured, and

(B) requirements comparable to the requirements of paragraph (2) are met with respect to such consent. . . .

(7) For purposes of this subsection, the term "applicable election period" means—

(A) in the case of an election to waive the qualified joint and survivor annuity form of benefit, the 180-day period ending on the annuity starting date, or

(B) in the case of an election to waive the qualified preretirement survivor annuity, the period which begins on the first day of the plan year in which the participant attains age 35 and ends on the date of the participant's death.

In the case of a participant who is separated from service, the applicable election period under subparagraph (B) with respect to benefits accrued before the date of such separation from service shall not begin later than such date.

(8) Notwithstanding any other provision of this subsection—

(A)(i) A plan may provide the written explanation described in paragraph (3)(A) after the annuity starting date. In any case to which this subparagraph applies, the applicable election period under paragraph (7) shall not end before the 30th day after the date on which such explanation is provided. . . .

(B) A plan may permit a participant to elect (with any applicable spousal consent) to waive any requirement that the written explanation be provided at least 30 days before the annuity starting date (or to waive the 30-day requirement under subparagraph (A)) if the distribution commences more than 7 days after such explanation is provided.

(d) "Qualified joint and survivor annuity" defined. For purposes of this section, the term "qualified joint and survivor annuity" means an annuity—

(1) for the life of the participant with a survivor annuity for the life of the spouse which is not less than 50 percent of (and is not greater than 100 percent of) the amount of the annuity which is payable during the joint lives of the participant and the spouse, and

(2) which is the actuarial equivalent of a single annuity for the life of the participant.

Such term also includes any annuity in a form having the effect of an annuity described in the preceding sentence. . . .

(e) "Qualified preretirement survivor annuity" defined. For purposes of this section—

(1) Except as provided in paragraph (2), the term "qualified preretirement survivor annuity" means a survivor annuity for the life of the surviving spouse of the participant if—

(A) the payments to the surviving spouse under such annuity are not less than the amounts which would be payable as a survivor annuity under the qualified joint and survivor annuity under the plan (or the actuarial equivalent thereof) if—

(i) in the case of a participant who dies after the date on which the participant attained the earliest retirement age, such participant had retired with an immediate qualified joint and survivor annuity on the day before the participant's date of death, or

(ii) in the case of a participant who dies on or before the date on which the participant would have attained the earliest retirement age, such participant had—

(I) separated from service on the date of death,

(II) survived to the earliest retirement age,

(III) retired with an immediate qualified joint and survivor annuity at the earliest retirement age, and

(IV) died on the day after the day on which such participant would have attained the earliest retirement age, and

(B) under the plan, the earliest period for which the surviving spouse may receive a payment under such annuity is not later than the month in which the participant would have attained the earliest retirement age under the plan.

In the case of an individual who separated from service before the date of such individual's death, subparagraph (A)(ii)(I) shall not apply.

(2) In the case of any individual account plan or participant described in subparagraph (B) or (C) of subsection (b)(1) of this section, the term "qualified preretirement survivor annuity" means an annuity for the life of the surviving spouse the actuarial equivalent of which is not less than 50 percent of the portion of the account balance of the participant (as of the date of death) to which the participant had a nonforfeitable right (within the meaning of section 203).

(3) For purposes of paragraphs (1) and (2), any security interest held by the plan by reason of a loan outstanding to the participant shall be taken into account in determining the amount of the qualified preretirement survivor annuity.

(f) Marriage requirements for plan

(1) Except as provided in paragraph (2), a plan may provide that a qualified joint and survivor annuity (or a qualified preretirement survivor annuity) will not be provided unless the participant and spouse had been married throughout the 1-year period ending on the earlier of—

(A) the participant's annuity starting date, or

(B) the date of the participant's death.

(2) For purposes of paragraph (1), if—

(A) a participant marries within 1 year before the annuity starting date, and

(B) the participant and the participant's spouse in such marriage have been married for at least a 1-year period ending on or before the date of the participant's death, such participant and such spouse shall be treated as having been married throughout the 1-year period ending on the participant's annuity starting date. . . .

(h) Definitions. For purposes of this section—

(1) The term "vested participant" means any participant who has a nonforfeitable right (within the meaning of section 3(19)) to any portion of such participant's accrued benefit.

(2)(A) The term "annuity starting date" means—

(i) the first day of the first period for which an amount is payable as an annuity, or

(ii) in the case of a benefit not payable in the form of an annuity, the first day on which all events have occurred which entitle the participant to such benefit.

(B) For purposes of subparagraph (A), the first day of the first period for which a benefit is to be received by reason of disability shall be treated as the annuity starting date only if such benefit is not an auxiliary benefit.

(3) The term "earliest retirement age" means the earliest date on which, under the plan, the participant could elect to receive retirement benefits. . . .

(k) Spousal consent. No consent of a spouse shall be effective for purposes of subsection (g)(1) or (g)(2) of this section (as the case may be) unless requirements comparable to the requirements for spousal consent to an election under subsection (c)(1)(A) of this section are met. . . .

§ 206 [§ 1056]. Form and payment of benefits

(a) Commencement date for payment of benefits. Each pension plan shall provide that unless the participant otherwise elects, the payment of benefits under the plan to the participant shall begin not later than the 60th day after the latest of the close of the plan year in which—

(1) occurs the date on which the participant attains the earlier of age 65 or the normal retirement age specified under the plan,

(2) occurs the 10th anniversary of the year in which the participant commenced participation in the plan, or

(3) the participant terminates his service with the employer.

In the case of a plan which provides for the payment of an early retirement benefit, such plan shall provide that a participant who satisfied the service requirements for such early retirement benefit, but separated from the service (with any nonforfeitable right to an accrued benefit) before satisfying the age requirement for such early retirement benefit, is entitled upon satisfaction of such age requirement to receive a benefit not less than the benefit to which he would be entitled at the normal retirement age, actuarially reduced under regulations prescribed by the Secretary of the Treasury. . . .

(d) Assignment or alienation of plan benefits

(1) Each pension plan shall provide that benefits provided under the plan may not be assigned or alienated.

(2) For the purposes of paragraph (1) of this subsection, there shall not be taken into account any voluntary and revocable

assignment of not to exceed 10 percent of any benefit payment, or of any irrevocable assignment or alienation of benefits executed before September 2, 1974. The preceding sentence shall not apply to any assignment or alienation made for the purposes of defraying plan administration costs. For purposes of this paragraph a loan made to a participant or beneficiary shall not be treated as an assignment or alienation if such loan is secured by the participant's accrued nonforfeitable benefit and is exempt from the tax imposed by section 4975 of [the Internal Revenue Code] (relating to tax on prohibited transactions) by reason of section 4975(d)(1) of [the Internal Revenue Code].

(3)(A) Paragraph (1) shall apply to the creation, assignment, or recognition of a right to any benefit payable with respect to a participant pursuant to a domestic relations order, except that paragraph (1) shall not apply if the order is determined to be a qualified domestic relations order. Each pension plan shall provide for the payment of benefits in accordance with the applicable requirements of any qualified domestic relations order.

(B) For purposes of this paragraph—

(i) the term "qualified domestic relations order" means a domestic relations order—

(I) which creates or recognizes the existence of an alternate payee's right to, or assigns to an alternate payee the right to, receive all or a portion of the benefits payable with respect to a participant under a plan, and

(II) with respect to which the requirements of subparagraphs (C) and (D) are met, and

(ii) the term "domestic relations order" means any judgment, decree, or order (including approval of a property settlement agreement) which—

(I) relates to the provision of child support, alimony payments, or marital property rights to a spouse, former spouse, child, or other dependent of a participant, and

(II) is made pursuant to a State domestic relations law (including a community property law).

(C) A domestic relations order meets the requirements of this subparagraph only if such order clearly specifies—

(i) the name and the last known mailing address (if any) of the participant and the name and mailing address of each alternate payee covered by the order,

(ii) the amount or percentage of the participant's benefits to be paid by the plan to each such alternate payee, or the manner in which such amount or percentage is to be determined,

(iii) the number of payments or period to which such order applies, and

(iv) each plan to which such order applies.

(D) A domestic relations order meets the requirements of this subparagraph only if such order—

(i) does not require a plan to provide any type or form of benefit, or any option, not otherwise provided under the plan,

(ii) does not require the plan to provide increased benefits (determined on the basis of actuarial value), and

(iii) does not require the payment of benefits to an alternate payee which are required to be paid to another alternate payee under another order previously determined to be a qualified domestic relations order.

(E)(i) A domestic relations order shall not be treated as failing to meet the requirements of clause (i) of subparagraph (D) solely because such order requires that payment of benefits be made to an alternate payee—

(I) in the case of any payment before a participant has separated from service, on or after the date on which the participant attains (or would have attained) the earliest retirement age,

(II) as if the participant had retired on the date on which such payment is to begin under such order (but taking into account only the present value of benefits actually accrued and not taking into account the present value of any employer subsidy for early retirement), and

(III) in any form in which such benefits may be paid under the plan to the participant (other than in the form of a joint and survivor annuity with respect to the alternate payee and his or her subsequent spouse).

For purposes of subclause (II), the interest rate assumption used in determining the present value shall be the interest rate specified in the plan or, if no rate is specified, 5 percent.

(ii) For purposes of this subparagraph, the term "earliest retirement age" means the earlier of—

(I) the date on which the participant is entitled to a distribution under the plan, or

(II) the later of the date of the participant attains age 50 or the earliest date on which the participant could begin receiving benefits under the plan if the participant separated from service.

(F) To the extent provided in any qualified domestic relations order—

(i) the former spouse of a participant shall be treated as a surviving spouse of such participant for purposes of section 205 (and any spouse of the participant shall not be treated as a spouse of the participant for such purposes), and

(ii) if married for at least 1 year, the surviving former spouse shall be treated as meeting the requirements of section 205(f).

(G)(i) In the case of any domestic relations order received by a plan—

(I) the plan administrator shall promptly notify the participant and each alternate payee of the receipt of such order and the plan's procedures for determining the qualified status of domestic relations orders, and

(II) within a reasonable period after receipt of such order, the plan administrator shall determine whether such order is a qualified domestic relations order and notify the participant and each alternate payee of such determination.

(ii) Each plan shall establish reasonable procedures to determine the qualified status of domestic relations orders and to administer distributions under such qualified orders. Such procedures—

(I) shall be in writing,

(II) shall provide for the notification of each person specified in a domestic relations order as entitled to payment of benefits under the plan (at the address included in the domestic relations order) of such procedures promptly upon receipt by the plan of the domestic relations order, and

(III) shall permit an alternate payee to designate a representative for receipt of copies of notices that are sent to the alternate payee with respect to a domestic relations order.

(H)(i) During any period in which the issue of whether a domestic relations order is a qualified domestic relations order is being determined (by the plan administrator, by a court of competent jurisdiction, or otherwise), the plan administrator shall separately account for the amounts (hereinafter in this subparagraph referred to as the "segregated amounts") which would have been payable to the alternate payee during such period if the order had been determined to be a qualified domestic relations order.

(ii) If within the 18-month period described in clause (v) the order (or modification thereof) is determined to be a qualified domestic relations order, the plan administrator shall pay the segregated amounts (including any interest thereon) to the person or persons entitled thereto.

(iii) If within 18-month period described in clause (v)—

(I) it is determined that the order is not a qualified domestic relations order, or

(II) the issue as to whether such order is a qualified domestic relations order is not resolved,

then the plan administrator shall pay the segregated amounts (including any interest thereon) to the person or persons who would have been entitled to such amounts if there had been no order.

(iv) Any determination that an order is a qualified domestic relations order which is made after the close of the 18-month period described in clause (v) shall be applied prospectively only.

(v) For purposes of this subparagraph, the 18-month period described in this clause is the 18-month period beginning with the date on which the first payment would be required to be made under the domestic relations order.

(I) If a plan fiduciary acts in accordance with part 4 of this subtitle in—

(i) treating a domestic relations order as being (or not being) a qualified domestic relations order, or

(ii) taking action under subparagraph (H), then the plan's obligation to the participant and each alternate payee shall be discharged to the extent of any payment made pursuant to such Act.

(J) A person who is an alternate payee under a qualified domestic relations order shall be considered for purposes of any provision of this Act a beneficiary under the plan. Nothing in the preceding sentence shall permit a requirement under section 4001 of the payment of more than 1 premium with respect to a participant for any period.

(K) The term "alternate payee" means any spouse, former spouse, child, or other dependent of a participant who is recognized by a domestic relations order as having a right to receive all, or a portion of, the benefits payable under a plan with respect to such participant. . . .

(4) Paragraph (1) shall not apply to any offset of a participant's benefits provided under an employee pension benefit plan against an amount that the participant is ordered or required to pay to the plan if—

(A) the order or requirement to pay arises—

(i) under a judgment of conviction for a crime involving such plan,

(ii) under a civil judgment (including a consent order or decree) entered by a court in an action brought in connection with a violation (or alleged violation) of part 4 of this subtitle, or

(iii) pursuant to a settlement agreement between the Secretary and the participant, or a settlement agreement between the Pension Benefit Guaranty Corporation and the participant, in connection with a violation (or alleged violation) of part 4 of this subtitle by a fiduciary or any other person,

(B) the judgment, order, decree, or settlement agreement expressly provides for the offset of all or part of the amount ordered or required to be paid to the plan against the participant's benefits provided under the plan, and

(C) in a case in which the survivor annuity requirements of section 205 apply with respect to distributions from the plan to the participant, if the participant has a spouse at the time at which the offset is to be made—

(i) either—

(I) such spouse has consented in writing to such offset and such consent is witnessed by a notary public or representative of the plan (or it is established to the satisfaction of a plan representative that such consent may not be obtained by reason of circumstances described in section 205(c)(2)(B)), or

(II) an election to waive the right of the spouse to a qualified joint and survivor annuity or a qualified preretirement survivor annuity is in effect in accordance with the requirements of section 205(c),

(ii) such spouse is ordered or required in such judgment, order, decree, or settlement to pay an amount to the plan in connection with a violation of part 4 of this subtitle, or

(iii) in such judgment, order, decree, or settlement, such spouse retains the right to receive the survivor annuity under a qualified joint and survivor annuity provided pursuant to section 205(a)(1) and under a qualified preretirement survivor annuity provided pursuant to section 205(a)(2), determined in accordance with paragraph (5).

A plan shall not be treated as failing to meet the requirements of section 205 solely by reason of an offset under this paragraph.

(5)(A) The survivor annuity described in paragraph (4)(C)(iii) shall be determined as if—

(i) the participant terminated employment on the date of the offset,

(ii) there was no offset,

(iii) the plan permitted commencement of benefits only on or after normal retirement age,

(iv) the plan provided only the minimum-required qualified joint and survivor annuity, and

(v) the amount of the qualified preretirement survivor annuity under the plan is equal to the amount of the survivor annuity payable under the minimum-required qualified joint and survivor annuity.

(B) For purposes of this paragraph, the term "minimum-required qualified joint and survivor annuity" means the qualified joint and survivor annuity which is the actuarial equivalent of the participant's accrued benefit (within the meaning of section 3(23) and under which the survivor annuity is 50 percent of the amount of the annuity which is payable during the joint lives of the participant and the spouse.

(e) Limitation on distributions other than life annuities paid by plan.

(1) Notwithstanding any other provision of this part, the fiduciary of a pension plan that is subject to the additional funding requirements of section 302(d) shall not permit a prohibited payment to be made from a plan during a period in which such plan has a liquidity shortfall (as defined in Section 302(e)(5)). . . .

Part 3 – Funding

§ 301 [§ 1081]. Coverage

(a) Plans excepted from applicability of this part. This part shall apply to any employee pension benefit plan described in section 4(a), (and not exempted under section 4(b)), other than—

(1) an employee welfare benefit plan;

(2) an insurance contract plan described in subsection (b) of this section;

(3) a plan which is unfunded and is maintained by an employer primarily for the purpose of providing deferred compensation for a select group of management or highly compensated employees;

(4)(A) a plan which is established and maintained by a society, order, or association described in section 501(c)(8) or (9) of [the Internal Revenue Code], if no part of the contributions to or under such plan are made by employers of participants in such plan; or

(B) a trust described in section 501(c)(18) of [the Internal Revenue Code];

(5) a plan which has not at any time after September 2, 1974, provided for employer contributions;

(6) an agreement providing payments to a retired partner or deceased partner or a deceased partner's successor in interest as described in section 736 of [the Internal Revenue Code];

(7) an individual retirement account or annuity as described in section 408(a) of [the Internal Revenue Code], or a retirement bond described in section 409 of [the Internal Revenue Code] (as effective for obligations issued before January 1, 1984);

(8) an individual account plan (other than a money purchase plan) and a defined benefit plan to the extent it is treated as an individual account plan (other than a money purchase plan) under section 3(35)(B);

(9) an excess benefit plan; or

(10) any plan, fund or program under which an employer, all of whose stock is directly or indirectly owned by employees, former employees or their beneficiaries, proposes through an unfunded arrangement to compensate retired employees for benefits which were forfeited by such employees under a pension plan maintained by a former employer prior to the date such pension plan became subject to this Act. . . .

§ 302 [§ 1082]. Minimum funding standards

[This section and the following sections require employers to make minimum contributions to defined benefit plans to ensure that money will be available to fund the promised benefits when the time comes to pay them.]

Part 4 – Fiduciary Responsibility

§ 401 [§ 1101]. Coverage

(a) Scope of Coverage. This part shall apply to any employee benefit plan described in section 4(a) (and not exempted under section 4(b)), other than—

(1) a plan which is unfunded and is maintained by an employer primarily for the purpose of providing deferred compensation for a select group of management or highly compensated employees; or

(2) any agreement described in section 736 of [the Internal Revenue Code], which provides payments to a retired partner or deceased partner or a deceased partner's successor in interest.

(b) Securities or policies deemed to be included in plan assets. For purposes of this part:

(1) In the case of a plan which invests in any security issued by an investment company registered under the Investment Company Act of 1940 [15 U.S.C. §§ 80a-1 et seq.], the assets of such plan shall be deemed to include such security but shall not, solely by reason of such investment, be deemed to include any assets of such investment company.

(2) In the case of a plan to which a guaranteed benefit policy is issued by an insurer, the assets of such plan shall be deemed to include such policy, but shall not, solely by reason of the issuance of such policy, be deemed to include any assets of such insurer. For purposes of this paragraph:

(A) The term "insurer" means an insurance company, insurance service, or insurance organization, qualified to do business in a State.

(B) The term "guaranteed benefit policy" means an insurance policy or contract to the extent that such policy or contract provides for benefits the amount of which is guaranteed by the insurer. Such term includes any surplus in a separate account, but excludes any other portion of a separate account. . . .

§ 402 [§ 1102]. Establishment of plan

(a) Named fiduciaries

(1) Every employee benefit plan shall be established and maintained pursuant to a written instrument. Such instrument shall provide for one or more named fiduciaries who jointly or severally shall have authority to control and manage the operation and administration of the plan.

(2) For purposes of this title, the term "named fiduciary" means a fiduciary who is named in the plan instrument, or who, pursuant to a procedure specified in the plan, is identified as a fiduciary (A) by a person who is an employer or employee organization with respect to the plan or (B) by such an employer and such an employee organization acting jointly.

(b) Requisite features of plan. Every employee benefit plan shall—

(1) provide a procedure for establishing and carrying out a funding policy and method consistent with the objectives of the plan and the requirements of this title,

(2) describe any procedure under the plan for the allocation of responsibilities for the operation and administration of the plan (including any procedure described in section 405(c)(1)),

(3) provide a procedure for amending such plan, and for identifying the persons who have authority to amend the plan, and

(4) specify the basis on which payments are made to and from the plan. . .

§ 403 [§ 1103]. Establishment of trust

(a) Benefit plan assets to be held in trust; authority of trustees. Except as provided in subsection (b) of this section, all assets of an employee benefit plan shall be held in trust by one or more trustees. Such trustee or trustees shall be either named in the trust instrument or in the plan instrument described in section 402(a) or appointed by a person who is a named fiduciary, and upon acceptance of being named or appointed, the trustee or trustees shall have exclusive authority and discretion to manage and control the assets of the plan, except to the extent that—

(1) the plan expressly provides that the trustee or trustees are subject to the direction of a named fiduciary who is not a trustee, in which case the trustees shall be subject to proper directions of such fiduciary which are made in accordance with the terms of the plan and which are not contrary to this Act, or

(2) authority to manage, acquire, or dispose of assets of the plan is delegated to one or more investment managers pursuant to section 402(c)(3). . . .

(c) Assets of plan not to inure to benefit of employer

(1) Except as provided in paragraph (2), (3) or (4) or subsection (d), or under section 4042 and 4044 (relating to termination of insured plans), . . . the assets of a plan shall never inure to the benefit of any employer and shall be held for the exclusive purposes of providing benefits to participants in the plan and their beneficiaries and defraying reasonable expenses of administering the plan. . . .

§ 404 [§ 1104]. Fiduciary duties

(a) Prudent man standard of care

(1) Subject to sections 403(c) and (d), 4042, and 4044, a fiduciary shall discharge his duties with respect to a plan solely in the interest of the participants and beneficiaries and—

(A) for the exclusive purpose of:

(i) providing benefits to participants and their beneficiaries; and

(ii) defraying reasonable expenses of administering the plan;

(B) with the care, skill, prudence, and diligence under the circumstances then prevailing that a prudent man acting in a like capacity and familiar with such matters would use in the conduct of an enterprise of a like character and with like aims;

(C) by diversifying the investments of the plan so as to minimize the risk of large losses, unless under the circumstances it is clearly prudent not to do so; and

(D) in accordance with the documents and instruments governing the plan insofar as such documents and instruments are consistent with the provisions of this title and title III of this Act. . . .

(c) Control over assets by participant or beneficiary

(1)(A) In the case of a pension plan which provides for individual accounts and permits a participant or beneficiary to exercise control over the assets in his account, if a participant or beneficiary exercises control over the assets in his account . . .—

(i) such participant or beneficiary shall not be deemed to be a fiduciary by reason of such exercise, and

(ii) no person who is otherwise a fiduciary shall be liable under this part for any loss, or by reason of any breach, which results from such participant's or beneficiary's exercise of control, except that this clause shall not apply in connection with such participant or beneficiary for any blackout period during which the ability of such participant or beneficiary to direct the investment of the assets in his or her account is suspended by a plan sponsor or fiduciary. . . .

(2) In the case of a simple retirement account established pursuant to a qualified salary reduction arrangement under section 408(p) of [the Internal Revenue Code], a participant or beneficiary shall, for purposes of paragraph (1), be treated as exercising control over the assets in the account upon the earliest of—

(A) an affirmative election among investment options with respect to the initial investment of any contribution,

(B) a rollover to any other simple retirement account or individual retirement plan, or

(C) one year after the simple retirement account is established.

No reports, other than those required under section 101(g), shall be required with respect to a simple retirement account established pursuant to such a qualified salary reduction arrangement. . . .

(5)(A) For purposes of paragraph (1), a participant or beneficiary in an individual account plan meting the notice requirements of subparagraph (B) shall be treated as exercising control over the assets in the account with respect to the amount of contributions and earnings which, in the absence of an investment election by the participant or beneficiary, are invested by the plan in accordance with regulations prescribed by the Secretary. The regulations under this subparagraph shall provide guidance on the appropriateness of designating default investments that include a mix of asset classes consistent with capital preservation or long-term capital appreciation, or a blend of both.

(B)(i) the requirements of this subparagraph are met if each participant or beneficiary—

(I) receives, within a reasonable period of time before each plan year, a notice explaining the employee's right under the plan to designate how contributions and earnings will be invested and explaining how, in the absence of any investment election by the participant or beneficiary, which contributions and earning will be invested, and

(II) has a reasonable period of time after receipt of such notice and before the beginning of the plan year to make such designation. . . .

§ 405 [§ 1105]. Liability for breach of co-fiduciary

(a) Circumstances giving rise to liability. In addition to any liability which he may have under any other provisions of this part, a fiduciary with respect to a plan shall be liable for a breach of fiduciary responsibility of another fiduciary with respect to the same plan in the following circumstances:

(1) if he participates knowingly in, or knowingly undertakes to conceal, an act or omission of such other fiduciary, knowing such act or omission is a breach;

(2) if, by his failure to comply with section 404 in the administration of his specific responsibilities which give rise to his status as a fiduciary, he has enabled such other fiduciary to commit a breach; or

(3) if he has knowledge of a breach by such other fiduciary, unless he makes reasonable efforts under the circumstances to remedy the breach.

(b) Assets held by two or more trustees

(1) Except as otherwise provided in subsection (d) of this section and in section 403(a)(1) and (2), if the assets of a plan are held by two or more trustees—

(A) each shall use reasonable care to prevent a co-trustee from committing a breach; and

(B) they shall jointly manage and control the assets of the plan, except that nothing in this subparagraph (B) shall preclude any agreement, authorized by the trust instrument, allocating specific responsibilities, obligations, or duties among trustees, in which event a trustee to whom certain responsibilities, obligations, or duties have not been allocated shall not be liable by reason of this subparagraph (B) either individually or as a trustee for any loss resulting to the plan arising from the acts or omissions on the part of another trustee to whom such responsibilities, obligations, or duties have been allocated.

(2) Nothing in this subsection shall limit any liability that a fiduciary may have under subsection (a) of this section or any other provision of this part.

(3)(A) In the case of a plan the assets of which are held in more than one trust, a trustee shall not be liable under paragraph (1) except with respect to an act or omission of a trustee of a trust of which he is a trustee.

(B) No trustee shall be liable under this subsection for following instructions referred to in section 403(a)(1).

(c) Allocation of fiduciary responsibility; designated persons to carry out fiduciary responsibilities

(1) The instrument under which a plan is maintained may expressly provide for procedures (A) for allocating fiduciary responsibilities (other than trustee responsibilities) among named fiduciaries, and (B) for named fiduciaries to designate persons other than named fiduciaries to carry out fiduciary responsibilities (other than trustee responsibilities) under the plan.

(2) If a plan expressly provides for a procedure described in paragraph (1), and pursuant to such procedure any fiduciary responsibility of a named fiduciary is allocated to any person, or a person is designated to carry out any such responsibility, then such named fiduciary shall not be liable for an act or omission of such person in carrying out such responsibility except to the extent that—

(A) the named fiduciary violated section 404(a)(1)—

(i) with respect to such allocation or designation,

(ii) with respect to the establishment or implementation of the procedure under paragraph (1), or

(iii) in continuing the allocation or designation; or

(B) the named fiduciary would otherwise be liable in accordance with subsection (a) of this section.

(3) For purposes of this subsection, the term "trustee responsibility" means any responsibility provided in the plan's trust instrument (if any) to manage or control the assets of the plan, other than a power under the trust instrument of a named fiduciary to appoint an investment manager in accordance with section 402(c)(3).

(d) Investment managers

(1) If an investment manager or managers have been appointed under section 402(c)(3), then, notwithstanding subsections (a)(2) and (3) and subsection (b) of this section, no trustee shall be liable for the acts or omissions of such investment manager or managers, or be under an obligation to invest or otherwise manage any asset of the plan which is subject to the management of such investment manager.

(2) Nothing in this subsection shall relieve any trustee of any liability under this part for any act of such trustee.

§ 406 [§ 1106]. Prohibited transactions . . .

(a) Transactions between plan and party in interest. Except as provided in section 408:

(1) A fiduciary with respect to a plan shall not cause the plan to engage in a transaction, if he knows or should know that such transaction constitutes a direct or indirect—

(A) sale, exchange, or leasing, of any property between the plan and a party in interest;

(B) lending of money or other extension of credit between the plan and a party in interest;

(C) furnishing of goods, services, or facilities between the plan and a party in interest;

(D) transfer to, or use by or for the benefit of, a party in interest, of any assets of the plan; or

(E) acquisition, on behalf of the plan, of any employer security or employer real property in violation of section 407(a). . . .

(b) Transactions between plan and fiduciary. A fiduciary with respect to a plan shall not—

(1) deal with the assets of the plan in his own interest or for his own account,

(2) in his individual or in any other capacity act in any transaction involving the plan on behalf of a party (or represent a party) whose interests are adverse to the interests of the plan or the interests of its participants or beneficiaries, or

(3) receive any consideration for his own personal account from any party dealing with such plan in connection with a transaction involving the assets of the plan. . . .

§ 407 [§ 1107]. Limitation with respect to acquisition and holding of employer securities and employer real property by certain plans

(a) Percentage limitation. Except as otherwise provided in this section and section 414 . . .

(2) A plan may not acquire any qualifying employer security or qualifying employer real property, if immediately after such acquisition the aggregate fair market value of employer securities and employer real property held by the plan exceeds 10 percent of the fair market value of the assets of the plan. . . .

§ 408 [§ 1108]. Exemptions from prohibited transactions

(a) Grant of exemptions. The Secretary shall establish an exemption procedure for purposes of this subsection. Pursuant to such procedure, he may grant a conditional or unconditional exemption of any fiduciary or transaction, or class of fiduciaries or transactions, from all or part of the restrictions imposed by sections 406 and 407(a). . . .

(b) Enumeration of transactions exempted from section 406 prohibitions. The prohibitions provided in section 406 shall not apply to any of the following transactions:

(1) Any loans made by the plan to parties in interest who are participants or beneficiaries of the plan if such loans (A) are available to all such participants and beneficiaries on a reasonably equivalent basis, (B) are not made available to highly compensated employees (within the meaning of section 414(q) of [the Internal Revenue Code]), in an amount greater than the amount made available to other employees, (C) are made in accordance with specific provisions regarding such loans set forth in the plan, (D) bear a reasonable rate of interest, and (E) are adequately secured. . . .

(13) Any transfer made before January 1, 2014, of excess pension assets from a defined benefit plan to a retiree health account in a qualified transfer permitted under section 420 of [the Internal Revenue Code](as in effect on August 17, 2006). . . .

(c) Fiduciary benefits and compensation not prohibited. Nothing in section 406 shall be construed to prohibit any fiduciary from—

(1) receiving any benefit to which he may be entitled as a participant or beneficiary in the plan, so long as the benefit is computed and paid on a basis which is consistent with the terms of the plan as applied to all other participants and beneficiaries;

(2) receiving any reasonable compensation for services rendered, or for the reimbursement of expenses properly and actually incurred, in the performance of his duties with the plan; except that no person so serving who already receives full-time pay from an employer or an association of employers, whose employees are participants in the plan, or from an employee organization whose members are participants in such plan shall receive compensation from such plan, except for reimbursement of expenses properly and actually incurred; or

(3) serving as a fiduciary in addition to being an officer, employee, agent, or other representative of a party in interest. . . .

§ 409 [§ 1109]. Liability for breach of fiduciary duty

(a) Any person who is a fiduciary with respect to a plan who breaches any of the responsibilities, obligations, or duties imposed upon fiduciaries by this title shall be personally liable to make good to such plan any losses to the plan resulting from each such breach, and to restore to such plan any profits of such fiduciary which have been made through use of assets of the plan by the fiduciary, and shall be subject to such other equitable or remedial relief as the court may deem appropriate, including removal of such fiduciary. A fiduciary may also be removed for a violation of section 411.

(b) No fiduciary shall be liable with respect to a breach of fiduciary duty under this title if such breach was committed before he became a fiduciary or after he ceased to be a fiduciary. . . .

§ 410 [§ 1110]. Exculpatory provisions; insurance

(a) Except as provided in sections 405(b)(1) and 405(d), any provision in an agreement or instrument which purports to relieve a fiduciary from responsibility or liability for any responsibility, obligation, or duty under this part shall be void as against public policy.

(b) Nothing in this subpart shall preclude—

(1) a plan from purchasing insurance for its fiduciaries or for itself to cover liability or losses occurring by reason of the act or omission of a fiduciary, if such insurance permits recourse by the insurer against the fiduciary in the case of a breach of a fiduciary obligation by such fiduciary;

(2) a fiduciary from purchasing insurance to cover liability under this part from and for his own account; or

(3) an employer or an employee organization from purchasing insurance to cover potential liability of one or more persons who serve in a fiduciary capacity with regard to an employee benefit plan. . . .

Part 5 – Administration and Enforcement

§ 501 [§ 1131]. Criminal penalties.

(a) Any person who willfully violates any provision of part 1 of this subtitle, or any regulation or order issued under any such provision, shall upon conviction be fined not more than $100,000 or imprisoned not more than 10 years, or both; except that in the case of such violation by a person not an individual, the fine imposed upon such person shall be a fine not exceeding $500,000. . . .

§ 502 [§ 1132]. Civil enforcement

(a) Persons empowered to bring a civil action. A civil action may be brought—

(1) by a participant or beneficiary—

(A) for the relief provided for in subsection (c) of this section, or

(B) to recover benefits due to him under the terms of his plan, to enforce his rights under the terms of the plan, or to clarify his rights to future benefits under the terms of the plan;

(2) by the Secretary, or by a participant, beneficiary or fiduciary for appropriate relief under section 409;

(3) by a participant, beneficiary, or fiduciary (A) to enjoin any act or practice which violates any provision of this title or the terms of the plan, or (B) to obtain other appropriate equitable relief (i) to redress such violations or (ii) to enforce any provisions of this title or the terms of the plan;

(4) by the Secretary, or by a participant, or beneficiary for appropriate relief in the case of a violation of [section] 105(c);

(5) except as otherwise provided in subsection (b) of this section, by the Secretary (A) to enjoin any act or practice which violates any provision of this title, or (B) to obtain other appropriate equitable relief (i) to redress such violation or (ii) to enforce any provision of this title;

(6) by the Secretary to collect any civil penalty under paragraph (2), (4), (5), (6), (7), (8), or (9) of subsection (c) of this section or under subsection (i) or (1) of this section;

(7) by a State to enforce compliance with a qualified medical child support order (as defined in Section 609); . . .

(9) in the event that the purchase of an insurance contract or insurance annuity in connection with termination of an individual's status as a participant covered under a pension plan with respect to all or any portion of the participant's pension benefit under such plan constitutes a violation of part 4 of this subtitle or the terms of the plan, by the Secretary, by any individual who was a participant or beneficiary at the time of the alleged violation, or by a fiduciary, to obtain appropriate relief, including the posting of security if necessary, to assure receipt by the participant or beneficiary of the amounts provided or to be provided by such insurance contract or annuity, plus reasonable prejudgment interest on such amounts. . . .

(c) Administrator's refusal to supply requested information; penalty for failure to provide annual report in complete form

(1) Any administrator (A) who fails to meet the requirements of paragraph (1) or (4) of section 606 or section 101(e)(1) with respect to a participant or beneficiary, or (B) who fails or refuses to comply with a request for any information which such administrator is required by this title to furnish to a participant or beneficiary (unless such failure or refusal results from matters reasonably beyond the control of the administrator) by mailing the material requested to the last known address of the requesting participant or beneficiary within 30 days after such request may in the court's discretion be personally liable to such participant or beneficiary in the amount of up to $100 a day from the date of such failure or refusal, and the court may in its discretion order such other relief as it deems proper. For purposes of this paragraph, each violation described in subparagraph (A) with respect to any single participant, and each violation described in

subparagraph (B) with respect to any single participant or beneficiary, shall be treated as a separate violation.

(2) The Secretary may assess a civil penalty against any plan administrator of up to $1,000 a day from the date of such plan administrator's failure or refusal to file the annual report required to be filed with the Secretary under section 101(b)(4). For purposes of this paragraph, an annual report that has been rejected under section 104(a)(4) for failure to provide material information shall not be treated as having been filed with the Secretary.

(3) Any employer maintaining a plan who fails to meet the notice requirement of section 101(d) with respect to any participant or beneficiary or who fails to meet the requirements of section 101(e)(2) with respect to any person may in the court's discretion be liable to such participant or beneficiary or to such person in the amount of up to $100 a day from the date of such failure, and the court may in its discretion order such other relief as it deems proper. . . .

(10) The Secretary may impose a penalty against any plan sponsor of a group health plan, or any health insurance issuer offering health insurance coverage in connection with the plan for any failure by such sponsor or issuer to meet the requirements of subsection (a)(1)(F), (b)(3), (c), or (d) of section 702 or section 701 or 702(b)(1) with respect to genetic information, in connection with the plan. . . .

(d) Status of employee benefit plan as entity

(1) An employee benefit plan may sue or be sued under this title as an entity. Service of summons, subpena, or other legal process of a court upon a trustee or an administrator of an employee benefit plan in his capacity as such shall constitute service upon the employee benefit plan. In a case where a plan has not designated in the summary plan description of the plan an agent for the service of legal process, service upon the Secretary shall constitute such service. The Secretary, not later than 15 days after receipt of service under the preceding sentence, shall notify the administrator or any trustee of the plan of receipt of such service.

(2) Any money judgment under this title against an employee benefit plan shall be enforceable only against the plan as an entity and shall not be enforceable against any other person unless liability against such person is established in his individual capacity under this title.

(e) Jurisdiction

(1) Except for actions under subsection (a)(1)(B) of this section, the district courts of the United States shall have exclusive jurisdiction of civil actions under this title brought by the Secretary or by a participant, beneficiary, fiduciary, or any person referred to in section 101(f)(1). State courts of competent jurisdiction and district courts

of the United States shall have concurrent jurisdiction of actions under paragraphs (1)(B) and (7) of subsection (a) of this section.

(2) Where an action under this title is brought in a district court of the United States, it may be brought in the district where the plan is administered, where the breach took place, or where a defendant resides or may be found, and process may be served in any other district where a defendant resides or may be found.

(f) Amount in controversy; citizenship of parties. The district courts of the United States shall have jurisdiction, without respect to the amount in controversy or the citizenship of the parties, to grant the relief provided for in subsection (a) of this section in any action.

(g) Attorney's fees and costs . . .

(1) In any action under this title (other than an action described in paragraph (2)) by a participant, beneficiary, or fiduciary, the court in its discretion may allow a reasonable attorney's fee and costs of action to either party. . . .

(h) Service upon Secretary of Labor and Secretary of Treasury. A copy of the complaint in any action under this title by a participant, beneficiary, or fiduciary (other than an action brought by one or more participants or beneficiaries under subsection (a)(1)(B) of this section which is solely for the purpose of recovering benefits due such participants under the terms of the plan) shall be served upon the Secretary and the Secretary of the Treasury by certified mail. Either Secretary shall have the right in his discretion to intervene in any action, except that the Secretary of the Treasury may not intervene in any action under part 4 of this subtitle. If the Secretary brings an action under subsection (a) of this section on behalf of a participant or beneficiary, he shall notify the Secretary of the Treasury.

(i) Administrative assessment of civil penalty. In the case of a transaction prohibited by section 406 by a party in interest with respect to a plan to which this part applies, the Secretary may assess a civil penalty against such party in interest. The amount of such penalty may not exceed 5 percent of the amount involved in each such transaction (as defined in section 4975(f)(4) of [the Internal Revenue Code]) for each year or part thereof during which the prohibited transaction continues, except that, if the transaction is not corrected (in such manner as the Secretary shall prescribe in regulations which shall be consistent with section 4975(f)(5) of [the Internal Revenue Code]) within 90 days after notice from the Secretary (or such longer period as the Secretary may permit), such penalty may be in an amount not more than 100 percent of the amount involved. This subsection shall not apply to a transaction with respect to a plan described in section 4975(e)(1) of [the Internal Revenue Code].

(j) Direction and control of litigation by Attorney General. In all civil actions under this title, attorneys appointed by the Secretary may represent the Secretary (except as provided in section 518(a) of Title 28), but all such litigation shall be subject to the direction and control of the Attorney General.

(k) Jurisdiction of actions against the Secretary of Labor. Suits by an administrator, fiduciary, participant, or beneficiary of an employee benefit plan to review a final order of the Secretary, to restrain the Secretary from taking any action contrary to the provisions of this Act, or to compel him to take action required under this title, may be brought in the district court of the United States for the district where the plan has its principal office, or in the United States District Court for the District of Columbia.

(l) Civil penalties on violations by fiduciaries

(1) In the case of—

(A) any breach of fiduciary responsibility under (or other violation of) part 4 by a fiduciary, or

(B) any knowing participation in such a breach or violation by any other person, the Secretary shall assess a civil penalty against such fiduciary or other person in an amount equal to 20 percent of the applicable recovery amount. . . .

(3) The Secretary may, in the Secretary's sole discretion, waive or reduce the penalty under paragraph (1) if the Secretary determines in writing that—

(A) the fiduciary or other person acted reasonably and in good faith, or

(B) it is reasonable to expect that the fiduciary or other person will not be able to restore all losses to the plan without severe financial hardship unless such waiver or reduction is granted. . . .

§ 503 [§ 1133]. Claims procedure. In accordance with regulations of the Secretary, every employee benefit plan shall—

(1) provide adequate notice in writing to any participant or beneficiary whose claim for benefits under the plan has been denied, setting forth the specific reasons for such denial, written in a manner calculated to be understood by the participant, and

(2) afford a reasonable opportunity to any participant whose claim for benefits has been denied for a full and fair review by the appropriate named fiduciary of the decision denying the claim. . . .

§ 510 [§ 1140]. Interference with protected rights. It shall be unlawful for any person to discharge, fine, suspend, expel, discipline, or discriminate against a participant or beneficiary for exercising any right to which he is entitled under the provisions of an employee benefit plan, this title, section 3001, or the Welfare and Pension Plans Disclosure Act [29 U.S.C. §§ 301 et seq.], or for the purpose of interfering with the attainment of any right to which such participant may become entitled under the plan, this title, or the

Welfare and Pension Plans Disclosure Act. It shall be unlawful for any person to discharge, fine, suspend, expel, or discriminate against any person because he has given information or has testified or is about to testify in any inquiry or proceeding relating to this Act or the Welfare and Pension Plans Disclosure Act. . . . The provisions of section 502 shall be applicable in the enforcement of this section. . . .

§ 514 [§ 1144]. Effect on other laws

(a) Supersedure; effective date. Except as provided in subsection (b) of this section, the provisions of this title and title III of this Act shall supersede any and all State laws insofar as they may now or hereafter relate to any employee benefit plan described in section 4(a) and not exempt under section 4(b). . . .

(b) Construction and application

(1) This section shall not apply with respect to any cause of action which arose, or any act or omission which occurred, before January 1, 1975.

(2)(A) Except as provided in subparagraph (B), nothing in this title shall be construed to exempt or relieve any person from any law of any State which regulates insurance, banking, or securities.

(B) Neither an employee benefit plan described in section 4(a), which is not exempt under section 4(b) (other than a plan established primarily for the purpose of providing death benefits), nor any trust established under such a plan, shall be deemed to be an insurance company or other insurer, bank, trust company, or investment company or to be engaged in the business of insurance or banking for purposes of any law of any State purporting to regulate insurance companies, insurance contracts, banks, trust companies, or investment companies.

(3) Nothing in this section shall be construed to prohibit use by the Secretary of services or facilities of a State agency as permitted under section 506.

(4) Subsection (a) of this section shall not apply to any generally applicable criminal law of a State.

(5) [S]ubsection (a) shall not apply to the Hawaii Prepaid Health Care Act [Haw. Rev. Stat §§ 393-1 through 393-51]. . . .

(7) Subsection (a) shall not apply to qualified domestic relations orders (within the meaning of section 206(d)(3)(B)(I)), qualified medical child support orders (within the meaning of section 609(a)(2)(A)), and the provisions of law referred to in section 609(a)(2)(B)(ii) to the extent enforced by qualified medical child support orders. . . .

(c) Definitions. For purposes of this section:

(1) The term "State law" includes all laws, decisions, rules, regulations, or other State action having the effect of law, of any State. A law of the United States applicable only to the District of Columbia shall be treated as a State law rather than a law of the United States.

(2) The term "State" includes a State, any political subdivisions thereof, or any agency or instrumentality of either, which purports to regulate, directly or indirectly, the terms and conditions of employee benefit plans covered by this title.

(d) Alteration, amendment, modification, invalidation, impairment, or supersedure of any law of United States prohibited. Nothing in this title shall be construed to alter, amend, modify, invalidate, impair, or supersede any law of the United States (except as provided in sections 111 and 507(b)) or any rule or regulation issued under any such law. . . .

Part 6 – Continuation Coverage and Additional Standards for Group Health Plans [COBRA]

§ 601 [§ 1161]. Plans must provide continuation coverage to certain individuals

(a) In general. The plan sponsor of each group health plan shall provide, in accordance with this part, that each qualified beneficiary who would lose coverage under the plan as a result of a qualifying event is entitled, under the plan, to elect, within the election period, continuation coverage under the plan.

(b) Exception for certain plans. Subsection (a) shall not apply to any group health plan for any calendar year if all employers maintaining such plan normally employed fewer than 20 employees on a typical business day during the preceding calendar year.

§ 602 [§ 1162]. Continuation coverage. For purposes of section 601, the term "continuation coverage" means coverage under the plan which meets the following requirements:

(1) Type of benefit coverage. The coverage must consist of coverage which, as of the time the coverage is being provided, is identical to the coverage provided under the plan to similarly situated beneficiaries under the plan with respect to whom a qualifying event has not occurred. If coverage is modified under the plan for any group of similarly situated beneficiaries, such coverage shall also be modified in the same manner for all individuals who are qualified beneficiaries under the plan pursuant to this part in connection with such group.

(2) Period of coverage. The coverage must extend for at least the period beginning on the date of the qualifying event and ending not earlier than the earliest of the following:

(A) Maximum required period.

(i) General rule for terminations and reduced hours. In the case of a qualifying event described in section

603(2), except as provided in clause (ii), the date which is 18 months after the date of the qualifying event.

(ii) **Special rule for multiple qualifying events**. If a qualifying event (other than a qualifying event described in section 603(6) occurs during the 18 months after the date of a qualifying event described in section 603(2), the date which is 36 months after the date of the qualifying event described in section 603(2).

(iii) **Special rule for certain bankruptcy proceedings**. In the case of a qualifying event described in section 603(6) (relating to bankruptcy proceedings), the date of the death of the covered employee or qualified beneficiary (described in section 607(3)(C)(iii), or in the case of the surviving spouse or dependent children of the covered employee, 36 months after the date of the death of the covered employee.

(iv) **General rule for other qualifying events**. In the case of a qualifying event not described in section 603(2) or 603(6), the date which is 36 months after the date of the qualifying event. . . .

(vii) **Medicare entitlement followed by qualifying event**. In the case of a qualifying event described in section 603(2) that occurs less than 18 months after the date the covered employee became entitled to benefits under title XVIII of the Social Security Act [42 U.S.C. §§ 1395 et seq.], the period of coverage for qualified beneficiaries other than the covered employee shall not terminate under this subparagraph before the close of the 36-month period beginning on the date the covered employee became so entitled. . . .

(B) **End of plan**. The date on which the employer ceases to provide any group health plan to any employee.

(C) **Failure to pay premium**. The date on which coverage ceases under the plan by reason of a failure to make timely payment of any premium required under the plan with respect to the qualified beneficiary. The payment of any premium (other than any payment referred to in the last sentence of paragraph (3)) shall be considered to be timely if made within 30 days after the date due or within such longer period as applies to or under the plan.

(D) **Group health plan coverage or Medicare entitlement**. The date on which the qualified beneficiary first becomes, after the date of the election—

(i) covered under any other group health plan (as an employee or otherwise) which does not contain any exclusion or limitation with respect to any preexisting condition of such beneficiary (other than such an exclusion or limitation which does not apply to (or is satisfied by) such beneficiary by reason of chapter 100 of [the Internal Revenue Code], part 7 of this subtitle [29 U.S.C. §§ 1181 et seq.], or title XXVII of the Public Health Service Act [42 U.S.C. §§ 300gg et seq], or

(ii) in the case of a qualified beneficiary other than a qualified beneficiary described in section 607(3)(C), entitled to benefits under title XVIII of the Social Security Act [42 U.S.C. § 1395 et seq.].

(E) Termination of extended coverage for disability. In the case of a qualified beneficiary who is disabled at any time during the first 60 days of continuation coverage under this part, the month that begins more than 30 days after the date of the final determination under title II or XVI of the Social Security Act that the qualified beneficiary is no longer disabled.

(3) Premium requirements. The plan may require payment of a premium for any period of continuation coverage, except that such premium—

(A) shall not exceed 102 percent of the applicable premium for such period, and

(B) may, at the election of the payor, be made in monthly installments.

In no event may the plan require the payment of any premium before the day which is 45 days after the day on which the qualified beneficiary made the initial election for continuation coverage. In the case of an individual described in the last sentence of paragraph (2)(A), any reference in subparagraph (A) of this paragraph to "102 percent" is deemed a reference to "150 percent" for any month after the 18th month of continuation coverage described in clause (i) or (ii) of paragraph (2)(A).

(4) No requirement of insurability. The coverage may not be conditioned upon, or discriminate on the basis of lack of, evidence of insurability.

(5) Conversion option. In the case of a qualified beneficiary whose period of continuation coverage expires under paragraph (2)(A), the plan must, during the 180-day period ending on such expiration date, provide to the qualified beneficiary the option of enrollment under a conversion health plan otherwise generally available under the plan.

§ 603 [§ 1163]. Qualifying event. For purposes of this part, the term "qualifying event" means, with respect to any covered employee, any of the following events which, but for the continuation coverage required under this part, would result in the loss of coverage of a qualified beneficiary:

(1) The death of the covered employee.

(2) The termination (other than by reason of such employee's gross misconduct), or reduction of hours, of the covered employee's employment.

(3) The divorce or legal separation of the covered employee from the employee's spouse.

(4) The covered employee becoming entitled to benefits under title XVIII of the Social Security Act.

(5) A dependent child ceasing to be a dependent child under the generally applicable requirements of the plan.

(6) A proceeding in a case under title 11, United States Code, commencing on or after July 1, 1986, with respect to the employer from whose employment the covered employee retired at any time.

In the case of an event described in paragraph (6), a loss of coverage includes a substantial elimination of coverage with respect to a qualified beneficiary described in section 607(3)(C) within one year before or after the date of commencement of the proceeding.

§ 604 [§ 1164]. Applicable premium. For purposes of this part—

(1) In general. The term "applicable premium" means, with respect to any period of continuation coverage of qualified beneficiaries, the cost to the plan for such period of the coverage for similarly situated beneficiaries with respect to whom a qualifying event has not occurred (without regard to whether such cost is paid by the employer or employee).

(2) Special rule for self-insured plans. To the extent that a plan is a self-insured plan—

(A) In general. Except as provided in subparagraph (B), the applicable premium for any period of continuation coverage of qualified beneficiaries shall be equal to a reasonable estimate of the cost of providing coverage for such period for similarly situated beneficiaries which—

(i) is determined on an actuarial basis, and

(ii) takes into account such factors as the Secretary may prescribe in regulations.

(B) Determination on basis of past cost. If an administrator elects to have this subparagraph apply, the applicable premium for any period of continuation coverage of qualified beneficiaries shall be equal to—

(i) the cost to the plan for similarly situated beneficiaries for the same period occurring during the preceding determination period under paragraph (3), adjusted by

(ii) the percentage increase or decrease in the implicit price deflator of the gross national product (calculated by the Department of Commerce and published in the Survey of Current Business) for the 12-month period ending on the last day of the sixth month of such preceding determination period.

(C) Subparagraph (B) not to apply where significant change. An administrator may not elect to have subparagraph (B) apply in any case in which there is any significant difference, between the determination period and the preceding determination period, in coverage under, or in employees covered by, the plan. The determination under the preceding sentence for any determination period shall be made at the same time as the determination under paragraph (3).

(3) Determination period. The determination of any applicable premium shall be made for a period of 12 months and shall be made before the beginning of such period.

§ 605 [§ 1165]. Election. For purposes of this part—

(1) Election period. The term "election period" means the period which—

(A) begins not later than the date on which coverage terminates under the plan by reason of a qualifying event,

(B) is of at least 60 days' duration, and

(C) ends not earlier than 60 days after the later of—

(i) the date described in subparagraph (A), or

(ii) in the case of any qualified beneficiary who receives notice under section 606(4), the date of such notice.

(2) Effect of election on other beneficiaries. Except as otherwise specified in an election, any election of continuation coverage by a qualified beneficiary described in subparagraph (A)(i) or (B) of section 607(3) shall be deemed to include an election of continuation coverage on behalf of any other qualified beneficiary who would lose coverage under the plan by reason of the qualifying event. If there is a choice among types of coverage under the plan, each qualified beneficiary is entitled to make a separate selection among such types of coverage. . . .

§ 606 [§ 1166]. Notice requirements

(a) In general. In accordance with regulations prescribed by the Secretary—

(1) the group health plan shall provide, at the time of commencement of coverage under the plan, written notice to each covered employee and spouse of the employee (if any) of the rights provided under this subsection [should read "part"],

(2) the employer of an employee under a plan must notify the administrator of a qualifying event described in paragraph (1), (2), (4), or (6) of section 603 within 30 days (or, in the case of a group health plan which is a multiemployer plan, such longer period of time as may be provided in the terms of the plan) of the date of the qualifying event,

(3) each covered employee or qualified beneficiary is responsible for notifying the administrator of the occurrence of any qualifying event described in paragraph (3) or (5) of section 603 within

60 days after the date of the qualifying event and each qualified beneficiary who is determined, under title II or XVI of the Social Security Act, to have been disabled at any time during the first 60 days of continuation coverage under this part is responsible for notifying the plan administrator of such determination within 60 days after the date of the determination and for notifying the plan administrator within 30 days after the date of any final determination under such title or titles that the qualified beneficiary is no longer disabled, and

(4) the administrator shall notify—

(A) in the case of a qualifying event described in paragraph (1), (2), (4), or (6) of section 603, any qualified beneficiary with respect to such event, and

(B) in the case of a qualifying event described in paragraph (3) or (5) of section 603 where the covered employee notifies the administrator under paragraph (3), any qualified beneficiary with respect to such event,of such beneficiary's rights under this subsection [should read "part"]. . . .

(c) **Rules relating to notification of qualified beneficiaries by plan administrator**. For purposes of subsection (a)(4), any notification shall be made within 14 days (or, in the case of a group health plan which is a multiemployer plan, such longer period of time as may be provided in the terms of the plan) of the date on which the administrator is notified under paragraph (2) or (3), whichever is applicable, and any such notification to an individual who is a qualified beneficiary as the spouse of the covered employee shall be treated as notification to all other qualified beneficiaries residing with such spouse at the time such notification is made.

§ 607 [§ 1167]. Definitions and special rules. For purposes of this part—

(1) **Group health plan**. The term "group health plan" means an employee welfare benefit plan providing medical care (as defined in section 213(d) of [the Internal Revenue Code]) to participants or beneficiaries directly or through insurance, reimbursement, or otherwise. . . .

(2) **Covered employee**. The term "covered employee" means an individual who is (or was) provided coverage under a group health plan by virtue of the performance of services by the individual for 1 or more persons maintaining the plan (including as an employee defined in section 401(c)(1) of [the Internal Revenue Code]).

(3) **Qualified beneficiary**

(A) **In general**. The term "qualified beneficiary" means, with respect to a covered employee under a group health plan, any other individual who, on the day before the qualifying event for that employee, is a beneficiary under the plan—

(i) as the spouse of the covered employee, or

(ii) as the dependent child of the employee.

Such term shall also include a child who is born to or placed for adoption with the covered employee during the period of continuation coverage under this part.

(B) **Special rule for terminations and reduced employment**. In the case of a qualifying event described in section 603(2), the term "qualified beneficiary" includes the covered employee.

(C) **Special rule for retirees and widows**. In the case of a qualifying event described in section 603(6), the term "qualified beneficiary" includes a covered employee who had retired on or before the date of substantial elimination of coverage and any other individual who, on the day before such qualifying event, is a beneficiary under the plan—

(i) as the spouse of the covered employee,

(ii) as the dependent child of the employee, or

(iii) as the surviving spouse of the covered employee.

(4) Employer. Subsection (n) (relating to leased employees) and subsection (t) (relating to application of controlled group rules to certain employee benefits) of section 414 of [the Internal Revenue Code] shall apply for purposes of this part in the same manner and to the same extent as such subsections apply for purposes of section 106 of such [Code]. Any regulations prescribed by the Secretary pursuant to the preceding sentence shall be consistent and coextensive with any regulations prescribed for similar purposes by the Secretary of the Treasury (or such Secretary's delegate) under such subsections.

(5) Optional extension of required periods. A group health plan shall not be treated as failing to meet the requirements of this part solely because the plan provides both—

(A) that the period of extended coverage referred to in section 602(2) commences with the date of the loss of coverage, and

(B) that the applicable notice period provided under section 606(a)(2) commences with the date of the loss of coverage.

§ 608 [§ 1168]. Regulations. The Secretary may prescribe regulations to carry out the provisions of this part.

§ 609 [§ 1169]. Additional standards for group health plans.

(a) Group health plan coverage pursuant to medical child support orders.

(1) Each group health plan shall provide benefits in accordance with the applicable requirements of any qualified medical child support order. A qualified medical child support order with respect to any participant or beneficiary shall be deemed to apply to each group health plan which has received such order, from which the participant

or beneficiary is eligible to receive benefits, and with respect to which the requirements of paragraph (4) are met.

(2) For purposes of this subsection—

(A) Qualified medical child support order. The term "qualified medical child support order" means a medical child support order—

(i) which creates or recognizes the existence of an alternate recipient's right to, or assigns to an alternate recipient the right to, receive benefits for which a participant or beneficiary is eligible under a group health plan, and

(ii) with respect to which the requirements of paragraphs (3) and (4) are met.

(B) The term "medical child support order" means any judgment, decree, or order (including approval of a settlement agreement) which—

(i) provides for child support with respect to a child of a participant under a group health plan or provides for health benefit coverage to such a child, is made pursuant to a State domestic relations law (including a community property law), and relates to benefits under such plan, or

(ii) is made pursuant to a law relating to medical child support described in section 1908 of the Social Security Act [42 U.S.C. § 1396g-1] with respect to a group health plan,if such judgment, decree, or order (I) is issued by a court of competent jurisdiction or (II) is issued through an administrative process established under State law and has the force and effect of law under applicable State law. For purposes of this subparagraph, an administrative notice which is issued pursuant to an administrative process referred to in subclause (II) of the preceding sentence and which has the effect of an order described in clause (i) or (ii) of the preceding sentence shall be treated as such an order.

(C) The term "alternate recipient" means any child of a participant who is recognized under a medical child support order as having a right to enrollment under a group health plan with respect to such participant.

(D) The term "child" includes any child adopted by, or placed for adoption with, a participant of a group health plan.

(3) A medical child support order meets the requirements of this paragraph only if such order clearly specifies—

(A) the name and the last known mailing address (if any) of the participant and the name and mailing address of each alternate recipient covered by the order, except that, to the extent provided in the order, the name and mailing address of an official of a State or a political subdivision thereof may be substituted for the mailing address of any such alternate recipient,

(B) a reasonable description of the type of coverage to be provided to each such alternate recipient, or the manner in which such type of coverage is to be determined, and

(C) the period to which such order applies.

(4) A medical child support order meets the requirements of this paragraph only if such order does not require a plan to provide any type or form of benefit, or any option, not otherwise provided under the plan, except to the extent necessary to meet the requirements of a law relating to medical child support described in section 1908 of the Social Security Act [42 U.S.C. § 1396g-1].

(5)(A) In the case of any medical child support order received by a group health plan—

(i) the plan administrator shall promptly notify the participant and each alternate recipient of the receipt of such order and the plan's procedures for determining whether medical child support orders are qualified medical child support orders, and

(ii) within a reasonable period after receipt of such order, the plan administrator shall determine whether such order is a qualified medical child support order and notify the participant and each alternate recipient of such determination.

(B) Each group health plan shall establish reasonable procedures to determine whether medical child support orders are qualified medical child support orders and to administer the provision of benefits under such qualified orders. Such procedures—

(i) shall be in writing,

(ii) shall provide for the notification of each person specified in a medical child support order as eligible to receive benefits under the plan (at the address included in the medical child support order) of such procedures promptly upon receipt by the plan of the medical child support order, and

(iii) shall permit an alternate recipient to designate a representative for receipt of copies of notices that are sent to the alternate recipient with respect to a medical child support order. . . .

(6) If a plan fiduciary acts in accordance with part 4 of this subtitle in treating a medical child support order as being (or not being) a qualified medical child support order, then the plan's obligation to the participant and each alternate recipient shall be discharged to the extent of any payment made pursuant to such act of the fiduciary. . .

(c) Group health plan coverage of dependent children in cases of adoption.

(1) In any case in which a group health plan provides coverage for dependent children of participants or beneficiaries, such plan shall provide benefits to dependent children placed with participants or beneficiaries for adoption under the same terms and conditions as apply in the case of dependent children who are natural children of participants or beneficiaries under the plan, irrespective of whether the adoption has become final.

(2) A group health plan may not restrict coverage under the plan of any dependent child adopted by a participant or beneficiary, or placed with a participant or beneficiary for adoption, solely on the basis of a preexisting condition of such child at the time that such child would otherwise become eligible for coverage under the plan, if the adoption or placement for adoption occurs while the participant or beneficiary is eligible for coverage under the plan.

(3) For purposes of this subsection—

(A) The term "child" means, in connection with any adoption, or placement for adoption, of the child, an individual who has not attained age 18 as of the date of such adoption or placement for adoption.

(B) The term "placement", or being "placed", for adoption, in connection with any placement for adoption of a child with any person, means the assumption and retention by such person of a legal obligation for total or partial support of such child in anticipation of adoption of such child. The child's placement with such person terminates upon the termination of such legal obligation.

(d) Continued coverage of costs of a pediatric vaccine under group health plans. A group health plan may not reduce its coverage of the costs of pediatric vaccines below the coverage it provided as of May 1, 1993. . . .

Part 7 – Group Health Plan Requirements
Subpart A – Requirements Relating to Portability, Access, and Renewability [HIPAA]

§ 701 [§ 1181]. Increased portability through limitation on preexisting condition exclusions

(a) Limitation on preexisting condition exclusion period; crediting for periods of previous coverage. Subject to subsection (d) of this section, a group health plan, and a health insurance issuer offering group health insurance coverage, may, with respect to a participant or beneficiary, impose a preexisting condition exclusion only if—

(1) such exclusion relates to a condition (whether physical or mental), regardless of the cause of the condition, for which medical advice, diagnosis, care, or treatment was recommended or received within the 6-month period ending on the enrollment date;

(2) such exclusion extends for a period of not more than 12 months (or 18 months in the case of a late enrollee) after the enrollment date; and

(3) the period of any such preexisting condition exclusion is reduced by the aggregate of the periods of creditable coverage (if any, as defined in subsection (c)(1) of this section) applicable to the participant or beneficiary as of the enrollment date.

(b) Definitions. For purposes of this part—

(1) Preexisting condition exclusion

(A) In general. The term "preexisting condition exclusion" means, with respect to coverage, a limitation or exclusion of benefits relating to a condition based on the fact that the condition was present before the date of enrollment for such coverage, whether or not any medical advice, diagnosis, care, or treatment was recommended or received before such date.

(B) Treatment of genetic information. Genetic information shall not be treated as a condition described in subsection (a)(1) of this section in the absence of a diagnosis of the condition related to such information.

(2) Enrollment date. The term "enrollment date" means, with respect to an individual covered under a group health plan or health insurance coverage, the date of enrollment of the individual in the plan or coverage or, if earlier, the first day of the waiting period for such enrollment.

(3) Late enrollee. The term "late enrollee" means, with respect to coverage under a group health plan, a participant or beneficiary who enrolls under the plan other than during—

(A) the first period in which the individual is eligible to enroll under the plan, or

(B) a special enrollment period under subsection (f) of this section.

(4) Waiting period. The term "waiting period" means, with respect to a group health plan and an individual who is a potential participant or beneficiary in the plan, the period that must pass with respect to the individual before the individual is eligible to be covered for benefits under the terms of the plan.

(c) Rules relating to crediting previous coverage

(1) **Creditable coverage defined.** For purposes of this part, the term "creditable coverage" means, with respect to an individual, coverage of the individual under any of the following:

(A) A group health plan.

(B) Health insurance coverage.

(C) Part A or part B of title XVIII of the Social Security Act [42 U.S.C. §1395c et seq. or § 1395j et seq.].

(D) Title XIX of the Social Security Act [42 U.S.C. § 1396 et seq.], other than coverage consisting solely of benefits under section 1928 [42 U.S.C. § 1396s].

(E) Chapter 55 of Title 10.

(F) A medical care program of the Indian Health Service or of a tribal organization.

(G) A State health benefits risk pool.

(H) A health plan offered under chapter 89 of Title 5.

(I) A public health plan (as defined in regulations).

(J) A health benefit plan under section 2504(e) of Title 22.

Such term does not include coverage consisting solely of coverage of excepted benefits (as defined in section 733(c).

(2) Not counting periods before significant breaks in coverage

(A) In general. A period of creditable coverage shall not be counted, with respect to enrollment of an individual under a group health plan, if, after such period and before the enrollment date, there was a 63-day period during all of which the individual was not covered under any creditable coverage.

(B) Waiting period not treated as a break in coverage. For purposes of subparagraph (A) and subsection (d)(4) of this section, any period that an individual is in a waiting period for any coverage under a group health plan (or for group health insurance coverage) or is in an affiliation period (as defined in subsection (g)(2) of this section) shall not be taken into account in determining the continuous period under subparagraph (A). . . .

(3) Method of crediting coverage

(A) Standard method. Except as otherwise provided under subparagraph (B), for purposes of applying subsection (a)(3) of this section, a group health plan, and a health insurance issuer offering group health insurance coverage, shall count a period of creditable coverage without regard to the specific benefits covered during the period.

(B) **Election of alternative method.** A group health plan, or a health insurance issuer offering group health insurance coverage, may elect to apply subsection (a)(3) of this section based on coverage of benefits within each of several classes or categories of benefits specified in regulations rather than as provided under subparagraph (A). Such election shall be made on a uniform basis for all participants and beneficiaries. Under such election a group health plan or issuer shall count a period of creditable coverage with respect to any class or category of benefits if any level of benefits is covered within such class or category.

(C) **Plan notice.** In the case of an election with respect to a group health plan under subparagraph (B) (whether or not health insurance coverage is provided in connection with such plan), the plan shall—

(i) prominently state in any disclosure statements concerning the plan, and state to each enrollee at the time of enrollment under the plan, that the plan has made such election, and

(ii) include in such statements a description of the effect of this election.

(4) **Establishment of period.** Periods of creditable coverage with respect to an individual shall be established through presentation of certifications described in subsection (e) of this section or in such other manner as may be specified in regulations.

(d) Exceptions

(1) **Exclusion not applicable to certain newborns.** Subject to paragraph (4), a group health plan, and a health insurance issuer offering group health insurance coverage, may not impose any preexisting condition exclusion in the case of an individual who, as of the last day of the 30-day period beginning with the date of birth, is covered under creditable coverage.

(2) **Exclusion not applicable to certain adopted children.** Subject to paragraph (4), a group health plan, and a health insurance issuer offering group health insurance coverage, may not impose any preexisting condition exclusion in the case of a child who is adopted or placed for adoption before attaining 18 years of age and who, as of the last day of the 30-day period beginning on the date of the adoption or placement for adoption, is covered under creditable coverage. The previous sentence shall not apply to coverage before the date of such adoption or placement for adoption.

(3) **Exclusion not applicable to pregnancy.** A group health plan, and health insurance issuer offering group health insurance coverage, may not impose any preexisting condition exclusion relating to pregnancy as a preexisting condition.

(4) **Loss if break in coverage.** Paragraphs (1) and (2) shall no longer apply to an individual after the end of the first 63-day period during all of which the individual was not covered under any creditable coverage.

(e) Certifications and disclosure of coverage

(1) Requirement for certification of period of creditable coverage

(A) In general. A group health plan, and a health insurance issuer offering group health insurance coverage, shall provide the certification described in subparagraph (B)—

(i) at the time an individual ceases to be covered under the plan or otherwise becomes covered under a COBRA continuation provision,

(ii) in the case of an individual becoming covered under such a provision, at the time the individual ceases to be covered under such provision, and

(iii) on the request on behalf of an individual made not later than 24 months after the date of cessation of the coverage described in clause (i) or (ii), whichever is later.

The certification under clause (i) may be provided, to the extent practicable, at a time consistent with notices required under any applicable COBRA continuation provision.

(B) Certification. The certification described in this subparagraph is a written certification of—

(i) the period of creditable coverage of the individual under such plan and the coverage (if any) under such COBRA continuation provision, and

(ii) the waiting period (if any) (and affiliation period, if applicable) imposed with respect to the individual for any coverage under such plan.

(C) Issuer compliance. To the extent that medical care under a group health plan consists of group health insurance coverage, the plan is deemed to have satisfied the certification requirement under this paragraph if the health insurance issuer offering the coverage provides for such certification in accordance with this paragraph.

(2) Disclosure of information on previous benefits. In the case of an election described in subsection (c)(3)(B) of this section by a group health plan or health insurance issuer, if the plan or issuer enrolls an individual for coverage under the plan and the individual provides a certification of coverage of the individual under paragraph (1)—

(A) upon request of such plan or issuer, the entity which issued the certification provided by the individual shall promptly disclose to such requesting plan or issuer information on coverage of classes and categories of health benefits available under such entity's plan or coverage, and

(B) such entity may charge the requesting plan or issuer for the reasonable cost of disclosing such information.

(3) Regulations. The Secretary shall establish rules to prevent an entity's failure to provide information under paragraph (1) or (2) with respect to previous coverage of an individual from adversely affecting any subsequent coverage of the individual under another group health plan or health insurance coverage.

(f) Special enrollment periods

(1) Individuals losing other coverage. A group health plan, and a health insurance issuer offering group health insurance coverage in connection with a group health plan, shall permit an employee who is eligible, but not enrolled, for coverage under the terms of the plan (or a dependent of such an employee if the dependent is eligible, but not enrolled, for coverage under such terms) to enroll for coverage under the terms of the plan if each of the following conditions is met:

(A) The employee or dependent was covered under a group health plan or had health insurance coverage at the time coverage was previously offered to the employee or dependent.

(B) The employee stated in writing at such time that coverage under a group health plan or health insurance coverage was the reason for declining enrollment, but only if the plan sponsor or issuer (if applicable) required such a statement at such time and provided the employee with notice of such requirement (and the consequences of such requirement) at such time.

(C) The employee's or dependent's coverage described in subparagraph (A)—

(i) was under a COBRA continuation provision and the coverage under such provision was exhausted; or

(ii) was not under such a provision and either the coverage was terminated as a result of loss of eligibility for the coverage (including as a result of legal separation, divorce, death, termination of employment, or reduction in the number of hours of employment) or employer contributions toward such coverage were terminated.

(D) Under the terms of the plan, the employee requests such enrollment not later than 30 days after the date of exhaustion of coverage described in subparagraph (C)(i) or termination of coverage or employer contribution described in subparagraph (C)(ii).

(2) For dependent beneficiaries

(A) In general. If—

(i) a group health plan makes coverage available with respect to a dependent of an individual,

(ii) the individual is a participant under the plan (or has met any waiting period applicable to becoming a participant under the plan and is eligible to be enrolled under the plan but for a failure to enroll during a previous enrollment period), and

(iii) a person becomes such a dependent of the individual through marriage, birth, or adoption or placement for adoption,

the group health plan shall provide for a dependent special enrollment period described in subparagraph (B) during which the person (or, if not otherwise enrolled, the individual) may be enrolled under the plan as a dependent of the individual, and in the case of the birth or adoption of a child, the spouse of the individual may be enrolled as a dependent of the individual if such spouse is otherwise eligible for coverage.

(B) Dependent special enrollment period. A dependent special enrollment period under this subparagraph shall be a period of not less than 30 days and shall begin on the later of—

(i) the date dependent coverage is made available, or

(ii) the date of the marriage, birth, or adoption or placement for adoption (as the case may be) described in subparagraph (A)(iii).

(C) No waiting period. If an individual seeks to enroll a dependent during the first 30 days of such a dependent special enrollment period, the coverage of the dependent shall become effective—

(i) in the case of marriage, not later than the first day of the first month beginning after the date the completed request for enrollment is received;

(ii) in the case of a dependent's birth, as of the date of such birth; or

(iii) in the case of a dependent's adoption or placement for adoption, the date of such adoption or placement for adoption. . . .

(g) Use of affiliation period by HMOs as alternative to preexisting condition exclusion

(1) In general. In the case of a group health plan that offers medical care through health insurance coverage offered by a health maintenance organization, the plan may provide for an affiliation period with respect to coverage through the organization only if—

(A) no preexisting condition exclusion is imposed with respect to coverage through the organization,

(B) the period is applied uniformly without regard to any health status- related factors, and

(C) such period does not exceed 2 months (or 3 months in the case of a late enrollee).

(2) Affiliation period

(A) Defined. For purposes of this part, the term "affiliation period" means a period which, under the terms of the health insurance coverage offered by the health maintenance organization, must expire before the health insurance coverage becomes effective. The organization is not required to provide health care services or benefits during such period and no premium shall be charged to the participant or beneficiary for any coverage during the period.

(B) Beginning. Such period shall begin on the enrollment date.

(C) Runs concurrently with waiting periods. An affiliation period under a plan shall run concurrently with any waiting period under the plan.

(3) Alternative methods. A health maintenance organization described in paragraph (1) may use alternative methods, from those described in such paragraph, to address adverse selection as approved by the State insurance commissioner or official or officials designated by the State to enforce the requirements of part A of title XXVII of the Public Health Service Act [42 U.S.C. §§ 300gg et seq.] for the State involved with respect to such issuer.

§ 702 [§ 1182]. Prohibiting discrimination against individual participants and beneficiaries based on health status. . .

(a) In eligibility to enroll

(1) In general. Subject to paragraph (2), a group health plan, and a health insurance issuer offering group health insurance coverage in connection with a group health plan, may not establish rules for eligibility (including continued eligibility) of any individual to enroll under the terms of the plan based on any of the following health status-related factors in relation to the individual or a dependent of the individual:

(A) Health status.

(B) Medical condition (including both physical and mental illnesses).

(C) Claims experience.

(D) Receipt of health care.

(E) Medical history.

(F) Genetic information.

(G) Evidence of insurability (including conditions arising out of acts of domestic violence).

(H) Disability.

(2) No application to benefits or exclusions. To the extent consistent with section 701, paragraph (1) shall not be construed—

(A) to require a group health plan, or group health insurance coverage, to provide particular benefits other than those provided under the terms of such plan or coverage, or

(B) to prevent such a plan or coverage from establishing limitations or restrictions on the amount, level, extent, or nature of the benefits or coverage for similarly situated individuals enrolled in the plan or coverage.

(3) Construction. For purposes of paragraph (1), rules for eligibility to enroll under a plan include rules defining any applicable waiting periods for such enrollment.

(b) In premium contributions

(1) In general. A group health plan, and a health insurance issuer offering health insurance coverage in connection with a group health plan, may not require any individual (as a condition of enrollment or continued enrollment under the plan) to pay a premium or contribution which is greater than such premium or contribution for a similarly situated individual enrolled in the plan on the basis of any health status-related factor in relation to the individual or to an individual enrolled under the plan as a dependent of the individual.

(2) Construction. Nothing in paragraph (1) shall be construed—

(A) to restrict the amount that an employer may be charged for coverage under a group health plan except as provided in paragraph (3); or

(B) to prevent a group health plan, and a health insurance issuer offering group health insurance coverage, from establishing premium discounts or rebates or modifying otherwise applicable copayments or deductibles in return for adherence to programs of health promotion and disease prevention.

(3) No group-based discrimination on basis of genetic information.

(A) For purposes of this section, a group health plan, and a health insurance issuer offering group health insurance coverage in connection with a group health plan, may not adjust premium or contribution amounts for the group covered under such plan on the basis of genetic information.

(B) Nothing in subparagraph (A) or paragraphs (1) and (2) of subsection (d) shall be construed to limit the ability of a health insurance issuer offering health insurance coverage in connection with a group health plan to increase the premium for an employer based on the manifestation of a disease or disorder of an individual who is enrolled in the plan. In such case, the manifestation of a disease or disorder in one individual cannot also be used as genetic information about other group members and to further increase the premium for hte employer.

(c) Genetic Testing

(1) A group health plan, and a health insurance issuer offering health insurance coverage in connection with a group health plan, shall not request or require an individual or a family member of such individual to undergo a genetic test. . . .

(d) Prohibition on collection of genetic information

(1) A group health plan, and a health insurance issuer offering health insurance coverage in connection with a group health plan, shall not request, require, or purchase genetic information for underwriting purposes . . .

(2) A group health plan, and a health insurance issuer offering health insurance coverage in connection with a group health plan, shall not request, require, or purchase genetic information with respect to any individual prior to such individual's enrollment under the plan or coverage in connection with such enrollment. . . .

Subpart B – Other Requirements

§ 711 [§ 1185]. Standards relating to benefits for mothers and newborns

(a) Requirements for minimum hospital stay following birth

(1) **In general**. A group health plan, and a health insurance issuer offering group health insurance coverage, may not—

(A) except as provided in paragraph (2)—

(i) restrict benefits for any hospital length of stay in connection with childbirth for the mother or newborn child, following a normal vaginal delivery, to less than 48 hours, or

(ii) restrict benefits for any hospital length of stay in connection with childbirth for the mother or newborn child, following a cesarean section, to less than 96 hours; or

(B) require that a provider obtain authorization from the plan or the issuer for prescribing any length of stay required under subparagraph (A) (without regard to paragraph (2)).

(2) Exception. Paragraph (1)(A) shall not apply in connection with any group health plan or health insurance issuer in any case in which the decision to discharge the mother or her newborn child prior to the expiration of the minimum length of stay otherwise required under paragraph (1)(A) is made by an attending provider in consultation with the mother.

(b) Prohibitions. A group health plan, and a health insurance issuer offering group health insurance coverage in connection with a group health plan, may not—

(1) deny to the mother or her newborn child eligibility, or continued eligibility, to enroll or to renew coverage under the terms of the plan, solely for the purpose of avoiding the requirements of this section;

(2) provide monetary payments or rebates to mothers to encourage such mothers to accept less than the minimum protections available under this section;

(3) penalize or otherwise reduce or limit the reimbursement of an attending provider because such provider provided care to an individual participant or beneficiary in accordance with this section;

(4) provide incentives (monetary or otherwise) to an attending provider to induce such provider to provide care to an individual participant or beneficiary in a manner inconsistent with this section; or

(5) subject to subsection (c)(3) of this section, restrict benefits for any portion of a period within a hospital length of stay required under subsection (a) of this section in a manner which is less favorable than the benefits provided for any preceding portion of such stay.

(c) Rules of construction

(1) Nothing in this section shall be construed to require a mother who is a participant or beneficiary—

(A) to give birth in a hospital; or

(B) to stay in the hospital for a fixed period of time following the birth of her child.

(2) This section shall not apply with respect to any group health plan, or any group health insurance coverage offered by a health insurance issuer, which does not provide benefits for hospital lengths of stay in connection with childbirth for a mother or her newborn child.

(3) Nothing in this section shall be construed as preventing a group health plan or issuer from imposing deductibles, coinsurance, or other cost-sharing in relation to benefits for hospital lengths of stay in connection with childbirth for a mother or newborn child under the plan (or under health insurance coverage offered in connection with a group health plan), except that such coinsurance or other cost-sharing for any portion of a period within a hospital length of stay required under subsection (a) of this section may not be greater than such coinsurance or cost-sharing for any preceding portion of such stay.

(d) Notice under group health plan. The imposition of the requirements of this section shall be treated as a material modification in the terms of the plan described in section 102(a)(1), for purposes of assuring notice of such requirements under the plan; except that the summary description required to be provided under the last sentence of section 104(b)(1) with respect to such modification shall be provided by not later than 60 days after the first day of the first plan year in which such requirements apply.

(e) Level and type of reimbursements. Nothing in this section shall be construed to prevent a group health plan or a health insurance issuer offering group health insurance coverage from negotiating the level and type of reimbursement with a provider for care provided in accordance with this section.

(f) Preemption; exception for health insurance coverage in certain states

(1) In general. The requirements of this section shall not apply with respect to health insurance coverage if there is a State law . . . for a State that regulates such coverage that is described in any of the following subparagraphs:

(A) Such State law requires such coverage to provide for at least a 48-hour hospital length of stay following a normal vaginal delivery and at least a 96-hour hospital length of stay following a caesarean section.

(B) Such State law requires such coverage to provide for maternity and pediatric care in accordance with guidelines established by the American College of Obstetricians and Gynecologists, the American Academy of Pediatrics, or other established professional medical associations.

(C) Such State law requires, in connection with such coverage for maternity care, that the hospital length of stay for such care is left to the decision of (or required to be made by) the attending provider in consultation with the mother.

(2) **Construction.** Section 731(a)(1) shall not be construed as superseding a State law described in paragraph (1).

§ 712 [§ 1185a]. Parity in mental health and substance abuse disorder benefits

(a) In general

(1) **Aggregate lifetime limits.** In the case of a group health plan (or health insurance coverage offered in connection with such a plan) that provides both medical and surgical benefits and mental health benefits or substance use disorder benefits—

(A) **No lifetime limit.** If the plan or coverage does not include an aggregate lifetime limit on substantially all medical and surgical benefits, the plan or coverage may not impose any aggregate lifetime limit on mental health or substance use disorder benefits.

(B) **Lifetime limit.** If the plan or coverage includes an aggregate lifetime limit on substantially all medical and surgical benefits (in this paragraph referred to as the "applicable lifetime limit"), the plan or coverage shall either—

(i) apply the applicable lifetime limit both to the medical and surgical benefits to which it otherwise would apply and to mental health and substance use disorder benefits and not distinguish in the application of such limit between such medical and surgical benefits and mental health and substance use disorder benefits; or

(ii) not include any aggregate lifetime limit on mental health or substance use disorder benefits that is less than the applicable lifetime limit.

(C) **Rule in case of different limits.** In the case of a plan or coverage that is not described in subparagraph (A) or (B) and that includes no or different aggregate lifetime limits on different categories of medical and surgical benefits, the Secretary shall establish rules under which subparagraph (B) is applied to such plan or coverage with respect to mental health and substance use disorder benefits by substituting for the applicable lifetime limit an average aggregate lifetime limit that is computed taking into account the weighted average of the aggregate lifetime limits applicable to such categories.

(2) **Annual limits**. In the case of a group health plan (or health insurance coverage offered in connection with such a plan) that provides both medical and surgical benefits and mental health or substance use disorder benefits—

(A) **No annual limit**. If the plan or coverage does not include an annual limit on substantially all medical and surgical benefits, the plan or coverage may not impose any annual limit on mental health or substance use disorder benefits.

(B) **Annual limit.** If the plan or coverage includes an annual limit on substantially all medical and surgical benefits (in this paragraph referred to as the "applicable annual limit"), the plan or coverage shall either—

(i) apply the applicable annual limit both to medical and surgical benefits to which it otherwise would apply and to mental health and substance use disorder benefits and not distinguish in the application of such limit between such medical and surgical benefits and mental health and substance use disorder benefits; or

(ii) not include any annual limit on mental health or substance use disorder benefits that is less than the applicable annual limit.

(C) **Rule in case of different limits.** In the case of a plan or coverage that is not described in subparagraph (A) or (B) and that includes no or different annual limits on different categories of medical and surgical benefits, the Secretary shall establish rules under which subparagraph (B) is applied to such plan or coverage with respect to mental health and substance use disorder benefits by substituting for the applicable annual limit an average annual limit that is computed taking into account the weighted average of the annual limits applicable to such categories.

(3) **Financial requirements and treatment limitations**

(A) In the case of a group health plan . . . that provides both medical and surgical benefits and mental health or substance use disorder benefits, such plan or coverage shall ensure that—

(i) the financial requirements applicable to such mental health or substance use disorder benefits are no more restrictive than the predominant financial requirements applied to substantially all medical and surgical benefits covered by the plan (or coverage), and there are no separate cost sharing requirements that are applicable only with respect to mental health or substance use disorder benefits; and

(ii) the treatment limitations applicable to such mental health or substance use disorder benefits are no more restrictive than the predominant treatment limitations applied to substantially all medical and surgival benefits covered by the plan (or coverage) and there are no separate treatment limitations that are applicable only with respect to mental health or substance use disorder benefits.

(B) In this paragraph:

(i) The term "financial requirement" incldues deductibles, copayments, coinsurance, and out-of-pocket expenses, but excludes an aggregate lifetime limit and an annual limti subject to paragraphs (1) and (2),

(ii) A financial requirement or treatment limit is considered to be predominant if it is the most common or frequest of such type of limit or requirement.

(iii) The term "treatment limitation" includes limits on the frequency of treatment, number of visits, days of coverage, or other similar limits on the scope or duration of treatment. . . .

(b) Construction. Nothing in this section shall be construed—

(1) as requiring a group health plan (or health insurance coverage offered in connection with such a plan) to provide any mental health or substance use disorder benefits; or

(2) in the case of a group health plan (or health insurance coverage offered in connection with such a plan) that provides mental health or substance use disorder benefits, as affecting the terms and conditions of the plan or coverage relating to such benefits under the plan or coverage, except as provided in subsection (a).

(c) Exemptions

(1) Small employer exemption

(A) In general. This section shall not apply to any group health plan (and group health insurance coverage offered in connection with a group health plan) for any plan year of a small employer.

(B) Small employer. For purposes of subparagraph (A), the term "small employer" means, in connection with a group health plan with respect to a calendar year and a plan year, an employer who employed an average of at least 2 (or 1 in the case of an employer residing in a State that permits small groups to include a single individual) but not more than 50 employees on business days during the preceding calendar year.

(C) **Application of certain rules in determination of employer size**. For purposes of this paragraph—

(i) **Application of aggregation rule for employers.** Rules similar to the rules under subsections (b), (c), (m), and (o) of section 414 [of the Internal Revenue Code] shall apply for purposes of treating persons as a single employer.

(ii) **Employers not in existence in preceding year.** In the case of an employer which was not in existence throughout the preceding calendar year, the determination of whether such employer is a small employer shall be based on the average number of employees that it is reasonably expected such employer will employ on business days in the current calendar year.

(iii) **Predecessors.** Any reference in this paragraph to an employer shall include a reference to any predecessor of such employer.

(2) **Cost exemption**.

(A) **In general.** With respect to a group health plan . . ., if the application of this section to such plan (or coverage) results in an increase for the plan year involved of the actual total costs of coverage with respect to medical and surgical benefits and mental health and substance use disorder benefits under the plan . . . by an amount that exceeds the applicable percentage described in subparagraph (B) of the actual total plan costs, the provisions of this section shall not apply to such plan (or coverage) during the following plan year, and such exemption shall apply to the plan (or coverage) for 1 plan year. An employer may elect to continue to apply mental health and substance use disorder parity pursuant to this section with respect to the group health plan (or coverage) involved regardless of any increase in total costs.

(B) **Applicable percentage.** With respect to a plan (or coverage), the applicable percentage described in this subparagraph shall be—

(i) 1 percent in the case of the first plan year to which this section is applied; and

(ii) 1 percent in the case of each subsequent plan year. . . .

(e) **Definitions**. For purposes of this section—

(1) **Aggregate lifetime limit**. The term "aggregate lifetime limit" means, with respect to benefits under a group health plan or health insurance coverage, a dollar limitation on the total amount that may be paid with respect to such benefits under the plan or health insurance coverage with respect to an individual or other coverage unit.

(2) **Annual limit**. The term "annual limit" means, with respect to benefits under a group health plan or health insurance coverage, a dollar limitation on the total amount of benefits that may be paid with respect to such benefits in a 12-month period under the plan or health insurance coverage with respect to an individual or other coverage unit.

(3) **Medical or surgical benefits**. The term "medical or surgical benefits" means benefits with respect to medical or surgical services, as defined under the terms of the plan or coverage (as the case may be), but does not include mental health benefits.

(4) **Mental health benefits**. The term "mental health benefits" means benefits with respect to mental health services, as defined under the terms of the plan and in accorance with applicable Federal and State law.

(5) **Substance use disorder benefits.** The term "substance use disorder benefits" means benefits with respect to services for substance use disorder, as defined under the terms of the plan and in accordance with applicable Federal and State law. . . .

§ 713 [§ 1185b]. Required coverage for reconstructive surgery following mastectomies

(a) **In general**. A group health plan, and a health insurance issuer providing health insurance coverage in connection with a group health plan, that provides medical and surgical benefits with respect to a mastectomy shall provide, in a case of a participant or beneficiary who is receiving benefits in connection with a mastectomy and who elects breast reconstruction in connection with such mastectomy, coverage for—

(1) all stages of reconstruction of the breast on which the mastectomy has been performed;

(2) surgery and reconstruction of the other breast to produce a symmetrical appearance; and

(3) prostheses and physical complications of mastectomy, including lymphedemas;

in a manner determined in consultation with the attending physician and the patient. Such coverage may be subject to annual deductibles and coinsurance provisions as may be deemed appropriate and as are consistent with those established for other benefits under the plan or coverage. Written notice of the availability of such coverage shall be delivered to the participant upon enrollment and annually thereafter.

(b) Notice. A group health plan, and a health insurance issuer providing health insurance coverage in connection with a group health plan shall provide notice to each participant and beneficiary under such plan regarding the coverage required by this section in accordance with regulations promulgated by the Secretary. Such notice shall be in writing and prominently positioned in any literature or correspondence made available or distributed by the plan or issuer and shall be transmitted—

(1) in the next mailing made by the plan or issuer to the participant or beneficiary;

(2) as part of any yearly informational packet sent to the participant or beneficiary; or

(3) not later than January 1, 1999; whichever is earlier.

(c) Prohibitions. A group health plan, and a health insurance issuer offering group health insurance coverage in connection with a group health plan, may not—

(1) deny to a patient eligibility, or continued eligibility, to enroll or to renew coverage under the terms of the plan, solely for the purpose of avoiding the requirements of this section; and

(2) penalize or otherwise reduce or limit the reimbursement of an attending provider, or provide incentives (monetary or otherwise) to an attending provider, to induce such provider to provide care to an individual participant or beneficiary in a manner inconsistent with this section.

(d) Rule of construction. Nothing in this section shall be construed to prevent a group health plan or a health insurance issuer offering group health insurance coverage from negotiating the level and type of reimbursement with a provider for care provided in accordance with this section.

(e) Preemption, relation to State laws

(1) In general. Nothing in this section shall be construed to preempt any State law in effect on October 21, 1998 with respect to health insurance coverage that requires coverage of at least the coverage of reconstructive breast surgery otherwise required under this section.

(2) ERISA. Nothing in this section shall be construed to affect or modify the provisions of section 514 with respect to group health plans.

Subpart C – General Provisions

§ 731 [§ 1191]. Preemption; State flexibility; construction

(a) Continued applicability of State law with respect to health insurance issuers

(1) **In general.** Subject to paragraph (2) and except as provided in subsection (b) of this section, this part shall not be construed to supersede any provision of State law which establishes, implements, or continues in effect any standard or requirement solely relating to health insurance issuers in connection with group health insurance coverage except to the extent that such standard or requirement prevents the application of a requirement of this part.

(2) **Continued preemption with respect to group health plans.** Nothing in this part shall be construed to affect or modify the provisions of section 514 with respect to group health plans.

(b) Special rules in case of portability requirements

(1) **In general.** Subject to paragraph (2), the provisions of this part relating to health insurance coverage offered by a health insurance issuer supersede any provision of State law which establishes, implements, or continues in effect a standard or requirement applicable to imposition of a preexisting condition exclusion specifically governed by section 701 which differs from the standards or requirements specified in such section.

(2) **Exceptions.** Only in relation to health insurance coverage offered by a health insurance issuer, the provisions of this part do not supersede any provision of State law to the extent that such provision—

(A) substitutes for the reference to "6-month period" in section 701(a)(1) a reference to any shorter period of time;

(B) substitutes for the reference to "12 months" and "18 months" in section 701(a)(2) a reference to any shorter period of time;

(C) substitutes for the references to "63 days" in sections 701(c)(2)(A) and (d)(4)(A) a reference to any greater number of days;

(D) substitutes for the reference to "30-day period" in sections 701(b)(2) and (d)(1) a reference to any greater period;

(E) prohibits the imposition of any preexisting condition exclusion in cases not described in section 701(d) or expands the exceptions described in such section;

(F) requires special enrollment periods in addition to those required under section 701(f); or

(G) reduces the maximum period permitted in an affiliation period under section 701(g)(1)(B).

(c) **Rules of construction**. Except as provided in section 711, nothing in this part shall be construed as requiring a group health plan or health insurance coverage to provide specific benefits under the terms of such plan or coverage.

(d) Definitions. For purposes of this section—

(1) **State law.** The term "State law" includes all laws, decisions, rules, regulations, or other State action having the effect of law, of any State. A law of the United States applicable only to the District of Columbia shall be treated as a State law rather than a law of the United States.

(2) **State.** The term "State" includes a State, the Northern Mariana Islands, any political subdivisions of a State or such Islands, or any agency or instrumentality of either.

§ 732 [§ 1191a]. Special rules relating to group health plans

(a) General exception for certain small group health plans. The requirements of this part (other than section 711) shall not apply to any group health plan (and group health insurance coverage offered in connection with a group health plan) for any plan year if, on the first day of such plan year, such plan has less than 2 participants who are current employees. . . .

§ 733 [§ 1191b]. Definitions

(a) Group health plan. For purposes of this part—

(1) **In general**. The term "group health plan" means an employee welfare benefit plan to the extent that the plan provides medical care (as defined in paragraph (2) and including items and services paid for as medical care) to employees or their dependents (as defined under the terms of the plan) directly or through insurance, reimbursement, or otherwise.

(2) **Medical care.** The term "medical care" means amounts paid for—

(A) the diagnosis, cure, mitigation, treatment, or prevention of disease, or amounts paid for the purpose of affecting any structure or function of the body,

(B) amounts paid for transportation primarily for and essential to medical care referred to in subparagraph (A), and

(C) amounts paid for insurance covering medical care referred to in subparagraphs (A) and (B).

(b) Definitions relating to health insurance. For purposes of this part—

(1) **Health insurance coverage**. The term "health insurance coverage" means benefits consisting of medical care (provided directly, through insurance or reimbursement, or otherwise and including items and services paid for as medical care) under any hospital or medical service policy or certificate, hospital or medical service plan contract, or health maintenance organization contract offered by a health insurance issuer.

(2) **Health insurance issuer**. The term "health insurance issuer" means an insurance company, insurance service, or insurance organization (including a health maintenance organization, as defined in paragraph (3)) which is licensed to engage in the business of insurance in a State and which is subject to State law which regulates insurance (within the meaning of section 514(b)(2)). Such term does not include a group health plan.

(3) **Health maintenance organization**. The term "health maintenance organization" means—

(A) a federally qualified health maintenance organization (as defined in section 300e(a) of Title 42),

(B) an organization recognized under State law as a health maintenance organization, or

(C) a similar organization regulated under State law for solvency in the same manner and to the same extent as such a health maintenance organization.

(4) **Group health insurance coverage.** The term "group health insurance coverage" means, in connection with a group health plan, health insurance coverage offered in connection with such plan.

(c) Excepted benefits. For purposes of this part, the term "excepted benefits" means benefits under one or more (or any combination thereof) of the following:

(1) **Benefits not subject to requirements**.

(A) Coverage only for accident, or disability income insurance, or any combination thereof.

(B) Coverage issued as a supplement to liability insurance.

(C) Liability insurance, including general liability insurance and automobile liability insurance.

(D) Workers' compensation or similar insurance.

(E) Automobile medical payment insurance.

(F) Credit-only insurance.

(G) Coverage for on-site medical clinics.

(H) Other similar insurance coverage, specified in regulations, under which benefits for medical care are secondary or incidental to other insurance benefits.

(2) **Benefits not subject to requirements if offered separately**

(A) Limited scope dental or vision benefits.

(B) Benefits for long-term care, nursing home care, home health care, community-based care, or any combination thereof.

(C) Such other similar, limited benefits as are specified in regulations.

(3) Benefits not subject to requirements if offered as independent, noncoordinated benefits

(A) Coverage only for a specified disease or illness.

(B) Hospital indemnity or other fixed indemnity insurance.

(4) Benefits not subject to requirements if offered as separate insurance policy. Medicare supplemental health insurance (as defined under section 1395ss(g)(1) of this title, coverage supplemental to the coverage provided under chapter 55 of Title 10, and similar supplemental coverage provided to coverage under a group health plan.

(d) Other definitions. For purposes of this part—

(1) COBRA continuation provision. The term "COBRA continuation provision" means any of the following:

(A) Part 6 of this subtitle.

(B) Section 4980B of Title 26, other than subsection (f)(1) of such section insofar as it relates to pediatric vaccines.

(C) Title XXII of the Public Health Service Act [42 U.S.C. §§ 300bb-1 et seq.].

(2) Health status-related factor. The term "health status-related factor" means any of the factors described in section 702(a)(1).

(3) Network plan. The term "network plan" means health insurance coverage offered by a health insurance issuer under which the financing and delivery of medical care (including items and services paid for as medical care) are provided, in whole or in part, through a defined set of providers under contract with the issuer.

(4) Placed for adoption. The term "placement", or being "placed", for adoption, has the meaning given such term in section 609(c)(3)(B).

(5) Family member. The term "family member" means, with respect to an individual—

(A) a dependent (as such term is used for purposes of section 701(f)(2)) of such individual, and

(B) any other individual who is a first-degree, second-degree, third-degree, or fourth-degree relative of such individual or of an individual described in subparagraph (A).

(6) Genetic information.

(A) The term "genetic information" means, with respect to any individual, information about—

(i) such individual's genetic tests,

(ii) the genetic tests of family members of such individual, and

(iii) the manifestation of a disease or disorder in family members of such individual. . . .

(C) The term "genetic information" shall not include information about the sex or age of any individual.

(7) Genetic Test.

(A) The term "genetic test" means an analysis of human DNA, RNA, chromosomes, proteins, or metabolites, that detects genotypes, mutations, or chromosomal changes.

(B) The term genetic test" does not mean—

(i) an analysis of proteins or metabolites that does not detect genotypes, mutations, or chromosomal changes; or

(ii) an analysis of proteins or metabolites that is directly related to a manifested disease, disorder, or pathological condition that could reasonable be detected by a health care professional with appropriate training and expertise in the field of medicine involved.

(8) Genetic services. The term "genetic services" means—

(A) a genetic test;

(B) genetic counseling (including obtaining, interpreting, or assessing genetic information); or

(C) genetic education. . . .

§ 734 [§ 1191c]. Regulations. The Secretary, consistent with section 104 of the Health Care Portability and Accountability Act of 1996 [42 U.S.C. § 300gg-92], may promulgate such regulations as may be necessary or appropriate to carry out the provisions of this part. The Secretary may promulgate any interim final rules as the Secretary determines are appropriate to carry out this part. . . .

Title IV – Plan Termination Insurance
Subtitle A – Pension Benefit Guaranty Corporation

§ 4001 [§ 1301]. Definitions

(a) For purposes of this title, the term—

(1) "administrator" means the person or persons described in paragraph (16) of section 3; . . .

(4) "corporation", except where the context clearly requires otherwise, means the Pension Benefit Guaranty Corporation established under section 4002; . . .

(6) "basic benefits" means benefits guaranteed under section 4022 (other than under section 4022(c)), or under section 4022a (other than under section 4022a(g));

(7) "non-basic benefits" means benefits guaranteed under section 4022(c) or 4022a(g);

(8) "nonforfeitable benefit" means, with respect to a plan, a benefit for which a participant has satisfied the conditions for entitlement under the plan or the requirements of this Act (other than submission of a formal application, retirement, completion of a required waiting period, or death in the case of a benefit which returns all or a portion of a participant's accumulated mandatory employee contributions upon the participant's death), whether or not the benefit may subsequently be reduced or suspended by a plan amendment, an occurrence of any condition, or operation of this title or [the Internal Revenue Code]; . . .

(13) "contributing sponsor", of a single-employer plan, means a person described in section 302(c)(11)(A) of this Act (without regard to section 302(c)(11)(B) of this Act) or section 412(c)(11)(A) of [the Internal Revenue Code] (without regard to section 412(c)(11)(B) of [the Internal Revenue Code]).

(14) in the case of a single-employer plan—

(A) "controlled group" means, in connection with any person, a group consisting of such person and all other persons under common control with such person; [and]

(B) the determination of whether two or more persons are under "common control" shall be made under regulations of the corporation which are consistent and coextensive with regulations prescribed for similar purposes by the Secretary of the Treasury under subsections (b) and (c) of section 414 of [the Internal Revenue Code.]

(15) "single-employer plan" means any defined benefit plan (as defined in section 3(35)) which is not a multiemployer plan;

(16) "benefit liabilities" means the benefits of employees and their beneficiaries under the plan (within the meaning of section 401(a)(2) of [the Internal Revenue Code]);

(17) "amount of unfunded guaranteed benefits", of a participant or beneficiary as of any date under a single-employer plan, means an amount equal to the excess of—

(A) the actuarial present value (determined as of such date on the basis of assumptions prescribed by the corporation for purposes of section 4044) of the benefits of the participant or beneficiary under the plan which are guaranteed under section 4022, over

(B) the current value (as of such date) of the assets of the plan which are required to be allocated to those benefits under section 4044;

(18) "amount of unfunded benefit liabilities" means, as of any date, the excess (if any) of—

(A) the value of the benefit liabilities under the plan (determined as of such date on the basis of assumptions prescribed by the corporation for purposes of section 4044), over

(B) the current value (as of such date) of the assets of the plan;

(19) "outstanding amount of benefit liabilities" means, with respect to any plan, the excess (if any) of—

(A) the value of the benefit liabilities under the plan (determined as of the termination date on the basis of assumptions prescribed by the corporation for purposes of section 4044), over

(B) the value of the benefit liabilities which would be so determined by only taking into account benefits which are guaranteed under section 4022 or to which assets of the plan are allocated under section 4044;

(20) "person" has the meaning set forth in section 3(9);

(21) "affected party" means, with respect to a plan—

(A) each participant in the plan,

(B) each beneficiary under the plan who is a beneficiary of a deceased participant or who is an alternate payee (within the meaning of section 206(d)(3)(K)) under an applicable qualified domestic relations order (within the meaning of section 206(d)(3)(B)(i)).

(C) each employee organization representing participants in the plan, and

(D) the corporation,

except that, in connection with any notice required to be provided to the affected party, if an affected party has designated, in writing, a person to receive such notice on behalf of the affected party, any reference to the affected party shall be construed to refer to such person. . . .

§ 4002 [§ 1302]. Pension Benefit Guaranty Corporation

(a) Establishment within Department of Labor. There is established within the Department of Labor a body corporate to be known as the Pension Benefit Guaranty Corporation. In carrying out its functions under this title, the corporation shall be administered by the chairman of the board of directors in accordance with policies established by the board. The purposes of this title, which are to be carried out by the corporation, are—

(1) to encourage the continuation and maintenance of voluntary private pension plans for the benefit of their participants,

(2) to provide for the timely and uninterrupted payment of pension benefits to participants and beneficiaries under plans to which this title applies, and

(3) to maintain premiums established by the corporation under section 4006 at the lowest level consistent with carrying out its obligations under this title. . . .

§ 4006 [§ 1306]. Premium rates

(a) Schedules for premium rates and bases for application; establishment, coverage, etc.

(1) The corporation shall prescribe such schedule or premium rates and bases for the application of those rates as may be necessary to provide sufficient revenue to the fund for the corporation to carry out its functions under this title. . . .

(3)(A) Except as provided in subparagraph (C), the annual premium rate payable to the corporation by all plans for basic benefits guaranteed under this title is—

(i) in the case of a single-employer plan, for plan years beginning after December 31, 2005, an amount equal to the sum of $30 plus the additional premium (if any) determined under subparagraph (E) for each individual who is a participant in such plan during the plan year. . . .

(E)(i) Except as provided in subparagraph (H), the additional premium determined under this subparagraph with respect to any plan for any plan year shall be an amount equal to the amount determined under clause (ii) divided by the number of participants in such plan as of the close of the preceding plan year.

(ii) The amount determined under this clause for any plan year shall be an amount equal to $9.00 for each $1,000 (or fraction thereof) of unfunded vested benefits under the plan as of the close of the preceding plan year. . . .

(H)(i) In the case of an employer who has 25 or fewer employees on the first day of the plan year, the additional premium determined under subparagraph (E) for each participant shall not exceed $5 multiplied by the number of participants in the plan as of the close of the preceding plan year. . . .

Subtitle B – Coverage

§ 4021 [§ 1321]. Coverage

(a) Plans covered. Except as provided in subsection (b) of this section, this title applies to any plan (including a successor plan) which, for a plan year—

(1) is an employee pension benefit plan (as defined in paragraph (2) of section 3) established or maintained—

(A) by an employer engaged in commerce or in any industry or activity affecting commerce, or

(B) by any employee organization, or organization representing employees, engaged in commerce or in any industry or activity affecting commerce, or

(C) by both,

which has, in practice, met the requirements of part I of subchapter D of chapter 1 of [the Internal Revenue Code] (as in effect for the preceding 5 plan years of the plan) applicable to plans described in paragraph (2) for the preceding 5 plan years; or

(2) is, or has been determined by the Secretary of the Treasury to be, a plan described in section 401(a) of [the Internal Revenue Code], or which meets, or has been determined by the Secretary of the Treasury to meet, the requirements of section 404(a)(2) of [the Internal Revenue Code]. . . .

(b) Plans not covered. This section does not apply to any plan—

(1) which is an individual account plan, as defined in paragraph (34) of section 3,

(2) established and maintained for its employees by the Government of the United States, by the government of any State or political subdivision thereof, or by any agency or instrumentality of any of the foregoing, or to which the Railroad Retirement Act of 1935 or 1937 [45 U.S.C. §§ 231 et seq.] applies and which is financed by contributions required under that Act,

(3) which is a church plan as defined in section 414(e) of [the Internal Revenue Code], unless that plan has made an election under section 410(d) of [the Internal Revenue Code], and has notified the corporation in accordance with procedures prescribed by the corporation, that it wishes to have the provisions of this part apply to it,

(4)(A) established and maintained by a society, order, or association described in section 501(c)(8) or (9) of [the Internal Revenue Code], if no part of the contributions to or under the plan is made by employers of participants in the plan, or

(B) of which a trust described in section 501(c)(18) of [the Internal Revenue Code] is a part;

(5) which has not at any time after September 2, 1974, provided for employer contributions;

(6) which is unfunded and which is maintained by an employer primarily for the purpose of providing deferred compensation for a select group of management or highly compensated employees;

(7) which is established and maintained outside of the United States primarily for the benefit of individuals substantially all of whom are nonresident aliens;

(8) which is maintained by an employer solely for the purpose of providing benefits for certain employees in excess of the limitations on contributions and benefits imposed by section 415 of [the Internal Revenue Code] on plans to which that section applies, without regard to whether the plan is funde d, and, to the extent that a separable part of a plan (as determined by the corporation) maintained by an employer is maintained for such purpose, that part shall be treated for purposes of this title, as a separate plan which is an excess benefit plan;

(9) which is established and maintained exclusively for substantial owners;

(10) of an international organization which is exempt from taxation under the International Organizations Immunities Act [22 U.S.C. §§ 288 et seq.];

(11) maintained solely for the purpose of complying with applicable workmen's compensation laws or unemployment compensation or disability insurance laws;

(12) which is a defined benefit plan, to the extent that it is treated as an individual account plan under paragraph (35)(B) of section 3; or

(13) established and maintained by a professional service employer which does not at any time after September 2, 1974, have more than 25 active participants in the plan. . . .

§ 4022 [§ 1322]. Single-employer plan benefits guaranteed

(a) Nonforfeitable benefits. Subject to the limitations contained in subsection (b), the corporation shall guarantee, in accordance with this section, the payment of all nonforfeitable benefits (other than benefits becoming nonforfeitable solely on account of the termination of a plan) under a single-employer plan which terminates at a time when this title applies to it.

(b) Exceptions

(1) Except to the extent provided in paragraph (7)—

(A) no benefits provided by a plan which has been in effect for less than 60 months at the time the plan terminates shall be guaranteed under this section, and

(B) any increase in the amount of benefits under a plan resulting from a plan amendment which was made, or became effective, whichever is later, within 60 months before the date on which the plan terminates shall be disregarded. . . .

(3) The amount of monthly benefits described in subsection (a) of this section provided by a plan, which are guaranteed under this section with respect to a participant, shall not have an actuarial value which exceeds the actuarial value of a monthly benefit in the form of a life annuity commencing at age 65 equal to the lesser of—

(A) his average monthly gross income from his employer during the 5 consecutive calendar year period (or, if less, during the number of calendar years in such period in which he actively participates in the plan) during which his gross income from that employer was greater than during any other such period with that employer determined by dividing 1/12 of the sum of all such gross income by the number of such calendar years in which he had such gross income, or

(B) $750 multiplied by a fraction, the numerator of which is the contribution and benefit base (determined under section 230 of [the Social Security Act]) in effect at the time the plan terminates and the denominator of which is such contribution and benefit base in effect in calendar year 1974.

The provisions of this paragraph do not apply to non-basic benefits. . . .

(7) Benefits described in paragraph (1) are guaranteed only to the extent of the greater of—

(A) 20 percent of the amount which, but for the fact that the plan or amendment has not been in effect for 60 months or more, would be guaranteed under this section, or

(B) $20 per month,

multiplied by the number of years (but not more than 5) the plan or amendment, as the case may be, has been in effect. . . . This paragraph does not apply to benefits payable under a plan unless the corporation finds substantial evidence that the plan was terminated for a reasonable business purpose and not for the purpose of obtaining the payment of benefits by the corporation under this title. . . .

Subtitle C – Terminations

§ 4041 [§ 1341]. Termination of single-employer plans

(a) General rules governing single-employer plan termination

(1) **Exclusive means of plan termination.** Except in the case of a termination for which proceedings are otherwise instituted by the corporation as provided in section 4042, a single-employer

plan may be terminated only in a standard termination under subsection (b) of this section or a distress termination under subsection (c) of this section.

(2) 60-day notice of intent to terminate. Not less than 60 days before the proposed termination date of a standard termination under subsection (b) of this section or a distress termination under subsection (c) of this section, the plan administrator shall provide to each affected party (other than the corporation in the case of a standard termination) a written notice of intent to terminate stating that such termination is intended and the proposed termination date. The written notice shall include any related additional information required in regulations of the corporation.

(3) Adherence to collective bargaining agreements. The corporation shall not proceed with a termination of a plan under this section if the termination would violate the terms and conditions of an existing collective bargaining agreement. Nothing in the preceding sentence shall be construed as limiting the authority of the corporation to institute proceedings to involuntarily terminate a plan under section 4042.

(b) Standard termination of single-employer plans

(1) General requirements. A single-employer plan may terminate under a standard termination only if—

(A) the plan administrator provides the 60-day advance notice of intent to terminate to affected parties required under subsection (a)(2) of this section,

(B) the requirements of subparagraphs (A) and (B) of paragraph (2) are met,

(C) the corporation does not issue a notice of noncompliance under subparagraph (C) of paragraph (2), and

(D) when the final distribution of assets occurs, the plan is sufficient for benefit liabilities (determined as of the termination date).

(2) Termination procedure

(A) Notice to corporation. As soon as practicable after the date on which the notice of intent to terminate is provided pursuant to subsection (a)(2) of this section, the plan administrator shall send a notice to the corporation setting forth—

(i) certification by an enrolled actuary—

(I) of the projected amount of the assets of the plan (as of a proposed date of final distribution of assets),

(II) of the actuarial present value (as of such date) of the benefit liabilities (determined as of the proposed termination date) under the plan, and

(III) that the plan is projected to be sufficient (as of such proposed date of final distribution) for such benefit liabilities,

(ii) such information as the corporation may prescribe in regulations as necessary to enable the corporation to make determinations under subparagraph (C), and

(iii) certification by the plan administrator that—

(I) the information on which the enrolled actuary based the certification under clause (i) is accurate and complete, and

(II) the information provided to the corporation under clause (ii) is accurate and complete.

Clause (i) and clause (iii)(I) shall not apply to a plan described in section 412(i) of [the Internal Revenue Code].

(B) Notice to participants and beneficiaries of benefit commitments. No later than the date on which a notice is sent by the plan administrator under subparagraph (A), the plan administrator shall send a notice to each person who is a participant or beneficiary under the plan—

(i) specifying the amount of the benefit liabilities (if any) attributable to such person as of the proposed termination date and the benefit form on the basis of which such amount is determined, and

(ii) including the following information used in determining such benefit liabilities:

(I) the length of service,

(II) the age of the participant or beneficiary,

(III) wages,

(IV) the assumptions, including the interest rate, and

(V) such other information as the corporation may require.

Such notice shall be written in such manner as is likely to be understood by the participant or beneficiary and as may be prescribed in regulations of the corporation.

(C) Notice from corporation of noncompliance

(i) In general. Within 60 days after receipt of the notice under subparagraph (A), the corporation shall issue a notice of noncompliance to the plan administrator if—

(I) it determines, based on the notice sent under paragraph (2)(A) of subsection (b) that the plan is not sufficient for benefit liabilities,

(II) it otherwise determines, on the basis of information provided by affected parties or otherwise obtained by the corporation, that there is reason to believe that the plan is not sufficient for benefit liabilities, or

(III) it determines that any other requirement of subparagraph (A) or (B) of this paragraph or of subsection (a)(2) has not been met, unless it further determines that the issuance of such notice would be inconsistent with the interests of participants and beneficiaries.

(ii) Extension. The corporation and the plan administrator may agree to extend the 60-day period referred to in clause (i) by a written agreement signed by the corporation and the plan administrator before the expiration of the 60-day period. The 60-day period shall be extended as provided in the agreement and may be further extended by subsequent written agreements signed by the corporation and the plan administrator made before the expiration of a previously agreed upon extension of the 60-day period. Any extension may be made upon such terms and conditions (including the payment of benefits) as are agreed upon by the corporation and the plan administrator.

(D) Final distribution of assets in absence of notice of noncompliance. The plan administrator shall commence the final distribution of assets pursuant to the standard termination of the plan as soon as practicable after the expiration of the 60-day (or extended) period referred to in subparagraph (C), but such final distribution may occur only if—

(i) the plan administrator has not received during such period a notice of noncompliance from the corporation under subparagraph (C), and

(ii) when such final distribution occurs, the plan is sufficient for benefit liabilities (determined as of the termination date).

(3) Methods of final distribution of assets

(A) **In general.** In connection with any final distribution of assets pursuant to the standard termination of the plan under this subsection, the plan administrator shall distribute the assets in accordance with section 4044. In distributing such assets, the plan administrator shall—

(i) purchase irrevocable commitments from an insurer to provide all benefit liabilities under the plan, or

(ii) in accordance with the provisions of the plan and any applicable regulations, otherwise fully provide all benefit liabilities under the plan. . . .

(B) Certification to corporation of final distribution of assets. Within 30 days after the final distribution of assets is completed pursuant to the standard termination of the plan under this subsection, the plan administrator shall send a notice to the corporation certifying that the assets of the plan have been distributed in accordance with the provisions of subparagraph (A) so as to pay all benefit liabilities under the plan.

(4) **Continuing authority.** Nothing in this section shall be construed to preclude the continued exercise by the corporation, after the termination date of a plan terminated in a standard termination under this subsection, of its authority under section 4003 with respect to matters relating to the termination. A certification under paragraph (3)(B) shall not affect the corporation's obligations under section 4022. . . .

(c) Distress termination of single-employer plans

(1) **In general.** A single-employer plan may terminate under a distress termination only if—

(A) the plan administrator provides the 60-day advance notice of intent to terminate to affected parties required under subsection (a)(2) of this section,

(B) the requirements of subparagraph (A) of paragraph (2) are met, and

(C) the corporation determines that the requirements of subparagraph (B) and (D) of paragraph (2) are met.

(2) Termination requirements

(A) Information submitted to corporation. As soon as practicable after the date on which the notice of intent to terminate is provided pursuant to subsection (a)(2) of this section, the plan administrator shall provide the corporation, in such form as may be prescribed by the corporation in regulations, the following information:

(i) such information as the corporation may prescribe by regulation as necessary to make determinations under subparagraph (B) and paragraph (3);

(ii) unless the corporation determines the information is not necessary for purposes of paragraph (3)(A) or section 4062, certification by an enrolled actuary of—

(I) the amount (as of the proposed termination date and, if applicable, the proposed distribution date) of the current value of the assets of the plan,

(II) the actuarial present value (as of such dates) of the benefit liabilities under the plan,

(III) whether the plan is sufficient for benefit liabilities as of such dates,

(IV) the actuarial present value (as of such dates) of benefits under the plan guaranteed under section 4022, and

(V) whether the plan is sufficient for guaranteed benefits as of such dates;

(iii) in any case in which the plan is not sufficient for benefit liabilities as of such date—

(I) the name and address of each participant and beneficiary under the plan as of such date, and

(II) such other information as shall be prescribed by the corporation by regulation as necessary to enable the corporation to be able to make payments to participants and beneficiaries as required under section 4022(c); and

(iv) certification by the plan administrator that—

(I) the information on which the enrolled actuary based the certifications under clause (ii) is accurate and complete, and

(II) the information provided to the corporation under clauses (i) and (iii) is accurate and complete.

Clause (ii) and clause (iv)(I) shall not apply to a plan described in section 412(i) of [the Internal Revenue Code].

(B) Determination by corporation of necessary distress criteria. Upon receipt of the notice of intent to terminate required under subsection (a)(2) of this section and the information required under subparagraph (A), the corporation shall determine whether the requirements of this subparagraph are met as provided in clause (i), (ii), or (iii). The requirements of this subparagraph are met if each person who is (as of the proposed termination date) a contributing sponsor of such plan or a member of such sponsor's controlled group meets the requirements of any of the following clauses:

(i) Liquidation in bankruptcy or insolvency proceedings. The requirements of this clause are met by a person if—

(I) such person has filed or has had filed against such person, as of the proposed termination date, a petition seeking liquidation in a case under Title 11, or under any similar federal law or law of a State or political subdivision of a State (or a case described in clause (ii) filed by or against such person has been converted, as of such date, to a case in which liquidation is sought), and

(II) such case has not, as of the proposed termination date, been dismissed.

(ii) Reorganization in bankruptcy or insolvency proceedings. The requirements of this clause are met by a person if—

(I) such person has filed, or has had filed against such person, as of the proposed termination date, a petition seeking reorganization in a case under Title 11, or under any similar law of a State or political subdivision of a State (or a case described in clause (i) filed by or against such person has been converted, as of such date, to such a case in which reorganization is sought),

(II) such case has not, as of the proposed termination date, been dismissed,

(III) such person timely submits to the corporation any request for the approval of the bankruptcy court (or other appropriate court in a case under such similar law of a State or political subdivision) of the plan termination, and

(IV) the bankruptcy court (or such other appropriate court) determines that, unless the plan is terminated, such person will be unable to pay all its debts pursuant to a plan of reorganization and will be unable to continue in business outside the chapter 11 reorganization process and approves the termination.

(iii) Termination required to enable payment of debts while staying in business or to avoid unreasonably burdensome pension costs caused by declining workforce. The requirements of this clause are met by a person if such person demonstrates to the satisfaction of the corporation that—

(I) unless a distress termination occurs, such person will be unable to pay such person's debts when due and will be unable to continue in business, or

(II) the costs of providing pension coverage have become unreasonably burdensome to such person, solely as a result of a decline of such person's workforce covered as participants under all single-employer plans of which such person is a contributing sponsor.

(C) Notification of determinations by corporation. The corporation shall notify the plan administrator as soon as practicable of its determinations made pursuant to subparagraph (B). . . .

(3) Termination procedure

(A) Determinations by corporation relating to plan sufficiency for guaranteed benefits and for benefit liabilities. If the corporation determines that the requirements for a distress termination set forth in paragraphs (1) and (2) are met, the corporation shall—

(i) determine that the plan is sufficient for guaranteed benefits (as of the termination date) or that the corporation is unable to make such determination on the basis of information made available to the corporation,

(ii) determine that the plan is sufficient for benefit liabilities (as of the termination date) or that the corporation is unable to make such determination on the basis of information made available to the corporation, and

(iii) notify the plan administrator of the determinations made pursuant to this subparagraph as soon as practicable.

(B) Implementation of termination. After the corporation notifies the plan administrator of its determinations under subparagraph (A), the termination of the plan shall be carried out as soon as practicable, as provided in clause (i), (ii), or (iii).

(i) Cases of sufficiency for benefit liabilities. In any case in which the corporation determines that the plan is sufficient for benefit liabilities, the plan administrator shall proceed to distribute the plan's assets, and make certification to the corporation with respect to such distribution, in the manner described in subsection (b)(3) of this section, and shall take such other actions as may be appropriate to carry out the termination of the plan.

(ii) Cases of sufficiency for guaranteed benefits without a finding of sufficiency for benefit liabilities. In any case in which the corporation determines that the plan is sufficient for guaranteed benefits, but further determines that it is unable to determine that the plan is sufficient for benefit liabilities on the basis of the information made available to it, the plan administrator shall proceed to distribute the plan's assets in the manner described in subsection (b)(3) of this section, make certification to the corporation that the distribution has occurred, and take such actions as may be appropriate to carry out the termination of the plan.

(iii) Cases without any finding of sufficiency. In any case in which the corporation determines that it is unable to determine that the plan is sufficient for guaranteed benefits on the basis of the information made available to it, the corporation shall commence proceedings in accordance with section 4042.

(C) Finding after authorized commencement of termination that plan is unable to pay benefits

(i) Finding with respect to benefit liabilities which are not guaranteed benefits. If, after the plan administrator has begun to terminate the plan as authorized under subparagraph (B)(i), the plan administrator finds that the plan is unable, or will be unable, to pay benefit liabilities which are not benefits guaranteed by the corporation under section 4022, the plan administrator shall notify the corporation of such finding as soon as practicable thereafter.

(ii) Finding with respect to guaranteed benefits. If, after the plan administrator has begun to terminate the plan as authorized by subparagraph (B)(i) or (ii), the plan administrator finds that the plan is unable, or will be unable, to pay all benefits under the plan which are guaranteed by the corporation under section 4022, the plan administrator shall notify the corporation of such finding as soon as practicable thereafter. If the corporation concurs in the finding of the plan administrator (or the corporation itself makes such a finding), the corporation shall institute appropriate proceedings under section 4042.

(D) Administration of plan during interim period

(i) In general. The plan administrator shall—

(I) meet the requirements of clause (ii) for the period commencing on the date on which the plan administrator provides a notice of distress termination to the corporation under subsection (a)(2) of this section and ending on the date on which the plan administrator receives notification from the corporation of its determinations under subparagraph (A), and

(II) meet the requirements of clause (ii) commencing on the date on which the plan administrator or the corporation makes a finding under subparagraph (C)(ii).

(ii) Requirements. The requirements of this clause are met by the plan administrator if the plan administrator—

(I) refrains from distributing assets or taking any other actions to carry out the proposed termination under this subsection,

(II) pays benefits attributable to employer contributions, other than death benefits, only in the form of an annuity,

(III) does not use plan assets to purchase irrevocable commitments to provide benefits from an insurer, and

(IV) continues to pay all benefit liabilities under the plan, but, commencing on the proposed termination date, limits the payment of benefits under the plan to those benefits which are guaranteed by the corporation under section 4022 or to which assets are required to be allocated under section 4044.

In the event the plan administrator is later determined not to have met the requirements for distress termination, any benefits which are not paid solely by reason of compliance with subclause (IV) shall be due and payable immediately (together with interest, at a reasonable rate, in accordance with regulations of the corporation).

(d) Sufficiency

For purposes of this section—

(1) **Sufficiency for benefit liabilities.** A single-employer plan is sufficient for benefit liabilities if there is no amount of unfunded benefit liabilities under the plan.

(2) **Sufficiency for guaranteed benefits.** A single-employer plan is sufficient for guaranteed benefits if there is no amount of unfunded guaranteed benefits under the plan.

(e) Limitation on conversion of defined benefit plan to defined contribution plan. The adoption of an amendment to a plan which causes the plan to become a plan described in section 4021(b)(1) constitutes a termination of the plan. Such an amendment may take effect only after the plan satisfies the requirements for standard termination under subsection (b) of this section or distress termination under subsection (c) of this section. . . .

§ 4042 [§ 1342]. Institution of termination proceedings by corporation

(a) Authority to institute proceedings to terminate plan. The corporation may institute proceedings under this section to terminate a plan whenever it determines that—

(1) the plan has not met the minimum funding standard required under section 412 of [the Internal Revenue Code], or has been notified by the Secretary of the Treasury that a notice of deficiency under section 6212 of [the Internal Revenue Code] has been mailed with respect to the tax imposed under section 4971(a) of [the Internal Revenue Code],

(2) the plan will be unable to pay benefits when due,

(3) the reportable event described in section 4043(c)(7) has occurred, or

(4) the possible long-run loss of the corporation with respect to the plan may reasonably be expected to increase unreasonably if the plan is not terminated.

The corporation shall as soon as practicable institute proceedings under this section to terminate a single-employer plan whenever the corporation determines that the plan does not have assets available to pay benefits which are currently due under the terms of the plan. The corporation may prescribe a simplified procedure to follow in terminating small plans as long as that procedure includes substantial safeguards for the rights of the participants and beneficiaries under the plans, and for the employers who maintain such plans (including the requirement for a court decree under subsection (c) of this section). Notwithstanding any other provision of this title, the corporation is authorized to pool assets of terminated plans for purposes of administration, investment, payment of liabilities of all such terminated plans, and such other purposes as it determines to be appropriate in the administration of this title.

(b) Appointment of trustee

(1) Whenever the corporation makes a determination under subsection (a) of this section with respect to a plan or is required under subsection (a) of this section to institute proceedings under this section, it may, upon notice to the plan, apply to the appropriate United States district court for the appointment of a trustee to administer the plan with respect to which the determination is made pending the issuance of a decree under subsection (c) of this section ordering the termination of the plan. If within 3 business days after the filing of an application under this subsection, or such other period as the court may order, the administrator of the plan consents to the appointment of a trustee, or fails to show why a trustee should not be appointed, the court may grant the application and appoint a trustee to administer the plan in accordance with its terms until the corporation determines that the plan should be terminated or that termination is unnecessary. The corporation may request that it be appointed as trustee of a plan in any case.

(2) Notwithstanding any other provision of this title—

(A) upon the petition of a plan administrator or the corporation, the appropriate United States district court may appoint a trustee in accordance with the provisions of this section if the interests of the plan participants would be better served by the appointment of the trustee, and

(B) upon the petition of the corporation, the appropriate United States district court shall appoint a trustee proposed by the corporation for a multiemployer plan which is in reorganization or to which section 4041A(d) applies, unless such appointment would be adverse to the interests of the plan participants and beneficiaries in the aggregate.

(3) The corporation and plan administrator may agree to the appointment of a trustee without proceeding in accordance with the requirements of paragraphs (1) and (2).

(c) Adjudication that plan must be terminated.

(1) If the corporation is required under subsection (a) of this section to commence proceedings under this section with respect to a plan or, after issuing a notice under this section to a plan administrator, has determined that the plan should be terminated, it may, upon notice to the plan administrator, apply to the appropriate United States district court for a decree adjudicating that the plan must be terminated in order to protect the interests of the participants or to avoid any unreasonable deterioration of the financial condition of the plan or any unreasonable increase in the liability of the fund. If the trustee appointed under subsection (b) of this section disagrees with the determination of the corporation under the preceding sentence he may intervene in the proceeding relating to the application for the decree, or make application for such decree himself. Upon granting a decree for which the corporation or trustee has applied under this subsection the court shall authorize the trustee appointed under subsection (b) of this section (or appoint a trustee if one has not been appointed under such subsection and authorize him) to terminate the plan in accordance with the provisions of this subtitle. If the corporation and the plan administrator agree that a plan should be terminated and agree to the appointment of a trustee without proceeding in accordance with the requirements of this subsection (other than this sentence) the trustee shall have the power described in subsection (d)(1) of this section and, in addition to any other duties imposed on the trustee under law or by agreement between the corporation and the plan administrator, the trustee is subject to the duties described in subsection (d)(3) of this section. Whenever a trustee appointed under this title is operating a plan with discretion as to the date upon which final distribution of the assets is to be commenced, the trustee shall notify the corporation at least 10 days before the date on which he proposes to commence such distribution.

(2) In the case of a proceeding initiated under this section, the plan administrator shall provide the corporation, upon the request of the corporation, the information described in clauses (ii), (iii), and (iv) of section 4041(c)(2)(A). . . .

(e) Filing of application notwithstanding pendency of other proceedings. An application by the corporation under this section may be filed notwithstanding the pendency in the same or any other court of any bankruptcy, mortgage foreclosure, or equity receivership proceeding, or any proceeding to reorganize, conserve, or liquidate such plan or its property, or any proceeding to enforce a lien against property of the plan. . . .

§ 4044 [§ 1344]. Allocation of assets

(a) Order of priority of participants and beneficiaries. In the case of the termination of a single-employer plan, the plan administrator shall allocate the assets of the plan (available to provide benefits) among the participants and beneficiaries of the plan in the following order:

(1) First, to that portion of each individual's accrued benefit which is derived from the participant's contributions to the plan which were not mandatory contributions.

(2) Second, to that portion of each individual's accrued benefit which is derived from the participant's mandatory contributions.

(3) Third, in the case of benefits payable as an annuity—

(A) in the case of the benefit of a participant or beneficiary which was in pay status as of the beginning of the 3-year period ending on the termination date of the plan, to each such benefit, based on the provisions of the plan (as in effect during the 5-year period ending on such date) under which such benefit would be the least,

(B) in the case of a participant's or beneficiary's benefit (other than a benefit described in subparagraph (A)) which would have been in pay status as of the beginning of such 3-year period if the participant had retired prior to the beginning of the 3-year period and if his benefits had commenced (in the normal form of annuity under the plan) as of the beginning of such period, to each such benefit based on the provisions of the plan (as in effect during the 5-year period ending on such date) under which such benefit would be the least.

For purposes of subparagraph (A), the lowest benefit in pay status during a 3-year period shall be considered the benefit in pay status for such period.

(4) Fourth—

(A) to all other benefits (if any) of individuals under the plan guaranteed under this title (determined without regard to section 4022B(a)), and

(B) to the additional benefits (if any) which would be determined under subparagraph (A) if section 4022(b)(5) did not apply.

For purposes of this paragraph, section 4021 shall be applied without regard to subsection (c) thereof.

(5) Fifth, to all other nonforfeitable benefits under the plan.

(6) Sixth, to all other benefits under the plan. . . .

(d) Distribution of residual assets . . .

(1) Subject to paragraph (3), any residual assets of a single-employer plan may be distributed to the employer if—

(A) all liabilities of the plan to participants and their beneficiaries have been satisfied,

(B) the distribution does not contravene any provision of law, and

(C) the plan provides for such a distribution in these circumstances.

(2)(A) In determining the extent to which a plan provides for the distribution of plan assets to the employer for purposes of paragraph (1)(C), any such provision, and any amendment increasing the amount which may be distributed to the employer, shall not be treated as effective before the end of the fifth calendar year following the date of the adoption of such provision or amendment.

(B) A distribution to the employer from a plan shall not be treated as failing to satisfy the requirements of this paragraph if the plan has been in effect for fewer than 5 years and the plan has provided for such a distribution since the effective date of the plan. . . .

(3)(A) Before any distributions from a plan pursuant to paragraph (1), if any assets of the plan attributable to employee contributions remain after satisfaction of all liabilities described in subsection (a) of this section, such remaining assets shall be equitably distributed to the participants who made such contributions or their beneficiaries. . . .

§ 4045 [§ 1345]. Recapture of payments

(a) Authorization to recover benefits. Except as provided in subsection (c) of this section, the trustee is authorized to recover for the benefit of a plan from a participant the recoverable amount (as defined in subsection (b) of this section) of all payments from the plan to him which commenced within the 3-year period immediately preceding the time the plan is terminated.

(b) Recoverable amount. For purposes of subsection (a) of this section the recoverable amount is the excess of the amount determined under paragraph (1) over the amount determined under paragraph (2).

(1) The amount determined under this paragraph is the sum of the amount of the actual payments received by the participant within the 3-year period.

(2) The amount determined under this paragraph is the sum of—

(A) the sum of the amount such participant would have received during each consecutive 12-month period within the 3 years if the participant received the benefit in the form described in paragraph (3),

(B) the sum for each of the consecutive 12-month periods of the lesser of—

(i) the excess, if any, of $10,000 over the benefit in the form described in paragraph (3), or

(ii) the excess of the actual payment, if any, over the benefit in the form described in paragraph (3), and

(C) the present value at the time of termination of the participant's future benefits guaranteed under this title as if the benefits commenced in the form described in paragraph (3).

(3) The form of benefit for purposes of this subsection shall be the monthly benefit the participant would have received during the consecutive 12-month period, if he had elected at the time of the first payment made during the 3- year period, to receive his interest in the plan as a monthly benefit in the form of a life annuity commencing at the time of such first payment. . . .

§ 4047 [§ 1347]. Restoration of plans. Whenever the corporation determines that a plan which is to be terminated under section 4041 or 4042, or which is in the process of being terminated under section 4041 or 4042, should not be terminated under section 4041 or 4042 as a result of such circumstances as the corporation determines to be relevant, the corporation is authorized to cease any activities undertaken to terminate the plan, and to take whatever action is necessary and within its power to restore the plan to its status prior to the determination that the plan was to be terminated under section 4041 or 4042. In the case of a plan which has been terminated under section 4041 or 4042 the corporation is authorized in any such case in which the corporation determines such action to be appropriate and consistent with its duties under this title, to take such action as may be necessary to restore the plan to its pretermination status, including, but not limited to, the transfer to the employer or a plan administrator of control of part or all of the remaining assets and liabilities of the plan. . . .

Subtitle D – Liability

§ 4061 [§ 1361]. Amounts payable by corporation. The corporation shall pay benefits under a single-employer plan terminated under this title subject to the limitations and requirements of subtitle B of this title. The corporation shall provide financial assistance to pay benefits under a multiemployer plan which is insolvent under section 4245 or 4281(d)(2)(A), subject to the limitations and requirements of subtitles B, C, and E of this title. Amounts guaranteed by the corporation under sections 4022 and 4022A shall be paid by the corporation only out of the appropriate fund. The corporation shall make payments under the supplemental program to reimburse multiemployer plans for uncollectible withdrawal liability only out of the fund established under section 4005(e).

§ 4062 [§ 1362]. Liability for termination of single-employer plans under a distress termination or a termination by corporation

(a) In general. In any case in which a single-employer plan is terminated in a distress termination under section 4041(c) or a termination otherwise instituted by the corporation under section 4042, any person who is, on the termination date, a contributing sponsor of the plan or a member of such a contributing sponsor's controlled group shall incur liability under this section. The liability under this section of all such persons shall be joint and several. The liability under this section consists of—

(1) liability to the corporation, to the extent provided in subsection (b) of this section, and

(2) liability to the trustee appointed under subsection (b) or (c) of section 4042, to the extent provided in subsection (c) of this section.

(b) Liability of corporation

(1) Amount of liability

(A) In general. Except as provided in subparagraph (B), the liability to the corporation of a person described in subsection (a) of this section shall be the total amount of the unfunded benefit liabilities (as of the termination date) to all participants and beneficiaries under the plan, together with interest (at a reasonable rate) calculated from the termination date in accordance with regulations prescribed by the corporation.

(B) Special rule in case of subsequent insufficiency. For purposes of subparagraph (A), in any case described in section 4041(c)(3)(C)(ii), actuarial present values shall be determined as of the date of the notice to the corporation (or the finding by the corporation) described in such section.

(2) Payment of liability

(A) In general. Except as provided in subparagraph (B), the liability to the corporation under this subsection shall be due and payable to the corporation as of the termination date, in cash or securities acceptable to the corporation. . . .

PART VIII.

WORKPLACE INJURIES AND DISEASES

NEW YORK WORKERS' COMPENSATION LAW

Chapter 67

ARTICLE 1. Short Title; Definitions; Application

§ 1. Short title

a. This chapter shall be known as the "workers' compensation law."

b. Reference in this chapter or in any other law to the workmen's compensation law shall be deemed to mean and refer to the workers' compensation law. The terms "workman" or "workmen" appearing in this chapter shall be deemed to mean "worker" or "workers," respectively. The terms "he," "his," or "him," appearing in this chapter shall be deemed to mean "he or she," "his or her," and "him or her."

§ 2. Definitions. As used in this chapter,

1. "Hazardous employment" means a work or occupation described in section three of this chapter.

2. "Department" means the department of labor of the state of New York; "Chairman" means the chairman of the workmen's compensation board of the state of New York; "Commissioner" means the industrial commissioner of the state of New York; "Board" means the workmen's compensation board of the state of New York; "Commissioners" means the commissioners of the state insurance fund of the department of labor of the state of New York.

3. "Employer," except when otherwise expressly stated, means a person, partnership, association, corporation, and the legal representatives of a deceased employer, or the receiver or trustee of a person, partner-ship, association or corporation, having one or more persons in employment, including the state, a municipal corporation, fire district or other political subdivision of the state, and every authority or commission heretofore or hereafter continued or created by the public authorities law. For the purposes of this chapter only "employer" shall also mean a person, partnership, association, corporation, and the legal representatives of a deceased employer, or the receiver or trustee of a person, partnership, association or corporation who delivers or causes to be delivered newspapers or periodicals for delivering or selling and delivering by a newspaper carrier under the age of eighteen years as defined in section thirty-two hundred twenty-eight of the education law. For the purpose of this chapter only, "employer" shall also mean a person, partnership, association, or corporation who leases or otherwise contracts with an operator or lessee for the purpose of driving, operating or leasing a taxicab as so defined in section one hundred forty-eight-a of the vehicle and traffic law, except where such person is an owner-operator of such taxicab who personally regularly operates such vehicle an average of forty or more hours per week and leases such taxi-cab for some portion of the remaining time. For the purposes of this section only, such an owner-operator shall be deemed to be an employer if he controls, directs, supervises, or has the power to hire or terminate such other person who leases the vehicle. . . .

4. "Employee" means a person engaged in one of the occupations enumerated in section three or who is in the service of an employer whose principal business is that of carrying on or conducting a hazardous employment upon the premises or at the plant, or in the course of his employment away from the plant of his employer; "employee" shall also mean for the purposes of this chapter civil defense volunteers who are personnel of volunteer agencies sponsored or authorized by a local office under regulations of the civil defense commission, to the extent of the provisions of groups seventeen and nineteen; "employee" shall at the election of a municipal corporation made pursuant to local law duly enacted also mean a member of an auxiliary police organization authorized by local law; and for the purposes of this chapter only a newspaper carrier under the age of eighteen years as defined in section thirty-two hundred twenty-eight of the education law, and shall not include domestic servants except as provided in section three of this chapter, and except where the employer has elected to bring such employees under the law by securing compensation in accordance with the terms of section fifty of this chapter. The term "employee" shall not include persons who are members of a supervised amateur athletic activity operated on a non-profit basis, provided that said members are not also otherwise engaged or employed by any person, firm or corporation participating in said athletic activity, nor shall it include the spouse or minor child of an employer who is a farmer unless the services of such spouse or minor child shall be engaged by said employer under an express contract of hire nor shall it include an executive officer of a corporation who at all times during the period involved owns all of the issued and outstanding stock of the corporation and holds all of the offices pursuant to paragraph (e) of section seven hundred fifteen of the business corporation law or two executive officers of a corporation who at all times during the period involved between them own all of the issued and outstanding stock of such corporation and hold all such offices except as provided in subdivision six of section fifty-four of this chapter provided, however, that where there are two executive officers of a corporation each officer must own at least one share of stock, nor shall it include a self-employed person or a partner of a partnership as defined in section ten of the partnership law who is not covered under a compensation insurance contract or a certificate of self-insurance as provided in subdivision eight of section fifty-four of this chapter, nor shall it include farm laborers except as provided in group fourteen-b of section three of this chapter. If a farm labor contractor recruits or supplies farm laborers for work on a farm, such farm laborers shall for the purposes of this chapter be deemed to be employees of the owner or lessee of such farm. The term "employee" shall not include baby sitters as defined in subdivision three of section one hundred thirty-one and subdivision three of section one hundred thirty-two of the labor law or minors fourteen years of age or over engaged in casual employment consisting of yard work and household chores in and about a one family owner-occupied residence or the premises of a non-profit, non-commercial organization, not involving the use of power-driven machinery. The term "employee" shall not include persons engaged by the owner in casual employment consisting of yard work, household chores and

making repairs to or painting in and about a one-family owner-occupied residence. The term "employee" shall not include the services of a licensed real estate broker or sales associate. . . .

"Employee" shall also mean, for purposes of this chapter, an infant rendering services for the public good as prescribed in sections seven hundred fifty-eight-a and 353.6 of the family court act. For the purpose of this chapter only, "employee" shall also mean a driver, operator or lessee who contracts with an owner, operator or lessor for the purpose of operating a taxicab as so defined in section one hundred forty-eight-a of the vehicle and traffic law, except where such person leases the taxicab from a person who personally, regularly operates such vehicle an average of forty or more hours per week. For the purposes of this section only, such person shall be deemed to be an employee of the owner-operator if the owner-operator controls, directs, supervises, or has the power to hire or terminate such person.

"Employee" shall also mean, for purposes of this chapter, a professional musician or a person otherwise engaged in the performing arts who performs services as such for a television or radio station or network, a film production, a theatre, hotel, restaurant, night club or similar establishment unless, by written contract, such musician or person is stipulated to be an employee of another employer covered by this chapter. "Engaged in the performing arts" shall mean performing service in connection with the production of or performance in any artistic endeavor which requires artistic or technical skill or expertise. . . .

"Employee" shall also mean, for purposes of this chapter, a professional model, who: (a) performs modeling services for; or (b) consents in writing to the transfer of his or her exclusive legal right to the use of his or her name, portrait, picture or image, for advertising purposes or for the purposes of trade, directly to a retail store, a manufacturer, an advertising agency, a photographer, a publishing company or any other such person or entity, which dictates such professional model's assignments, hours of work or performance locations and which compensates such professional model in return for a waiver of such professional model's privacy rights enumerated above, unless such services are performed pursuant to a written contract wherein it is stated that such professional model is the employee of another employer covered by this chapter. For the purposes of this paragraph, the term "professional model" means a person who, in the course of his or her trade, occupation or profession, performs modeling services. For purposes of this paragraph, the term "modeling services" means the appearance by a professional model in photographic sessions or the engagement of such model in live, filmed or taped modeling performances for remuneration. . . .

5. "Employment" includes employment in a trade, business or occupation carried on by the employer for pecuniary gain, or in connection therewith, except where the employer elects to bring his employees within the provisions of this chapter as provided in section three, and except employment as a domestic worker as provided in section three, and except where a town

elects to have the provisions of this chapter apply to the town superintendent of highways. "Employment" shall also include, in connection with the civil defense effort and for purposes of this chapter the service of a civil defense volunteer in authorized activities of a volunteer agency sponsored or authorized by a local office as defined in a state defense emergency act. "Employment" shall also include participation with an auxiliary police effort made within a municipal corporation which elected to include auxiliary policemen within the definition of "employee" as authorized by subdivision four of this section and for purposes of this chapter, the services of members or volunteers in activities authorized by local law. The service of a civil defense volunteer who is also an employee recompensed by an employer for service to such employer, shall not be deemed to be in employment of a local office when he is performing civil defense service in his employment or in relation thereto. For the purposes of this chapter only "employment" shall also include the delivery or sale and delivery of newspapers or periodicals by a newspaper carrier as defined in section thirty-two hundred twenty-eight of the education law. . . .

For the purpose of this chapter only, "employment" shall also include the service of a driver, operator or lessee of a taxicab as so defined in section one hundred forty-eight-a of the vehicle and traffic law, except where a person leases a taxicab from an owner-operator of a taxicab who, regularly operates the vehicle an average of forty or more hours per week. Such a lessee shall be deemed to be in employment if the lessor controls, directs, supervises, or has the power to hire or terminate the lessee. . . .

6. "Compensation" means the money allowance payable to an employee or to his dependents as provided for in this chapter, and includes funeral benefits provided therein.

7. "Injury" and "personal injury" mean only accidental injuries arising out of and in the course of employment and such disease or infection as may naturally and unavoidably result therefrom. The terms "injury"and "personal injury" shall not include an injury which is solely mental and is based on workrelated stress if such mental injury is a direct consequence of a lawful personnel decision involving a disciplinary action, work evaluation, job transfer, demotion, or termination taken in good faith by the employer.

8. "Death" when mentioned as a basis for the right to compensation means only death resulting from such injury.

9. "Wages" means the money rate at which the service rendered is recompensed under the contract of hiring in force at the time of the accident, including the reasonable value of board, rent, housing, lodging or similar advantage received from the employer, or in the case of (a) a civil defense volunteer, (b) a volunteer worker in a state department as provided in group sixteen of subdivision one of section three of this chapter, (c) a volunteer worker for a social services district as provided in group seventeen of subdivision one of section three of this chapter, (d) a county fire coordinator, a deputy county fire coordinator or a comparable county official to whom the provisions of group fifteen-a of subdivision one of section three of this chapter are applicable, who

is also a volunteer firefighter or ambulance worker, (e) a fire district officer whether elective or appointive and whether or not he is compensated for his services or a paid fire or ambulance district employee, (f) a state fire instructor whose compensation is paid in whole or in part by the state, (g) an enrolled member of a fire company who, is not a volunteer firefighter, receives compensation for his services and is not a full-time fireman, known as a "call fireman", (h) persons who are performing services for a public or not-for-profit corporation, association, institution or agency organized as an unincorporated association or duly incorporated under the laws of this state in fulfillment of a sentence of probation or of conditional discharge, or persons performing such services pursuant to the provisions of section 170.55 or 170.56 of the criminal procedure law, (i) an auxiliary policeman in a municipal corporation which elected to include such persons within the definition of "employee" as authorized by subdivision four of this section, or (j) a duly appointed member of a regional hazardous materials incidents team recognized under section two hundred ninety of the general municipal law, such money rate applying in his regular vocation or the amount of the regular earnings of such volunteer, coordinator, instructor, or comparable officer, fire or ambulance district officer or employee or call fireman, or team member as the case may be, in his regular vocation, plus any amount earned as such a coordinator, instructor or comparable officer, or as such a fire or ambulance district officer or employee or call fireman or team member, provided, however, that in no event shall the average weekly wage be fixed at less than thirty dollars regardless of whether or not such volunteer, coordinator, instructor or comparable officer or fire or ambulance district officer or employee or call fireman or team member had gainful employment elsewhere at the time of the injury.

10. "State fund" means the state insurance fund provided for in article five of this chapter.

11. "Child" shall include a posthumous child, a child legally adopted prior to the injury of the employee; and a step-child or child born out of wedlock dependent upon the deceased.

12. "Insurance carrier" shall include the state fund, stock corporations, mutual corporations or reciprocal insurers with which employers have insured, and employers permitted to pay compensation directly under the provisions of subdivisions three, three-a or four of section fifty.

13. "Manufacture, " "construction, " "operation" and "installation" shall include "repair, " "demolition," "fabrication" and "alteration" and shall include all work done in connection with the repair of plants, buildings, grounds and approaches of all places where any of the hazardous employments are being carried on, operated or conducted.

14. "Minor" means a person who has not attained the age of eighteen years.

15. "Occupational disease" means a disease resulting from the nature of employment and contracted therein.

§ 3. Application

1. **Hazardous employments**. Compensation shall be payable for injuries or death incurred by employees in the following employments. . . .

Group 14a. On and after January first, nineteen hundred sixty-two, any other employment in a trade, business, or occupation carried on by the employer for pecuniary gain in which one or more employees other than farm laborers are employed.

Group 14-b. Employment as a farm laborer as provided herein. A farmer shall provide coverage under this chapter for all farm laborers employed during any part of the twelve consecutive months beginning April first of any calendar year preceded by a calendar year in which the cash remuneration paid to all farm laborers aggregated twelve hundred dollars or more.

Group 15. Employment as a keeper, guard, resident physician, nurse, interne, resident interne, assistant resident interne or orderly in a prison reformatory, hospital for the mentally ill or hospital maintained or operated by a municipal corporation or other subdivision of the state, notwithstanding the definitions of the terms "employment," "employer" or "employee" in subdivisions three, four and five of section two of this chapter.

Group 15-a. Employment as a county fire coordinator or as a deputy county fire coordinator pursuant to section two hundred twenty-five-a or section four hundred one of the county law, notwithstanding the definitions of the terms "employer", "employee" or "employment" in subdivisions three, four and five of section two of this chapter. . . .

Group 16. Any employment by the state, including the employment of all elected and appointed public officers, notwithstanding the definitions of the terms "employment," "employer" or "employee," in subdivisions three, four and five of section two of this chapter;. . . .

Group 17. Any employment carried on by a municipal corporation or other subdivision of the state and enumerated in the foregoing groups one to fourteen, inclusive, and on and after July first, nineteen hundred fifty-one, other such employment to the extent of authorized services related to civil defense and performed by employees in the course of employment or in relation thereto; and the sheriff and undersheriff of any county and the duly appointed regular deputies of the sheriff, notwithstanding the definition of the term "employment" in subdivision five of section two of this chapter; but employment in the department of sanitation of the city of New York in the sanitation service classification of the classified civil service of such city shall not be within the coverage of this chapter. . . .

Group 18. All other employments, except persons engaged in a teaching or nonmanual capacity in or for a religious, charitable or educational institution, notwithstanding the definition of employment in subdivision five of section two, not hereinbefore enumerated, carried on by any person, firm or corporation in which there are engaged or employed one or more employees regularly, in the same business or in or about the same establishment either upon the premises or at the plant or away from the plant of the employer, under any contract of hire, express or implied, oral or written, except farm laborers and domestics other than those within the coverage of this chapter pursuant to groups fourteen-b and twelve respectively of this subdivision, unless the employer has elected to bring such employees under the law by securing compensation in accordance with the terms of section fifty of this chapter and persons engaged in voluntary service not under contract of hire. A duly ordained, commissioned or licensed minister, priest or rabbi, a sexton, a christian science reader, or a member of a religious order, shall not be deemed to be employed or engaged in employment under the terms of this section. Recipients of charitable aid from a religious or charitable institution who perform work in or for the institution which is incidental to or in return for the aid conferred, and not under any express contract of hire, shall not be deemed to be employed or engaged in employment under the terms of this section. All persons who are members of a supervised amateur athletic activity operated on a non-profit basis shall not be deemed to be employed or engaged in employment under the terms of this section, provided that said members are not also otherwise engaged or employed by any person, firm or corporation participating in said athletic activity. The terms "religious, charitable or educational institution" mean a corporation, unincorporated association, community chest, fund or foundation organized and operated exclusively for religious, charitable or educational purposes, no part of the net earnings of which inure to the benefit of any private shareholder or individual.

Group 19. An employer may bring an employment that is not listed in this section within the coverage of this chapter by securing compensation to his employee or employees engaged in such employment in accordance with section fifty of this chapter. . . .

Group 20. In a city having a population of one million or more, teachers, regular or substitute, of shop work, manual training, industrial or trade subjects, mechanic arts, textiles, machine shop assistants, laboratory assistants, laboratory specialists, laboratory technicians, and teachers of any subject, trade, or employment requiring, for instruction purposes, use of tools or machinery for which protective, guarding or safety devices are required by the labor law, may elect to receive the benefits prescribed by this chapter provided they are not qualified to receive benefits even if eligible to apply for retirement under the teachers' retirement system in said city. An election to come within this chapter shall constitute a waiver of any right to receive absence refunds from the board of education of said city. But a teacher shall, if incapacitated to teach by reason of his injuries, be entitled to the refund of his accumulated deductions in the teachers' retirement system or in lieu thereof he may elect to receive an annuity which shall be the actuarial equivalent of said accumulated deductions. Any election or choice provided for herein may be made for the teacher by one acting in the teacher's behalf if said teacher is incapacitated to act for himself.

Group 20-a. For the purposes of this chapter, the work of any person employed as a school aide by school authorities of any school district, notwithstanding the definitions of the terms "employer," "employee" or "employment" in subdivisions three, four and five of section two of this chapter.

Group 20-b. For the purposes of this chapter, the work of any person employed in a nonpedagogical capacity by school authorities within a city having a population of one million or more, notwithstanding the definitions of the terms "employer", "employee" or "employment" in subdivisions three, four and five of section two of this chapter.

Group 21. For the purposes of this chapter, on and after January first, nineteen hundred sixty-two, the work of a newspaper carrier as defined in section thirty-two hundred twenty-eight of the education law for an employer of one or more employees as defined in subdivisions three and four of section two of this chapter.

Group 22. Employment as a teacher in a public school or place of instruction maintained or operated by a board of education or trustees of a school district, other than a school district located in a city having a population of more than one million, no twithstanding the definitions of the terms "employment," "employer" or "employee" in subdivisions three, four and five of section two of this chapter.

Group 23. For the purposes of this chapter, the work of any person employed to direct vehicular traffic at any street crossing or highway intersection crossed by pupils in going to and returning from any school in this state, whose chief duty primarily is to guard the life and safety of such pupils.

Group 24. For the purposes of this chapter, employment of any person appointed by the board of water supply of the city of New York pursuant to the provisions of section K 51-36.0 of the administrative code of the city of New York, notwithstanding the definitions of the terms "employment", "employer", or "employee", in subdivisions three, four and five of section two of this chapter.

2. Occupational diseases. Compensation shall be payable for disabilities sustained or death incurred by an employee resulting from the following occupational diseases:

COLUMN ONE DESCRIPTION OF DISEASES	COLUMN TWO DESCRIPTION OF PROCESS
1. Anthrax.	1. Handling of wool, hair, bristles, hides or skins.
2. Lead poisoning or its sequelae.	2. Any process involving the use of or direct contact with lead or its preparations or compounds.
3. Zinc poisoning or its sequelae.	3. Any process involving the use of or direct contact with zinc or its preparations or compounds or alloys.
4. Mercury poisoning or its sequelae.	4. Any process involving the use of or direct contact with mercury or its preparations or compounds.
5. Phosphorous poisoning or its sequelae.	5. Any process involving the use of or direct contact with phosphorous or its preparations or compounds.
6. Arsenic poisoning or its sequelae.	6. Any process involving the use of or direct contact with arsenic or its preparations or compounds.
7. Poisoning by wood alcohol.	7. Any process involving the use of wood alcohol or any preparation containing wood alcohol.
8. Poisoning by benzol or nitro-, hydro-, hydroxy-, and amido-derivatives of benzene (dinitro-benzol, anilin, and others), or its sequelae.	8. Any process involving the use of or direct contact with benzol or nitro-, hydro-, hydroxyl-, or amido-derivatives benzene or its preparations or compounds.
9. Poisoning by carbon bisulphide or its sequelae, or any sulphide.	9. Any process involving the use of or direct contact with carbon bisulphide or its preparations or compound, or any sulphide.
10. Poisoning by nitrous fumes or its sequelae.	10. Any process in which nitrous fumes are evolved.
11. Poisoning by nickel carbonyl or its sequelae.	11. Any process in which nickel carbonyl is evolved.
12. Dope poisoning (poisoning by tetrachlor-methane or any substance used as or in conjunction with a solvent of cellulose or nitro cellulose, or its sequelae).	12. Any process involving the use of or direct contact with any substance used as or in conjunction with a solvent for acetate of cellulose or nitro cellulose.
13. Poisoning by formaldehyde and its preparations.	13. Any process involving the use of preparations or direct contact with formaldehyde and its preparations.

14. Chrome ulceration or its sequelae.	14. Any process involving the use of or direct contact with chromic acid or by-chromate of ammonium, potassium or sodium, or their preparations.
15. Epitheliomatous cancer or ulceration of the skin or eye, due to tar, pitch, bitumen, mineral oil, or paraffin, or any compound, residue of any of these substances.	15. Handling or use of tar, pitch, bitumen, mineral oil, or of the paraffin or any product or compound, product or residue of any of these substances.
16. Glanders.	16. Care of handling of any equine animal or the carcass of any such animal.
17. Compressed air illness or its sequelae.	17. Any process carried on in compressed air.
18. Miners' diseases, including only celluitis, bursitis, ankylostomiasis, tenosynovitis and nystagmus.	18. Any process involving mining.
19. Cataract in glassworkers.	19. Processes in the manufacture of glass involving exposure to the glare of molten glass.
20. Radium poisoning or disability due to radioactive properties of sub-substances or to Roentgen rays (X-rays) or exposure to ionizing radiation.	20. Any process involving the use of or direct contact with radium or radioactive substance or the use of or direct exposure to Roentgen rays (X-rays) or ionizing radiation.
21. Methyl chloride poisoning.	21. Any process involving the use of or direct contact with methyl chloride or its preparations or compounds.
22. Carbon monoxide poisoning.	22. Any process involving direct exposure to carbon monoxide in buildings, sheds or enclosed places.
23. Poisoning by sulphuric, hydrochloric or hydrofluoric acid.	23. Any process involving the use of or direct contact with sulphuric, hydrochloric or hydrofluoric acids or their fumes.
24. Respiratory, gastro-intestinalor physiological nerve and eye disorders due to contact with petroleum products and their fumes.	24. Any process involving the use of or direct contact with petroleum or petroleum products and their fumes.
25. Disability arising from blisters or abrasions.	25. Any process involving continuous friction, rubbing or vibration causing blisters or abrasions.

26. Disability arising from bursitis or synovitis.	26. Any process involving continuous rubbing, pressure or vibration of the parts affected.
27. Dermatitis (venenata).	27. Any process involving the use of or direct contact with acids, alkalies, acids or oils, or with brick, cement, lime, concrete or mortar capable of causing dermatitis.
28. Byssinosis.	28. Any process involving exposure to raw cotton.
29. Silicosis or other dust diseases.	29. Any process involving exposure to silica or other harmful dust.
30. Any and all occupational diseases.	30. Any and all employments enumerated in subdivision one of section three of this chapter.

Nothing in paragraph thirty of this subdivision shall be construed to apply to any disability or death due to any disease described in paragraph twenty-nine of this subdivision.

ARTICLE 2. Compensation

§ 10. Liability for compensation

1. Every employer subject to this chapter shall in accordance with this chapter, except as otherwise provided in section twenty-five-a hereof, secure compensation to his employees and pay or provide compensation for their disability or death from injury arising out of and in the course of the employment without regard to fault as a cause of the injury, except that there shall be no liability for compensation under this chapter when the injury has been solely occasioned by intoxication from alcohol or a controlled substance of the injured employee while on duty; or by wilful intention of the injured employee to bring about the injury or death of himself or another; or where the injury was sustained in or caused by voluntary participation in an off-duty athletic activity not constituting part of the employee's work related duties unless the employer (a) requires the employee to participate in such activity, (b) compensates the employee for participating in such activity or (c) otherwise sponsors the activity.

2. Notwithstanding any other provisions of this chapter, an injury incurred by an individual currently employed as an emergency medical technician or an advanced emergency medical technician who is certified pursuant to section three thousand two of the public health law, while voluntarily and without expectation of monetary compensation rendering medical assistance at the scene of an accident shall be deemed to have arisen out of and in the course of the employment with that emergency medical technician or advanced emergency medical technician's current employer. . . .

§ **11. Alternative remedy.** The liability of an employer prescribed by the last preceding section shall be exclusive and in place of any other liability whatsoever, to such employee, his or her personal representatives, spouse, parents, dependents, distributees, or any person otherwise entitled to recover damages, contribution or indemnity, at common law or otherwise, on account of such injury or death or liability arising therefrom, except that if an employer fails to secure the payment of compensation for his or her injured employees and their dependents as provided in section fifty of this chapter, an injured employee, or his or her legal representative in case death results from the injury, may, at his or her option, elect to claim compensation under this chapter, or to maintain an action in the courts for damages on account of such injury; and in such an action it shall not be necessary to plead or prove freedom from contributory negligence nor may the defendant plead as a defense that the injury was caused by the negligence of a fellow servant nor that the employee assumed the risk of his or her employment, nor that the injury was due to the contributory negligence of the employee. . . .

For purposes of this section the terms "indemnity" and "contribution" shall not include a claim or cause of action for contribution or indemnification based upon a provision in a written contract entered into prior to the accident or occurrence by which the employer had expressly agreed to contribution to or indemnification of the claimant or person asserting the cause of action for the type of loss suffered.

An employer shall not be liable for contribution or indemnity to any third person based upon liability for injuries sustained by an employee acting within the scope of his or her employment for such employer unless such third person proves through competent medical evidence that such employee has sustained a "grave injury" which shall mean only one or more of the following: death, permanent and total loss of use or amputation of an arm, leg, hand or foot, loss of multiple fingers, loss of multiple toes, paraplegia or quadriplegia, total and permanent blindness, total and permanent deafness, loss of nose, loss of ear, permanent and severe facial disfigurement, loss of an index finger or an acquired injury to the brain caused by an external physical force resulting in permanent total disability.

For purposes of this section "person" means any individual, firm, company, partnership, corporation, joint venture, joint-stock association, association, trust or legal entity. . . .

§ **12. Compensation not allowed for first seven days.** No compensation shall be allowed for the first seven days of disability, except the benefits provided for in section thirteen of this chapter, provided, however, that in case the injury results in disability of more than fourteen days, the compensation shall be allowed from the date of the disability.

§ **13. Treatment and care of injured employees**

(a) The employer shall promptly provide for an injured employee such medical, surgical, optometric or other attendance or treatment, nurse and hospital service, medicine, optometric services, crutches, eye-glasses, false teeth, artificial eyes, orthotics, functional assistive and adaptive devices and apparatus for such period as the nature of the injury or the process of recovery may require. The employer shall be liable for the payment of the expenses of medical, surgical, optometric or other attendance or treatment, nurse and hospital service, medicine, optometric services, crutches, eye-glasses, false teeth, artificial eyes, orthotics, functional assistive and adaptive devices and apparatus, as well as artificial members of the body or other devices or appliances necessary in the first instance to replace, support or relieve a portion or part of the body resulting from and necessitated by the injury of an employee, for such period as the nature of the injury or the process of recovery may require, and the employer shall also be liable for replacements or repairs of such artificial members of the body or such other devices, eye-glasses, false teeth, artificial eyes, orthotics, functional assistive and adaptive devices or appliances necessitated by ordinary wear or loss or damage to a prosthesis without bodily injury to the employee. Damage to or loss of a prosthetic device shall be deemed an injury except that no disability benefits shall be payable with respect to such injury under section fifteen of this article. Such a replacement or repair of artificial members of the body or such other devices, eye-glasses, false teeth, artificial eyes, orthotics, functional assistive and adaptive devices or appliances or the providing of medical treatment and care as defined herein shall not constitute the payment of compensation under section twenty-five-a of this chapter. All fees and other charges for such treatment and services shall be limited to such charges as prevail in the same community for similar treatment of injured persons of a like standard of living.

The chair shall prepare and establish a schedule for the state, or schedules limited to defined localities, of charges and fees for such medical treatment and care, to be determined in accordance with and to be subject to change pursuant to rules promulgated by the chair. . . .

The chair shall also prepare and establish a schedule for the state, or schedules limited to defined localities, of charges and fees for outpatient hospital services not covered under the medical fee schedule previously referred to in this subdivision, to be determined in accordance with and to be subject to change pursuant to rules promulgated by the chair. . . .

The amounts payable by the employer for such treatment and services shall be the fees and charges established by such schedule. Nothing in this schedule, however, shall prevent voluntary payment of amounts higher or lower than the fees and charges fixed therein, but no physician rendering medical treatment or care, and no physical or occupational therapist rendering their respective physical or occupational therapy services may receive payment in any higher amount unless such increased amount has been authorized by the employer, or by decision as provided in section thirteen-g herein. Nothing in this section shall be construed as preventing the employment of a duly authorized physician on a salary basis by an authorized compensation medical bureau or laboratory. . . .

(d)(1) In the event that an insurer or health benefits plan make payments for medical and/or hospital services for or on behalf of an injured employee they shall be entitled to be reimbursed for such payments by the carrier or employer within the limits of the medical and hospital fee schedules if the board determines that the claim is compensable. . . .

(2) An insurer or health benefits plan entitled to reimbursement pursuant to paragraph one of this subdivision shall receive copies of the hearing and decision notices and shall develop with the carrier or employer its own mechanisms and standard operating procedures for payment of undisputed claims for reimbursement.

(e) The board, on its own motion, or a referee, upon the recommendation of the compensation medical director for the board, hearing a claim for compensation may require examination of any claimant, or of the testimony, reports and exhibits, or both, by a physician especially qualified with respect to the diagnosis or treatment of the disability for which compensation is claimed; and may require a report from such physician on the diagnosis, the causal relationship between the alleged injury and subsequent disability or death, proper treatment, and the extent of the disability of such claimant. The employer or his or her insurance carrier shall pay for such examination in an amount to be directed by the chairman.

The chairman may in his discretion designate physicians of outstanding qualifications in such fields of medicine as he deems essential in order to ascertain the diagnosis, the causal relationship between the alleged injury and subsequent disability, the type of medical care and operative procedure requisite in particular cases where such matters are not readily determinable by the regularly employed medical examiners of the board. Each of such physicians shall have had, prior to his or her designation, at least five years of practice in the field with respect to which he or she is designated, and shall receive a fee for each case, or shall be paid on a per diem basis, as determined by the chairman. Claimants may be required to submit to examination by such physicians in the manner hereinbefore specified. The contents of reports of designated physicians when introduced in evidence shall constitute prima facie evidence of fact as to the matter contained therein, and the makers of such reports shall be subject to examination upon demand and shall be paid an additional fee, as determined by the chairman, for testifying in each case.

(f) Copies of medical reports of claimant's attending physician or medical consultant, made pursuant to this chapter subsequent to the date of the request provided for in this subdivision and antedating not more than thirty days, shall be transmitted by the physician or consultant to the claimant's licensed representative or attorney representing the claimant before the board upon his written request therefore accompanied by a notice of his retainer and consent to such transmittal signed by the claimant.

(g) Every hospital operating in the state shall, within twenty days of receiving a written request by a claimant, claimant's representative, employer, carrier or special fund created under this chapter, provide to such claimant, claimant's representative, employer, carrier or special fund for use in board proceedings the medical records of an employee who has received treatment in such hospital and who is claiming benefits under this chapter. . . .

(h)(1) The chair shall require the performance of computer searches to identify injured employees who, with respect to the same injury or illness, have filed claims under the provisions of this chapter and made claims to, or on their behalf with, a payor of medical payments eligible for reimbursement pursuant to this section. Such searches shall be done at least quarterly upon request of payors and upon submission to the board of computer tapes containing the information the chair shall need to identify injured employees who file dual claims under this section. At least quarterly, the chair shall identify injured employees who have filed dual claims by social security number and workers' compensation board number and shall notify the payor of such results.

(2) Such payor shall use the information of dual filings solely for the purpose of reimbursement from the carrier or employer. The chair, upon a finding that such entity has used the information for purposes other than reimbursement from the carrier or employer, may, after hearing, impose a penalty of not more than ten thousand dollars and may prohibit such entity from receiving information under this subdivision for up to three years. . .

§ 13-a. Selection of authorized physician by employee

(1) An injured employee may, when care is required, select to treat him or her any physician authorized by the chair to render medical care, as hereafter provided. If for any reason during the period when medical treatment and care is required, the employee wishes to transfer his or her treatment and care to another authorized physician, he or she may do so, in accordance with rules prescribed by the chair. In such instance the remuneration of the physician whose services are being dispensed with shall be limited to the value of treatment rendered at fees as established in the schedule for his or her location, unless payment in higher amounts has been approved as authorized in section thirteen, paragraph a. If a claimant shall receive treatment in any hospital or other institution operated in whole or in part by the state of New York, the employer shall be liable for food, clothing and maintenance furnished by the hospital or other institution to such employee. If the employee is unable due to the nature of the injury to select such authorized physician and the emergency nature of the injury requires immediate medical treatment and care, or if he or she does not desire to select a physician, and in writing so advises the employer, the employer shall promptly provide him or her with the necessary medical care, provided however, that nothing herein contained shall operate to prevent such employee, when subsequently able to do so, from selecting for continuance of any medical treatment or care required, any physician authorized by the chair to render medical care as hereinafter provided.

(2) The chairman shall prescribe the form of a notice informing employees of their privilege under this chapter, and such notice shall be posted and maintained by the employer in a conspicuous place or places in and about his place or places of business.

(3) The employer shall have the right to transfer the care of an injured employee from the attending physician, whether chosen originally by the employee or by the employer, to another authorized physician (1) if the interest of the injured employee necessitates the transfer or (2) if the physician has not been authorized to treat injured employees under this act or (3) if he has not been authorized under this act to treat the particular injury or condition as provided by section thirteen-b (2). An authorized physician from whom the case has been transferred shall have the right of appeal to an arbitration committee as provided in subdivision two of section thirteen-g and if said arbitration committee finds that the transfer was not authorized by this section, said employer shall pay to the physician a sum equal to the total fee earned by the physician to whom the care of the injured employee has been transferred, or such proportion of said fee as the arbitration committee shall deem adequate.

(4)(a) No claim for medical or surgical treatment shall be valid and enforceable, as against such employer, or employee, unless within forty-eight hours following the first treatment the physician giving such treatment furnish to the employer and directly to the chairman a preliminary notice of such injury and treatment, within fifteen days thereafter a more complete report and subsequent thereto progress reports if requested in writing by the chairman, board, employer or insurance carrier at intervals of not less than three weeks apart or at less frequent intervals if requested on forms prescribed by the chairman. The board may excuse failure to give such notices within the designated periods when it finds it to be in the interest of justice to do so.

(b) Upon receipt of the notice provided for by paragraph (a) of this subdivision, the employer, the carrier, and the claimant each shall be entitled to have the claimant examined by a physician. . . .

(5) No claim for specialist consultations, surgical operations, physiotherapeutic or occupational therapy procedures, x-ray examinations or special diagnostic laboratory tests costing more than five hundred dollars shall be valid and enforceable, as against such employer, unless such special services shall have been authorized by the employer or by the board, or unless such authorization has been unreasonably withheld, or withheld for a period of more than thirty calendar days from receipt of a request for authorization, or unless such special services are required in an emergency, provided, however, that the basis for a denial of such authorization by the employer must be based on a conflicting second opinion rendered by a physician authorized by the workers' compensation board.

(6) Any interference by any person with the selection by an injured employee of an authorized physician to treat him, except when the selection is made pursuant to article 10-A of this chapter, and the improper influencing or attempt by any person improperly to influence the medical opinion of any physician who has treated or examined an injured employee, shall be a misdemeanor; provided, however, that it shall not constitute interference or improper influence if, in the presence of such injured employee's physician, an employer, his carrier or agent should recommend or provide information concerning rehabilitation services or the availability thereof to an injured employee or his family.

§ 13-aa. Medical appeals unit

1. There is hereby created a medical appeals unit. Such medical appeals unit shall consist of three physicians licensed to practice in this state and known to represent the schools of medical practice eligible to practice under this chapter. The members of the medical appeals unit shall be appointed by the governor. . . .

3. The medical appeals unit shall

(a) consider all matters connected with the practice of medicine submitted to it by the workmen's compensation board or the chairman thereof;

(b) prescribe rules and regulations to govern the procedure of investigations and hearings by the medical societies or boards of charges against authorized physicians and licensed compensation medical bureaus, laboratories and bureaus engaged in x-ray diagnosis or treatment, in clinical diagnosis or in physiotherapy or other therapeutic procedures, as provided in section thirteen-d and thirteen-e of this chapter;

(c) review, upon request, charges made by a physician, compensation medical bureau or laboratory or bureau engaged in x-ray diagnosis or treatment, in clinical diagnosis, or in physiotherapy or other therapeutic procedures, that any medical society or board has improperly refused to recommend authorization of the physician, compensation medical bureau or laboratory or bureau to do compensation work, and if it sustain the charges, recommend such authorization to the chairman;

(d) review, upon request, charges made by a physician, compensation medical bureau or laboratory or bureau engaged in x-ray diagnosis or treatment, in clinical diagnosis, or in physiotherapy or other therapeutic procedures, that any medical society or board has improperly recommended that his or its authorization to do compensation work be revoked, and if it sustain the charges, recommend to the chairman that such authorization not be revoked.

In each case arising under this subdivision the medical appeals unit may re-open the matter and receive further evidence, and its decision and recommendation shall be advisory to the chairman and shall not be binding or conclusive upon him. . . .

§ 13-b. Authorization of physicians, medical bureaus and laboratories by chairman

1. Upon the recommendation of the medical society of the county in which the physician's office is located or of a board designated by such county society or of a board representing duly licensed physicians of any other school of medical practice in such county, the chairman may authorize physicians licensed to practice medicine in the state of New York to render medical care under this chapter. If, within sixty days after the chairman requests such recommendations the medical society of such county or board fails to act, or if there is no such society in such county, the chairman shall designate a board of three outstanding physicians, who shall make the requisite recommendations . . . .

§ 13-c. Licensing of compensation medical bureaus and laboratories

1. The chairman may, upon the recommendation of the medical society of the county or of a board as provided in section thirteen-b, authorize and license compensation medical bureaus in such counties operated by qualified physicians wholly or principally for the diagnosis and treatment of industrial injuries or illnesses in respect to which they are authorized to render medical care under this chapter. . . .

§ 13-d. Removal of physicians from lists of those authorized to render medical care

1. The medical society of the county in which the physician's office is located at the time or a board designated by such county society or a board representing duly licensed physicians of any other school of medical practice in such county shall investigate, hear and make findings with respect to all charges as to professional or other misconduct of any authorized physician as herein provided under rules and procedure to be prescribed by the medical appeals unit. . . .

2. The chairman shall remove from the list of physicians authorized to render medical care under this chapter . . . the name of any physician who he shall find after reasonable investigation is disqualified. . . .

§ 13-e. Revocation of licenses of compensation medical bureaus and laboratories.

The chairman may revoke the license of any compensation medical bureau or laboratory upon a finding certified to him by the medical society of the county in which such bureau or laboratory is located, or by a board designated by such medical society or otherwise, as provided under section thirteen-b, or by the medical appeals unit, that such bureau or laboratory has been guilty of professional or other misconduct, or of violation of the provisions of this chapter, or that the personnel of such bureau is not properly qualified under this chapter, or that the equipment of such bureau or laboratory is inadequate for the proper rendering of medical care. . . .

§ 13-f. Payment of medical fees

(1) Fees for medical services shall be payable only to a physician or other qualified person permitted by sections thirteen-b, thirteen-k, thirteen-l and thirteen-m of this chapter or other authorized provider of health care under the education law or the public health law permitted to render medical care or treatment under this chapter, or to the agent, executor or administrator of the estate of such physician or such other qualified person. . . .

(2) Whenever his attendance at a hearing is required, the physician of the injured employee shall be entitled to receive a fee from the employer, or carrier, in an amount to be fixed by the board in addition to any fee payable under section eight thousand one of the civil practice law and rules.

§ 13-g. Payment of bills for medical care

(1) Within forty-five days after a bill has been rendered to the employer by the hospital, physician, or self-employed physical therapist or occupational therapist who has rendered treatment pursuant to a referral from the injured employee's authorized physician or authorized podiatrist for treatment to the injured employee, such employer must pay the bill or notify the hospital, physician or self-employed physical or occupational therapist in writing that the bill is not being paid and explain the reasons for non-payment. In the event that the employer fails to make payment or notify the hospital, physician or self-employed physical or occupational therapist within such forty-five day period that payment is not being made, the hospital, physician, self-employed physical therapist or self-employed occupational therapist may notify the chair in writing that the bill has not been paid and request that the board make an award for payment of such bill. The board or the chair may make an award not in excess of the established fee schedules for any such bill or part thereof which remains unpaid after said forty-five day period or thirty days after all other questions duly and timely raised in accordance with the provisions of this chapter, relating to the employer's liability for the payment of such amount, shall have been finally determined adversely to the employer, whichever is later. . . .

(2) If the parties fail to agree as to the value of medical aid rendered under this chapter, such value shall be decided by an arbitration committee consisting of one physician designated by the president of the medical society of the county in which the medical services were rendered, one physician who is a member of the medical society of the state of New York, appointed by the employer or carrier, and one physician, also a member of the medical society of the state of New York, appointed by the chairman of the workers' compensation board. . . .

§ 13-h. Ombudsman for injured workers

1. The office of ombudsman for injured workers is created within the workers' compensation board. The ombudsman shall report directly to the chair. The ombudsman shall act as an advocate for injured workers by accepting complaints concerning matters related to workers' compensation, investigating them and attempting to resolve them. The ombudsman shall also provide information to injured workers to enable them to protect their rights in the workers' compensation system.

2. The office of ombudsman for small business is created within the workers' compensation board. The ombudsman shall report directly to the chair. The ombudsman shall provide information and assistance to small businesses with regard to workers' compensation insurance and claim processing matters.

§ 13-i. Solicitation prohibited. Any person who shall make it a business to solicit employment for any person authorized by this chapter to render medical care to an injured employee in connection with any claim under this chapter, shall be guilty of a misdemeanor, except that the employer shall have the right subject to regulations prescribed by the chairman, to recommend to the injured employee the names of enrolled physicians who he believes to be competent to treat him.

§ 13-j. Medical or surgical treatment by insurance carriers and employers

1. An insurance carrier shall not participate in the treatment of injured workmen, except, that it may employ medical inspectors to examine compensation cases periodically, while under treatment, and report upon the adequacy of medical care, and other matters relative to the medical conduct of the case, a copy of which report shall be filed directly with the chairman within ten days, and that it may maintain rehabilitation bureaus operated by qualified physicians if authorized by the chairman in accordance with section thirteen-c of this chapter. (2) An employer may maintain a compensation medical bureau at the place or places of employment, if such bureau is required because of the nature of the industrial hazards, or the frequency of injuries to employees arising out of industry. Such bureau or bureaus shall be authorized and licensed pursuant to section thirteen-c, and their use by an injured employee shall be optional in accordance with the provisions of section thirteen-a.

§ 13-l. Care and treatment of injured employees by duly licenses chiropractors

2. An injured employee injured under circumstances which make such injury compensable under this article, when care is required for an injury which consists solely of a condition which may lawfully be treated by a chiropractor as defined in section sixty-five hundred fifty-one of the education law may select to treat him or her, any duly registered and licensed chiropractor of the state of New York, authorized by the chair to render chiropractic care as hereinafter provided. . . .

§ 13-m. Care and treatment of injured employees by duly licensed psychologists

2.(a) An injured employee, injured under circumstances which make such injury compensable under this article, may lawfully be treated, upon the referral of an authorized physician, by a psychologist, duly registered and licensed by the state of New York, authorized by the chairman to render psychological care pursuant to this section. . . .

§ 14. Weekly wages basis of compensation. Except as otherwise provided in this chapter, the average weekly wages of the injured employee at the time of the injury shall be taken as the basis upon which to compute compensation or death benefits, and shall be determined as follows:

1. If the injured employee shall have worked in the employment in which he was working at the time of the accident, whether for the same employer or not, during substantially the whole of the year immediately preceding his injury, his average annual earnings shall consist of three hundred times the average daily wage or salary for a six-day worker, and two hundred sixty times the average daily wage or salary for a five-day worker, which he shall have earned in such employment during the days when so employed;

2. If the injured employee shall not have worked in such employment during substantially the whole of such year, his average annual earnings, if a six-day worker, shall consist of three hundred times the average daily wage or salary, and, if a five-day worker, two hundred and sixty times the average daily wage or salary, which an employee of the same class working substantially the whole of such immediately preceding year in the same or in a similar employment in the same or a neighboring place shall have earned in such employment during the days when so employed;

3. If either of the foregoing methods of arriving at the annual average earnings of an injured employee cannot reasonably and fairly be applied, such annual average earnings shall be such sum as, having regard to the previous earnings of the injured employee and of other employees of the same or most similar class, working in the same or most similar employment, or other employment as defined in this chapter, in the same or neighboring locality, shall reasonably represent the annual earning capacity of the injured employee in the employment in which he was working at the time of the accident, provided, however, his average annual earnings shall consist of not less than two hundred times the average daily wage or salary which he shall have earned in such employment during the days when so employed, further provided, however, that if the injured employee shall have been in the military or naval service of the United States or of the state of New York within twelve months prior to his injury, and his average annual earnings cannot be fairly determined under subdivisions one and two, then the average annual earnings shall be determined by multiplying his average daily wage during the days so employed by not less than two hundred and forty;

4. The average weekly wages of an employee shall be one-fifty-second part of his average annual earnings;

5. If it be established that the injured employee was under the age of twenty-five when injured, and that under normal conditions his wages would be expected to increase, that fact may be considered in arriving at his average weekly wages;

6. If the injured employee is concurrently engaged in more than one employment at the time of injury, the employee's average weekly wages shall be calculated upon the basis of wages earned from all concurrent employments covered under this chapter. The employer in whose employment the employee was injured shall be liable for the benefits that would have been payable if the employee had had no other employment. Any additional benefits resulting from the increase in average weekly wages due to the employee's concurrent employments shall be payable in the first instance by the employer in whose employment the employee was injured and shall be reimbursed by the special disability fund created under subdivision eight of section fifteen of this article. The employer in whose employment the employee was injured shall be liable for all medical costs;

7. The average weekly wages of a jockey, apprentice jockey or exercise person shall be computed based upon all of the earnings of the jockey, apprentice jockey or exercise person, including those derived from outside of the state.

§ 14-a. Double compensation and death benefits when minors illegally employed

1. Compensation, death benefits, and awards to the commissioner of taxation and finance in accordance with subdivision nine of section fifteen and section twenty-five-a, as provided in this article, shall be double the amount otherwise payable if the injured employee at the time of the accident is a minor employed, permitted or suffered to work in violation of any provision of the labor law or in violation of any rule heretofore or hereafter adopted by the board of standards and appeals pursuant to subdivision four of section one hundred thirty-three of said law.

An employer who knowingly permits or suffers a newspaper carrier to work in violation of section thirty-two hundred twenty-eight of the education law, shall be liable for the increased awards provided by this section.

2. The employer alone and not the insurance carrier shall be liable for the increased compensation, increased death benefits, or awards to the commissioner of taxation and finance provided for by this section. Any provision in an insurance policy undertaking to relieve an employer from such increased liability shall be void. . . .

§ 15. Schedule in case of disability. The following schedule of compensation is hereby established:

1. **Permanent total disability**. In case of total disability adjudged to be permanent sixty-six and two-thirds per centum of the average

weekly wages shall be paid to the employee during the continuance of such total disability. Loss of both hands, or both arms, or both feet, or both legs, or both eyes, or of any two thereof shall, in the absence of conclusive proof to the contrary, constitute permanent total disability. In all other cases permanent total disability shall be determined in accordance with the facts. Notwithstanding any other provision of this chapter, an injured employee disabled due to the loss or total loss of use of both eyes, or both hands, or both arms, or both feet, or both legs, or of any two thereof shall not suffer any diminution of his compensation by engaging in business or employment provided his earnings or wages, when combined with his compensation, shall not be in excess of the wage base on which the maximum weekly compensation benefit is computed under the law in effect at the time of such earning; further provided, that if the combination exceeds such wage base, the compensation shall be diminished to an amount which, together with his earnings or wages, shall equal the wage base; and further provided that the application of this subdivision shall not result in reduction of compensation which an injured employee who is disabled due to the loss or total loss of use of both eyes, or both hands, or both arms, or both feet, or both legs or of any two thereof, would otherwise be entitled to under any other provision of this section.

2. **Temporary total disability**. In case of temporary total disability, sixty-six and two-thirds per centum of the average weekly wages shall be paid to the employee during the continuance thereof, except as otherwise provided in this chapter.

3. **Permanent partial disability**. In case of disability partial in character but permanent in quality the compensation shall be sixty-six and two-thirds per centum of the average weekly wages and shall be paid to the employee for the period named in this subdivision, as follows:

Member lost	Number of weeks' compensation
a. Arm	312
b. Leg	288
c. Hand	244
d. Foot	205
e. Eye	160
f. Thumb	75
g. First finger	46
h. Great toe	38
i. Second finger	30
j. Third finger	25
k. Toe other than great toe	16
l. Fourth finger	15

m. Loss of hearing. Compensation for the complete loss of the hearing of one ear, for sixty weeks, for the loss of hearing of both ears, for one hundred and fifty weeks.

n. Phalanges. Compensation for the loss of more than one phalange of a digit shall be the same as for loss of the entire digit. Compensation for loss of the first phalange shall be one-half of the compensation for loss of the entire digit.

o. Amputated arm or leg. Compensation for an arm or a leg, if amputated at or above the wrist or ankle, shall be for the proportionate loss of the arm or leg.

p. Binocular vision or per centum of vision. Compensation for loss of binocular vision or for eighty per centum or more of the vision of an eye shall be the same as for loss of the eye.

q. Two or more digits. Compensation for loss or loss of use of two or more digits, or one or more phalanges of two or more digits, of a hand or foot may be proportioned to the loss of use of the hand or foot occasioned thereby but shall not exceed the compensation for loss of a hand or foot.

r. Total loss of use. Compensation for permanent total loss of use of a member shall be the same as for loss of the member.

s. Partial loss or partial loss of use. Compensation for permanent partial loss or loss of use of a member may be for proportionate loss or loss of use of the member. Compensation for permanent partial loss or loss of use of an eye shall be awarded on the basis of uncorrected loss of vision or corrected loss of vision resulting from an injury whichever is the greater.

t. Disfigurement.

1. The board may award proper and equitable compensation for serious facial or head disfigurement, not to exceed twenty thousand dollars, including a disfigurement continuous in length which is partially in the facial area and also extends into the neck region as described in paragraph two hereof.

2. The board, if in its opinion the earning capacity of an employee has been or may in the future be impaired, may award compensation for any serious disfigurement in the region above the sterno clavicular articulations anterior to and including the region of the sterno cleido mastoid muscles on either side, but no award under subdivisions one and two shall, in the aggregate, exceed twenty thousand dollars.

3. Notwithstanding any other provision hereof, two or more serious disfigurements, not continuous in length, resulting from the same injury, if partially in the facial area and partially in the neck region as described in paragraph two hereof, shall be deemed to be a facial disfigurement.

u. Total or partial loss or loss of use of more than one member or parts of members. In any case in which there shall be a loss or loss of use of more than one member or parts of more than one member set forth in paragraphs a to t, both inclusive, of this subdivision, but not amounting to permanent total disability, the board shall award compensation for the loss or loss of use of each such member or part thereof, which awards shall run consecutively.

v. Additional compensation for impairment of wage earning capacity in certain permanent partial disabilities. Notwithstanding any other provision of this subdivision, additional compensation shall be payable for impairment of wage earning capacity for any period after the termination of an award under paragraphs a, b, c, or d, of this subdivision for the loss or loss of use of fifty per centum or more of a member, provided such impairment of earning capacity shall be due solely thereto. Such additional compensation shall be determined in accordance with paragraph w of this subdivision. The additional compensation shall be reduced by fifty per centum of any amount of disability benefits which the disabled employee is receiving or entitled to receive for the same period under the social security act, and shall cease on the date the disabled employee receives or is entitled to receive old-age insurance benefits under the social security act. As soon as practicable after the injury, the worker shall be required to participate in a board approved rehabilitation program; or shall have demonstrated cooperation with efforts to institute such a board approved program and shall have been determined by the board not to be a feasible candidate for rehabilitation; such rehabilitation shall constitute treatment and care as provided in this chapter.

w. Other cases. In all other cases of permanent partial disability, the compensation shall be sixty-six and two-thirds percent of the difference between the injured employee's average weekly wages and his or her wage-earning capacity thereafter in the same employment or otherwise. Compensation under this paragraph shall be payable during the continuance of such permanent partial disability, but subject to reconsideration of the degree of such impairment by the board on its own motion or upon application of any party in interest however, all compensation payable under this paragraph shall not exceed (i) five hundred twenty-five weeks in cases in which the loss of wage-earning capacity is greater than ninety-five percent; (ii) five hundred weeks in cases in which the loss of wage-earning capacity is greater than ninety percent but not more than ninety-five percent; (iii) four hundred seventy-five weeks in cases in which the loss of wage-earning capacity is greater than eighty-five percent but not more than ninety percent; (iv) four hundred fifty weeks in cases in which the loss of wage-earning capacity is greater than eighty percent but not more than eighty-five percent; (v) four hundred twenty-five weeks in cases in which the loss of wage-earning capacity is greater than seventy-five percent but not more than eighty percent; (vi) four hundred weeks in cases in which the loss of wage-earning capacity is greater than seventy percent but not more than seventy-five percent; (vii) three hundred seventy-five weeks in cases in which the loss of wage-earning capacity is greater than sixty percent but not more than seventy percent; (viii) three hundred fifty weeks in cases in which the loss of wage-earning capacity is greater than fifty percent but not more than sixty percent; (ix) three hundred weeks in cases in which the loss of wage-earning capacity is greater than forty percent but not more than fifty percent; (x) two hundred seventy-five weeks in cases in which the loss of wage earning capacity is greater than thirty percent but not more than forty percent; (xi) two hundred fifty weeks in cases in which the loss of wage-earning capacity is greater than fifteen percent but not more than thirty percent; and (xii) two hundred twenty-five weeks in cases in which the loss of wage-earning capacity is fifteen percent or less. For those claimants classified as permanently partially disabled who no longer receive indemnity payments because they have surpassed their number of maximum benefit weeks, the following provisions will apply:

(1) There will be a presumption that medical services shall continue notwithstanding the completion of the time period for compensation set forth in this section and the burden of going forward and the burden of proof will lie with the carrier, self-insured employer or state insurance fund in any application before the board to discontinue or suspend such services. Medical services will continue during the pendency of any such application and any appeals thereto.

(2) The board is directed to promulgate regulations that establish an independent review and appeal by an outside agent or entity of the board's choosing of any administrative law judge's determination to discontinue or suspend medical services before a final determination of the board.

4. Effect of award. An award made to a claimant under subdivision three shall in case of death arising from causes other than the injury be payable to and for the benefit of the persons following:

a. If there be a surviving spouse and no child of the deceased under the age of eighteen years, to such spouse.

b. If there be a surviving spouse and surviving child or children of the deceased under the age of eighteen years, one-half shall be payable to the surviving spouse and the other half to the surviving child or children. The board may in its discretion require the appointment of a guardian for the purpose of receiving the compensation of the minor child. In the absence of such a requirement by the board the appointment for such a purpose shall not be necessary.

c. If there be a surviving child or children of the deceased under the age of eighteen years, but no surviving spouse then to such child or children.

d. If there be no surviving spouse and no surviving child or children of the deceased under the age of eighteen years, then to such dependent or dependents as defined in section sixteen of this chapter, as directed by the board; and if there be no such dependents, then to the estate of such deceased in an amount not exceeding reasonable funeral expenses as provided in subdivision one of section sixteen of this chapter, or, if there be no estate, to the person or persons paying the funeral expenses of such deceased in an amount not exceeding reasonable funeral expenses as provided in subdivision one of section sixteen of this chapter.

An award for disability may be made after the death of the injured employee.

4-a. Protracted temporary total disability in connection with permanent partial disability. In case of temporary total disability and permanent partial disability both resulting from the same injury, if the temporary total disability continues for a longer period than the number of weeks set forth in the following schedule, the period of temporary total disability in excess of such number of weeks shall be added to the compensation period provided in subdivision three of this section: Arm, thirty-two weeks; leg, forty weeks; hand, thirty-two weeks; foot, thirty-two weeks; ear, twenty-five weeks; eye, twenty weeks; thumb, twenty-four weeks; first finger, eighteen weeks; great toe, twelve weeks; second finger, twelve weeks; third finger, eight weeks; fourth finger, eight weeks; toe other than great toe, eight weeks.

In any case resulting in loss or partial loss of use of arm, leg, hand, foot, ear, eye, thumb, finger or toe, where the temporary total disability does not extend beyond the periods above mentioned for such injury, compensation shall be limited to the schedule contained in subdivision three.

5. Temporary partial disability. In case of temporary partial disability resulting in decrease of earning capacity, the compensation shall be two-thirds of the difference between the injured employee's average weekly wages before the accident and his wage earning capacity after the accident in the same or other employment.

5-a. Determination of wage earning capacity. The wage earning capacity of an injured employee in cases of partial disability shall be determined by his actual earnings, provided, however, that if he has no such actual earnings the board may in the interest of justice fix such wage earning capacity as shall be reasonable, but not in excess of seventy-five per centum of his former full time actual earnings, having due regard to the nature of his injury and his physical impairment.

5-b. Non-schedule adjustments. Notwithstanding any other provision of this chapter, in any case coming within the provisions of subdivisions three or five of this section, in which the right to compensation has been established and compensation has been paid for not less than three months, in which the continuance of disability and of future earning capacity cannot be ascertained with reasonable certainty, the board may, in the interest of justice, approve a non-schedule adjustment agreed to between the claimant and the employer or his insurance carrier. The board shall require, before approving any such agreement, that there be an examination of the claimant in accordance with section nineteen of this chapter, and such approval shall only be given when it is found that the adjustment is fair and in the best interest of the claimant. The board may, in such case, order all future compensation to be paid in one or more lump sums or periodically, and any such adjustment shall be regarded as a closing of the claim unless the board find upon proof that there has been a change in condition or in the degree of disability of claimant not found in the medical evidence and, therefore, not contemplated at the time of the adjustment.

6. Maximum and minimum compensation for disability

(a) . . . Compensation for permanent or temporary partial disability, or for permanent or temporary total disability due to an accident or disablement resulting from an occupational disease that occurs (1) on or after July first, two thousand seven shall not exceed five hundred dollars per week, (2) on or after July first, two thousand eight shall not exceed five hundred fifty dollars per week, (3) on or after July first, two thousand nine shall not exceed six hundred dollars per week, and (4) on or after July first, two thousand ten, and on or after July first of each succeeding year, shall not exceed two-thirds of the New York state average weekly wage for the year in which it is reported. Compensation for permanent or temporary partial disability, or for permanent or temporary total disability due to an accident or disablement resulting from an occupational disease that occurs on or after July first, two thousand seven shall not be less than one hundred dollars per week except that if the employee's wages at the time of injury are less than one hundred dollars per week, the employee shall receive his or her full wages. In no event shall compensation when combined with decreased earnings or earning capacity exceed the amount of wages the employee was receiving at the time the injury occurred. . . .

6-a. Reclassification of disabilities. Subject to the limitations set forth in sections twenty-five-a and one hundred twenty-three of this chapter, the board may, at any time, without regard to the date of accident, upon its own motion, or on application of any party in interest, reclassify a disability upon proof that there has been a change in condition, or that the previous classification was erroneous and not in the interest of justice.

7. Previous disability. The fact that an employee has suffered previous disability or received compensation therefor shall not preclude him from compensation for a later injury nor preclude compensation for death resulting therefrom; but in determining compensation for the later injury or death his average weekly wages shall be such sum as will reasonably represent his earning capacity at the time of the later injury, provided, however, that an employee who is suffering from a previous disability shall not receive compensation for a later injury in excess of the compensation allowed for such injury when considered by itself and not in conjunction with the previous disability except as hereinafter provided in subdivision eight of this section.

8. Disability following previous permanent physical impairment

(a) Declaration of policy and legislative intent. As a guide to the interpretation and application of this subdivision, the policy and intent of this legislature is declared to be as follows:

First: That every person in this state who works for a living is entitled to a reasonable opportunity to maintain his independence and self-respect through self-support even after he/she has been physically handicapped by injury or disease;

Second: That any plan which will reasonably, equitably and practically operate to break down hindrances and remove obstacles to the employment of partially disabled persons honorably discharged from our armed forces, or any other physically handicapped persons, is of vital importance to the state and its people and is of concern to this legislature;

Third: That it is the considered judgment of this legislature that the system embodied in this subdivision, which makes a logical and equitable adjustment of the liability under the worker's compensation law which an employer must assume in hiring employees, constitutes a practical and reasonable approach to a solution of the problem for the employment of physically handicapped persons.

Moreover, because of the insidious nature of slowly developing diseases such as silicosis and other dust diseases and because of the reluctance on the part of employers to employ persons previously exposed to silica or other harmful dust, means should also be provided whereby employers will be encouraged to employ and to continue the employment of such persons, by apportioning liability fairly between the employer and industry as a whole without at the same time removing any incentive for the prevention of harmful dust diseases.

(b) Definition. As used in this subdivision, "permanent physical impairment" means any permanent condition due to previous accident or disease or any congenital condition which is or is likely to be a hindrance or obstacle to employment.

(c) Permanent total disability after permanent partial disability. Notwithstanding the provisions of paragraph (d) of this subdivision, if an employee who has previously incurred permanent partial disability through the loss of one hand, one arm, one foot, one leg, or one eye, incurs permanent total disability through the loss of another member or organ, he/she shall be paid, in addition to the compensation for permanent partial disability provided in this section and after the cessation of the payments for the prescribed period of weeks special additional compensation during the continuance of such total disability to the amount of sixty-six and two-thirds per centum of the average weekly wage earned by him/her at the time the total permanent disability was incurred. If such employee shall establish an earning capacity by employment he shall be paid during the period of such employment, instead of the additional compensation above provided, two-thirds of the difference between his average weekly wages at the time the total disability was incurred and his wage earning capacity as determined by his actual earnings in such employment, subject to the limitations in subdivision six of this section. Such additional compensation, and expense as in this subdivision provided, shall be paid out of the special disability fund and in the manner as hereinafter in this subdivision provided.

(d) If an employee of an employer who has secured the payment of compensation as required under the provisions of section fifty of this chapter, who has a total or partial loss or loss of use of one hand, one arm, one foot, one leg or one eye, or who has other permanent physical impairment incurs a subsequent disability by accident arising out of and in the course of his employment or an occupational disease arising therefrom, resulting in a permanent disability caused by both conditions that is materially and substantially greater than that which would have resulted from the subsequent injury or occupational disease alone, the employer or his insurance carrier shall in the first instance pay all awards of compensation and all medical expense provided by this chapter, but such employer or his insurance carrier, except as specifically provided in paragraph (ee) of this subdivision, shall be reimbursed from the special disability fund created by this subdivision for all compensation and medical benefits subsequent to those payable for the first one hundred four weeks of disability for claims where the date of accident or date of disablement occurred prior to August first, nineteen hundred ninety-four, and two hundred sixty weeks of disability for claims where the date of accident or date of disablement occurred on or after August first, nineteen hundred ninety-four, regardless of knowledge on the part of the employer as to the existence of such pre-existing permanent physical impairment. . . .

(f) Any award under this subdivision shall be made against the employer or his or her insurance carrier, but if such employer or insurance carrier be entitled to reimbursement as provided in this subdivision, notice or claim of the right to such reimbursement shall be filed with the board in writing prior to the final determination that the resulting disability is permanent, but in no case more than one hundred four weeks after the date of disability or death or fifty-two weeks after the date that a claim for compensation is filed with the chair, whichever is later, or in the event of the reopening of a case theretofore closed, no later than the determination of permanency upon such reopening.

The employer or his or her insurance carrier shall in the first instance make the payments of compensation and medical expenses provided by this subdivision. Whenever for any reason payments are not made by the employer or his or her insurance carrier at any time after the payments have been made for the first one hundred four weeks for claims where the date of accident or date of disablement occurred prior to August first, nineteen hundred ninety-four, and two hundred sixty weeks of disability for claims where the date of accident or date of disablement occurred on or after August first, nineteen hundred ninety-four, the payments of subsequent compensation and medical expenses shall be made out of the special disability fund by the commissioner of taxation and finance upon vouchers approved by the chair of the workers' compensation board. . . .

(g) Upon the making of a determination that an employer or insurance carrier is entitled to reimbursement from the special disability fund in any case where the employer or insurance carrier has made payment into the aggregate trust fund, as provided in section twenty-seven of this chapter, or where payment of compensation has been commuted into one or more lump sum payments, the employer or insurance carrier shall be reimbursed forthwith for the sums paid in excess of those payable for one hundred four weeks for claims where the date of accident or date of disablement occurred prior to August first, nineteen hundred ninety-four, and two hundred sixty weeks of disability for claims where the date of accident or date of disablement occurred on or after August first, nineteen hundred ninety-four, in a silicosis or other dust disease case as provided in paragraph (ee) of this subdivision, exclusive of administrative and loading charges paid pursuant to section twenty-seven, in accordance with the decision and order of the board. In all other cases such employer or insurance carrier shall, periodically every six months from the decision and order of the board, be reimbursed from such special disability fund for all compensation and medical expense in accordance with the provisions of paragraph (f) of this subdivision.

(h) **Special disability fund. . . .**

(i) When an application for apportionment of compensation is made under this subdivision, the chair of the workmen's compensation board shall appoint a representative of such fund in such proceedings, but whenever it shall appear that, through any committee, board or organization representative of the interest of employers or insurance carriers, an attorney has been appointed to act for and on behalf of such employers and insurance carriers generally to represent such fund in any proceedings brought hereunder, the chair of the board may designate such attorney as the representative of such special disability fund in proceedings involving claims against such fund. Such representative shall thereafter be given notice of all hearings or proceedings involving the rights or obligations of such fund. Such representative may apply to the chair of the board for authority to hire such medical and other experts and to defray the expense thereof and of such witnesses as may be necessary to a proper defense of any claim, within an amount in the discretion of the chair and, if authorized, such amount shall be a charge against such special disability fund. . . .

(k) The additional compensation required to be paid by an employer in the case of the injury of a minor illegally employed, in accordance with the provisions of subdivisions one and two of section fourteen-a of this chapter, shall not be reimbursable under the provisions of this subdivision.

(l) Notwithstanding anything to the contrary in this subdivision, when an employer or carrier shall have paid additional benefits to an employee pursuant to subdivision six of section fourteen of this article as a result of the employee's increased average weekly wages from wages earned in concurrent employment, reimbursement for all such additional benefits shall be made to the employer or carrier from the special disability fund created by this subdivision. It shall not be required that the employee had, either at the time of hiring or during the employment, any previous physical condition or disability, nor shall it be required that the employee's disability be permanent in nature. Notice of the right to reimbursement shall be filed with the board in writing prior to the decision making an award, and reimbursement shall be made periodically, every six months from the decision of the board.

9. Expenses for rehabilitating injured employees. An employee, who as a result of injury is or may be expected to be totally or partially incapacitated for a remunerative occupation and who, under the direction of the state education department is being rendered fit to engage in a remunerative occupation, may receive additional compensation necessary for his rehabilitation, not more than thirty dollars per week of which may be expended for maintenance. Such expense and such of the administrative expenses of the state education department as are properly assignable to the expenses of rehabilitating employees entitled to compensation as a result of injuries under this chapter, shall be paid out of a special fund created in the following manner: The employer, or if insured, his insurance carrier, shall pay into the vocational rehabilitation fund for every case of injury causing death, in which there are no persons entitled to compensation, the sum of five hundred dollars where such injury occurred prior to July first, nineteen hundred sixty-three and the sum of one thousand dollars where such injury shall occur on or after July first, nineteen hundred sixty-three and the sum of two thousand dollars where such injury shall occur on or after September first, nineteen hundred seventy-eight. . . .

Disbursements from the vocational rehabilitation fund for the additional compensation provided for by this section shall be paid by the commissioner of taxation and finance on warrants drawn by the state comptroller upon vouchers signed by the commissioner of education or the deputy commissioner of education provided that the compensation claim number of an injured employee undergoing vocational rehabilitation has been verified by the chairman. . . .

§ 16. Death benefits. If the injury causes death, the compensation shall be known as a death benefit and shall be payable in the amount and to or for the persons following:

1. Funeral expenses. The chair shall prepare and establish a schedule for the state or schedules limited to defined localities of maximum charges and fees for such funeral expenses, to be determined in accordance with, and to be subject to change pursuant to, rules promulgated by the chair.

Before preparing such schedule for the state or schedules for limited localities, the chair shall request the president of the New York state funeral directors' association to submit to the chair a report on the amount of remuneration deemed by such association to be fair and adequate for the types of funeral services rendered under this chapter, but consideration shall also be given to the views of other interested parties. The amounts payable by the employer for such services shall be the actual fees and charges up to the maximum established by such schedule. Provided, however, no such schedule of charges and fees shall apply where a firefighter dies from injuries received in the line of duty as a direct result of firefighting, where such funeral expenses are reasonable. If such funeral expenses shall have been paid by the claimants entitled to compensation under this section or by others, the funeral expenses awarded shall be made payable to such claimants or others, otherwise they shall be made payable to the undertaker who shall have provided burial. Funeral expenses shall be awarded in case of all injuries causing death including cases in which there are no persons entitled to other compensation under this chapter.

1-a. For the purpose of this section, (1) the term dependent blind or physically disabled as used herein in relation to dependent children shall be deemed to mean totally blind or physically disabled children whose disablement is total and permanent, (2) the term surviving spouse shall be deemed to mean the legal spouse but shall not include a spouse who has abandoned the deceased, and (3) the term abandoned shall be deemed to mean such an abandonment as would be sufficient under section two hundred of the domestic relations law to sustain a judgment of separation on that ground.

1-b. If there be a surviving spouse and no child of the deceased under the age of eighteen years and no child of any age dependent blind or physically disabled, and the death occurs on or after July first, nineteen hundred forty-eight, and prior to January first, nineteen hundred seventy-eight, to such spouse forty per centum of the average wages of the deceased during widowhood or widowerhood with two years' compensation in one sum, upon remarriage; and where the death occurred prior to July first, nineteen hundred forty-eight, to such wife (or dependent husband) thirty per centum of such wages during widowhood (or dependent widowerhood) with two years' compensation in one sum, upon remarriage.

1-c. If there be a surviving spouse and no child of the deceased under the age of eighteen years or under the age of twenty-three years if enrolled and attending as a full time student in an accredited educational institution and such enrollment and full time attendance is certified by such institution and no child of any age dependent blind or physically disabled, and the death occurs on or after January first, nineteen hundred seventy-eight, to such spouse sixty-six and two-thirds per centum of the average wages of the deceased during widowhood or widowerhood with two years' compensation, in one sum, upon remarriage. Where the death occurs on or after January first, nineteen hundred seventy-eight, and the spouse is receiving the survivors insurance benefits under the social security act, the death benefit payable under this section shall be reduced in accordance with the provisions of table No. 1 below by five per centum of the spouse's share of the survivor's insurance benefits under the social security act for each ten dollars of deceased's average weekly wage in excess of one hundred dollars provided that in no case shall such reduction exceed fifty per centum of said spouse's share of the survivors insurance benefits under the social security act.

TABLE No. I

Offset provisions applicable in death benefits where there is a sole surviving spouse

AVERAGE WEEKLY WAGE	PERCENTAGE OF SPOUSE'S SHARE OF SURVIVORS INSURANCE BENEFITS
over $100 up to and including $110	5
over $110 up to and including $120	10
over $120 up to and including $130	15
over $130 up to and including $140	20
over $140 up to and including $150	25
over $150 up to and including $160	30
over $160 up to and including $170	35
over $170 up to and including $180	40
over $180 up to and including $190	45
over $190 up to and including $200	50
over $200	50

2. If there be a surviving spouse and a surviving child or children of the deceased under the age of eighteen years or a surviving child or children of any age dependent blind or physically disabled, and the death occurs on or after July first, nineteen hundred forty-eight, and prior to January first, nineteen hundred seventy-eight, to such spouse thirty per centum of the average wages of the deceased during widowhood or widowerhood with two years' compensation in one sum, upon remarriage; and the additional amount of twenty per centum of such wages for each such child until the age of eighteen years or until the removal of the dependency of the blind or physically disabled child or children; in case of the subsequent death or remarriage of such surviving spouse any surviving child of the deceased employee, at the time under

eighteen years of age or dependent through mental or physical infirmity, shall have his compensation increased to thirty per centum of such wages, and the same shall be payable until he shall reach the age of eighteen years or until such dependent blind or physically disabled condition shall have been removed; provided that the total amount payable shall in no case exceed sixty-six and two-thirds per centum of such wages. Upon statutory termination of compensation payments to all such children, the compensation of the surviving spouse shall be increased to forty per centum of such wages with two years' compensation, at such rate, in one sum, upon remarriage. . . .

> 2-a. If there be a surviving spouse and a surviving child under the age of eighteen years or under the age of twenty-three years if enrolled and attending as a full time student in an accredited educational institution and such enrollment and full time attendance is certified by such institution or a surviving child of any age dependent blind or physically disabled and the death occurs on or after January first, nineteen hundred seventy-eight, to such spouse thirty-six and two-thirds per centum of the average wages of the deceased during widowhood or widowerhood with two years' compensation in one sum, upon remarriage; and thirty per centum of such wages to such child under the age of eighteen years or under the age of twenty-three years if enrolled and attending as a full time student in an accredited educational institution and such enrollment and full time attendance is certified by such institution or a surviving child of any age dependent blind or physically disabled; in the case of the subsequent death of such surviving spouse the surviving child shall have his compensation increased to sixty-six and two-thirds per centum of such wages and the same shall be payable so long as he is under the age of eighteen years or under the age of twenty-three years if enrolled and attending as a full time student in an accredited educational institution and such enrollment and full time attendance is certified by such institution or a surviving child of any age dependent blind or physically disabled; upon statutory termination of compensation payable to such child, the compensation of the surviving spouse shall be increased to sixty-six and two-thirds per centum of such wages with two years' compensation, at such rate, in one sum, upon remarriage. Upon remarriage of such surviving spouse, the surviving child shall continue to receive thirty per centum of such wages. Where the death occurs on or after January first, nineteen hundred seventy-eight and the spouse is receiving survivors insurance benefits under the social security act, the death benefit payable under this section shall be reduced by five per centum of the spouse's share of the survivors insurance benefits under the social security act for each ten dollars of deceased's average weekly wage in excess of one hundred dollars provided that in no case shall such reduction exceed fifty per centum of said spouse's share of the survivors insurance benefits under the social security act as set forth in table No. I below.

TABLE No. I

Offset provisions applicable in death benefits where there is a surviving spouse and one child

AVERAGE WEEKLY WAGE	PERCENTAGE OF SPOUSE'S SHARE OF SURVIVORS INSURANCE BENEFITS
over $100 up to and including $110	5
over $110 up to and including $120	10
over $120 up to and including $130	15
over $130 up to and including $140	20
over $140 up to and including $150	25
over $150 up to and including $160	30
over $160 up to and including $170	35
over $170 up to and including $180	40
over $180 up to and including $190	45
over $190 up to and including $200	50
over $200	50

§ **17. Aliens**. Compensation under this chapter to aliens not residents or about to become nonresidents of the United States or Canada, shall be the same in amount as provided for residents, except that dependents in any foreign country shall be limited to surviving spouse and child or children, or, if there is no surviving spouse or child or children, to surviving father or mother whom the employee has supported, either wholly or in part, for the period of one year prior to the date of the accident.

§ **18. Notice of injury or death**. Notice of an injury or death for which compensation is payable under this chapter shall be given to the employer within thirty days after the accident causing such injury, and also in case of the death of the employee resulting from such injury, within thirty days after such death. Such notice may be given by any person claiming to be entitled to compensation, or by some one in his behalf. The notice shall be in writing, and contain the name and address of the employee, and state in ordinary language the time, place, nature and cause of the injury, and be signed by him or by a person on his behalf or, in case of death, by any one or more of his dependents, or by a person, on their behalf. It shall be given to the employer by delivering it to him or sending it by mail, by registered letter, addressed to the employer at his or its last known place of business; provided that, if the employer be a partnership then such notice may be so given to any one of the partners, and if the employer be a corporation, then such notice may be given to any agent or officer thereof upon whom legal process may be served, or any agent in charge of his business in the place where the injury occurred. The failure to give notice of injury or notice of death unless excused by the board either on the ground that notice for some sufficient reason could not have been given, or on the ground that the employer, or his or its agents in charge of the business in the place where the accident occurred or having immediate supervision of the employee to whom the accident happened, had knowledge of the accident or death, or on the ground that the employer has not been prejudiced thereby, shall be a bar to any claim under this chapter, but the employer and the insurance carrier shall be deemed to have waived such notice unless the objection to the failure to give such notice or the insufficiency thereof, is raised before the board on the first hearing of the claim filed by such injured employee, or his or her dependents at which all parties in interest are present, or represented, and at which the claimant, or principal beneficiary, testifies. . . .

§ **19. Physical examination.** An injured employee claiming or entitled to compensation shall submit to such physical examination as the chairman or the board may require. The place, or places, shall be reasonably convenient for him. No physician selected by the employer, carrier or employee shall be present at or participate in any manner in such examination, but such employer or carrier shall, upon request, be entitled to have the employee examined immediately thereafter and upon the same premises by a qualified physician or physicians in the presence of such physician as the employee may select, if any. Proceedings shall be suspended and no compensation shall be payable for any period during which the employee may refuse to submit to examination.

§ **19-a. Physicians not to accept fees from carriers.** No physician or surgeon in the employ of the board for the purpose of making the examinations required by section nineteen of this chapter, shall, during such employment, be employed by or accept or participate in any fee from any insurance company authorized to write workmen's compensation insurance in this state or from any self-insurer, if such employment or fee relates to a workmen's compensation claim or otherwise except as herein provided. Any physician or surgeon so employed by the board who violates the provisions of this section shall be guilty of a misdemeanor. . . .

§ **20. Determination of claims for compensation**

1. At any time after the expiration of the first seven days of disability on the part of an injured employee, or at any time after the employee's death, a claim for compensation may be presented to the employer or to the chair. The board shall have full power and authority to determine all questions in relation to the payment of claims presented to it for compensation under the provisions of this chapter. The chair or board shall make or cause to be made such investigation as it deems necessary, and upon application of either party, shall order a hearing, and within thirty days after a claim for compensation is submitted under this section, or such hearing closed, shall make or deny an award, determining such claim for compensation, and file the same in the office of the chair. Immediately after such filing the chair shall send to the parties a copy of the decision. Upon a hearing pursuant to this section either party may present evidence and be represented by counsel. The decision of the board shall be final

as to all questions of fact, and, except as provided in section twenty-three, as to all questions of law. Except as provided in section twenty-seven of this article, all awards of the board shall draw simple interest from thirty days after the making thereof at the rate provided in section five thousand four of the civil practice law and rules. Whenever a hearing or proceeding for the determination of a claim for compensation is begun before a referee, pursuant to the provisions of this chapter, such hearing or proceeding or any adjourned hearing thereon shall continue before the same referee until a final determination awarding or denying compensation, except in the absence, inability or disqualification to act of such referee, or for other good cause, in which event such hearing or proceeding may be continued before another referee by order of the chair or board. . . .

§ **21. Presumptions.** In any proceeding for the enforcement of a claim for compensation under this chapter, it shall be presumed in the absence of substantial evidence to the contrary

1. That the claim comes within the provision of this chapter;
2. That sufficient notice thereof was given;
3. That the injury was not occasioned by the willful intention of the injured employee to bring about the injury or death of himself or of another;
4. That the injury did not result solely from the intoxication of the injured employee while on duty;
5. That the contents of medical and surgical reports introduced in evidence by claimants for compensation shall constitute prima facie evidence of fact as to the matter contained therein.

§ **21-a. Temporary payment of compensation.**

1. Notwithstanding any other provision of this chapter to the contrary, in any instance in which an employer is unsure of the extent of its liability for a claim for compensation by an injured employee pursuant to this chapter, such employer may initiate compensation payments and continue such payments for one year, without prejudice and without admitting liability, in accordance with a notice of temporary payment of compensation, on a form prescribed by the board.

2. The notice of temporary payment of compensation authorized by subdivision one of this section shall be delivered to the injured employee and the board. Such notice shall notify the injured employee that the temporary payment of compensation shall not be deemed to be an admission of liability by the employer for the injury or injuries to the employee. The board, upon receipt of a notice of temporary payment of compensation, shall send a notice to the injured employee stating that: (a) the board has received a notice of temporary payment of compensation relating to such injured employee; (b) the payment of temporary compensation and the injured employee's acceptance of such temporary compensation shall not be an admission of liability by the employer, nor prejudice the claim of the injured employee; (c) the payment of temporary compensation shall terminate on the elapse of: one year, or the

employer's contesting of the injured employee's claim for compensation, or the board determination of the injured employee's claim, whichever is first; and (d) the injured employee may be required to enter into an agreement with the employer to ensure the continuation of payments of temporary compensation.

3. An employer may cease making temporary payments of compensation if such employer delivers within five days after the last payment, to the injured employee and the board, a notice of termination of temporary payments of compensation on a form prescribed by the board. Such notice shall inform the injured employee that the employer is ceasing temporary payment of compensation. Upon the cessation of temporary payments of compensation, all parties to any action pursuant to this chapter shall retain all rights, defenses and obligations they would otherwise have pursuant to this chapter without regard for the temporary payment of compensation.

4. The failure of an employer to provide the notice of termination, pursuant to subdivision three of this section, within one year of the commencement of temporary payment of compensation shall be deemed to be an admission of liability by the employer and the notice of temporary payment of compensation shall be converted to a notice of compensation payable.

§ 22. **Modification of awards, decisions or orders.** Upon its own motion or upon the application of any party in interest, on the ground of a change in conditions or proof of erroneous wage rate, the board may at any time, subject to the limitations set forth in sections twenty-five-a and one hundred and twenty-three of this chapter, review any award, decision or order and, on such review, may make an award ending, diminishing or increasing the compensation previously awarded, subject to the maximum or minimum provided in this chapter, and shall immediately send to the parties a copy of its decision, which shall include a statement of the facts which formed the basis of its action. No such review shall affect such award as regards any moneys already paid, except that an award increasing the compensation rate may be made effective from date of injury, and except that if any part of the compensation due or to become due is unpaid, an award decreasing the compensation rate may be made effective from the date of injury, and any payments made prior thereto in excess of such decreased rate shall be deducted from any unpaid compensation, in such manner and by such methods as may be determined by the board.

§ 23. **Appeals.** An award or decision of the board shall be final and conclusive upon all questions within its jurisdiction, as against the state fund or between the parties, unless reversed or modified on appeal therefrom as hereinafter provided. Any party may within thirty days after notice of the filing of an award or a decision of a referee, file with the board an application in writing for a modification or rescission or review of such award or decision, as provided in this chapter. The board shall render its decision upon such application in writing and shall include in such decision a statement of the facts which formed the basis of its action on the issues raised before it on such application. Within thirty days after notice of the decision of the board upon such application has been served upon the parties, or within thirty days after notice of an administrative redetermination review decision by the chair pursuant to subdivision five of section fifty-two of this chapter has been served upon any party in interest, an appeal may be taken therefrom to the appellate division of the supreme court, third department, by any party in interest, including an employer insured in the state fund; provided, however, that if the decision or determination was that of a panel of the board and there was a dissent from such decision or determination other than a dissent the sole basis of which is to refer the case to an impartial specialist, any party in interest may within thirty days after notice of the filing of the board panel's decision with the secretary of the board, make application in writing for review thereof by the full board, and the full board shall review and affirm, modify or rescind such decision or determination in the same manner as herein above provided for an award or decision of a referee. Failure to apply for such review by the full board shall not bar any party in interest from taking an appeal directly to the court as above provided. The board may also, in its discretion certify to such appellate division of the supreme court, questions of law involved in its decision. Such appeals and the question so certified shall be heard in a summary manner and shall have precedence over all other civil cases in such court. The board shall be deemed a party to every such appeal from its decision upon such application, and the chair shall be deemed a party to every such appeal from an administrative redetermination review decision pursuant to subdivision five of section fifty-two of this chapter. The attorney general shall represent the board and the chair thereon. An appeal may also be taken to the court of appeals in the same manner and subject to the same limitations not inconsistent herewith as is now provided in the civil practice law and rules. It shall not be necessary to file exceptions to the rulings of the board. An appeal to the appellate division of the supreme court, third department, or to the court of appeals, shall not operate as a stay of the payment of compensation required by the terms of the award or of the payment of the doctors' bills found to be fair and reasonable. Where such award is modified or rescinded upon appeal, the appellant shall be entitled to reimbursement in a sum equal to the compensation in dispute paid to the respondent in addition to a sum equal to the amount of the doctors' bills paid by the appellant pending adjudication of the appeal. Such reimbursement shall be paid from administration expenses as provided in section one hundred fifty-one of this chapter upon audit and warrant of the comptroller upon vouchers approved by the chair. Where such award is subject to the provisions of section twenty-seven of this article, the appellant shall pay directly to the claimant all compensation as it becomes due during the pendency of the appeal, and upon affirmance shall be entitled to credit for such payments. Neither the chair, the board, the commissioners of the state insurance fund nor the claimant shall be required to file a bond upon an appeal to the court of appeals. Upon final determination of such an appeal, the board or chair, as the case may be, shall enter an order in accordance therewith. Whenever a notice of appeal is served or an application made to the board by the employer or insurance carrier for a modification or rescission or review of an award or decision, and the board shall find that such notice of appeal was served or such application was made for the purpose of delay or upon frivolous grounds, the board shall impose a penalty in the amount of two hundred fifty dollars upon the employer or insurance carrier, which penalty shall be added to the compensation and paid to the claimant. The penalties provided herein shall be collected in like manner as compensation. A party against whom an award of compensation shall be made may appeal from a part of such award. In such a case the payment of such part of the award as is not appealed from shall not prejudice any rights of such party on appeal, nor be taken as an admission against such party. Any appeal by an employer from an administrative redetermination review decision pursuant to subdivision five of section fifty-two of this chapter shall in no way serve to relieve the employer from the obligation to timely pay compensation and benefits otherwise payable in accordance with the provisions of this chapter.

Nothing herein contained shall be construed to inhibit the continuing jurisdiction of the board as provided in section one hundred twenty-three of this chapter.

§ 24-a. Representation before the workers' compensation board

1. No person, firm or corporation, other than an attorney and counsellor-at-law, shall appear on behalf of any claimant or person entitled to the benefits of this chapter, before the board or any officer, agent or employee of the board assigned to conduct any hearing, investigation or inquiry relative to a claim for compensation or benefits under this chapter, unless he or she shall be a citizen of the United States or an alien lawfully admitted for permanent residence in the United States, and shall have obtained from the board a license authorizing him or her to appear in matters or proceedings before the board. Such license shall be issued by the board in accordance with the rules established by it. Any person, firm or corporation violating the aforesaid provisions shall be guilty of a misdemeanor. The board, in its rules, shall provide for the issuance of licenses to representatives of charitable and welfare organizations, and to associations who employ a representative to appear for members of such association, upon certification of the proper officer of such association or organization, which licenses shall issue without charge; and may provide for a license fee in the case of all other persons, firms or corporations in an amount to be fixed by said rules, not exceeding the sum of one hundred dollars a year. All license fees collected under the provisions of this section shall be paid into the state treasury. The board shall have such tests of character and fitness with respect to applicants for licenses, and such rules governing the conduct of those licensed, as aforesaid, as it may deem necessary. . . .

§ 28. Limitation of right to compensation. The right to claim compensation under this chapter shall be barred, except as hereinafter provided, unless within two years after the accident, or if death results therefrom within two years after such death, a claim for compensation shall be filed with the chairman, but the employer and insurance carrier shall be deemed to have waived the bar of the statute unless the objection to the failure to file the claim within two years is raised on the first hearing on such claim at which all parties in interest are present. The right of an employee to claim compensation under this chapter for disablement caused by any occupational disease including but not limited to compressed air illness or its sequelae, silicosis or other dust disease, latent or delayed pathological bone, blood or lung changes or malignancies due to occupational exposure to or contact with arsenic, benzol, beryllium, zirconium, cadmium, chrome, lead or fluorine or to exposure to x-rays, radium, ionizing radiation, radio-active substances, or any other chemical compound shall not be barred by the failure of the employee to file a claim within such period of two years, provided such claim shall be filed after such period of two years and within two years after disablement and after the claimant knew or should have known that the disease is or was due to the nature of the employment. No case in which an advance payment is made to an employee or to his dependents in case of death shall be barred by the failure of the employee or his dependents to file a claim, and the board may at any time order a hearing on any such case in the same manner as though a claim for compensation had been filed.

§ 29. Remedies of employees; subrogation

1. If an employee entitled to compensation under this chapter be injured or killed by the negligence or wrong of another not in the same employ, such injured employee, or in case of death, his dependents, need not elect whether to take compensation and medical benefits under this chapter or to pursue his remedy against such other but may take such compensation and medical benefits and at any time either prior thereto or within six months after the awarding of compensation or within nine months after the enactment of a law or laws creating, establishing or affording a new or additional remedy or remedies, pursue his remedy against such other subject to the provisions of this chapter. . . .

§ 31. Agreement for contribution by employee void. No agreement by an employee to pay any portion of the premium paid by his employer to the state insurance fund or to contribute to a benefit fund or department maintained by such employer or to the cost of mutual insurance or other insurance, maintained for or carried for the purpose of providing compensation as herein required, shall be valid, and any employer who makes a deduction for such purpose from the wages or salary of any employee entitled to the benefits of this chapter shall be guilty of a misdemeanor.

§ 32. Waiver agreements. No agreement by an employee to waive his right to compensation under this chapter shall be valid. . . .

§ 33. Assignments; exemptions. Compensation or benefits due under this chapter shall not be assigned, released or commuted except as provided by this chapter. . . .

ARTICLE 3. Occupational Diseases

§ 37. Definitions. Whenever used in this article:

1. "Disability" means the state of being disabled from earning full wages at the work at which the employee was last employed.

2. "Disablement" means the act of becoming so disabled as defined in subdivision one.

§ 38. Disablement treated as accident. The disablement of an employee resulting from an occupational disease described in subdivision two of section three shall be treated as the happening of an accident within the meaning of this chapter and the procedure and practice provided in this chapter shall apply to all proceedings under this article, except where specifically otherwise provided herein.

§ 39. Right to compensation. If an employee is disabled or dies and his disability or death is caused by one of the diseases mentioned in subdivision two of section three, and the disease is due to the nature of the corresponding employment as described in such subdivision in which such employee was engaged and was contracted therein, he or his dependents shall be entitled to compensation for the duration of his disablement or for his death in accordance with the provisions of articles two and three of this chapter, provided, however, that if it shall be determined that an employee so disabled is able to earn wages at another occupation which shall be neither unhealthful nor injurious, and such wages do not equal his full wages prior to the date of his disablement, the compensation payable shall be computed pursuant to the provisions of article two of this chapter.

§ 44. Liability of employer. The total compensation due shall be recoverable from the employer who last employed the employee in the employment to the nature of which the disease was due and in which it was contracted. If, however, such disease, except silicosis or other dust disease and compressed air illness or its sequelae, was contracted while such employee was in the employment of a prior employer, the employer who is made liable for the total compensation as provided by this section, may appeal to the board for an apportionment of such compensation among the several employers who since the contraction of such disease shall have employed such employee in the employment to the nature of which the disease was due. Such apportionment shall be proportioned to the time such employee was employed in the service of such employers, and shall be determined only after a hearing, notice of the time and place of which shall have been given to every employer alleged to be liable for any portion of such compensation. If the board finds that any portion of such compensation is payable by an employer prior to the employer who is made liable for the total compensation as provided by this section, it shall make an award accordingly in favor of the last employer, and such award may be enforced in the same manner as an award for compensation.

§ 45. Notice to employers. The employer to whom notice of death or disability is to be given, or against whom claim is to be made by the employee, shall be the employer who last employed the employee in the employment to the nature of which the disease was due and such notice and claim shall be deemed seasonable as against prior employers. The requirements as to notice as to occupational disease and death resulting therefrom shall be the same as required in section eighteen of this chapter, except that the notice shall be given to the employer within two years after the disablement or after the claimant knew or should have known that the disease is due to the nature of the employment, whichever is the later date. . . .

§ 47. Presumption as to the cause of disease. If the employee, at or immediately before the date of disablement, was employed in any process mentioned in the second column of the schedule of diseases in subdivision two of section three, and his disease is the disease in the first column of such schedule set opposite the description of the process, the disease presumptively shall be deemed to have been due to the nature of that employment. Any exposure to the hazards of compressed air, after July first, nineteen hundred forty-six shall be presumed, in the absence of substantial evidence to the contrary, to be injurious exposure. Any exposure to the hazards of harmful dust in this state for a period of sixty days after September first, nineteen hundred thirty-five, shall be presumed, in the absence of substantial evidence to the contrary, to be an injurious exposure.

§ 48. Diseases which are accidents. Nothing in this article shall affect the rights of an employee to recover compensation in respect to a disease to which this article does not apply if the disease is an accidental personal injury within the meaning of subdivision seven of section two of this chapter.

ARTICLE 3-A. Occupational Loss of Hearing

§ 49-aa. Declaration of purpose. The compensability of claims for loss of hearing resulting from exposure to industrial noise has created a problem in this state which is a matter of grave concern to the legislature. The legislature, therefore, finds and declares that the public interest can best be served by providing that compensation for occupational loss of hearing shall be paid only as provided in this article and subject to the conditions and limitations hereinafter set forth.

§ 49-bb. Waiting period; date of disablement; payment of compensation. Notwithstanding any other inconsistent provisions of this chapter, compensation for occupational loss of hearing shall become due and payable at the employee's choice three months after (1) removal from exposure to harmful noise in employment (removal from exposure to harmful noise in employment for the three month waiting period may be achieved by use of effective ear protection devices provided at the expense of the employer) or (2) separation from work for the last employer in whose employment the employee was at anytime during such employment exposed to harmful noise. The last day of such period of removal from such exposure or of separation from such work shall be the date of disablement. Such disablement shall be treated as the happening of an accident within the meaning of this chapter and the procedure and practice provided in the chapter shall apply to all proceedings as set forth in this article except where specifically otherwise provided herein. . . .

ARTICLE 7. Miscellaneous Provisions

§ 110. Record and report of injuries by employers

1. An employer, or a third party designated by the employer, shall record any injury or illness incurred by one of its employees in the course of employment using the form prescribed by the chair for reporting injuries under subdivision two of this section. Such form, a copy of which shall be provided to the injured employee upon request, shall be maintained by the employer, or a third party designated by the employer, for at least eighteen years, and shall be subject to review by the chair at any time. Such form need not be filed with the chair unless the status of such injury or illness changes resulting in the loss of time from regular duties or in medical treatment which would require reporting in accordance with subdivision two of this subsection.

2. An employer, or a third party designated by the employer, shall file with the chair of the worker's compensation board and with the carrier if the employer is insured, upon a form prescribed by the chair, a report of any accident resulting in personal injury which has caused or will cause a loss of time from regular duties of one day beyond the working day or shift on which the accident occurred, or which has required or will require medical treatment beyond ordinary first aid or more than two treatments by a person rendering first aid. . . .

§ 118. Technical rules of evidence or procedure not required. The chairman or board in making an investigation or inquiry or conducting a hearing shall not be bound by common law or statutory rules of evidence or by technical or formal rules of procedure, except as provided by this chapter; but may make such investigation or inquiry or conduct such hearing in such manner as to ascertain the substantial rights of the parties. Declarations of a deceased employee concerning the accident shall be received in evidence and shall, if corroborated by circumstances or other evidence, be sufficient to establish the accident and the injury.

§ 120. Discrimination against employees who bring proceedings. It shall be unlawful for any employer or his or her duly authorized agent to discharge or in any other manner discriminate against an employee as to his or her employment because such employee has claimed or attempted to claim compensation from such employer, or because he or she has testified or is about to testify in a proceeding under this chapter and no other valid reason is shown to exist for such action by the employer. . . .

§ 125. Job discrimination prohibited based on prior receipt of benefits.

1. It shall be unlawful for any employer to inquire into, or to consider for the purpose of assessing fitness or capability for employment, whether a job applicant has filed for or received benefits under this chapter, or to discriminate against a job applicant with regard to employment on the basis of that claimant having filed for or received benefits under this chapter. An individual

aggrieved under this subdivision may initiate proceedings in a court of competent jurisdiction seeking damages, including reasonable attorney fees, for violation of this subdivision.

2. An employer who violates the provisions of subdivision one of this section shall be guilty of a misdemeanor, and upon conviction shall be punished, except as in this chapter or in the penal law otherwise provided, by a fine of not more than one thousand dollars.

ARTICLE 8. Administration

§ 140. Workmen's Compensation Board. The workmen's compensation board in the department of labor is hereby continued. Such board shall consist of thirteen members, at least four of whom shall be attorneys and counsellors-at-law duly admitted to practice in this state. The members of the board shall be appointed by the governor, by and with the advice and consent of the senate. . . .

The members next appointed, except to fill a vacancy created otherwise than by expiration of term, shall be appointed for terms of seven years. The governor shall designate one of the members of the board as chairman and another as vice-chairman.

§ 141. General powers and duties of the chairman. The chairman shall be the administrative head of the workers' compensation board and shall exercise the powers and perform the duties in relation to the administration of this chapter heretofore vested in the commissioner of labor by chapter fifty of the laws of nineteen hundred twenty-one, and acts amendatory thereof, and by this chapter excepting article six thereof, and except in so far as such powers and duties are vested by this chapter in the workers' compensation board. . . .

§ 142. General powers and duties of the workmen's compensation board

1. The workmen's compensation board shall have power to hear and determine all claims for compensation or benefits or relating to special funds created under the provisions of this chapter, in the manner provided by this chapter; to require medical service for injured employees as provided by this chapter; to approve and fix attorney's fees and claims for medical service to the extent provided in this chapter; to excuse failure to give notice either of injury or death of an employee, to approve agreements, to modify or rescind awards, to make conclusions of fact and rulings of law, to certify questions to the appellate division of the supreme court, to enter orders in appealed cases, to determine the time for the payment of compensation, to order the reimbursement of employers for amounts advanced, to assess penalties, to commute awards, to compromise actions for the collection of awards, to require or permit employers to deposit the present value of awards in the aggregate trust fund of the state fund, to determine by rule the assignment of a minor's right to sue a third party, to require guardianship for minor dependents, to hear and

determine claims under the occupational disease act, to order physical examinations, to take testimony by depositions; and to have and exercise all other powers and duties, exclusive of purely administrative functions, originally conferred or imposed upon the workmen's compensation commission. . . .

2. Any review, hearing, rehearing, inquiry or investigation required or authorized to be conducted or made by the workers' compensation board may be conducted or made by any panel of the board consisting of not less than three members thereof, and the order, decision or determination of a majority of the members of a panel shall be deemed the order, decision or determination of the board from the date of filing thereof with the secretary of the board, unless the board on its own motion, or on application by a party in interest for a full board review, shall modify or rescind such order, decision or determination. Four panels shall be constituted at all times, and the chair shall assign the members to the panels upon which they shall serve. At least one member on each panel shall be an attorney and counsellor-at-law, but the absence of an attorney on any panel shall not invalidate the order, decision or determination of a majority of the members of the panel if at least two affirmative votes are cast in favor of such action. The panels shall be constituted so that the members of the board shall alternate in their periods of service together thereon. Whenever a number of proceedings remains pending before the board for a period in excess of thirty days, members of the board shall hold hearings and otherwise act in the discharge of their duties evenings and at other convenient times on all days of the week except Sundays, in addition to the times when they would perform such duties in the ordinary conduct of the business of the board, in order to expedite the disposal thereof. The chair may and shall, when directed by the governor, prescribe the hours and the times for such additional performance of duty by the members of the board and the period or periods for the continuance thereof. . . .

§ 150. Referees and secretary

(a) The chair shall appoint as many persons as may be necessary to be referees to perform the duties prescribed by this section. All positions of referee now in existence shall remain in the exempt class of the classified civil service, except as otherwise provided herein. The term of referees appointed to positions in the exempt class shall be seven years from the date of appointment; provided, however, that referees may be removed by the chair for cause after notice of charges and an opportunity to be heard. . . .

(b) It shall be the duty of a referee, under rules adopted by the board, to hear and determine claims for compensation, and to conduct such hearings and investigations and to make such orders, decisions and determinations as may be required by any general or special rule or order of the board under the provisions of this chapter. The decision of a referee on such a claim shall be deemed the decision of the board from the date of the filing thereof in the office of the secretary of the board unless the board, on its own motion or on application duly made to it, modify or rescind such decision. . . .

ARKANSAS WORKERS' COMPENSATION LAW

Ark. Code Chapter 9, §§ 11-9-101 - 11-9-1001

§ 11-9-102. Definitions. As used in this chapter: . . .

(5)(A) "Compensable injury" means:

(i) An accidental injury causing internal or external physical harm to the body or accidental injury to prosthetic appliances, including eyeglasses, contact lenses, or hearing aids, arising out of and in the course of employment and which requires medical services or results in disability or death. An injury is "accidental" only if it is caused by a specific incident and is identifiable by time and place of occurrence;

(ii) An injury causing internal or external physical harm to the body and arising out of and in the course of employment if it is not caused by a specific incident or is not identifiable by time and place of occurrence, if the injury is:

(a) Caused by rapid repetitive motion. Carpal tunnel syndrome is specifically categorized as a compensable injury falling within this definition;

(b) A back injury which is not caused by a specific incident or which is not identifiable by time and place of occurrence;

(c) Hearing loss which is not caused by a specific incident or which is not identifiable by time and place of occurrence;

(iii) Mental illness as set out in § 11-9-113;

(iv) Heart, cardiovascular injury, accident, or disease as set out in § 11-9-114;

(v) A hernia as set out in § 11-9-523.

(B) "Compensable injury" does not include:

(i) Injury to any active participant in assaults or combats which, although they may occur in the workplace, are the result of nonemployment-related hostility or animus of one, both, or all of the combatants, and which said assault or combat amounts to a deviation from customary duties; further, except for innocent victims, injuries caused by horseplay shall not be considered to be compensable injuries;

(ii) Injury incurred while engaging in or performing, or as the result of engaging in or performing, any recreational or social activities for the employee's personal pleasure;

(iii) Injury which was inflicted upon the employee at a time when employment services were not being performed, or before the employee was hired or after the employment relationship was terminated;

(iv) Injury where the accident was substantially occasioned by the use of alcohol, illegal drugs, or prescription drugs used in contravention of physician's orders.

The presence of alcohol, illegal drugs, or prescription drugs used in contravention of a physician's orders shall create a rebuttable presumption that the injury or accident was substantially occasioned by the use of alcohol, illegal drugs, or prescription drugs used in contravention of physician's orders.

Every employee is deemed by his performance of services to have impliedly consented to reasonable and responsible testing by properly trained medical or law enforcement personnel for the presence of any of the aforementioned substances in the employee's body.

An employee shall not be entitled to compensation unless it is proved by a preponderance of the evidence that the alcohol, illegal drugs, or prescription drugs utilized in contravention of the physician's orders did not substantially occasion the injury or accident.

(C) The definition of "compensable injury" as set forth herein above shall not be deemed to limit or abrogate the right to recover for mental injuries as set forth in § 11-9-113 or occupational diseases as hereinafter set forth in § 11-9-601 et seq.

(D) A compensable injury must be established by medical evidence, supported by "objective findings" as defined in subdivision (16) of this section.

(E) Burden of Proof. The burden of proof of a compensable injury shall be on the employee and shall be as follows:

(i) For injuries falling within the definition of compensable injury under subdivision (5)(A)(i) of this section, the burden of proof shall be a preponderance of the evidence;

(ii) For injuries falling within the definition of compensable injury under subdivision (5)(A)(ii) of this section, the burden of proof shall be by a preponderance of the evidence, and the resultant condition is compensable only if the alleged compensable injury is the major cause of the disability or need for treatment.

(F) Benefits

(i) When an employee is determined to have a compensable injury, the employee is entitled to medical and temporary disability as provided by this chapter.

(ii) Permanent benefits shall be awarded only upon a determination that the compensable injury was the major cause of the disability or impairment. If any compensable injury combines with a preexisting disease or condition or the natural process of aging to cause or prolong disability or a need for treatment, permanent benefits shall be payable for the resultant condition only if the compensable injury is the major cause of the permanent disability or need for treatment.

(iii) Under subdivision (5)(F) of this section, benefits shall not be payable for a condition which results from a nonwork-related independent intervening cause following a compensable injury which causes or prolongs disability or a need for treatment. A nonwork-related independent intervening cause does not require negligence or recklessness on the part of a claimant.

(iv) Nothing in this section shall limit the payment of rehabilitation benefits or benefits for disfigurement as set forth in this chapter; . . .

(14) "Major cause" means more than fifty percent (50%) of the cause. A finding of major cause shall be established according to the preponderance of the evidence;

(16) "Objective findings" are those findings which cannot come under the voluntary control of the patient. When determining physical or anatomical impairment, neither a physician, any other medical provider, an administrative law judge, the Workers' Compensation Commission, nor the courts may consider complaints of pain. For the purpose of making physical or anatomical impairment ratings to the spine, straight-leg-raising tests or range-of-motion tests shall not be considered objective findings. Medical opinions addressing compensability and permanent impairment must be stated within a reasonable degree of medical certainty.

§ 11-9-107. Penalties for discrimination for filing claim

(a)(1) Any employer who willfully discriminates in regard to the hiring or tenure of work or any term or condition of work of any individual on account of the individual's claim for benefits under this chapter, or who in any manner obstructs or impedes the filing of claims for benefits under this chapter, shall be subject to a fine of up to ten thousand dollars ($10,000) as determined by the Workers' Compensation Commission.

(2) This fine shall be payable to the Second Injury Trust Fund and paid by the employer and not by the carrier.

(b) In addition, the prevailing party shall be entitled to recover costs and a reasonable attorney's fee payable from the fine. Provided, however, if the employee is the nonprevailing party, the attorney's fee and costs shall, at the election of the employer, be paid by the employee or deducted from future workers' compensation benefits.

(c) The employer may also be guilty of a Class D felony.

(d) This section shall not be construed as establishing an exception to the "employment at will" doctrine.

(e) A purpose of this section is to preserve the exclusive remedy doctrine and specifically annul any case law inconsistent herewith. . . .

§ 11-9-113. Mental injury or illness

(a)(1) A mental injury or illness is not a compensable injury unless it is caused by physical injury to the employee's body, and shall not be considered an injury arising out of and in the course of employment or compensable unless it is demonstrated by a preponderance of the evidence; provided, however, that this physical injury limitation shall not apply to any victim of a crime of violence.

(2) No mental injury or illness under this section shall be compensable unless it is also diagnosed by a licensed psychiatrist or psychologist and unless the diagnosis of the condition meets the criteria established in the most current issue of the Diagnostic and Statistical Manual of Mental Disorders.

(b)(1) Notwithstanding any other provision of this chapter, where a claim is by reason of mental injury or illness, the employee shall be limited to twenty-six (26) weeks of disability benefits.

(2)(A) In case death results directly from the mental injury or illness within a period of one (1) year, compensation shall be paid the dependents as provided in other death cases under this chapter.

(B) Death directly or indirectly related to the mental injury or illness occurring one (1) year or more from the incident resulting in the mental injury or illness shall not be a compensable injury.

§ 11-9-509. Medical services and supplies – Amounts and time periods.

The amounts payable or time periods allowable for authorized medical, hospital, and other services and treatment furnished under §§ 11-9-508 – 11-9-516, unless waived by the employer-respondent or approved by the commission and warranted by the preponderance of the evidence on the basis of the record as a whole, are:

(1) Six (6) months if the claimant lost no compensable time from work as a result of his injury;

(2) Six (6) months following the return to work by an injured employee who has been receiving authorized medical or hospital or other services or treatment;

(3) Ten thousand dollars ($10,000) aggregate for all authorized medical, hospital, and other services and treatment, including any amounts paid under subdivisions (1) and (2) of this section.

§ 11-9-1001. Legislative declaration [1993].

The Seventy-Ninth General Assembly realizes that the Arkansas workers' compensation statutes must be revised and amended from time to time. Unfortunately, many of the changes made by this act were necessary because administrative law judges, the Workers' Compensation Commission, and the Arkansas courts have continually broadened the scope and eroded the purpose of the workers' compensation statutes of this state. The Seventy-Ninth General Assembly intends to restate that the major and controlling purpose of workers' compensation is to pay timely temporary and permanent disability benefits to all legitimately injured workers that suffer an injury or disease arising out of and in the course of their employment, to pay reasonable and necessary medical expenses resulting therefrom, and then to return the worker to the work force. When, and if, the workers' compensation statutes of this state need to be changed, the General Assembly acknowledges its responsibility to do so. It is the specific intent of the Seventy-Ninth General Assembly to repeal, annul, and hold for naught all prior opinions or decisions of any administrative law judge, the Workers' Compensation Commission, or courts of this state contrary to or in conflict with any provision in this act. In the future, if such things as the statute of limitations, the standard of review by the Workers' Compensation Commission or courts, the extent to which any physical condition, injury, or disease should be excluded from or added to coverage by the law, or the scope of the workers' compensation statutes need to be liberalized, broadened, or narrowed, those things shall be addressed by the General Assembly and should not be done by administrative law judges, the Workers' Compensation Commission, or the courts.

CALIFORNIA WORKERS' COMPENSATION LAW

Cal. Labor Code §§ 3200–5303

§ 3201.5. Collective bargaining agreement provision establishing alternative dispute resolution systems

(a) Except as provided in subdivisions (b) and (c), the Department of Industrial Relations and the courts of this state shall recognize as valid and binding any provision in a collective bargaining agreement between a private employer or groups of employers engaged in construction, construction maintenance, or activities limited to rock, sand, gravel, cement and asphalt operations, heavy-duty mechanics, surveying, and construction inspection and a union that is the recognized or certified exclusive bargaining representative that establishes any of the following:

> (1) An alternative dispute resolution system governing disputes between employees and employers or their insurers that supplements or replaces all or part of those dispute resolution processes contained in this division, including, but not limited to, mediation and arbitration. Any system of arbitration shall provide that the decision of the arbiter or board of arbitration is subject to review by the appeals board in the same manner as provided for reconsideration of a final order, decision, or award made and filed by a workers' compensation judge. . . . The findings of fact, award, order, or decision of the arbitrator shall have the same force and effect as an award, order, or decision of a workers' compensation judge. . . .

(2) The use of an agreed list of providers of medical treatment that may be the exclusive source of all medical treatment provided under this division.

(3) The use of an agreed, limited list of qualified medical evaluators and agreed medical evaluators that may be the exclusive source of qualified medical evaluators and agreed medical evaluators under this division.

(4) Joint labor management safety committees.

(5) A light-duty, modified job or return-to-work program.

(6) A vocational rehabilitation or retraining program utilizing an agreed list of providers of rehabilitation services that may be the exclusive source of providers of rehabilitation services under this division.

(b) Nothing in this section shall allow a collective bargaining agreement that diminishes the entitlement of an employee to compensation payments for total or partial disability, temporary disability, vocational rehabilitation, or medical treatment fully paid by the employer as otherwise provided in this division. The portion of any agreement that violates this subdivision shall be declared null and void. . . .

§ 4653. Temporary total disability. If the injury causes temporary total disability, the disability payment is two-thirds of the average weekly earnings during the period of such disability, consideration being given to the ability of the injured employee to compete in an open labor market.

§ 4654. Temporary partial disability. If the injury causes temporary partial disability, the disability payment is two-thirds of the weekly loss in wages during the period of such disability. However, such disability payment shall be reduced by the sum of unemployment compensation benefits and extended duration benefits received by the employee during the period of temporary partial disability.

§ 4658. Permanent disability; Computation; Benefits schedules; Increase or decrease in disability payments depending on offer or termination of regular, modified or alternative work . . .

(b) This subdivision shall apply to injuries occurring on or after January 1, 1992. If the injury causes permanent disability, the percentage of disability to total disability shall be determined, and the disability payment computed and allowed, according to paragraph (1). However, in no event shall the disability payment allowed be less than the disability payment computed according to paragraph (2).

Column 1 Range of percentage of permanent disability incurred:	**Column 2** Number of weeks for which two-thirds of average weekly earnings allowed for each 1 percent of permanent disability within percentage range:
Under 10	3
10 - 19.75	4
20 - 24.75	5
25 - 29.75	6
30 - 49.75	7
50 - 69.75	8
70 - 99.75	9

(1) The numbers set forth in column 2 above are based upon the percentage of permanent disability set forth in column 1 above and shall be cumulative, and shall increase with the severity of the disability in the manner illustrated in subdivision (a).

(2) Two-thirds of the average weekly earnings for four weeks for each 1 percent of disability, where, for the purposes of this subdivision, the average weekly earnings shall be taken at not more than seventy-eight dollars and seventy-five cents ($78.75).

(c) This subdivision shall apply to injuries occurring on or after January 1, 2004. If the injury causes permanent disability, the percentage of disability to total disability shall be determined, and the disability payment computed and allowed as follows:

Column 1 Range of percentage of permanent disability incurred:	**Column 2** Number of weeks for which two-thirds of average weekly earnings allowed for each 1 percent of permanent disability within percentage range:
Under 10	4
10 - 19.75	5
20 - 24.75	5
25 - 29.75	6
30 - 49.75	7
50 - 69.75	8
70 - 99.75	9

The numbers set forth in column 2 above are based upon the percentage of permanent disability set forth in column 1 above and shall be cumulative, and shall increase with the severity of the disability in the manner illustrated in subdivision (a).

(d)(1) This subdivision shall apply to injuries occurring on or after the effective date of the revised permanent disability schedule adopted by the administrative director pursuant to Section 4660. If the injury causes permanent disability, the percentage of disability to total disability shall be determined, and the basic disability payment computed as follows:

Column 1 Range of percentage of permanent disability incurred:	**Column 2** Number of weeks for which two-thirds of average weekly earnings allowed for each 1 percent of permanent disability within percentage range:
.25 - 9.75	3
10 - 14.75	4
15 - 24.75	5
25 - 29.75	6
30 - 49.75	7
50 - 69.75	8
70 - 99.75	16

The numbers set forth in column 2 above are based upon the percentage of permanent disability set forth in column 1 above and shall be cumulative, and shall increase with the severity of the disability in the manner illustrated in subdivision (a).

(2) If, within 60 days of a disability becoming permanent and stationary, an employer does not offer the injured employee regular work, modified work, or alternative work, in the form and manner prescribed by the administrative director, for a period of at least 12 months, each disability payment remaining to be paid to the injured employee from the date of the end of the 60-day period shall be paid in accordance with paragraph (1) and increased by 15 percent. This paragraph shall not apply to an employer that employs fewer than 50 employees.

(3)(A) If, within 60 days of a disability becoming permanent and stationary, an employer offers the injured employee regular work, modified work, or alternative work, in the form and manner prescribed by the administrative director, for a period of at least 12 months, and regardless of whether the injured employee accepts or rejects the offer, each disability payment remaining to be paid to the injured employee from the date the offer was made shall be paid in accordance with paragraph (1) and decreased by 15 percent.

(B) If the regular work, modified work, or alternative work is terminated by the employer before the end of the period for which disability payments are due the injured employee, the amount of each of the remaining disability payments shall be paid in accordance with paragraph (1) and increased by 15 percent. An employee who voluntarily terminates employment shall not be eligible for payment under this subparagraph. This paragraph shall not apply to an employer that employs fewer than 50 employees. . .

§ 4660. Percentages of permanent disability; How determined; Adjusted rating schedule; Amendments and revisions to schedule

(a) In determining the percentages of permanent disability, account shall be taken of the nature of the physical injury or disfigurement, the occupation of the injured employee, and his or her age at the time of the injury, consideration being given to an employee's diminished future earning capacity.

(b)(1) For purposes of this section, the "nature of the physical injury or disfigurement" shall incorporate the descriptions and measurements of physical impairments and the corresponding percentages of impairments published in the American Medical Association (AMA) Guides to the Evaluation of Permanent Impairment (5th Edition).

(2) For purposes of this section, an employee's diminished future earning capacity shall be a numeric formula based on empirical data and findings that aggregate the average percentage of long-term loss of income resulting from each type of injury for similarly situated employees. The administrative director shall formulate the adjusted rating schedule based on empirical data and findings from the Evaluation of California's Permanent Disability Rating Schedule, Interim Report (December 2003), prepared by the RAND Institute for Civil Justice, and upon data from additional empirical studies.

(c) The administrative director shall amend the schedule for the determination of the percentage of permanent disability in accordance with this section at least once every five years. This schedule shall be available for public inspection and, without formal introduction in evidence, shall be prima facie evidence of the percentage of permanent disability to be attributed to each injury covered by the schedule.

(d) The schedule shall promote consistency, uniformity, and objectivity. The schedule and any amendment thereto or revision thereof shall apply prospectively and shall apply to and govern only those permanent disabilities that result from compensable injuries received or occurring on and after the effective date of the adoption of the schedule, amendment or revision, as the fact may be. For compensable claims arising before January 1, 2005, the schedule as revised pursuant to changes made in legislation enacted during the 2003-04 Regular and Extraordinary Sessions shall apply to the determination of permanent disabilities when there has been either no comprehensive medical-legal report or no report by a treating physician indicating the existence of permanent disability, or when the employer is not required to provide the notice required by Section 4061 to the injured worker.

(e) On or before January 1, 2005, the administrative director shall adopt regulations to implement the changes made to this section by the act that added this subdivision.

§ 4663. Apportionment of permanent disability; Causation as basis; Physician's report; Apportionment determination; Disclosure by employee; Applicability

(a) Apportionment of permanent disability shall be based on causation.

(b) Any physician who prepares a report addressing the issue of permanent disability due to a claimed industrial injury shall in that report address the issue of causation of the permanent disability.

(c) In order for a physician's report to be considered complete on the issue of permanent disability, the report must include an apportionment determination. A physician shall make an apportionment determination by finding what approximate percentage of the permanent disability was caused by the direct result of injury arising out of and occurring in the course of employment and what approximate percentage of the permanent disability was caused by other factors both before and subsequent to the industrial injury, including prior industrial injuries. If the physician is unable to include an apportionment determination in his or her report, the physician shall state the specific reasons why the physician could not make a determination of the effect of that prior condition on the permanent disability arising from the injury. The physician shall then consult with other physicians or refer the employee to another physician from whom the employee is authorized to seek treatment or evaluation in accordance with this division in order to make the final determination.

(d) An employee who claims an industrial injury shall, upon request, disclose all previous permanent disabilities or physical impairments. . . .

§ 4664. Liability of employer for percentage of permanent disability directly caused by injury; Conclusive presumption from prior award of permanent disability; Accumulation of permanent disability awards

(a) The employer shall only be liable for the percentage of permanent disability directly caused by the injury arising out of and occurring in the course of employment.

(b) If the applicant has received a prior award of permanent disability, it shall be conclusively presumed that the prior permanent disability exists at the time of any subsequent industrial injury. This presumption is a presumption affecting the burden of proof.

(c)(1) The accumulation of all permanent disability awards issued with respect to any one region of the body in favor of one individual employee shall not exceed 100 percent over the employee's lifetime unless the employee's injury or illness is conclusively presumed to be total in character pursuant to Section 4662. As used in this section, the regions of the body are the following:

(A) Hearing.

(B) Vision.

(C) Mental and behavioral disorders.

(D) The spine.

(E) The upper extremities, including the shoulders.

(F) The lower extremities, including the hip joints.

(G) The head, face, cardiovascular system, respiratory system, and all other systems or regions of the body not listed in subparagraphs (A) to (F), inclusive.

(2) Nothing in this section shall be construed to permit the permanent disability rating for each individual injury sustained by an employee arising from the same industrial accident, when added together, from exceeding 100 percent.

FLORIDA WORKERS' COMPENSATION LAW

Fla. Stat. ch. 440

§ 440.02. Definitions. When used in this chapter, unless the context clearly requires otherwise, the following terms shall have the following meanings:

(1) "Accident" means only an unexpected or unusual event or result that happens suddenly. Disability or death due to the accidental acceleration or aggravation of a venereal disease or of a disease due to the habitual use of alcohol or controlled substances or narcotic drugs, or a disease that manifests itself in the fear of or dislike for an individual because of the individual's race, color, religion, sex, national origin, age, or handicap is not an injury by accident arising out of the employment. Subject to § 440.15(5), if a preexisting disease or anomaly is accelerated or aggravated by an accident arising out of and in the course of employment, only acceleration of death or acceleration or aggravation of the preexisting condition reasonably attributable to the accident is compensable, with respect to any compensation otherwise payable under this chapter. . . .

(19) "Injury" means personal injury or death by accident arising out of and in the course of employment, and such diseases or infection as naturally or unavoidably result from such injury. Damage to dentures, eyeglasses, prosthetic devices, and artificial limbs may be included in this definition only when the damage is shown to be part of, or in conjunction with, an accident. This damage must specifically occur as the result of an accident in the normal course of employment. . . .

(36) "Arising out of" pertains to occupational causation. An accidental injury or death arises out of employment if work performed in the course and scope of employment is the major contributing cause of the injury or death. . . .

§ 440.15. Compensation for disability. Compensation for disability shall be paid to the employee, subject to the limits provided in § 440.12(2), as follows:

(1) *Permanent Total Disability.*

In case of total disability adjudged to be permanent, 66 2/3 percent of the average weekly wages shall be paid to the employee during the continuance of such total disability. No compensation shall be payable under this section if the employee is engaged in, or is physically capable of engaging in, at least sedentary employment.

(b) In the following cases, an injured employee is presumed to be permanently and totally disabled unless the employer or carrier establishes that the employee is physically capable of engaging in at least sedentary employment within a 50-mile radius of the employee's residence:

1. Spinal cord injury involving severe paralysis of an arm, a leg, or the trunk;

2. Amputation of an arm, a hand, a foot, or a leg involving the effective loss of use of that appendage;

3. Severe brain or closed-head injury as evidenced by:

a. Severe sensory or motor disturbances;

b. Severe communication disturbances;

c. Severe complex integrated disturbances of cerebral function;

d. Severe episodic neurological disorders; or

e. Other severe brain and closed-head injury conditions at least as severe in nature as any condition provided in sub-subparagraphs a.-d.;

4. Second-degree or third-degree burns of 25 percent or more of the total body surface or third-degree burns of 5 percent or more to the face and hands; or

5. Total or industrial blindness.

In all other cases, in order to obtain permanent total disability benefits, the employee must establish that he or she is not able to engage in at least sedentary employment, within a 50-mile radius of the employee's residence, due to his or her physical limitation. Entitlement to such benefits shall cease when the employee reaches age 75, unless the employee is not eligible for social security benefits under 42 U.S.C. § 402 or § 423 because the employee's compensable injury has prevented the employee from working sufficient quarters to be eligible for such benefits, notwithstanding any age limits. If the accident occurred on or after the employee reaches age 70, benefits shall be payable during the continuance of permanent total disability, not to exceed 5 years following the determination of permanent total disability. Only claimants with catastrophic injuries or claimants who are incapable of engaging in employment, as described in this paragraph, are eligible for permanent total benefits. In no other case may permanent total disability be awarded. . . .

(2) *Temporary Total Disability.*

Subject to subsection (7), in case of disability total in character but temporary in quality, 66 2/3 percent of the average weekly wages shall be paid to the employee during the continuance thereof, not to exceed 104 weeks except as provided in this subsection, § 440.12(1), and § 440.14(3). Once the employee reaches the maximum number of weeks allowed, or the employee reaches the date of maximum medical improvement, whichever occurs earlier, temporary disability benefits shall cease and the injured worker's permanent impairment shall be determined.

(b) Notwithstanding the provisions of paragraph (a), an employee who has sustained the loss of an arm, leg, hand, or foot, has been rendered a paraplegic, paraparetic, quadriplegic, or quadriparetic, or has lost the sight of both eyes shall be paid temporary total disability of 80 percent of her or his average weekly wage. The increased temporary total disability compensation provided for in this paragraph must not extend beyond 6 months from the date of the accident; however, such benefits shall not be due or payable if the employee is eligible for, entitled to, or collecting permanent total disability benefits. The compensation provided by this paragraph is not subject to the limits provided in § 440.12(2), but instead is subject to a maximum weekly compensation rate of $ 700. If, at the conclusion of this period of increased temporary total disability compensation, the employee is still temporarily totally disabled, the employee shall continue to receive temporary total disability compensation as set forth in paragraphs (a) and (c). The period of time the employee has received this increased compensation will be counted as part of, and not in addition to, the maximum periods of time for which the employee is entitled to compensation under paragraph (a) but not paragraph (c).

(c) Temporary total disability benefits paid pursuant to this subsection shall include such period as may be reasonably necessary for training in the use of artificial members and appliances, and shall include such period as the employee may be receiving training and education under a program pursuant to § 440.491. . . .

(3) *Permanent Impairment Benefits.*

Once the employee has reached the date of maximum medical improvement, impairment benefits are due and payable within 14 days after the carrier has knowledge of the impairment.

(b) The three-member panel, in cooperation with the department, shall establish and use a uniform permanent impairment rating schedule. This schedule must be based on medically or scientifically demonstrable findings as well as the systems and criteria set forth in the American Medical Association's Guides to the Evaluation of Permanent Impairment; the Snellen Charts, published by the American Medical Association Committee for Eye Injuries; and the Minnesota Department of Labor and Industry Disability Schedules. The schedule must be based upon objective findings. . . .

(c) All impairment income benefits shall be based on an impairment rating using the impairment schedule referred to in paragraph (b). Impairment income benefits are paid biweekly at the rate of 75 percent of the employee's average weekly temporary total disability benefit not to exceed the maximum weekly benefit under § 440.12; provided, however, that such benefits shall be reduced by 50 percent for each week in which the employee has earned income equal to or in excess of the employee's average weekly wage. An employee's entitlement to impairment income benefits begins the day after the employee reaches maximum medical improvement or the expiration of temporary benefits, whichever occurs earlier, and continues until the earlier of:

1. The expiration of a period computed at the rate of 3 weeks for each percentage point of impairment; or

2. The death of the employee.

Impairment income benefits as defined by this subsection are payable only for impairment ratings for physical impairments. If objective medical findings can substantiate a permanent psychiatric impairment resulting from the accident, permanent impairment benefits are limited for the permanent psychiatric impairment to 1-percent permanent impairment. . . .

(g) Notwithstanding paragraph (c), for accidents occurring on or after October 1, 2003, an employee's entitlement to impairment income benefits begins the day after the employee reaches maximum medical improvement or the expiration of temporary benefits, whichever occurs earlier, and continues for the following periods:

1. Two weeks of benefits are to be paid to the employee for each percentage point of impairment from 1 percent up to and including 10 percent.

2. For each percentage point of impairment from 11 percent up to and including 15 percent, 3 weeks of benefits are to be paid.

3. For each percentage point of impairment from 16 percent up to and including 20 percent, 4 weeks of benefits are to be paid.

4. For each percentage point of impairment from 21 percent and higher, 6 weeks of benefits are to be paid.

(4) *Temporary Partial Disability*.

(a) Subject to subsection (7), in case of temporary partial disability, compensation shall be equal to 80 percent of the difference between 80 percent of the employee's average weekly wage and the salary, wages, and other remuneration the employee is able to earn postinjury, as compared weekly; however, weekly temporary partial disability benefits may not exceed an amount equal to 66 2/3 percent of the employee's average weekly wage at the time of accident. . . .

§ 440.211. Authorization of collective bargaining agreement

(1) Subject to the limitation stated in subsection (2), a provision that is mutually agreed upon in any collective bargaining agreement filed with the division between an individually self-insured employer or other employer upon consent of the employer's carrier and a recognized or certified exclusive bargaining representative establishing any of the following shall be valid and binding:

(a) An alternative dispute resolution system to supplement, modify, or replace the provisions of this chapter which may include, but is not limited to, conciliation, mediation, and arbitration. Arbitration held pursuant to this section shall be binding on the parties.

(b) The use of an agreed-upon list of certified health care providers of medical treatment which may be the exclusive source of all medical treatment under this chapter.

(c) The use of a limited list of physicians to conduct independent medical examinations which the parties may agree shall be the exclusive source of independent medical examiners pursuant to this chapter.

(d) A light-duty, modified-job, or return-to-work program.

(e) A vocational rehabilitation or retraining program.

(2) Nothing in this section shall allow any agreement that diminishes an employee's entitlement to benefits as otherwise set forth in this chapter. Any such agreement in violation of this provision shall be null and void.

OREGON WORKERS' COMPENSATION LAW

Or. Rev. Stat. Chapter 656

§656.005. Definitions

(7)(a) A "compensable injury" is an accidental injury, or accidental injury to prosthetic appliances, arising out of and in the course of employment requiring medical services or resulting in disability or death; an injury is accidental if the result is an accident, whether or not due to accidental means, if it is established by medical evidence supported by objective findings, subject to the following limitations:

(A) No injury or disease is compensable as a consequence of a compensable injury unless the compensable injury is the major contributing cause of the consequential condition.

(B) If an otherwise compensable injury combines at any time with a preexisting condition to cause or prolong disability or a need for treatment, the combined condition is compensable only if, so long as and to the extent that the otherwise compensable injury is the major contributing cause of the disability of the combined condition or the major contributing cause of the need for treatment of the combined condition.

(b) "Compensable injury" does not include:

(A) Injury to any active participant in assaults or combats which are not connected to the job assignment and which amount to a deviation from customary duties;

(B) Injury incurred while engaging in or performing, or as the result of engaging in or performing, any recreational or social activities primarily for the worker's personal pleasure; or

(C) Injury the major contributing cause of which is demonstrated to be by a preponderance of the evidence the injured worker's consumption of alcoholic beverages or the unlawful consumption of any controlled substance, unless the employer permitted, encouraged or had actual knowledge of such consumption.

(c) A "disabling compensable injury" is an injury which entitles the worker to compensation for disability or death. An injury is not disabling if no temporary benefits are due and payable, unless there is a reasonable expectation that permanent disability will result from the injury.

(d) A "nondisabling compensable injury" is any injury which requires medical services only. . . .

§ 656.018. Effect of providing coverage; exclusive remedy.

(1)(a) The liability of every employer who satisfies the duty required by ORS 656.017 (1) is exclusive and in place of all other liability arising out of injuries, diseases, symptom complexes or similar conditions arising out of and in the course of employment that are sustained by subject workers, the workers' beneficiaries and anyone otherwise entitled to recover damages from the employer on account of such conditions or claims resulting therefrom, specifically including claims for contribution or indemnity asserted by third persons from whom damages are sought on account of such conditions, except as specifically provided otherwise in this chapter. . . .

(2) The rights given to a subject worker and the beneficiaries of the subject worker under this chapter for injuries, diseases, symptom complexes or similar conditions arising out of and in the course of employment are in lieu of any remedies they might otherwise have for such injuries, diseases, symptom complexes or similar conditions against the worker's employer under ORS 654.305 to 654.335 or other laws, common law or statute, except to the extent the worker is expressly given the right under this chapter to bring suit against the employer of the worker for an injury, disease, symptom complex or similar condition.

(3) The exemption from liability given an employer under this section is also extended to the employer's insurer, the self-insured employer's claims administrator, the Department of Consumer and Business Services, and the contracted agents, employees, officers and directors of the employer, the employer's insurer, the self-insured employer's claims administrator and the department, except that the exemption from liability shall not apply:

> (a) Where the injury, disease, symptom complex or similar condition is proximately caused by willful and unprovoked aggression by the person otherwise exempt under this subsection;
>
> (b) Where the worker and the person otherwise exempt under this subsection are not engaged in the furtherance of a common enterprise or the accomplishment of the same or related objectives; or
>
> (c) Where the injury, disease, symptom complex or similar condition is proximately caused by failure of the employer to comply with the notice posted pursuant to ORS 654.082.

(4) The exemption from liability given an employer under this section applies to a worker leasing company and the client to whom workers are provided when the worker leasing company and the client comply with ORS 656.850 (3).

> (5)(a) The exemption from liability given an employer under this section applies to a temporary service provider, as that term is used in ORS 656.850, and also extends to the client to whom workers are provided when the temporary service provider complies with ORS 656.017.
>
> (b) The exemption from liability given a client under paragraph (a) of this subsection is also extended to the client's insurer, the self-insured client's claims administrator, the department, and the

contracted agents, employees, officers and directors of the client, the client's insurer, the self-insured client's claims administrator and the department, except that the exemption from liability shall not apply:

(A) When the injury, disease, symptom complex or similar condition is proximately caused by willful and unprovoked aggression by the person otherwise exempt under this subsection;

(B) When the worker and the person otherwise exempt under this subsection are not engaged in the furtherance of a common enterprise or the accomplishment of the same or related objectives; or

(C) When the injury, disease, symptom complex or similar condition is proximately caused by failure of the client to comply with the notice posted pursuant to ORS 654.082.

(6) Nothing in this chapter shall prohibit payment, voluntarily or otherwise, to injured workers or their beneficiaries in excess of the compensation required to be paid under this chapter.

(7) The exclusive remedy provisions and limitation on liability provisions of this chapter apply to all injuries and to diseases, symptom complexes or similar conditions of subject workers arising out of and in the course of employment whether or not they are determined to be compensable under this chapter.

Note: The amendments to §656.018 by § 4, chapter 6, Oregon Laws 1999, that were to become operative December 31, 2004, would have eliminated §656.018(c)(7). The 1999 amendment was repealed by § 23, chapter 865, Oregon Laws 2001.

§ 656.802. Occupational disease defined

(1)(a) As used in this chapter, "occupational disease" means any disease or infection arising out of and in the course of employment caused by substances or activities to which an employee is not ordinarily subjected or exposed other than during a period of regular actual employment therein, and which requires medical services or results in disability or death, including:

(A) Any disease or infection caused by ingestion of, absorption of, inhalation of or contact with dust, fumes, vapors, gases, radiation or other substances.

(B) Any mental disorder, whether sudden or gradual in onset, which requires medical services or results in physical or mental disability or death.

(C) Any series of traumatic events or occurrences which requires medical services or results in physical disability or death.

(b) As used in this chapter, a "mental disorder" includes any physical disorder caused or worsened by mental stress.

(2)(a) The worker must prove that employment conditions were the major contributing cause of the disease.

(b) If the occupational disease claim is based on the worsening of a preexisting disease or condition pursuant to ORS 656.005 (7), the worker must prove that employment conditions were the major contributing cause of the combined condition and pathological worsening of the disease.

(c) Occupational diseases shall be subject to all of the same limitations and exclusions as accidental injuries under ORS 656.005 (7).

(d) Existence of an occupational disease or worsening of a preexisting disease must be established by medical evidence supported by objective findings.

(e) Preexisting conditions shall be deemed causes in determining major contributing cause under this section.

(3) Notwithstanding any other provision of this chapter, a mental disorder is not compensable under this chapter unless the worker establishes all of the following:

(a) The employment conditions producing the mental disorder exist in a real and objective sense.

(b) The employment conditions producing the mental disorder are conditions other than conditions generally inherent in every working situation or reasonable disciplinary, corrective or job performance evaluation actions by the employer, or cessation of employment or employment decisions attendant upon ordinary business or financial cycles.

(c) There is a diagnosis of a mental or emotional disorder which is generally recognized in the medical or psychological community.

(d) There is clear and convincing evidence that the mental disorder arose out of and in the course of employment.

(4) Death, disability or impairment of health of firefighters of any political division who have completed five or more years of employment as firefighters, caused by any disease of the lungs or respiratory tract, hypertension or cardiovascular-renal disease, and resulting from their employment as firefighters is an "occupational disease." Any condition or impairment of health arising under this subsection shall be presumed to result from a firefighter's employment. However, any such firefighter must have taken a physical examination upon becoming a firefighter, or subsequently thereto, which failed to reveal any evidence of such condition or impairment of health which preexisted employment. Denial of a claim for any condition or impairment of health arising under this subsection must be on the basis of clear and convincing medical evidence that the cause of the condition or impairment is unrelated to the firefighter's employment.

WISCONSIN WORKERS' COMPENSATION LAW

Wis. Stat. ch. 102

§ 102.42. Incidental compensation

(1) Treatment of employee.

The employer shall supply such medical, surgical, chiropractic, psychological, podiatric, dental, and hospital treatment, medicines, medical and surgical supplies, crutches, artificial members, appliances, and training in the use of artificial members and appliances, or, at the option of the employee, Christian Science treatment in lieu of medical treatment, medicines, and medical supplies, as may be reasonably required to cure and relieve from the effects of the injury, and to attain efficient use of artificial members and appliances, and in case of the employers neglect or refusal seasonably to do so, or in emergency until it is practicable for the employee to give notice of injury, the employer shall be liable for the reasonable expense incurred by or on behalf of the employee in providing such treatment, medicines, supplies, and training. When the employer has knowledge of the injury and the necessity for treatment, the employers failure to tender the necessary treatment, medicines, supplies, and training constitutes such neglect or refusal. The employer shall also be liable for reasonable expense incurred by the employee for necessary treatment to cure and relieve the employee from the effects of occupational disease prior to the time that the employee knew or should have known the nature of his or her disability and its relation to employment, and as to such treatment subs. (2) and (3) shall not apply. The obligation to furnish such treatment and appliances shall continue as required to prevent further deterioration in the condition of the employee or to maintain the existing status of such condition whether or not healing is completed.

(1m) Liability for unnecessary treatment.

If an employee who has sustained a compensable injury undertakes in good faith invasive treatment that is generally medically acceptable, but that is unnecessary, the employer shall pay disability indemnity for all disability incurred as a result of that treatment. An employer is not liable for disability indemnity for any disability incurred as a result of any unnecessary treatment undertaken in good faith that is noninvasive or not medically acceptable. This subsection applies to all findings that an employee has sustained a compensable injury, whether the finding results from a hearing, the default of a party, or a compromise or stipulation confirmed by the department.

(2) Choice of practitioner.

(a) When the employer has notice of an injury and its relationship to the employment, the employer shall offer to the injured employee his or her choice of any physician, chiropractor, psychologist, dentist, physician assistant, advanced practice nurse prescriber, or podiatrist licensed to practice and practicing in this state for treatment of the injury. By mutual agreement, the employee may have the choice of any qualified practitioner not licensed in this state. In case of emergency, the employer may arrange for treatment without tendering a choice. After the emergency has passed the employee shall be given his or her choice of attending practitioner at the earliest opportunity. The employee has the right to a 2nd choice of attending practitioner on notice to the employer or its insurance carrier. Any further choice shall be by mutual agreement. Partners and clinics are considered to be one practitioner. Treatment by a practitioner on referral from another practitioner is considered to be treatment by one practitioner.

(b) The employer is liable for the expense of reasonable travel to obtain treatment at the same rate as is provided for state officers and employees under *s. 20.916 (8)* The employer is not liable for the expense of unreasonable travel to obtain treatment.

(3) Practitioner choice unrestricted.

If the employer fails to tender treatment as provided in sub. (1) or choice of an attending practitioner as provided in sub. (2), the employees right to choose the attending practitioner is not restricted and the employer is liable for the reasonable and necessary expense thereof.

(4) Christian Science.

The liability of an employer for the cost of Christian Science treatment provided to an injured employee is limited to the usual and customary charge for that treatment.

(5) Artificial members.

Liability for repair and replacement of prosthetic devices is limited to the effects of normal wear and tear. Artificial members furnished at the end of the healing period for cosmetic purposes only need not be duplicated.

(6) Treatment rejected by employee.

Unless the employee shall have elected Christian Science treatment in lieu of medical, surgical, dental or hospital treatment, no compensation shall be payable for the death or disability of an employee, if the death be caused, or insofar as the disability may be aggravated, caused or continued by an unreasonable refusal or neglect to submit to or follow any competent and reasonable medical, surgical or dental treatment or, in the case of tuberculosis, by refusal or neglect to submit to or follow hospital or medical treatment when found by the department to be necessary. The right to compensation accruing during a period of refusal or neglect to submit to or follow hospital or medical treatment when found by the department to be necessary in the case of tuberculosis shall be barred, irrespective of whether disability was aggravated, caused or continued thereby. . . .

(8) Award to state employee.

Whenever an award is made by the department in behalf of a state employee, the department of workforce development shall file duplicate copies of the award with the department of administration. Upon receipt of the copies of the award, the department of administration shall promptly issue a voucher in payment of the award from the proper appropriation under s. 20.865 (1) (fm), (kr) or (ur), and shall transmit one copy of the voucher and the award to the officer, department or agency by whom the affected employee is employed.

(9) Rehabilitation; physical and vocational.

(a) One of the primary purposes of this chapter is restoration of an injured employee to gainful employment. To this end, the department shall employ a specialist in physical, medical and vocational rehabilitation.

(b) Such specialist shall study the problems of rehabilitation, both physical and vocational and shall refer suitable cases to the department for vocational evaluation and training. The specialist shall investigate and maintain a directory of such rehabilitation facilities, private and public, as are capable of rendering competent rehabilitation service to seriously injured employees.

(c) The specialist shall review and evaluate reported injuries for potential cases in which seriously injured employees may be in need of physical and medical rehabilitation and may confer with the injured employee, employer, insurance carrier or attending practitioner regarding treatment and rehabilitation.

§ 102.44. Maximum limitations. Section 102.43 shall be subject to the following limitation: . . .

(2) In case of permanent total disability aggregate indemnity shall be weekly indemnity for the period that the employee may live. Total impairment for industrial use of both eyes, or the loss of both arms at or near the shoulder, or of both legs at or near the hip, or of one arm at the shoulder and one leg at the hip, constitutes permanent total disability. This enumeration is not exclusive, but in other cases the department shall find the facts.

(3) For permanent partial disability not covered by ss. 102.52 to 102.56, the aggregate number of weeks of indemnity shall bear such relation to 1,000 weeks as the nature of the injury bears to one causing permanent total disability and shall be payable at the rate of two-thirds of the average weekly earnings of the employee, the earnings to be computed as provided in s. 102.11. The weekly indemnity shall be in addition to compensation for the healing period and shall be for the period that the employee may live, not to exceed 1,000 weeks. . . .

(6)(a) Where an injured employee claiming compensation for disability under sub. (2) or (3) has returned to work for the employer for whom he or she worked at the time of the injury, the permanent disability award shall be based upon the physical limitations resulting from the injury without regard to loss of earning capacity unless the actual wage loss in comparison with earnings at the time of injury equals or exceeds 15%.

(b) If, during the period set forth in s. 102.17(4) the employment relationship is terminated by the employer at the time of the injury, or by the employee because his or her physical or mental limitations prevent his or her continuing in such employment, or if during such period a wage loss of 15% or more occurs the department may reopen any award and make a redetermination taking into account loss of earning capacity. . . .

(g) For purposes of this subsection, if the employer in good faith makes an offer of employment which is refused by the employee without reasonable cause, the employee is considered to have returned to work with the earnings the employee would have received had it not been for the refusal. . . .

§ **102.57. Violations of safety provisions, penalty**. If injury is caused by the failure of the employer to comply with any statute or any lawful order of the department, compensation and death benefits provided in this chapter shall be increased 15% but the total increase may not exceed $15,000. Failure of an employer reasonably to enforce compliance by employees with that statute or order of the department constitutes failure by the employer to comply with that statute or order.

§102.58. Decreased compensation. If injury is caused by the failure of the employee to use safety devices which are provided in accordance with any statute or lawful order of the department and are adequately maintained, and the use of which is reasonably enforced by the employer, or if injury results from the employee's failure to obey any reasonable rule adopted and reasonably enforced by the employer for the safety of the employee and of which the employee has notice, or if injury results from the intoxication of the employee by alcohol beverages, as defined in s. 125.02(1), or use of a controlled substance, as defined in s. 961.01(4), or a controlled substance analog, as defined in s. 961.01(4m), the compensation and death benefit provided in this chapter shall be reduced 15% but the total reduction may not exceed $15,000.

OCCUPATIONAL SAFETY AND HEALTH ACT OF 1970

29 U.S.C. §§ 651-678

§ 651 (§2). Congressional Findings and Purpose

(a) The Congress finds that personal injuries and illnesses arising out of work situations impose a substantial burden upon, and are a hindrance to, interstate commerce in terms of lost production, wage loss, medical expenses, and disability compensation payments.

(b) The Congress declares it to be its purpose and policy, through the exercise of its powers to regulate commerce among the several States and with foreign nations and to provide for the general welfare, to assure so far as possible every working man and woman in the Nation safe and healthful working conditions and to preserve our human resources—

(1) by encouraging employers and employees in their efforts to reduce the number of occupational safety and health hazards at their places of employment, and to stimulate employers and employees to institute new and to perfect existing programs for providing safe and healthful working conditions;

(2) by providing that employers and employees have separate but dependent responsibilities and rights with respect to achieving safe and healthful working conditions;

(3) by authorizing the Secretary of Labor to set mandatory occupational safety and health standards applicable to businesses affecting interstate commerce, and by creating an Occupational and Health Review Commission for carrying out adjudicatory functions under the Act;

(4) by building upon advances already made through employer and employee initiative for providing safe and healthful working conditions;

(5) by providing for research in the field of occupational safety and health, including the psychological factors involved, and by developing innovative methods, techniques, and approaches for dealing with occupational safety and health problems;

(6) by exploring ways to discover latent diseases, establishing causal connections between diseases and work in environmental conditions, and conducting other research relating to health problems, in recognition of the fact that occupational health standards present problems often different from those involved in occupational safety;

(7) by providing medical criteria which will assure insofar as practicable that no employee will suffer diminished health, functional capacity, or life expectancy as a result of his work experience;

(8) by providing for training programs to increase the number and competence of personnel engaged in the field of occupational safety and health; affecting the OSH Act since its passage in 1970 through January 1, 2004.

(9) by providing for the development and promulgation of occupational safety and health standards;

(10) by providing an effective enforcement program which shall include a prohibition against giving advance notice of any inspection and sanctions for any individual violating this prohibition;

(11) by encouraging the States to assume the fullest responsibility for the administration and enforcement of their occupational safety and health laws by providing grants to the States to assist in identifying their needs and responsibilities in the area of occupational safety and health, to develop plans in accordance with the provisions of this Act, to improve the administration and enforcement of State occupational safety and health laws, and to conduct experimental and demonstration projects in connection therewith;

(12) by providing for appropriate reporting procedures with respect to occupational safety and health which procedures will help achieve the objectives of this Act and accurately describe the nature of the occupational safety and health problem;

(13) by encouraging joint labor-management efforts to reduce injuries and disease arising out of employment.

§ 652 (§3). Definitions. For the purposes of this Act—

(1) The term "Secretary" means the Secretary of Labor.

(2) The term "Commission" means the Occupational Safety and Health Review Commission established under this Act.

(3) The term "commerce" means trade, traffic, commerce, transportation, or communication among the several States, or between a State and any place outside thereof, or within the District of Columbia, or a possession of the United States (other than the Trust Territory of the Pacific Islands), or between points in the same State but through a point outside thereof.

(4) The term "person" means one or more individuals, partnerships, associations, corporations, business trusts, legal representatives, or any organized group of persons.

(5) The term "employer" means a person engaged in a business affecting commerce who has employees, but does not include the United States (not including the United States Postal Service) or any State or political subdivision of a State.

(6) The term "employee" means an employee of an employer who is employed in a business of his employer which affects commerce.

(7) The term "State" includes a State of the United States, the District of Columbia, Puerto Rico, the Virgin Islands, American Samoa, Guam, and the Trust Territory of the Pacific Islands.

(8) The term "occupational safety and health standard" means a standard which requires conditions, or the adoption or use of one or more practices, means, methods, operations, or processes, reasonably necessary or appropriate to provide safe or healthful employment and places of employment.

(9) The term "national consensus standard" means any occupational safety and health standard or modification thereof which (1), has been adopted and promulgated by a nationally recognized standards-producing organization under procedures whereby it can be determined by the Secretary that persons

interested and affected by the scope or provisions of the standard have reached substantial agreement on its adoption, (2) was formulated in a manner which afforded an opportunity for diverse views to be considered and (3) has been designated as such a standard by the Secretary, after consultation with other appropriate Federal agencies.

(10) The term "established Federal standard" means any operative occupational safety and health standard established by any agency of the United States and presently in effect, or contained in any Act of Congress in force on the date of enactment of this Act.

(11) The term "Committee" means the National Advisory Committee on Occupational Safety and Health established under this Act.

(12) The term "Director" means the Director of the National Institute for Occupational Safety and Health.

(13) The term "Institute" means the National Institute for Occupational Safety and Health established under this Act.

(14) The term "Workmen's Compensation Commission" means the National Commission on State Workmen's Compensation Laws established under this Act.

§ 653 (§4). Applicability of This Act

(a) This Act shall apply with respect to employment performed in a workplace in a State, the District of Columbia, the Commonwealth of Puerto Rico, the Virgin Islands, American Samoa, Guam, the Trust Territory of the Pacific Islands, Wake Island, Outer Continental Shelf lands defined in the Outer Continental Shelf Lands Act, Johnston Island, and the Canal Zone. The Secretary of the Interior shall, by regulation, provide for judicial enforcement of this Act by the courts established for areas in which there are no United States district courts having jurisdiction.

(b)(1) Nothing in this Act shall apply to working conditions of employees with respect to which other Federal agencies, and State agencies acting under section 274 of the Atomic Energy Act of 1954, as amended (42 U.S.C. § 2021), exercise statutory authority to prescribe or enforce standards or regulations affecting occupational safety or health.

(2) The safety and health standards promulgated under the Act of June 30, 1936, commonly known as the Walsh-Healey Act (41 U.S.C. §§ 35 et seq.), the Service Contract Act of 1965 (41 U.S.C. §§ 351 et seq), Public Law 91-54, Act of August 9, 1969 (40 U.S.C. § 333), Public Law 85-742, Act of August 23, 1958 (33 U.S.C. § 941), and the National Foundation on Arts and Humanities Act (20 U.S.C. 951 et seq.) are superseded on the effective date of corresponding standards, promulgated under this Act, which are determined by the Secretary to be more effective. Standards issued under the laws listed in this paragraph and in effect on or after the effective date of this Act shall be deemed to be

occupational safety and health standards issued under this Act, as well as under such other Acts.

(3) The Secretary shall, within three years after the effective date of this Act, report to the Congress his recommendations for legislation to avoid unnecessary duplication and to achieve coordination between this Act and other Federal laws.

(4) Nothing in this Act shall be construed to supersede or in any manner affect any workmen's compensation law or to enlarge or diminish or affect in any other manner the common law or statutory rights, duties, or liabilities of employers and employees under any law with respect to injuries, diseases, or death of employees arising out of, or in the course of, employment.

§ 654 (§5). Duties

(a) Each employer—

(1) shall furnish to each of his employees employment and a place of employment which are free from recognized hazards that are causing or are likely to cause death or serious physical harm to his employees;

(2) shall comply with occupational safety and health standards promulgated under this Act.

(b) Each employee shall comply with occupational safety and health standards and all rules, regulations, and orders issued pursuant to this Act which are applicable to his own actions and conduct.

§ 655 (§6). Occupational Safety and Health Standards

(a) Without regard to chapter 5 of title 5 or to the other subsections of this section, the Secretary shall, as soon as practicable during the period beginning with the effective date of this Act and ending two years after such date, by rule promulgate as an occupational safety or health standard any national consensus standard, and any established Federal standard, unless he determines that the promulgation of such a standard would not result in improved safety or health for specifically designated employees. In the event of conflict among any such standards, the Secretary shall promulgate the standard which assures the greatest protection of the safety or health of the affected employees.

(b) The Secretary may by rule promulgate, modify, or revoke any occupational safety or health standard in the following manner:

(1) Whenever the Secretary, upon the basis of information submitted to him in writing by an interested person, a representative of any organization of employers or employees, a nationally recognized standards-producing organization, the Secretary of Health and Human Services, the National Institute for Occupational Safety and Health, or a State or political subdivision, or on the basis of information developed

by the Secretary or otherwise available to him, determines that a rule should be promulgated in order to serve the objectives of this Act, the Secretary may request the recommendations of an advisory committee appointed under section 7 of this Act [29 USCS § 656]. The Secretary shall provide such an advisory committee with any proposals of his own or of the Secretary of Health and Human Services, together with all pertinent factual information developed by the Secretary or the Secretary of Health and Human Services, or otherwise available, including the results of research, demonstrations, and experiments. An advisory committee shall submit to the Secretary its recommendations regarding the rule to be promulgated within ninety days from the date of its appointment or within such longer or shorter period as may be prescribed by the Secretary, but in no event for a period which is longer than two hundred and seventy days.

(2) The Secretary shall publish a proposed rule promulgating, modifying, or revoking an occupational safety or health standard in the Federal Register and shall afford interested persons a period of thirty days after publication to submit written data or comments. Where an advisory committee is appointed and the Secretary determines that a rule should be issued, he shall publish the proposed rule within sixty days after the submission of the advisory committee's recommendations or the expiration of the period prescribed by the Secretary for such submission.

(3) On or before the last day of the period provided for the submission of written data or comments under paragraph (2), any interested person may file with the Secretary written objections to the proposed rule, stating the grounds therefor and requesting a public hearing on such objections. Within thirty days after the last day for filing such objections, the Secretary shall publish in the Federal Register a notice specifying the occupational safety or health standard to which objections have been filed and a hearing requested, and specifying a time and place for such hearing.

(4) Within sixty days after the expiration of the period provided for the submission of written data or comments under paragraph (2), or within sixty days after the completion of any hearing held under paragraph (3), the Secretary shall issue a rule promulgating, modifying, or revoking an occupational safety or health standard or make a determination that a rule should not be issued. Such a rule may contain a provision delaying its effective date for such period (not in excess of ninety days) as the Secretary determines may be necessary to insure that affected employers and employees will be informed of the existence of the standard and of its terms and that employers affected are given an opportunity to familiarize themselves and their employees with the existence of the requirements of the standard.

(5) The Secretary, in promulgating standards dealing with toxic materials or harmful physical agents under this subsection, shall set the standard which most adequately assures, to the extent feasible, on the basis of the best available evidence, that no employee will suffer material impairment of health or functional capacity even if such employee has regular exposure to the hazard dealt with by such standard for the period of his working life. Development of standards under this subsection shall be based upon research, demonstrations, experiments, and such other information as may be appropriate. In addition to the attainment of the highest degree of health and safety protection for the employee, other considerations shall be the latest available scientific data in the field, the feasibility of the standards, and experience gained under this and other health and safety laws. Whenever practicable, the standard promulgated shall be expressed in terms of objective criteria and of the performance desired.

(6)(A) Any employer may apply to the Secretary for a temporary order granting a variance from a standard or any provision thereof promulgated under this section. Such temporary order shall be granted only if the employer files an application which meets the requirements of clause (B) and establishes that (i) he is unable to comply with a standard by its effective date because of unavailability of professional or technical personnel or of materials and equipment needed to come into compliance with the standard or because necessary construction or alteration of facilities cannot be completed by the effective date, (ii) he is taking all available steps to safeguard his employees against the hazards covered by the standard, and (iii) he has an effective program for coming into compliance with the standard as quickly as practicable.

Any temporary order issued under this paragraph shall prescribe the practices, means, methods, operations, and processes which the employer must adopt and use while the order is in effect and state in detail his program for coming into compliance with the standard. Such a temporary order may be granted only after notice to employees and an opportunity for a hearing: Provided, That the Secretary may issue one interim order to be effective until a decision is made on the basis of the hearing. No temporary order may be in effect for longer than the period needed by the employer to achieve compliance with the standard or one year, whichever is shorter, except that such an order may be renewed not more than twice (I) so long as the requirements of this paragraph are met and (II) if an application for renewal is filed at least 90 days prior to the expiration date of the order. No interim renewal of an order may remain in effect for longer than 180 days.

(B) An application for a temporary order under this paragraph (6) shall contain:

(i) a specification of the standard or portion thereof from which the employer seeks a variance,

(ii) a representation by the employer, supported by representations from qualified persons having firsthand knowledge of the facts represented, that he is unable to comply with the standard or portion thereof and a detailed statement of the reasons therefor,

(iii) a statement of the steps he has taken and will take (with specific dates) to protect employees against the hazard covered by the standard,

(iv) a statement of when he expects to be able to comply with the standard and what steps he has taken and what steps he will take (with dates specified) to come into compliance with the standard, and

(v) a certification that he has informed his employees of the application by giving a copy thereof to their authorized representative, posting a statement giving a summary of the application and specifying where a copy may be examined at the place or places where notices to employees are normally posted, and by other appropriate means.

A description of how employees have been informed shall be contained in the certification. The information to employees shall also inform them of their right to petition the Secretary for a hearing.

(C) The Secretary is authorized to grant a variance from any standard or portion thereof whenever he determines, or the Secretary of Health and Human Services certifies, that such variance is necessary to permit an employer to participate in an experiment approved by him or the Secretary of Health and Human Services designed to demonstrate or validate new and improved techniques to safeguard the health or safety of workers.

(7) Any standard promulgated under this subsection shall prescribe the use of labels or other appropriate forms of warning as are necessary to insure that employees are apprised of all hazards to which they are exposed, relevant symptoms and appropriate emergency treatment, and proper conditions and precautions of safe use or exposure. Where appropriate, such standard shall also prescribe suitable protective equipment and control or technological procedures to be used in connection with such hazards and shall provide for monitoring or measuring employee exposure at such locations and intervals, and in such manner as may be necessary for the protection of employees. In

addition, where appropriate, any such standard shall prescribe the type and frequency of medical examinations or other tests which shall be made available, by the employer or at his cost, to employees exposed to such hazards in order to most effectively determine whether the health of such employees is adversely affected by such exposure. In the event such medical examinations are in the nature of research, as determined by the Secretary of Health and Human Services, such examinations may be furnished at the expense of the Secretary of Health and Human Services. The results of such examinations or tests shall be furnished only to the Secretary or the Secretary of Health and Human Services, and, at the request of the employee, to his physician. The Secretary, in consultation with the Secretary of Health and Human Services, may by rule promulgated pursuant to section 553 of title 5, United States Code [5 USCS § 533], make appropriate modifications in the foregoing requirements relating to the use of labels or other forms of warning, monitoring or measuring, and medical examinations, as may be warranted by experience, information, or medical or technological developments acquired subsequent to the promulgation of the relevant standard.

(8) Whenever a rule promulgated by the Secretary differs substantially from an existing national consensus standard, the Secretary shall, at the same time, publish in the Federal Register a statement of the reasons why the rule as adopted will better effectuate the purposes of this Act than the national consensus standard.

(c)(1) The Secretary shall provide, without regard to the requirements of chapter 5, title 5 for an emergency temporary standard to take immediate effect upon publication in the Federal Register if he determines (A) that employees are exposed to grave danger from exposure to substances or agents determined to be toxic or physically harmful or from new hazards, and (B) that such emergency standard is necessary to protect employees from such danger.

(2) Such standard shall be effective until superseded by a standard promulgated in accordance with the procedures prescribed in paragraph (3) of this subsection.

(3) Upon publication of such standard in the Federal Register the Secretary shall commence a proceeding in accordance with section 6(b) of this Act [subsec. (b) of this section], and the standard as published shall also serve as a proposed rule for the proceeding. The Secretary shall promulgate a standard under this paragraph no later than six months after publication of the emergency standard as provided in paragraph (2) of this subsection.

(d) Any affected employer may apply to the Secretary for a rule or order for a variance from a standard promulgated under this section. Affected employees shall be given notice of each such application and an opportunity to participate in a hearing. The Secretary shall issue such rule or order if he determines on the record, after opportunity for an inspection where appropriate and a hearing, that the proponent of the variance has demonstrated by a preponderance of the evidence that the conditions, practices, means, methods, operations, or processes used or proposed to be used by an employer will provide employment and places of employment to his employees which are as safe and healthful as those which would prevail if he complied with the standard. The rule or order so issued shall prescribe the conditions the employer must maintain, and the practices, means, methods, operations, and processes which he must adopt and utilize to the extent they differ from the standard in question. Such a rule or order may be modified or revoked upon application by an employer, employees, or by the Secretary on his own motion, in the manner prescribed for its issuance under this subsection at any time after six months from its issuance.

(e) Whenever the Secretary promulgates any standard, makes any rule, order, or decision, grants any exemption or extension of time, or compromises, mitigates, or settles any penalty assessed under this Act he shall include a statement of the reasons for such action, which shall be published in the Federal Register.

(f) Any person who may be adversely affected by a standard issued under this section may at any time prior to the sixtieth day after such standard is promulgated file a petition challenging the validity of such standard with the United States court of appeals for the circuit wherein such person resides or has his principal place of business, for a judicial review of such standard. A copy of the petition shall be forthwith transmitted by the clerk of the court to the Secretary. The filing of such petition shall not, unless otherwise ordered by the court, operate as a stay of the standard. The determinations of the Secretary shall be conclusive if supported by substantial evidence in the record considered as a whole.

(g) In determining the priority for establishing standards under this section, the Secretary shall give due regard to the urgency of the need for mandatory safety and health standards for particular industries, trades, crafts, occupations, businesses, workplaces or work environments. The Secretary shall also give due regard to the recommendations of the Secretary of Health and Human Services regarding the need for mandatory standards in determining the priority for establishing such standards.

§ 656 (§7). Advisory Committees; Administration

(a)(1) There is hereby established a National Advisory Committee on Occupational Safety and Health consisting of twelve members appointed by the Secretary, four of whom are to be designated by the Secretary of Health and Human Services, without regard to the provisions of title 5 governing appointments in the competitive service, and composed of representatives of management, labor, occupational safety and occupational health professions, and of the public. The Secretary shall designate one of the public members as Chairman. The members shall be selected upon the basis of their experience and competence in the field of occupational safety and health.

(2) The Committee shall advise, consult with, and make recommendations to the Secretary and the Secretary of Health and Human Services on matters relating to the administration of the Act. The Committee shall hold no fewer than two meetings during each calendar year. All meetings of the Committee shall be open to the public and a transcript shall be kept and made available for public inspection.

(3) The members of the Committee shall be compensated in accordance with the provisions of section 3109 of title 5.

(4) The Secretary shall furnish to the Committee an executive secretary and such secretarial, clerical, and other services as are deemed necessary to the conduct of its business.

(b) An advisory committee may be appointed by the Secretary to assist him in his standard-setting functions under section 6 of this Act. Each such committee shall consist of not more than fifteen members and shall include as a member one or more designees of the Secretary of Health and Human Services, and shall include among its members an equal number of persons qualified by experience and affiliation to present the viewpoint of the employers involved, and of persons similarly qualified to present the viewpoint of the workers involved, as well as one or more representatives of health and safety agencies of the States. An advisory committee may also include such other persons as the Secretary may appoint who are qualified by knowledge and experience to make a useful contribution to the work of such committee, including one or more representatives of professional organizations of technicians or professionals specializing in occupational safety or health, and one or more representatives of nationally recognized standards-producing organizations, but the number of persons so appointed to any such advisory committee shall not exceed the number appointed to such committee as representatives of Federal and State agencies. Persons appointed to advisory committees from private life shall be compensated in the same manner as consultants or experts under section 3109 of title 5. The Secretary shall pay to any State which is the employer of a member of such a committee who is a representative of the health or safety agency of that State, reimbursement sufficient to cover the actual cost to the State resulting from such representative's membership on such committee. Any meeting of such committee shall be open to the public and an accurate record shall be kept and made available to the public. No member of such committee (other than representatives of employers and employees) shall have an economic interest in any proposed rule.

(c) In carrying out his responsibilities under this Act, the Secretary is authorized to—

(1) use, with the consent of any Federal agency, the services, facilities, and personnel of such agency, with or without reimbursement, and with the consent of any State or political subdivision

thereof, accept and use the services, facilities, and personnel of any agency of such State or subdivision with reimbursement; and

(2) employ experts and consultants or organizations thereof as authorized by section 3109 of title 5 except that contracts for such employment may be renewed annually; compensate individuals so employed at rates not in excess of the rate specified at the time of service for grade GS-18 under section 5332 of title 5, including traveltime, and allow them while away from their homes or regular places of business, travel expenses (including per diem in lieu of subsistence) as authorized by section 5703 of title 5 for persons in the Government service employed intermittently, while so employed.

§ 657 (§8). Inspections, Investigations, and Recordkeeping

(a) In order to carry out the purposes of this Act, the Secretary, upon presenting appropriate credentials to the owner, operator, or agent in charge, is authorized—

(1) to enter without delay and at reasonable times any factory, plant, establishment, construction site, or other area, workplace or environment where work is performed by an employee of an employer; and

(2) to inspect and investigate during regular working hours and at other reasonable times, and within reasonable limits and in a reasonable manner, any such place of employment and all pertinent conditions, structures, machines, apparatus, devices, equipment, and materials therein, and to question privately any such employer, owner, operator, agent or employee.

(b) In making his inspections and investigations under this Act the Secretary may require the attendance and testimony of witnesses and the production of evidence under oath. Witnesses shall be paid the same fees and mileage that are paid witnesses in the courts of the United States. In case of a contumacy, failure, or refusal of any person to obey such an order, any district court of the United States or the United States courts of any territory or possession, within the jurisdiction of which such person is found, or resides or transacts business, upon the application by the Secretary, shall have jurisdiction to issue to such person an order requiring such person to appear to produce evidence if, as, and when so ordered, and to give testimony relating to the matter under investigation or in question, and any failure to obey such order of the court may be punished by said court as a contempt thereof.

(c)(1) Each employer shall make, keep and preserve, and make available to the Secretary or the Secretary of Health and Human Services, such records regarding his activities relating to this Act as the Secretary, in cooperation with the Secretary of Health and Human Services, may prescribe by regulation as necessary or appropriate for the enforcement of this Act or for developing information regarding the causes and prevention of occupational accidents and illnesses. In order to carry out the provisions of this paragraph such regulations may include provisions requiring employers to conduct periodic inspections. The Secretary shall also issue regulations requiring that employers, through posting of notices or other appropriate means, keep their employees informed of their protections and obligations under this Act, including the provisions of applicable standards.

(2) The Secretary, in cooperation with the Secretary of Health and Human Services, shall prescribe regulations requiring employers to maintain accurate records of, and to make periodic reports on, work-related deaths, injuries and illnesses other than minor injuries requiring only first aid treatment and which do not involve medical treatment, loss of consciousness, restriction of work or motion, or transfer to another job.

(3) The Secretary, in cooperation with the Secretary of Health and Human Services, shall issue regulations requiring employers to maintain accurate records of employee exposures to potentially toxic materials or harmful physical agents which are required to be monitored or measured under section 6. Such regulations shall provide employees or their representatives with an opportunity to observe such monitoring or measuring, and to have access to the records thereof. Such regulations shall also make appropriate provision for each employee or former employee to have access to such records as will indicate his own exposure to toxic materials or harmful physical agents. Each employer shall promptly notify any employee who has been or is being exposed to toxic materials or harmful physical agents in concentrations or at levels which exceed those prescribed by an applicable occupational safety and health standard promulgated under section 6, and shall inform any employee who is being thus exposed of the corrective action being taken.

(d) Any information obtained by the Secretary, the Secretary of Health and Human Services, or a State agency under this chapter shall be obtained with a minimum burden upon employers, especially those operating small businesses. Unnecessary duplication of efforts in obtaining information shall be reduced to the maximum extent feasible.

(e) Subject to regulations issued by the Secretary, a representative of the employer and a representative authorized by his employees shall be given an opportunity to accompany the Secretary or his authorized representative during the physical inspection of any workplace under subsection (a) for the purpose of aiding such inspection. Where there is no authorized employee representative, the Secretary or his authorized representative shall consult with a reasonable number of employees concerning matters of health and safety in the workplace.

(f)(1) Any employees or representative of employees who believe that a violation of a safety or health standard exists that threatens physical harm, or that an imminent danger exists, may request an inspection by giving notice to the Secretary or his authorized representative of such violation or danger. Any such notice shall be reduced to writing, shall set forth with reasonable particularity the grounds for the notice, and shall be signed by the employees or representative of employees, and a copy shall be provided the employer or his agent no later than at the time of inspection, except that, upon the request of the person giving such notice, his name and the names of individual employees referred to therein shall not appear in such copy or on any record published, released, or made available pursuant to subsection (g) of this section. If upon receipt of such notification the Secretary determines there are reasonable grounds to believe that such violation or danger exists, he shall make a special inspection in accordance with the provisions of this section as soon as practicable, to determine if such violation or danger exists. If the Secretary determines there are no reasonable grounds to believe that a violation or danger exists he shall notify the employees or representative of the employees in writing of such determination.

(2) Prior to or during any inspection of a workplace, any employees or representative of employees employed in such workplace may notify the Secretary or any representative of the Secretary responsible for conducting the inspection, in writing, of any violation of this Act which they have reason to believe exists in such workplace. The Secretary shall, by regulation, establish procedures for informal review of any refusal by a representative of the Secretary to issue a citation with respect to any such alleged violation and shall furnish the employees or representative of employees requesting such review a written statement of the reasons for the Secretary's final disposition of the case.

(g)(1) The Secretary and Secretary of Health and Human Services are authorized to compile, analyze, and publish, either in summary or detailed form, all reports or information obtained under this section.

(2) The Secretary and the Secretary of Health and Human Services shall each prescribe such rules and regulations as he may deem necessary to carry out their responsibilities under this Act, including rules and regulations dealing with the inspection of an employer's establishment.

(h) The Secretary shall not use the results of enforcement activities, such as the number of citations issued or penalties assessed, to evaluate employees directly involved in enforcement activities under this Act or to impose quotas or goals with regard to the results of such activities.

§ 658 (§9). Citations

(a) If, upon inspection or investigation, the Secretary or his authorized representative believes that an employer has violated a requirement of section 5 of this Act, of any standard, rule or order promulgated pursuant to section 6 of this Act, or of any regulations prescribed pursuant to this Act, he shall with reasonable promptness issue a citation to the employer. Each citation shall be in writing and shall describe with particularity the nature of the violation, including a reference to the provision of the Act, standard, rule, regulation, or order alleged to have been violated. In addition, the citation shall fix a reasonable time for the abatement of the violation. The Secretary may prescribe procedures for the issuance of a notice in lieu of a citation with respect to de minimis violations which have no direct or immediate relationship to safety or health.

(b) Each citation issued under this section, or a copy or copies thereof, shall be prominently posted, as prescribed in regulations issued by the Secretary, at or near such place a violation referred to in the citation occurred.

(c) No citation may be issued under this section after the expiration of six months following the occurrence of any violation.

§ 659 (§10). Procedure for Enforcement

(a) If, after an inspection or investigation, the Secretary issues a citation under section 9(a), he shall, within a reasonable time after the termination of such inspection or investigation, notify the employer by certified mail of the penalty, if any, proposed to be assessed under section 17 and that the employer has fifteen working days within which to notify the Secretary that he wishes to contest the citation or proposed assessment of penalty. If, within fifteen working days from the receipt of the notice issued by the Secretary the employer fails to notify the Secretary that he intends to contest the citation or proposed assessment of penalty, and no notice is filed by any employee or representative of employees under subsection (c) within such time, the citation and the assessment, as proposed, shall be deemed a final order of the Commission and not subject to review by any court or agency.

(b) If the Secretary has reason to believe that an employer has failed to correct a violation for which a citation has been issued within the period permitted for its correction (which period shall not begin to run until the entry of a final order by the Commission in the case of any review proceedings under this section initiated by the employer in good faith and not solely for delay or avoidance of penalties), the Secretary shall notify the employer by certified mail of such failure and of the penalty proposed to be assessed under section 17 by reason of such failure, and that the employer has fifteen working days within which to notify the Secretary that he wishes to contest the Secretary's notification or the proposed assessment of penalty. If, within fifteen working days from the receipt of notification issued by the Secretary, the employer fails to notify the Secretary that he intends to contest the notification or proposed assessment of penalty, the notification and assessment, as proposed, shall be deemed a final order of the Commission and not subject to review by any court or agency.

(c) If an employer notifies the Secretary that he intends to contest a citation issued under section 9(a) or notification issued under subsection (a) or (b) of this section, or if, within fifteen working days of the issuance of a citation under section 9(a), any employee or representative of employees files a notice with the Secretary alleging that the period of time fixed in the citation for the abatement of the violation is unreasonable, the Secretary shall immediately advise the Commission of such notification, and the Commission shall afford an opportunity for a hearing (in accordance with section 554 of title 5, but without regard to subsection (a)(3) of such section). The Commission shall thereafter issue an order, based on findings of fact, affirming, modifying, or vacating the Secretary's citation or proposed penalty, or directing other appropriate relief, and such order shall become final thirty days after its issuance. Upon a showing by an employer of a good faith effort to comply with the abatement requirements of a citation, and that abatement has not been completed because of factors beyond his reasonable control, the Secretary, after an opportunity for a hearing as provided in this subsection, shall issue an order affirming or modifying the abatement requirements in such citation. The rules of procedure prescribed by the Commission shall provide affected employees or representatives of affected employees an opportunity to participate as parties to hearings under this subsection.

§ 660 (§11). Judicial Review

(a) Any person adversely affected or aggrieved by an order of the Commission issued under subsection (c) of section 10 may obtain a review of such order in any United States court of appeals for the circuit in which the violation is alleged to have occurred or where the employer has its principal office, or in the Court of Appeals for the District of Columbia Circuit, by filing in such court within sixty days following the issuance of such order a written petition praying that the order be modified or set aside. A copy of such petition shall be forthwith transmitted by the clerk of the court to the Commission and to the other parties, and thereupon the Commission shall file in the court the record in the proceeding as provided in section 2112 of title 28. Upon such filing, the court shall have jurisdiction of the proceeding and of the question determined therein, and shall have power to grant such temporary relief or restraining order as it deems just and proper, and to make and enter upon the pleadings, testimony, and proceedings set forth in such record a decree affirming, modifying, or setting aside in whole or in part, the order of the Commission and enforcing the same to the extent that such order is affirmed or modified. The commencement of proceedings under this subsection shall not, unless ordered by the court, operate as a stay of the order of the Commission. No objection that has not been urged before the Commission shall be considered by the court, unless the failure or neglect to urge such objection shall be excused because of extraordinary circumstances. The findings of the Commission with respect to questions of fact, if supported by substantial evidence on the record considered as a whole, shall be conclusive. If any party shall apply to the court for leave to adduce additional evidence and shall show to the satisfaction of the court that such additional evidence is material and that there were reasonable grounds for the failure to adduce such evidence in the hearing before the Commission, the court may order such additional evidence to be taken before the Commission and to be made a part of the record. The Commission may modify its findings as to the facts, or make new findings, by reason of additional evidence so taken and filed, and it shall file such modified or new findings, which findings with respect to questions of fact, if supported by substantial evidence on the record considered as a whole, shall be conclusive, and its recommendations, if any, for the modification or setting aside of its original order. Upon the filing of the record with it, the jurisdiction of the court shall be exclusive and its judgment and decree shall be final, except that the same shall be subject to review by the Supreme Court of the United States, as provided in section 1254 of title 28.

(b) The Secretary may also obtain review or enforcement of any final order of the Commission by filing a petition for such relief in the United States court of appeals for the circuit in which the alleged violation occurred or in which the employer has its principal office, and the provisions of subsection (a) shall govern such proceedings to the extent applicable. If no petition for review, as provided in subsection (a), is filed within sixty days after service of the Commission's order, the Commission's findings of fact and order shall be conclusive in connection with any petition for enforcement which is filed by the Secretary after the expiration of such sixty-day period. In any such case, as well as in the case of a noncontested citation or notification by the Secretary which has become a final order of the Commission under subsection (a) or (b) of section 10 of this Act, the clerk of the court, unless otherwise ordered by the court, shall forthwith enter a decree enforcing the order and shall transmit a copy of such decree to the Secretary and the employer named in the petition. In any contempt proceeding brought to enforce a decree of a court of appeals entered pursuant to this subsection or subsection (a), the court of appeals may assess the penalties provided in section 17, in addition to invoking any other available remedies.

(c)(1) No person shall discharge or in any manner discriminate against any employee because such employee has filed any complaint or instituted or caused to be instituted any proceeding under or related to this Act or has testified or is about to testify in any such proceeding or because of the exercise by such employee on behalf of himself or others of any right afforded by this Act.

(2) Any employee who believes that he has been discharged or otherwise discriminated against by any person in violation of this subsection may, within thirty days after such violation occurs, file a complaint with the Secretary alleging such discrimination. Upon receipt of such complaint, the Secretary shall cause such investigation to be made as he deems appropriate. If upon such investigation, the Secretary determines that the provisions of this subsection have been violated, he shall bring an action in any appropriate United States district court against such person. In any such action the United States district courts shall have jurisdiction, for cause shown to restrain violations of paragraph (1) of this subsection and order all appropriate relief including rehiring or reinstatement of the employee to his former position with back pay.

(3) Within 90 days of the receipt of a complaint filed under this subsection the Secretary shall notify the complainant of his determination under paragraph 2 of this subsection.

§ 661 (§12). The Occupational Safety and Health Review Commission

(a) The Occupational Safety and Health Review Commission is hereby established. The Commission shall be composed of three members who shall be appointed by the President, by and with the advice and consent of the Senate, from among persons who by reason of training, education, or experience are qualified to carry out the functions of the Commission under this Act. The President shall designate one of the members of the Commission to serve as Chairman.

(b) The terms of members of the Commission shall be six years except that (1) the members of the Commission first taking office shall serve, as designated by the President at the time of appointment, one for a term of two years, one for a term of four years, and one for a term of six years, and (2) a vacancy caused by the death, resignation, or removal of a member prior to the expiration of the term for which he was appointed shall be filled only for the remainder of such unexpired term. A member of the Commission may be removed by the President for inefficiency, neglect of duty, or malfeasance in office.

(c) Omitted.

(d) The principal office of the Commission shall be in the District of Columbia. Whenever the Commission deems that the convenience of the public or of the parties may be promoted, or delay or expense may be minimized, it may hold hearings or conduct other proceedings at any other place.

(e) The Chairman shall be responsible on behalf of the Commission for the administrative operations of the Commission and shall appoint such administrative law judges and other employees as he deems necessary to assist in the performance of the Commission's functions and to fix their compensation in accordance with the provisions of chapter 51 and subchapter III of chapter 53 of title 5 relating to classification and General Schedule pay rates: Provided, That assignment, removal and compensation of administrative law judges shall be in accordance with sections 3105, 3344, 5372, and 7521 of title 5.

(f) For the purpose of carrying out its functions under this Act, two members of the Commission shall constitute a quorum and official action can be taken only on the affirmative vote of at least two members.

(g) Every official act of the Commission shall be entered of record, and its hearings and records shall be open to the public. The Commission is authorized to make such rules as are necessary for the orderly transaction of its proceedings. Unless the Commission has adopted a different rule, its proceedings shall be in accordance with the Federal Rules of Civil Procedure.

(h) The Commission may order testimony to be taken by deposition in any proceedings pending before it at any state of such proceeding. Any person may be compelled to appear and depose, and to produce books, papers, or documents, in the same manner as witnesses may be compelled to appear and testify and produce like documentary evidence before the Commission. Witnesses whose depositions are taken under this subsection, and the persons taking such depositions, shall be entitled to the same fees as are paid for like services in the courts of the United States.

(i) For the purpose of any proceeding before the Commission, the provisions of section 11 of the National Labor Relations Act (29 U.S.C. §161) are hereby made applicable to the jurisdiction and powers of the Commission.

(j) An administrative law judge appointed by the Commission shall hear, and make a determination upon, any proceeding instituted before the Commission and any motion in connection therewith, assigned to such administrative law judge by the Chairman of the Commission, and shall make a report of any such determination which constitutes his final disposition of the proceedings. The report of the administrative law judge shall become the final order of the Commission within thirty days after such report by the administrative law judge, unless within such period any Commission member has directed that such report shall be reviewed by the Commission.

(k) Except as otherwise provided in this Act the administrative law judges shall be subject to the laws governing employees in the classified civil service, except that appointments shall be made without regard to section 5108 of title 5. Each administrative law judge shall receive compensation at a rate not less than that prescribed for GS-16 under section 5332 of title 5.

§ 662 (§13). Procedures to Counteract Imminent Danger

(a) The United States district courts shall have jurisdiction, upon petition of the Secretary, to restrain any conditions or practices in any place of employment which are such that a danger exists which could reasonably be expected to cause death or serious physical harm immediately or before the imminence of such danger can be eliminated through the enforcement procedures otherwise provided by this Act. Any order issued under this section may require such steps to be taken as may be necessary to avoid, correct, or remove such imminent danger and prohibit the employment or presence of any individual in locations or under conditions where such imminent danger exists, except individuals whose presence is necessary to avoid, correct, or remove such imminent danger or to maintain the capacity of a continuous process operation to resume normal operations without a complete cessation of operations, or where a cessation of operations is necessary, to permit such to be accomplished in a safe and orderly manner.

(b) Upon the filing of any such petition the district court shall have jurisdiction to grant such injunctive relief or temporary restraining order pending the outcome of an enforcement proceeding pursuant to this Act. The proceeding shall be as provided by Rule 65 of the Federal Rules, Civil Procedure, except that no temporary restraining order issued without notice shall be effective for a period longer than five days.

(c) Whenever and as soon as an inspector concludes that conditions or practices described in subsection (a) exist in any place of employment, he shall inform the affected employees and employers of the danger and that he is recommending to the Secretary that relief be sought.

(d) If the Secretary arbitrarily or capriciously fails to seek relief under this section, any employee who may be injured by reason of such failure, or the representative of such employees, might bring an action against the Secretary in the United States district court for the district in which the imminent danger is alleged to exist or the employer has its principal office, or for the District of Columbia, for a writ of mandamus to compel the Secretary to seek such an order and for such further relief as may be appropriate.

§ 663 (§14). Representation in Civil Litigation.

Except as provided in section 518(a) of title 28 relating to litigation before the Supreme Court, the Solicitor of Labor may appear for and represent the Secretary in any civil litigation brought under this Act but all such litigation shall be subject to the direction and control of the Attorney General.

§ 664 (§15). Confidentiality of Trade Secrets.

All information reported to or otherwise obtained by the Secretary or his representative in connection with any inspection or proceeding under this Act which contains or which might reveal a trade secret referred to in section 1905 of title 18 of the United States Code shall be considered confidential for the purpose of that section, except that such information may be disclosed to other officers or employees concerned with carrying out this Act or when relevant in any proceeding under this Act. In any such proceeding the Secretary, the Commission, or the court shall issue such orders as may be appropriate to protect the confidentiality of trade secrets.

§ 665 (§16). Variations, Tolerances, and Exemptions

The Secretary, on the record, after notice and opportunity for a hearing may provide such reasonable limitations and may make such rules and regulations allowing reasonable variations, tolerances, and exemptions to and from any or all provisions of this Act as he may find necessary and proper to avoid serious impairment of the national defense. Such action shall not be in effect for more than six months without notification to affected employees and an opportunity being afforded for a hearing.

§ 666 (§17). Penalties

(a) Any employer who willfully or repeatedly violates the requirements of section 5 of this Act, any standard, rule, or order promulgated pursuant to section 6 of this Act, or regulations prescribed pursuant to this Act may be assessed a civil penalty of not more than $70,000 for each violation, but not less than $5,000 for each willful violation.

(b) Any employer who has received a citation for a serious violation of the requirements of section 5 of this Act, of any standard, rule, or order promulgated pursuant to section 6 of this Act, or of any regulations prescribed pursuant to this Act, shall be assessed a civil penalty of up to $7,000 for each such violation.

(c) Any employer who has received a citation for a violation of the requirements of section 5 of this Act, of any standard, rule, or order promulgated pursuant to section 6 of this Act, or of regulations prescribed pursuant to this Act, and such violation is specifically determined not to be of a serious nature, may be assessed a civil penalty up to $7,000 for each such violation.

(d) Any employer who fails to correct a violation for which a citation has been issued under section 9(a) within the period permitted for its correction (which period shall not begin to run until the date of the final order of the Commission in the case of any review proceeding under section 10 initiated by the employer in good faith and not solely for delay or avoidance of penalties), may be assessed a civil penalty of not more than $7,000 for each day during which such failure or violation continues.

(e) Any employer who willfully violates any standard, rule, or order promulgated pursuant to section 6 of this Act, or of any regulations prescribed pursuant to this Act, and that violation caused death to any employee, shall, upon conviction, be punished by a fine of not more than $10,000 or by imprisonment for not more than six months, or by both; except that if the conviction is for a violation committed after a first conviction of such person, punishment shall be by a fine of not more than $20,000 or by imprisonment for not more than one year, or by both.

(f) Any person who gives advance notice of any inspection to be conducted under this Act without authority from the Secretary or his designees, shall, upon conviction, be punished by a fine of not more than $1,000 or by imprisonment for not more than six months, or by both.

(g) Whoever knowingly makes any false statement, representation, or certification in any application, record, report, plan, or other document filed or required to be maintained pursuant to this Act shall, upon conviction, be punished by a fine of not more than $10,000, or by imprisonment for not more than six months, or by both.

(h) Omitted

(i) Any employer who violates any of the posting requirements, as prescribed under the provisions of this Act shall be assessed a civil penalty of up to $7,000 for each violation.

(j) The Commission shall have authority to assess all civil penalties provided in this section, giving due consideration to the appropriateness of the penalty with respect to the size of the business of the employer being charged, the gravity of the violation, the good faith of the employer, and the history of previous violations.

(k) For purposes of this section, a serious violation shall be deemed to exist in a place of employment if there is a substantial probability that death or serious physical harm could result from a condition which exists, or from one or more practices, means, methods, operations, or processes which have been adopted or are in use, in such place of employment unless the employer did not, and could not with the exercise of reasonable diligence, know of the presence of the violation.

(l) Civil penalties owed under this Act shall be paid to the Secretary for deposit into the Treasury of the United States and shall accrue to the United States and may be recovered in a civil action in the name of the United States brought in the United States district court for the district where the violation is alleged to have occurred or where the employer has its principal office.

§ 667 (§18). State Jurisdiction and State Plans

(a) Nothing in this Act shall prevent any State agency or court from asserting jurisdiction under State law over any occupational safety or health issue with respect to which no standard is in effect under section 6.

(b) Any State which, at any time, desires to assume responsibility for development and enforcement therein of occupational safety and health standards relating to any occupational safety or health issue with respect to which a Federal standard has been promulgated under section 6 shall submit a State plan for the development of such standards and their enforcement.

(c) The Secretary shall approve the plan submitted by a State under subsection (b), or any modification thereof, if such plan in his judgment—

(1) designates a State agency or agencies as the agency or agencies responsible for administering the plan throughout the State,

(2) provides for the development and enforcement of safety and health standards relating to one or more safety or health issues, which standards (and the enforcement of which standards) are or will be at least as effective in providing safe and healthful employment and places of employment as the standards promulgated under section 6 which relate to the same issues, and which standards, when applicable to products which are distributed or used in interstate commerce, are required by compelling local conditions and do not unduly burden interstate commerce,

(3) provides for a right of entry and inspection of all workplaces subject to the Act which is at least as effective as that provided in section 8, and includes a prohibition on advance notice of inspections,

(4) contains satisfactory assurances that such agency or agencies have or will have the legal authority and qualified personnel necessary for the enforcement of such standards,

(5) gives satisfactory assurances that such State will devote adequate funds to the administration and enforcement of such standards,

(6) contains satisfactory assurances that such State will, to the extent permitted by its law, establish and maintain an effective and comprehensive occupational safety and health program applicable to all employees of public agencies of the State and its political subdivisions, which program is as effective as the standards contained in an approved plan,

(7) requires employers in the State to make reports to the Secretary in the same manner and to the same extent as if the plan were not in effect, and

(8) provides that the State agency will make such reports to the Secretary in such form and containing such information, as the Secretary shall from time to time require.

(d) If the Secretary rejects a plan submitted under subsection (b), he shall afford the State submitting the plan due notice and opportunity for a hearing before so doing.

(e) After the Secretary approves a State plan submitted under subsection (b), he may, but shall not be required to, exercise his authority under sections 8, 9, 10, 13 and 17 with respect to comparable standards promulgated under section 6, for the period specified in the next sentence. The Secretary may exercise the authority referred to above until he determines, on the basis of actual operations under the State plan, that the criteria set forth in subsection (c) are being applied, but he shall not make such determination for at least three years after the plan's approval under subsection (c). Upon making the determination referred to in the preceding sentence, the provisions of sections 5(a)(2), 8 (except for the purpose of carrying out subsection (f) of this section), 9, 10, 13, and 17, and standards promulgated under section 6 of this Act, shall not apply with respect to any occupational safety or health issues covered under the plan, but the Secretary may retain jurisdiction under the above provisions in any proceeding commenced under section 9 or 10 before the date of determination.

(f) The Secretary shall, on the basis of reports submitted by the State agency and his own inspections make a continuing evaluation of the manner in which each State having a plan approved under this section is carrying out such plan. Whenever the Secretary finds, after affording due notice and opportunity for a hearing, that in the administration of the State plan there is a failure to comply substantially with any provision of the State plan (or any assurance contained therein), he shall notify the State agency of his withdrawal of approval of such plan and upon receipt of such notice such plan shall cease to be in effect, but the State may retain jurisdiction in any case commenced before the withdrawal of the plan in order to enforce standards under the plan whenever the issues involved do not relate to the reasons for the withdrawal of the plan.

(g) The State may obtain a review of a decision of the Secretary withdrawing approval of or rejecting its plan by the United States court of appeals for the circuit in which the State is located by filing in such court within thirty days following receipt of notice of such decision a petition to modify or set aside in whole or in part the action of the Secretary. A copy of such petition shall forthwith be served upon the Secretary, and thereupon the Secretary shall certify and file in the court the record upon which the decision complained of was issued as provided in section 2112 of title 28. Unless the court finds that the Secretary's decision in rejecting a proposed State plan or withdrawing his approval of such a plan is not supported by substantial evidence the court shall affirm the Secretary's decision. The judgment of the court shall be subject to review by the Supreme Court of the United States upon certiorari or certification as provided in section 1254 of title 28.

(h) The Secretary may enter into an agreement with a State under which the State will be permitted to continue to enforce one or more occupational health and safety standards in effect in such State until final action is taken by the Secretary with respect to a plan submitted by a State under subsection (b) of this section, or two years from the date of enactment of this Act [enacted Dec. 29, 1970], whichever is earlier.

§ 668 (§19). Federal Agency Safety Programs and Responsibilities

(a) It shall be the responsibility of the head of each Federal agency (not including the United States Postal Service) to establish and maintain an effective and comprehensive occupational safety and health program which is consistent with the standards promulgated under section 6. The head of each agency shall (after consultation with representatives of the employees thereof)—

(1) provide safe and healthful places and conditions of employment, consistent with the standards set under section 6;

(2) acquire, maintain, and require the use of safety equipment, personal protective equipment, and devices reasonably necessary to protect employees;

(3) keep adequate records of all occupational accidents and illnesses for proper evaluation and necessary corrective action;

(4) consult with the Secretary with regard to the adequacy as to form and content of records kept pursuant to subsection (a)(3) of this section; and

(5) make an annual report to the Secretary with respect to occupational accidents and injuries and the agency's program under this section. Such report shall include any report submitted under section 7902(e)(2) of title 5, United States Code.

(b) The Secretary shall report to the President a summary or digest of reports submitted to him under subsection (a)(5) of this section, together with his evaluations of and recommendations derived from such reports.

(c) Omitted

(d) The Secretary shall have access to records and reports kept and filed by Federal agencies pursuant to subsections (a) (3) and (5) of this section unless those records and reports are specifically required by Executive order to be kept secret in the interest of the national defense or foreign policy, in which case the Secretary shall have access to such information as will not jeopardize national defense or foreign policy.

§ 669 (§20). Research and Related Activities

(a)(1) The Secretary of Health and Human Services, after consultation with the Secretary and with other appropriate Federal departments or agencies, shall conduct (directly or by grants or contracts) research, experiments, and demonstrations relating to occupational safety and health, including studies of psychological factors involved, and relating to innovative methods, techniques, and approaches for dealing with occupational safety and health problems.

(2) The Secretary of Health and Human Services shall from time to time consult with the Secretary in order to develop specific plans for such research, demonstrations, and experiments as are necessary to produce criteria, including criteria identifying toxic substances, enabling the Secretary to meet his responsibility for the formulation of safety and health standards under this Act and the Secretary of Health and Human Services, on the basis of such research, demonstrations, and experiments and any other information available to him, shall develop and publish at least annually such criteria as will effectuate the purpose of this Act.

(3) The Secretary of Health and Human Services, on the basis of such research, demonstrations, and experiments, and any other information available to him, shall develop criteria dealing with toxic materials and harmful physical agents and substances which will describe exposure levels that are safe for various periods of employment, including but not limited to the exposure levels at which no employee will suffer impaired health or functional capacities or diminished life expectancy as a result of his work experience.

(4) The Secretary of Health and Human Services shall also conduct special research, experiments, and demonstrations relating to occupational safety and health as are necessary to explore new problems, including those created by new technology in occupational safety and health, which may require ameliorative action beyond that which is otherwise provided for in the operating provisions of this Act. The Secretary of Health and Human Services shall also conduct research into the motivational and behavioral factors relating to the field of occupational safety and health.

(5) The Secretary of Health and Human Services, in order to comply with his responsibilities under paragraph (2), and in order to develop needed information regarding potentially toxic substances or harmful physical agents, may prescribe regulations requiring employers to measure, record, and make reports on the exposure of employees to

substances or physical agents which the Secretary of Health and Human Services reasonably believes may endanger the health or safety of employees. The Secretary of Health and Human Services also is authorized to establish such programs of medical examinations and tests as may be necessary for determining the incidence of occupational illnesses and the susceptibility of employees to such illnesses. Nothing in this or any other provision of this Act shall be deemed to authorize or require medical examination, immunization, or treatment for those who object thereto on religious grounds, except where such is necessary for the protection of the health or safety of others. Upon the request of any employer who is required to measure and record exposure of employees to substances or physical agents as provided under this subsection, the Secretary of Health and Human Services shall furnish full financial or other assistance to such employer for the purpose of defraying any additional expense incurred by him in carrying out the measuring and recording as provided in this subsection.

(6) The Secretary of Health and Human Services shall publish within six months of enactment of this Act and thereafter as needed but at least annually a list of all known toxic substances by generic family or other useful grouping, and the concentrations at which such toxicity is known to occur. He shall determine following a written request by any employer or authorized representative of employees, specifying with reasonable particularity the grounds on which the request is made, whether any substance normally found in the place of employment has potentially toxic effects in such concentrations as used or found; and shall submit such determination both to employers and affected employees as soon as possible. If the Secretary of Health and Human Services determines that any substance is potentially toxic at the concentrations in which it is used or found in a place of employment, and such substance is not covered by an occupational safety or health standard promulgated under section 6, the Secretary of Health and Human Services shall immediately submit such determination to the Secretary, together with all pertinent criteria.

(7) Within two years of enactment of this Act [enacted Dec. 29, 1970], and annually thereafter the Secretary of Health and Human Services shall conduct and publish industrywide studies of the effect of chronic or low-level exposure to industrial materials, processes, and stresses on the potential for illness, disease, or loss of functional capacity in aging adults.

(b) The Secretary of Health and Human Services is authorized to make inspections and question employers and employees as provided in section 8 of this Act in order to carry out his functions and responsibilities under this section.

(c) The Secretary is authorized to enter into contracts, agreements, or other arrangements with appropriate public agencies or private organizations for the purpose of conducting studies relating to his responsibilities under this Act. In carrying out his responsibilities under this subsection, the Secretary shall cooperate with the Secretary of Health and Human Services in order to avoid any duplication of efforts under this section.

(d) Information obtained by the Secretary and the Secretary of Health and Human Services under this section shall be disseminated by the Secretary to employers and employees and organizations thereof.

(e) The functions of the Secretary of Health and Human Services under this Act shall, to the extent feasible, be delegated to the Director of the National Institute for Occupational Safety and Health established by section 22 of this Act.

§ 669 (§20). Expanded Research on Worker Safety and Health

(a)(1) The Secretary of Health and Human Services (referred to in this section as the "Secretary"), acting through the Director of the National Institute of Occupational Safety and Health, shall enhance and expand research as deemed appropriate on the health and safety of workers who are at risk for bioterrorist threats or attacks in the workplace, including research on the health effects of measures taken to treat or protect such workers for diseases or disorders resulting from a bioterrorist threat or attack. Nothing in this section may be construed as establishing new regulatory authority for the Secretary or the Director to issue or modify any occupational safety and health rule or regulation.

§ 670 (§21). Training and Employee Education

(a) The Secretary of Health and Human Services, after consultation with the Secretary and with other appropriate Federal departments and agencies, shall conduct, directly or by grants or contracts (1) education programs to provide an adequate supply of qualified personnel to carry out the purposes of this Act, and (2) informational programs on the importance of and proper use of adequate safety and health equipment.

(b) The Secretary is also authorized to conduct, directly or by grants or contracts, short-term training of personnel engaged in work related to his responsibilities under this Act.

(c) The Secretary, in consultation with the Secretary of Health and Human Services, shall (1) provide for the establishment and supervision of programs for the education and training of employers and employees in the recognition, avoidance, and prevention of unsafe or unhealthful working conditions in employments covered by this Act, and (2) consult with and advise employers and employees, and organizations representing employers and employees as to effective means of preventing occupational injuries and illnesses.

(d)(1) The Secretary shall establish and support cooperative agreements with the States under which employers subject to this Act may consult with State personnel with respect to—

(A) the application of occupational safety and health requirements under this Act or under State plans approved under section 18 [29 U.S.C. § 667]; and

(B) voluntary efforts that employers may undertake to establish and maintain safe and healthful employment and places of employment.

Such agreements may provide, as a condition of receiving funds under such agreements, for contributions by States towards meeting the costs of such agreements.

(2) Pursuant to such agreements the State shall provide on-site consultation at the employer's worksite to employers who request such assistance. The State may also provide other education and training programs for employers and employees in the State. The State shall ensure that on-site consultations conducted pursuant to such agreements include provision for the participation by employees.

(3) Activities under this subsection shall be conducted independently of any enforcement activity. If an employer fails to take immediate action to eliminate employee exposure to an imminent danger identified in a consultation or fails to correct a serious hazard so identified within a reasonable time, a report shall be made to the appropriate enforcement authority for such action as is appropriate.

(4) The Secretary shall, by regulation after notice and opportunity for comment, establish rules under which an employer—

(A) which requests and undergoes an on-site consultative visit provided under this subsection;

(B) which corrects the hazards that have been identified during the visit within the time frames established by the State and agrees to request a subsequent consultative visit if major changes in working conditions or work processes occur which introduce new hazards in the workplace; and

(C) which is implementing procedures for regularly identifying and preventing hazards regulated under this Act and maintains appropriate involvement of, and training for, management and non-management employees in achieving safe and healthful working conditions, may be exempt from an inspection (except an inspection requested under section 8(f) or an inspection to determine the cause of a workplace accident which resulted in the death of one or more employees or hospitalization for three or more employees) for a period of 1 year from the closing of the consultative visit.

(5) A State shall provide worksite consultations under paragraph (2) at the request of an employer. Priority in scheduling such consultations shall be assigned to requests from small businesses which are in higher hazard industries or have the most hazardous conditions at issue in the request.

§ 671 (§22). National Institute for Occupational Safety and Health

(a) It is the purpose of this section to establish a National Institute for Occupational Safety and Health in the Department of Health, Education, and Welfare in order to carry out the policy set forth in section 2 of this Act and to perform the functions of the Secretary of Health and Human Services under sections 20 and 21 of this Act.

(b) There is hereby established in the Department of Health, Education, and Welfare a National Institute for Occupational Safety and Health. The Institute shall be headed by a Director who shall be appointed by the Secretary of Health and Human Services, and who shall serve for a term of six years unless previously removed by the Secretary of Health and Human Services.

(c) The Institute is authorized to—

(1) develop and establish recommended occupational safety and health standards; and

(2) perform all functions of the Secretary of Health and Human Services under sections 20 and 21 of this Act.

(d) Upon his own initiative, or upon the request of the Secretary or the Secretary of Health and Human Services, the Director is authorized (1) to conduct such research and experimental programs as he determines are necessary for the development of criteria for new and improved occupational safety and health standards, and (2) after consideration of the results of such research and experimental programs make recommendations concerning new or improved occupational safety and health standards. Any occupational safety and health standard recommended pursuant to this section shall immediately be forwarded to the Secretary of Labor, and to the Secretary of Health and Human Services.

(e) In addition to any authority vested in the Institute by other provisions of this section, the Director, in carrying out the functions of the Institute, is authorized to—

(1) prescribe such regulations as he deems necessary governing the manner in which its functions shall be carried out;

(2) receive money and other property donated, bequeathed, or devised, without condition or restriction other than that it be used for the purposes of the Institute and to use, sell, or otherwise dispose of such property for the purpose of carrying out its functions;

(3) receive (and use, sell, or otherwise dispose of, in accordance with paragraph (2)), money and other property donated, bequeathed, or devised to the Institute with a condition or restriction, including a condition that the Institute use other funds of the Institute for the purposes of the gift;

(4) in accordance with the civil service laws, appoint and fix the compensation of such personnel as may be necessary to carry out the provisions of this section;

(5) obtain the services of experts and consultants in accordance with the provisions of section 3109 of title 5, United States Code;

(6) accept and utilize the services of voluntary and noncompensated personnel and reimburse them for travel expenses, including per diem, as authorized by section 5703 of title 5, United States Code;

(7) enter into contracts, grants or other arrangements, or modifications hereof to carry out the provisions of this section, and such contracts or modifications thereof may be entered into without performance or other bonds, and without regard to section 3709 of the Revised Statutes, as amended (41 U.S.C. 5), or any other provision of law relating to competitive bidding;

(8) make advance, progress, and other payments which the Director deems necessary under this title without regard to the provisions of section 3324(a) and (b) of Title 31; and

(9) make other necessary expenditures.

(f) The Director shall submit to the Secretary of Health and Human Services, to the President, and to the Congress an annual report of the operations of the Institute under this Act, which shall include a detailed statement of all private and public funds received and expended by it, and such recommendations as he deems appropriate.

(g) Omitted.

§ 672 (§23). Grants to the States

(a) The Secretary is authorized, during the fiscal year ending June 30, 1971, and the two succeeding fiscal years, to make grants to the States which have designated a State agency under section 18 to assist them—

(1) in identifying their needs and responsibilities in the area of occupational safety and health,

(2) in developing State plans under section 18, or

(3) in developing plans for—

(A) establishing systems for the collection of information concerning the nature and frequency of occupational injuries and diseases;

(B) increasing the expertise and enforcement capabilities of their personnel engaged in occupational safety and health programs; or

(C) otherwise improving the administration and enforcement of State occupational safety and health laws, including standards thereunder, consistent with the objectives of this Act.

(b) The Secretary is authorized, during the fiscal year ending June 30, 1971, and the two succeeding fiscal years, to make grants to the States for experimental and demonstration projects consistent with the objectives set forth in subsection (a) of this section.

(c) The Governor of the State shall designate the appropriate State agency for receipt of any grant made by the Secretary under this section.

(d) Any State agency designated by the Governor of the State desiring a grant under this section shall submit an application therefor to the Secretary.

(e) The Secretary shall review the application, and shall, after consultation with the Secretary of Health and Human Services, approve or reject such application.

(f) The Federal share for each State grant under subsection (a) or (b) of this section may not exceed 90 per centum of the total cost of the application. In the event the Federal share for all States under either such subsection is not the same, the differences among the States shall be established on the basis of objective criteria.

(g) The Secretary is authorized to make grants to the States to assist them in administering and enforcing programs for occupational safety and health contained in State plans approved by the Secretary pursuant to section 18 of this Act. The Federal share for each State grant under this subsection may not exceed 50 per centum of the total cost to the State of such a program. The last sentence of subsection (f) shall be applicable in determining the Federal share under this subsection.

(h) Prior to June 30, 1973, the Secretary shall, after consultation with the Secretary of Health and Human Services, transmit a report to the President and to the Congress, describing the experience under the grant programs authorized by this section and making any recommendations he may deem appropriate.

§ 673 (§24). Statistics

(a) In order to further the purposes of this Act, the Secretary, in consultation with the Secretary of Health and Human Services, shall develop and maintain an effective program of collection, compilation, and analysis of occupational safety and health statistics. Such program may cover all employments whether or not subject to any other provisions of this Act but shall not cover employments excluded by section 4 of the Act [29 USCS § 653]. The Secretary shall compile accurate statistics on work injuries and illnesses which shall include all disabling, serious, or significant injuries and illnesses, whether or not involving loss of time from work, other than minor injuries requiring only first aid treatment and which do not involve medical treatment, loss of consciousness, restriction of work or motion, or transfer to another job.

(b) To carry out his duties under subsection (a) of this section, the Secretary may—

(1) promote, encourage, or directly engage in programs of studies, information and communication concerning occupational safety and health statistics;

(2) make grants to States or political subdivisions thereof in order to assist them in developing and administering programs dealing with occupational safety and health statistics; and

(3) arrange, through grants or contracts, for the conduct of such research and investigations as give promise of furthering the objectives of this section.

(c) The Federal share for each grant under subsection (b) of this section may be up to 50 per centum of the State's total cost.

(d) The Secretary may, with the consent of any State or political subdivision thereof, accept and use the services, facilities, and employees of the agencies of such State or political subdivision, with or without reimbursement, in order to assist him in carrying out his functions under this section.

(e) On the basis of the records made and kept pursuant to section 8(c) of this Act, employers shall file such reports with the Secretary as he shall prescribe by regulation, as necessary to carry out his functions under this Act.

(f) Agreements between the Department of Labor and States pertaining to the collection of occupational safety and health statistics already in effect on the effective date of this Act shall remain in effect until superseded by grants or contracts made under this Act.

§ 674 (§25). Audits

(a) Each recipient of a grant under this Act shall keep such records as the Secretary or the Secretary of Health and Human Services shall prescribe, including records which fully disclose the amount and disposition by such recipient of the proceeds of such grant, the total cost of the project or undertaking in connection with which such grant is made or used, and the amount of that portion of the cost of the project or undertaking supplied by other sources, and such other records as will facilitate an effective audit.

(b) The Secretary or the Secretary of Health and Human Services, and the Comptroller General of the United States, or any of their duly authorized representatives, shall have access for the purpose of audit and examination to any books, documents, papers, and records of the recipients of any grant under this Act that are pertinent to any such grant.

§ 675 (§26). Annual Report

Within one hundred and twenty days following the convening of each regular session of each Congress, the Secretary and the Secretary of Health and Human Services shall each prepare and submit to the President for transmittal to the Congress a report upon the subject matter of this Act, the progress toward achievement of the purpose of this Act, the needs and requirements in the field of occupational safety and health, and any other relevant information. Such reports shall include information regarding occupational safety and health standards, and criteria for such standards, developed during the preceding year; evaluation of standards and criteria previously developed under this Act, defining areas of emphasis for new criteria and standards; an evaluation of the degree of observance of applicable occupational safety and health standards, and a summary of inspection and enforcement activity undertaken; analysis and evaluation of research activities for which results have been obtained under governmental and nongovernmental sponsorship; an analysis of major occupational diseases; evaluation of available control and measurement technology for hazards for which standards or criteria have been developed during the preceding year; description of cooperative efforts undertaken between Government agencies and other interested parties in the implementation of this Act during the preceding year; a progress report on the development of an adequate supply of trained manpower in the field of occupational safety and health, including estimates of future needs and the efforts being made by Government and others to meet those needs; listing of all toxic substances in industrial usage for which labeling requirements, criteria, or standards have not yet been established; and such recommendations for additional legislation as are deemed necessary to protect the safety and health of the worker and improve the administration of this Act.

§ 676. (§27) Omitted

§ 677. (§32) Separability.

If any provision of this Act, or the application of such provision to any person or circumstance, shall be held invalid, the remainder of this Act, or the application of such provision to persons or circumstances other than those as to which it is held invalid, shall not be affected thereby.

§ 678. (§33) Appropriations.

There are authorized to be appropriated to carry out this Act for each fiscal year such sums as the Congress shall deem necessary.

(§34) Effective Date.

The Act shall take effect one hundred and twenty days after the date of its enactment. Approved December 29, 1970.

ADMINISTRATIVE PROCEDURES ACT

5 U.S.C. § 706

§ 706. Scope of review

To the extent necessary to decision and when presented, the reviewing court shall decide all relevant questions of law, interpret constitutional and statutory provisions, and determine the meaning or applicability of the terms of an agency action. The reviewing court shall—

(1) compel agency action unlawfully withheld or unreasonably delayed; and

(2) hold unlawful and set aside agency action, findings, and conclusions found to be—

(A) arbitrary, capricious, an abuse of discretion, or otherwise not in accordance with law;

(B) contrary to constitutional right, power, privilege, or immunity;

(C) in excess of statutory jurisdiction, authority, or limitations, or short of statutory right;

(D) without observance of procedure required by law;

(E) unsupported by substantial evidence in a case subject to sections 556 and 557 of this title [5 U.S.C. §§ 556 and 557] or otherwise reviewed on the record of an agency hearing provided by statute; or

(F) unwarranted by the facts to the extent that the facts are subject to trial de novo by the reviewing court.

In making the foregoing determinations, the court shall review the whole record or those parts of it cited by a party, and due account shall be taken of the rule of prejudicial error.

FEDERAL RULES OF EVIDENCE

ARTICLE VII. OPINIONS AND EXPERT TESTIMONY

Rule 702. Testimony by Experts

If scientific, technical, or other specialized knowledge will assist the trier of fact to understand the evidence or to determine a fact in issue, a witness qualified as an expert by knowledge, skill, experience, training, or education, may testify thereto in the form of an opinion or otherwise, if (1) the testimony is based upon sufficient facts or data, (2) the testimony is the product of reliable principles and methods, and (3) the witness has applied the principles and methods reliably to the facts of the case.

Amendment of Rule 702, effective December 1, 2011. By order dated April 26, 2011, the Supreme Court of the United States approved the following amendments to Rule 702, effective December 1, 2011, and authorized their transmission to Congress in accordance with 28 U.S.C. § 2072:

Rule 702. Testimony by Expert Witnesses

A witness who is qualified as an expert by knowledge, skill, experience, training, or education may testify in the form of an opinion or otherwise if:

(a) the expert's scientific, technical, or other specialized knowledge will help the trier of fact to understand the evidence or to determine a fact in issue;

(b) the testimony is based on sufficient facts or data;

(c) the testimony is the product of reliable principles and methods; and

(d) the expert has reliably applied the principles and methods to the facts of the case.

PART IX.

ENFORCEMENT OF EMPLOYMENT RIGHTS

FEDERAL ARBITRATION ACT

9 U.S.C. §§ 1 et seq.

CHAPTER 1. GENERAL PROVISIONS

§ 1. "Maritime transactions" and "commerce" defined; exceptions to operation of title. "Maritime transactions", as herein defined, means charter parties, bills of lading of water carriers, agreements relating to wharfage, supplies furnished vessels or repairs to vessels, collisions, or any other matters in foreign commerce which, if the subject of controversy, would be embraced within admiralty jurisdiction; "commerce", as herein defined, means commerce among the several States or with foreign nations, or in any Territory of the United States or in the District of Columbia, or between any such Territory and another, or between any such Territory and any State or foreign nation, or between the District of Columbia and any State or Territory or foreign nation, but nothing herein contained shall apply to contracts of employment of seamen, railroad employees, or any other class of workers engaged in foreign or interstate commerce.

§ 2. Validity, irrevocability, and enforcement of agreements to arbitrate. A written provision in any maritime transaction or a contract evidencing a transaction involving commerce to settle by arbitration a controversy thereafter arising out of such contract or transaction, or the refusal to perform the whole or any part thereof, or an agreement in writing to submit to arbitration an existing controversy arising out of such a contract, transaction, or refusal, shall be valid, irrevocable, and enforceable, save upon such grounds as exist at law or in equity for the revocation of any contract.

§ 3. Stay of proceedings where issue therein referable to arbitration. If any suit or proceeding be brought in any of the courts of the United States upon any issue referable to arbitration under an agreement in writing for such arbitration, the court in which such suit is pending, upon being satisfied that the issue involved in such suit or proceeding is referable to arbitration under such an agreement, shall on application of one of the parties stay the trial of the action until such arbitration has been had in accordance with the terms of the agreement, providing the applicant for the stay is not in default in proceeding with such arbitration.

§ 4. Failure to arbitrate under agreement; petition to United States court having jurisdiction for order to compel arbitration; notice and service thereof; hearing and determination. A party aggrieved by the alleged failure, neglect, or refusal of another to arbitrate under a written agreement for arbitration may petition any United States district court which, save for such agreement, would have jurisdiction under Title 28, in a civil action or in admiralty of the subject matter of a suit arising out of the controversy between the parties, for an order directing that such arbitration proceed in the manner provided for in such agreement. Five days' notice in writing of such application shall be served upon the party in default. Service thereof shall be made in the manner provided by the Federal Rules of Civil Procedure. The court shall hear the parties, and upon being satisfied that the making of the agreement for arbitration or the failure to comply therewith is not in issue, the court shall make an order directing the parties to proceed to arbitration in accordance with the terms of the agreement. The hearing and proceedings, under such agreement, shall be within the district in which the petition for an order directing such arbitration is filed. If the making of the arbitration agreement or the failure, neglect, or refusal to perform the same be in issue, the court shall proceed summarily to the trial thereof. If no jury trial be demanded by the party alleged to be in default, or if the matter in dispute is within admiralty jurisdiction, the court shall hear and determine such issue. Where such an issue is raised, the party alleged to be in default may, except in cases of admiralty, on or before the return day of the notice of application, demand a jury trial of such issue, and upon such demand the court shall make an order referring the issue or issues to a jury in the manner provided by the Federal Rules of Civil Procedure, or may specially call a jury for that purpose. If the jury find that no agreement in writing for arbitration was made or that there is no default in proceeding thereunder, the proceeding shall be dismissed. If the jury find that an agreement for arbitration was made in writing and that there is a default in proceeding thereunder, the court shall make an order summarily directing the parties to proceed with the arbitration in accordance with the terms thereof.

§ **5. Appointment of arbitrators or umpire.** If in the agreement provision be made for a method of naming or appointing an arbitrator or arbitrators or an umpire, such method shall be followed; but if no method be provided therein, or if a method be provided and any party thereto shall fail to avail himself of such method, or if for any other reason there shall be a lapse in the naming of an arbitrator or arbitrators or umpire, or in filling a vacancy, then upon the application of either party to the controversy the court shall designate and appoint an arbitrator or arbitrators or umpire, as the case may require, who shall act under the said agreement with the same force and effect as if he or they had been specifically named therein; and unless otherwise provided in the agreement the arbitration shall be by a single arbitrator.

§ **6. Application heard as motion.** Any application to the court hereunder shall be made and heard in the manner provided by law for the making and hearing of motions, except as otherwise herein expressly provided.

§ **7. Witnesses before arbitrators; fees; compelling attendance.** The arbitrators selected either as prescribed in this title or otherwise, or a majority of them, may summon in writing any person to attend before them or any of them as a witness and in a proper case to bring with him or them any book, record, document, or paper which may be deemed material as evidence in the case. The fees for such attendance shall be the same as the fees of witnesses before masters of the United States courts. Said summons shall issue in the name of the arbitrator or arbitrators, or a majority of them, and shall be signed by the arbitrators, or a majority of them, and shall be directed to the said person and shall be served in the same manner as subpoenas to appear and testify before the court; if any person or persons so summoned to testify shall refuse or neglect to obey said summons, upon petition the United States district court for the district in which such arbitrators, or a majority of them, are sitting may compel the attendance of such person or persons before said arbitrator or arbitrators, or punish said person or persons for contempt in the same manner provided by law for securing the attendance of witnesses or their punishment for neglect or refusal to attend in the courts of the United States.

§ **8. Proceedings begun by libel in admiralty and seizure of vessel or property.** If the basis of jurisdiction be a cause of action otherwise justiciable in admiralty, then, notwithstanding anything herein to the contrary, the party claiming to be aggrieved may begin his proceeding hereunder by libel and seizure of the vessel or other property of the other party according to the usual course of admiralty proceedings, and the court shall then have jurisdiction to direct the parties to proceed with the arbitration and shall retain jurisdiction to enter its decree upon the award.

§ 9. Award of arbitrators; confirmation; jurisdiction; procedure. If the parties in their agreement have agreed that a judgment of the court shall be entered upon the award made pursuant to the arbitration, and shall specify the court, then at any time within one year after the award is made any party to the arbitration may apply to the court so specified for an order confirming the award, and thereupon the court must grant such an order unless the award is vacated, modified, or corrected as prescribed in sections 10 and 11 of this title. If no court is specified in the agreement of the parties, then such application may be made to the United States court in and for the district within which such award was made. Notice of the application shall be served upon the adverse party, and thereupon the court shall have jurisdiction of such party as though he had appeared generally in the proceeding. If the adverse party is a resident of the district within which the award was made, such service shall be made upon the adverse party or his attorney as prescribed by law for service of notice of motion in an action in the same court. If the adverse party shall be a nonresident, then the notice of the application shall be served by the marshal of any district within which the adverse party may be found in like manner as other process of the court.

§ 10. Same; vacation; grounds; rehearing.

(a) In any of the following cases the United States court in and for the district wherein the award was made may make an order vacating the award upon the application of any party to the arbitration—

(1) where the award was procured by corruption, fraud, or undue means;

(2) where there was evident partiality or corruption in the arbitrators, or either of them;

(3) where the arbitrators were guilty of misconduct in refusing to postpone the hearing, upon sufficient cause shown, or in refusing to hear evidence pertinent and material to the controversy; or of any other misbehavior by which the rights of any party have been prejudiced; or

(4) where the arbitrators exceeded their powers, or so imperfectly executed them that a mutual, final, and definite award upon the subject matter submitted was not made.

(b) If an award is vacated and the time within which the agreement required the award to be made has not expired, the court may, in its discretion, direct a rehearing by the arbitrators.

(c) The United States district court for the district wherein an award was made that was issued pursuant to section 580 of title 5 may make an order vacating the award upon the application of a person, other than a party to the arbitration, who is adversely affected or aggrieved by the award, if the use of arbitration or the award is clearly inconsistent with the factors set forth in section 572 of title 5.

§ 11. Same; modification or correction; grounds; order. In either of the following cases the United States court in and for the district wherein the award was made may make an order modifying or correcting the award upon the application of any party to the arbitration—

(a) Where there was an evident material miscalculation of figures or an evident material mistake in the description of any person, thing, or property referred to in the award.

(b) Where the arbitrators have awarded upon a matter not submitted to them, unless it is a matter not affecting the merits of the decision upon the matter submitted.

(c) Where the award is imperfect in matter of form not affecting the merits of the controversy.

The order may modify and correct the award, so as to effect the intent thereof and promote justice between the parties.

§ 12. Notice of motions to vacate or modify; service; stay of proceedings. Notice of a motion to vacate, modify, or correct an award must be served upon the adverse party or his attorney within three months after the award is filed or delivered. If the adverse party is a resident of the district within which the award was made, such service shall be made upon the adverse party or his attorney as prescribed by law for service of notice of motion in an action in the same court. If the adverse party shall be a nonresident then the notice of the application shall be served by the marshal of any district within which the adverse party may be found in like manner as other process of the court. For the purposes of the motion any judge who might make an order to stay the proceedings in an action brought in the same court may make an order, to be served with the notice of motion, staying the proceedings of the adverse party to enforce the award.

§ 13. Papers filed with order on motions; judgment; docketing; force and effect; enforcement. The party moving for an order confirming, modifying, or correcting an award shall, at the time such order is filed with the clerk for the entry of judgment thereon, also file the following papers with the clerk:

(a) The agreement; the selection or appointment, if any, of an additional arbitrator or umpire; and each written extension of the time, if any, within which to make the award.

(b) The award.

(c) Each notice, affidavit, or other paper used upon an application to confirm, modify, or correct the award, and a copy of each order of the court upon such an application. The judgment shall be docketed as if it was rendered in an action. The judgment so entered shall have the same force and effect, in all respects, as, and be subject to all the provisions of law relating to, a judgment in an action; and it may be enforced as if it had been rendered in an action in the court in which it is entered.

§ 14. Contracts not affected. This title shall not apply to contracts made prior to January 1, 1926.

§ 15. Inapplicability of the Act of State doctrine. Enforcement of arbitral agreements, confirmation of arbitral awards, and execution upon judgments based on orders confirming such awards shall not be refused on the basis of the Act of State doctrine.

§ 16. Appeals.

(a) An appeal may be taken from—

(1) an order—

(A) refusing a stay of any action under section 3 of this title,

(B) denying a petition under section 4 of this title to order arbitration to proceed,

(C) denying an application under section 206 of this title to compel arbitration,

(D) confirming or denying confirmation of an award or partial award, or

(E) modifying, correcting, or vacating an award;

(2) an interlocutory order granting, continuing, or modifying an injunction against an arbitration that is subject to this title; or

(3) a final decision with respect to an arbitration that is subject to this title.

(b) Except as otherwise provided in section 1292(b) of title 28, an appeal may not be taken from an interlocutory order—

(1) granting a stay of any action under section 3 of this title;

(2) directing arbitration to proceed under section 4 of this title;

(3) compelling arbitration under section 206 of this title; or

(4) refusing to enjoin an arbitration that is subject to this title.

[Chapter 2. Convention on the Recognition and Enforcement of Foreign Arbitral Awards omitted]

[Chapter 3. Inter-American Convention on International Commercial Arbitration omitted]